D0376358

ART AND ITS
SIGNIFICANCE

Third Edition

ART AND ITS SIGNIFICANCE

An Anthology of Aesthetic Theory

THIRD EDITION

Edited by

Stephen David Ross

STATE UNIVERSITY OF NEW YORK PRESS

Published by
State University of New York Press, Albany

© 1994 State University of New York, THIRD EDITION

For information, contact State University of New York Press, Albany, NY
www.sunypress.edu

Production by Marilyn P. Semerad
Marketing by Nancy Farrell

Library of Congress Cataloging-in-Publication Data

Art and its significance : an anthology of aesthetic theory / edited
    by Stephen David Ross. — 3rd ed.
        p.   cm.
    Includes bibliographical references.
    ISBN: 978-0-7914-1852-9

    1. Aesthetics. 2. Art—Philosophy. I. Ross, Stephen David.
BH39.A69 1994
701′.17–dc20   93-43609
                                                              CIP

30 29 28 27 26 25 24 23 22 21 20

CONTENTS

II. RECENT SYSTEMATIC THEORIES

III. INTERPRETATION AND CRITICISM

IV. DISCUSSIONS

PREFACE

The philosophy of art, including the theory of interpretation, has been among the most productive branches of philosophy in the latter half of the twentieth century. Remarkable, interesting, and important work has emerged from both sides of the Atlantic, and elsewhere, from all the sources of philosophic thought. A collection is needed that includes the best of contemporary writings as well as the most important works of the past hundred years and the major writings from the Western tradition. This collection has been designed to fill that need.

There is enough here for more than one course on the theory of art. Material drawn from the most important Continental writers is supplemented by the historical selections and the writings of psychologists and artists; some important and interesting works of contemporary Anglo-American writers are included. But the course that this collection is specifically designed to serve is one that draws from every available source for our understanding of art: from the major writings in the Western philosophical tradition, from contemporary American, Continental, British, and nonWestern philosophers, and from psychologists and artists.

This is primarily a theory-based collection. I have chosen works less for the conflict of their arguments and more for the theories they offer concerning the nature of art and how we are to understand it. There are, however, a few less theoretical selections in Part IV that are important in contemporary discussions of the philosophy of art.

The selections in Part I from the history of philosophy include the most important writers and, in the selections from Plato and Kant, a major portion of the relevant writings. I would have liked to include in this edition all of *Phaedrus*, which I believe offers a wonderful treatment of the relation between *erôs* and *technē*. Instead, I have expanded the material from Kant, including more of his writing on aesthetical ideas and the sublime. I would have liked to include selections from Augustine and Plotinus and to expand the selections from Hegel and Nietzsche but, due to limited space, I have omitted important historical writings in order to include more contemporary discussions. In Part II, there are significant selections from Dewey, Langer, Goodman, Heidegger, and Merleau-Ponty. Again, I would have preferred more, but I believe I have included the most important philosophical writings of the last hundred years on the theory of art. The selections in Part III, on the nature of interpretation, from Hirsch and Gadamer, but also from Derrida, Foucault, and Ricoeur, are important in contemporary Continental discussions. The selections from Derrida have been updated and considerably expanded for this edition, primarily from *The Truth in Painting*, also including one of his most interesting provocations, his letter to Peter Eisenman on architecture.

Part IV has again been expanded for this edition to include a wider range of contemporary discussions. All the selections from Part IV of the second edition have been retained except for the substitution of a chapter from Irigaray's *Speculum of the Other Woman* for Cixous's "Laugh of the Medusa," a difficult choice, but in my view raising a wider range of issues relevant to feminist views of art. The major addition to Part IV is a complete new section on multicultural theory. These selections range from discussions of art in other cultures to discussions of the appropriation of nonWestern art in Western cultures. Some of this material is very controversial. It also raises important issues.

The materials from artists that close the anthology remain relatively limited, primarily from manifestoes in early twentieth-century plastic art, to introduce questions, largely of a political nature, concerning the relationship of art to society and human experience. There are more illuminating writings by artists, but few that are quite so provocative as the ones included here, and few that so sharply define "modernism." I have limited the writings of artists to the plastic arts to focus them more tightly.

I remain convinced that minimal editorial intervention is best, even with such difficult readings, that strong editorial readings may interfere with the relation of the reader to the text or of the teacher to the class. Very minor changes in introductory material have been made for this edition.

I have made great efforts to provide a comprehensive collection. I hope even more to have made it interesting.

Finally, a topic of grave importance for art of our time and for humanity is not addressed in this collection, and its absence cannot be left in silence. AIDS, its thought and its reality, has opened deep wounds in communities concerned with art and culture, especially in the West. The deaths of so many people from AIDS is a tragedy worldwide. The loss of so many artists, performers, and critics is a cultural disaster. In the age of AIDS, Western artists face death incessantly.

ACKNOWLEDGMENTS

Oxford University Press

Reprinted by permission of Oxford University Press: from G. W. F. Hegel, *Aesthetics: Lectures on Fine Art*, translated by T. M. Knox, 2 vols., copyright 1975 by Oxford University Press; from Leo Tolstoy, *What is Art?*, translated by Louise and Aylmer Maude, 1930; from R. G. Collingwood, *The Principles of Art*, 1938; from *The Dialogues of Plato*, translated by Benjamin Jowett, 3rd ed., 1892; from *The Oxford Translation of Aristotle*, edited by W. D. Ross, vol. 9, 1925 (*Nicomachean Ethics*, translated by W. D. Ross; *Poetics*, translated by Ingram Bywater), reprinted in the United States, with the permission of Oxford University Press, by Random House, New York.

Macmillan

Reprinted by permission of Macmillan Publishers, Inc., New York, from Immanuel Kant, *Critique of Judgment*, translated by J. H. Bernard, Hafner, 1951.

Random House

Reprinted by permission of Random House, Inc., New York: from Michel Foucault, *The Order of Things: An Archaeology of the Human Sciences*, translation of *Les mots et les choses*, Pantheon, 1970; from Friedrich Nietzsche, *The Birth of Tragedy and The Case of Wagner*, translated by Walter Kaufmann, 1967.

Putnam

Reprinted by permission of G. P. Putnam's Sons, New York, from Clive Bell, *Art*, originally published 1914, reprinted Capricorn, 1958; from John Dewey, *Art as Experience*, copyright 1934 by John Dewey, renewed 1962.

British Psychological Society

Reprinted by permission of the British Psychological Society, from "'Psychical Distance' as a Factor in Art and as an Aesthetic Principle," *British Journal of Psychology*, 1912, pp. 87-98.

Journal of Philosophy

"The Artworld," reprinted by permission of the *Journal of Philosophy*, 1964, pp. 571-584.

Basic Books

Reprinted by permission of Basic Books, Inc., New York, from Sigmund Freud, "The Relation of the Poet to Day-dreaming," translated by I. F. Grant Duff, in *Collected Papers*, vol. 4, pp. 173-183.

Harcourt Brace Jovanovich

Reprinted by permission of Harcourt Brace Jovanovich, New York, from Carl G. Jung, "Psychology and Literature," translated by W. S. Dell and Cary F. Baynes, in *Modern Man in Search of a Soul*, 1955. Reprinted by permission of Harcourt Brace Jovanovich and Jonathan Cape Ltd., from *Illuminations* by Walter Benjamin, translated by Harry Zohn, English copyright © 1968.

MIT Press

Reprinted by permission of MIT Press, Cambridge, Massachusetts, from Lev Vygotsky, *Psychology of Art*, 1971. From James Clifford, "On Collecting Art and Culture," in *Out There: Marginalization and Contemporary Culture*. Edited by Russell Ferguson, Martha Bever, Trinh T. Minh-ha, Cornell West. Foreword by Marcia Tucker. Copyright © 1990 by The New Museum of Contemporary Art and MIT Press. Reprinted by permission of MIT Press and *Assemblage*, from Jacques Derrida, "A Letter to Peter Eisenman," in *Assemblage* (12), 7-13.

Beacon Press

Reprinted by permission of Beacon Press, Boston, from Herbert Marcuse, *The Aesthetic Dimension*, 1978. Reprinted by permission of Beacon Press and The Women's Press Ltd., from Heide Göttner-Abendroth, "Nine Principles of a Matriarchal Aesthetic," in *Feminist Aesthetics*, edited by Gisela Ecker. Introduction and Collection © Gisela Ecker 1985; translation © Harriet Anderson 1985.

University of California Press

Reprinted by permission of University of California Press, Berkeley and Los Angeles, from *Theories of Modern Art*, edited by Hershel B. Chipp, 1968.

Scribner

Reprinted by permission of Charles Scribner's Sons, New York, from Susanne K. Langer, *Feeling and Form: A Theory of Art*, copyright 1953 by Charles Scribner's Sons; renewed 1981 by Susanne K. Langer.

Hackett

Reprinted by permission of Nelson Goodman and Hackett Publishing Company, Inc., Indianapolis, Indiana, from Nelson Goodman, *Ways of World-making*, 1978, and *Languages of Art*, 2nd ed., 1976.

Harper & Row

Reprinted by permission of Harper & Row Publishers, Inc., New York, from Martin Heidegger, "The Origin of the Work of Art," in *Poetry, Language, Thought*, translated by Albert Hofstadter, 1975.

Northwestern University Press

Reprinted by permission of Northwestern University Press, Evanston, Illinois: from Maurice Merleau-Ponty, "Eye and Mind," in *The Primacy of Perception*, translation by Carleton Dallery, edited by James M. Edie, 1964; from Paul Ricoeur, "The Problem of Double Meaning as Hermeneutic Problem and as Semantic Problem," translated by Kathleen McLaughlin, in *The Conflict of Interpretations*, 1974.

Indiana University Press

Reprinted by permission of Indiana University Press, Bloomington, Indiana, from Stephen Pepper, *The Work of Art*, 1955. From V. Y. Mudimbe, *The Invention of Africa*. Copyright © 1988 by V. Y. Mudimbe; from Trinh T. Minh-ha, *Woman, Native, Other: Writing Postcoloniality and Feminism*. Copyright © 1989 by Trinh T. Minh-ha.

Yale University Press

Reprinted by permission of Yale University Press, New Haven, Connecticut, from E. D. Hirsch, Jr., *Validity in Interpretation*, 1967.

Crossroad

Reprinted by permission of Crossroad Publishing Company, New York, from Hans-Georg Gadamer, *Truth and Method*, English translation, copyright 1975 by Sheed & Ward Ltd., London.

LeWitt

Reprinted by permission of Sol LeWitt from Sol LeWitt, "Sentences on Conceptual Art," in *Six Years: The Dematerialization of the Art Object from 1966 to 1972*, edited by Lucy R. Lippard, Praeger, New York, 1973.

The Continuum Publishing Company

Reprinted by permission of The Continuum Publishing Company, from Theodor W. Adorno, "On the Fetish-Character in Music and the Regression of Listening," in *The Essential Frankfurt School Reader*, edited by Andrew Arato and Eike Gebhardt, © 1982 by the Continuum Publishing Company.

University of Texas Press

Reprinted by permission of the University of Texas Press, from M. M. Bakhtin, *The Dialogic Imagination: Four Essays*, edited by Michael Holquist. Translated by Caryl Emerson and Michael Holquist. Copyright © 1981 by the University of Texas Press.

University of Chicago Press

Reprinted by permission of the University of Chicago Press, from Jacques Derrida, *The Truth in Painting*. Translated by Geoff Bennington and Ian McLeod. Copyright © 1987 by the University of Chicago Press. With the permission of the author.

University of Minnesota Press

Reprinted by permission of the University of Minnesota Press, from Jean-François Lyotard, *The Postmodern Condition: A Report on Knowledge*, translated by Geoff Bennington and Brian Massumi. Copyright © 1984 by the University of Minnesota Press.

Bay Press

Reprinted by permission of Bay Press, from Craig Owens, "The Discourse of Others: Feminists and Postmodernism," in *The Anti-Aesthetic: Essays on Postmodern Culture*, edited by Hal Foster. Copyright © 1983 by Bay Press.

Tony Fry and Anne-Marie Willis

Reprinted by permission of Tony Fry and Anne-Marie Willis, from Tony Fry and Anne-Marie Willis, "Aboriginal Art: Symptom or Success?," in *Art in America* (July 1989).

Cornell University Press

Reprinted by permission of Cornell University Press, from Luce Irigaray, *Speculum of the Other Woman*. Translated by Gillian C. Gill. Copyright © 1985 by Cornell University Press.

INTRODUCTION

What is art and how are we to understand it? These are interesting and difficult questions, for art is a fascinating and complex subject. Universal in its scope, throughout all human cultures art has taken a bewildering multiplicity of forms, in the many arts—story-telling, painting and sculpture, music, dance—and in the immense variety of forms within any art—song, instrumental music, opera, symphony, string quartet, brass ensemble, sonata, fantasy, but also ceremonial, folk, popular, dance, and classical music, and much more. It is controversial whether there is a common essence to art that pervades the many arts and genres in Western cultures, and far more controversial when we include other cultures. There have been periods when the notion of an essence to art was rejected, when emphasis in criticism was placed on understanding individual works of art, but where a general, philosophical understanding of art was held to be impossible. Yet even emphasizing the individual work of art is frequently inappropriate to nonWestern cultures, where art is often ceremonial and communal.

The selections in this collection do not take so particular and pessimistic a view toward understanding the nature of art, but compose a wide and frequently insightful array of views on the nature and importance of art in human experience. The variety is so great, however, that bewilderment may seem the most natural response. Yet the variety of different points of view is testimony not only to the imaginative inventiveness of philosophers confronted with the complexity of artistic achievements, but to the complexity and variety of artistic works themselves. Art is so difficult to understand because it has taken so many forms, because artists have utilized their powers in remarkably diverse and accomplished ways.

Art is interesting and important enough. But the question of the nature of art, particularly of the way we are to understand it, is a far more complex question than one addressing art alone. How we are to understand art raises

1

questions both about the nature of our understanding of so rich a phenomenon and about the singularity and uniqueness of that phenomenon in the context of other human achievements, even our understanding of the natural world.

A natural view is that art tells us something about the world. This is the fundamental impulse behind mimetic theory. But if so, then what art tells us is either similar to and testable against what science and philosophy tell us, leading to direct confrontation, or else is entirely different, raising possibilities of alternative realities and of alternative pathways to their realization. An equally natural view, given the remarkable emotional power of many works of art, is that art speaks to the emotions, that the purpose of art is to arouse our feelings and to give us pleasure. A difficulty here is that many of the greatest works cause us pain or make us weep, and that the gaining of pleasure, however desirable, seems to have no great importance, is at best a minor achievement.

If we believe that understanding the nature of reality is the highest achievement of which human beings are capable, then it is natural to suppose that if art is important, it offers such an understanding, or else is unimportant if it cannot do so. To understand art here is to understand something about understanding itself as well as the world surrounding us. In his dialogues, Plato sometimes suggests that art cannot give adequate knowledge of reality: therefore, art is minor, however tantalizing, and distracts us from those activities that offer adequate knowledge. In other places, in myths and stories, and in the dramatic form of his dialogues, Plato seems to suggest that the truth of poetry and myth is the highest that we can know.

If we believe that gratification and pleasure are the best we can achieve in our lives, that all our activities either are or should be devoted to gaining pleasure and avoiding pain, then art also is to be judged by the pleasures and pains it produces. Works that do not please us may be discarded. Works that fail to arouse our emotions are weak and empty.

There is another alternative, that art is neither a form of understanding competitive with science and philosophy nor a form of activity devoted to gratification. Art is rather a unique and singular form of human spirituality. If we take this view, however, we have the responsibility for explaining and making intelligible what this form of activity may be, given that it is neither a form of knowledge nor a form of action. The most famous and influential theory of the singularity and uniqueness of art is Kant's, and anyone who would attempt to understand the nature of art is forced to come to terms with Kant's theory. Kant emphasizes that art achieves a beauty that we share in common, through taste, but is not rule-governed, leading to Romanticism's view of genius. Kant also develops a theory of the sublime in art, that art can give us a sense of what surpasses any possibility of representation. Both of these are possibilities in art that Kant claims can be found neither in scientific understanding nor moral reason. It is worth remembering that Kant developed his theory of art relatively late in life, that before his *Critique of Judgment* he held essentially an anthropological position on art, maintaining that we can classify and analyze the ways in which different human beings respond to different works of art in different societies, but that there is no singular essence to art, no concepts fundamental to aesthetic experience.

Kant exerted a powerful influence on Western views of art, and until the middle of the twentieth century, art was considered neither a form of knowledge nor a form of practice. One of the most important views in this context is that art is expressive, primarily of emotion, but that expression is to be distinguished both from knowledge of emotion and from the production or elicitation of emotions in an audience. Tolstoy's status in the history of the theory of art is guaranteed by his having, virtually alone, taken a forthright and consistent position on the importance of arousing and transmitting emotions through art.

Recent writings, in both Europe and the United States, have returned to the view that art provides important truths of human experience and nature. Some of the most striking Anglo-American theories, such as Goodman's, are symbolic: artistic symbols function cognitively but with singular properties that distinguish them from symbols in science and propositional language. Continental writers share this view in part, but frequently subscribe to a profound suspicion of the limits of scientific understanding and a conviction that there are forms of knowledge that plumb the depths of the human condition and the world—forms, like art, which can tolerate an ambiguity and indeterminateness in nature and truth that are incompatible with propositional discourse. Such discussions follow a different line in Kant's *Critique of Judgment,* much closer to the sublime, concerned with the limits of representation. On such views, propositional discourse is a form of representation. Nietzsche found in Kant's sublime the idea of a truth at or beyond the limits of representation, pertaining to art. On such a view of truth, truth works not by correspondence or representation, but by opening nature to language and thought, an event much closer to art on this view than science.

The emergence of such views of the truth of art has been accompanied by a critique of the priority of the scientific world view. One of the major factors in this change of perspective is an emphasis, prominent in Wittgenstein and Heidegger, upon the social and human conditions of any human activity, including science and art. This has had profound consequences for the theory of art and the interpretation of works of art. In particular, recent philosophers have emphasized the cultural and social milieux in which works of art are produced and interpreted. Feminist writings have made enduring contributions to how we understand art and science in cultural and social terms. More recently, multicultural writings have brought claims that art and other cultural forms have been understood in Western writing to the detriment of non-Western artists. Many multicultural writers suggest that our entire understanding of art is distorted in favor of Western institutions.

Not only are works of art almost infinitely various but interpretations of works of art are also extraordinarily diverse, in many cases appearing to admit no norms and criteria that would allow us to choose among incompatible interpretations. Thus, whatever our view of the relation between art and truth, there is the further question of whether we can know what is true about works of art so that we can interpret them correctly.

The literature on criticism and interpretation of works of art turns almost entirely on this question. There are those who believe that interpretive questions are scientific and descriptive questions, that we should be able, taking the human context into account, looking to both artist and audience, to resolve all interpretive questions satisfactorily in principle. Others are more impressed by the diversity of incompatible interpretations of works of art. At the extreme, we find the plurality of interpretations inherent in art paradigmatic for all understanding, leading both to Gadamer's general hermeneutic epistemological theory, in which all knowledge is treated as analogous to the interpretation of texts, striving among divergent perspectives for an authoritative interpretation, and to Derrida's far more extreme position, in which no standards and norms can be considered authoritative. Derrida's writing manifests great suspicion of every authority, demanding an unrelenting critical alertness in interpretation and understanding. Such a view of understanding and criticism requires all the resources we can muster and invent, and demands endless reinterpretation.

Art is one of the major achievements of the human spirit. As Gadamer argues, it is our fundamental concern to understand art in terms that reflect the truly magnificent achievement it is. However, the question of the importance of art is inseparable from the question of what else is important in human experience—questions of the nature of humanity and the world. From this perspective, questions of the nature of art and of how we are to understand it are among the most important questions concerning the nature of who we are, what we are capable of, and where we dwell. That is surely a primary motive behind our concern with understanding art.

I

Historical Background

PLATO

WHITEHEAD CLAIMS, in one of his most memorable remarks, that the history of philosophy is but a series of footnotes to Plato. Overstated as this claim may be, it forcefully expresses the influence of Plato's writings upon the history of Western philosophy. What Plato has to say about art is no less important, and it is both colored and augmented by the fact that Plato was a supreme artist himself: his dialogues are incomparable dramatic achievements, and he used a great many literary devices, the most prominent of which is Platonic irony, a form unique in the history of writing in affirming and negating truth at many different levels simultaneously.

The dramatic form of Plato's dialogues, the complexity introduced by the fact that Socrates, who wrote nothing himself, was both Plato's teacher and his dramatic protagonist, makes it impossible to tell what position is Plato's own. There are critics who believe, indeed, that Plato had no authoritative position, and that exploration of the process of inquiry, of philosophical dialectic, was Plato's supreme achievement.

In connection with art, Plato presents a great number of different views, several of which are represented here. Among them, we can discern many of the central issues that involve the importance of art in the context of human life. The *Republic*, perhaps Plato's most influential work, addresses the nature of justice. Responding to the question of why a person should be just, Socrates sets himself the task of describing an ideal state. The passages from Books II and III present his view of the kinds of stories and music that should be made available to children who are being educated to defend the state and from whose ranks the philosopher king will be chosen. The entire discussion presupposes the view of art as *technē*, the employment of the best means to produce desirable ends.

Socrates' answer to the question of justice is that justice is an ideal order, in the state and in the individual soul, governed by reason. This emphasis on reason is the basis for making the philosopher ruler of the state. The question for art is what role it can have relative to an ideal governed by reason. It is a question of the truthful possibilities of art and of the corruption in the soul produced by works of art that are not grounded in reason.

There is a far more profound argument in the *Republic*, in Book X, where Socrates criticizes art for being a "mere" imitation where what we desire is knowledge of reality. In contemporary terms, this is the question of why we should waste our time with art when we could spend it pursuing knowledge of the world.

These do not complete Plato's views on art, for in other places he shows a far greater sympathy for the possibilities realizable through art. *Ion* is frequently read as supporting the view that poetry is not based on knowledge and provides no understanding. Yet it may also be read as suggesting that the understanding Ion lacks is *technē*, while he possesses truth through divine inspiration, something that far exceeds any human understanding. For as Socrates says, speaking of the Muse that inspires poets as a magnet attracts iron rings, "the poet is a light and winged and holy thing, and there is no invention in him until he has been inspired and is out of his senses." Such themes of what surpasses *technē* continue in *Symposium* and *Phaedrus*, where *erōs* and madness cross between heaven and earth, and Plato presents Socrates as drawing a magnificent and eloquent parallel between love of beauty and love of the Forms. These different views may not exhaust all the different philosophical positions taken on art, but given our concern with the nature of reality and with understanding that reality they come close to covering the question of the importance of art.

PLATO

*Republic, Books II, III, X**

BOOK II

[Steph. 376] He who is to be a really good and noble guardian of the State will require to unite in himself philosophy and spirit and swiftness and strength?

Undoubtedly.

Then we have found the desired natures; and now that we have found them, how are they to be reared and educated? Is not this an enquiry which may be expected to throw light on the greater enquiry which is our final end—How do justice and injustice grow up in States? for we do not want either to omit what is to the point or to draw out the argument to an inconvenient length.

Adeimantus thought that the enquiry would be of great service to us.

Then, I said, my dear friend, the task must not be given up, even if somewhat long.

Certainly not.

Come then, and let us pass a leisure hour in story-telling, and our story shall be the education of our heroes.

By all means.

And what shall be their education? Can we find a better than the traditional sort?—and this has two divisions, gymnastic for the body, and music for the soul.

True.

---

* Plato, *The Dialogues of Plato*, translated by Benjamin Jowett, 3rd ed. (London: Oxford University Press, 1892), pp. 639-648, 852-866. (Footnotes omitted.)

Shall we begin education with music, and go on to gymnastic afterwards?

By all means.

And when you speak of music, do you include literature or not?

I do.

And literature may be either true or false?

Yes.

[377] And the young should be trained in both kinds, and we begin with the false?

I do not understand your meaning, he said.

You know, I said, that we begin by telling children stories which, though not wholly destitute of truth, are in the main fictitious; and these stories are told them when they are not of an age to learn gymnastics.

Very true.

That was my meaning when I said that we must teach music before gymnastics.

Quite right, he said.

You know also that the beginning is the most important part of any work, especially in the case of a young and tender thing; for that is the time at which the character is being formed and the desired impression is more readily taken.

Quite true.

And shall we just carelessly allow children to hear any casual tales which may be devised by casual persons, and to receive into their minds ideas for the most part the very opposite of those which we should wish them to have when they are grown up?

We cannot.

Then the first thing will be to establish a censorship of the writers of fiction, and let the censors receive any tale of fiction which is good, and reject the bad; and we will desire mothers and nurses to tell their children the authorised ones only. Let them fashion the mind with such tales, even more fondly than they mould the body with their hands; but most of those which are now in use must be discarded.

Of what tales are you speaking? he said.

You may find a model of the lesser in the greater, I said; for they are necessarily of the same type, and there is the same spirit in both of them.

Very likely, he replied; but I do not as yet know what you would term the greater.

Those, I said, which are narrated by Homer and Hesiod, and the rest of the poets, who have ever been the great story-tellers of mankind.

But which stories do you mean, he said; and what fault do you find with them?

A fault which is most serious, I said; the fault of telling a lie, and, what is more, a bad lie.

But when is this fault committed?

Whenever an erroneous representation is made of the nature of gods and heroes,—as when a painter paints a portrait not having the shadow of a likeness to the original.

Yes, he said, that sort of thing is certainly very blameable; but what are the stories which you mean?

First of all, I said, there was that greatest of all lies, in high places, which the poet told about Uranus, and which was a bad lie too,—I mean what Hesiod says that Uranus did, and how Cronus [378] retaliated on him. The doings of Cronus, and the sufferings which in turn his son inflicted upon him, even if they were true, ought certainly not to be lightly told to young and thoughtless persons; if possible, they had better be buried in silence. But if there is an absolute necessity for their mention, a chosen few might hear them in a mystery, and they should sacrifice not a common [Eleusinian] pig, but some huge and unprocurable victim; and then the number of the hearers will be very few indeed.

Why, yes, said he, those stories are extremely objectionable.

Yes, Adeimantus, they are stories not to be repeated in our State; the young man should not be told that in committing the worst of crimes he is far from doing anything outrageous; and that even if he chastises his father when he does wrong, in whatever manner, he will only be following the example of the first and greatest among the gods.

I entirely agree with you, he said; in my opinion those stories are quite unfit to be repeated.

Neither, if we mean our future guardians to regard the habit of quarrelling among themselves as of all things the basest, should any word be said to them of the wars in heaven, and of the plots and fightings of the gods against one another, for they are not true. No, we shall never mention the battles of the giants, or let them be embroidered on garments; and we shall be silent about the innumerable other quarrels of gods and heroes with their friends and relatives. If they would only believe us we would tell them that quarrelling is unholy, and that never up to this time has there been any quarrel between citizens; this is what old men and old women should begin by telling children; and when they grow up, the poets also should be told to compose for them in a similar spirit. But the narrative of Hephaestus binding Here his mother, or how on another occasion Zeus sent him flying for taking her part when she was being beaten, and all the battles of the gods in Homer—these tales must not be admitted into our State, whether they are supposed to have an allegorical meaning or not. For a young person cannot judge what is allegorical and what is literal; anything that he receives into his mind at that age is likely to become indelible and unalterable; and therefore it is most important that the takes which the young first hear should be models of virtuous thoughts.

There you are right, he replied; but if any one asks where are such models to be found and of what tales are you speaking—how shall we answer him?

[379] I said to him, You and I, Adeimantus, at this moment are not poets, but founders of a State: now the founders of a State ought to know the general forms in which poets should cast their tales, and the limits which must be observed by them, but to make the tales is not their business.

Very true, he said; but what are these forms of theology which you mean?

Something of this kind, I replied:—God is always to be represented as he truly is, whatever be the sort of poetry, epic, lyric or tragic, in which the representation is given.

Right.

And is he not truly good? and must he not be represented as such?

Certainly.

And no good thing is hurtful?

No, indeed.

And that which is not hurtful hurts not?

Certainly not.

And that which hurts not does no evil?

No.

And can that which does no evil be a cause of evil?

Impossible.

And the good is advantageous?

Yes.

And therefore the cause of well-being?

Yes.

It follows therefore that the good is not the cause of all things, but of the good only?

Assuredly.

Then God, if he be good, is not the author of all things, as the many assert, but he is the cause of a few things only, and not of most things that occur to men. For few are the goods of human life, and many are the evils, and the good is to be attributed to God alone; of the evils the causes are to be sought elsewhere, and not in him.

That appears to me to be most true, he said.

Then we must not listen to Homer or to any other poet who is guilty of the folly of saying that two casks

Lie at the threshold of Zeus, full of lots, one of good, the other of evil lots,

and that he to whom Zeus gives a mixture of the two

Sometimes meets with evil fortune, at other times with good;

but that he to whom is given the cup of unmingled ill,

Him wild hunger drives o'er the beauteous earth.

And again—

> Zeus, who is the dispenser of good and evil to us.

And if any one asserts that the violation of oaths and treaties, which was really the work of Pandarus, was brought about by Athene and Zeus, or that the strife and contention of the gods was instigated by Themis and Zeus, he shall not have our approval; neither will we allow our young men to hear the words of Aeschylus that

> [380] God plants guilt among men when he desires utterly to destroy a house.

And if a poet writes of the sufferings of Niobe—the subject of the tragedy in which these iambic verses occur—or of the house of Pelops, or of the Trojan war or on any similar theme, either we must not permit him to say that these are the works of God, or if they are of God, he must devise some explanation of them such as we are seeking; he must say that God did what was just and right, and they were the better for being punished; but that those who are punished are miserable, and that God is the author of their misery—the poet is not to be permitted to say; though he may say that the wicked are miserable because they require to be punished, and are benefited by receiving punishment from God; but that God being good is the author of evil to any one is to be strenuously denied, and not to be said or sung or heard in verse or prose by any one whether old or young in any well-ordered commonwealth. Such a fiction is suicidal, ruinous, impious.

I agree with you, he replied, and am ready to give my assent to the law.

Let this then be one of our rules and principles concerning the gods, to which our poets and reciters will be expected to conform—that God is not the author of all things, but of good only.

That will do, he said.

And what do you think of a second principle? Shall I ask you whether God is a magician, and of a nature to appear insidiously now in one shape, and now in another—sometimes himself changing and passing into many forms, sometimes deceiving us with the semblance of such transformations; or is he one and the same immutably fixed in his own proper image?

I cannot answer you, he said, without more thought.

Well, I said; but if we suppose a change in anything, that change must be effected either by the thing itself, or by some other thing?

Most certainly.

And things which are at their best are also least liable to be altered or discomposed; for example, when healthiest and strongest, the human frame is least liable to be affected by meats and drinks, and the plant which is in the fullest vigour also suffers least from winds or the heat of the sun or any similar causes.

Of course.

[381] And will not the bravest and wisest soul be least confused or deranged by any external influence?

True.

And the same principle, as I should suppose, applies to all composite things—furniture, houses, garments: when good and well made, they are least altered by time and circumstances.

Very true.

Then everything which is good, whether made by art or nature, or both, is least liable to suffer change from without?

True.

But surely God and the things of God are in every way perfect?

Of course they are.

Then he can hardly be compelled by external influence to take many shapes?

He cannot.

But may he not change and transform himself?

Clearly, he said, that must be the case if he is changed at all.

And will he then change himself for the better and fairer, or for the worse and more unsightly?

If he change at all he can only change for the worse, for we cannot suppose him to be deficient either in virtue or beauty.

Very true, Adeimantus; but then, would any one, whether God or man, desire to make himself worse?

Impossible.

Then it is impossible that God should ever be willing to change; being, as is supposed, the fairest and best that is conceivable, every God remains absolutely and for ever in his own form.

That necessarily follows, he said, in my judgment.

Then, I said, my dear friend, let none of the poets tell us that

> The gods, taking the disguise of strangers from other lands, walk up and down cities in all sorts of forms,

and let no one slander Proteus and Thetis, neither let any one, either in tragedy or in any other kind of poetry, introduce Here disguised in the likeness of a priestess asking an alms

> For the life-giving daughters of Inachus the river of Argos;

—let us have no more lies of that sort. Neither must we have mothers under the influence of the poets scaring their children with a bad version of these myths—telling how certain gods, as they say, 'Go about by night in the likeness of so many strangers and in divers forms;' but let them take heed lest they make cowards of their children, and at the same time speak blasphemy against the gods.

Heaven forbid, he said.

But although the gods are themselves unchangeable, still by witchcraft and deception they may make us think that they appear in various forms?

Perhaps, he replied.

Well, but can you imagine that God will be willing to lie, whether in word or deed, or to put forth a phantom of himself?

[382] I cannot say, he replied.

Do you not know, I said, that the true lie, if such an expression may be allowed, is hated of gods and men?

What do you mean? he said.

I mean that no one is willingly deceived in that which is the truest and highest part of himself, or about the truest and highest matters; there, above all, he is most afraid of a lie having possession of him.

Still, he said, I do not comprehend you.

The reason is, I replied, that you attribute some profound meaning to my words; but I am only saying that deception, or being deceived or uninformed about the highest realities in the highest part of themselves, which is the soul, and in that part of them to have and to hold the lie, is what mankind least like;—that, I say, is what they utterly detest.

There is nothing more hateful to them.

And, as I was just now remarking, this ignorance in the soul of him who is deceived may be called the true lie; for the lie in words is only a kind of imitation and shadowy image of a previous affection of the soul, not pure unadulterated falsehood. Am I not right?

Perfectly right.

The true lie is hated not only by the gods, but also by men?

Yes.

Whereas the lie in words is in certain cases useful and not hateful; in dealing with enemies—that would be an instance; or again, when those whom we call our friends in a fit of madness or illusion are going to do some harm, then it is useful and is a sort of medicine or preventive; also in the tales of mythology, of which we were just now speaking—because we do not know the truth about ancient times, we make falsehood as much like truth as we can, and so turn it to account.

Very true, he said.

But can any of these reasons apply to God? Can we suppose that he is ignorant of antiquity, and therefore has recourse to invention?

That would be ridiculous, he said.

Then the lying poet has no place in our idea of God?

I should say not.

Or perhaps he may tell a lie because he is afraid of enemies?

That is inconceivable.

But he may have friends who are senseless or mad?

But no mad or senseless person can be a friend of God.

Then no motive can be imagined why God should lie?

None whatever.

Then the superhuman and divine is absolutely incapable of falsehood?

Yes.

Then is God perfectly simple and true both in word and deed; he changes not; he deceives not, either by sign or word, by dream or waking vision.

[383] Your thoughts, he said, are the reflection of my own.

You agree with me then, I said, that this is the second type or form in which we should write and speak about divine things. The gods are not magicians who transform themselves, neither do they deceive mankind in any way.

I grant that.

Then, although we are admirers of Homer, we do not admire the lying dream which Zeus sends to Agamemnon; neither will we praise the verses of Aeschylus in which Thetis says that Apollo at her nuptials

> Was celebrating in song her fair progeny whose days were to be long, and to know no sickness. And when he had spoken of my lot as in all things blessed of heaven he raised a note of triumph and cheered my soul. And I thought that the word of Phoebus, being divine and full of prophecy, would not fail. And now he himself who uttered the strain, he who was present at the banquet, and who said this—he it is who has slain my son.

These are the kind of sentiments about the gods which will arouse our anger; and he who utters them shall be refused a chorus; neither shall we allow teachers to make use of them in the instruction of the young, meaning, as we do, that our guardians, as far as men can be, should be true worshippers of the gods and like them.

I entirely agree, he said, in these principles, and promise to make them my laws.

BOOK III

[386] Such then, I said, are our principles of theology—some tales are to be told, and others are not to be told to our disciples from their youth upwards, if we mean them to honour the gods and their parents, and to value friendship with one another.

Yes; and I think that our principles are right, he said.

But if they are to be courageous, must they not learn other lessons besides these, and lessons of such a kind as will take away the fear of death? Can any man be courageous who has the fear of death in him?

Certainly not, he said.

And can he be fearless of death, or will he choose death in battle rather than defeat and slavery, who believes the world below to be real and terrible?

Impossible.

Then we must assume a control over the narrators of this class of tales as well as over the others, and beg them not simply to revile, but rather to commend the world below, intimating to them that their descriptions are untrue, and will do harm to our future warriors.

That will be our duty, he said.

Then, I said, we shall have to obliterate many obnoxious passages, beginning with the verses,

> I would rather be a serf on the land of a poor and portionless man than rule over all the dead who have come to nought.

We must also expunge the verse, which tells us how Pluto feared,

> Lest the mansions grim and squalid which the gods abhor should be seen both of mortals and immortals.

And again:—

> O heavens! verily in the house of Hades there is soul and ghostly form but no mind at all!

Again of Tiresias:—

> [To him even after death did Persephone grant mind,] that he alone should be wise; but the other souls are flitting shades.

Again:—

> The soul flying from the limbs had gone to Hades, lamenting her fate, leaving manhood and youth.

Again:—

> [387] And the soul, with shrilling cry, passed like smoke beneath the earth.

And,—

> As bats in hollow of mystic cavern, whenever any of them has dropped out of the string and falls from the rock, fly shrilling and cling to one another, so did they with shrilling cry hold together as they moved.

And we must beg Homer and the other poets not to be angry if we strike out these and similar passages, not because they are unpoetical, or unattractive to the popular ear, but because the greater the poetical charm of them, the less are they meet for the ears of boys and men who are meant to be free, and who should fear slavery more than death.

Undoubtedly.

Also we shall have to reject all the terrible and appalling names which describe the world below—Cocytus and Styx, ghosts under the earth, and sapless shades, and any similar words of which the very mention causes a shudder to pass through the inmost soul of him who hears them. I do not say that these horrible stories may not have a use of some kind; but there is a danger that the nerves of our guardians may be rendered too excitable and effeminate by them.

There is a real danger, he said.

Then we must have no more of them.

True.

Another and a nobler strain must be composed and sung by us.

Clearly.

And shall we proceed to get rid of the weepings and wailings of famous men?

They will go with the rest.

But shall we be right in getting rid of them? Reflect: our principle is that the good man will not consider death terrible to any other good man who is his comrade.

Yes; that is our principle.

And therefore he will not sorrow for his departed friend as though he had suffered anything terrible?

He will not.

Such an one, as we further maintain, is sufficient for himself and his own happiness, and therefore is least in need of other men.

True, he said.

And for this reason the loss of a son or brother, or the deprivation of fortune, is to him of all men least terrible.

Assuredly.

And therefore he will be least likely to lament, and will bear with the greatest equanimity any misfortune of this sort which may befall him.

Yes, he will feel such a misfortune far less than another.

Then we shall be right in getting rid of the lamentations of famous men, and making them over to women (and not even to women [388] who are good for anything), or to men of a baser sort, that those who are being educated by us to be the defenders of their country may scorn to do the like.

That will be very right.

Then we will once more entreat Homer and the other poets not to depict Achilles, who is the son of a goddess, first lying on his side, then on his back, and then on his face; then starting up and sailing in a frenzy along the shores of the barren sea; now taking the sooty ashes in both his hands and pouring them over his head, or weeping and wailing in the various modes which Homer has delineated. Nor should he describe Priam the kinsman of the gods as praying and beseeching,

> Rolling in the dirt, calling each man loudly by his name.

Still more earnestly will we beg of him at all events not to introduce the gods lamenting and saying,

> Alas! my misery! Alas! that I bore the bravest to my sorrow.

But if he must introduce the gods, at any rate let him not dare so completely to misrepresent the greatest of the gods, as to make him say—

> O heavens! with my eyes verily I behold a dear friend of mine chased round and round the city, and my heart is sorrowful.

Or again:—

> Woe is me that I am fated to have Sarpedon, dearest of men to me, subdued at the hands of Patroclus the son of Menoetius.

For if, my sweet Adeimantus, our youth seriously listen to such unworthy representations of the gods, instead of laughing at them as they ought, hardly will any of them deem that he himself, being but a man, can be dishonoured by similar actions; neither will he rebuke any inclination which may arise in his mind to say and do the like. And instead of having any shame or self-control, he will be always whining and lamenting on slight occasions.

Yes, he said, that is most true.

Yes, I replied; but that surely is what ought not to be, as the argument has just proved to us; and by that proof we must abide until it is disproved by a better.

It ought not to be.

Neither ought our guardians to be given to laughter. For a fit of laughter which has been indulged to excess almost always produces a violent reaction.

So I believe.

Then persons of worth, even if only mortal men, must not be represented as overcome by laughter, and still less must such a representation of the gods be allowed.

[389] Still less of the gods, as you say, he replied.

Then we shall not suffer such an expression to be used about the gods as that of Homer when he describes how

> Inextinguishable laughter arose among the blessed gods, when they saw Hephaestus bustling about the mansion.

On your views, we must not admit them.

On my views, if you like to father them on me; that we must not admit them is certain.

Again, truth should be highly valued; if, as we were saying, a lie is useless to the gods, and useful only as a medicine to men, then the use of such medicines should be restricted to physicians; private individuals have no business with them.

Clearly not, he said.

Then if any one at all is to have the privilege of lying, the rulers of the State should be the persons; and they, in their dealings either with enemies or with their own citizens, may be allowed to lie for the public good. But nobody else should meddle with anything of the kind; and although the rulers have this privilege, for a private man to lie to them in return is to be deemed a more heinous fault than for the patient or the pupil of a gymnasium not to speak the truth about his own bodily illnesses to the physician or to the trainer, or for a sailor not to tell the captain what is happening about the ship and the rest of the crew, and how things are going with himself or his fellow sailors.

Most true, he said.

If, then, the ruler catches anybody beside himself lying in the State,

Any of the craftsmen, whether he be priest or physician or carpenter,

he will punish him for introducing a practice which is equally subversive and destructive of ship or State.

Most certainly, he said, if our idea of the State is ever carried out.

In the next place our youth must be temperate?

Certainly.

Are not the chief elements of temperance, speaking generally, obedience to commanders and self-control in sensual pleasures?

True.

Then we shall approve such language as that of Diomede in Homer,

Friend, sit still and obey my word,

and the verses which follow,

The Greeks marched breathing prowess,
. . . in silent awe of their leaders,

and other sentiments of the same kind.

We shall.

What of this line,

O heavy with wine, who hast the eyes of a dog and the heart of a stag,

[390] and of the words which follow? Would you say that these, or any similar impertinences which private individuals are supposed to address to their rulers, whether in verse or prose, are well or ill spoken?

They are ill spoken.

They may very possibly afford some amusement, but they do not conduce to temperance. And therefore they are likely to do harm to our young men—you would agree with me there?

Yes.

And then, again, to make the wisest of men say that nothing in his opinion is more glorious than

> When the tables are full of bread and meat, and the cup-bearer carries round wine which he draws from the bowl and pours into the cups,

is it fit or conducive to temperance for a young man to hear such words? Or the verse

> The saddest of fates is to die and meet destiny from hunger?

What would you say again to the tale of Zeus, who, while other gods and men were asleep and he the only person awake, lay devising plans, but forgot them all in a moment through his lust, and was so completely overcome at the sight of Here that he would not even go into the hut, but wanted to lie with her on the ground, declaring that he had never been in such a state of rapture before, even when they first met one another

> Without the knowledge of their parents,

or that other tale of how Hephaestus, because of similar goings on, cast a chain around Ares and Aphrodite?

Indeed, he said, I am strongly of opinion that they ought not to hear that sort of thing.

But any deeds of endurance which are done or told by famous men, these they ought to see and hear; as, for example, what is said in the verses,

> He smote his breast, and thus reproached his heart,
> Endure, my heart; far worse hast thou endured!

Certainly, he said.

In the next place, we must not let them be receivers of gifts or lovers of money.

Certainly not.

Neither must we sing to them of

> Gifts persuading gods, and persuading reverend kings.

Neither is Phoenix, the tutor of Achilles, to be approved or deemed to have given his pupil good counsel when he told him that he should take the gifts of the Greeks and assist them; but that without a gift he should not lay aside his anger. Neither will we believe or acknowledge Achilles himself to have been such a lover of money that he took Agamemnon's gifts, or that when he had received payment he restored the dead body of Hector, but that without payment he was unwilling to do so.

[391] Undoubtedly, he said, these are not sentiments which can be approved.

Loving Homer as I do, I hardly like to say that in attributing these feelings to Achilles, or in believing that they are truly attributed to him, he is guilty of downright impiety. As little can I believe the narrative of his insolence to Apollo, where he says,

> Thou hast wronged me, O far-darter, most abominable of deities. Verily I would be even with thee, if I had only the power,

or his insubordination to the river-god, on whose divinity he is ready to lay hands; or his offering to the dead Patroclus of his own hair, which had been previously dedicated to the other river-god Spercheius, and that he actually performed this vow; or that he dragged Hector round the tomb of Patroclus, and slaughtered the captives at the pyre; of all this I cannot believe that he was guilty, any more than I can allow our citizens to believe that he, the wise Cheiron's pupil, the son of a goddess and of Peleus who was the gentlest of men and third in descent from Zeus, was so disordered in his wits as to be at one time the slave of two seemingly inconsistent passions, meanness, not untainted by avarice, combined with overweening contempt of gods and men.

You are quite right, he replied.

And let us equally refuse to believe, or allow to be repeated, the tale of Theseus son of Poseidon, or of Peirithous son of Zeus, going forth as they did to perpetrate a horrid rape; or of any other hero or son of a god daring to do such impious and dreadful things as they falsely ascribe to them in our day: and let us further compel the poets to declare either that these acts were not done by them, or that they were not the sons of gods;—both in the same breath they shall not be permitted to affirm. We will not have them trying to persuade our youth that the gods are the authors of evil, and that heroes are no better than men—sentiments which, as we were saying, are neither pious nor true, for we have already proved that evil cannot come from the gods.

Assuredly not.

And further they are likely to have a bad effect on those who hear them; for everybody will begin to excuse his own vices when he is convinced that similar wickednesses are always being perpetrated by—

> The kindred of the gods, the relatives of Zeus, whose ancestral altar, the altar of Zeus, is aloft in air on the peak of Ida,

and who have

the blood of deities yet flowing in their veins.

And therefore let us put an end to such tales, lest they engender laxity of morals among the young.

[392] By all means, he replied.

But now that we are determining what classes of subjects are or are not to be spoken of, let us see whether any have been omitted by us. The manner in which gods and demigods and heroes and the world below should be treated has been already laid down.

Very true.

And what shall we say about men? That is clearly the remaining portion of our subject.

Clearly so.

But we are not in a condition to answer this question at present, my friend.

Why not?

Because, if I am not mistaken, we shall have to say that about men poets and story-tellers are guilty of making the gravest misstatements when they tell us that wicked men are often happy, and the good miserable; and that injustice is profitable when undetected, but that justice is a man's own loss and another's gain—these things we shall forbid them to utter, and command them to sing and say the opposite.

To be sure we shall, he replied.

But if you admit that I am right in this, then I shall maintain that you have implied the principle for which we have been all along contending.

I grant the truth of your inference.

That such things are or are not to be said about men is a question which we cannot determine until we have discovered what justice is, and how naturally advantageous to the possessor, whether he seems to be just or not.

Most true, he said.

Enough of the subjects of poetry: let us now speak of the style; and when this has been considered, both matter and manner will have been completely treated.

I do not understand what you mean, said Adeimantus.

Then I must make you understand; and perhaps I may be more intelligible if I put the matter in this way. You are aware, I suppose, that all mythology and poetry is a narration of events, either past, present, or to come?

Certainly, he replied.

And narration may be either simple narration, or imitation, or a union of the two?

That again, he said, I do not quite understand.

I fear that I must be a ridiculous teacher when I have so much difficulty in making myself apprehended. Like a bad speaker, therefore, I will not take the whole of the subject, but will break a piece off in illustration of my meaning. You know the first lines of the Iliad, in which the poet says that Chryses prayed Agamemnon to release his [393] daughter, and that Agamemnon flew into a passion with him; whereupon Chryses, failing of his object, invoked the anger of the God against the Achaeans. Now as far as these lines,

> And he prayed all the Greeks, but especially the two sons of Atreus, the chiefs of the people,

the poet is speaking in his own person; he never leads us to suppose that he is any one else. But in what follows he takes the person of Chryses, and then he does all that he can to make us believe that the speaker is not Homer, but the aged priest himself. And in this double form he has cast the entire narrative of the events which occurred at Troy and in Ithaca and throughout the Odyssey.

Yes.

And a narrative it remains both in the speeches which the poet recites from time to time and in the intermediate passages?

Quite true.

But when the poet speaks in the person of another, may we not say that he assimilates his style to that of the person who, as he informs you, is going to speak?

Certainly.

And this assimilation of himself to another, either by the use of voice or gesture, is the imitation of the person whose character he assumes?

Of course.

Then in this case the narrative of the poet may be said to proceed by way of imitation?

Very true.

Or, if the poet everywhere appears and never conceals himself, then again the imitation is dropped, and his poetry becomes simple narration. However, in order that I may make my meaning quite clear, and that you may no more say, 'I don't understand,' I will show how the change might be effected. If Homer had said, 'The priest came, having his daughter's ransom in his hands, supplicating the Achaeans, and above all the kings;' and then if, instead of speaking in the person of Chryses, he had continued in his own person, the words would have been, not imitation, but simple narration. The passage would have run as follows (I am no poet, and therefore I drop the metre), 'The priest came and prayed the gods on behalf of the Greeks that they might capture Troy and return safely home, but begged that they would give him back his daughter, and take the ransom which he brought, and respect the God. Thus he spoke, and the other Greeks revered the priest and assented. But Agamemnon was wroth, and bade him depart and not come again, lest the staff and chaplets of the God should be of no avail to him—the daughter of Chryses should not be released, he said—she should grow old with him in Argos. And then he told him to go away and not to provoke him, if he intended to get home unscathed. And the old man went away in fear and silence, and, [394] when he had left the camp, he called upon Apollo by his many names, reminding him of everything which he had done pleasing to him, whether in building his temples, or in offering sacrifice, and praying that his good deeds might be returned to him, and that the Achaeans might expiate his tears by the arrows of the god,'—and so on. In this way the whole becomes simple narrative.

I understand, he said.

Or you may suppose the opposite case—that the intermediate passages are omitted, and the dialogue only left.

That also, he said, I understand; you mean, for example, as in tragedy.

You have conceived my meaning perfectly; and if I mistake not, what you failed to apprehend before is now made clear to you, that poetry and mythology are, in some cases, wholly imitative—instances of this are supplied by tragedy and comedy; there is likewise the opposite style, in which the poet is the only speaker—of this the dithyramb affords the best example; and the combination of both is found in epic, and in several other styles of poetry. Do I take you with me?

Yes, he said; I see now what you meant.

I will ask you to remember also what I began by saying, that we had done with the subject and might proceed to the style.

Yes, I remember.

In saying this, I intended to imply that we must come to an understanding about the mimetic art,—whether the poets, in narrating their stories, are to be allowed by us to imitate, and if so, whether in whole or in part, and if the latter, in what parts; or should all imitation be prohibited?

You mean, I suspect, to ask whether tragedy and comedy shall be admitted into our State?

Yes, I said; but there may be more than this in question: I really do not know as yet, but whither the argument may blow, thither we go.

And go we will, he said.

Then, Adeimantus, let me ask you whether our guardians ought to be imitators; or rather, has not this question been decided by the rule already laid down that one man can only do one thing well, and not many; and that if he attempt many, he will altogether fail of gaining much reputation in any?

Certainly.

And this is equally true of imitation; no one man can imitate many things as well as he would imitate a single one?

He cannot.

[395] Then the same person will hardly be able to play a serious part in life, and at the same time to be an imitator and imitate many other parts as well; for even when two species of imitation are nearly allied, the same persons cannot succeed in both, as, for example, the writers of tragedy and comedy—did you not just now call them imitations?

Yes, I did; and you are right in thinking that the same persons cannot succeed in both.

Any more than they can be rhapsodists and actors at once?

True.

Neither are comic and tragic actors the same; yet all these things are but imitations.

They are so.

And human nature, Adeimantus, appears to have been coined into yet smaller pieces, and to be as incapable of imitating many things well, as of performing well the actions of which the imitations are copies.

Quite true, he replied.

If then we adhere to our original notion and bear in mind that our guardians, setting aside every other business, are to dedicate themselves wholly to the maintenance of freedom in the State, making this their craft, and engaging in no work which does not bear on this end, they ought not to practise or imitate anything else; if they imitate at all, they should imitate from youth upward only those characters which are suitable to their profession—the courageous, temperate, holy, free, and the like; but they should not depict or be skilful at imitating any kind of illiberality or baseness, lest from imitation they should come to be what they imitate. Did you never observe how imitations, beginning in early youth and continuing far into life, at length grow into habits and become a second nature, affecting body, voice, and mind?

Yes, certainly, he said.

Then, I said, we will not allow those for whom we profess a care and of whom we say that they ought to be good men, to imitate a woman, whether young or old, quarrelling with her husband, or striving and vaunting against the gods in conceit of her happiness, or when she is in affliction, or sorrow, or weeping; and certainly not one who is in sickness, love, or labour.

Very right, he said.

Neither must they represent slaves, male or female, performing the offices of slaves?

They must not.

And surely not bad men, whether cowards or any others, who do the reverse of what we have just been prescribing, who scold or mock or revile one another in drink or out of drink, or who in any other manner sin against themselves and their neighbors in word or deed, as the manner of such is. Neither should they be trained [396] to imitate the action or speech of men or women who are mad or bad; for madness, like vice, is to be known but not to be practised or imitated.

Very true, he replied.

Neither may they imitate smiths or other artificers, or oarsmen, or boatswains, or the like?

How can they, he said, when they are not allowed to apply their minds to the callings of any of these?

Nor may they imitate the neighing of horses, the bellowing of bulls, the murmur of rivers and roll of the ocean, thunder, and all that sort of thing?

Nay, he said, if madness be forbidden, neither may they copy the behaviour of madmen.

You mean, I said, if I understand you aright, that there is one sort of narrative style which may be employed by a truly good man when he has anything to say, and that another sort will be used by a man of an opposite character and education.

And which are these two sorts? he asked.

Suppose, I answered, that a just and good man in the course of a narration comes on some saying or action of another good man,—I should imagine that he will like to personate him, and will not be ashamed of this sort of imitation: he will be most ready to play the part of the good man when he is acting firmly and wisely; in a less degree when he is overtaken by illness or love or drink, or has met with any other disaster. But when he comes to a character which is unworthy of him, he will not make a study of that; he will disdain such a person, and will assume his likeness, if at all, for a moment only when he is performing some good action; at other times he will be ashamed to play a part which he has never practised, nor will he like to fashion and frame himself after the baser models; he feels the employment of such an art, unless in jest, to be beneath him, and his mind revolts at it.

So I should expect, he replied.

Then he will adopt a mode of narration such as we have illustrated out of Homer, that is to say, his style will be both imitative and narrative; but there will be very little of the former, and a great deal of the latter, Do you agree?

Certainly, he said; that is the model which such a speaker must [397] necessarily take.

But there is another sort of character who will narrate anything, and, the worse he is, the more unscrupulous he will be; nothing will be too bad for him: and he will be ready to imitate anything, not as a joke, but in right good earnest, and before a large company. As I was just now saying, he will attempt to represent the roll of thunder, the noise of wind and hail, or the creaking of wheels, and pulleys, and the various sounds of flutes, pipes, trumpets, and all sorts of instruments: he will bark like a dog, bleat like a sheep, or crow like a cock; his entire art will consist in imitation of voice and gesture, and there will be very little narration.

That, he said, will be his mode of speaking.

These, then, are the two kinds of style?

Yes.

And you would agree with me in saying that one of them is simple and has but slight changes; and if the harmony and rhythm are also chosen for their simplicity, the result is that the speaker, if he speaks correctly, is always pretty much the same in style, and he will keep within the limits of a single harmony (for the changes are not great), and in like manner he will make use of nearly the same rhythm?

That is quite true, he said.

Whereas the other requires all sorts of harmonies and all sorts of rhythms, if the music and the style are to correspond, because the style has all sorts of changes.

That is also perfectly true, he replied.

And do not the two styles, or the mixture of the two, comprehend all poetry, and every form of expression in words? No one can say anything except in one or other of them or in both together.

They include all, he said.

And shall we receive into our State all the three styles, or one only of the two unmixed styles? or would you include the mixed?

I should prefer only to admit the pure imitator of virtue.

Yes, I said, Adeimantus; but the mixed style is also very charming: and indeed the pantomimic, which is the opposite of the one chosen by you, is the most popular style with children and their attendants, and with the world in general.

I do not deny it.

But I suppose you would argue that such a style is unsuitable to our State, in which human nature is not twofold or manifold, for one man plays one part only?

Yes; quite unsuitable.

And this is the reason why in our State, and in our State only, we shall find a shoemaker to be a shoemaker and not a pilot also, and a husbandman to be a husbandman and not a dicast also, and a soldier a soldier and not a trader also, and the same throughout?

True, he said.

[398] And therefore when any one of these pantomimic gentlemen, who are so clever that they can imitate anything, comes to us, and makes a proposal to exhibit himself and his poetry, we will fall down and worship him as a sweet and holy and wonderful being; but we must also inform him that in our State such as he are not permitted to exist; the law will not allow them. And so when we have anointed him with myrrh, and set a garland of wool upon his head, we shall send him away to another city. For we mean to employ for our souls' health the rougher and severer poet or storyteller, who will imitate the style of the virtuous only, and will follow those models which we prescribed at first when we began the education of our soldiers.

We certainly will, he said, if we have the power.

Then now, my friend, I said, that part of music or literary education which relates to the story or myth may be considered to be finished; for the matter and manner have both been discussed.

I think so too, he said.

Next in order will follow melody and song.

That is obvious.

Every one can see already what we ought to say about them, if we are able to be consistent with ourselves.

I fear, said Glaucon, laughing, that the word 'every one' hardly includes me, for I cannot at the moment say what they should be; though I may guess.

At any rate you can tell that a song or ode has three parts—the words, the melody, and the rhythm; that degree of knowledge I may presuppose?

Yes, he said; so much as that you may.

And as for the words, there will surely be no difference between words which are and which are not set to music; both will conform to the same laws, and these have been already determined by us?

Yes.

And the melody and rhythm will depend upon the words?

Certainly.

We were saying, when we spoke of the subject-matter, that we had no need of lamentations and strains of sorrow?

True.

And which are the harmonies expressive of sorrow? You are musical, and can tell me.

The harmonies which you mean are the mixed or tenor Lydian, and the full-toned or bass Lydian, and such like.

These then, I said, must be banished; even to women who have a character to maintain they are of no use, and much less to men.

Certainly.

In the next place, drunkenness and softness and indolence are utterly unbecoming the character of our guardians.

Utterly unbecoming.

And which are the soft or drinking harmonies?

[399] The Ionian, he replied, and the Lydian; they are termed 'relaxed.'

Well, and are these of any military use?

Quite the reverse, he replied; and if so the Dorian and the Phrygian are the only ones which you have left.

I answered: Of the harmonies I know nothing, but I want to have one warlike, to sound the note or accent which a brave man utters in the hour of danger and stern resolve, or when his cause is failing, and he is going to wounds or death or is overtaken by some other evil, and at every such crisis meets the blows of fortune with firm step and a determination to endure; and another to be used by him in times of peace and freedom of action, when there is no pressure of necessity, and he is seeking to persuade God by prayer, or man by instruction and admonition, or on the other hand, when he is expressing his willingness to yield to persuasion or entreaty or admonition, and which represents him when by prudent conduct he has attained his end, not carried away by his success, but acting moderately and wisely under the circumstances, and acquiescing in the event. These two harmonies I ask you to leave; the strain of necessity and the strain of freedom, the strain of the unfortunate and the strain of the fortunate, the strain of courage, and the strain of temperance; these, I say, leave.

And these, he replied, are the Dorian and Phrygian harmonies of which I was just now speaking.

Then, I said, if these and these only are to be used in our songs and melodies, we shall not want multiplicity of notes or a panharmonic scale?

I suppose not.

Then we shall not maintain the artificers of lyres with three corners and complex scales, or the makers of any other many-stringed curiously-harmonised instruments?

Certainly not.

But what do you say to flute-makers and flute-players? Would you admit them into our State when you reflect that in this composite use of harmony the flute is worse than all the stringed instruments put together; even the panharmonic music is only an imitation of the flute?

Clearly not.

There remain then only the lyre and the harp for use in the city, and the shepherds may have a pipe in the country.

That is surely the conclusion to be drawn from the argument.

The preferring of Apollo and his instruments to Marsyas and his instruments is not at all strange, I said.

Not at all, he replied.

And so, by the dog of Egypt, we have been unconsciously purging the State, which not long ago we termed luxurious.

And we have done wisely, he replied.

Then let us now finish the purgation, I said. Next in order to harmonies, rhythms will naturally follow, and they should be subject to the same rules, for we ought not to seek out complex systems of metre, or metres of every kind, but rather to discover what rhythms are the expressions of a courageous and harmonious life; [400] and when we have found them, we shall adapt the foot and the melody to words having a like spirit, not the words to the foot and melody. To say what these rhythms are will be your duty—you must teach me them, as you have already taught me the harmonies.

But, indeed, he replied, I cannot tell you. I only know that there are some three principles of rhythm out of which metrical systems are framed, just as in sounds there are four notes out of which all the harmonies are composed: that is an observation which I have made. But of what sort of lives they are severally the imitations I am unable to say.

Then, I said, we must take Damon into our counsels; and he will tell us what rhythms are expressive of meanness, or insolence, or fury, or other unworthiness, and what are to be reserved for the expression of opposite feelings. And I think that I have an indistinct recollection of his mentioning a complex Cretic rhythm; also a dactylic or heroic, and he arranged them in some manner which I do not quite understand, making the rhythms equal in the rise and fall of the foot, long and short alternating; and, unless I am mistaken, he spoke of an iambic as well as of a trochaic rhythm, and assigned to them short and long quantities. Also in some cases he appeared to praise or censure the movement of the foot quite as much as the rhythm; or perhaps a combination of the two; for I am not certain what he meant.

These matters, however, as I was saying, had better be referred to Damon himself, for the analysis of the subject would be difficult, you know?

Rather so, I should say.

But there is no difficulty in seeing that grace or the absence of grace is an effect of good or bad rhythm.

None at all.

And also that good and bad rhythm naturally assimilate to a good and bad style; and that harmony and discord in like manner follow style; for our principle is that rhythm and harmony are regulated by the words, and not the words by them.

Just so, he said, they should follow the words.

And will not the words and the character of the style depend on the temper of the soul?

Yes.

And everything else on the style?

Yes.

Then beauty of style and harmony and grace and good rhythm depend on simplicity,—I mean the true simplicity of a rightly and nobly ordered mind and character, not that other simplicity which is only an euphemism for folly?

Very true, he replied.

And if our youth are to do their work in life, must they not make these graces and harmonies their perpetual aim?

They must.

[401] And surely the art of the painter and every other creative and constructive art are full of them,—weaving, embroidery, architecture, and every kind of manufacture; also nature, animal and vegetable,—in all of them there is grace or the absence of grace. And ugliness and discord and inharmonious motion are nearly allied to ill words and ill nature, as grace and harmony are the twin sisters of goodness and virtue and bear their likeness.

That is quite true, he said.

But shall our superintendence go no further, and are the poets only to be required by us to express the image of the good in their works, on pain, if they do anything else, of expulsion from our State? Or is the same control to be extended to other artists, and are they also to be prohibited from exhibiting the opposite forms of vice and intemperance and meanness and indecency in sculpture and building and the other creative arts; and is he who cannot conform to this rule of ours to be prevented from practising his art in our State, lest the taste of our citizens be corrupted by him? We would not have our guardians grown up amid images of moral deformity, as in some noxious pasture, and there browse and feed upon many a baneful herb and flower day by day, little by little, until they silently gather a festering mass of corruption in their own soul. Let our artists rather be those who are gifted to discern the true nature of the beautiful and graceful; then will our youth dwell in a land of health, amid fair sights and sounds, and receive the good in everything; and beauty, the effluence of fair works, shall flow into the eye and ear, like a health-giving breeze from a purer region, and insensibly draw the soul from earliest years into likeness and sympathy with the beauty of reason.

There can be no nobler training than that, he replied.

And therefore, I said, Glaucon, musical training is a more potent instrument than any other, because rhythm and harmony find their way into the inward places of the soul, on which they mightily fasten, imparting grace, and making the soul of him who is rightly educated graceful, or of him who is ill-educated ungraceful; and also because he who has received this true education of the inner being will most shrewdly perceive omissions or faults in art and nature, and with a true taste, while he praises and rejoices over [402] and receives into his soul the good, and becomes noble and good, he will justly blame and hate the bad, now in the days of his youth, even before he is able to know the reason why; and when reason comes he will recognise and salute the friend with whom his education has made him long familiar.

Yes, he said, I quite agree with you in thinking that our youth should be trained in music and on the grounds which you mention. . . .

BOOK X

Of the many excellences which I perceive in the order of our [595] State, there is none which upon reflection pleases me better than the rule about poetry.

To what do you refer?

To the rejection of imitative poetry, which certainly ought not to be received; as I see far more clearly now that the parts of the soul have been distinguished.

What do you mean?

Speaking in confidence, for I should not like to have my words repeated to the tragedians and the rest of the imitative tribe—but I do not mind saying to you, that all poetical imitations are ruinous to the understanding of the hearers, and that the knowledge of their true nature is the only antidote to them.

Explain the purport of your remark.

Well, I will tell you, although I have always from my earliest youth had an awe and love of Homer, which even now makes the words falter on my lips, for he is the great captain and teacher of the whole of that charming tragic company; but a man is not to be reverenced more than the truth, and therefore I will speak out.

Very good, he said.

Listen to me then, or rather, answer me.

Put your question.

Can you tell me what imitation is? for I really do not know.

A likely thing, then, that I should know.

[596] Why not? for the duller eye may often see a thing sooner than the keener.

Very true, he said; but in your presence, even if I had any faint notion, I could not muster courage to utter it. Will you enquire yourself?

Well then, shall we begin the enquiry in our usual manner: Whenever a number of individuals have a common name, we assume them to have also a corresponding idea or form:—do you understand me?

I do.

Let us take any common instance; there are beds and tables in the world—plenty of them, are there not?

Yes.

But there are only two ideas or forms of them—one the idea of a bed, the other of a table.

True.

And the maker of either of them makes a bed or he makes a table for our use, in accordance with the idea—that is our way of speaking in this and similar instances—but no artificer makes the ideas themselves: how could he?

Impossible.

And there is another artist,—I should like to know what you would say of him.

Who is he?

One who is the maker of all the works of all other workmen.

What an extraordinary man!

Wait a little, and there will be more reason for your saying so. For this is he who is able to make not only vessels of every kind, but plants and animals, himself and all other things—the earth and heaven, and the things which are in heaven or under the earth; he makes the gods also.

He must be a wizard and no mistake.

Oh! you are incredulous, are you? Do you mean that there is no such maker or creator, or that in one sense there might be a maker of all these things but in another not? Do you see that there is a way in which you could make them all yourself?

What way?

An easy way enough; or rather, there are many ways in which the feat might be quickly and easily accomplished, none quicker than that of turning a mirror round and round—you would soon enough make the sun and the heavens, and the earth and yourself, and other animals and plants, and all the other things of which we were just now speaking, in the mirror.

Yes, he said; but they would be appearances only.

Very good, I said, you are coming to the point now. And the painter too is, as I conceive, just such another—a creator of appearances, is he not?

Of course.

But then I suppose you will say that what he creates is untrue. And yet there is a sense in which the painter also creates a bed?

Yes, he said, but not a real bed.

[597] And what of the maker of the bed? were you not saying that he too makes, not the idea which, according to our view, is the essence of the bed, but only a particular bed?

Yes, I did.

Then if he does not make that which exists he cannot make true existence, but only some semblance of existence; and if any one were to say that the work of the maker of the bed, or of any other workman, has real existence, he could hardly be supposed to be speaking the truth.

At any rate, he replied, philosophers would say that he was not speaking the truth.

No wonder, then, that his work too is an indistinct expression of truth.

No wonder.

Suppose now that by the light of the examples just offered we enquire who this imitator is?

If you please.

Well then, here are three beds: one existing in nature, which is made by God, as I think that we may say—for no one else can be the maker?

No.

There is another which is the work of the carpenter?

Yes.

And the work of the painter is a third?

Yes.

Beds, then, are of three kinds, and there are three artists who superintend them: God, the maker of the bed, and the painter?

Yes, there are three of them.

God, whether from choice or from necessity, made one bed in nature and one only; two or more such ideal beds neither ever have been nor ever will be made by God.

Why is that?

Because even if He had made but two, a third would still appear behind them which both of them would have for their idea, and that would be the ideal bed and not the two others.

Very true, he said.

God knew this, and He desired to be the real maker of a real bed, not a particular maker of a particular bed, and therefore He created a bed which is essentially and by nature one only.

So we believe.

Shall we, then, speak of Him as the natural author or maker of the bed?

Yes, he replied; inasmuch as by the natural process of creation He is the author of this and of all other things.

And what shall we say of the carpenter—is not he also the maker of the bed?

Yes.

But would you call the painter a creator and maker?

Certainly not.

Yet if he is not the maker, what is he in relation to the bed?

I think, he said, that we may fairly designate him as the imitator of that which the others make.

Good, I said; then you call him who is third in the descent from nature an imitator?

Certainly, he said.

And the tragic poet is an imitator, and therefore, like all other imitators, he is thrice removed from the king and from the truth?

That appears to be so.

Then about the imitator we are agreed. And what about the painter?—I would like to know whether he may be thought to [598] imitate that which originally exists in nature, or only the creations of artists?

The latter.

As they are or as they appear? you have still to determine this.

What do you mean?

I mean, that you may look at a bed from different points of view, obliquely or directly or from any other point of view, and the bed will appear different, but there is no difference in reality. And the same of all things.

Yes, he said, the difference is only apparent.

Now let me ask you another question: Which is the art of painting designed to be—an imitation of things as they are, or as they appear—of appearance or of reality?

Of appearance.

Then the imitator, I said, is a long way off the truth, and can do all things because he lightly touches on a small part of them, and that part an image. For example: A painter will paint a cobbler, carpenter, or any other artist, though he knows nothing of their arts; and, if he is a good artist, he may deceive children or simple persons, when he shows them his picture of a carpenter from a distance, and they will fancy that they are looking at a real carpenter.

Certainly.

And whenever any one informs us that he has found a man who knows all the arts, and all things else that anybody knows, and every single thing with a higher degree of accuracy than any other man—whoever tells us this, I think that we can only imagine him to be a simple creature who is likely to have been deceived by some wizard or actor whom he met, and whom he thought all-knowing, because he himself was unable to analyse the nature of knowledge and ignorance and imitation.

Most true.

And so, when we hear persons saying that the tragedians, and Homer, who is at their head, know all the arts and all things human, virtue as well as vice, and divine things too, for that the good poet cannot compose well unless he knows his subject, and that he who has not this knowledge can never be a poet, we ought to consider whether here also there may not be a similar illusion. Perhaps they may have come across imitators and been deceived by them; they may not have remembered when they saw their works that these were but imitations thrice removed from the [599] truth, and could easily be made without any knowledge of the truth, because they are appearances only and not realities? Or, after all, they may be in the right, and poets do really know the things about which they seem to the many to speak so well?

The question, he said, should by all means be considered.

Now do you suppose that if a person were able to make the original as well as the image, he would seriously devote himself to the image-making branch? Would he allow imitation to be the ruling principle of his life, as if he had nothing higher in him?

I should say not.

The real artist, who knew what he was imitating, would be interested in realities and not in imitations; and would desire to leave as memorials of himself works many and fair; and, instead of being the author of encomiums, he would prefer to be the theme of them.

Yes, he said, that would be to him a course of much greater honor and profit.

Then, I said, we must put a question to Homer; not about medicine, or any of the arts to which his poems only incidentally refer: we are not going to ask him, or any other poet, whether he has cured patients like Asclepius, or left behind him a school of medicine such as the Asclepiads were, or whether he only talks about medicine and other arts at second-hand; but we have a right to know respecting military tactics, politics, education, which are the chiefest and noblest subjects of his poems, and we may fairly ask him about them. 'Friend Homer,' then we say to him, 'if you are only in the second remove from truth in what you say of virtue, and not in the third—not an image maker or imitator—and if you are able to discern what pursuits make men better or worse in private or public life, tell us what State was ever better governed by your help? The good order of Lacedaemon is due to Lycurgus, and many other cities great and small have been similarly benefited by others; but who says that you have been a good legislator to them and have done them any good? Italy and Sicily boast of Charondas, and there is Solon who is renowned among us; but what city has anything to say about you?' Is there any city which he might name?

I think not, said Glaucon; not even the Homerids themselves pretend that he was a legislator.

[600] Well, but is there any war on record which was carried on successfully by him, or aided by his counsels, when he was alive?

There is not.

Or is there any invention of his, applicable to the arts or to human life, such as Thales the Milesian or Anacharsis the Scythian, and other ingenious men have conceived, which is attributed to him?

There is absolutely nothing of the kind.

But, if Homer never did any public service, was he privately a guide or teacher of any? Had he in his lifetime friends who loved to associate with him, and who handed down to posterity an Homeric way of life, such as was established by Pythagoras who was so greatly beloved for his wisdom, and whose followers are to this day quite celebrated for the order which was named after him?

Nothing of the kind is recorded of him. For surely, Socrates, Creophylus, the companion of Homer, that child of flesh, whose name always makes us laugh, might be more justly ridiculed for his stupidity, if, as is said, Homer was greatly neglected by him and others in his own day when he was alive?

Yes, I replied, that is the tradition. But can you imagine, Glaucon, that if Homer had really been able to educate and improve mankind—if he had possessed knowledge and not been a mere imitator—can you imagine, I say, that he would not have had many followers, and been honoured and loved by them? Protagoras of Abdera, and Prodicus of Ceos, and a host of others, have only to whisper to their contemporaries: 'You will never be able to manage either your own house or your own State until you appoint us to be your ministers of education'—and this ingenious device of theirs has such an effect in making men love them that their companions all but carry them about on their shoulders. And is it conceivable that the contemporaries of Homer, or again of Hesiod, would have allowed either of them to go about as rhapsodists, if they had really been able to make mankind virtuous? Would they not have been as unwilling to part with them as with gold, and have compelled them to stay at home with them? Or, if the master would not stay, then the disciples would have followed him about everywhere, until they had got education enough?

Yes, Socrates, that, I think, is quite true.

Then must we not infer that all these poetical individuals, beginning with Homer, are only imitators; they copy images of virtue [601] and the like, but the truth they never reach? The poet is like a painter who, as we have already observed, will make a likeness of a cobbler though he understands nothing of cobbling; and his picture is good enough for those who know no more than he does, and judge only by colours and figures.

Quite so.

In like manner the poet with his words and phrases may be said to lay on the colours of the several arts, himself understanding their nature only enough to imitate them; and other people, who are as ignorant as he is, and judge only from his words, imagine that if he speaks of cobbling, or of military tactics, or of anything else, in metre and harmony and rhythm, he speaks very well—such is the sweet influence which melody and rhythm by nature have. And I think that you must have observed again and again what a poor appearance the tales of poets make when stripped of the colours which music puts upon them, and recited in simple prose.

Yes, he said.

They are like faces which were never really beautiful, but only blooming; and now the bloom of youth has passed away from them?

Exactly.

Here is another point: The imitator or maker of the image knows nothing of true existence; he knows appearances only. Am I not right?

Yes.

Then let us have a clear understanding, and not be satisfied with half an explanation.

Proceed.

Of the painter we say that he will paint reins, and he will paint a bit?

Yes.

And the worker in leather and brass will make them?

Certainly.

But does the painter know the right form of the bit and reins? Nay, hardly even the workers in brass and leather who make them; only the horseman who knows how to use them—he knows their right form.

Most true.

And may we not say the same of all things?

What?

That there are three arts which are concerned with all things: one which uses, another which makes, a third which imitates them?

Yes.

And the excellence or beauty or truth of every structure, animate or inanimate, and of every action of man, is relative to the use for which nature or the artist has intended them.

True.

Then the user of them must have the greatest experience of them, and he must indicate to the maker the good or bad qualities which develop themselves in use; for example, the flute-player will tell the flute-maker which of his flutes is satisfactory to the performer; he will tell him how he ought to make them, and the other will attend to his instructions?

Of course.

The one knows and therefore speaks with authority about the goodness and badness of flutes, while the other, confiding in him, will do what he is told by him?

True.

The instrument is the same, but about the excellence or badness of it the maker will only attain to a correct belief; and this he will gain from him who knows, by talking to him and being compelled to hear what he has to say, whereas the user will have knowledge. [602]

True.

But will the imitator have either? Will he know from use whether or no his drawing is correct or beautiful? or will he have right opinion from being compelled to associate with another who knows and gives him instructions about what he should draw?

Neither.

Then he will no more have true opinion than he will have knowledge about the goodness or badness of his imitations?

I suppose not.

The imitative artist will be in a brilliant state of intelligence about his own creations?

Nay, very much the reverse.

And still he will go on imitating without knowing what makes a thing good or bad, and may be expected therefore to imitate only that which appears to be good to the ignorant multitude?

Just so.

Thus far then we are pretty well agreed that the imitator has no knowledge worth mentioning of what he imitates. Imitation is only a kind of play or sport, and the tragic poets, whether they write in Iambic or in Heroic verse, are imitators in the highest degree?

Very true.

And now tell me, I conjure you, has not imitation been shown by us to be concerned with that which is thrice removed from the truth?

Certainly.

And what is the faculty in man to which imitation is addressed?

What do you mean?

I will explain: The body which is large when seen near, appears small when seen at a distance?

True.

And the same object appears straight when looked at out of the water, and crooked when in the water; and the concave becomes convex, owing to the illusion about colours to which the sight is liable. Thus every sort of confusion is revealed within us; and this is that weakness of the human mind on which the art of conjuring and of deceiving by light and shadow and other ingenious devices imposes, having an effect upon us like magic.

True.

And the arts of measuring and numbering and weighing come to the rescue of the human understanding—there is the beauty of them—and the apparent greater or less, or more or heavier, no longer have the mastery over us, but give way before calculation and measure and weight?

Most true.

And this, surely, must be the work of the calculating and rational principle in the soul?

To be sure.

And when this principle measures and certifies that some things are equal, or that some are greater or less than others, there occurs an apparent contradiction?

True.

But were we not saying that such a contradiction is impossible—[603] the same faculty cannot have contrary opinions at the same time about the same thing?

Very true.

Then that part of the soul which has an opinion contrary to measure is not the same with that which has an opinion in accordance with measure?

True.

And the better part of the soul is likely to be that which trusts to measure and calculation?

Certainly.

And that which is opposed to them is one of the inferior principles of the soul?

No doubt.

This was the conclusion at which I was seeking to arrive when I said that painting or drawing, and imitation in general, when doing their own proper work, are far removed from truth, and the companions and friends and associates of a principle within us which is equally removed from reason, and that they have no true or healthy aim.

Exactly.

The imitative art is an inferior who marries an inferior, and has inferior offspring.

Very true.

And is this confined to the sight only, or does it extend to the hearing also, relating in fact to what we term poetry?

Probably the same would be true of poetry.

Do not rely, I said, on a probability derived from the analogy of painting; but let us examine further and see whether the faculty with which poetical imitation is concerned is good or bad.

By all means.

We may state the question thus:—Imitation imitates the actions of men, whether voluntary or involuntary, on which, as they imagine, a good or bad result has ensued, and they rejoice or sorrow accordingly. Is there anything more?

No, there is nothing else.

But in all this variety of circumstances is the man at unity with himself— or rather, as in the instance of sight there was confusion and opposition in his opinions about the same things, so here also is there not strife and inconsistency in his life? Though I need hardly raise the question again, for I remember that all this has been already admitted; and the soul has been acknowledged by us to be full of these and ten thousand similar oppositions occurring at the same moment?

And we were right, he said.

Yes, I said, thus far we were right; but there was an omission which must now be supplied.

What was the omission?

Were we not saying that a good man, who has the misfortune to lose his son or anything else which is most dear to him, will bear the loss with more equanimity than another?

Yes.

But will he have no sorrow, or shall we say that although he cannot help sorrowing, he will moderate his sorrow?

The latter, he said, is the truer statement.

[604] Tell me: will he be more likely to struggle and hold out against his sorrow when he is seen by his equals, or when he is alone?

It will make a great difference whether he is seen or not.

When he is by himself he will not mind saying or doing many things which he would be ashamed of any one hearing or seeing him do?

True.

There is a principle of law and reason in him which bids him resist, as well as a feeling of his misfortune which is forcing him to indulge his sorrow?

True.

But when a man is drawn in two opposite directions, to and from the same object, this, as we affirm, necessarily implies two distinct principles in him?

Certainly.

One of them is ready to follow the guidance of the law?

How do you mean?

The law would say that to be patient under suffering is best, and that we should not give way to impatience, as there is no knowing whether such things are good or evil; and nothing is gained by impatience; also, because no human thing is of serious importance, and grief stands in the way of that which at the moment is most required.

What is most required? he asked.

That we should take counsel about what has happened, and when the dice have been thrown order our affairs in the way which reason deems best; not, like children who have had a fall, keeping hold of the part struck and wasting time in setting up a howl, but always accustoming the soul forthwith to apply a remedy, raising up that which is sickly and fallen, banishing the cry of sorrow by the healing art.

Yes, he said, that is the true way of meeting the attacks of fortune.

Yes, I said; and the higher principle is ready to follow this suggestion of reason?

Clearly.

And the other principle, which inclines us to recollection of our troubles and to lamentation, and can never have enough of them, we may call irrational, useless, and cowardly?

Indeed, we may.

And does not the latter—I mean the rebellious principle—furnish a great variety of materials for imitation? Whereas the wise and calm temperament, being always nearly equable, is not easy to imitate or to appreciate when imitated, especially at a public festival when a promiscuous crowd is assembled in a theatre. For the feeling represented is one to which they are strangers.

Certainly.

[605] Then the imitative poet who aims at being popular is not by nature made, nor is his art intended, to please or to affect the rational principle in the soul; but he will prefer the passionate and fitful temper, which is easily imitated?

Clearly.

And now we may fairly take him and place him by the side of the painter, for he is like him in two ways: first, inasmuch as his creations have an inferior degree of truth—in this, I say, he is like him; and he is also like him in being concerned with an inferior part of the soul; and therefore we shall be right in refusing to admit him into a well-ordered State, because he awakens and nourishes and strengthens the feelings and impairs the reason. As in a city when the evil are permitted to have authority and the good are put out of the way, so in the soul of man, as we maintain, the imitative poet implants an evil constitution, for he indulges the irrational nature which has no discernment of greater and less, but thinks the same thing at one time great and at another small—he is a manufacturer of images and is very far removed from the true.

Exactly.

But we have not yet brought forward the heaviest count in our accusation:—the power which poetry has of harming even the good (and there are very few who are not harmed), is surely an awful thing?

Yes, certainly, if the effect is what you say.

Hear and judge: The best of us, as I conceive, when we listen to a passage of Homer, or one of the tragedians, in which he represents some pitiful hero who is drawling out his sorrows in a long oration, or weeping, and smiting his breast—the best of us, you know, delight in giving way to sympathy, and are in raptures at the excellence of the poet who stirs our feelings most.

Yes, of course I know.

But when any sorrow of our own happens to us, then you may observe that we pride ourselves on the opposite quality—we would fain be quiet and patient; this is the manly part, and the other which delighted us in the recitation is now deemed to be the part of a woman.

Very true, he said.

Now can we be right in praising and admiring another who is doing that which any one of us would abominate and be ashamed of in his own person?

No, he said, that is certainly not reasonable.

[606] Nay, I said, quite reasonable from one point of view.

What point of view?

If you consider, I said, that when in misfortune we feel a natural hunger and desire to relieve our sorrow by weeping and lamentation, and that this feeling which is kept under control in our own calamities is satisfied and delighted by the poets;—the better nature in each of us, not having been sufficiently trained by reason or habit, allows the sympathetic element to break loose because the sorrow is another's; and the spectator fancies that there can be no disgrace to himself in praising and pitying any one who comes telling him what a good man he is, and making a fuss about his troubles; he thinks that the pleasure is a gain, and why should he be supercilious and lose this and the poem too? Few persons ever reflect, as I should imagine, that from the evil of other men something of evil is communicated to themselves. And so the feeling of sorrow which has gathered strength at the sight of the misfortunes of others is with difficulty repressed in our own.

How very true!

And does not the same hold also of the ridiculous? There are jests which you would be ashamed to make yourself, and yet on the comic stage, or indeed in private, when you hear them, you are greatly amused by them, and are not at all disgusted at their unseemliness;—the case of pity is repeated;—there is a principle in human nature which is disposed to raise a laugh, and this which you once restrained by reason, because you were afraid of being thought a buffoon, is now let out again; and having stimulated the risible faculty at the theatre, you are betrayed unconsciously to yourself into playing the comic poet at home.

Quite true, he said.

And the same may be said of lust and anger and all the other affections, of desire and pain and pleasure, which are held to be inseparable from every action—in all of them poetry feeds and waters the passions instead of drying them up; she lets them rule, although they ought to be controlled, if mankind are ever to increase in happiness and virtue.

I cannot deny it.

Therefore, Glaucon, I said, whenever you meet with any of the eulogists of Homer declaring that he has been the educator of Hellas, and that he is profitable for education and for the ordering of human things, and that you should take him up again and again [607] and get to know him and regulate your whole life according to him, we may love and honour those who say these things—they are excellent people, as far as their lights extend; and we are ready to acknowledge that Homer is the greatest of poets and first of tragedy writers; but we must remain firm in our conviction that hymns to the gods and praises of famous men are the only poetry which ought to be admitted into our State. For if you go beyond this and allow the honeyed muse to enter, either in epic or lyric verse, not law and the reason of mankind, which by common consent have ever been deemed best, but pleasure and pain will be the rulers in our State.

That is most true, he said.

And now since we have reverted to the subject of poetry, let this our defence serve to show the reasonableness of our former judgment in sending away out of our State an art having the tendencies which we have described; for reason constrained us. But that she may not impute to us any harshness or want of politeness, let us tell her that there is an ancient quarrel between philosophy and poetry; of which there are many proofs, such as the saying of 'the yelping hound howling at her lord,' or of one 'mighty in the vain talk of fools,' and 'the mob of sages circumventing Zeus,' and the 'subtle thinkers who are beggars after all'; and there are innumerable other signs of ancient enmity between them. Notwithstanding this, let us assure our sweet friend and the sister arts of imitation, that if she will only prove her title to exist in a well-ordered State we shall be delighted to receive her—we are very conscious of her charms; but we may not on that account betray the truth. I dare say, Glaucon, that you are as much charmed by her as I am, especially when she appears in Homer?

Yes, indeed, I am greatly charmed.

Shall I propose, then, that she be allowed to return from exile, but upon this condition only—that she makes a defence of herself in lyrical or some other metre?

Certainly.

And we may further grant to those of her defenders who are lovers of poetry and yet not poets the permission to speak in prose on her behalf: let them show not only that she is pleasant but also useful to States and to human life, and we will listen in a kindly spirit; for if this can be proved we shall surely be the gainers—I mean, if there is a use in poetry as well as a delight?

Certainly, he said, we shall be the gainers.

If her defence fails, then, my dear friend, like other persons who are enamoured of something, but put a restraint upon themselves when they think their desires are opposed to their interests, so too must we after the manner of lovers give her up, though not without a struggle. We too are inspired by that love of poetry which the education of noble [608] States has implanted in us, and therefore we would have her appear at her best and truest; but so long as she is unable to make good her defence, this argument of ours shall be a charm to us, which we will repeat to ourselves while we listen to her strains; that we may not fall away into the childish love of her which captivates the many. At all events we are well aware that poetry being such as we have described is not to be regarded seriously as attaining to the truth; and he who listens to her, fearing for the safety of the city which is within him, should be on his guard against her seductions and make our words his law.

PLATO

Ion *

[530] *Socrates.* Welcome, Ion. Are you from your native city of Ephesus?

Ion. No, Socrates; but from Epidaurus, where I attended the festival of Asclepius.

Soc. And do the Epidaurians have contests of rhapsodes at the festival?

Ion. O yes; and all sorts of musical performers.

Soc. And were you one of the competitors—and did you succeed?

Ion. I obtained the first prize of all, Socrates.

Soc. Well done; and I hope that you will do the same for us at the Panathenaea.

Ion. And I will, please heaven.

Soc. I often envy the profession of a rhapsode, Ion; for you have always to wear fine clothes, and to look as beautiful as you can is a part of your art. Then, again, you are obliged to be continually in the company of many good poets; and especially of Homer, who is the best and most divine of them; and to understand him, and not merely learn his words by rote, is a thing greatly to be envied. And no man can be a rhapsode who does not understand the meaning of the poet. For the rhapsode ought to interpret the mind of the poet to his hearers, but how can he interpret him well unless he knows what he means? All this is greatly to be envied.

Ion. Very true, Socrates; interpretation has certainly been the most laborious part of my art; and I believe myself able to speak about Homer better than any man; and that neither Metrodorus of Lampsacus, nor Stesimbrotus

* Plato, *The Dialogues of Plato*, translated by Benjamin Jowett, 3rd ed. (London: Oxford University Press, 1892), pp. 285-297. (Footnotes omitted.)

of Thasos, nor Glaucon, nor any one else who ever was, had as good ideas about Homer as I have, or as many.

Soc. I am glad to hear you say so, Ion; I see that you will not refuse to acquaint me with them.

Ion. Certainly, Socrates; and you really ought to hear how exquisitely I render Homer. I think that the Homeridae should give me a golden crown.

Soc. I shall take an opportunity of hearing your embellishments of him at some other time. But just now I should like to ask [531] you a question: Does your art extend to Hesiod and Archilochus, or to Homer only?

Ion. To Homer only; he is in himself quite enough.

Soc. Are there any things about which Homer and Hesiod agree?

Ion. Yes; in my opinion there are a good many.

Soc. And can you interpret better what Homer says, or what Hesiod says, about these matters in which they agree?

Ion. I can interpret them equally well, Socrates, where they agree.

Soc. But what about matters in which they do not agree?—for example, about divination, of which both Homer and Hesiod have something to say,—

Ion. Very true:

Soc. Would you or a good prophet be a better interpreter of what these two poets say about divination, not only when they agree, but when they disagree?

Ion. A prophet.

Soc. And if you were a prophet, would you be able to interpret them when they disagree as well as when they agree?

Ion. Clearly.

Soc. But how did you come to have this skill about Homer only, and not about Hesiod or the other poets? Does not Homer speak of the same themes which all other poets handle? Is not war his great argument? and does he not speak of human society and of intercourse of men, good and bad, skilled and unskilled, and of the gods conversing with one another and with mankind, and about what happens in heaven and in the world below, and the generations of gods and heroes? Are not these the themes of which Homer sings?

Ion. Very true, Socrates.

Soc. And do not the other poets sing of the same?

Ion. Yes, Socrates; but not in the same way as Homer.

Soc. What, in a worse way?

Ion. Yes, in a far worse.

Soc. And Homer in a better way?

Ion. He is incomparably better.

Soc. And yet surely, my dear friend Ion, in a discussion about arithmetic, where many people are speaking, and one speaks better than the rest, there is somebody who can judge which of them is the good speaker?

Ion. Yes.

Soc. And he who judges of the good will be the same as he who judges of the bad speakers?

Ion. The same.

Soc. And he will be the arithmetician?

Ion. Yes.

Soc. Well, and in discussions about the wholesomeness of food, when many persons are speaking, and one speaks better than the rest, will he who recognizes the better speaker be a different person from him who recognizes the worse, or the same?

Ion. Clearly the same.

Soc. And who is he, and what is his name?

Ion. The physician.

Soc. And speaking generally, in all discussions in which the subject is the same and many men are speaking, will not he who knows the good know the bad speaker also? For if he does not know the [532] bad, neither will he know the good when the same topic is being discussed.

Ion. True.

Soc. Is not the same person skilful in both?

Ion. Yes.

Soc. And you say that Homer and the other poets, such as Hesiod and Archilochus, speak of the same things, although not in the same way; but the one speaks well and the other not so well?

Ion. Yes; and I am right in saying so.

Soc. And if you knew the good speaker, you would also know the inferior speakers to be inferior?

Ion. That is true.

Soc. Then, my dear friend, can I be mistaken in saying that Ion is equally skilled in Homer and in other poets, since he himself acknowledges that the same person will be a good judge of all those who speak of the same things; and that almost all poets do speak of the same things?

Ion. Why then, Socrates, do I lose attention and go to sleep and have absolutely no ideas of the least value, when any one speaks of any other poet; but when Homer is mentioned, I wake up at once and am all attention and have plenty to say?

Soc. The reason, my friend, is obvious. No one can fail to see that you speak of Homer without any art or knowledge. If you were able to speak of him by rules of art, you would have been able to speak of all other poets; for poetry is a whole.

Ion. Yes.

Soc. And when any one acquires any other art as a whole, the same may be said of them. Would you like me to explain my meaning, Ion?

Ion. Yes, indeed, Socrates; I very much wish that you would: for I love to hear you wise men talk.

Soc. O that we were wise, Ion, and that you could truly call us so; but you rhapsodes and actors, and the poets whose verses you sing, are wise; whereas I am a common man, who only speak the truth. For consider what a very commonplace and trivial thing is this which I have said—a thing which any man might say: that when a man has acquired a knowledge of a whole art, the enquiry into good and bad is one and the same. Let us consider this matter; is not the art of painting a whole?

Ion. Yes.

Soc. And there are and have been many painters good and bad?

Ion. Yes.

Soc. And did you ever know any one who was skilful in pointing out the excellences and defects of Polygnotus the son of Aglaophon, [533] but incapable of criticizing other painters; and when the work of any other painter was produced, went to sleep and was at a loss, and had no ideas; but when he had to give his opinion about Polygnotus, or whoever the painter might be, and about him only, woke up and was attentive and had plenty to say?

Ion. No indeed, I have never known such a person.

Soc. Or did you ever know of any one in sculpture, who was skilful in expounding the merits of Daedalus the son of Metion, or of Epeius the son of Panopeus, or of Theodorus the Samian, or of any individual sculptor; but when the works of sculptors in general were produced, was at a loss and went to sleep and had nothing to say?

Ion. No indeed; no more than the other.

Soc. And if I am not mistaken, you never met with any one among flute-players or harp-players or singers to the harp or rhapsodes who was able to discourse of Olympus or Thamyras or Orpheus, or Phemius the rhapsode of Ithaca, but was at a loss when he came to speak of Ion of Ephesus, and had no notion of his merits or defects?

Ion. I cannot deny what you say, Socrates. Nevertheless I am conscious in my own self, and the world agrees with me in thinking that I do speak better and have more to say about Homer than any other man. But I do not speak equally well about others—tell me the reason of this.

Soc. I perceive, Ion; and I will proceed to explain to you what I imagine to be the reason of this. The gift which you possess of speaking excellently about Homer is not an art, but, as I was just saying, an inspiration; there is a divinity moving you, like that contained in the stone which Euripides calls a magnet, but which is commonly known as the stone of Heraclea. This stone not only attracts iron rings, but also imparts to them a similar power of attracting other rings; and sometimes may see a number of pieces of iron and rings suspended from one another so as to form quite a long chain: and all of them derive their power of suspension from the original stone. In like manner the Muse first of all inspires men herself; and from these inspired persons a chain of other persons is suspended, who take the inspiration. For all good poets, epic as well as lyric, compose their beautiful poems not by art, but because they are inspired and possessed. And as the Corybantian revellers when they dance are not in their right mind, so the lyric [534] poets are not in their right mind when they are composing their beautiful strains: but when falling under the power of music and metre they are inspired and possessed; like Bacchic maidens who draw milk and honey from the rivers when they are under the influence of Dionysus but not when they are in their right mind. And the soul of the lyric poet does the same, as they themselves say; for they tell us that they bring songs from honeyed fountains, culling them out of the gardens and dells of the Muses; they, like the bees, winging their way from flower to flower. And this is true. For the poet is a light and winged and holy thing, and there is no invention in him until he has been inspired and is out of his senses, and the mind is no longer in him: when he has not attained to this state, he is powerless and is unable to utter his oracles. Many are the noble words in which poets speak concerning the actions of men; but like yourself when speaking about Homer, they do not speak of them by any rules of art: they are simply inspired to utter that to which the Muse impels them, and that only; and when inspired, one of them will make dithyrambs, another hymns of praise, another choral strains, another epic or iambic verses—and he who is good at one is not good at any other kind of verse: for not by art does the poet sing, but by power divine. Had he learned by rules of art, he would have known how to speak not of one theme only, but of all; and therefore God takes away the minds of poets, and uses them as his ministers, as he also uses diviners and holy prophets, in order that we who hear them may know them to be speaking not of themselves who utter these priceless words in a state of unconsciousness, but that God himself is the speaker, and that through them he is conversing with us. And Tynnichus the Chalcidian affords a striking instance of what I am saying: he wrote nothing that any one would care to remember but the famous paean which is in every one's mouth, one of the finest poems ever written, simply an invention of the Muses, as he himself says. For in this way the God would seem to indicate to us and not allow us to doubt that these beautiful poems are not human, or the work of man, but divine and the work of God; and that the poets are only the interpreters of the Gods by whom they are severally possessed. Was not this the lesson which the God intended to [535] teach when by the mouth of the worst of poets he sang the best of songs? Am I not right, Ion?

Ion. Yes, indeed, Socrates, I feel that you are; for your words touch my soul, and I am persuaded that good poets by a divine inspiration interpret the things of the Gods to us.

Soc. And you rhapsodists are the interpreters of the poets?

Ion. There again you are right.

Soc. Then you are the interpreters of interpreters?

Ion. Precisely.

Soc. I wish you would frankly tell me, Ion, what I am going to ask of you: When you produce the greatest effect upon the audience in the recitation of some striking passage, such as the apparition of Odysseus leaping forth on the floor, recognized by the suitors and casting his arrows at his feet, or the description of Achilles rushing at Hector, or the sorrows of Andromache, Hecuba, or Priam,—are you in your right mind? Are you not carried out of yourself, and does not your soul in an ecstasy seem to be among the persons or places of which you are speaking, whether they are in Ithaca or in Troy or whatever may be the scene of the poem?

Ion. That proof strikes home to me, Socrates. For I must frankly confess that at the tale of pity my eyes are filled with tears, and when I speak of horrors, my hair stands on end and my heart throbs.

Soc. Well, Ion, and what are we to say of a man who at a sacrifice or festival, when he is dressed in holiday attire, and has golden crowns upon his head, of which nobody has robbed him, appears weeping or panic-stricken in the presence of more than twenty thousand friendly faces, when there is no one despoiling or wronging him;—is he in his right mind or is he not?

Ion. No indeed, Socrates, I must say that, strictly speaking, he is not in his right mind.

Soc. And are you aware that you produce similar effects on most spectators?

Ion. Only too well; for I look down upon them from the stage, and behold the various emotions of pity, wonder, sternness, stamped upon their countenances when I am speaking: and I am obliged to give my very best attention to them; for if I make them cry I myself shall laugh, and if I make them laugh I myself shall cry when the time of payment arrives.

Soc. Do you know that the spectator is the last of the rings which, as I am saying, receive the power of the original magnet from one another? The rhapsode like yourself and the actor are intermediate links, and the poet himself is the first of them. [536] Through all these the God sways the souls of men in any direction which he pleases, and makes one man hang down from another. Thus there is a vast chain of dancers and masters and undermasters of choruses, who are suspended, as if from the stone, at the side of the rings which hang down from the Muse. And every poet has some Muse from whom he is suspended, and by whom he is said to be possessed, which is nearly the same thing; for he is taken hold of. And from these first rings, which are the poets, depend others, some deriving their inspiration from Orpheus, others from Musaeus; but the greater number are possessed and held by Homer. Of whom, Ion, you are one, and are possessed by Homer; and when any one repeats the words of another poet you go to sleep, and know not what to say; but when any one recites a strain of Homer you wake up in a moment, and your soul leaps within you, and you have plenty to say; for not by art or knowledge about Homer do you say what you say, but by divine inspiration and by possession; just as the Corybantian revellers too have a quick perception of that strain only which is appropriated to the God by whom they are possessed, and have plenty of dances and words for that, but take no heed of any other. And you, Ion, when the name of Homer is mentioned have plenty to say, and have nothing to say of others. You ask, 'Why is this?' The answer is that you praise Homer not by art but by divine inspiration.

Ion. That is good, Socrates; and yet I doubt whether you will ever have eloquence enough to persuade me that I praise Homer only when I am mad and possessed; and if you could hear me speak of him I am sure you would never think this to be the case.

Soc. I should like very much to hear you, but not until you have answered a question which I have to ask. On what part of Homer do you speak well?—not surely about every part.

Ion. There is no part, Socrates, about which I do not speak well: of that I can assure you.

Soc. Surely not about things in Homer of which you have no knowledge?

Ion. And what is there in Homer of which I have no knowledge?

Soc. Why, does not Homer speak in many passages about arts? [537] For example, about driving; if I can only remember the lines I will repeat them.

Ion. I remember, and will repeat them.

Soc. Tell me then, what Nestor says to Antilochus, his son, where he bids him be careful of the turn at the horse-race in honour of Patroclus.

Ion. 'Bend gently,' he says, 'in the polished chariot to the left of them, and urge the horse on the right hand with whip and voice; and slacken the rein. And when you are at the goal, let the left horse draw near, yet so that the nave of the well-wrought wheel may not even seem to touch the extremity; and avoid catching the stone.'

Soc. Enough. Now, Ion, will the charioteer or the physician be the better judge of the propriety of these lines?

Ion. The charioteer, clearly.

Soc. And will the reason be that this is his art, or will there be any other reason?

Ion. No, that will be the reason.

Soc. And every art is appointed by God to have knowledge of a certain work; for that which we know by the art of the pilot we do not know by the art of medicine?

Ion. Certainly not.

Soc. Nor do we know by the art of the carpenter that which we know by the art of medicine?

Ion. Certainly not.

Soc. And this is true of all the arts;—that which we know with one art we do not know with the other? But let me ask a prior question: You admit that there are differences of arts?

Ion. Yes.

Soc. You would argue, as I should, that when one art is of one kind of knowledge and another of another, they are different?

Ion. Yes.

Soc. Yes, surely; for if the subject of knowledge were the same, there would be no meaning in saying that the arts were different,—if they both gave the same knowledge. For example, I know that here are five fingers, and you know the same. And if I were to ask whether I and you became acquainted with this fact by the help of the same art of arithmetic, you would acknowledge that we did?

Ion. Yes.

[538] *Soc.* Tell me, then, what I was intending to ask you,—whether this holds universally? Must the same art have the same subject of knowledge, and different arts other subjects of knowledge?

Ion. That is my opinion, Socrates.

Soc. Then he who has no knowledge of a particular art will have no right judgment of the sayings and doings of that art?

Ion. Very true.

Soc. Then which will be a better judge of the lines which you were reciting from Homer, you or the charioteer?

Ion. The charioteer.

Soc. Why, yes, because you are a rhapsode and not a charioteer.

Ion. Yes.

Soc. And the art of the rhapsode is different from that of the charioteer?

Ion. Yes.

Soc. And if a different knowledge, then a knowledge of different matters?

Ion. True.

Soc. You know the passage in which Hecamede, the concubine of Nestor, is described as giving to the wounded Machaon a posset, as he says,

> Made with Pramnian wine; and she grated cheese of goat's milk with a grater of bronze, and at his side placed an onion which gives a relish to drink.

Now would you say that the art of the rhapsode or the art of medicine was better able to judge of the propriety of these lines?

Ion. The art of medicine.

Soc. And when Homer says,

> And she descended into the deep like a leaden plummet, which, set in the horn of ox that ranges in the fields, rushes along carrying death among the ravenous fishes,—

will the art of the fisherman or of the rhapsode be better able to judge whether these lines are rightly expressed or not?

Ion. Clearly, Socrates, the art of the fisherman.

Soc. Come now, suppose that you were to say to me: 'Since you, Socrates, are able to assign different passages in Homer to their corresponding arts, I wish that you would tell me what are the passages of which the excellence ought to be judged by the prophet and prophetic art'; and you will see how readily and truly I shall answer you. For there are many such passages, particularly in the Odyssee; as, for example, the passage in which Theoclymenus the prophet of the house of Melampus says to the suitors:—

> [539] Wretched men! what is happening to you? Your heads and your faces and your limbs underneath are shrouded in night; and the voice of lamen-

tation bursts forth, and your cheeks are wet with tears. And the vestibule is full, and the court is full, of ghosts descending into the darkness of Erebus, and the sun has perished out of heaven, and an evil mist is spread abroad.

And there are many such passages in the Iliad also; as for example in the description of the battle near the rampart, where he says:—

> As they were eager to pass the ditch, there came to them an omen: a soaring eagle, holding back the people on the left, bore a huge bloody dragon in his talons, still living and panting; nor had he yet resigned the strife, for he bent back and smote the bird which carried him on the breast by the neck, and he in pain let him fall from him to the ground into the midst of the multitude. And the eagle, with a cry, was borne afar on the wings of the wind.

These are the sort of things which I should say that the prophet ought to consider and determine.

Ion. And you are quite right, Socrates, in saying so.

Soc. Yes, Ion, and you are right also. And as I have selected from the Iliad and Odyssee for you passages which describe the office of the prophet and the physician and the fisherman, do you, who know Homer so much better than I do, Ion, select for me passages which relate to the rhapsode and the rhapsode's art, and which the rhapsode ought to examine and judge of better than other men.

Ion. All passages, I should say, Socrates.

Soc. Not all, Ion, surely. Have you already forgotten what you were saying? A rhapsode ought to have a better memory.

[540] *Ion.* Why, what am I forgetting?

Soc. Do you not remember that you declared the art of the rhapsode to be different from the art of the charioteer?

Ion Yes, I remember.

Soc. And you admitted that being different they would have different subjects of knowledge?

Ion. Yes.

Soc. Then upon your own showing the rhapsode, and the art of the rhapsode, will not know everything?

Ion. I should exclude certain things, Socrates.

Soc. You mean to say that you would exclude pretty much the subjects of the other arts. As he does not know all of them, which of them will he know?

Ion. He will know what a man and what a woman ought to say, and what a freeman and what a slave ought to say, and what a ruler and what a subject.

Soc. Do you mean that a rhapsode will know better than the pilot what the rule of a sea-tossed vessel ought to say?

Ion. No, the pilot will know best.

Soc. Or will the rhapsode know better than the physician what the ruler of a sick man ought to say?

Ion. He will not.

Soc. But he will know what a slave ought to say?

Ion. Yes.

Soc. Suppose the slave to be a cowherd; the rhapsode will know better than the cowherd what he ought to say in order to soothe the infuriated cows?

Ion. No, he will not.

Soc. But he will know what a spinning-woman ought to say about the working of wool?

Ion. No.

Soc. At any rate he will know what a general ought to say when exhorting his soldiers?

Ion. Yes, that is the sort of thing which the rhapsode will be sure to know.

Soc. Well, but is the art of the rhapsode the art of the general?

Ion. I am sure that I should know what a general ought to say.

Soc. Why, yes, Ion, because you may possibly have a knowledge of the art of the general as well as of the rhapsode; and you may also have a knowledge of horsemanship as well as of the lyre: and then you would know when horses were well or ill managed. But suppose I were to ask you: By the help of which art, Ion, do you know whether horses are well managed, by your skill as a horseman or as a performer on the lyre—what would you answer?

Ion. I should reply, by my skill as a horseman.

Soc. And if you judged of performers on the lyre, you would admit that you judged of them as a performer on the lyre, and not as a horseman?

Ion. Yes.

Soc. And in judging of the general's art, do you judge of it as a general or a rhapsode?

Ion. To me there appears to be no difference between them.

[541] *Soc.* What do you mean? Do you mean to say that the art of the rhapsode and of the general is the same?

Ion. Yes, one and the same.

Soc. Then he who is a good rhapsode is also a good general?

Ion. Certainly, Socrates.

Soc. And he who is a good general is also a good rhapsode?

Ion. No; I do not say that.

Soc. But you do say that he who is a good rhapsode is also a good general.

Ion. Certainly.

Soc. And you are the best of Hellenic rhapsodes?

Ion. Far the best, Socrates.

Soc. And you are the best general, Ion?

Ion. To be sure, Socrates; and Homer was my master.

Soc. But then, Ion, what in the name of goodness can be the reason why you, who are the best of generals as well as the best of rhapsodes in all Hellas, go about as a rhapsode when you might be a general? Do you think that the Hellenes want a rhapsode with his golden crown, and do not want a general?

Ion. Why, Socrates, the reason is, that my countrymen, the Ephesians, are the servants and soldiers of Athens, and do not need a general; and you and Sparta are not likely to have me, for you think that you have enough generals of your own.

Soc. My good Ion, did you never hear of Apollodorus of Cyzicus?

Ion. Who may he be?

Soc. One who, though a foreigner, has often been chosen their general by the Athenians: and there is Phanosthenes of Andros, and Heraclides of Clazomenae, whom they have also appointed to the command of their armies and to other offices, although aliens, after they had shown their merit. And will they not choose Ion the Ephesian to be their general, and honour him, if he prove himself worthy? Were not the Ephesians originally Athenians, and Ephesus is no mean city? But, indeed, Ion, if you are correct in saying that by art and knowledge you are able to praise Homer, you do not deal fairly with me, and after all your professions of knowing many glorious things about Homer, and promises that you would exhibit them, you are only a deceiver, and so far from exhibiting the art of which you are a master, will not, even after my repeated entreaties, explain to me the nature of it. You have literally as many forms as Proteus; and now you go all manner of ways, twisting and turning, and, like Proteus, become all manner of people at once, and at last slip away from me in the disguise of a [542] general, in order that you may escape exhibiting your Homeric lore. And if you have art, then, as I was saying, in falsifying your promise that you would exhibit Homer, you are not dealing fairly with me. But if, as I believe, you have no art, but speak all these beautiful words about Homer unconsciously under his inspiring influence, then I acquit you of dishonesty, and shall only say that you are inspired. Which do you prefer to be thought, dishonest or inspired?

Ion. There is a great difference, Socrates, between the two alternatives; and inspiration is by far the nobler.

Soc. Then, Ion, I shall assume the nobler alternative; and attribute to you in your praises of Homer inspiration, and not art.

PLATO

Symposium *

[201] And now, taking my leave of you, I will rehearse a tale of love which I heard from Diotima of Mantineia, a woman wise in this and in many other kinds of knowledge, who in the days of old, when the Athenians offered sacrifice before the coming of the plague, delayed the disease ten years. She was my instructress in the art of love, and I shall repeat to you what she said to me, beginning with the admissions made by Agathon, which are nearly if not quite the same which I made to the wise woman when she questioned me: I think that this will be the easiest way, and I shall take both parts myself as well as I can. As you, Agathon, suggested, I must speak first of the being and nature of Love, and then of his works. First I said to her in nearly the same words which he used to me, that Love was a mighty god, and likewise fair; and she proved to me as I proved to him that, by my own showing, Love was neither fair nor good. 'What do you mean, Diotima,' I said, 'is love then evil and foul?' 'Hush,' she cried; 'must that be foul which is not fair?' 'Certainly,' I said. 'And is that which is not wise, ignorant? [202] do you not see that there is a mean between wisdom and ignorance?' 'And what may that be?' I said. 'Right opinion,' she replied; 'which, as you know, being incapable of giving a reason, is not knowledge (for how can knowledge be devoid of reason? nor again, ignorance, for neither can ignorance attain the truth), but is clearly something which is a mean between ignorance and wisdom.' 'Quite true,' I replied. 'Do not then insist,' she said, 'that what is not fair is of necessity foul, or what is not good evil; or infer that because love is not fair and good he is

* Plato, *The Dialogues of Plato*, translated by Benjamin Jowett, 3rd ed. (London: Oxford University Press, 1892), pp. 327-335. (Footnotes omitted.)

therefore foul and evil; for he is in a mean between them.' 'Well,' I said, 'Love is surely admitted by all to be a great god.' 'By those who know or by those who do not know?' 'By all.' 'And how, Socrates,' she said with a smile, 'can Love be acknowledged to be a great god by those who say that he is not a god at all?' 'And who are they?' I said. 'You and I are two of them,' she replied. 'How can that be?' I said. 'It is quite intelligible,' she replied; 'for you yourself would acknowledge that the gods are happy and fair—of course you would—would you dare to say that any god was not?' 'Certainly not,' I replied. 'And you mean by the happy, those who are the possessors of things good or fair?' 'Yes.' 'And you admitted that Love, because he was in want, desires those good and fair things of which he is in want?' 'Yes, I did.' 'But how can he be a god who has no portion in what is either good or fair?' 'Impossible.' 'Then you see that you also deny the divinity of Love.'

'What then is Love?' I asked; 'Is he mortal?' 'No.' 'What then?' 'As in the former instance, he is neither mortal nor immortal, but in a mean between the two.' 'What is he, Diotima?' 'He is a great spirit (daimon), and like all spirits he is intermediate between the divine and the mortal.' 'And what,' I said, 'is his power?' 'He interprets,' she replied, 'between gods and men, conveying and taking across to the gods the prayers and sacrifices of men, and to men the commands and replies of the gods; he is the mediator who spans the chasm which divides them, and therefore in him all is bound together, and through him the arts of the prophet and the [203] priest, their sacrifices and mysteries and charms, and all prophecy and incantation, find their way. For God mingles not with man; but through Love all the intercourse and converse of god with man, whether awake or asleep, is carried on. The wisdom which understands this is spiritual; all other wisdom, such as that of arts and handicrafts, is mean and vulgar. Now these spirits or intermediate powers are many and diverse, and one of them is Love.' 'And who,' I said, 'was his father, and who his mother?' 'The tale,' she said, 'will take time; nevertheless I will tell you. On the birthday of Aphrodite there was a feast of the gods, at which the god Poros or Plenty, who is the son of Metis or Discretion, was one of the guests. When the feast was over, Penia or Poverty, as the manner is on such occasions, came about the doors to beg. Now Plenty, who was the worse for nectar (there was no wine in those days), went into the garden of Zeus and fell into a heavy sleep; and Poverty considering her own straitened circumstances, plotted to have a child by him, and accordingly she lay down at his side and conceived Love, who partly because he is naturally a lover of the beautiful, and because Aphrodite is herself beautiful, and also because he was born on her birthday, is her follower and attendant. And as his parentage is, so also are his fortunes. In the first place he is always poor, and anything but tender and fair, as the many imagine him; and he is rough and squalid, and has no shoes, nor a house to dwell in; on the bare earth exposed he lies under the open heaven, in the streets, or at the doors of houses, taking his rest; and like his mother he is always in distress. Like his father too, whom he also partly resembles, he is always plotting against the fair and good; he is bold, enterprising, strong, a mighty hunter, always weaving some intrigue or other, keen in the pursuit of wisdom, fertile in resources; a philosopher at all times, terrible as an enchanter, sorcerer, sophist. He is by nature neither mortal nor immortal, but alive and flourishing at one moment when he is in plenty, and dead at another moment, and again alive by reason of his father's nature. But that which is always flowing in is always flowing.out, and so he is never in want and never in wealth; and, further, he is in a mean between ignorance and knowledge. The truth of the matter is this: No god is a philosopher or seeker after wisdom, for he is wise already; nor does any man who is wise seek after wisdom. Neither do the ignorant seek after wisdom. For herein is the evil of [204] ignorance, that he who is neither good nor wise is nevertheless satisfied with himself: he has no desire for that of which he feels no want.' 'But who then, Diotima,' I said, 'are the lovers of wisdom, if they are neither the wise nor the foolish?' 'A child may answer that question,' she replied; 'they are those who are in a mean between the two; Love is one of them. For wisdom is a most beautiful thing, and Love is of the beautiful; and therefore Love is also a philosopher or lover of wisdom, and being a lover of wisdom is in a mean between the wise and the ignorant. And of this too his birth is the cause; for his father is wealthy and wise, and his mother poor and foolish. Such, my dear Socrates, is the nature of the spirit Love. The error in your conception of him was very natural, and as I imagine from what you say, has arisen out of a confusion of love and the beloved, which made you think that love was all beautiful. For the beloved is the truly beautiful, and delicate, and perfect, and blessed; but the principle of love is of another nature, and is such as I have described.'

I said: 'O thou stranger woman, thou sayest well; but, assuming Love to be such as you say, what is the use of him to men?' 'That, Socrates,' she replied, 'I will attempt to unfold: of his nature and birth I have already spoken; and you acknowledge that love is of the beautiful. But some one will say: Of the beautiful in what, Socrates and Diotima?—or rather let me put the question more clearly, and ask: When a man loves the beautiful, what does he desire?' I answered her 'That the beautiful may be his.' 'Still,' she said, 'the answer suggests a further question: What is given by the possession of beauty?' 'To what you have asked,' I replied, 'I have no answer ready.' 'Then,' she said, 'let me put the word "good" in the place of the beautiful, and repeat the question once more: If he who loves loves the good, what is it then that he loves?' 'The possession of the good,' I said. 'And what does he gain who possesses the good?' 'Happiness,' I replied; 'there is less difficulty in answering that question.' 'Yes,' she said, 'the happy are made happy by [205] the acquisition of good things. Nor is there any need to ask why a man desires happiness; the answer is already final.' 'You are right,' I said. 'And is this wish and this desire common to all? and do all men always desire their own good, or only some men?—what say you?' 'All men,' I replied; 'the desire is common to all.' 'Why, then,' she rejoined, 'are not all men, Socrates, said to love, but only some of them? whereas you say that all men are always loving the same things.' 'I myself wonder,' I said, 'why this is.' 'There is nothing to wonder at,' she replied; 'the reason is that one part of love is separated off and receives the name of the whole, but the other parts have other names.' 'Give an illustration,' I said. She answered me as follows: 'There is poetry, which, as you know, is complex and manifold. All creation or passage of non-being into being is poetry or making, and the processes of all art are creative; and the masters of arts are all poets or makers.' 'Very true.' 'Still,' she said, 'you know that they are not called poets, but have other names; only that portion of the art which is separated off from the rest, and is concerned with music and metre, is termed poetry, and they who possess poetry in this sense of the word are called poets.' 'Very true,' I said. 'And the same holds of love. For you may say generally that all desire of good and happiness is only the great and subtle power of love; but they who are drawn towards him by any other path, whether the path of money-making or gymnastics or philosophy, are not called lovers—the name of the whole is appropriated to those whose affection takes one form only—they alone are said to love, or to be lovers.' 'I dare say,' I replied, 'that you are right.' 'Yes,' she added, 'and you hear people say that lovers are seeking for their other half; but I say that they are seeking neither for the half of themselves, nor for the whole, unless the half or the whole be also a good. And they will cut off their own hands and feet and cast them away, if they are evil; for they love not what is their own, unless perchance there be some one who calls what belongs to [206] him the good, and what belongs to another the evil. For there is nothing which men love but the good. Is there anything?' 'Certainly, I should say, that there is nothing.' 'Then,' she said, 'the simple truth is, that men love the good.' 'Yes,' I said. 'To which must be added that they love the possession of the good?' 'Yes, that must be added.' 'And not only the possession, but the everlasting possession of the good?' 'That must be added too.' 'Then love,' she said, 'may be described generally as the love of the everlasting possession of the good?' 'That is most true.'

'Then if this be the nature of love, can you tell me further,' she said, 'what is the manner of the pursuit? what are they doing who show all this eagerness and heat which is called love? and what is the object which they have in view? Answer me.' 'Nay, Diotima,' I replied, 'if I had known, I should not have wondered at your wisdom, neither should I have come to learn from you about this very matter.' 'Well,' she said, 'I will teach you:—The object which they have in view is birth in beauty, whether of body or soul.' 'I do not understand you,' I said; 'the oracle requires an explanation.' 'I will make my meaning clearer,' she replied. 'I mean to say, that all men are bringing to the birth in their bodies and in their souls. There is a certain age at which human nature is desirous of procreation—procreation which must be in beauty and not in deformity; and this procreation is the union of man and woman, and is a divine thing; for conception and generation are an immortal principle in the mortal creature, and in the inharmonious they can never be. But the deformed is always inharmonious with the divine, and the beautiful harmonious. Beauty, then, is the destiny or goddess of parturition who presides at

birth, and therefore, when approaching beauty, the conceiving power is pro-
pitious, and diffusive, and benign, and begets and bears fruit: at the sight of
ugliness she frowns and contracts and has a sense of pain, and turns away, and
shrivels up, and not without a pang refrains from conception. And this is the
reason why, when the hour of conception arrives, and the teeming nature is
full, there is such a flutter and ecstasy about beauty whose approach is the alleviation of the pain of travail. For love, Socrates, is not, as you imagine, the love
of the beautiful only.' 'What then?' 'The love of generation and of birth in
beauty.' 'Yes,' I said. 'Yes, indeed,' she replied. 'But why of generation?'
'Because to the mortal creature, generation is a sort of eternity and immortality,' she replied; 'and if, as has been already admitted, love is of the everlasting possession of the good, all men will necessarily desire immortality
together with good: Wherefore [207] love is of immortality.'

All this she taught me at various times when she spoke of love. And I
remember her once saying to me, 'What is the cause, Socrates, of love, and the
attendant desire? See you not how all animals, birds, as well as beasts, in their
desire of procreation, are in agony when they take the infection of love, which
begins with the desire of union; whereto is added the care of offspring, on
whose behalf the weakest are ready to battle against the strongest even to
the uttermost, and to die for them, and will let themselves be tormented with
hunger or suffer anything in order to maintain their young. Man may be supposed to act thus from reason; but why should animals have these passionate
feelings? Can you tell me why?' Again I replied that I did not know. She said to
me: 'And do you expect ever to become a master in the art of love, if you do
not know this?' 'But I have told you already, Diotima, that my ignorance is the
reason why I come to you; for I am conscious that I want a teacher; tell me
then the cause of this and of the other mysteries of love.' 'Marvel not,' she
said, 'if you believe that love is of the immortal, as we have several times
acknowledged; for here again, and on the same principle too, the mortal
nature is seeking as far as is possible to be everlasting and immortal: and this
is only to be attained by generation, because generation always leaves behind
a new existence in the place of the old. Nay even in the life of the same individual there is succession and not absolute unity: a man is called the same, and
yet in the short interval which elapses between youth and age, and in which
every animal is said to have life and identity, he is undergoing a perpetual process of loss and reparation—hair, flesh, bones, blood, and the whole body are
always changing. Which is true not only of the body, but also of the soul,
whose habits, tempers, opinions, desires, pleasures, pains, fears, never remain
the same in any one of us, but are always coming and going; and equally true
of knowledge, and what is still more surprising [208] to us mortals, not only
do the sciences in general spring up and decay, so that in respect of them we
are never the same; but each of them individually experiences a like change.
For what is implied in the word "recollection," but the departure of knowledge, which is ever being forgotten, and is renewed and preserved by recollection, and appears to be the same although in reality new, according to

that law of succession by which all mortal things are preserved, not absolutely the same, but by substitution, the old worn-out mortality leaving another new and similar existence behind—unlike the divine, which is always the same and not another? And in this way, Socrates, the mortal body, or mortal anything, partakes of immortality; but the immortal in another way. Marvel not then at the love which all men have of their offspring; for that universal love and interest is for the sake of immortality.'

I was astonished at her words, and said: 'Is this really true, O thou wise Diotima?' And she answered with all the authority of an accomplished sophist: 'Of that, Socrates, you may be assured;—think only of the ambition of men, and you will wonder at the senselessness of their ways, unless you consider how they are stirred by the love of an immortality of fame. They are ready to run all risks greater far than they would have run for their children, and to spend money and undergo any sort of toil, and even to die, for the sake of leaving behind them a name which shall be eternal. Do you imagine that Alcestis would have died to save Admetus, or Achilles to avenge Patroclus, or your own Codrus in order to preserve the kingdom for his sons, if they had not imagined that the memory of their virtues, which still survives among us, would be immortal? Nay,' she said, 'I am persuaded that all men do all things, and the better they are the more they do them, in hope of the glorious fame of immortal virtue; for they desire the immortal.

'Those who are pregnant in the body only, betake themselves to women and beget children—this is the character of their love; their offspring, as they hope, will preserve their memory and give them the blessedness and immortality which they desire in the future. But souls which are pregnant—for there certainly are men who are [209] more creative in their souls than in their bodies—conceive that which is proper for the soul to conceive or contain. And what are these conceptions?—wisdom and virtue in general. And such creators are poets and all artists who are deserving of the name inventor. But the greatest and fairest sort of wisdom by far is that which is concerned with the ordering of states and families, and which is called temperance and justice. And he who in youth has the seed of these implanted in him and is himself inspired, when he comes to maturity desires to beget and generate. He wanders about seeking beauty that he may beget offspring—for in deformity he will beget nothing—and naturally embraces the beautiful rather than the deformed body; above all when he finds a fair and noble and well-nurtured soul, he embraces the two in one person, and to such an one he is full of speech about virtue and the nature and pursuits of a good man; and he tries to educate him; and at the touch of the beautiful which is ever present to his memory, even when absent, he brings forth that which he had conceived long before, and in company with him tends that which he brings forth; and they are married by a far nearer tie and have a closer friendship than those who beget mortal children, for the children who are their common offspring are fairer and more immortal. Who, when he thinks of Homer and Hesiod and other great poets, would not rather have their children than ordinary human ones? Who would not emulate them in the creation of children such as theirs, which have preserved their memory and given them everlasting glory? Or who would not have such children as Lycurgus left behind him to be the saviours, not only of Lacedaemon, but of Hellas, as one may say? There is Solon, too, who is the revered father of Athenian laws; and many others there are in many other places, both among Hellenes and barbarians, who have given to the world many noble works, and have been the parents of virtue of every kind; and many temples have been raised in their honour for the sake of children such as theirs; which were never raised in honour of any one, for the sake of his mortal children.

'These are the lesser mysteries of love, into which even you, Socrates, [210] may enter; to the greater and more hidden ones which are the crown of these, and to which, if you pursue them in a right spirit, they will lead, I know not whether you will be able to attain. But I will do my utmost to inform you, and do you follow if you can. For he who would proceed aright in this matter should begin in youth to visit beautiful forms; and first, if he be guided by his instructor aright, to love one such form only—out of that he should create fair thoughts; and soon he will of himself perceive that the beauty of one form is akin to the beauty of another; and then if beauty of form in general is his pursuit, how foolish would he be not to recognize that the beauty in every form is one and the same! And when he perceives this he will abate his violent love of the one, which he will despise and deem a small thing, and will become a lover of all beautiful forms; in the next stage he will consider that the beauty of the mind is more honourable than the beauty of the outward form. So that if a virtuous soul have but a little comeliness, he will be content to love and tend him, and will search out and bring to the birth thoughts which may improve the young, until he is compelled to contemplate and see the beauty of institutions and laws, and to understand that the beauty of them all is of one family, and that personal beauty is a trifle; and after laws and institutions he will go on to the sciences, that he may see their beauty, being not like a servant in love with the beauty of one youth or man or institution, himself a slave mean and narrow-minded, but drawing towards and contemplating the vast sea of beauty, he will create many fair and noble thoughts and notions in boundless love of wisdom; until on that shore he grows and waxes strong, and at last the vision is revealed to him of a single science, which is the science of beauty everywhere. To this I will proceed; please to give me your very best attention:

'He who has been instructed thus far in the things of love, and who has learned to see the beautiful in due order and succession, when he comes toward the end will suddenly perceive a nature of [211] wondrous beauty (and this, Socrates, is the final cause of all our former toils)—a nature which in the first place is everlasting, not growing and decaying, or waxing and waning; secondly, not fair in one point of view and foul in another, or at one time or in one relation or at one place fair, at another time or in another relation or at another place foul, as if fair to some and foul to others, or in the likeness of a face or hands or any other part of the bodily frame, or in any form of speech or knowledge, or existing in any other being, as for example, in an animal, or in heaven, or in earth, or in any other place; but beauty absolute, separate, simple, and everlasting, which without diminution and without increase, or any change, is imparted to the ever-growing and perishing beauties of all other things. He who from these ascending under the influence of true love, begins to perceive that beauty, is not far from the end. And the true order of going, or being led by another, to the things of love, is to begin from the beauties of earth and mount upwards for the sake of that other beauty, using these as steps only, and from one going on to two, and from two to all fair forms, and from fair forms to fair practices, and from fair practices to fair notions, until from fair notions he arrives at the notion of absolute beauty, and at last knows what the essence of beauty is. This, my dear Socrates,' said the stranger of Mantineia, 'is that life above all others which man should live, in the contemplation of beauty absolute; a beauty which if you once beheld, you would see not to be after the measure of gold, and garments, and fair boys and youths, whose presence now entrances you; and you and many a one would be content to live seeing them only and conversing with them without meat or drink, if that were possible—you only want to look at them and to be with them. But what if man had eyes to see the true beauty—the divine beauty, I mean, pure and clear and unalloyed, not clogged with the pollutions of mortality and all the colours and vanities of human life—thither looking, and holding converse with the true beauty simple and divine? Remember how in that [212] communion only, beholding beauty with the eye of the mind, he will be enabled to bring forth, not images of beauty, but realities (for he has hold not of an image but of a reality), and bringing forth and nourishing true virtue to become the friend of God and be immortal, if mortal man may. Would that be an ignoble life?'

Such, Phaedrus—and I speak not only to you, but to all of you—were the words of Diotima; and I am persuaded of their truth. And being persuaded of them, I try to persuade others, that in the attainment of this end human nature will not easily find a helper better than love. And therefore, also, I say that every man ought to honour him as I myself honour him, and walk in his ways, and exhort others to do the same, and praise the power and spirit of love according to the measure of my ability now and ever.

ARISTOTLE

SOCRATES WAS PLATO'S TEACHER, as well as his dramatic protagonist; Plato in turn was Aristotle's teacher and no less important in his life and work. Aristotle may well be the most influential philosopher in the history of philosophy, not least because of his importance to science.

With respect to art, Aristotle's writings in the *Poetics* are the most important presentation and defense of *mimēsis*, not as Plato describes painting in Book X of the *Republic*, an imitation of particular things, but a concern with reality, "to describe, not the thing that has happened, but a kind of thing that might happen." Aristotle answers Plato on two counts: the value of imitation and the benefits of the kinds of emotional gratifications we receive from poetry. Whether the answer he gives is satisfactory for all art is an important question, especially considering nonrepresentational art of the twentieth century.

In addition to the selections from the *Poetics*, there is a brief selection from the *Nicomachean Ethics* in which Aristotle explores the nature of art as production, as *technē*. This may be read in connection with Aristotle's description of nature, *physis*, as that which moves of itself, from within itself. Natural things are the source of their own production. Artificial things, produced by *technē*, are not. The principle of their production lies outside them, in something else.

We may therefore find in Aristotle three modes of production, one by nature, from within, distinguished from *technē*, production from without; then, within *technē*, between production by design or according to an end, and *poiēsis*, bringing into being from nonbeing.

ARISTOTLE

*Poetics**

[1447ᵃ]1 Our subject being Poetry, I propose to speak not only of the art in general but also of its species and their respective capacities; of the structure of plot required for a good poem; of the number and nature of the constituent parts of a poem; and likewise of any other matters in the same line of inquiry. Let us follow the natural order and begin with the primary facts.

Epic poetry and Tragedy, as also Comedy, Dithyrambic poetry, and most flute-playing and lyre-playing, are all, viewed as a whole, modes of imitation. But at the same time they differ from one another in three ways, either by a difference of kind in their means, or by differences in the objects, or in the manner of their imitations.

I. Just as colour and form are used as means by some, who (whether by art or constant practice) imitate and portray many things by their aid, and the voice is used by others; so also in the above-mentioned group of arts, the means with them as a whole are rhythm, language, and harmony—used, however, either singly or in certain combinations. A combination of harmony and rhythm alone is the means in flute-playing and lyre-playing, and any other arts there may be of the same description, e.g. imitative piping. Rhythm alone, without harmony, is the means in the dancer's imitations; for even he, by the rhythms of his attitudes, may represent men's characters, as well as what they do and suffer. There is further an art which imitates by language alone, without harmony, in prose or in verse, and if in verse, either in some one or in a plurality of metres. [1447ᵇ] This form of imitation is to this day without a

* Aristotle, *The Oxford Translation of Aristotle*, edited by W. D. Ross, vol. 9 (*Poetics* translated by Ingram Bywater) (New York: Random House), pp. 1455-1465. (Footnotes omitted.)

name. We have no common name for a mime of Sophron or Xenarchus and a Socratic Conversation; and we should still be without one even if the imitation in the two instances were in trimeters or elegiacs or some other kind of verse—though it is the way with people to tack on 'poet' to the name of a metre, and talk of elegiac-poets and epic-poets, thinking that they call them poets not by reason of the imitative nature of their work, but indiscriminately by reason of the metre they write in. Even if a theory of medicine or physical philosophy be put forth in a metrical form, it is usual to describe the writer in this way; Homer and Empedocles, however, have really nothing in common apart from their metre; so that, if the one is to be called a poet, the other should be termed a physicist rather than a poet. We should be in the same position also, if the imitation in these instances were in all the metres, like the *Centaur* (a rhapsody in a medley of all metres) of Chaeremon; and Chaeremon one has to recognize as a poet. So much, then, as to these arts. There are, lastly, certain other arts, which combine all the means enumerated, rhythm, melody, and verse, e.g. Dithyrambic and Nomic poetry, Tragedy and Comedy; with this difference, however, that the three kinds of means are in some of them all employed together, and in others brought in separately, one after the other. These elements of difference in the above arts I term the means of their imitation.

[1448ᵃ] 2 II. The objects the imitator represents are actions, with agents who are necessarily either good men or bad—the diversities of human character being nearly always derivative from this primary distinction, since the line between virtue and vice is one dividing the whole of mankind. It follows, therefore, that the agents represented must be either above our own level of goodness, or beneath it, or just such as we are; in the same way as, with the painters, the personages of Polygnotus are better than we are, those of Pauson worse, and those of Dionysius just like ourselves. It is clear that each of the above-mentioned arts will admit of these differences, and that it will become a separate art by representing objects with this point of difference. Even in dancing, flute-playing, and lyre-playing such diversities are possible; and they are also possible in the nameless art that uses language, prose or verse without harmony, as its means; Homer's personages, for instance, are better than we are; Cleophon's are on our own level; and those of Hegemon of Thasos, the first writer of parodies, and Nicochares, the author of the *Diliad,* are beneath it. The same is true of the Dithyramb and the Nome: the personages may be presented in them with the difference exemplified in the . . . of . . . and Argas, and in the Cyclopses of Timotheus and Philoxenus. This difference it is that distinguishes Tragedy and Comedy also; the one would make its personages worse, and the other better, than the men of the present day.

3 III. A third difference in these arts is in the manner in which each kind of object is represented. Given both the same means and the same kind of object for imitation, one may either (1) speak at one moment in narrative and

at another in an assumed character, as Homer does; or (2) one may remain the same throughout, without any such change; or (3) the imitators may represent the whole story dramatically, as though they were actually doing the things described.

As we said at the beginning, therefore, the differences in the imitation of these arts come under three heads, their means, their objects, and their manner.

So that as an imitator Sophocles will be on one side akin to Homer, both portraying good men; and on another to Aristophanes, since both present their personages as acting and doing. This in fact, according to some, is the reason for plays being termed dramas, because in a play the personages act the story. Hence too both Tragedy and Comedy are claimed by the Dorians as their discoveries; Comedy by the Megarians—by those in Greece as having arisen when Megara became a democracy, and by the Sicilian Megarians on the ground that the poet Epicharmus was of their country, and a good deal earlier than Chionides and Magnes; even Tragedy also is claimed by certain of the Peloponnesian Dorians. In support of this claim they point to the words 'comedy' and 'drama'. Their word for the outlying hamlets, they say, is *comae*, whereas Athenians call them *demes*—thus assuming that comedians got the name not from their *comoe* or revels, but from their strolling from hamlet to hamlet, lack of appreciation keeping them out of the city. Their word also [1448^b] for 'to act', they say, is *dran*, whereas Athenians use *prattein*.

So much, then, as to the number and nature of the points of difference in the imitation of these arts.

4 It is clear that the general origin of poetry was due to two causes, each of them part of human nature. Imitation is natural to man from childhood, one of his advantages over the lower animals being this, that he is the most imitative creature in the world, and learns at first by imitation. And it is also natural for all to delight in works of imitation. The truth of this second point is shown by experience: though the objects themselves may be painful to see, we delight to view the most realistic representations of them in art, the forms for example of the lowest animals and of dead bodies. The explanation is to be found in a further fact: to be learning something is the greatest of pleasures not only to the philosopher but also to the rest of mankind, however small their capacity for it; the reason of the delight in seeing the picture is that one is at the same time learning—gathering the meaning of things, e.g. that the man there is so-and-so; for if one has not seen the thing before, one's pleasure will not be in the picture as an imitation of it, but will be due to the execution or colouring or some similar cause. Imitation, then, being natural to us—as also the sense of harmony and rhythm, the metres being obviously species of rhythms—it was through their original aptitude, and by a series of improvements for the most part gradual on their first efforts, that they created poetry out of their improvisations.

Poetry, however, soon broke up into two kinds according to the differences of character in the individual poets; for the graver among them would represent noble actions, and those of noble personages; and the meaner sort the actions of the ignoble. The latter class produced invectives at first, just as others did hymns and panegyrics. We know of no such poem by any of the pre-Homeric poets, though there were probably many such writers among them; instances, however, may be found from Homer downwards, e.g. his *Margites,* and the similar poems of others. In this poetry of invective its natural fitness brought an iambic metre into use; hence our present term 'iambic', because it was the metre of their 'iambs' or invectives against one another. The result was that the old poets became some of them writers of heroic and others of iambic verse. Homer's position, however, is peculiar: just as he was in the serious style the poet of poets, standing alone not only through the literary excellence, but also through the dramatic character of his imitations, so too he was the first to outline for us the general forms of Comedy by producing not a dramatic invective, but a dramatic picture of the Ridiculous; his *Margites* in fact stands in the same relation to our comedies [1449ª] as the *Iliad* and *Odyssey* to our tragedies. As soon, however, as Tragedy and Comedy appeared in the field, those naturally drawn to the one line of poetry became writers of comedies instead of iambs, and those naturally drawn to the other, writers of tragedies instead of epics, because these new modes of art were grander and of more esteem than the old.

If it be asked whether Tragedy is now all that it need be in its formative elements, to consider that, and decide it theoretically and in relation to the theatres, is a matter of another inquiry.

It certainly began in improvisations—as did also Comedy; the one originating with the authors of the Dithyramb, the other with those of the phallic songs, which still survive as institutions in many of our cities. And its advance after that was little by little, through their improving on whatever they had before them at each stage. It was in fact only after a long series of changes that the movement of Tragedy stopped on its attaining to its natural form. (1) The number of actors was first increased to two by Aeschylus, who curtailed the business of the Chorus, and made the dialogue, or spoken portion, take the leading part in the play. (2) A third actor and scenery were due to Sophocles. (3) Tragedy acquired also its magnitude. Discarding short stories and a ludicrous diction, through its passing out of its satyric stage, it assumed, though only at a late point in its progress, a tone of dignity; and its metre changed then from trochaic to iambic. The reason for their original use of the trochaic tetrameter was that their poetry was satyric and more connected with dancing than it now is. As soon, however, as a spoken part came in, nature herself found the appropriate metre. The iambic, we know, is the most speakable of metres, as is shown by the fact that we very often fall into it in conversation, whereas we rarely talk hexameters, and only when we depart from the speaking tone of voice. (4) Another change was a plurality of episodes or acts. As for the remaining matters, the superadded embellishments and the account of their introduction, these must be taken as said, as it would probably be a long piece of work to go through the details.

5 As for Comedy, it is (as has been observed) an imitation of men worse than the average; worse, however, not as regards any and every sort of fault, but only as regards one particular kind, the Ridiculous, which is a species of the Ugly. The Ridiculous may be defined as a mistake or deformity not productive of pain or harm to others; the mask, for instance, that excites laughter, is something ugly and distorted without causing pain.

Though the successive changes in Tragedy and their authors are not unknown, we cannot say the same of Comedy; its early stages passed unnoticed, because it was not as yet taken up in a serious [1449ᵇ] way. It was only at a late point in its progress that a chorus of comedians was officially granted by the archon; they used to be mere volunteers. It had also already certain definite forms at the time when the record of those termed comic poets begins. Who it was who supplied it with masks, or prologues, or a plurality of actors and the like, has remained unknown. The invented Fable, or Plot, however, originated in Sicily with Epicharmus and Phormis; of Athenian poets Crates was the first to drop the Comedy of invective and frame stories of a general and non-personal nature, in other words, Fables or Plots.

Epic poetry, then, has been seen to agree with Tragedy to this extent, that of being an imitation of serious subjects in a grand kind of verse. It differs from it, however, (1) in that it is in one kind of verse and in narrative form; and (2) in its length—which is due to its action having no fixed limit of time, whereas Tragedy endeavours to keep as far as possible within a single circuit of the sun, or something near that. This, I say, is another point of difference between them, though at first the practice in this respect was just the same in tragedies as in epic poems. They differ also (3) in their constituents, some being common to both and others peculiar to Tragedy—hence a judge of good and bad in Tragedy is a judge of that in epic poetry also. All the parts of an epic are included in Tragedy; but those of Tragedy are not all of them to be found in the Epic.

6 Reserving hexameter poetry and Comedy for consideration hereafter, let us proceed now to the discussion of Tragedy; before doing so, however, we must gather up the definition resulting from what has been said. A tragedy, then, is the imitation of an action that is serious and also, as having magnitude, complete in itself; in language with pleasurable accessories, each kind brought in separately in the parts of the work; in a dramatic, not in a narrative form; with incidents arousing pity and fear, wherewith to accomplish its catharsis of such emotions. Here by 'language with pleasurable accessories' I mean that with rhythm and harmony or song superadded; and by 'the kinds separately' I mean that some portions are worked out with verse only, and others in turn with song.

I. As they act the stories, it follows that in the first place the Spectacle (or stage-appearance of the actors) must be some part of the whole; and in the second Melody and Diction, these two being the means of their imitation. Here by 'Diction' I mean merely this, the composition of the verses; and by 'Melody', what is too completely understood to require explanation. But further: the subject represented also is an action; and the action involves agents, who must necessarily have their distinctive qualities both of character and [1450ᵃ] thought, since it is from these that we ascribe certain qualities to their actions. There are in the natural order of things, therefore, two causes, Thought and Character, of their actions, and consequently of their success or failure in their lives. Now the action (that which was done) is represented in the play by the Fable or Plot. The Fable, in our present sense of the term, is simply this, the combination of the incidents, or things done in the story; whereas Character is what makes us ascribe certain moral qualities to the agents; and Thought is shown in all they say when proving a particular point or, it may be, enunciating a general truth. There are six parts consequently of every tragedy, as a whole (that is) of such or such quality, viz. a Fable or Plot, Characters, Diction, Thought, Spectacle, and Melody; two of them arising from the means, one from the manner, and three from the objects of the dramatic imitation; and there is nothing else besides these six. Of these, its formative elements, then, not a few of the dramatists have made due use, as every play, one may say, admits of Spectacle, Character, Fable, Diction, Melody, and Thought.

II. The most important of the six is the combination of the incidents of the story. Tragedy is essentially an imitation not of persons but of action and life, of happiness and misery. All human happiness or misery takes the form of action; the end for which we live is a certain kind of activity, not a quality. Character gives us qualities, but it is in our actions—what we do—that we are happy or the reverse. In a play accordingly they do not act in order to portray the Characters; they include the Characters for the sake of the action. So that it is the action in it, i.e. its Fable or Plot, that is the end and purpose of the tragedy; and the end is everywhere the chief thing. Besides this, a tragedy is impossible without action, but there may be one without Character. The tragedies of most of the moderns are characterless—a defect common among poets of all kinds, and with its counterpart in painting in Zeuxis as compared with Polygnotus; for whereas the latter is strong in character, the work of Zeuxis is devoid of it. And again: one may string together a series of characteristic speeches of the utmost finish as regards Diction and Thought, and yet fail to produce the true tragic effect; but one will have much better success with a tragedy which, however inferior in these respects, has a Plot, a combination of incidents, in it. And again: the most powerful elements of attraction in Tragedy, the Peripeties and Discoveries, are parts of the Plot. A further proof is in the fact that beginners succeed earlier with the Diction and Characters than with the construction of a story; and the same may be said of nearly all the early dramatists. We maintain, therefore, that the first essential, the life and soul, so to speak, of Tragedy is the Plot; and that the Characters come second—compare the parallel in painting, [1450ᵇ] where the most beautiful colours laid on without order will not give one the same pleasure as a simple black-and-white sketch of a portrait. We maintain that Tragedy is primarily an imitation of action and that it is mainly for the sake of the action that it imitates the personal agents. Third comes the element of Thought, i.e. the power of saying whatever can be said, or what is appropriate to the occasion. This is what, in the speeches in Tragedy, falls under the arts of Politics and Rhetoric; for the older poets make their personages discourse like statesmen, and the modern like rhetoricians. One must not confuse it with Character. Character in a play is that which reveals the moral purpose of the agents, i.e. the sort of thing they seek or avoid, where that is not obvious—hence there is no room for Character in a speech on a purely indifferent subject. Thought, on the other hand, is shown in all they say when proving or disproving some particular point, or enunciating some universal proposition. Fourth among the literary elements is the Diction of the personages, i.e., as before explained, the expression of their thoughts in words, which is practically the same thing with verse as with prose. As for the two remaining parts, the Melody is the greatest of the pleasurable accessories of Tragedy. The Spectacle, though an attraction, is the least artistic of all the parts, and has least to do with the art of poetry. The tragic effect is quite possible without a public performance and actors; and besides, the getting-up of the Spectacle is more a matter for the costumier than the poet.

7 Having thus distinguished the parts, let us now consider the proper construction of the Fable or Plot, as that is at once the first and the most important thing in Tragedy. We have laid it down that a tragedy is an imitation of an action that is complete in itself, as a whole of some magnitude; for a whole may be of no magnitude to speak of. Now a whole is that which has beginning, middle, and end. A beginning is that which is not itself necessarily after anything else, and which has naturally something else after it; an end is that which is naturally after something itself, either as its necessary or usual consequent, and with nothing else after it; and a middle, that which is by nature after one thing and has also another after it. A well-constructed Plot, therefore, cannot either begin or end at any point one likes; beginning and end in it must be of the forms just described. Again: to be beautiful, a living creature, and every whole made up of parts, must not only present a certain order in its arrangement of parts, but also be of a certain definite magnitude. Beauty is a matter of size and order, and therefore impossible either (1) in a very minute creature, since our perception becomes indistinct as it approaches instantaneity; or (2) in a creature of vast size—one, say, 1,000 miles long—as in that case, instead of the object being seen [1451^a] all at once, the unity and wholeness of it is lost to the beholder. Just in the same way, then, as a beautiful whole made up of parts, or a beautiful living creature, must be of some size, but a size to be taken in by the eye, so a story or Plot must be of some length, but of a length to be taken in by the memory. As for the limit of its length, so far as that is relative to public performances and spectators, it does not fall within the theory of poetry. If they had to perform a

hundred tragedies, they would be timed by water-clocks, as they are said to have been at one period. The limit, however, set by the actual nature of the thing is this: the longer the story, consistently with its being comprehensible as a whole, the finer it is by reason of its magnitude. As a rough general formula, 'a length which allows of the hero passing by a series of probable or necessary stages from misfortune to happiness, or from happiness to misfortune', may suffice as a limit for the magnitude of the story.

8 The Unity of a Plot does not consist, as some suppose, in its having one man as its subject. An infinity of things befall that one man, some of which it is impossible to reduce to unity; and in like manner there are many actions of one man which cannot be made to form one action. One sees, therefore, the mistake of all the poets who have written a *Heracleid*, a *Theseid*, or similar poems; they suppose that, because Heracles was one man, the story also of Heracles must be one story. Homer, however, evidently understood this point quite well, whether by art or instinct, just in the same way as he excels the rest in every other respect. In writing an *Odyssey*, he did not make the poem cover all that ever befell his hero—it befell him, for instance, to get wounded on Parnassus and also to feign madness at the time of the call to arms, but the two incidents had no necessary or probable connexion with one another—instead of doing that, he took as the subject of the *Odyssey*, as also of the *Iliad*, an action with a Unity of the kind we are describing. The truth is that, just as in the other imitative arts one imitation is always of one thing, so in poetry the story, as an imitation of action, must represent one action, a complete whole, with its several incidents so closely connected that the transposal or withdrawal of any one of them will disjoin and dislocate the whole. For that which makes no perceptible difference by its presence or absence is no real part of the whole.

9 From what we have said it will be seen that the poet's function is to describe, not the thing that has happened, but a kind of thing that might happen, i.e. what is possible as being probable or necessary. The distinction between historian and poet is not in the one [1451^b] writing prose and the other verse—you might put the work of Herodotus into verse, and it would still be a species of history; it consists really in this, that the one describes the thing that has been, and the other a kind of thing that might be. Hence poetry is something more philosophic and of graver import than history, since its statements are of the nature rather of universals, whereas those of history are singulars. By a universal statement I mean one as to what such or such a kind of man will probably or necessarily say or do—which is the aim of poetry, though it affixes proper names to the characters; by a singular statement, one as to what, say, Alcibiades did or had done to him. In Comedy this has become clear by this time; it is only when their plot is already made up of probable incidents that they give it a basis of proper names, choosing for the purpose any names that may occur to them, instead of writing like the old

iambic poets about particular persons. In Tragedy, however, they still adhere to the historic names; and for this reason: what convinces is the possible; now whereas we are not yet sure as to the possibility of that which has not happened, that which has happened is manifestly possible, else it would not have come to pass. Nevertheless even in Tragedy there are some plays with but one or two known names in them, the rest being inventions; and there are some without a single known name, e.g. Agathon's *Antheus*, in which both incidents and names are of the poet's invention; and it is no less delightful on that account. So that one must not aim at a rigid adherence to the traditional stories on which tragedies are based. It would be absurd, in fact, to do so, as even the known stories are only known to a few, though they are a delight none the less to all.

It is evident from the above that the poet must be more the poet of his stories or Plots than of his verses, inasmuch as he is a poet by virtue of the imitative element in his work, and it is actions that he imitates. And if he should come to take a subject from actual history, he is none the less a poet for that; since some historic occurrences may very well be in the probable and possible order of things; and it is in that aspect of them that he is their poet.

Of simple Plots and actions the episodic are the worst. I call a Plot episodic when there is neither probability nor necessity in the sequence of its episodes. Actions of this sort bad poets construct through their own fault, and good ones on account of the players. His work being for public performance, a good poet often stretches out a Plot beyond its capabilities, and is thus obliged to twist the sequence of incident.

[1452ª] Tragedy, however, is an imitation not only of a complete action, but also of incidents arousing pity and fear. Such incidents have the very greatest effect on the mind when they occur unexpectedly and at the same time in consequence of one another; there is more of the marvellous in them then than if they happened of themselves or by mere chance. Even matters of chance seem most marvellous if there is an appearance of design as it were in them; as for instance the statue of Mitys at Argos killed the author of Mitys' death by falling down on him when a looker-on at a public spectacle; for incidents like that we think to be not without a meaning. A Plot, therefore, of this sort is necessarily finer than others.

ARISTOTLE

*Nicomachean Ethics**

[1140ª] Things which admit of being other than they are include both things made and things done. Production is different from action—for that point we can rely even on our less technical discussions. Hence, the characteristic of acting rationally is different from the characteristic of producing rationally. It also follows that one does not include the other, for action is not production nor production action. Now, building is an art or applied science, and it is essentially a characteristic or trained ability of rationally producing. In fact, there is no art that is not a characteristic or trained ability of rationally producing, nor is there a characteristic or trained ability of rationally producing that is not an art. It follows that art is identical with the characteristic of producing under the guidance of true reason. All art is concerned with the realm of coming-to-be, i.e., with contriving and studying how something which is capable both of being and of not being may come into existence, a thing whose starting point or source is in the producer and not in the thing produced. For art is concerned neither with things which exist or come into being by necessity, nor with things produced by nature: these have their source of motion within themselves.

Since production and action are different, it follows that art deals with production and not with action. In a certain sense, fortune and art are concerned with the same things, as Agathon says: "Fortune loves art and art fortune." So, as we have said, art is a characteristic of producing under the guid-

* Aristotle, *The Oxford Translation of Aristotle*, edited by W. D. Ross, vol. 9 (*Nicomachean Ethics* translated by W. D. Ross) (New York: Random House), pp. 151-152. (Footnotes omitted.)

ance of true reason, and lack of art, on the contrary, is a characteristic of producing under the guidance of false reason; and both of them deal with what admits of being other than it is.

DAVID HUME

HUME IS THE MOST PROMINENT spokesman for empiricism. He is best known for his powerful and effective arguments that all our knowledge comes from experience but that experience offers no unassailable foundation for knowledge. He argues that causation can only be understood as constant conjunction, the linking of events in the mind based on its past experience. Similarly, he argues that morality is founded on internal principles of sympathy and sentiments toward others. The constant theme of Hume's position is a reliance on mechanisms internal to the mind and a skepticism toward the foundations underlying experience.

His theory of art is consistent with his general position. Taste is the primary notion, for there is no authority beyond taste for the evaluation of works of art. A standard of taste, however, can be derived from the workings of the mind.

To many philosophers, this kind of analysis is psychologistic, and offers no foundation for a theory of art. We may say, then, that Hume poses the central problem of the philosophy of art, whether any theory can do more than describe the workings of the human mind when confronted with works of beauty and power.

DAVID HUME

*Of the Standard of Taste**

The great variety of Taste, as well as of opinion, which prevails in the world, is too obvious not to have fallen under every one's observation. Men of the most confined knowledge are able to remark a difference of taste in the narrow circle of their acquaintance, even where the persons have been educated under the same government, and have early imbibed the same prejudices. But those, who can enlarge their view to contemplate distant nations and remote ages, are still more surprized at the great inconsistence and contrariety. We are apt to call *barbarous* whatever departs widely from our own taste and apprehension: But soon find the epithet of reproach retorted on us. And the highest arrogance and self-conceit is at last startled, on observing an equal assurance on all sides, and scruples, amidst such a contest of sentiment, to pronounce positively in its own favour.

As this variety of taste is obvious to the most careless enquirer; so will it be found, on examination, to be still greater in reality than in appearance. The sentiments of men often differ with regard to beauty and deformity of all kinds, even while their general discourse is the same. There are certain terms in every language, which import blame, and others praise; and all men, who use the same tongue, must agree in their application of them. Every voice is united in applauding elegance, propriety, simplicity, spirit in writing; and in blaming fustian, affectation, coldness, and a false brilliancy: But when critics come to particulars, this seeming unanimity vanishes; and it is found, that they had affixed a very different meaning to their expressions. In all matters of

* David Hume, "Of the Standard of Taste," from *Essays, Moral, Political and Literary*, edited by T. H. Green and T. H. Grose, vol. I, pp. 266-284 (London: Longmans, Green & Co., Ltd., 1882).

opinion and science, the case is opposite: The difference among men is there oftener found to lie in generals than in particulars; and to be less in reality than in appearance. An explanation of the terms commonly ends the controversy; and the disputants are surprized to find, that they had been quarreling, while at bottom they agreed in their judgment.

Those who found morality on sentiment, more than on reason, are inclined to comprehend ethics under the former observation, and to maintain, that, in all questions, which regard conduct and manners, the difference among men is really greater than at first sight it appears. It is indeed obvious, that writers of all nations and all ages concur in applauding justice, humanity, magnanimity, prudence, veracity; and in blaming the opposite qualities. Even poets and other authors, whose compositions are chiefly calculated to please the imagination, are yet found, from HOMER down to FENELON, to inculcate the same moral precepts, and to bestow their applause and blame on the same virtues and vices. This great unanimity is usually ascribed to the influence of plain reason; which, in all these cases, maintains similar sentiments in all men, and prevents those controversies, to which the abstract sciences are so much exposed. So far as the unanimity is real, this account may be admitted as satisfactory: But we must also allow that some part of the seeming harmony in morals may be accounted for from the very nature of language. The word *virtue*, with its equivalent in every tongue, implies praise; as that of *vice* does blame: And no one, without the most obvious and grossest impropriety, could affix reproach to a term, which in general acceptation is understood in a good sense; or bestow applause, where the idiom requires disapprobation. HOMER's general precepts, where he delivers any such will never be controverted; but it is obvious, that, when he draws particular pictures of manners, and represents heroism in ACHILLES and prudence in ULYSSES, he intermixes a much greater degree of ferocity in the former, and of cunning and fraud in the latter, than FENELON would admit of. The sage ULYSSES in the GREEK poet seems to delight in lies and fictions; and often employs them without any necessity or even advantage: But his more scrupulous son, in the FRENCH epic writer, exposes himself to the most imminent perils, rather than depart from the most exact line of truth and veracity.

The admirers and followers of the ALCORAN insist on the excellent moral precepts interspersed throughout that wild and absurd performance. But it is to be supposed, that the ARABIC words, which correspond to the ENGLISH, equity, justice, temperance, meekness, charity, were such as, from the constant use of that tongue, must always be taken in a good sense; and it would have argued the greatest ignorance, not of morals, but of language, to have mentioned them with any epithets, besides those of applause and approbation. But would we know, whether the pretended prophet had really attained a just sentiment of morals? Let us attend to his narration; and we shall soon find, that he bestows praise on such instances of treachery, inhumanity, cruelty, revenge, bigotry, as are utterly incompatible with civilized society. No steady rule of right seems there to be attended to; and every action is blamed or praised, so far only as it is beneficial or hurtful to the true believers.

The merit of delivering true general precepts in ethics is indeed very small. Whoever recommends any moral virtues, really does no more than is implied in the terms themselves. That people, who invented the word *charity*, and used it in a good sense, inculcated more clearly and much more efficaciously, the precept, *be charitable*, than any pretended legislator or prophet, who should insert such a *maxim* in his writings. Of all expressions, those, which, together with their other meaning, imply a degree either of blame or approbation, are the least liable to be perverted or mistaken.

It is natural for us to seek a *Standard of Taste;* a rule, by which the various sentiments of men may be reconciled; at least, a decision, afforded, confirming one sentiment, and condemning another.

There is a species of philosophy, which cuts off all hopes of success in such an attempt, and represents the impossibility of ever attaining any standard of taste. The difference, it is said, is very wide between judgment and sentiment. All sentiment is right; because sentiment has a reference to nothing beyond itself, and is always real, wherever a man is conscious of it. But all determinations of the understanding are not right; because they have a reference to something beyond themselves, to wit, real matter of fact; and are not always conformable to that standard. Among a thousand different opinions which different men may entertain of the same subject, there is one, and but one, that is just and true; and the only difficulty is to fix and ascertain it. On the contrary, a thousand different sentiments, excited by the same object, are all right: Because no sentiment represents what is really in the object. It only marks a certain conformity or relation between the object and the organs or faculties of the mind; and if that conformity did not really exist, the sentiment could never possibly have being. Beauty is no quality in things themselves: It exists merely in the mind which contemplates them; and each mind perceives a different beauty. One person may even perceive deformity, where another is sensible of beauty; and every individual ought to acquiesce in his own sentiment, without pretending to regulate those of others. To seek the real beauty, or real deformity, is as fruitless an enquiry, as to pretend to ascertain the real sweet or real bitter. According to the disposition of the organs, the same object may be both sweet and bitter; and the proverb has justly determined it to be fruitless to dispute concerning tastes. It is very natural, and even quite necessary, to extend this axiom to mental, as well as bodily taste; and thus common sense, which is so often at variance with philosophy, especially with the skeptical kind, is found, in one instance at least, to agree in pronouncing the same decision.

But though this axiom, by passing into a proverb, seems to have attained the sanction of common sense; there is certainly a species of common sense which opposes it, at least serves to modify and restrain it. Whoever would assert an equality of genius and elegance between OGILBY and MILTON, or BUNYAN and ADDISON, would be thought to defend no less an extravagance, than if he had maintained a mole-hill to be as high as TENERIFFE, or a pond as extensive as the ocean. Though there may be found persons, who give the preference to the former authors; no one pays attention to such a taste; and we pronounce without scruple the sentiment of these pretended critics to be absurd and ridiculous. The principle of the natural equality of tastes is then totally forgot, and while we admit it on some occasions, where the objects seem near an equality, it appears an extravagant paradox, or rather a palpable absurdity, where objects so disproportioned are compared together.

It is evident that none of the rules of composition are fixed by reasonings *a priori,* or can be esteemed abstract conclusions of the understanding, from comparing those habitudes and relations of ideas, which are eternal and immutable. Their foundation is the same with that of all the practical sciences, experience; nor are they any thing but general observations, concerning what has been universally found to please in all countries and in all ages. Many of the beauties of poetry and even of eloquence are founded on falsehood and fiction, on hyperboles, metaphors, and an abuse or perversion of terms from their natural meaning. To check the sallies of the imagination, and to reduce every expression to geometrical truth and exactness, would be the most contrary to the laws of criticism; because it would produce a work, which, by universal experience, has been found the most insipid and disagreeable. But though poetry can never submit to exact truth, it must be confined by rules of art, discovered to the author either by genius or observation. If some negligent or irregular writers have pleased, they have not pleased by their transgressions of rule or order, but in spite of these transgressions: They have possessed other beauties, which were conformable to just criticism; and the force of these beauties has been able to overpower censure, and give the mind a satisfaction superior to the disgust arising from the blemishes. ARIOSTO pleases; but not by his monstrous and improbable fictions, by his bizarre mixture of the serious and comic styles, by the want of coherence in his stories, or by the continual interruptions of his narration. He charms by the force and clearness of his expression, by the readiness and variety of his inventions, and by his natural pictures of the passions, especially those of the gay and amorous kind: And however his faults may diminish our satisfaction, they are not able entirely to destroy it. Did our pleasure really arise from those parts of his poem, which we denominate faults, this would be no objection to criticism in general: It would only be an objection to those particular rules of criticism, which would establish such circumstances to be faults, and would represent them as universally blameable. If they are found to please, they cannot be faults; let the pleasure, which they produce, be ever so unexpected and unaccountable.

But though all the general rules of art are founded only on experience and on the observation of the common sentiments of human nature, we must not imagine, that, on every occasion, the feelings of men will be conformable to these rules. Those finer emotions of the mind are of a very tender and delicate nature, and require the concurrence of many favourable circumstances to make them play with facility and exactness, according to their general and established principles. The least exterior hindrance to such small springs, or the least internal disorder, disturbs their motion, and confounds the operation of the whole machine. When we would make an experiment of this nature, and would try the force of any beauty or deformity, we must choose with care a proper time and place, and bring the fancy to a suitable situation and disposition. A perfect serenity of mind, a recollection of thought, a due attention to the object; if any of these circumstances be wanting, our experiment will be fallacious, and we shall be unable to judge of the catholic and universal beauty. The relation, which nature has placed between the form and the sentiment will at least be more obscure; and it will require greater accuracy to trace and discern it. We shall be able to ascertain its influence not so much from the operation of each particular beauty, as from the durable admiration, which attends those works, that have survived all the caprices of mode and fashion, all the mistakes of ignorance and envy.

The same HOMER, who pleased at ATHENS and ROME two thousand years ago, is still admired at PARIS and at LONDON. All the changes of climate, government, religion, and language, have not been able to obscure his glory. Authority or prejudice may give a temporary vogue to a bad poet or orator; but his reputation will never be durable or general. When his compositions are examined by posterity or by foreigners, the enchantment is dissipated, and his faults appear in their true colours. On the contrary, a real genius, the longer his works endure, and the more wide they are spread, the more sincere is the admiration which he meets with. Envy and jealousy have too much place in a narrow circle; and even familiar acquaintance with his person may diminish the applause due to his performances. But when these obstructions are removed, the beauties, which are naturally fitted to excite agreeable sentiments, immediately display their energy and while the world endures, they maintain their authority over the minds of men.

It appears then, that, amidst all the variety and caprice of taste, there are certain general principles of approbation or blame, whose influence a careful eye may trace in all operations of the mind. Some particular forms or qualities, from the original structure of the internal fabric, are calculated to please, and others to displease; and if they fail of their effect in any particular instance, it is from some apparent defect or imperfection in the organ. A man in a fever would not insist on his palate as able to decide concerning flavours; nor would one, affected with the jaundice, pretend to give a verdict with regard to colours. In each creature, there is a sound and a defective state; and the former alone can be supposed to afford us a true standard of taste and sentiment. If, in the sound state of the organ, there be an entire or a considerable uniformity of sentiment among men, we may thence derive an idea of the perfect beauty; in like manner as the appearance of objects in daylight, to the eye of a man in health, is denominated their true and real colour, even while colour is allowed to be merely a phantasm of the senses.

Many and frequent are the defects in the internal organs, which prevent or weaken the influence of those general principles, on which depends our sentiment of beauty or deformity. Though some objects, by the structure of the mind, be naturally calculated to give pleasure, it is not to be expected, that in every individual the pleasure will be equally felt. Particular incidents and situations occur, which either throw a false light on the objects, or hinder the true from conveying to the imagination the proper sentiment and perception.

One obvious cause, why many feel not the proper sentiment of beauty, is the want of that *delicacy* of imagination, which is requisite to convey a sensibility of those finer emotions. This delicacy every one pretends to: Every one talks of it; and would reduce every kind of taste or sentiment to its standard. But as our intention in this essay is to mingle some light of the understanding with the feelings of sentiment, it will be proper to give a more accurate definition of delicacy, than has hitherto been attempted. And not to draw our philosophy from too profound a source, we shall have recourse to a noted story in DON QUIXOTE.

It is with good reason, says SANCHO to the squire with the great nose, that I pretend to have a judgment in wine: This is a quality hereditary in our family. Two of my kinsmen were once called to give their opinion of a hogshead, which was supposed to be excellent, being old and of a good vintage. One of them tastes it; considers it; and after mature reflection pronounces the wine to be good, were it not for a small taste of leather, which he perceived in it. The other, after using the same precautions, gives also his verdict in favour of the wine; but with the reserve of a taste of iron, which he could easily distinguish. You cannot imagine how much they were both ridiculed for their judgment. But who laughed in the end? On emptying the hogshead, there was found at the bottom, an old key with a leathern thong tied to it.

The great resemblance between mental and bodily taste will easily teach us to apply this story. Though it be certain, that beauty and deformity, more than sweet and bitter, are not qualities in objects, but belong entirely to the sentiment, internal or external; it must be allowed, that there are certain qualities in objects, which are fitted by nature to produce those particular feelings. Now as these qualities may be found in a small degree, or may be mixed and confounded with each other, it often happens, that the taste is not affected with such minute qualities, or is not able to distinguish all the particular flavours, amidst the disorder, in which they are presented. Where the organs are so fine, as to allow nothing to escape them; and at the same time so exact as to perceive every ingredient in the composition: This we call delicacy of taste, whether we employ these terms in the literal or metaphorical sense. Here then the general rules of beauty are of use; being drawn from established models, and from the observation of what pleases or displeases, when presented singly and in a high degree: And if the same qualities, in a continued composition and in a smaller degree, affect not the organs with a sensible delight or uneasiness, we exclude the person from all pretensions to this delicacy. To produce these general rules or avowed patterns of composition is like finding the key with the leathern thong; which justified the verdict of

SANCHO's kinsmen, and confounded those pretended judges who had condemned them. Though the hogshead had never been emptied, the taste of the one was still equally delicate, and that of the other equally dull and languid: But it would have been more difficult to have proved the superiority of the former, to the conviction of every by-stander. In like manner, though the beauties of writing had never been methodized, or reduced to general principles; though no excellent models had ever been acknowledged; the different degrees of taste would still have subsisted, and the judgment of one man had been preferable to that of another; but it would not have been so easy to silence the bad critic, who might always insist upon his particular sentiment, and refuse to submit to his antagonist. But when we show him an avowed principle of art; when we illustrate this principle by examples, whose operation, from his own particular taste, he acknowledges to be conformable to the principle; when we prove, that the same principle may be applied to the present case, where he did not perceive or feel its influence: He must conclude, upon the whole, that the fault lies in himself, and that he wants the delicacy, which is requisite to make him sensible of every beauty and every blemish, in any composition or discourse.

It is acknowledged to be the perfection of every sense or faculty, to perceive with exactness its most minute objects, and allow nothing to escape its notice and observation. The smaller the objects are, which become sensible to the eye, the finer is that organ, and the more elaborate its make and composition. A good palate is not tried by strong flavours; but by a mixture of small ingredients, where we are still sensible of each part, notwithstanding its minuteness and its confusion with the rest. In like manner, a quick and acute perception of beauty and deformity must be the perfection of our mental taste; nor can a man be satisfied with himself while he suspects, that any excellence or blemish in a discourse has passed him unobserved. In this case, the perfection of the man, and the perfection of the sense or feeling, are found to be united. A very delicate palate, on many occasions, may be a great inconvenience both to a man himself and to his friends: But a delicate taste of wit or beauty must always be a desirable quality; because it is the source of all the finest and most innocent enjoyments, of which human nature is susceptible. In this decision the sentiments of all mankind are agreed. Wherever you can ascertain a delicacy of taste, it is sure to meet with approbation; and the best way of ascertaining it is to appeal to those models and principles, which have been established by the uniform consent and experience of nations and ages.

But though there be naturally a wide difference in point of delicacy between one person and another, nothing tends further to encrease and improve this talent, than *practice* in a particular art, and the frequent survey or contemplation of a particular species of beauty. When objects of any kind are first presented to the eye or imagination, the sentiment, which attends them, is obscure and confused; and the mind is, in a great measure, incapable of pronouncing concerning their merits or defects. The taste cannot perceive the several excellences of the performance; much less distinguish the particular character of each excellency, and ascertain its quality and degree. If it pronounce the whole in general to be beautiful or deformed, it is the utmost that can be expected; and even this judgment, a person, so unpractised, will be apt to deliver with great hesitation and reserve. But allow him to acquire experience in those objects, his feeling becomes more exact and nice: He not only perceives the beauties and defects of each part, but marks the distinguishing species of each quality, and assigns it suitable praise or blame. A clear and distinct sentiment attends him through the whole survey of the objects; and he discerns that very degree and kind of approbation or displeasure, which each part is naturally fitted to produce. The mist dissipates, which seemed formerly to hang over the object: The organ acquires greater perfection in its operations; and can pronounce, without danger of mistake, concerning the merits of every performance. In a word, the same address and dexterity, which practice gives to the execution of any work, is also acquired by the same means, in the judging of it.

So advantageous is practice to the discernment of beauty, that, before we can give judgment on any work of importance, it will even be requisite, that that very individual performance be more than once perused by us, and be surveyed in different lights with attention and deliberation. There is a flutter or hurry of thought which attends the first perusal of any piece, and which confounds the genuine sentiment of beauty. The relation of the parts is not discerned: The true characters of style are little distinguished: The several perfections and defects seem wrapped up in a species of confusion, and present themselves indistinctly to the imagination. Not to mention, that there is a species of beauty, which, as it is florid and superficial, pleases at first; but being found incompatible with a just expression either of reason or passion, soon palls upon the taste, and is then rejected with disdain, at least rated at a much lower value.

It is impossible to continue in the practice of contemplating any order of beauty, without being frequently obliged to form *comparisons* between the several species and degrees of excellence, and estimating their proportion to each other. A man, who has had no opportunity of comparing the different kinds of beauty, is indeed totally unqualified to pronounce an opinion with regard to any object presented to him. By comparison alone we fix the epithets of praise or blame, and learn how to assign the due degree of each. The coarsest daubing contains a certain lustre of colours and exactness of imitation, which are so far beauties, and would affect the mind of a peasant or Indian with the highest admiration. The most vulgar ballads are not entirely destitute of harmony or nature; and not but a person, familiarized to superior beauties, would pronounce their numbers harsh, or narration uninteresting. A great inferiority of beauty gives pain to a person conversant in the highest excellence of the kind, and is for that reason pronounced a deformity: As the most finished object, with which we are acquainted, is naturally supposed to have reached the pinnacle of perfection, and to be entitled to the highest applause. One accustomed to see, and examine, and weigh the several performances, admired in different ages and nations, can only rate the merits of a work exhibited to his view, and assign its proper rank among the productions of genius.

But to enable a critic the more fully to execute this undertaking, he must preserve his mind free from all *prejudice*, and allow nothing to enter into his consideration, but the very object which is submitted to his examination. We may observe, that every work of art, in order to produce its due effect on the mind, must be surveyed in a certain point of view, and cannot be fully relished by persons, whose situation, real or imaginary, is not conformable to that which is required by the performance. An orator addresses himself to a particular audience, and must have a regard to their particular genius, interests, opinions, passions, and prejudices; otherwise he hopes in vain to govern their resolutions, and inflame their affections. Should they even have entertained some prepossessions against him, however unreasonable, he must not overlook this disadvantage; but, before he enters upon the subject, must endeavour to conciliate their affection, and acquire their good graces. A critic of a different age or nation, who should peruse this discourse, must have all these circumstances in his eye, and must place himself in the same situation as the audience, in order to form a true judgment of the oration. In like manner, when any work is addressed to the public, though I should have a friendship or enmity with the author, I must depart from this situation; and considering myself as a man in general, forget, if possible, my individual being and my peculiar circumstances. A person influenced by prejudice, complies not with this condition; but obstinately maintains his natural position, without placing himself in that point of view, which the performance supposes. If the work be addressed to persons of a different age or nation, he makes no allowance for their peculiar views and prejudices; but, full of the manners of his own age and country, rashly condemns what seemed admirable in the eyes of those for whom alone the discourse was calculated. If the work be executed for the public, he never sufficiently enlarges his comprehension, or forgets his interest as a friend or enemy, as a rival or commentator. By this means, his sentiments are perverted; nor have the same beauties and blemishes the same influence upon him, as if he had imposed a proper violence on his imagination, and had forgotten himself for a moment. So far his taste evidently departs from the true standard; and of consequence loses all credit and authority.

It is well known, that in all questions, submitted to the understanding, prejudice is destructive of sound judgment, and perverts all operations of the intellectual faculties: It is no less contrary to good taste; nor has it less influence to corrupt our sentiment of beauty. It belongs to *good sense* to check its influence in both cases; and in this respect, as well as in many others, reason, if not an essential part of taste, is at least requisite to the operations of this latter faculty. In all the nobler productions of genius, there is a mutual relation and correspondence of parts; nor can either the beauties or blemishes be perceived by him, whose thought is not capacious enough to comprehend all those parts, and compare them with each other, in order to perceive the consistence and uniformity of the whole. Every work of art has also a certain end or purpose, for which it is calculated; and is to be deemed more or less perfect, as it is more or less fitted to attain this end. The object of eloquence is to persuade, of history to instruct, of poetry to please by means of the passions and the imagination. These ends we must carry constantly in our view, when we peruse any performance; and we must be able to judge how far the means employed are adapted to their respective purposes. Besides, every kind of composition, even the most poetical, is nothing but a chain of propositions and reasonings; not always, indeed, the justest and most exact, but still plausible and specious, however disguised by the colouring of the imagination. The persons introduced in tragedy and epic poetry, must be represented as reasoning, and thinking, and concluding, and acting, suitably to their character and circumstances; and without judgment, as well as taste and invention, a poet can never hope to succeed in so delicate an undertaking. Not to mention, that the same excellence of faculties which contributes to the improvement of reason, the same clearness of conception, the same exactness of distinction, the same vivacity of apprehension, are essential to the operations of true taste, and are its infallible concomitants. It seldom, or never happens, that a man of sense, who has experience in any art, cannot judge of its beauty; and it is no less rare to meet with a man who has a just taste without a sound understanding.

Thus, though the principles of taste be universal, and, nearly, if not entirely the same in all men; yet few are qualified to give judgment on any work of art, or establish their own sentiment as the standard of beauty. The organs of internal sensation are seldom so perfect as to allow the general principles their full play, and produce a feeling correspondent to those principles. They either labour under some defect, or are vitiated by some disorder; and by that means, excite a sentiment, which may be pronounced erroneous. When the critic has no delicacy, he judges without any distinction, and is only affected by the grosser and more palpable qualities of the object: The finer touches pass unnoticed and disregarded. Where he is not aided by practice, his verdict is attended with confusion and hesitation. Where no comparison has been employed, the most frivolous beauties, such as rather merit the name of defects, are the object of his admiration. Where he lies under the influence of prejudice, all his natural sentiments are perverted. Where good sense is wanting, he is not qualified to discern the beauties of design and reasoning, which are the highest and most excellent. Under some or other of these imperfections, the generality of men labour; and hence a true judge in the finer arts is observed, even during the most polished ages, to be so rare a character: Strong sense, united to delicate sentiment, improved by practice, perfected by comparison, and cleared of all prejudice, can alone entitle critics to this valuable character; and the joint verdict of such, wherever they are to be found, is the true standard of taste and beauty.

But where are such critics to be found? By what marks are they to be known? How distinguish them from pretenders? These questions are embarrassing; and seem to throw us back into the same uncertainty, from which, during the course of this essay, we have endeavoured to extricate ourselves.

But if we consider the matter aright, these are questions of fact, not of sentiment. Whether any particular person be endowed with good sense and a delicate imagination, free from prejudice, may often be the subject of dispute, and be liable to great discussion and enquiry: But that such a character is valuable and estimable will be agreed in by all mankind. Where these doubts occur, men can do no more than in other disputable questions, which are submitted to the understanding: They must produce the best arguments, that their invention suggests to them; they must acknowledge a true and decisive standard to exist somewhere, to wit, real existence and matter of fact; and they must have indulgence to such as differ from them in their appeals to this standard. It is sufficient for our present purpose, if we have proved, that the taste of all individuals is not upon an equal footing, and that some men in general, however difficult to be particularly pitched upon, will be acknowledged by universal sentiment to have a preference above others.

But in reality the difficulty of finding, even in particulars, the standard of taste, is not so great as it is represented. Though in speculation, we may readily avow a certain criterion in science and deny it in sentiment, the matter is found in practice to be much more hard to ascertain in the former case than in the latter. Theories of abstract philosophy, systems of profound theology, have prevailed during one age: In a successive period, these have been universally exploded: Their absurdity has been detected: Other theories and systems have supplied their place, which again gave place to their successors: And nothing has been experienced more liable to the revolutions of chance and fashion than these pretended decisions of science. The case is not the same with the beauties of eloquence and poetry. Just expressions of passion and nature are sure, after a little time, to gain public applause, which they maintain for ever. ARISTOTLE, and PLATO, and EPICURUS, and DESCARTES, may successively yield to each other: But TERENCE and VIRGIL maintain an universal, undisputed empire over the minds of men. The abstract philosophy of CICERO has lost its credit: The vehemence of his oratory is still the object of our admiration.

Though men of delicate taste be rare, they are easily to be distinguished in society, by the soundness of their understanding and the superiority of their faculties above the rest of mankind. The ascendant, which they acquire, gives a prevalence to that lively approbation, with which they receive any productions of genius, and renders it generally predominant. Many men, when left to themselves, have but a faint and dubious perception of beauty, who yet are capable of relishing any fine stroke, which is pointed out to them. Every convert to the admiration of the real poet or orator is the cause of some new conversion. And though prejudices may prevail for a time, they never unite in celebrating any rival to the true genius, but yield at last to the force of nature and just sentiment. Thus, though a civilized nation may easily be mistaken in the choice of their admired philosopher, they never have been found long to err, in their affection for a favorite epic or tragic author.

But notwithstanding all our endeavours to fix a standard of taste, and reconcile the discordant apprehensions of men, there still remain two sources of variation, which are not sufficient indeed to confound all the boundaries of beauty and deformity, but will often serve to produce a difference in the degrees of our approbation or blame. The one is the different humours of particular men; the other, the particular manners and opinions of our age and country. The general principles of taste are uniform in human nature: Where men vary in their judgments, some defect or perversion in the faculties may commonly be remarked; proceeding either from prejudice, from want of practice, or want of delicacy; and there is just reason for approving one taste, and condemning another. But where there is such a diversity in the internal frame or external situation as is entirely blameless on both sides, and leaves no room to give one the preference above the other; in that case a certain degree of diversity in judgment is unavoidable, and we seek in vain for a standard, by which we can reconcile the contrary sentiments.

A young man, whose passions are warm, will be more sensibly touched with amorous and tender images, than a man more advanced in years, who takes pleasure in wise, philosophical reflections concerning the conduct of life and moderation of the passions. At twenty, OVID may be the favourite author; HORACE at forty; and perhaps TACITUS at fifty. Vainly would we, in such cases, endeavour to enter into the sentiments of others, and divest ourselves of those propensities, which are natural to us. We choose our favourite author as we do our friend, from a conformity of humour and disposition. Mirth or passion, sentiment or reflection; whichever of these most predominates in our temper, it gives us a peculiar sympathy with the writer who resembles us.

One person is more pleased with the sublime; another with the tender; a third with raillery. One has a strong sensibility to blemishes, and is extremely studious of correctness: Another has a more lively feeling of beauties, and pardons twenty absurdities and defects for one elevated or pathetic stroke. The ear of this man is entirely turned towards conciseness and energy; that man is delighted with a copious, rich, and harmonious expression. Simplicity is affected by one; ornament by another. Comedy, tragedy, satire, odes, have each its partizans, who prefer that particular species of writing to all others. It is plainly an error in a critic, to confine his approbation to one species or style of writing, and condemn all the rest. But it is almost impossible not to feel a predilection for that which suits our particular turn and disposition. Such preferences are innocent and unavoidable, and can never reasonably be the object of dispute, because there is no standard, by which they can be decided.

For a like reason, we are more pleased, in the course of our reading, with pictures and characters, that resemble objects which are found in our own age or country, than with those which describe a different set of customs. It is not without some effort, that we reconcile ourselves to the simplicity of ancient manners, and behold princesses carrying water from the spring, and kings and heroes dressing their own victuals. We may allow in general, that the representation of such manners is no fault in the author, nor deformity in the piece; but we are not so sensibly touched with them. For this reason, comedy is not easily transferred from one age or nation to another. A FRENCHMAN or ENGLISHMAN is not pleased with the ANDRIA of TERENCE, or CLITIA of MACHIAVEL; where the fine lady, upon whom all the play turns, never once appears to the spectators, but is always kept behind the scenes, suitably to the reserved humour of the ancient GREEKS and modern ITALIANS. A man of learning and reflection can make allowance for these peculiarities of manners; but a common audience can never divest themselves so far of their usual ideas and sentiments, as to relish pictures which in no wise resemble them.

But here there occurs a reflection, which may, perhaps, be useful in examining the celebrated controversy concerning ancient and modern learning; where we often find the one side excusing any seeming absurdity in the ancients from the manners of the age, and the other refusing to admit this excuse, or at least, admitting it only as an apology for the author, not for the performance. In my opinion, the proper boundaries in this subject have seldom been fixed between the contending parties. Where any innocent peculiarities of manners are represented, such as those above mentioned, they ought certainly to be admitted; and a man, who is shocked with them, gives an evident proof of false delicacy and refinement. The poet's *monument more durable than brass,* must fall to the ground like common brick or clay, were men to make no allowance for the continual revolutions of manners and customs, and would admit of nothing but what was suitable to the prevailing fashion. Must we throw aside the pictures of our ancestors, because of their ruffs and fardingales? But where the ideas of morality and decency alter from one age to another, and where vicious manners are described, without being marked with the proper characters of blame and disapprobation; this must be allowed to disfigure the poem, and to be a real deformity. I cannot, nor is it proper I should, enter into such sentiments; and however I may excuse the poet, on account of the manners in his age, I never can relish the composition. The want of humanity and of decency, so conspicuous in the characters drawn by several of the ancient poets, even sometimes by HOMER and the GREEK tragedians, diminishes considerably the merit of their noble performances, and gives modern authors an advantage over them. We are not interested in the fortunes and sentiments of such rough heroes: We are displeased to find the limits of vice and virtue so much confounded: And whatever indulgence we may give to the writer on account of his prejudices, we cannot prevail on ourself to enter into his sentiments, or bear an affection to characters, which we plainly discover to be blameable.

The case is not the same with moral principles, as with speculative opinions of any kind. These are in continual flux and revolution. The son embraces a different system from the father. Nay, there scarcely is any man, who can boast of great constancy and uniformity in this particular. Whatever speculative errors may be found in the polite writings of any age or country, they detract but little from the value of those compositions. There needs but a certain turn of thought or imagination to make us enter into all the opinions, which then prevailed, and relish the sentiments or conclusions derived from them. But a very violent effort is requisite to change our judgment of manners, and excite sentiments of approbation or blame, love or hatred, different from those to which the mind from long custom has been familiarized. And where a man is confident of the rectitude of that moral standard, by which he judges, he is justly jealous of it, and will not pervert the sentiments of his heart for a moment, in complaisance to any writer whatsoever.

Of all speculative errors, those, which regard religion, are the most excusable in compositions of genius; nor is it ever permitted to judge of the civility or wisdom of any people, or even of single persons, by the grossness or refinement of their theological principles. The same good sense, that directs men in the ordinary occurrences of life, is not harkened to in religious matters, which are supposed to be placed altogether above the cognizance of human reason. On this account, all the absurdities of the pagan system of theology must be overlooked by every critic, who would pretend to form a just notion of ancient poetry; and our posterity, in their turn, must have the same indulgence to their forefathers. No religious principles can ever be imputed as a fault to any poet, while they remain merely principles, and take not such strong possession of his heart, as to lay him under the imputation of *bigotry* or *superstition*. Where that happens, they confound the sentiments of morality, and alter the natural boundaries of vice and virtue. They are therefore eternal blemishes, according to the principle above mentioned; nor are the prejudices and false opinions of the age sufficient to justify them.

It is essential to the ROMAN catholic religion to inspire a violent hatred of every other worship, and to represent all pagans, mahometans, and heretics as the objects of divine wrath and vengeance. Such sentiments, though they are in reality very blameable, are considered as virtues by the zealots of that communion, and are represented in their tragedies and epic poems as a kind of divine heroism. This bigotry has disfigured two very fine tragedies of the FRENCH theatre, POLIEUCTE and ATHALIA; where an intemperate zeal for particular modes of worship is set off with all the pomp imaginable, and forms the predominant character of the heroes. 'What is this,' says the sublime JOAD to JOSABET, finding her in discourse with MATHAN, the priest of BAAL, 'Does the daughter of DAVID speak to this traitor? Are you not afraid, lest the earth should open and pour forth flames to devour you both? Or lest these holy walls should fall and crush you together? What is his purpose? Why comes that enemy of God hither to poison the air, which we breath, with his horrid presence?' Such sentiments are received with great applause on the theatre of PARIS; but at LONDON the spectators would be full as much pleased to hear ACHILLES tell AGAMEMNON, that he was a dog in his forehead, and a deer in his heart, or JUPITER threaten JUNO with a sound drubbing, if she will not be quiet.

RELIGIOUS principles are also a blemish in any polite composition, when they rise up to superstition, and intrude themselves into every sentiment, however remote from any connection with religion. It is no excuse for the poet, that the customs of his country had burthened life with so many religious ceremonies and observances, that no part of it was exempt from that yoke. It must for ever be ridiculous in PETRARCH to compare his mistress LAURA, to JESUS CHRIST. Nor is it less ridiculous in that agreeable libertine, BOCCACE, very seriously to give thanks to GOD ALMIGHTY and the ladies, for their assistance in defending him against his enemies.

Immanuel Kant

KANT'S *CRITIQUE OF JUDGMENT* is probably the most important and influential work in Western aesthetic theory, and it is not difficult to understand why. His general theory may be read as a response to the problems raised by Hume concerning the necessity in scientific understanding or morality. Kant's theory may equally be interpreted as a synthetic resolution of the central problems of modern philosophy. He argues at great length that there are fundamental principles in the human mind that constitute its cognitive powers, that enable it to synthesize its manifold experiences into unity. Thus, space and time are forms under which we must experience our surroundings in order to experience them at all.

Kant's first critique, the *Critique of Pure Reason*, may therefore be read as an analysis of the principles that define the concepts whereby we can experience and understand the world surrounding us. His second critique, the *Critique of Practical Reason*, is an analysis of the principles that define the concepts of moral obligation and duty. In effect then the first *Critique* defines understanding under causal necessity, and the second *Critique* defines reason under the concept of freedom.

Into this general system, Kant brings fundamental questions concerning the nature of art. He denies that art falls under the concepts of necessity or freedom, denies that art is a form of understanding or morality. In other words, he offers a powerful argument for the uniqueness and autonomy of art by denying that aesthetic judgment and taste are objective. Nevertheless, although subjective, judgments of beauty must be universal, shareable by everyone who possesses good taste. In relation to beauty, Kant offers a community of taste ungoverned by concepts. But Kant also offers a theory of the sublime, where the infinite, beyond concepts, appears in art, and of genius, the capacity to produce apart from rules.

The autonomy of art is attained at an enormous price in Kant, since art can offer neither knowledge nor morality, though it may be conjoined with them in impure arts. Kant's theory of taste has had enormous influence, supporting a view of art for art's sake, independent of the human or natural world. Yet there is much more to the *Critique of Judgment* than this. His view of genius was deeply influential in Romanticism. His view of the sublime was important for Hegel and Nietzsche, greatly influencing most late Continental writing. We should also note Kant's view of the beautiful as the symbol of the good, and his conception of the aesthetic as the free play of imagination. Delight in the beautiful and sublime is a delight in the cognitive faculties of imagination and judgment freed from their subservience to reason and the understanding—that is, freed from the constraints of propositional discourse. This notion of freedom in the cognitive faculties had an enormous influence on Kant's German followers, especially Schelling and Hegel.

IMMANUEL KANT

IMMANUEL KANT

*Critique of Judgment**

INTRODUCTION

III. OF THE CRITIQUE OF JUDGMENT AS A MEANS OF COMBINING THE TWO PARTS OF PHILOSOPHY INTO A WHOLE. The critique of the cognitive faculties, as regards what they can furnish *a priori*, has, properly speaking, no realm in respect of objects, because it is not a doctrine, but only has to investigate whether and how, in accordance with the state of these faculties, a doctrine is possible by their means. Its field extends to all their pretensions, in order to confine them within their legitimate bounds. But what cannot enter into the division of philosophy may yet enter, as a chief part, into the critique of the pure faculty of cognition in general, viz. if it contains principles which are available neither for theoretical nor for practical use.

The natural concepts, which contain the ground of all theoretical knowledge *a priori*, rest on the legislation of the understanding. The concept of freedom, which contains the ground of all sensuously unconditioned practical precepts *a priori*, rests on the legislation of the reason. Both faculties, therefore, besides being capable of application as regards their logical form to principles of whatever origin, have also as regards their content, their special legislations above which there is no other *(a priori)*, and hence the division of philosophy into theoretical and practical is justified.

But in the family of the supreme cognitive faculties there is a middle term between the understanding and the reason. This is the *judgment*, of

---

* Immanuel Kant, *Critique of Judgment*, translated by J. H. Bernard (Hafner, 1951), pp. 12-17, 37-51, 54-56, 59, 61-62, 68-77, 82-89, 93-94, 99-101, 122-133, 150-158, 183-187, 196-200. (Titles for "First Division" preceding §1 and "Second Division" preceding §56 have been deleted. Footnotes have been renumbered.)

which we have cause for supposing according to analogy that it may contain in itself, if not a special legislation, yet a special principle of its own to be sought according to law, though merely subjective *a priori*. This principle, even if it have no field of objects as its realm, yet may have somewhere a territory with a certain character for which no other principle can be valid.

But besides (to judge by analogy), there is a new ground for bringing the judgment into connection with another arrangement of our representative faculties, which seems to be of even greater importance than that of its relationship with the family of the cognitive faculties. For all faculties or capacities of the soul can be reduced to three, which cannot be any further derived from one common ground: *the faculty of knowledge,* the *feeling of pleasure and pain,* and the *faculty of desire.*[1] For the faculty of knowledge the understanding is alone legislative, if (as must happen when it is considered by itself without confusion with the faculty of desire) this faculty is referred to nature as the faculty of *theoretical knowledge;* for in respect of nature (as phenomenon) it is alone possible for us to give laws by means of natural concepts *a priori*, i.e. by pure concepts of understanding. For the faculty of desire, as a supreme faculty according to the concept of freedom, the reason (in which alone this concept has a place) is alone *a priori* legislative. Now between the faculties of knowledge and desire there is the feeling of pleasure, just as the judgment mediates between the understanding and the reason. We may therefore suppose provisionally that the judgment likewise contains in itself an *a priori* principle. And as pleasure or pain is necessarily combined with the faculty of desire (either preceding this principle, as in the lower desires, or following it, as in the higher, when the desire is determined by the moral law), we may also suppose that the judgment will bring about a transition from the pure faculty of knowledge, the realm of natural concepts, to the realm of the concept of freedom, just as in its logical use it makes possible the transition from understanding to reason.

Although, then, philosophy can be divided only into two main parts, the theoretical and the practical, and although all that we may be able to say of the special principles of judgment must be counted as belonging in it to the theoretical part, i.e. to rational cognition in accordance with natural concepts, yet the critique of pure reason, which must decide all this, as regards the possibility of the system before undertaking it, consists of three parts: the critique of pure understanding, of pure judgment, and of pure reason, which faculties are called pure because they are legislative *a priori*.

IV. OF JUDGMENT AS A FACULTY LEGISLATING A PRIORI. Judgment in general is the faculty of thinking the particular as contained under the universal. If the universal (the rule, the principle, the law) be given, the judgment which subsumes the particular under it (even if, as transcendental judgment, it furnishes, *a priori*, the conditions in conformity with which subsumption under that universal is alone possible) is *determinant*. But if only the particular be given for which the universal has to be found, the judgment is merely *reflective*.

The determinant judgment only subsumes under universal transcendental laws given by the understanding; the law is marked out for it, *a priori*, and it has therefore no need to seek a law for itself in order to be able to subordinate the particular in nature to the universal. But the forms of nature are so manifold, and there are so many modifications of the universal transcendental natural concepts left undetermined by the laws given, *a priori*, by the pure understanding—because these only concern the possibility of a nature in general (as an object of sense)—that there must be laws for these [forms] also. These, as empirical, may be contingent from the point of view of *our* understanding; and yet, if they are to be called laws (as the concept of a nature requires), they must be regarded as necessary in virtue of a principle of the unity of the manifold, though it be unknown to us. The reflective judgment, which is obliged to ascend from the particular in nature to the universal, requires on that account a principle that it cannot borrow from experience, because its function is to establish the unity of all empirical principles under higher ones, and hence to establish the possibility of their systematic subordination. Such a transcendental principle, then, the reflective judgment can only give as a law from and to itself. It cannot derive it from outside (because then it would be the determinant judgment); nor can it prescribe it to nature, because reflection upon the laws of nature adjusts itself by nature, and not nature by the conditions according to which we attempt to arrive at a concept of it which is quite contingent in respect of nature.

This principle can be no other than the following: As universal laws of nature have their ground in our understanding, which prescribes them to nature (although only according to the universal concept of it as nature), so particular empirical laws, in respect of what is in them left undetermined by these universal laws, must be considered in accordance with such a unity as they would have if an understanding (although not our understanding) had furnished them to our cognitive faculties, so as to make possible a system of experience according to particular laws of nature. Not as if, in this way, such an understanding must be assumed as actual (for it is only our reflective judgment to which this idea serves as a principle—for reflecting, not for determining); but this faculty thus gives a law only to itself, and not to nature.

Now the concept of an object, so far as it contains the ground of the actuality of this object, is the *purpose;* and the agreement of a thing with that constitution of things which is only possible according to purposes is called the *purposiveness* of its form. Thus the principle of judgment, in respect of the form of things of nature under empirical laws generally, is the *purposiveness of nature* in its variety. That is, nature is represented by means of this concept as if an understanding contained the ground of the unity of the variety of its empirical laws.

The purposiveness of nature is therefore a particular concept, *a priori*, which has its origin solely in the reflective judgment. For we cannot ascribe to natural products anything like a reference of nature in them to purposes; we can only use this concept to reflect upon such products in respect of the connection of phenomena which is given in them according to empirical laws. This concept is also quite different from practical purposiveness (in human art or in morals), though it is certainly thought according to the analogy of these last. . . .

FIRST BOOK
ANALYTIC OF THE BEAUTIFUL

FIRST MOMENT
Of the Judgment of Taste,[2] *According to Quality*

§ 1. THE JUDGMENT OF TASTE IS AESTHETICAL. In order to distinguish whether anything is beautiful or not, we refer to the representation, not by the understanding to the object for cognition, but by the imagination (perhaps in conjunction with the understanding) to the subject and its feeling of pleasure or pain. The judgment of taste is therefore not a judgment of cognition, and is consequently not logical but aesthetical, by which we understand that whose determining ground can be *no other than subjective.* Every reference of representations, even that of sensations, may be objective (and then it signifies the real [element] of an empirical representation), save only the reference to the feeling of pleasure and pain, by which nothing in the object is signified, but through which there is a feeling in the subject as it is affected by the representation.

To apprehend a regular, purposive building by means of one's cognitive faculty (whether in a clear or a confused way of representation) is something quite different from being conscious of this representation as connected with the sensation of satisfaction. Here the representation is altogether referred to the subject and to its feeling of life, under the name of the feeling of pleasure or pain. This establishes a quite separate faculty of distinction and of judgment, adding nothing to cognition, but only comparing the given representation in the subject with the whole faculty of representations, of which the mind is conscious in the feeling of its state. Given representations in a judgment can be empirical (consequently, aesthetical); but the judgment which is formed by means of them is logical, provided they are referred in the judgment to the object. Conversely, if the given representations are rational, but are referred in a judgment simply to the subject (to its feeling), the judgment is so far always aesthetical.

§ 2. THE SATISFACTION WHICH DETERMINES THE JUDGMENT OF TASTE IS DISINTERESTED. The satisfaction which we combine with the representation of the existence of an object is called "interest." Such satisfaction always has reference to the faculty of desire, either as its determining ground or as necessarily connected with its determining ground. Now when the question is if a thing is beautiful, we do not want to know whether anything depends or can depend on the existence of the thing, either for myself or for anyone else, but how we judge it by mere observation (intuition or reflection). If anyone asks me if I find that palace beautiful which I see before me, I may answer: I do not like things of that kind which are made merely to be stared at. Or I can answer like that Iroquois Sachem, who was pleased in Paris by nothing more than the cook shops. Or again, after the manner of Rousseau, I may rebuke the vanity of the great who waste the sweat of the people on such superfluous things. In fine, I could easily convince myself that if I found myself on an uninhabited island without the hope of ever again coming among men, and could conjure up just such a splendid building by my mere wish, I should not even give myself the trouble if I had a sufficiently comfortable hut. This may all be admitted and approved, but we are not now talking of this. We wish only to know if this mere representation of the object is accompanied in me with satisfaction, however indifferent I may be as regards the existence of the object of this representation. We easily see that, in saying it is *beautiful* and in showing that I have taste, I am concerned, not with that in which I depend on the existence of the object, but with that which I make out of this representation in myself. Everyone must admit that a judgment about beauty, in which the least interest mingles, is very partial and is not a pure judgment of taste. We must not be in the least prejudiced in favor of the existence of the things, but be quite indifferent in this respect, in order to play the judge in things of taste.

We cannot, however, better elucidate this proposition, which is of capital importance, than by contrasting the pure disinterested[3] satisfaction in judgments of taste with that which is bound up with an interest, especially if we can at the same time be certain that there are no other kinds of interest than those which are to be now specified.

§ 3. THE SATISFACTION IN THE PLEASANT IS BOUND UP WITH INTEREST. *That which pleases the senses in sensation is "pleasant."* Here the opportunity presents itself of censuring a very common confusion of the double sense which the word "sensation" can have, and of calling attention to it. All satisfaction (it is said or thought) is itself sensation (of a pleasure). Consequently everything that pleases is pleasant because it pleases (and according to its different degrees or its relations to other pleasant sensations it is *agreeable, lovely, delightful, enjoyable,* etc.). But if this be admitted, then impressions of sense which determine the inclination, fundamental propositions of reason which determine the will, mere reflective forms of intuition which determine the judgment, are quite the same as regards the effect upon the feeling of pleasure. For this would be pleasantness in the sensation of one's state; and since in the end all the operations of our faculties must issue in the practical and unite in it as their goal, we could suppose no other way of estimating things and their worth than that which consists in the gratification that they promise. It is of no consequence at all how this is attained, and since then the choice of means alone could make a difference, men could indeed blame one another for stupidity and indiscretion, but never for baseness and wickedness. For thus they all, each according to his own way of seeing things, seek one goal, that is, gratification.

If a determination of the feeling of pleasure or pain is called sensation, this expression signifies something quite different from what I mean when I call the representation of a thing (by sense, as a receptivity belonging to the cognitive faculty) sensation. For in the latter case the representation is referred to the object, in the former simply to the subject, and is available for no cognition whatever, not even for that by which the subject *cognizes* itself.

In the above elucidation we understand by the word "sensation" an objective representation of sense; and, in order to avoid misinterpretation, we shall call that which must always remain merely subjective and can constitute absolutely no representation of an object by the ordinary term "feeling." The green color of the meadows belongs to *objective* sensation, as a perception of an object of sense; the pleasantness of this belongs to *subjective* sensation by which no object is represented, i.e. to feeling, by which the object is considered as an object of satisfaction (which does not furnish a cognition of it).

Now that a judgment about an object by which I describe it as pleasant expresses an interest in it, is plain from the fact that by sensation it excites a desire for objects of that kind; consequently the satisfaction presupposes, not the mere judgment about it, but the relation of its existence to my state, so far as this is affected by such an object. Hence we do not merely say of the pleasant, *it pleases,* but, *it gratifies.* I give to it no mere assent, but inclination is aroused by it; and in the case of what is pleasant in the most lively fashion there is no judgment at all upon the character of the object, for those [persons] who always lay themselves out for enjoyment (for that is the word describing intense gratification) would fain dispense with all judgment.

§ 4. THE SATISFACTION IN THE GOOD IS BOUND UP WITH INTEREST. Whatever by means of reason pleases through the mere concept is *good.* That which pleases only as a means we call *good for something* (the useful), but that which pleases for itself is *good in itself.* In both there is always involved the concept of a purpose, and consequently the relation of reason to the (at least possible) volition, and thus a satisfaction in the *presence* of an object or an action, i.e. some kind of interest.

In order to find anything good, I must always know what sort of a thing the object ought to be, i.e. I must have a concept of it. But there is no need of this to find a thing beautiful. Flowers, free delineations, outlines intertwined with one another without design and called [conventional] foliage, have no meaning, depend on no definite concept, and yet they please. The satisfaction in the beautiful must depend on the reflection upon an object, leading to any concept (however indefinite), and it is thus distinguished from the pleasant, which rests entirely upon sensation.

It is true, the pleasant seems in many cases to be the same as the good. Thus people are accustomed to say that all gratification (especially if it lasts) is good in itself, which is very much the same as to say that lasting pleasure and the good are the same. But we can soon see that this is merely a confusion of words, for the concepts which properly belong to these expressions can in no way be interchanged. The pleasant, which, as such, represents the object simply in relation to sense, must first be brought by the concept of a purpose under principles of reason, in order to call it good, as an object of the will. But that there is [involved] a quite different relation to satisfaction in calling that which gratifies at the same time *good* may be seen from the fact that, in the case of the good, the question always is whether it is mediately or immediately good (useful or good in itself); but on the contrary in the case of the pleasant, there can be no question about this at all, for the word always signifies something which pleases immediately. (The same is applicable to what I call beautiful.)

Even in common speech men distinguish the pleasant from the good. Of a dish which stimulates the taste by spices and other condiments we say unhesitatingly that it is pleasant, though it is at the same time admitted not to be good; for though it immediately *delights* the senses, yet mediately, i.e. considered by reason which looks to the after results, it displeases. Even in the judging of health we may notice this distinction. It is immediately pleasant to everyone possessing it (at least negatively, i.e. as the absence of all bodily pains). But in order to say that it is good, it must be considered by reason with reference to purposes, viz. that it is a state which makes us fit for all our business. Finally, in respect of happiness, everyone believes himself entitled to describe the greatest sum of the pleasantness of life (as regards both their number and their duration) as a true, even as the highest, good. However, reason is opposed to this. Pleasantness is enjoyment. And if we were concerned with this alone, it would be foolish to be scrupulous as regards the means which procure it for us, or [to care] whether it is obtained passively by the bounty of nature or by our own activity and work. But reason can never be persuaded that the existence of a man who merely lives for *enjoyment* (however busy he may be in this point of view) has a worth in itself, even if he at the same time is conducive as a means to the best enjoyment of others and shares in all their gratifications by sympathy. Only what he does, without reference to enjoyment, in full freedom and independently of what nature can procure for him passively, gives an [absolute][4] worth to his presence [in the world] as the existence of a person; and happiness, with the whole abundance of its pleasures, is far from being an unconditioned good.[5]

However, notwithstanding all this difference between the pleasant and the good, they both agree in this that they are always bound up with an interest in their object; so are not only the pleasant (§ 3), and the mediate good (the useful) which is pleasing as a means toward pleasantness somewhere, but also that which is good absolutely and in every aspect, viz. moral good, which brings with it the highest interest. For the good is the object of will (i.e. of a faculty of desire determined by reason). But to wish for something and to have a satisfaction in its existence, i.e. to take an interest in it, are identical.

§ 5. COMPARISON OF THE THREE SPECIFICALLY DIFFERENT KINDS OF SATISFAC-
TION. The pleasant and the good have both a reference to the faculty of
desire, and they bring with them, the former a satisfaction pathologically conditioned (by impulses, *stimuli*), the latter a pure practical satisfaction which is
determined not merely by the representation of the object but also by the represented connection of the subject with the existence of the object. [It is not
merely the object that pleases, but also its existence.][6] On the other hand,
the judgment of taste is merely *contemplative;* i.e., it is a judgment which,
indifferent as regards the existence of an object, compares its character with
the feeling of pleasure and pain. But this contemplation itself is not directed
to concepts; for the judgment of taste is not a cognitive judgment (either theoretical or practical), and thus is not *based* on concepts, nor has it concepts as
its *purpose.*

The pleasant, the beautiful, and the good designate then three different
relations of representations to the feeling of pleasure and pain, in reference to
which we distinguish from one another objects or methods of representing
them. And the expressions corresponding to each, by which we mark our
complacency in them, are not the same. That which *gratifies* a man is called
pleasant; that which merely *pleases* him is *beautiful;* that which is *esteemed* [or
approved][7] by him, i.e. that to which he accords an objective worth, is *good.*
Pleasantness concerns irrational animals also, but beauty only concerns men,
i.e. animal, but still rational, beings—not merely *qua* rational (e.g. spirits), but
qua animal also—and the good concerns every rational being in general. This
is a proposition which can only be completely established and explained in the
sequel. We may say that, of all these three kinds of satisfaction, that of taste in
the beautiful is alone a disinterested and *free* satisfaction; for no interest,
either of sense or of reason, here forces our assent. Hence we may say of
satisfaction that it is related in the three aforesaid cases to *inclination,* to *favor,*
or to *respect.* Now *favor* is the only free satisfaction. An object of inclination
and one that is proposed to our desire by a law of reason leave us no freedom
in forming for ourselves anywhere an object of pleasure. All interest presupposes or generates a want, and, as the determining ground of assent, it leaves
the judgment about the object no longer free.

As regards the interest of inclination in the case of the pleasant, everyone says that hunger is the best sauce, and everything that is eatable is relished
by people with a healthy appetite; and thus a satisfaction of this sort shows no
choice directed by taste. It is only when the want is appeased that we can distinguish which of many men has or has not taste. In the same way there may
be manners (conduct) without virtue, politeness without good will, decorum
without modesty, etc. For where the moral law speaks there is no longer,
objectively, a free choice as regards what is to be done; and to display taste in
its fulfillment (or in judging of another's fulfillment of it) is something quite
different from manifesting the moral attitude of thought. For this involves a
command and generates a want, while moral taste only plays with the objects
of satisfaction, without attaching itself to one of them.

Explanation of the Beautiful Resulting from the First Moment

Taste is the faculty of judging of an object or a method of representing it by an *entirely disinterested* satisfaction or dissatisfaction. The object of such satisfaction is called *beautiful*.[8]

SECOND MOMENT
Of the Judgment of Taste, According to Quantity

§ 6. THE BEAUTIFUL IS THAT WHICH APART FROM CONCEPTS IS REPRESENTED AS THE OBJECT OF A UNIVERSAL SATISFACTION. This explanation of the beautiful can be derived from the preceding explanation of it as the object of an entirely disinterested satisfaction. For the fact of which everyone is conscious, that the satisfaction is for him quite disinterested, implies in his judgment a ground of satisfaction for all men. For since it does not rest on any inclination of the subject (nor upon any other premeditated interest), but since the person who judges feels himself quite *free* as regards the satisfaction which he attaches to the object, he cannot find the ground of this satisfaction in any private conditions connected with his own subject, and hence it must be regarded as grounded on what he can presuppose in every other person. Consequently he must believe that he has reason for attributing a similar satisfaction to everyone. He will therefore speak of the beautiful as if beauty were a characteristic of the object and the judgment logical (constituting a cognition of the object by means of concepts of it), although it is only aesthetical and involves merely a reference of the representation of the object to the subject. For it has this similarity to a logical judgment that we can presuppose its validity for all men. But this universality cannot arise from concepts; for from concepts there is no transition to the feeling of pleasure or pain (except in pure practical laws, which bring an interest with them such as is not bound up with the pure judgment of taste). Consequently the judgment of taste, accompanied with the consciousness of separation from all interest, must claim validity for every man, without this universality depending on objects. That is, there must be bound up with it a title to subjective universality.

§ 7. COMPARISON OF THE BEAUTIFUL WITH THE PLEASANT AND THE GOOD BY MEANS OF THE ABOVE CHARACTERISTIC. As regards the pleasant, everyone is content that his judgment, which he bases upon private feeling and by which he says of an object that it pleases him, should be limited merely to his own person. Thus he is quite contented that if he says, "Canary wine is pleasant," another man may correct his expression and remind him that he ought to say, "It is pleasant *to me.*" And this is the case not only as regards the taste of the tongue, the palate, and the throat, but for whatever is pleasant to anyone's eyes and ears. To one, violet color is soft and lovely; to another, it is washed out and dead. One man likes the tone of wind instruments, another that of strings. To strive here with the design of reproving as incorrect another man's judgment which is different from our own, as if the judgments were logically opposed, would be folly. As regards the pleasant, therefore, the fundamental proposition is valid; *everyone has his own taste* (the taste of sense).

The case is quite different with the beautiful. It would (on the contrary) be laughable if a man who imagined anything to his own taste thought to justify himself by saying: "This object (the house we see, the coat that person wears, the concert we hear, the poem submitted to our judgment) is beautiful *for me.*" For he must not call it *beautiful* if it merely pleases him. Many things may have for him charm and pleasantness—no one troubles himself at that— but if he gives out anything as beautiful, he supposes in others the same sat- isfaction; he judges not merely for himself, but for everyone, and speaks of beauty as if it were a property of things. Hence he says "the *thing is* beautiful"; and he does not count on the agreement of others with this his judgment of satisfaction, because he has found this agreement several times before, but he *demands* it of them. He blames them if they judge otherwise and he denies them taste, which he nevertheless requires from them. Here, then, we cannot say that each man has his own particular taste. For this would be as much as to say that there is no taste whatever, i.e. no aesthetical judgment which can make a rightful claim upon everyone's assent.

At the same time we find as regards the pleasant that there is an agree- ment among men in their judgments upon it in regard to which we deny taste to some and attribute it to others, by this not meaning one of our organic senses, but a faculty of judging in respect of the pleasant generally. Thus we say of a man who knows how to entertain his guests with pleasures (of enjoyment for all the senses), so that they are all pleased, "he has taste." But here the universality is only taken comparatively; and there emerge rules which are only *general* (like all empirical ones), and not *universal,* which latter the judgment of taste upon the beautiful undertakes or lays claim to. It is a judgment in reference to sociability, so far as this rests on empirical rules. In respect of the good it is true that judgments make rightful claim to validity for everyone; but the good is represented only *by means of a concept* as the object of a universal satisfaction, which is the case neither with the pleasant nor with the beautiful.

§ 8. THE UNIVERSALITY OF THE SATISFACTION IS REPRESENTED IN A JUDGMENT OF TASTE ONLY AS SUBJECTIVE. This particular determination of the universal- ity of an aesthetical judgment, which is to be met with in a judgment of taste, is noteworthy, not indeed for the logician, but for the transcendental philoso- pher. It requires no small trouble to discover its origin, but we thus detect a property of our cognitive faculty which without this analysis would remain unknown.

First, we must be fully convinced of the fact that in a judgment of taste (about the beautiful) the satisfaction in the object is imputed to *everyone,* with- out being based on a concept (for then it would be the good). Further, this claim to universal validity so essentially belongs to a judgment by which we describe anything as *beautiful* that, if this were not thought in it, it would never come into our thoughts to use the expression at all, but everything which pleases without a concept would be counted as pleasant. In respect of the latter, everyone has his own opinion; and no one assumes in another agreement with his judgment of taste, which is always the case in a judgment of taste about beauty. I may call the first the taste of sense, the second the taste of reflection, so far as the first lays down mere private judgments and the second judgments supposed to be generally valid (public), but in both cases aesthetical (not practical) judgments about an object merely in respect of the relation of its representation to the feeling of pleasure and pain. Now here is something strange. As regards the taste of sense, not only does experience show that its judgment (of pleasure or pain connected with anything) is not valid universally, but everyone is content not to impute agreement with it to others (although actually there is often found a very extended concurrence in these judgments). On the other hand, the taste of reflection has its claim to the universal validity of its judgments (about the beautiful) rejected often enough, as experience teaches, although it may find it possible (as it actually does) to represent judgments which can demand this universal agreement. In fact it imputes this to everyone for each of its judgments of taste, without the persons that judge disputing as to the possibility of such a claim, although in particular cases they cannot agree as to the correct application of this faculty.

Here we must, in the first place, remark that a universality which does not rest on concepts of objects (not even on empirical ones) is not logical but aesthetical; i.e. it involves no objective quantity of the judgment, but only that which is subjective. For this I use the expression *general validity*, which signifies the validity of the reference of a representation, not to the cognitive faculty, but to the feeling of pleasure and pain for every subject. (We can avail ourselves also of the same expression for the logical quantity of the judgment, if only we prefix "objective" to "universal validity," to distinguish it from that which is merely subjective and aesthetical.)

A judgment with *objective universal validity* is also always valid subjectively; i.e. if the judgment holds for everything contained under a given concept, it holds also for everyone who represents an object by means of this concept. But from a *subjective universal validity*, i.e. aesthetical and resting on no concept, we cannot infer that which is logical because that kind of judgment does not extend to the object. But, therefore, the aesthetical universality which is ascribed to a judgment must be of a particular kind, because it does not unite the predicate of beauty with the concept of the object, considered in its whole logical sphere, and yet extends it to the whole sphere of judging persons.

In respect of logical quantity, all judgments of taste are *singular* judgments. For because I must refer the object immediately to my feeling of pleasure and pain, and that not by means of concepts, they cannot have the quantity of objective generally valid judgments. Nevertheless, if the singular representation of the object of the judgment of taste, in accordance with the conditions determining the latter, were transformed by comparison into a concept, a logically universal judgment could result therefrom. E.g., I describe by a judgment of taste the rose that I see as beautiful. But the judgment which results from the comparison of several singular judgments, "Roses in general are beautiful," is no longer described simply as aesthetical, but as a logical judgment based on an aesthetical one. Again the judgment, "The rose is pleasant" (to use) is, although aesthetical and singular, not a judgment of taste but of sense. It is distinguished from the former by the fact that the judgment of taste carries with it an *aesthetic quantity* of universality, i.e. of validity for everyone, which cannot be found in a judgment about the pleasant. It is only judgments about the good which, although they also determine satisfaction in an object, have logical and not merely aesthetical universality, for they are valid of the object as cognitive of it, and thus are valid for everyone.

If we judge objects merely according to concepts, then all representation of beauty is lost. Thus there can be no rule according to which anyone is to be forced to recognize anything as beautiful. We cannot press [upon others] by the aid of any reasons or fundamental propositions our judgment that a coat, a house, or a flower is beautiful. People wish to submit the object to their own eyes, as if the satisfaction in it depended on sensation; and yet, if we then call the object beautiful, we believe that we speak with a universal voice, and we claim the assent of everyone, although on the contrary all private sensation can only decide for the observer himself and his satisfaction.

We may see now that in the judgment of taste nothing is postulated but such a *universal voice*, in respect of the satisfaction without the intervention of concepts, and thus the *possibility* of an aesthetical judgment that can, at the same time, be regarded as valid for everyone. The judgment of taste itself does not *postulate* the agreement of everyone (for that can only be done by a logically universal judgment because it can adduce reasons); it only *imputes* this agreement to everyone, as a case of the rule in respect of which it expects, not confirmation by concepts, but assent from others. The universal voice is, therefore, only an idea (we do not yet inquire upon what it rests). It may be uncertain whether or not the man who believes that he is laying down a judgment of taste is, as a matter of fact, judging in conformity with that idea; but that he refers his judgment thereto, and consequently that it is intended to be a judgment of taste, he announces by the expression "beauty." He can be quite certain of this for himself by the mere consciousness of the separating off everything belonging to the pleasant and the good from the satisfaction which is left; and this is all for which he promises himself the agreement of everyone—a claim which would be justifiable under these conditions, provided only he did not often make mistakes, and thus lay down an erroneous judgment of taste. . . .

Explanation of the Beautiful Resulting from the Second Moment

The *beautiful* is that which pleases universally without [requiring] a concept.

THIRD MOMENT
Of Judgments of Taste, According to the Relation of the
Purposes Which Are Brought into Consideration in Them

§ 10. OF PURPOSIVENESS IN GENERAL. If we wish to explain what a purpose is according to its transcendental determinations (without presupposing anything empirical like the feeling of pleasure), [we say that] the purpose is the object of a concept, in so far as the concept is regarded as the cause of the object (the real ground of its possibility); and the causality of a *concept* in respect of its *object* is its purposiveness (*forma finalis*). Where then not merely the cognition of an object but the object itself (its form and existence) is thought as an effect only possible by means of the concept of this latter, there we think a purpose. The representation of the effect is here the determining ground of its cause and precedes it. The consciousness of the causality of a representation, for *maintaining* the subject in the same state, may here generally denote what we call pleasure; while on the other hand pain is that representation which contains the ground of the determination of the state of representations into their opposite [of restraining or removing them].[9]

The faculty of desire, so far as it is determinable to act only through concepts, i.e. in conformity with the representation of a purpose, would be the will. But an object, or a state of mind, or even an action is called purposive, although its possibility does not necessarily presuppose the representation of a purpose, merely because its possibility can be explained and conceived by us only so far as we assume for its ground a causality according to purposes, i.e. in accordance with a will which has regulated it according to the representation of a certain rule. There can be, then, purposiveness without[10] purpose, so far as we do not place the causes of this form in a will, but yet can only make the explanation of its possibility intelligible to ourselves by deriving it from a will. Again, we are not always forced to regard what we observe (in respect of its possibility) from the point of view of reason. Thus we can at least observe a purposiveness according to form, without basing it on a purpose (as the material of the *nexus finalis*), and remark it in objects, although only by reflection.

§ 11. THE JUDGMENT OF TASTE HAS NOTHING AT ITS BASIS BUT THE FORM OF THE PURPOSIVENESS OF AN OBJECT OR OF ITS MODE OF REPRESENTATION. Every purpose, if it be regarded as a ground of satisfaction, always carries with it an interest—as the determining ground of the judgment—about the object of pleasure. Therefore no subjective purpose can lie at the basis of the judgment of taste. But also the judgment of taste can be determined by no representation of an objective purpose, i.e. of the possibility of the object itself in accordance with principles of purposive combination, and consequently by no concept of the good, because it is an aesthetical and not a cognitive judgment. It therefore has to do with no *concept* of the character and internal or external possibility of the object by means of this or that cause, but merely with the relation of the representative powers to one another, so far as they are determined by a representation.

Now this relation in the determination of an object as beautiful is bound up with the feeling of pleasure, which is declared by the judgment of taste to be valid for everyone; hence a pleasantness [merely] accompanying the representation can as little contain the determining ground [of the judgment] as the representation of the perfection of the object and the concept of the good can. Therefore it can be nothing else than the subjective purposiveness in the representation of an object without any purpose (either objective or subjective), and thus it is the mere form of purposiveness in the representation by which an object is *given* to us, so far as we are conscious of it, which constitutes the satisfaction that we without a concept judge to be universally communicable; and, consequently, this is the determining ground of the judgment of taste. . . .

§ 14. ELUCIDATION BY MEANS OF EXAMPLES. Aesthetical judgments can be divided just like theoretical (logical) judgments into empirical and pure. The first assert pleasantness or unpleasantness; the second assert the beauty of an object or of the manner of representing it. The former are judgments of sense (material aesthetical judgments); the latter [as formal][11] are alone strictly judgments of taste.

A judgment of taste is therefore pure only so far as no merely empirical satisfaction is mingled with its determining ground. But this always happens if charm or emotion have any share in the judgment by which anything is to be described as beautiful. . . .

Even what we call "ornaments" [*parerga*],[12] i.e. those things which do not belong to the complete representation of the object internally as elements, but only externally as complements, and which augment the satisfaction of taste, do so only by their form; as, for example, [the frames of pictures[13] or] the draperies of statues or the colonnades of palaces. But if the ornament does not itself consist in beautiful form, and if it is used as a golden frame is used, merely to recommend the painting by its *charm*, it is then called *finery* and injures genuine beauty.

Emotion, that is a sensation in which pleasantness is produced by means of a momentary checking and a consequent more powerful outflow of the vital force, does not belong at all to beauty. But sublimity [with which the feeling of emotion is bound up][14] requires a different standard of judgment from that which is at the foundation of taste; and thus a pure judgment of taste has for its determining ground neither charm nor emotion—in a word, no sensation as the material of the aesthetical judgment. . . .

§ 17. OF THE IDEAL OF BEAUTY. There can be no objective rule of taste which shall determine by means of concepts what is beautiful. For every judgment from this source is aesthetical; i.e. the feeling of the subject, and not a concept of the object, is its determining ground. To seek for a principle of taste which shall furnish, by means of definite concepts, a universal criterion of the beautiful is fruitless trouble, because what is sought is impossible and self-contradictory. The universal communicability of sensation (satisfaction or dissatisfaction) without the aid of a concept—the agreement, as far as is possible, of all times and peoples as regards this feeling in the representation of certain objects—this is the empirical criterion, although weak and hardly sufficing for probability, of the derivation of a taste, thus confirmed by examples, from the deep-lying general grounds of agreement in judging of the forms under which objects are given.

Hence we consider some products of taste as *exemplary*. Not that taste can be acquired by imitating others, for it must be an original faculty. He who imitates a model shows no doubt, in so far as he attains to it, skill; but only shows taste in so far as he can judge of this model itself.[15] It follows from hence that the highest model, the archetype of taste, is a mere idea, which everyone must produce in himself and according to which he must judge every object of taste, every example of judgment by taste, and even the taste of everyone. *Idea* properly means a rational concept, and *ideal* the representation of an individual being, regarded as adequate to an idea.[16] Hence that archetype of taste, which certainly rests on the indeterminate idea that reason has of a maximum, but which cannot be represented by concepts but only in an individual presentation, is better called the ideal of the beautiful. Although we are not in possession of this, we yet strive to produce it in ourselves. But it can only be an ideal of the imagination, because it rests on a presentation and not on concepts, and the imagination is the faculty of presentation. How do we arrive at such an ideal of beauty? *A priori*, or empirically? Moreover, what species of the beautiful is susceptible of an ideal?

First, it is well to remark that the beauty for which an ideal is to be sought cannot be *vague* beauty, but is *fixed* by a concept of objective purposiveness; and thus it cannot appertain to the object of a quite pure judgment of taste, but to that of a judgment of taste which is in part intellectual. That is, in whatever grounds of judgment an ideal is to be found, an idea of reason in accordance with definite concepts must lie at its basis, which determines *a priori* the purpose on which the internal possibility of the object rests. An ideal of beautiful flowers, of a beautiful piece of furniture, of a beautiful view, is inconceivable. But neither can an ideal be represented of a beauty dependent on definite purposes, e.g. of a beautiful dwelling house, a beautiful tree, a beautiful garden, etc.; presumably because their purpose is not sufficiently determined and fixed by the concept, and thus the purposiveness is nearly as free as in the case of *vague* beauty. The only being which has the purpose of its existence in itself is *man*, who can determine his purposes by reason; or, where he must receive them from external perception, yet can compare them with essential and universal purposes and can judge this their accordance aesthetically. This *man* is, then, alone of all objects in the world, susceptible of an ideal of *beauty*, as it is only *humanity* in his person, as an intelligence, that is susceptible of the ideal of *perfection*.

But there are here two elements. *First*, there is the aesthetical *normal idea*, which is an individual intuition (of the imagination), representing the standard of our judgment [upon man] as a thing belonging to a particular animal species. *Secondly*, there is the *rational idea* which makes the purposes of humanity, so far as they cannot be sensibly represented the principle for judging of a figure through which, as their phenomenal effect, those purposes are revealed. The normal idea of the figure of an animal of a particular race must take its elements from experience. But the greatest purposiveness in the construction of the figure that would be available for the universal standard of aesthetical judgment upon each individual of these species—the image which is as it were designedly at the basis of nature's technique, to which only the whole race and not any isolated individual is adequate—this lies merely in the idea of the judging [subject]. And this, with its proportions as an aesthetical idea, can be completely presented *in concreto* in a model. In order to make intelligible in some measure (for who can extract her whole secret from nature?) how this comes to pass, we shall attempt a psychological explanation.

We must remark that, in a way quite incomprehensible by us, the imagination cannot only recall on occasion the signs for concepts long past, but can also reproduce the image of the figure of the object out of an unspeakable number of objects of different kinds or even of the same kind. Further, if the mind is concerned with comparisons, the imagination can, in all probability, actually, though unconsciously, let one image glide into another; and thus, by the concurrence of several of the same kind, come by an average, which serves as the common measure of all. Everyone has seen a thousand full-grown men. Now if you wish to judge their normal size, estimating it by means of comparison, the imagination (as I think) allows a great number of images (perhaps the whole thousand) to fall on one another. If I am allowed to apply here the analogy of optical presentation, it is in the space where most of them are combined and inside the contour, where the place is illuminated with the most vivid colors, that the *average size* is cognizable, which, both in height and breadth, is equally far removed from the extreme bounds of the greatest and smallest stature. And this is the stature of a beautiful man. (We could arrive at the same thing mechanically by adding together all thousand magnitudes, heights, breadths, and thicknesses, and dividing the sum by a thousand. But the imagination does this by means of a dynamical effect, which arises from the various impressions of such figures on the organ of internal sense.) If now, in a similar way, for this average man we seek the average head, for this head the average nose, etc., such figure is at the basis of the normal idea in the country where the comparison is instituted. Thus necessarily under these empirical conditions a Negro must have a different normal idea of the beauty of the [human figure] from a white man, a Chinaman a different normal idea from a European, etc. And the same is the case with the model of a beautiful horse or dog (of a certain breed). This *normal idea* is not derived from proportions gotten from experience [and regarded] as *definite rules*, but in accordance with it rules for judging become in the first instance possible. It is the image for the whole race, which floats among all the variously different intuitions of individuals, which nature takes as archetype in her production of the same species, but which appears not to be fully reached in any individual case. It is by no means the whole *archetype of beauty* in the race, but only the form constituting the indispensable condition of all beauty, and thus merely *correctness* in the [mental] presentation of the race. It is, like the celebrated "Doryphorus" of Polycletus,[17] the *rule* (Myron's[18] Cow might also be used thus for its kind). It can therefore contain nothing specifically characteristic, for otherwise it would not be the *normal idea* for the race. Its presentation pleases, not by its beauty, but merely because it contradicts no condition, under which alone a thing of this kind can be beautiful. The presentation is merely correct.[19]

We must yet distinguish the *normal idea* of the beautiful from the *ideal*, which latter, on grounds already alleged, we can only expect in the *human* figure. In this the ideal consists in the expression of the *moral*, without which the object would not please universally and thus positively (not merely negatively in an accurate presentation). The visible expression of moral ideas that rule men inwardly can indeed only be gotten from experience; but to make its connection with all which our reason unites with the morally good in the idea of the highest purposiveness—goodness of heart, purity, strength, peace, etc.—visible as it were in bodily manifestation (as the effect of that which is internal) requires a union of pure ideas of reason with great imaginative power even in him who wishes to judge of it, still more in him who wishes to present it. The correctness of such an ideal of beauty is shown by its permitting no sensible charm to mingle with the satisfaction in the object, and yet allowing us to take a great interest therein. This shows that a judgment in accordance with such a standard can never be purely aesthetical, and that a judgment in accordance with an ideal of beauty is not a mere judgment of taste.

Explanation of the Beautiful Derived from this Third Moment

Beauty is the form of the *purposiveness* of an object, so far as this is perceived in it *without any representation of a purpose*.[20]

FOURTH MOMENT
Of the Judgment of Taste, According to the Modality of the Satisfaction in the Object

§ 18. WHAT THE MODALITY IN A JUDGMENT OF TASTE IS. I can say of every representation that it is at least *possible* that (as a cognition) it should be bound up with a pleasure. Of a representation that I call *pleasant* I say that it *actually* excites pleasure in me. But the *beautiful* we think as having a *necessary* reference to satisfaction. Now this necessity is of a peculiar kind. It is not a theoretical objective necessity, in which case it would be cognized *a priori* that everyone *will feel* this satisfaction in the object called beautiful by me. It is not a practical necessity, in which case, by concepts of a pure rational will serving as a rule for freely acting beings, the satisfaction is the necessary result of an objective law and only indicates that we absolutely (without any further design) ought to act in a certain way. But the necessity which is thought in an aesthetical judgment can only be called exemplary, i.e. a necessity of the assent of *all* to a judgment which is regarded as the example of a universal rule that we cannot state. Since an aesthetical judgment is not an objective cognitive judgment, this necessity cannot be derived from definite concepts and is therefore not apodictic. Still less can it be inferred from the universality of experience (of a complete agreement of judgments as to the beauty of a certain object). For not only would experience hardly furnish sufficiently numerous vouchers for this, but also, on empirical judgments, we can base no concept of the necessity of these judgments.

§ 19. THE SUBJECTIVE NECESSITY, WHICH WE ASCRIBE TO THE JUDGMENT OF TASTE, IS CONDITIONED. The judgment of taste requires the agreement of everyone, and he who describes anything as beautiful claims that everyone *ought* to give his approval to the object in question and also describe it as beautiful. The *ought* in the aesthetical judgment is therefore pronounced in accordance with all the data which are required for judging, and yet is only conditioned. We ask for the agreement of everyone else, because we have for it a ground that is common to all; and we could count on this agreement, provided we were always sure that the case was correctly subsumed under that ground as rule of assent.

§ 20. THE CONDITION OF NECESSITY WHICH A JUDGMENT OF TASTE ASSERTS IS THE IDEA OF A COMMON SENSE. If judgments of taste (like cognitive judgments) had a definite objective principle, then the person who lays them down in accordance with this latter would claim an unconditioned necessity for his judgment. If they were devoid of all principle, like those of the mere taste of sense, we would not allow them in thought any necessity whatever. Hence they must have a subjective principle which determines what pleases or displeases only by feeling and not by concepts, but yet with universal validity. But such a principle could only be regarded as a *common sense*, which is essentially different from common understanding which people sometimes call common sense *(sensus communis);* for the latter does not judge by feeling but always by concepts, although ordinarily only as by obscurely represented principles.

Hence it is only under the presupposition that there is a common sense (by which we do not understand an external sense, but the effect resulting from the play of our cognitive powers)—it is only under this presupposition, I say, that the judgment of taste can be laid down.

. . . .

§ 22. THE NECESSITY OF THE UNIVERSAL AGREEMENT THAT IS THOUGHT IN A JUDGMENT OF TASTE IS A SUBJECTIVE NECESSITY, WHICH IS REPRESENTED AS OBJECTIVE UNDER THE PRESUPPOSITION OF A COMMON SENSE. In all judgments by which we describe anything as beautiful, we allow no one to be of another opinion, without, however, grounding our judgment on concepts, but only on our feeling, which we therefore place at its basis, not as a private, but as a common feeling. Now this common sense cannot be grounded on experience, for it aims at justifying judgments which contain an *ought*. It does not say that everyone *will* agree with my judgment, but that he *ought*. And so common sense, as an example of whose judgment I here put forward my judgment of taste and on account of which I attribute to the latter an *exemplary* validity, is a mere ideal norm, under the supposition of which I have a right to make into a rule for everyone a judgment that accords therewith, as well as the satisfaction in an object expressed in such judgment. For the principle which concerns the agreement of different judging persons, although only subjective, is yet assumed as subjectively universal (an idea necessary for everyone), and thus can claim universal assent (as if it were objective) provided we are sure that we have correctly subsumed [the particulars] under it.

This indeterminate norm of a common sense is actually presupposed by us, as is shown by our claim to lay down judgments of taste. Whether there is in fact such a common sense, as a constitutive principle of the possibility of experience, or whether a yet higher principle of reason makes it only into a regulative principle for producing in us a common sense for higher purposes; whether, therefore, taste is an original and natural faculty or only the idea of an artificial one yet to be acquired, so that a judgment of taste with its assumption of a universal assent in fact is only a requirement of reason for producing such harmony of sentiment; whether the ought, i.e. the objective necessity of the confluence of the feeling of any one man with that of every other, only signifies the possibility of arriving at this accord, and the judgment of taste only affords an example of the application of this principle—these questions we have neither the wish nor the power to investigate as yet; we have now only to resolve the faculty of taste into its elements in order to unite them at last in the idea of a common sense.

Explanation of the Beautiful Resulting from the Fourth Moment

The *beautiful* is that which without any concept is cognized as the object of a *necessary* satisfaction. . . .

SECOND BOOK
ANALYTIC OF THE SUBLIME

§ 23. TRANSITION FROM THE FACULTY WHICH JUDGES OF THE BEAUTIFUL TO THAT WHICH JUDGES OF THE SUBLIME. The beautiful and the sublime agree in this that both please in themselves. Further, neither presupposes a judgment of sense nor a judgment logically determined, but a judgment of reflection. Consequently the satisfaction [belonging to them] does not depend on a sensation, as in the case of the pleasant, nor on a definite concept, as in the case of the good; but it is nevertheless referred to concepts, although indeterminate ones. And so the satisfaction is connected with the mere presentation [of the object] or with the faculty of presentation, so that in the case of a given intuition this faculty or the imagination is considered as in agreement with the *faculty of concepts* of understanding or reason, regarded as promoting these latter. Hence both kinds of judgments are *singular,* and yet announce themselves as universally valid for every subject; although they lay claim merely to the feeling of pleasure, and not to any cognition of the object.

But there are also remarkable differences between the two. The beautiful in nature is connected with the form of the object, which consists in having [definite] boundaries. The sublime, on the other hand, is to be found in a formless object, so far as in it or by occasion of it *boundlessness* is represented, and yet its totality is also present to thought. Thus the beautiful seems to be regarded as the presentation of an indefinite concept of understanding, the sublime as that of a like concept of reason. Therefore the satisfaction in the one case is bound up with the representation of *quality,* in the other with that of *quantity.* And the latter satisfaction is quite different in kind from the former, for this [the beautiful][21] directly brings with it a feeling of the furtherance of life, and thus is compatible with charms and with the play of the imagination. But the other [the feeling of the sublime][22] is a pleasure that arises only indirectly; viz. it is produced by the feeling of a momentary checking of the vital powers and a consequent stronger outflow of them, so that it seems to be regarded as emotion—not play, but earnest in the exercise of the imagination. Hence it is incompatible with [physical] charm; and as the mind is not merely attracted by the object but is ever being alternately repelled, the satisfaction in the sublime does not so much involve a positive pleasure as admiration or respect, which rather deserves to be called negative pleasure.

But the inner and most important distinction between the sublime and beautiful is, certainly, as follows. (Here, as we are entitled to do, we only bring under consideration in the first instance the sublime in natural objects, for the sublime of art is always limited by the conditions of agreement with nature.) Natural beauty (which is independent) brings with it a purposiveness in its form by which the object seems to be, as it were, preadapted to our judgment, and thus constitutes in itself an object of satisfaction. On the other hand, that which excites in us, without any reasoning about it, but in the mere apprehension of it, the feeling of the sublime may appear, as regards its form, to violate purpose in respect of the judgment, to be unsuited to our presentative faculty, and as it were to do violence to the imagination; and yet it is judged to be only the more sublime.

Now we may see from this that, in general, we express ourselves incorrectly if we call any *object of nature* sublime, although we can quite correctly call many objects of nature beautiful. For how can that be marked by an expression of approval which is apprehended in itself as being a violation of purpose? All that we can say is that the object is fit for the presentation of a sublimity which can be found in the mind, for no sensible form can contain the sublime properly so-called. This concerns only ideas of the reason, which, although no adequate presentation is possible for them, by this inadequateness that admits of sensible presentation are aroused and summoned into the mind. Thus the wide ocean, disturbed by the storm, cannot be called sublime. Its aspect is horrible; and the mind must be already filled with manifold ideas if it is to be determined by such an intuition to a feeling itself sublime, as it is incited to abandon sensibility and to busy itself with ideas that involve higher purposiveness.

Independent natural beauty discovers to us a technique of nature which represents it as a system in accordance with laws, the principle of which we do not find in the whole of our faculty of understanding. That principle is the principle of purposiveness, in respect of the use of our judgment in regard to phenomena, [which requires] that these must not be judged as merely belonging to nature in its purposeless mechanism, but also as belonging to something analogous to art. It therefore actually extends, not indeed our cognition of natural objects, but our concept of nature, [which is now not regarded] as mere mechanism but as art. This leads to profound investigations as to the possibility of such a form. But in what we are accustomed to call sublime there is nothing at all that leads to particular objective principles and forms of nature corresponding to them; so far from it that, for the most part, nature excites the ideas of the sublime in its chaos or in its wildest and most irregular disorder and desolation, provided size and might are perceived. Hence, we see that the concept of the sublime is not nearly so important or rich in consequences as the concept of the beautiful; and that, in general, it displays nothing purposive in nature itself, but only in that possible use of our intuitions of it by which there is produced in us a feeling of a purposiveness quite independent of nature. We must seek a ground external to ourselves for the beautiful of nature, but seek it for the sublime merely in ourselves and in our attitude of thought, which introduces sublimity into the representation of nature. This is a very needful preliminary remark, which quite separates the ideas of the sublime from that of a purposiveness of *nature* and makes the theory of the sublime a mere appendix to the aesthetical judging of that purposiveness, because by means of it no particular form is represented in nature, but there is only developed a purposive use which the imagination makes of its representation. . . .

A. OF THE MATHEMATICALLY SUBLIME

§ 25. EXPLANATION OF THE TERM SUBLIME. We call that *sublime* which is *absolutely great*. But to be great and to be a great something are quite different concepts (*magnitudo* and *quantitas*). In like manner to say simply *(simpliciter)* that anything is great is quite different from saying that it is *absolutely great (absolute, non comparative magnum)*. The latter is *what is great beyond all comparison*. What now is meant by the expression that anything is great or small or of medium size? It is not a pure concept of understanding that is thus signified; still less is it an intuition of sense; and just as little is it a concept of reason, because it brings with it no principle of cognition. It must therefore be a concept of judgment or derived from one, and a subjective purposiveness of the representation in reference to the judgment must lie at its basis. That anything is a magnitude *(quantum)* may be cognized from the thing itself, without any comparison of it with other things, viz. if there is a multiplicity of the homogeneous constituting one thing. But to cognize *how great* it is always requires some other magnitude as a measure. But because the judging of magnitude depends, not merely on multiplicity (number), but also on the magnitude of the unit (the measure), and since, to judge of the magnitude of this latter again requires another as measure with which it may be compared, we see that the determination of the magnitude of phenomena can supply no absolute concept whatever of magnitude, but only a comparative one.

If now I say simply that anything is great, it appears that I have no comparison in view, at least none with an objective measure, because it is thus not determined at all how great the object is. But although the standard of comparison is merely subjective, yet the judgment nonetheless claims universal assent; "this man is beautiful" and "he is tall" are judgments, not limited merely to the judging subject, but, like theoretical judgments, demanding the assent of everyone.

In a judgment by which anything is designated simply as great, it is not merely meant that the object has a magnitude, but that this magnitude is superior to that of many other objects of the same kind, without, however, any exact determination of this superiority. Thus there is always at the basis of our judgment a standard which we assume as the same for everyone; this, however, is not available for any logical (mathematically definite) judging of magnitude, but only for aesthetical judging of the same, because it is a merely subjective standard lying at the basis of the reflective judgment upon magnitude. It may be empirical, as, e.g., the average size of the men known to us, of animals of a certain kind, trees, houses, mountains, etc. Or it may be a standard given *a priori* which, through the defects of the judging subject, is limited by the subjective conditions of presentation *in concreto*, as, e.g., in the practical sphere, the greatness of a certain virtue or of the public liberty and justice in a country, or, in the theoretical sphere, the greatness of the accuracy or the inaccuracy of an observation or measurement that has been made, etc.

Here it is remarkable that, although we have no interest whatever in an object—i.e. its existence is indifferent to us—yet its mere size, even if it is considered as formless, may bring a satisfaction with it that is universally communicable and that consequently involves the consciousness of a subjective purposiveness in the use of our cognitive faculty. This is not indeed a satisfaction in the object (because it may be formless), as in the case of the beautiful, in which the reflective judgment finds itself purposively determined in reference to cognition in general, but [a satisfaction] in the extension of the imagination by itself.

If (under the above limitation) we say simply of an object "it is great," this is no mathematically definite judgment, but a mere judgment of reflection upon the representation of it, which is subjectively purposive for a certain use of our cognitive powers in the estimation of magnitude; and we always then bind up with the representation a kind of respect, as also a kind of contempt, for what we simply call "small." Further, the judging of things as great or small extends to everything, even to all their characteristics; thus we describe beauty as great or small. The reason of this is to be sought in the fact that whatever we present in intuition according to the precept of the judgment (and thus represent aesthetically) is always a phenomenon, and thus a quantum.

But if we call anything, not only great, but absolutely great in every point of view (great beyond all comparison), i.e. sublime, we soon see that it is not permissible to seek for an adequate standard of this outside itself, but merely in itself. It is a magnitude which is like itself alone. It follows hence that the sublime is not to be sought in the things of nature, but only in our ideas; but in which of them it lies must be reserved for the "Deduction."

The foregoing explanation can be thus expressed: *the sublime is that in comparison with which everything else is small.* Here we easily see that nothing can be given in nature, however great it is judged by us to be, which could not, if considered in another relation, be reduced to the infinitely small; and conversely there is nothing so small which does not admit of extension by our imagination to the greatness of a world if compared with still smaller standards. Telescopes have furnished us with abundant material for making the first remark, microscopes for the second. Nothing, therefore, which can be an object of the senses is, considered on this basis, to be called sublime. But because there is in our imagination a striving toward infinite progress and in our reason a claim for absolute totality, regarded as a real idea, therefore this very inadequateness for that idea in our faculty for estimating the magnitude of things of sense excites in us the feeling of a supersensible faculty. And it is not the object of sense, but the use which the judgment naturally makes of certain objects on behalf of this latter feeling that is absolutely great, and in comparison every other use is small. Consequently it is the state of mind produced by a certain representation with which the reflective judgment is occupied, and not the object, that is to be called sublime.

We can therefore append to the preceding formulas explaining the sublime this other: *the sublime is that, the mere ability to think which shows a faculty of the mind surpassing every standard of sense.* . . .

. . . I only remark that if the aesthetical judgment is *pure* (i.e. *mingled with no teleological judgment* or judgment of reason) and is to be given as a completely suitable example of the critique of the *aesthetical* judgment, we must not exhibit the sublime in products of art (e.g. buildings, pillars, etc.) where human purpose determines the form as well as the size, nor yet in things of nature *the concepts of which bring with them a definite purpose* (e.g. animals with a known natural destination), but in rude nature (and in this only in so far as it does not bring with it any charm or emotion produced by actual danger) merely as containing magnitude. For in this kind of representation nature contains nothing monstrous (either magnificent or horrible); the magnitude that is apprehended may be increased as much as you wish, provided it can be comprehended in a whole by the imagination. An object is *monstrous* if, by its size, it destroys the purpose which constitutes the concept of it. But the mere presentation of a concept is called *colossal,* which is almost too great for any presentation (bordering on the relatively monstrous), because the purpose of the presentation of a concept is made hard [to carry out] by the intuition of the object being almost too great for our faculty of apprehension. A pure judgment upon the sublime must, however, have no purpose of the object as its determining ground if it is to be aesthetical and not mixed up with any judgment of understanding or reason. . . .

But the infinite is absolutely (not merely comparatively) great. Compared with it everything else (of the same kind of magnitudes) is small. And what is most important is that to be able only to think it as *a whole* indicates a faculty of mind which surpasses every standard of sense. For [to represent it sensibly] would require a comprehension having for unit a standard bearing a definite relation, expressible in numbers, to the infinite, which is impossible. Nevertheless, *the bare capability of thinking* this infinite without contradiction requires in the human mind a faculty itself supersensible. For it is only by means of this faculty and its idea of a noumenon—which admits of no intuition, but which yet serves as the substrate for the intuition of the world, as a mere phenomenon—that the infinite of the world of sense, in the pure intellectual estimation of magnitude, can be *completely* comprehended *under* one concept, although in the mathematical estimation of magnitude by means of *concepts of number* it can never be completely thought. The faculty of being able to think the infinite of supersensible intuition as given (in its intelligible substrate) surpasses every standard of sensibility and is great beyond all comparison even with the faculty of mathematical estimation, not, of course, in a theoretical point of view and on behalf of the cognitive faculty, but as an extension of the mind which feels itself able in another (practical) point of view to go beyond the limits of sensibility.

Nature is therefore sublime in those of its phenomena whose intuition brings with it the idea of its infinity. This last can only come by the inadequacy of the greatest effort of our imagination to estimate the magnitude of an object. But now, in mathematical estimation of magnitude, the imagination is equal to providing a sufficient measure for every object, because the numerical concepts of the understanding, by means of progression, can make any measure adequate to any given magnitude. Therefore it must be the *aesthetical* estimation of magnitude in which the effort toward comprehension surpasses the power of the imagination. Here it is felt that we can comprehend in a whole of intuition the progressive apprehension, and at the same time we perceive the inadequacy of this faculty, unbounded in its progress, for grasping and using any fundamental measure available for the estimation of magnitude with the easiest application of the understanding. Now the proper unchangeable fundamental measure of nature is its absolute whole, which, regarding nature as a phenomenon, would be infinity comprehended. But since this fundamental measure is a self-contradictory concept (on account of the impossibility of the absolute totality of an endless progress), that magnitude of a natural object on which the imagination fruitlessly spends its whole faculty of comprehension must carry our concept of nature to a supersensible substrate (which lies at its basis and also at the basis of our faculty of thought). As this, however, is great beyond all standards of sense, it makes us judge as *sublime*, not so much the object, as our own state of mind in the estimation of it. . . .

B. OF THE DYNAMICALLY SUBLIME IN NATURE

§ 28. OF NATURE REGARDED AS MIGHT. *Might* is that which is superior to great hindrances. It is called *dominion* if it is superior to the resistance of that which itself possesses might. Nature, considered in an aesthetical judgment as might that has no dominion over us, is *dynamically sublime.*

If nature is to be judged by us as dynamically sublime, it must be represented as exciting fear (although it is not true conversely that every object which excites fear is regarded in our aesthetical judgment as sublime). For in aesthetical judgments (without the aid of concepts) superiority to hindrances can only be judged according to the greatness of the resistance. Now that which we are driven to resist is an evil and, if we do not find our faculties a match for it, is an object of fear. Hence nature can be regarded by the aesthetical judgment as might, and consequently as dynamically sublime, only so far as it is considered an object of fear.

But we can regard an object as *fearful* without being afraid of it, viz. if we judge of it in such a way that we merely *think* a case in which we would wish to resist it and yet in which all resistance would be altogether vain. Thus the virtuous man fears God without being afraid of Him, because to wish to resist Him and His commandments he thinks is a case that he need not apprehend. But in every such case that he thinks as not impossible, he cognizes Him as fearful.

He who fears can form no judgment about the sublime in nature, just as he who is seduced by inclination and appetite can form no judgment about the beautiful. The former flies from the sight of an object which inspires him with awe, and it is impossible to find satisfaction in a terror that is seriously felt. Hence the pleasurableness arising from the cessation of an uneasiness is *a state of joy*. But this, on account of the deliverance from danger [which is involved], is a state of joy when conjoined with the resolve that we shall no more be exposed to the danger; we cannot willingly look back upon our sensations [of danger], much less seek the occasion for them again.

Bold, overhanging, and as it were threatening rocks; clouds piled up in the sky, moving with lightning flashes and thunder peals; volcanoes in all their violence of destruction; hurricanes with their track of devastation; the boundless ocean in a state of tumult; the lofty waterfall of a mighty river, and such like—these exhibit our faculty of resistance as insignificantly small in comparison with their might. But the sight of them is the more attractive, the more fearful it is, provided only that we are in security; and we willingly call these objects sublime, because they raise the energies of the soul above their accustomed height and discover in us a faculty of resistance of a quite different kind, which gives us courage to measure ourselves against the apparent almightiness of nature.

Now, in the immensity of nature and in the insufficiency of our faculties to take in a standard proportionate to the aesthetical estimation of the magnitude of its *realm*, we find our own limitation, although at the same time in our rational faculty we find a different, nonsensuous standard, which has that infinity itself under it as a unity, in comparison with which everything in nature is small, and thus in our mind we find a superiority to nature even in its immensity. And so also the irresistibility of its might, while making us recognize our own [physical][23] impotence, considered as beings of nature, discloses to us a faculty of judging independently of and a superiority over nature, on which is based a kind of self-preservation entirely different from that which can be attacked and brought into danger by external nature. Thus humanity in our person remains unhumiliated, though the individual might have to submit to this dominion. In this way nature is not judged to be sublime in our aesthetical judgments in so far as it excites fear, but because it calls up that power in us (which is not nature) of regarding as small the things about which we are solicitous (goods, health, and life), and of regarding its might (to which we are no doubt subjected in respect of these things) as nevertheless without any dominion over us and our personality to which we must bow where our highest fundamental propositions, and their assertion or abandonment, are concerned. Therefore nature is here called sublime merely because it elevates the imagination to a presentation of those cases in which the mind can make felt the proper sublimity of its destination, in comparison with nature itself. . . .

§ 31. OF THE METHOD OF DEDUCTION OF JUDGMENTS OF TASTE. A deduction, i.e. the guarantee of the legitimacy of a class of judgments, is only obligatory if the judgment lays claim to necessity. This it does if it demands even subjective universality or the agreement of everyone, although it is not a judgment of cognition, but only one of pleasure or pain in a given object, i.e. it assumes a subjective purposiveness thoroughly valid for everyone, which must not be based on any concept of the thing, because the judgment is one of taste.

We have before us in the latter case no cognitive judgment—neither a theoretical one based on the concept of a *nature* in general formed by the understanding, nor a (pure) practical one based on the idea of *freedom*, as given *a priori* by reason. Therefore we have to justify *a priori* the validity, neither of a judgment which represents what a thing is, nor of one which prescribes that I ought to do something in order to produce it. We have merely to prove for the judgment generally the *universal validity* of a singular judgment that expresses the subjective purposiveness of an empirical representation of the form of an object, in order to explain how it is possible that a thing can please in the mere act of judging it (without sensation or concept) and how the satisfaction of one man can be proclaimed as a rule for every other, just as the act of judging of an object for the sake of a *cognition* in general has universal rules.

If, now, this universal validity is not to be based on any collecting of the suffrages of others or on any questioning of them as to the kind of sensations they have, but is to rest, as it were, on an autonomy of the judging subject in respect of the feeling of pleasure (in the given representation), i.e. on his own taste, and yet is not to be derived from concepts, then a judgment like this—such as the judgment of taste is, in fact—has a twofold logical peculiarity. First, there is its *a priori* universal validity, which is not a logical universality in accordance with concepts, but the universality of a singular judgment. Secondly, it has a necessity (which must always rest on *a priori* grounds), which however does not depend on any *a priori* grounds of proof, through the representation of which the assent that everyone concedes to the judgment of taste could be exacted.

The explanation of these logical peculiarities, wherein a judgment of taste is different from all cognitive judgments—if we at the outset abstract from all content, viz. from the feeling of pleasure, and merely compare the aesthetical form with the form of objective judgments as logic prescribes it—is sufficient by itself for the deduction of this singular faculty. We shall then represent and elucidate by examples these characteristic properties of taste.

§ 32. FIRST PECULIARITY OF THE JUDGMENT OF TASTE. The judgment of taste determines its object in respect of satisfaction (in its beauty) with an accompanying claim for the assent of *everyone*, just as if it were objective.

To say that "this flower is beautiful" is the same as to assert its proper claim to satisfy everyone. By the pleasantness of its smell it has no such claim. A smell which one man enjoys gives another a headache. Now what are we to presume from this except that beauty is to be regarded as a property of the flower itself, which does not accommodate itself to any diversity of persons or of their sensitive organs, but to which these must accommodate themselves if they are to pass any judgment upon it? And yet this is not so. For a judgment of taste consists in calling a thing beautiful just because of that characteristic in respect of which it accommodates itself to our mode of apprehension.

Moreover, it is required of every judgment which is to prove the taste of the subject that the subject shall judge by himself, without needing to grope about empirically among the judgments of others, and acquaint himself previously as to their satisfaction or dissatisfaction with the same object; thus his judgment should be pronounced *a priori*, and not be a mere limitation, because the thing actually gives universal pleasure. However, we ought to think that an *a priori* judgment must contain a concept of the object for the cognition of which it contains the principle, but the judgment of taste is not based upon concepts at all and is in general, not a cognitive, but an aesthetical judgment.

Thus a young poet does not permit himself to be dissuaded out of his conviction that his poem is beautiful, by the judgment of the public or of his friends; and if he gives ear to them he does so, not because he now judges differently, but because, although (in regard to him) the whole public has false taste, in his desire for applause he finds reason for accommodating himself to the common error (even against his judgment). It is only at a later time, when his judgment has been sharpened by exercise, that he voluntarily departs from his former judgments, just as he proceeds with those of his judgments which rest upon reason. Taste [merely][24] claims autonomy. To make the judgments of others the determining grounds of his own would be heteronomy.

That we, and rightly, recommend the works of the ancients as models and call their authors classical, thus forming among writers a kind of noble class who give laws to the people by their example, seems to indicate *a posteriori* sources of taste and to contradict the autonomy of taste in every subject. But we might just as well say that the old mathematicians—who are regarded up to the present day as supplying models not easily to be dispensed with for the supreme profundity and elegance of their synthetical methods—prove that our reason is only imitative and that we have not the faculty of producing from it, in combination with intuition, rigid proofs by means of the construction of concepts.[25] There is no use of our powers, however free, no use of reason itself (which must create all its judgments *a priori* from common sources) which would not give rise to faulty attempts if every subject had always to begin anew from the rude basis of his natural state and if others had not preceded him with their attempts. Not that these make mere imitators of those who come after them, but rather by their procedure they put others on the track of seeking in themselves principles and so of pursuing their own course, often a better one. Even in religion—where certainly everyone has to derive the rule of his conduct from himself, because he remains responsible for it and cannot shift the blame of his transgressions upon others, whether his teachers or his predecessors—there is never as much accomplished by means of universal precepts, either obtained from priests or philosophers or gotten from oneself, as by means of an example of virtue or holiness which, exhibited in history, does not dispense with the autonomy of virtue based on the proper and original idea of morality *(a priori)* or change it into a mechanical imitation. *Following,* involving something precedent, not "imitation," is the right expression for all influence that the products of an exemplary author may have upon others. And this only means that we draw from the same sources as our predecessor did and learn from him only the way to avail ourselves of them. But of all faculties and talents, taste, because its judgment is not determinable by concepts and precepts, is just that one which most needs examples of what has in the progress of culture received the longest approval, that it may not become again uncivilized and return to the crudeness of its first essays.

§ 33. SECOND PECULIARITY OF THE JUDGMENT OF TASTE. The judgment of taste is not determinable by grounds of proof, just as if it were merely *subjective*.

If a man, *in the first place*, does not find a building, a prospect, or a poem beautiful, a hundred voices all highly praising it will not force his inmost agreement. He may indeed feign that it pleases him, in order that he may not be regarded as devoid of taste; he may even begin to doubt whether he has formed his taste on a knowledge of a sufficient number of objects of a certain kind (just as one who believes that he recognizes in the distance as a forest something which all others regard as a town doubts the judgment of his own sight). But he clearly sees that the agreement of others gives no valid proof of the judgment about beauty. Others might perhaps see and observe for him; and what many have seen in one way, although he believes that he has seen it differently, might serve him as an adequate ground of proof of a theoretical and consequently logical judgment. But that a thing has pleased others could never serve as the basis of an aesthetical judgment. A judgment of others which is unfavorable to ours may indeed rightly make us scrutinize our own carefully, but it can never convince us of its incorrectness. There is therefore no empirical *ground of proof* which would force a judgment of taste upon anyone.

Still less, *in the second place*, can an *a priori* proof determine according to definite rules a judgment about beauty. If a man reads me a poem of his or brings me to a play which does not on the whole suit my taste, he may bring forward in proof of the beauty of his poem Batteux[26] or Lessing, or still more ancient and famous critics of taste, and all the rules laid down by them. Certain passages which displease me may agree very well with rules of beauty (as they have been put forth by these writers and are universally recognized); but I stop my ears, I will listen to no arguments and no reasoning; and I will rather assume that these rules of the critics are false, or at least that they do not apply to the case in question, than admit that my judgment should be determined by grounds of proof *a priori*. For it is to be a judgment of taste, and not of understanding or reason.

It seems that this is one of the chief reasons why this aesthetical faculty of judgment has been given the name of "taste." For though a man enumerate to me all the ingredients of a dish and remark that each is separately pleasant to me, and further extol with justice the wholesomeness of this particular food, yet am I deaf to all these reasons; I try the dish with *my* tongue and my palate, and thereafter (and not according to universal principles) do I pass my judgment.

In fact, the judgment of taste always takes the form of a singular judgment about an object. The understanding can form a universal judgment by comparing the object in point of the satisfaction it affords with the judgment of others upon it: e.g., "All tulips are beautiful." But then this is not a judgment of taste but a logical judgment, which takes the relation of an object to taste as the predicate of things of a certain species. That judgment, however, in which I find an individual given tulip beautiful, i.e. in which I find my satisfaction in the object to be universally valid, is alone a judgment of taste. Its peculiarity consists in the fact that, although it has merely subjective validity, it claims the assent of *all* subjects, exactly as it would do if it were an objective judgment resting on grounds of knowledge that could be established by a proof.

§ 34. THERE IS NO OBJECTIVE PRINCIPLE OF TASTE POSSIBLE. By a principle of taste I mean a principle under the condition of which we would subsume the concept of an object and thus infer, by means of a syllogism, that the object is beautiful. But that is absolutely impossible. For I must immediately feel pleasure in the representation of the object, and of that I can be persuaded by no grounds of proof whatever. Although, as Hume says,[27] all critics can reason more plausibly than cooks, yet the same fate awaits them. They cannot expect the determining ground of their judgment [to be derived] from the force of the proofs, but only from the reflection of the subject upon its own proper state (of pleasure or pain), all precepts and rules being rejected.

But although critics can and ought to pursue their reasonings so that our judgments of taste may be corrected and extended, it is not with a view to set forth the determining ground of this kind of aesthetical judgments in a universally applicable formula, which is impossible; but rather to investigate the cognitive faculties and their exercise in these judgments, and to explain by examples the reciprocal subjective purposiveness, the form of which, as has been shown above, in a given representation, constitutes the beauty of the object. Therefore the critique of taste is only subjective as regards the representation through which an object is given to us, viz. it is the art or science of reducing to rules the reciprocal relation between the understanding and the imagination in the given representation (without reference to any preceding sensation or concept). That is, it is the art or science of reducing to rules their accordance or discordance, and of determining the conditions of this. It is an *art*, if it only shows this by examples; it is a *science* if it derives the possibility of such judgments from the nature of these faculties, as cognitive faculties in general. We have here, in Transcendental Critique, only to do with the latter. It should develop and justify the subjective principle of taste, as an *a priori* principle of the judgment. This critique, as an art, merely seeks to apply, in the judging of objects, the physiological (here psychological), and therefore empirical, rules according to which taste actually proceeds (without taking any account of their possibility); and it criticizes the products of beautiful art just as, regarded as a science, it criticizes the faculty by which they are judged.

§ 35. THE PRINCIPLE OF TASTE IS THE SUBJECTIVE PRINCIPLE OF JUDGMENT IN GEN-
ERAL. The judgment of taste is distinguished from a logical judgment in this
that the latter subsumes a representation under the concept of the object,
while the former does not subsume it under any concept; because otherwise
the necessary universal agreement [in these judgments] would be capable of
being compelled by proofs. Nevertheless it is like the latter in this that it
claims universality and necessity, though not according to concepts of the
object, and consequently a merely subjective necessity. Now because the concepts in a judgment constitute its content (what belongs to the cognition of
the object), but the judgment of taste is not determinable by concepts, it is
based only on the subjective formal condition of a judgment in general. The
subjective condition of all judgments is the faculty of judgment itself. This,
when used with reference to a representation by which an object is given,
requires the accordance of two representative powers, viz. imagination (for the
intuition and comprehension of the manifold) and understanding (for the
concept as a representation of the unity of this comprehension). Now because
no concept of the object lies here at the basis of the judgment, it can only consist in the subsumption of the imagination itself (in the case of a representation by which an object is given), under the conditions that the understanding
requires to pass from intuition to concepts. That is, because the freedom of
the imagination consists in the fact that it schematizes without any concept,
the judgment of taste must rest on a mere sensation of the reciprocal activity
of the imagination in its *freedom* and the understanding with its *conformity to
law*. It must therefore rest on a feeling, which makes us judge the object by the
purposiveness of the representation (by which an object is given) in respect of
the furtherance of the cognitive faculty in its free play. Taste, then, as subjective judgment, contains a principle of subsumption, not of intuitions under
concepts, but of the *faculty* of intuitions or presentations (i.e. the imagination)
under the *faculty* of the concepts (i.e. the understanding), so far as the former
in its freedom harmonizes with the latter *in its conformity to law*.

   In order to discover this ground of legitimacy by a deduction of the
judgments of taste, we can only take as a clue the formal peculiarities of this
kind of judgments, and consequently can only consider their logical form.

§ 36. OF THE PROBLEM OF A DEDUCTION OF JUDGMENTS OF TASTE. The concept
of an object in general can immediately be combined with the perception of
an object, containing its empirical predicates, so as to form a cognitive judgment; and it is thus that a judgment of experience is produced.[28] At the basis
of this lie *a priori* concepts of the synthetical unity of the manifold of intuition, by which the manifold is thought as the determination of an object.
These concepts (the categories) require a deduction, which is given in the *Critique of Pure Reason*; and by it we can get the solution of the problem: how are
synthetical *a priori* cognitive judgments possible? This problem concerns
then the *a priori* principles of the pure understanding and its theoretical
judgments.

But with a perception there can also be combined a feeling of pleasure (or pain) and a satisfaction, that accompanies the representation of the object and serves instead of its predicate; thus there can result an aesthetical noncognitive judgment. At the basis of such a judgment—if it is not a mere judgment of sensation but a formal judgment of reflection, which imputes the same satisfaction necessarily to everyone—must lie some *a priori* principle, which may be merely subjective (if an objective one should prove impossible for judgments of this kind), but also as such may need a deduction, that we may thereby comprehend how an aesthetical judgment can lay claim to necessity. On this is founded the problem with which we are now occupied: how are judgments of taste possible? This problem, then, has to do with the *a priori* principles of the pure faculty of judgment in *aesthetical* judgments, i.e. judgments in which it has not (as in theoretical ones) merely to subsume under objective concepts of understanding and in which it is subject to a law, but in which it is itself, subjectively, both object and law.

This problem then may be thus represented: how is a judgment possible in which merely from *our own* feeling of pleasure in an object, independently of its concept, we judge that this pleasure attaches to the representation of the same object *in every other subject*, and that *a priori* without waiting for the accordance of others?

It is easy to see that judgments of taste are synthetical, because they go beyond the concept and even beyond the intuition of the object, and add to that intuition as predicate something that is not a cognition, viz. a feeling of pleasure (or pain). Although the predicate (of the *personal* pleasure bound up with the representation) is empirical, nevertheless, as concerns the required assent of *everyone* the judgments are *a priori*, or desire to be regarded as such; and this is already involved in the expressions of this claim. Thus this problem of the *Critique of Judgment* belongs to the general problem of transcendental philosophy: how are synthetical *a priori* judgments possible?

§ 37. WHAT IS PROPERLY ASSERTED A PRIORI OF AN OBJECT IN A JUDGMENT OF TASTE. That the representation of an object is immediately bound up with pleasure can only be internally perceived; and if we did not wish to indicate anything more than this, it would give a merely empirical judgment. For I cannot combine a definite feeling (of pleasure or pain) with any representation, except where there is at bottom an *a priori* principle in the reason determining the will. In that case the pleasure (in the moral feeling) is the consequence of the principle, but cannot be compared with the pleasure in taste, because it requires a definite concept of law; and the latter pleasure, on the contrary, must be bound up with the mere act of judging, prior to all concepts. Hence also all judgments of taste are singular judgments, because they do not combine their predicate of satisfaction with a concept, but with a given individual empirical representation.

And so it is not the pleasure, but the *universal validity of this pleasure*, perceived as mentally bound up with the mere judgment upon an object, which is represented *a priori* in a judgment of taste as a universal rule for the judgment and valid for everyone. It is an empirical judgment [to say] that I perceive and judge an object with pleasure. But it is an *a priori* judgment [to say] that I find it beautiful, i.e. I attribute this satisfaction necessarily to everyone.

§ 38. DEDUCTION OF JUDGMENTS OF TASTE. If it be admitted that, in a pure judgment of taste, the satisfaction in the object is combined with the mere act of judging its form, it is nothing else than its subjective purposiveness for the judgment which we feel to be mentally combined with the representation of the object. The judgment, as regards the formal rules of its action, apart from all matter (whether sensation or concept), can only be directed to the subjective conditions of its employment in general (it is applied[29] neither to a particular mode of sense nor to a particular concept of the understanding), and consequently to that subjective [element] which we can presuppose in all men (as requisite for possible cognition in general). Thus the agreement of a representation with these conditions of the judgment must be capable of being assumed as valid *a priori* for everyone. That is, we may rightly impute to everyone the pleasure or the subjective purposiveness of the representation for the relation between the cognitive faculties in the act of judging a sensible object in general.[25]

Remark

This deduction is thus easy, because it has no need to justify the objective reality of any concept, for beauty is not a concept of the object and the judgment of taste is not cognitive. It only maintains that we are justified in presupposing universally in every man those subjective conditions of the judgment which we find in ourselves; and further, that we have rightly subsumed the given object under these conditions. The latter has indeed unavoidable difficulties which do not beset the logical judgment. There we subsume under concepts, but in the aesthetical judgment under a merely sensible relation between the imagination and understanding mutually harmonizing in the representation of the form of the object—in which case the subsumption may easily be deceptive. Yet the legitimacy of the claim of the judgment in counting upon universal assent is not thus annulled; it reduces itself merely to judging as valid for everyone the correctness of the principle from subjective grounds. For as to the difficulty or doubt concerning the correctness of the subsumption under that principle, it makes the legitimacy of the claim of an aesthetical judgment in general to such validity and the principle of the same as little doubtful as the alike (though neither so commonly nor readily) faulty subsumption of the logical judgment under its principle can make the latter, an objective principle, doubtful. But if the question were to be, "How is it possible to assume nature *a priori* to be a complex of objects of taste?" this problem has reference to teleology, because it must be regarded as a purpose of nature essentially belonging to its concept to exhibit forms that are purposive for our judgment. But the correctness of this latter assumption is very doubtful, whereas the efficacy of natural beauties is patent to experience. . . .

§ 46. BEAUTIFUL ART IS THE ART OF GENIUS. *Genius* is the talent (or natural gift) which gives the rule to art. Since talent, as the innate productive faculty of the artist, belongs itself to nature, we may express the matter thus: Genius is the innate mental disposition *(ingenium) through which* nature gives the rule to art.

Whatever may be thought of this definition, whether it is merely arbitrary or whether it is adequate to the concept that we are accustomed to combine with the word *genius* (which is to be examined in the following paragraphs), we can prove already beforehand that, according to the signification of the word here adopted, beautiful arts must necessarily be considered as arts of *genius.*

For every art presupposes rules by means of which in the first instance a product, if it is to be called artistic, is represented as possible. But the concept of beautiful art does not permit the judgment upon the beauty of a product to be derived from any rule which has a *concept* as its determining ground, and therefore has at its basis a concept of the way in which the product is possible. Therefore beautiful art cannot itself devise the rule according to which it can bring about its product. But since at the same time a product can never be called art without some precedent rule, nature in the subject must (by the harmony of its faculties) give the rule to art; i.e. beautiful art is only possible as a product of genius.

We thus see (1) that genius is a *talent* for producing that for which no definite rule can be given; it is not a mere aptitude for what can be learned by a rule. Hence *originality* must be its first property. (2) But since it also can produce original nonsense, its products must be models, i.e. *exemplary,* and they consequently ought not to spring from imitation, but must serve as a standard or rule of judgment for others. (3) It cannot describe or indicate scientifically how it brings about its products, but it gives the rule just as nature does. Hence the author of a product for which he is indebted to his genius does not know himself how he has come by his ideas; and he has not the power to devise the like at pleasure or in accordance with a plan, and to communicate it to others in precepts that will enable them to produce similar products. (Hence it is probable that the word "genius" is derived from *genius,* that peculiar guiding and guardian spirit given to a man at his birth, from whose suggestion these original ideas proceed.) (4) Nature, by the medium of genius, does not prescribe rules to science but to art, and to it only in so far as it is to be beautiful art.

§ 47. ELUCIDATION AND CONFIRMATION OF THE ABOVE EXPLANATION OF GENIUS. Everyone is agreed that genius is entirely opposed to the *spirit of imitation.* Now since learning is nothing but imitation, it follows that the greatest ability and teachableness (capacity) regarded *qua* teachableness cannot avail for genius. Even if a man thinks or composes for himself and does not merely take in what others have taught, even if he discovers many things in art and science, this is not the right ground for calling such a (perhaps great) *head* a genius (as opposed to him who, because he can only learn and imitate, is called a *shallowpate*). For even these things could be learned; they lie in the natural path of him who investigates and reflects according to rules, and they do not differ specifically from what can be acquired by industry through imitation. Thus we can readily learn all that Newton has set forth in his immortal work on the *Principles of Natural Philosophy,* however great a head was required to discover it, but we cannot learn to write spirited poetry, however express may be the precepts of the art and however excellent its models. The reason is that Newton could make all his steps, from the first elements of geometry to his own great and profound discoveries, intuitively plain and definite as regards consequence, not only to himself but to everyone else. But a Homer or a Wieland cannot show how his ideas, so rich in fancy and yet so full of thought, come together in his head, simply because he does not know and therefore cannot teach others. In science, then, the greatest discoverer only differs in degree from his laborious imitator and pupil, but he differs specifically from him whom nature has gifted for beautiful art. And in this there is no depreciation of those great men to whom the human race owes so much gratitude, as compared with nature's favorites in respect of the talent for beautiful art. For in the fact that the former talent is directed to the ever advancing greater perfection of knowledge and every advantage depending on it, and at the same time to the imparting this same knowledge to others—in this it has a great superiority over [the talent of] those who deserve the honor of being called geniuses. For art stands still at a certain point; a boundary is set to it beyond which it cannot go, which presumably has been reached long ago and cannot be extended further. Again, artistic skill cannot be communicated; it is imparted to every artist immediately by the hand of nature; and so it dies with him, until nature endows another in the same way, so that he only needs an example in order to put in operation in a similar fashion the talent of which he is conscious.

If now it is a natural gift which must prescribe its rule to art (as beautiful art), of what kind is this? It cannot be reduced to a formula and serve as a precept, for then the judgment upon the beautiful would be determinable according to concepts; but the rule must be abstracted from the fact, i.e. from the product, on which others may try their own talent by using it as a model, not to be *copied* but to be *imitated.* How this is possible is hard to explain. The ideas of the artist excite like ideas in his pupils if nature had endowed them with a like proportion of their mental powers. Hence models of beautiful art are the only means of handing down these ideas to posterity. This cannot be done by mere descriptions, especially not in the case of the arts of speech; and in this latter classical models are only to be had in the old dead languages, now preserved only as "the learned languages."

Although mechanical and beautiful art are very different, the first being a mere art of industry and learning and the second of genius, yet there is no beautiful art in which there is not a mechanical element that can be comprehended by rules and followed accordingly, and in which therefore there must be something *scholastic* as an essential condition. For [in every art] some purpose must be conceived; otherwise we could not ascribe the product to art at all; it would be a mere product of chance. But in order to accomplish a purpose, definite rules from which we cannot dispense ourselves are requisite. Now since the originality of the talent constitutes an essential (though not the only) element in the character of genius, shallow heads believe that they cannot better show themselves to be full-blown geniuses than by throwing off the constraint of all rules; they believe, in effect, that one could make a braver show on the back of a wild horse than on the back of a trained animal. Genius can only furnish rich *material* for products of beautiful art; its execution and its *form* require talent cultivated in the schools, in order to make such a use of this material as will stand examination by the judgment. But it is quite ridiculous for a man to speak and decide like a genius in things which require the most careful investigation by reason. One does not know whether to laugh more at the imposter who spreads such a mist round him that we cannot clearly use our judgment, and so use our imagination the more, or at the public which naïvely imagines that his inability to recognize clearly and to comprehend the masterpiece before him arises from new truths crowding in on him in such abundance that details (duly weighed definitions and accurate examination of fundamental propositions) seem but clumsy work.

§ 48. OF THE RELATION OF GENIUS TO TASTE. For *judging* of beautiful objects as such, *taste* is requisite; but for beautiful art, i.e. for the *production* of such objects, *genius* is requisite.

If we consider genius as the talent for beautiful art (which the special meaning of the word implies) and in this point of view analyze it into the faculties which must concur to constitute such a talent, it is necessary in the first instance to determine exactly the difference between natural beauty, the judging of which requires only taste, and artificial beauty, the possibility of which (to which reference must be made in judging such an object) requires genius.

A natural beauty is a *beautiful thing*; artificial beauty is a *beautiful representation* of a thing.

In order to judge of a natural beauty as such, I need not have beforehand a concept of what sort of thing the object is to be; i.e. I need not know its material purposiveness (the purpose), but its mere form pleases by itself in the act of judging it without any knowledge of the purpose. But if the object is given as a product of art and as such is to be declared beautiful, then, because art always supposes a purpose in the cause (and its causality), there must be at bottom in the first instance a concept of what the thing is to be. And as the agreement of the manifold in a thing with its inner destination, its purpose, constitutes the perfection of the thing, it follows that in judging of artificial beauty the perfection of the thing must be taken into account; but in judging of natural beauty (as *such*), there is no question at all about this. It is true that in judging of objects of nature, especially objects endowed with life, e.g.

a man or a horse, their objective purposiveness also is commonly taken into consideration in judging of their beauty; but then the judgment is no longer purely aesthetical, i.e. a mere judgment of taste. Nature is no longer judged inasmuch as it appears like art, but in so far as it *is* actual (although superhuman) art; and the teleological judgment serves as the basis and condition of the aesthetical, as a condition to which the latter must have respect. In such a case, e.g. if it is said "That is a beautiful woman," we think nothing else than this: nature represents in her figure the purposes in view of the shape of a woman's figure. For we must look beyond the mere form to a concept, if the object is to be thought in such a way by means of a logically conditioned aesthetical judgment.

Beautiful art shows its superiority in this, that it describes as beautiful things which may be in nature ugly or displeasing.[31] The Furies, diseases, the devastations of war, etc., may [even regarded as calamitous][32] be described as very beautiful, as they are represented in a picture. There is only one kind of ugliness which cannot be represented in accordance with nature without destroying all aesthetical satisfaction, and consequently artificial beauty, viz. that which excites *disgust.* For in this singular sensation, which rests on mere imagination, the object is represented as it were obtruding itself for our enjoyment, while we strive against it with all our might. And the artistic representation of the object is no longer distinguished from the nature of the object itself in our sensation, and thus it is impossible that it can be regarded as beautiful. The art of sculpture again, because in its products art is almost interchangeable with nature, excludes from its creations the immediate representation of ugly objects; e.g. it represents death by a beautiful genius, the warlike spirit of Mars, and permits [all such things] to be represented only by an allegory or attribute[33] that has a pleasing effect, and thus only indirectly by the aid of the interpretation of reason, and not for the mere aesthetical judgment.

So much for the beautiful representation of an object, which is properly only the form of the presentation of a concept, by means of which this latter is communicated universally. But to give this form to the product of beautiful art, mere taste is requisite. By taste the artist estimates his work after he has exercised and corrected it by manifold examples from art or nature, and after many, often toilsome, attempts to content himself he finds that form which satisfies him. Hence this form is not, as it were, a thing of inspiration or the result of a free swing of the mental powers, but of a slow and even painful process of improvement, by which he seeks to render it adequate to his thought, without detriment to the freedom of the play of his powers.

But taste is merely a judging and not a productive faculty, and what is appropriate to it is therefore not a work of beautiful art. It can only be a product belonging to useful and mechanical art or even to science, produced according to definite rules that can be learned and must be exactly followed. But the pleasing form that is given to it is only the vehicle of communication and a mode, as it were, of presenting it, in respect of which we remain free to a certain extent, although it is combined with a definite purpose. Thus we desire that table appointments, a moral treatise, even a sermon, should have in themselves this form of beautiful art, without it seeming to be *sought;* but we do not therefore call these things works of beautiful art. Under the latter class are reckoned a poem, a piece of music, a picture gallery, etc.; and in some works of this kind asserted to be works of beautiful art we find genius without taste, while in others we find taste without genius.

§ 49 OF THE FACULTIES OF THE MIND THAT CONSTITUTE GENIUS. We say of certain products of which we expect that they should at least in part appear as beautiful art, they are without *spirit,*[34] although we find nothing to blame in them on the score of taste. A poem may be very neat and elegant, but without spirit. A history may be exact and well arranged, but without spirit. A festal discourse may be solid and at the same time elaborate, but without spirit. Conversation is often not devoid of entertainment, but it is without spirit; even of a woman we say that she is pretty, an agreeable talker, and courteous, but without spirit. What then do we mean by spirit?

Spirit, in an aesthetical sense, is the name given to the animating principle of the mind. But that by means of which this principle animates the soul, the material which it applies to that [purpose], is what puts the mental powers purposively into swing, i.e. into such a play as maintains itself and strengthens the mental powers in their exercise.

Now I maintain that this principle is no other than the faculty of presenting *aesthetical ideas.* And by an aesthetical idea I understand that representation of the imagination which occasions much thought, without however any definite thought, i.e. any *concept,* being capable of being adequate to it; it consequently cannot be completely compassed and made intelligible by language. We easily see that it is the counterpart (pendant) of a *rational idea,* which conversely is a concept to which no *intuition* (or representation of the imagination) can be adequate.

The imagination (as a productive faculty of cognition) is very powerful in creating another nature, as it were, out of the material that actual nature gives it. We entertain ourselves with it when experience becomes too commonplace, and by it we remold experience, always indeed in accordance with analogical laws, but yet also in accordance with principles which occupy a higher place in reason (laws, too, which are just as natural to us as those by which understanding comprehends empirical nature). Thus we feel our freedom from the law of association (which attaches to the empirical employment of imagination), so that the material supplied to us by nature in accordance with this law can be worked up into something different which surpasses nature.

Such representations of the imagination we may call *ideas,* partly because they at least strive after something which lies beyond the bounds of experience and so seek to approximate to a presentation of concepts of reason (intellectual ideas), thus giving to the latter the appearance of objective reality, but especially because no concept can be fully adequate to them as internal intu-itions. The poet ventures to realize to sense, rational ideas of invisible beings, the kingdom of the blessed, hell, eternity, creation, etc.; or even if he deals with things of which there are examples in experience—e.g. death, envy and all vices, also love, fame, and the like—he tries, by means of imagination, which emulates the play of reason in its quest after a maximum, to go beyond the limits of experience and to present them to sense with a completeness of which there is no example in nature. This is properly speaking the art of the poet, in which the faculty of aesthetical ideas can manifest itself in its entire strength. But this faculty, considered in itself, is properly only a talent (of the imagination).

If now we place under a concept a representation of the imagination belonging to its presentation, but which occasions in itself more thought than can ever be comprehended in a definite concept and which consequently aesthetically enlarges the concept itself in an unbounded fashion, the imagi-nation is here creative, and it brings the faculty of intellectual ideas (the rea-son) into movement; i.e. by a representation more thought (which indeed belongs to the concept of the object) is occasioned than can in it be grasped or made clear. . . .

§ 56. REPRESENTATION OF THE ANTINOMY OF TASTE. The first commonplace of taste is contained in the proposition, with which every tasteless person pro-poses to avoid blame: *everyone has his own taste*. That is as much as to say that the determining ground of this judgment is merely subjective (gratification or grief), and that the judgment has no right to the necessary assent of others.

The second commonplace invoked even by those who admit for judg-ments of taste the right to speak with validity for everyone is: *there is no dis-puting about taste*. That is as much as to say that the determining ground of a judgment of taste may indeed be objective, but that it cannot be reduced to definite concepts; and that consequently about the judgment itself nothing can be *decided* by proofs, although much may rightly be *contested*. For *contesting* [quarreling] and *disputing* [controversy] are doubtless the same in this, that, by means of the mutual opposition of judgments they seek to produce their accordance, but different in that the latter hopes to bring this about according to definite concepts as determining grounds, and consequently assumes *objec-tive concepts* as grounds of the judgment. But where this is regarded as imprac-ticable, controversy is regarded as alike impracticable.

We easily see that, between these two commonplaces, there is a propo-sition wanting which, though it has not passed into a proverb, is yet familiar to everyone, viz. *there may be a quarrel about taste* (although there can be no con-troversy). But this proposition involves the contradictory of the former one. For wherever quarreling is permissible, there must be a hope of mutual rec-onciliation; and consequently we can count on grounds of our judgment that have not merely private validity, and therefore are not merely subjective. And to this the proposition, *everyone has his own taste*, is directly opposed.

There emerges therefore in respect of the principle of taste the following antinomy:

(1) *Thesis.* The judgment of taste is not based upon concepts, for otherwise it would admit of controversy (would be determinable by proofs).

(2) *Antithesis.* The judgment of taste is based on concepts, for otherwise, despite its diversity, we could not quarrel about it (we could not claim for our judgment the necessary assent of others).

§ 57. SOLUTION OF THE ANTINOMY OF TASTE. There is no possibility of removing the conflict between these principles that underlie every judgment of taste (which are nothing else than the two peculiarities of the judgment of taste exhibited above in the Analytic), except by showing that the concept to which we refer the object in this kind of judgment is not taken in the same sense in both maxims of the aesthetical judgment. This twofold sense or twofold point of view is necessary to our transcendental judgment, but also the illusion which arises from the confusion of one with the other is natural and unavoidable.

The judgment of taste must refer to some concept; otherwise it could make absolutely no claim to be necessarily valid for everyone. But it is not therefore capable of being proved *from* a concept, because a concept may be either determinable or in itself undetermined and undeterminable. The concepts of the understanding are of the former kind; they are determinable through predicates of sensible intuition which can correspond to them. But the transcendental rational concept of the supersensible, which lies at the basis of all sensible intuition, is of the latter kind, and therefore cannot be theoretically determined further.

Now the judgment of taste is applied to objects of sense, but not with a view of determining a *concept* of them for the understanding; for it is not a cognitive judgment. It is thus only a private judgment, in which a singular representation intuitively perceived is referred to the feeling of pleasure, and so far would be limited as regards its validity to the individual judging. The object is *for me* an object of satisfaction; by others it may be regarded quite differently—everyone has his own taste.

Nevertheless there is undoubtedly contained in the judgment of taste a wider reference of the representation of the object (as well as of the subject), whereon we base an extension of judgments of this kind as necessary for everyone. At the basis of this there must necessarily be a concept somewhere, though a concept which cannot be determined through intuition. But through a concept of this sort we know nothing, and consequently it can *supply no proof* for the judgment of taste. Such a concept is the mere pure rational concept of the supersensible which underlies the object (and also the subject judging it), regarded as an object of sense and thus as phenomenal. For if we do not admit such a reference, the claim of the judgment of taste to universal validity would not hold good. If the concept on which it is based were only a mere confused concept of the understanding, like that of perfection, with which we could bring the sensible intuition of the beautiful into correspondence, it would be at least possible in itself to base the judgment of taste on proofs, which contradicts the thesis.

But all contradiction disappears if I say: the judgment of taste is based on a concept (viz. the concept of the general ground of the subjective purposiveness of nature for the judgment); from which, however, nothing can be known and proved in respect of the object, because it is in itself undeterminable and useless for knowledge. Yet at the same time and on that very account the judgment has validity for everyone (though, of course, for each only as a singular judgment immediately accompanying his intuition), because its determining ground lies perhaps in the concept of that which may be regarded as the supersensible substrate of humanity.

The solution of an antinomy only depends on the possibility of showing that two apparently contradictory propositions do not contradict each other in fact, but that they may be consistent, although the explanation of the possibility of their concept may transcend our cognitive faculties. That this illusion is natural and unavoidable by human reason, and also why it is so and remains so, although it ceases to deceive after the analysis of the apparent contradiction, may be thus explained.

In the two contradictory judgments we take the concept on which the universal validity of a judgment must be based in the same sense, and yet we apply to it two opposite predicates. In the thesis we mean that the judgment of taste is not based upon *determinate* concepts, and the antithesis that the judgment of taste is based upon a concept, but an *indeterminate* one (viz. of the supersensible substrate of phenomena). Between these two there is no contradiction.

We can do nothing more than remove this conflict between the claims and counterclaims of taste. It is absolutely impossible to give a definite objective principle of taste in accordance with which its judgments could be derived, examined, and established, for then the judgment would not be one of taste at all. The subjective principle, viz. the indefinite idea of the supersensible in us, can only be put forward as the sole key to the puzzle of this faculty whose sources are hidden from us; it can be made no further intelligible.

The proper concept of taste, that is of a merely reflective aesthetical judgment, lies at the basis of the antinomy here exhibited and adjusted. Thus the two apparently contradictory principles are reconciled—*both can be true,* which is sufficient. If, on the other hand, we assume, as some do, *pleasantness* as the determining ground of taste (on account of the singularity of the representation which lies at the basis of the judgment of taste) or, as others will have it, the principle of perfection (on account of the universality of the same), and settle the definition of taste accordingly, then there arises an antinomy which it is absolutely impossible to adjust except by showing that *both* the contrary (not merely contradictory) *propositions are false.* And this would prove that the concept on which they are based is self-contradictory. Hence we see that the removal of the antinomy of the aesthetical judgment takes a course similar to that pursued by the critique in the solution of the anti-nomies of pure theoretical reason. And thus here, as also in the *Critique of Practical Reason*, antinomies force us against our will to look beyond the sensible and to seek in the supersensible the point of union for all our *a priori* faculties, because no other expedient is left to make our reason harmonious with itself. . . .

§ 59. OF BEAUTY AS THE SYMBOL OF MORALITY. Intuitions are always required to establish the reality of our concepts. If the concepts are empirical, the intuitions are called *examples*. If they are pure concepts of understanding, the intuitions are called *schemata*. If we desire to establish the objective reality of rational concepts, i.e. of ideas, on behalf of theoretical cognition, then we are asking for something impossible, because absolutely no intuition can be given which shall be adequate to them.

All *hypotyposis* (presentation, *subjectio sub adspectum*), or sensible illustration, is twofold. It is either *schematical*, when to a concept comprehended by the understanding the corresponding intuition is given, or it is *symbolical*. In the latter case, to a concept only thinkable by the reason, to which no sensible intuition can be adequate, an intuition is supplied with which accords a procedure of the judgment analogous to what it observes in schematism, i.e. merely analogous to the rule of this procedure, not to the intuition itself, consequently to the form of reflection merely and not to its content.

There is a use of the word *symbolical* that has been adopted by modern logicians which is misleading and incorrect, i.e. to speak of the *symbolical* mode of representation as if it were opposed to the *intuitive*, for the symbolical is only a mode of the intuitive. The latter (the intuitive, that is), may be divided into the *schematical* and *symbolical* modes of representation. Both are hypotyposes, i.e. presentations *(exhibitiones)*, not mere *characterizations* or designations of concepts by accompanying sensible signs which contain nothing belonging to the intuition of the object and only serve as a means for reproducing the concepts, according to the law of association of the imagination, and consequently in a subjective point of view. These are either words or visible (algebraical, even mimetical) signs, as mere expressions for concepts.[29]

All intuitions which we supply to concepts *a priori* are therefore either *schemata* or *symbols*, of which the former contain direct, the latter indirect, presentations of the concept. The former do this demonstratively; the latter by means of an analogy (for which we avail ourselves even of empirical intuitions) in which the judgment exercises a double function, first applying the concept to the object of a sensible intuition, and then applying the mere rule of the reflection made upon that intuition to a quite different object of which the first is only the symbol. Thus a monarchical state is represented by a living body if it is governed by national laws, and by a mere machine (like a hand mill) if governed by an individual absolute will; but in both cases only *symbolically*. For between a despotic state and a hand mill there is, to be sure, no similarity; but there is a similarity in the rules according to which we reflect upon these two things and their causality. This matter has not been sufficiently analyzed hitherto, for it deserves a deeper investigation; but this is not the place to linger over it. Our language [i.e. German] is full of indirect presentations of this sort, in which the expression does not contain the proper schema for the concept, but merely a symbol for reflection. Thus the words *ground* (support, basis), *to depend* (to be held up from above), *to flow* from something (instead of, to follow), *substance* (as Locke expresses it, the support of accidents), and countless others are not schematical but symbolical hypotyposes and expressions for concepts, not by means of a direct intuition, but only an analogy with it, i.e. by the transference of reflection upon an object of intuition to a quite different concept to which perhaps an intuition can never directly correspond. If we are to give the name of "cognition" to a mere mode of representation (which is quite permissible if the latter is not a principle of the theoretical determination of what an object is in itself, but of the practical determination of what the idea of it should be for us and for its purposive use), then all our knowledge of God is merely symbolical; and he who regards it as schematical, along with the properties of understanding, will, etc., which only establish their objective reality in beings of this world, falls into anthropomorphism, just as he who gives up every intuitive element falls into deism, by which nothing at all is cognized, not even in a practical point of view.

Now I say the beautiful is the symbol of the morally good, and that it is only in this respect (a reference which is natural to every man and which every man postulates in others as a duty) that it gives pleasure with a claim for the agreement of everyone else. By this the mind is made conscious of a certain ennoblement and elevation above the mere sensibility to pleasure received through sense, and the worth of others is estimated in accordance with a like maxim of their judgment. That is the *intelligible* to which, as pointed out in the preceding paragraph, taste looks, with which our higher cognitive faculties are in accord, and without which a downright contradiction would arise between their nature and the claims made by taste. In this faculty the judgment does not see itself, as in empirical judging, subjected to a heteronomy of empirical laws; it gives the law to itself in respect of the objects of so pure a satisfaction, just as the reason does in respect of the faculty of desire. Hence, both on account of this inner possibility in the subject and of the external possibility of a nature that agrees with it, it finds itself to be referred to something within the subject as well as without him, something which is neither nature nor freedom, but which yet is connected with the supersensible ground of the latter. In this supersensible ground, therefore, the theoretical faculty is bound together in unity with the practical in a way which, though common, is yet unknown. We shall indicate some points of this analogy, while at the same time we shall note the differences.

(1) The beautiful pleases *immediately* (but only in reflective intuition, not, like morality, in its concept). (2) It pleases *apart from any interest* (the morally good is indeed necessarily bound up with an interest, though not

with one which precedes the judgment upon the satisfaction, but with one which is first of all produced by it). (3) The *freedom* of the imagination (and therefore the sensibility of our faculty) is represented in judging the beautiful as harmonious with the conformity to law of the understanding (in the moral judgment the freedom of the will is thought as the harmony of the latter with itself, according to universal laws of reason). (4) The subjective principle in judging the beautiful is represented as *universal,* i.e. as valid for every man, though not cognizable through any universal concept. (The objective principle of morality is also expounded as universal, i.e. for every subject and for every action of the same subject, and thus as cognizable by means of a universal concept.) Hence the moral judgment is not only susceptible of definite constitutive principles, but is possible *only* by grounding its maxims on these in their universality.

A reference to this analogy is usual even with the common understanding [of men], and we often describe beautiful objects of nature or art by names that seem to put a moral appreciation at their basis. We call buildings or trees majestic and magnificent, landscapes laughing and gay; even colors are called innocent, modest, tender, because they excite sensations which have something analogous to the consciousness of the state of mind brought about by moral judgments. Taste makes possible the transition, without any violent leap, from the charm of sense to habitual moral interest, as it represents the imagination in its freedom as capable of purposive determination for the understanding, and so teaches us to find even in objects of sense a free satisfaction apart from any charm of sense.

NOTES

1. If we have cause for supposing that concepts which we use as empirical principles stand in relationship with the pure cognitive faculty *a priori,* it is profitable, because of this reference, to seek for them a transcendental definition, i.e., a definition through pure categories, so far as these by themselves adequately furnish the distinction of the concept in question from others. We here follow the example of the mathematician, who leaves undetermined the empirical data of his problem and only brings their relation in their pure synthesis under the concepts of pure arithmetic, and thus generalizes the solution. Objection has been brought against a similar procedure of mine (cf. the Preface to the *Critique of Practical Reason,* Abbott's translation, p. 94), and my definition of the faculty of desire has been found fault with, viz., that it is [the being's] *faculty of becoming, by means of its representations, the cause of the actuality of the objects of these representations;* for the desires might be mere *cravings,* and by means of these alone everyone is convinced the object cannot be produced. But this proves nothing more than that there are desires in man, by which he is in contradiction with himself. For here he strives for the production of the object by means of the representation *alone,* from which he can expect no result, because he is conscious that his mechanical powers (if I may so call those which are not psychological), which must be determined by that representation to bring about the object (mediately), are either not competent or even tend toward what is impossible, e.g. to reverse the past (*O mihi prae-*

teritos . . . etc.) or to annihilate in the impatience of expectation the interval before the wished for moment. Although in such fantastic desires we are conscious of the inadequacy (or even the unsuitability) of our representations for being *causes* of their objects, yet their reference as causes, and consequently the representation of the *causality*, is contained in every *wish*; and this is peculiarly evident if the wish is an affection or *longing*. For these [longings], by their dilatation and contraction of the heart and consequent exhaustion of powers, prove that these powers are continually kept on the stretch by representations, but that they perpetually let the mind, having regard to the impossibility [of the desire], fall back in exhaustion. Even prayers [offered up] to avert great and (as far as one can see) unavoidable evils, and many superstitious means for attaining in a natural way impossible purposes, point to the casual reference of representations to their objects, a reference which cannot at all be checked by the consciousness of the inadequacy of the effort to produce the effect. As to why there should be in our nature this propensity to desires which are consciously vain, that is an anthropologico-teleological problem. It seems that, if we were not determined to the application of our powers before we were assured of the adequacy of our faculties to produce an object, these powers would remain in great part unused. For we commonly learn to know our powers only by first making trial of them. This deception in the case of vain wishes is then only the consequence of a benevolent ordinance in our nature. [This note was added by Kant in the Second Edition.]

2. The definition of "taste" which is laid down here is that it is the faculty of judging of the beautiful. But the analysis of judgments of taste must show what is required in order to call an object beautiful. The moments to which the judgment has regard in its reflection I have sought in accordance with the guidance of the logical functions of judgment (for in a judgment of taste a reference to the understanding is always involved). I have considered the moment of quality first because the aesthetical judgment upon the beautiful first pays attention to it.

3. A judgment upon an object of satisfaction may be quite *disinterested*, but yet very *interesting*, i.e. not based upon an interest, but bringing an interest with it; of this kind are all pure moral judgments. Judgments of taste, however, do not in themselves establish any interest. Only in society is it *interesting* to have taste; the reason of this will be shown in the sequel.

4. [Second edition.]

5. An obligation to enjoyment is a manifest absurdity. Thus the obligation to all actions which have merely enjoyment for their aim can only be a pretended one, however spiritually it may be conceived (or decked out), even if it is a mystical, or socalled heavenly, enjoyment.

6. [Second edition.]

7. [Second edition.]

8. [Ueberweg points out (*History of Philosophy, II,* 528, English translation) that Mendelssohn had already called attention to the disinterestedness of our satisfaction in the beautiful. "It appears," says Mendelssohn, "to be a particular mark of the beautiful, that it is contemplated with quiet satisfaction, that it pleases, even though it be not in our possession, and even though we be never so far removed from the desire to put it

to our use." But, of course, as Ueberweg remarks, Kant's conception of disinterestedness extends far beyond the idea of merely not desiring to possess the object.]

9. [Second edition. Mr. Herbert Spencer expresses much more concisely what Kant has in his mind here. "Pleasure . . . is a feeling which we seek to bring into consciousness and retain there; pain is . . . a feeling which we seek to get out of consciousness and to keep out." *Principles of Psychology,* § 125.]

10. [The editions of Hartenstein and Kirchmann omit *"ohne"* before *"Zweck,"* which makes havoc of the sentence. It is correctly printed by Rosenkranz.]

11. [Second edition.]

12. [Second edition.]

13. [Second edition.]

14. [Second edition.]

15. Models of taste as regards the arts of speech must be composed in a dead and learned language. The first in order that they may not suffer that change which inevitably comes over living languages, in which noble expressions become flat, common ones antiquated, and newly created ones have only a short circulation. The second because learned languages have a grammar which is subject to no wanton change of fashion, but the rules of which are preserved unchanged.

16. [This distinction between an *idea* and an *ideal,* as also the further contrast between ideals of the reason and ideals of the imagination, had already been given by Kant in the *Critique of Pure Reason,* "Dialectic," Bk. II, Ch. 3, § 1.]

17. [Polycletus of Argos flourished about 430 B.C. His statue of the "Spearbearer" *(Doryphorus),* afterward became known as the "Canon," because in it the artist was supposed to have embodied a perfect representation of the ideal of the human figure.]

18. [This was a celebrated statue executed by Myron, a Greek sculptor, contemporary with Polycletus.]

19. It will be found that a perfectly regular countenance, such as a painter might wish to have for a model, ordinarily tells us nothing because it contains nothing characteristic, and therefore rather expresses the idea of the race than the specific [traits] of a person. The exaggeration of a characteristic of this kind, i.e. such as does violence to the normal idea (the purposiveness of the race), is called *caricature.* Experience also shows that these quite regular countenances commonly indicate internally only a mediocre man, presumably (if it may be assumed that external nature expresses the proportions of internal) because, if no mental disposition exceeds that proportion which is requisite in order to constitute a man free from faults, nothing can be expected of what is called *genius,* in which nature seems to depart from the ordinary relations of the mental powers on behalf of some special one.

20. It might be objected to this explanation that there are things in which we see a purposive form without cognizing any purpose in them, like the stone implements often gotten from old sepulchral tumuli with a hole in them, as if for a handle. These,

although they plainly indicate by their shape a purposiveness of which we do not know the purpose, are nevertheless not described as beautiful. But if we regard a thing as a work of art, that is enough to make us admit that its shape has reference to some design and definite purpose. And hence there is no immediate satisfaction in the contemplation of it. On the other hand a flower, e.g. a tulip, is regarded as beautiful, because in perceiving it we find a certain purposiveness which, in our judgment, is referred to no purpose at all.

21. [Second edition.]

22. [Second edition.]

23. [Second edition.]

24. [Second edition.]

25. [Cf. *Critique of Pure Reason,* "Methodology," Ch. I, § 1. "The construction of a concept is the *a priori* presentation of the corresponding intuition."]

26. [Charles Batteux (1713-1780), author of *Les Beauz Arts reduits à un même principe.*]

27. [Essay XVIII, "The Sceptic": "Critics can reason and dispute more plausibly than cooks or perfumers. We may observe, however, that this uniformity among human kind, hinders not, but that there is a considerable diversity in the sentiments of beauty and worth, and that education, custom, prejudice, caprice, and humour, frequently vary our taste of this kind. . . . Beauty and worth are merely of a relative nature, and consist in an agreeable sentiment, produced by an object in a particular mind, according to the peculiar structure and constitution of that mind." (In *Hume's Moral and Political Philosophy,* ed. Aiken, "Hafner Library of Classics" #3, 1948, pp. 338 ff.—Ed.)]

28. [For the distinction—an important one in Kant—between judgments of experience and judgments of perception, see his *Prolegomena,* § 18.]

29. [First edition has "limited."]

30. In order to be justified in claiming universal assent for an aesthetical judgment that rests merely on subjective grounds, it is sufficient to assume: (1) That the subjective conditions of the judgment, as regards the relation of the cognitive powers thus put into activity to a cognition in general, are the same in all men. This must be true, because otherwise men would not be able to communicate their representations or even their knowledge. (2) The judgment must merely have reference to this relation (consequently to the *formal condition* of the judgment) and be pure, i.e. not mingled either with concepts of the object or with sensations, as determining grounds. If there has been any mistake as regards this latter condition, then there is only an inaccurate application of the privilege, which a law gives us, to a particular case; but that does not destroy the privilege itself in general.

31. [Cf. Aristotle *Poetics* iv. 1448b: ha gar auta hlypērōs horōmen, toytōn tas eikonas tas malista ἠκριδωμένας chairomen theōroytes hoion therion te morphas tōn ἀτιμοτάτων kai nekrōn. (Though the objects themselves may be painful to see, we delight to view the most realistic representations of them in art, the forms for example

of the lowest animals and dead bodies.) Cf. also *Rhetoric* i. 11. 1371b; and Burke on the *Sublime and Beautiful,* Pt. I, § 16. Boileau *L'art poétique,* chant 3 makes a similar observation:

> Il n'est point de serpent ni de monstre odieux
> Qui, par l'art imité, ne puisse plaire aux yeux.
> D'un pinceau délicat l'artifice agréable
> Du plus affreux objet fait un objet aimable.]

32. [Second edition.]

33. [Cf. p. 158.]

34. [In English we would rather say "without soul," but I prefer to translate *"Geist"* consistently by "spirit," to avoid the confusion of it with *"Seele."*]

35. The intuitive in cognition must be opposed to the discursive (not to the symbolical). The former is either *schematical,* by *demonstration,* or *symbolical,* as a representation in accordance with a mere *analogy.*

G. W. F. HEGEL

HEGEL IS THE GIANT among Kant's immediate followers, enormously indebted to Kant for many of his central ideas, but developing his own important and novel view of history and thought. The notion in Kant that the principles of rationality and understanding are found within the nature of consciousness itself—in the conditions of any possible experience—are conjoined in Hegel with the principle of freedom as the giving of law to oneself. This synthesis produces a conception of history as a progression in consciousness, from consciousness to self-consciousness and then to self-consciousness of self-consciousness, the giving of law reflexively to oneself as lawgiver. The process of development in consciousness is conceived by Hegel as dialectical—opposing moments, conflicting principles, reconciled in a synthesis that supersedes each moment, only to undergo conflict itself and subsequent supersession. Each supersession includes the conflicting moments that gave rise to it. The fulfillment of the process is consciousness aware of itself as free cause of itself. This is Absolute Spirit, the Absolute Idea, realizable only through its own history, the Universal in the concrete.

Hegel's view of art is one of qualified admiration. For he regards art as unavoidably limited by its sensuous medium, incapable of rising to the full realization of self-consciousness and Spirit. He takes the highest period of art to be the classical period in which the universal is most completely realized in sensuous form. Later forms of art, especially Romanticism, show an understanding of art's origin in self-consciousness, but the result is a more limited artistic achievement.

The selection here emphasizes the three major forms and periods of art, the symbolic, where the Idea has not found its form, the classical, in which the Idea and form harmonize, and the romantic, emphasizing the inwardness of self-consciousness over harmony of form.

G. W. F. HEGEL

Philosophy of Fine Art *

[8] Division of the Subject

After the foregoing introductory remarks it is now time to pass on to the study of our subject itself. But the introduction, where we still are, can in this respect do no more than sketch for our apprehension a conspectus of the entire course of our subsequent scientific studies. But since we have spoken of art as itself proceeding from the absolute Idea, and have even pronounced its end to be the sensuous presentation of the Absolute itself, we must proceed, even in this conspectus, by showing, at least in general, how the particular parts of the subject emerge from the conception of artistic beauty as the presentation of the Absolute. Therefore we must attempt, in the most general way, to awaken an idea of this conception.

It has already been said that the content of art is the Idea, while its form is the configuration of sensuous material. Now art has to harmonize these two sides and bring them into a free reconciled totality. The *first* point here is the demand that the content which is to come into artistic representation should be in itself qualified for such representation. For otherwise we obtain only a bad combination, because in that case a content ill-adapted to figurativeness and external presentation is made to adopt this form, or, in other words, material explicitly prosaic is expected to find a really appropriate mode of presentation in the form antagonistic to its nature.

The *second* demand, derived from the first, requires of the content of art that it be not anything abstract in itself, but concrete, though not concrete in

* G. W. F. Hegel, from the "Introduction" to *Aesthetics: Lectures on Fine Art*, translated by T. M. Knox (London: Oxford University Press, 1975), pp. 69-90. (Footnotes omitted.)

the sense in which the sensuous is concrete when it is contrasted with everything spiritual and intellectual and these are taken to be simple and abstract. For everything genuine in spirit and nature alike is inherently concrete and, despite its universality, has nevertheless subjectivity and particularity in itself. If we say, for example, of God that he is simply *one*, the supreme being as such, we have thereby only enunciated a dead abstraction of the sub-rational Understanding. Such a God, not apprehended himself in his concrete truth, will provide no content for art, especially not for visual art. Therefore the Jews and the Turks have not been able by art to represent their God, who does not even amount to such an abstraction of the Understanding, in the positive way that the Christians have. For in Christianity God is set forth in his truth, and therefore as thoroughly concrete in himself, as person, as subject, and, more closely defined, as spirit. What he is as spirit is made explicit for religious apprehension as a Trinity of Persons, which yet at the same time is self-aware as *one*. Here we have essentiality or universality, and particularization, together with their reconciled unity, and only such unity is the concrete. Now since a content, in order to be true at all, must be of this concrete kind, art too demands similar concreteness, because the purely abstract universal has not in itself the determinate character of advancing to particularization and phenomenal manifestation and to unity with itself in these.

Now, *thirdly*, if a sensuous form and shape is to correspond with a genuine and therefore concrete content, it must likewise be something individual, in itself completely concrete and single. The fact that the concrete accrues to both sides of art, i.e. to both content and its presentation, is precisely the point in which both can coincide and correspond with one another; just as, for instance, the natural shape of the human body is such a sensuously concrete thing, capable of displaying spirit, which is concrete in itself, and of showing itself in conformity with it. Therefore, after all, we must put out of our minds the idea that it is purely a matter of chance that to serve as such a genuine shape an actual phenomenon of the external world is selected. For art does not seize upon this form either because it just finds it there or because there is no other; on the contrary, the concrete content itself involves the factor of external, actual, and indeed even sensuous manifestation. But then in return this sensuous concrete thing, which bears the stamp of an essentially spiritual content, is also essentially *for* our inner [apprehension]; the external shape, whereby the content is made visible and imaginable, has the purpose of existing solely for our mind and spirit. For this reason alone are content and artistic form fashioned in conformity with one another. The *purely* sensuously concrete—external nature as such—does not have this purpose for the sole reason of its origin. The variegated richly coloured plumage of birds shines even when unseen, their song dies away unheard; the torch-thistle, which blooms for only one night, withers in the wilds of the southern forests without having been admired, and these forests, jungles themselves of the most beautiful and luxuriant vegetation, with the most sweet-smelling and aromatic perfumes, rot and decay equally unenjoyed. But the work of art is not so naïvely self-centered; it is essentially a question, an address to the responsive breast, a call to the mind and the spirit.

Although illustration by art is not in this respect a matter of chance, it is, on the other hand, not the highest way of apprehending the spiritually concrete. The higher way, in contrast to representation by means of the sensuously concrete, is thinking, which in a relative sense is indeed abstract, but it must be concrete, not one-sided, if it is to be true and rational. How far a specific content has its appropriate form in sensuous artistic representation, or whether, owing to its own nature, it essentially demands a higher, more spiritual, form, is a question of the distinction which appears at once, for example, in a comparison between the Greek gods and God as conceived by Christian ideas. The Greek god is not abstract but individual, closely related to the natural [human] form. The Christian God too is indeed a concrete personality, but is *pure* spirituality and is to be known as *spirit* and in spirit. His medium of existence is therefore essentially inner knowledge and not the external natural form through which he can be represented only imperfectly and not in the whole profundity of his nature.

But since art has the task of presenting the Idea to immediate perception in a sensuous shape and not in the form of thinking and pure spirituality as such, and, since this presenting has its value and dignity in the correspondence and unity of both sides, i.e. the Idea and its outward shape, it follows that the loftiness and excellence of art in attaining a reality adequate to its Concept will depend on the degree of inwardness and unit in which Idea and shape appear fused into one.

In this point of higher truth, as the spirituality which the artistic formation has achieved in conformity with the Concept of spirit, there lies the basis for the division of the philosophy of art. For, before reaching the true Concept of its absolute essence, the spirit has to go through a course of stages, a series grounded in this Concept itself, and to this course of the content which the spirit gives to itself there corresponds a course, immediately connected therewith, of configurations of art, in the form of which the spirit, as artist, gives itself a consciousness of itself.

This course within the spirit of art has itself in turn, in accordance with its own nature, two sides. *First,* this development is itself a spiritual and universal one, since the sequence of definite conceptions of the world, as the definite but comprehensive consciousness of nature, man, and God, gives itself artistic shape. *Secondly,* this inner development of art has to give itself immediate existence and sensuous being, and the specific modes of the sensuous being of art are themselves a totality of necessary differences in art, i.e., the *particular arts.* Artistic configuration and its differences are, on the one hand, as spiritual, of a more universal kind and not bound to *one* material [e.g. stone or paint], and sensuous existence is itself differentiated in numerous ways; but since this existence, like spirit, has the Concept implicitly for its inner soul, a specific sensuous material does thereby, on the other hand, acquire a closer relation and a secret harmony with the spiritual differences and forms of artistic configuration.

However, in its completeness our science is divided into three main sections:

First, we acquire a *universal* part. This has for its content and subject both the universal Idea of artistic beauty as the Ideal, and also the nearer relation of the Ideal to nature on the one hand and to subjective artistic production on the other.

Secondly, there is developed out of the conception of artistic beauty a *particular* part, because the essential differences contained in this conception unfold into a sequence of particular forms of artistic configuration.

Thirdly, there is a *final* part which has to consider the individualization of artistic beauty, since art advances to the sensuous realization of its creations and rounds itself off in a system of single arts and their genera and species.

(I) THE IDEA OF THE BEAUTY OF ART OR THE IDEAL. In the first place, so far as the first and second parts are concerned, we must at once, if what follows is to be made intelligible, recall again that the Idea as the beauty of art is not the Idea as such, in the way that a metaphysical logic has to apprehend it as the Absolute, but the Idea as shaped forward into reality and as having advanced to immediate unit and correspondence with this reality. For the *Idea as such* is indeed the absolute truth itself, but the truth only in its not yet objectified universality, while the Idea as the *beauty of art* is the Idea with the nearer qualification of being both essentially individual reality and also an individual configuration of reality destined essentially to embody and reveal the Idea. Accordingly there is here expressed the demand that the Idea and its configuration as a concrete reality shall be made completely adequate to one another. Taken thus, the Idea as reality, shaped in accordance with the Concept of the Idea, is the *Ideal*.

The problem of such correspondence might in the first instance be understood quite formally in the sense that any Idea at all might serve, if only the actual shape, no matter which, represented precisely this specific Idea. But in that case the demanded *truth* of the Ideal is confused with mere *correctness* which consists in the expression of some meaning or other in an appropriate way and therefore the direct rediscovery of its sense in the shape produced. The Ideal is not to be thus understood. For any content can be represented quite adequately, judged by the standard of its own essence, without being allowed to claim the artistic beauty of the Ideal. Indeed, in comparison with ideal beauty, the representation will even appear defective. In this regard it may be remarked in advance, what can only be proved later, namely that the defectiveness of a work of art is not always to be regarded as due, as may be supposed, to the artist's lack of skill; on the contrary, defectiveness of *form* results from defectiveness of *content*. So, for example, the Chinese, Indians, and Egyptians, in their artistic shapes, images of gods, and idols, never get beyond formlessness or a bad and untrue definiteness of form. They could not master true beauty because their mythological ideas, the content and thought of their works of art, were still indeterminate, or determined badly, and so did not consist of the content which is absolute in itself. Works of art are all the more excellent in expressing true beauty, the deeper is the inner truth of their content and thought. And in this connection we are not merely to think, as others may, of any greater or lesser skill with which natural forms as they exist in the external world are apprehended and imitated. For, in certain stages of art-consciousness and presentation, the abandonment and distortion of natural formations is not unintentional lack of technical skill or practice, but intentional alteration which proceeds from and is demanded by what is in the artist's mind. Thus, from this point of view, there is imperfect art which in technical and other respects may be quite perfect in its *specific* sphere, and yet it is clearly defective in comparison with the concept of art itself and the Ideal.

Only in the highest art are Idea and presentation truly in conformity with one another, in the sense that the shape given to the Idea is in itself the absolutely true shape, because the content of the Idea which that shape expresses is itself the true and genuine content. Associated with this, as has already been indicated, is the fact that the Idea must be determined in and through itself as a concrete totality, and therefore possess in itself the principle and measure of its particularization and determinacy in external appearance. For example, the Christian imagination will be able to represent God in human form and its expression of *spirit*, only because God himself is here completely known in himself as *spirit*. Determinacy is, as it were, the bridge to appearance. Where this determinacy is not a totality emanating from the Idea itself, where the Idea is not presented as self-determining and self-particularizing, the Idea remains abstract and has its determinacy, and therefore the principle for its particular and solely appropriate mode of appearance, not in itself, but outside itself. On this account, then, the still abstract Idea has its shape also external to itself, not settled by itself. On the other hand, the inherently concrete Idea carries within itself the principle of its mode of appearance and is therefore its own free configurator. Thus the truly concrete Idea alone produces its true configuration, and this correspondence of the two is the Ideal.

(II) DEVELOPMENT OF THE IDEAL INTO THE PARTICULAR FORMS OF THE BEAUTY OF ART. But because the Idea is in this way a concrete unity, this unity can enter the art-consciousness only through the unfolding and then the reconciliation of the particularizations of the Idea, and, through this development, artistic beauty acquires a *totality of particular stages and forms*. Therefore, after studying artistic beauty in itself and on its own account, we must see how beauty as a whole decomposes into its particular determinations. This gives, as the *second* part of our study, the doctrine of the *forms of art*. These forms find their origin in the different ways of grasping the Idea as content, whereby a difference in the configuration in which the Idea appears is conditioned. Thus the forms of art are nothing but the different relations of meaning and shape, relations which proceed from the Idea itself and therefore provide the true basis for the division of this sphere. For division must always be implicit in the concept, the particularization and division of which is in question.

We have here to consider *three* relations of the Idea to its configuration.

(a) First, art begins when the Idea, still in its indeterminacy and obscurity, or in bad and untrue determinacy, is made the content of artistic shapes. Being indeterminate, it does not yet possess in itself that individuality which the Ideal demands; its abstraction and one-sidedness leave its shape externally defective and arbitrary. The first form of art is therefore rather a *mere search* for portrayal than a capacity for true presentation; the Idea has not found the form even in itself and therefore remains struggling and striving after it. We may call this form, in general terms, the *symbolic* form of art. In it the abstract Idea has its shape outside itself in the natural sensuous material from which the process of shaping starts and with which, in its appearance, this process is linked. Perceived natural objects are, on the one hand, primarily left as they are, yet at the same time the substantial Idea is imposed on them as their meaning so that they now acquire a vocation to express it and so are to be interpreted as if the Idea itself were present in them. A corollary of this is the fact that natural objects have in them an aspect according to which they are capable of representing a universal meaning. But since a complete correspondence is not yet possible, this relation can concern only an *abstract* characteristic, as when, for example, in a lion strength is meant.

On the other hand, the abstractness of this relation brings home to consciousness even so the foreignness of the Idea to natural phenomena, and the Idea, which has no other reality to express it, launches out in all these shapes, seeks itself in them in their unrest and extravagance, but yet does not find them adequate to itself. So now the Idea exaggerates natural shapes and the phenomena of reality itself into indefiniteness and extravagance; it staggers round in them, it bubbles and ferments in them, does violence to them, distorts and stretches them unnaturally, and tries to elevate their phenomenal appearance to the Idea by the diffuseness, immensity, and splendour of the formations employed. For the Idea is here still more or less indeterminate and unshapable, while the natural objects are thoroughly determinate in their shape.

In the incompatibility of the two sides to one another, the relation of the Idea to the objective world therefore becomes a *negative* one, since the Idea, as something inward, is itself unsatisfied by such externality, and, as the inner universal substance thereof, it persists *sublime* above all this multiplicity of shapes which do not correspond with it. In the light of this sublimity, the natural phenomena and human forms and events are accepted, it is true, and left as they are, but yet they are recognized at the same time as incompatible with their meaning which is raised far above all mundane content.

These aspects constitute in general the character of the early artistic pantheism of the East, which on the one hand ascribes absolute meaning to even the most worthless objects, and, on the other, violently coerces the phenomena to express its view of the world whereby it becomes bizarre, grotesque, and tasteless, or turns the infinite but abstract freedom of the substance [i.e., the one Lord] disdainfully against all phenomena as being null and evanescent. By this means the meaning cannot be completely pictured in the expression and, despite all striving and endeavour, the incompatibility of Idea and shape still remains unconquered.—This may be taken to be the first form of art, the symbolic form with its quest, its fermentation, its mysteriousness, and its sublimity.

(b) In the *second* form of art which we will call the *classical*, the double defect of the symbolic form is extinguished. The symbolic shape is imperfect because, (i) in it the Idea is presented to consciousness only as indeterminate or determined *abstractly*, and, (ii) for this reason the correspondence of meaning and shape is always defective and must itself remain purely abstract. The classical art-form clears up this double defect; it is the free and adequate embodiment of the Idea in the shape peculiarly appropriate to the Idea itself in its essential nature. With this shape, therefore, the Idea is able to come into free and complete harmony. Thus the classical art-form is the first to afford the production and vision of the completed Ideal and to present it as actualized in fact.

Nevertheless, the conformity of concept and reality in classical art must not be taken in the purely *formal* sense of a correspondence between a content and its external configuration, any more than this could be the case with the Ideal itself. Otherwise every portrayal of nature, every cast of features, every neighbourhood, flower, scene, etc., which constitutes the end and content of the representation, would at once be classical on the strength of such congruity between content and form. On the contrary, in classical art the peculiarity of the content consists in its being itself the concrete Idea, and as such the concretely spiritual, for it is the spiritual alone which is the truly inner [self]. Consequently, to suit such a content we must try to find out what in nature belongs to the spiritual in and for itself. The *original* Concept itself it must be which *invented* the shape for concrete spirit, so that now the *subjective* Concept—here the spirit of art—has merely *found* this shape and made it, as a natural shaped existent, appropriate to free individual spirituality. This shape, which the Idea as spiritual—indeed as individually determinate spirituality— assumes when it is to proceed out into a temporal manifestation, is the human form. Of course personification and anthropomorphism have often been maligned as a degradation of the spiritual, but in so far as art's task is to bring the spiritual before our eyes in a sensuous manner, it must get involved in this anthropomorphism, since spirit appears sensuously in a satisfying way only in its body. The transmigration of souls is in this respect an abstract idea and physiology should have made it one of its chief propositions that life in its development had necessarily to proceed to the human form as the one and only sensuous appearance appropriate to spirit.

But the human body in its form counts in classical art no longer as a merely sensuous existent, but only as the existence and natural shape of the spirit, and it must therefore be exempt from all the deficiency of the purely sensuous and from the contingent finitude of the phenomenal world. While in this way the shape is purified in order to express in itself a content adequate to itself, on the other hand, if the correspondence of meaning and shape is to be perfect, the spirituality, which is the content, must be of such a kind that it can express itself completely in the natural human form, without towering beyond and above this expression in sensuous and bodily terms. Therefore here the spirit is at once determined as particular and human, not as purely absolute and eternal, since in this latter sense it can proclaim and express itself only as spirituality.

This last point in its turn is the defect which brings about the dissolution of the classical art-form and demands a transition to a higher form, the *third*, namely the *romantic*.

(c) The romantic form of art cancels again the completed unification of the Idea and its reality, and reverts, even if in a higher way, to that difference and opposition of the two sides which in symbolic art remained unconquered. The classical form of art has attained the pinnacle of what illustration by art could achieve, and if there is something defective in it, the defect is just art itself and the restrictedness of the sphere of art. This restrictedness lies in the fact that art in general takes as its subject-matter the spirit (i.e. the *universal*, infinite and concrete in its nature) in a *sensuously* concrete form, and classical art presents the complete unification of spiritual and sensuous existence as the *correspondence* of the two. But in this blending of the two, spirit is not in fact represented in its *true nature*. For spirit is the infinite subjectivity of the Idea, which as absolute inwardness cannot freely and truly shape itself outwardly on condition of remaining moulded into a bodily existence as the one appropriate to it.

Abandoning this [classical] principle, the romantic form of art cancels the undivided unity of classical art because it has won a content which goes beyond and above the classical form of art and its mode of expression. This content—to recall familiar ideas—coincides with what Christianity asserts of God as a spirit, in distinction from the Greek religion which is the essential and most appropriate content for classical art. In classical art the concrete content is *implicitly* the unity of the divine nature with the human, a unity which, just because it is only immediate and implicit, is adequately manifested also in an immediate and sensuous way. The Greek god is the object of naïve intuition and sensuous imagination, and therefore his shape is the bodily shape of man. The range of his power and his being is individual and particular. Contrasted with the individual he is a substance and power with which the individual's inner being is only implicitly at one but without itself possessing this oneness as inward subjective knowledge. Now the higher state is the *knowledge* of that *implicit* unity which is the content of the classical art-form and is capable of perfect presentation in bodily shape. But this elevation of the implicit into self-conscious knowledge introduces a tremendous difference. It is the infinite difference which, for example, separates man from animals. Man is an animal, but even in his animal functions, he is not confined to the implicit, as the animal is; he becomes conscious of them, recognizes them, and lifts them, as, for instance, the process of digestion, into self-conscious science. In this way man breaks the barrier of his implicit and immediate character, so that precisely because he *knows* that he is an animal, he ceases to be an animal and attains knowledge of himself as spirit.

Now if in this way what was implicit at the previous stage, the unity of divine and human nature, is raised from an *immediate* to a *known* unity, the *true* element for the realization of this content is no longer the sensuous immediate existence of the spiritual in the bodily form of man, but instead the *inwardness of self-consciousness.* Now Christianity brings God before our imagination as spirit, not as an individual, particular spirit, but as absolute in spirit and in truth. For this reason it retreats from the sensuousness of imagination into spiritual inwardness and makes this, and not the body, the medium and the existence of truth's content. Thus the unity of divine and human nature is a known unity, one to be realized only by *spiritual* knowing and *in spirit.* The new content, thus won, is on this account not tied to sensuous presentation, as if that corresponded to it, but is freed from this immediate existence which must be set down as negative, overcome, and reflected into the spiritual unity. In this way romantic art is the self-transcendence of art but within its own sphere and in the form of art itself.

We may, therefore, in short, adhere to the view that at this third stage the subject-matter of art is *free concrete spirituality*, which is to be manifested as *spirituality* to the spiritually inward. In conformity with this subject-matter, art cannot work for sensuous intuition. Instead it must, on the one hand, work for the inwardness which coalesces with its object simply as if with itself, for subjective inner depth, for reflective emotion, for feeling which, as spiritual, strives for freedom in itself and seeks and finds its reconciliation only in the inner spirit. This *inner* world constitutes the content of the romantic sphere and must therefore be represented as this inwardness and in the pure appearance of this depth of feeling. Inwardness celebrates its triumph over the external and manifests its victory in and on the external itself, whereby what is apparent to the senses alone sinks into worthlessness.

On the other hand, however, this romantic form too, like all art, needs an external medium for its expression. Now since spirituality has withdrawn into itself out of the external world and immediate unity therewith, the sensuous externality of shape is for this reason accepted and represented, as in symbolic art, as something inessential and transient; and the same is true of the subjective finite spirit and will, right down to the particularity and caprice of individuality, character, action, etc., of incident, plot, etc. The aspect of external existence is consigned to contingency and abandoned to the adventures devised by an imagination whose caprice can mirror what is present to it, *exactly as it is*, just as readily as it can jumble the shapes of the external world and distort them grotesquely. For this external medium has its essence and meaning no longer, as in classical art, in itself and its own sphere, but in the heart which finds its manifestation in itself instead of in the external world and *its* form of reality, and this reconciliation with itself it can preserve or regain in every chance, in every accident that takes independent shape, in all misfortune and grief, and indeed even in crime.

Thereby the separation of Idea and shape, their difference and inadequacy to each other, come to the fore again, as in symbolic art, but with this essential difference, that, in romantic art, the Idea, the deficiency of which in the symbol brought with it deficiency of shape, now has to appear *perfected* in itself as spirit and heart. Because of this higher perfection, it is not susceptible of an adequate union with the external, since its true reality and manifestation it can seek and achieve only within itself.

This we take to be the general character of the symbolic, classical, and romantic forms of art, as the three relations of the Idea to its shape in the sphere of art. They consist in the striving for, the attainment, and the transcendence of the Ideal as the true Idea of beauty.

(III) THE SYSTEM OF THE INDIVIDUAL ARTS. Now the *third* part of our subject, in contradistinction from the two just described, presupposes the concept of the Ideal and also the three general forms of art, since it is only the realization of these in specific sensuous materials. Therefore we now no longer have to do with the inner development of artistic beauty in its general fundamental characteristics. Instead we have to consider how these characteristics pass into existence, are distinguished from one another externally, and actualize every feature in the conception of beauty independently and explicitly as a *work of art* and not merely as a *general form*. But since it is the differences immanent in the Idea of beauty, and proper to it, that art transfers into external existence, it follows that in this Part III the general forms of art must likewise be the fundamental principle for the articulation and determination of the individual arts; in other words, the kinds of art have the same essential distinctions in themselves which we came to recognize in the general forms of art. Now the *external* objectivity into which these forms are introduced through a sensuous and therefore *particular* material, makes these forms *fall apart* from one another independently, to become distinct ways of their realization, i.e. the particular arts. For each form finds its specific character also in a specific external material, and its adequate realization in the mode of portrayal which that material requires. But, on the other hand, these art-forms, universal as they are despite their determinateness, break the bounds of a *particular* realization through a *specific* kind of art and achieve their existence equally through the other arts, even if in a subordinate way. Therefore the particular arts belong, on the one hand, specifically to *one* of the general forms of art and they shape its adequate external artistic actuality, and, on the other hand, in their own individual way of shaping externality, they present the totality of the forms of art.

In general terms, that is to say, in Part III of our subject we have to deal with the beauty of art as it unfolds itself, in the arts and their productions, into a world of actualized beauty. The content of this world is the beautiful, and the true beautiful, as we saw, is spirituality given shape, the Ideal, and, more precisely, absolute spirit, the truth itself. This region of divine truth, artistically represented for contemplation and feeling, forms the centre of the whole world of art. It is the independent, free, and divine shape which has completely mastered the externality of form and material and wears it only as a manifestation of itself. Still, since the beautiful develops itself in this region as *objective* reality and therefore distinguishes within itself its single aspects and factors, granting them independent particularity, it follows that this centre now arrays its extremes, realized in their appropriate actuality, as contrasted with itself. One of these extremes therefore forms a still *spiritless objectivity*, the merely natural environment of God. Here the external as such takes shape as something having its spiritual end and content not in itself but in another.

The other extreme is the Divine as inward, as something known, as the variously particularized *subjective* existence of the Deity: the truth as it is effective and living in the sense, heart, and spirit of individual persons, not remaining poured out into its external shape, but returning into the subjective individual inner life. Thereby the Divine as such is at the same time distinguished from its pure manifestation as *Deity*, and thereby enters itself into the particularity characteristic of all individual subjective knowledge, emotion, perception, and feeling. In the analogous sphere of religion, with which art at its highest stage is immediately connected, we conceive this same difference as follows. *First*, earthly natural life in its finitude confronts us on one side; but then, *secondly*, our consciousness makes *God* its object wherein the difference of objectivity and subjectivity falls away, until, *thirdly*, and lastly, we advance from God as such to worship by the *community*, i.e. to God as living and present in subjective consciousness. These three fundamental differences arise also in the world of art in independent development.

(a) The *first* of the particular arts, the one with which we have to begin in accordance with this fundamental characterization of them, is *architecture* as a fine art. Its task consists in so manipulating external inorganic nature that, as an external world conformable to art, it becomes cognate to spirit. Its material is matter itself in its immediate externality as a mechanical heavy mass, and its forms remain the forms of inorganic nature, set in order according to relations of the abstract Understanding, i.e. relations of symmetry. In this material and in these forms the Ideal, as concrete spirituality, cannot be realized. Hence the reality presented in them remains opposed to the Idea, because it is something external not penetrated by the Idea or only in an abstract relation to it. Therefore the fundamental type of the art of building is the *symbolic* form of art. For architecture is the first to open the way for the adequate actuality of the god, and in his service it slaves away with objective nature in order to work it free from the jungle of finitude and the monstrosity of chance. Thereby it levels a place for the god, forms his external environment, and builds for him his temple as the place for the inner composure of the spirit and its direction on its absolute objects. It raises an enclosure for the assembly of the congregation, as protection against the threat of storm,

against rain, tempest, and wild animals, and it reveals in an artistic way, even if in an external one, the wish to assemble. This meaning it can build into its material and the forms thereof with greater or lesser effect, in proportion as the determinate character of the content for which it undertakes its work is more significant or insignificant, more concrete or abstract, more profoundly plumbing its own depths, or more obscure and superficial. Indeed in this respect architecture may itself attempt to go so far as to fashion in its forms and material an adequate artistic existence for that content; but in that event it has already stepped beyond its one sphere and is swinging over to sculpture, the stage above it. For its limitation lies precisely in retaining the spiritual, as something inner, over against its own external forms and thus pointing to what has soul only as to something distinct from these.

(*b*) But by architecture, after all, the inorganic external world has been purified, set in order symmetrically, and made akin to spirit, and the god's temple, the house of his community, stands there ready. Then into this temple, *secondly*, the god enters himself as the lightning-flash of individuality striking and permeating the inert mass, and the infinite, and no longer merely symmetrical, form of spirit itself concentrates and gives shape to something corporeal. This is the task of *sculpture*.

In so far as in sculpture the spiritual inner life, at which architecture can only hint, makes itself at home in the sensuous shape and its external material, and in so far as these two sides are so mutually formed that neither preponderates, sculpture acquires the *classical* art-form as its fundamental type. Therefore, no expression is left to the sensuous which is not an expression of spirit itself, just as, conversely, for sculpture no spiritual content can be perfectly represented unless it can be fully and adequately presented to view in bodily form. For through sculpture the spirit should stand before us in blissful tranquillity in its bodily form and in immediate unity therewith, and the form should be brought to life by the content of spiritual individuality. So the external sensuous material is no longer processed either according to its mechanical quality alone, as a mass possessing weight, or in forms of the inorganic world, or as indifferent to colour, etc., but in the ideal forms of the human figure and in all three spatial dimensions too. In this last respect we must claim for sculpture that in it the inward and the spiritual come into appearance for the first time in their eternal peace and essential self-sufficiency. To this peace and unity with itself only that external shape corresponds which itself persists in this unity and peace. This is shape according to its *abstract spatiality*. The spirit which sculpture presents is spirit compact in itself, not variously splintered into the play of accidents and passions. Consequently sculpture does not abandon spirit's external form to this variety of appearance, but picks up therein only this one aspect, abstract spatiality in the totality of its dimensions.

(*c*) Now when architecture has built its temple and the hand of sculpture has set up within it the statues of the god, this sensuously present god is confronted, *thirdly,* in the wide halls of his house, by the *community*. The community is the spiritual reflection into itself of this sensuous existent, and is animating subjectivity and inwardness. With these, therefore, it comes about that the determining principle, alike for the content of art and for the material that represents it outwardly, is particularization and individualization and their requisite subjective apprehension. The compact unity in itself which the god has in sculpture disperses into the plurality of the inner lives of individuals whose unity is not sensuous but purely ideal. And so only here is God himself truly spirit, spirit in his community, God as this to-and-fro, as this exchange of his inherent unity with his actualization in subjective knowing and its individualization as well as in the universality and union of the multitude. In the community God is released alike from the abstraction of undeveloped self-identity and from his sculptural representation as immediately immersed in a bodily medium; and he is raised to spirituality and knowledge, i.e. to spirit's mirror-image which essentially appears as inward and as subjectivity. Consequently the higher content is now the spiritual, the spiritual as absolute. But at the same time, owing to the dispersal mentioned just now, the spiritual appears here as *particular* spirituality, an individual mind. And it is not the self-sufficient peace of the god in himself, but appearance as such, being *for* another, that manifestation of the self, which comes to the fore here as the chief thing; so now what becomes on its own account an object of artistic representation is the most manifold subjectivity in its living movement and activity as human passion, action, and adventure, and, in general, the wide range of human feeling, willing, and neglect.

Now in conformity with this content the sensuous element in art has likewise to show itself particularized in itself and appropriate to subjective inwardness. Material for this is afforded by colour, musical sound, and finally sound as the mere indication of inner intuitions and ideas. And as modes of realizing the content in question by means of these materials we have painting, music, and poetry. Here the sensuous medium appears as particularized in itself and posited throughout as ideal. Thus it best corresponds with the generally spiritual content of art, and the connection of spiritual meaning with sensuous material grows into a deeper intimacy than was possible in architecture and sculpture. Nevertheless this is a more inner unity which lies entirely on the subjective side, and which, in so far as form and content have to particularize themselves and posit themselves as ideal, can only come about at the expense of the objective universality of the content and its fusion with the immediately sensuous element.

Now in these arts form and content raise themselves to ideality, and thus, since they leave behind symbolic architecture and the classical idea of sculpture, they acquire their type from the *romantic* form of art on whose mode of configuration they are adapted to impress themselves in the most appropriate manner. But they are a totality of arts, because the romantic is in itself the most concrete form of art.

The inner articulation of this *third sphere* of the individual arts may be established as follows:

(α) The *first* art, standing next to sculpture, is *painting.* It uses as material for its content, and its content's configuration, visibility as such, in so far as this is at the same time particularized, i.e. developed into colour. True, the material of architecture and sculpture is likewise visible and coloured, but it is not, as in painting, the making visible as such; it is not the simple light which, differentiating itself in its contrast with darkness, and in combination therewith, becomes colour. This quality of visibility inherently subjectivized and posited as ideal, needs neither the abstract mechanical difference of mass operative in heavy matter, as in architecture, nor the totality of sensuous spatiality which sculpture retains, even if concentrated and in organic shapes. On the contrary, the visibility and the making visible which belong to painting have their differences in a more ideal way, i.e. in the particular colours, and they free art from the *complete* sensuous spatiality of material things by being restricted to the dimensions of a *plane* surface.

On the other hand, the content too attains the widest particularization. Whatever can find room in the human breast as feeling, idea, and purpose, whatever it is capable of shaping into act, all this multiplex material can constitute the variegated content of painting. The whole realm of particularity from the highest ingredients of spirit right down to the most isolated natural objects finds its place here. For even finite nature in its particular scenes and phenomena can come on the stage in painting, if only some allusion to an element of spirit allies it more closely with thought and feeling.

(β) The *second* art through which the romantic form is actualized is, as contrasted with painting, *music.* Its material, though still sensuous, proceeds to still deeper subjectivity and particularization. I mean that music's positing of the sensuous as ideal is to be sought in the fact that it cancels, and idealizes into the individual singularity of one point, the indifferent self-externality of space, the total appearance of which is accepted by painting and deliberately simulated. But as this negativity, the point is concrete in itself and an active cancellation within the material by being a movement and tremor of the material body in itself in its relation to itself. This incipient ideality of matter, which appears no longer as spatial but as temporal ideality, is sound: the sensuous set down as negated with its abstract visibility changed into audibility, since sound releases the ideal, as it were, from its entanglement in matter.

Now this earliest inwardness and ensouling of matter affords the material for the still indefinite inwardness and soul of the spirit, and in its tones makes the whole gamut of the heart's feelings and passions resound and die away. In this manner, just as sculpture stands as the centre between architecture and the arts of romantic subjectivity, so music forms the centre of the romantic arts and makes the point of transition between the abstract spatial sensuousness of painting and the abstract spirituality of poetry. Like architecture, music has in itself, as an antithesis to feeling and inwardness, a relation of quantity conformable to the mathematical intellect; it also has as its basis a fixed conformity to law on the part of the notes and their combination and succession.

(γ) Finally, as for the *third*, most spiritual presentation of romantic art, we must look for it in *poetry*. Its characteristic peculiarity lies in the power with which it subjects to spirit and its ideas the sensuous element from which music and painting began to make art free. For sound, the last external material which poetry keeps, is in poetry no longer the feeling of sonority itself, but a *sign*, by itself void of significance, a sign of the idea which has become concrete in itself, and not merely of indefinite feeling and its nuances and gradations. Sound in this way becomes a *word* as a voice inherently articulated, the meaning of which is to indicate ideas and thoughts. The inherently negative point to which music had moved forward now comes forth as the completely concrete point, as the point of the spirit, as the self-conscious individual who out of his own resources unites the infinite *space* of his ideas with the *time* of sound. Yet this sensuous element, which in music was still immediately one with inwardness, is here cut free from the content of consciousness, while spirit determines this content on its own account and in itself and makes it into ideas. To express these it uses sound indeed, but only as a sign in itself without value or content. The sound, therefore, may just as well be a mere letter, since the audible, like the visible, has sunk into being a mere indication of spirit. Therefore the proper element of poetical representation is the poetical *imagination* and the illustration of spirit itself, and since this element is common to all the art-forms, poetry runs through them all and develops itself independently in each of them. Poetry is the universal art of the spirit which has become free in itself and which is not tied down for its realization to external sensuous material; instead, it launches out exclusively in the inner space and the inner time of ideas and feelings. Yet, precisely, at this highest stage, art now transcends itself, in that it forsakes the element of a reconciled embodiment of the spirit in sensuous form and passes over from the poetry of the imagination to the prose of thought.

This we may take to be the articulated totality of the particular arts: the external art of architecture, the objective art of sculpture, and the subjective art of painting, music, and poetry. Of course many other classifications have been attempted, since the work of art presents such a wealth of aspects that, as has often happened, now this one and now that can be made the basis of classification. Consider, for example, the sensuous material. In that case architecture is the crystallization, sculpture the organic configuration, of matter in its sensuous and spatial totality; painting is the coloured surface and line; while, in music, space as such passes over into the inherently filled point of time; until, finally, in poetry the external material is altogether degraded as worthless. Alternatively, these differences have been considered in their totally abstract aspect of space and time. But such abstract characteristics of the work of art may of course, like its material, be consistently pursued in their special features, but they cannot be carried through as the final basis of classification, because any such aspect derives its origin from a higher principle and therefore has to be subordinate thereto.

As this higher principle we have found the art-forms of the symbolical, the classical, and the romantic, which are themselves the universal moments of the Idea of beauty.

The concrete form of their relation to the individual arts is of such a kind that the several arts constitute the real existence of the art-forms. *Symbolic art* attains its most appropriate actuality and greatest application in *architecture*, where it holds sway in accordance with its whole conception and is not yet degraded to be the inorganic nature, as it were, dealt with by another art. For the *classical form*, on the other hand, *sculpture* is its unqualified realization, while it takes architecture only as something surrounding it, and it cannot yet develop painting and music as absolute forms for its content. Finally, the *romantic* art-form masters painting and music, and poetic representation like-wise, as modes of expression in a way that is substantive and unqualified. But poetry is adequate to all forms of the beautiful and extends over all of them, because its proper element is beautiful imagination, and imagination is indispensable for every beautiful production, no matter to what form of art it belongs.

Now, therefore, what the particular arts realize in individual works of art is, according to the Concept of art, only the universal forms of the self-unfolding Idea of beauty. It is as the external actualization of this idea that the wide Pantheon of art is rising. Its architect and builder is the self-comprehending spirit of beauty, but to complete it will need the history of the world in its development through thousands of years.

FRIEDRICH NIETZSCHE

SINCE HIS DEATH at the turn of the century, Nietzsche's influence has grown enormously, to the point where his views of art, ethics, and rationality mark a watershed in contemporary philosophic thought. It is possible to argue persuasively that divergences in much of contemporary thought turn on differences in reading Nietzsche. He argues that there are no secure standards of truth, but many truths, no secure standards of rationality or the good, but practices emergent within lived experience and historical and social events. He argues that values are created, not found in nature, and that such a creation can be successful only if we acknowledge both our own role as the source of values and the limitations of our understanding due to historical and social conditions. Such a view of truth and value brings them much closer to art, to genius and even the sublime, than other views of rational activities.

The Birth of Tragedy is an early work, perhaps ironically described by Nietzsche himself as "peripheral." It offers a view of art based on polarities and tensions rather than on delight and imitation. Nietzsche's polarities are those of order (Apollo) and frenzy (Dionysus). Each of these is natural in human beings; each is defective without the other. Tragedy requires their integration, and is one of the supreme achievements of humanity. Yet many human beings find the tensions and polarities of tragedy intolerable, and seek respite in rules, in the conviction that the world is orderly. The vitality of art is then replaced by the sterility of rational inquiry.

In his later writing, Nietzsche characterized both the demand for order and the yearning for disorder as overwhelming passions. The overwhelming passion for order gives rise to what he called the will to truth. Included here is Nietzsche's retrospective criticism of his youthful work, emphasizing its hidden concern with truth.

FRIEDRICH NIETZSCHE

The Birth of Tragedy *

1

We shall have gained much for the science of aesthetics, once we perceive not merely by logical inference, but with the immediate certainty of vision, that the continuous development of art is bound up with the *Apollinian* and *Dionysian* duality—just as procreation depends on the duality of the sexes, involving perpetual strife with only periodically intervening reconciliations. The terms Dionysian and Apollinian we borrow from the Greeks, who disclose to the discerning mind the profound mysteries of their view of art, not, to be sure, in concepts, but in the intensely clear figures of their gods. Through Apollo and Dionysus, the two art deities of the Greeks, we come to recognize that in the Greek world there existed a tremendous opposition, in origin and aims between the Apollinian art of sculpture, and the nonimagistic, Dionysian art of music. These two different tendencies run parallel to each other, for the most part openly at variance; and they continually incite each other to new and more powerful births, which perpetuate an antagonism, only superficially reconciled by the common term "art"; till eventually, by a metaphysical miracle of the Hellenic "will," they appear coupled with each other, and through this coupling ultimately generate an equally Dionysian and Apollinian form of art—Attic tragedy.

In order to grasp these two tendencies, let us first conceive of them as the separate art worlds of *dreams* and *intoxication*. These physiological phe-

---

* Friedrich Nietzsche, *The Birth of Tragedy and The Case of Wagner*, translated by Walter Kaufmann (New York: Random House, 1967), pp. 33-41. (Footnotes omitted.)

nomena present a contrast analogous to that existing between the Apollinian and the Dionysian. It was in dreams, says Lucretius, that the glorious divine figures first appeared to the souls of men; in dreams the great shaper beheld the splendid bodies of superhuman beings; and the Hellenic poet, if questioned about the mysteries of poetic inspiration, would likewise have suggested dreams and he might have given an explanation like that of Hans Sachs in the *Meistersinger:*

> The poet's task is this, my friend;
> to read his dreams and comprehend.
> The truest human fancy seems
> to be revealed to us in dreams;
> all poems and versification
> are but true dreams' interpretations.

The beautiful illusion of the dream worlds, in the creation of which every man is truly an artist, is the prerequisite of all plastic art, and, as we shall see, of an important part of poetry also. In our dreams we delight in the immediate understanding of figures; all forms speak to us; there is nothing unimportant or superfluous. But even when this dream reality is most intense, we still have, glimmering through it, the sensation that it is *mere appearance:* at least this is my experience, and for its frequency—indeed, normality—I could adduce many proofs, including the sayings of the poets.

Philosophical men even have a presentiment that the reality in which we live and have our being is also mere appearance, and that another, quite different reality lies beneath it. Schopenhauer actually indicates as the criterion of philosophical ability the occasional ability to view men and things as mere phantoms or dream images. Thus the aesthetically sensitive man stands in the same relation to the reality of dreams as the philosopher does to the reality of existence; he is a close and willing observer, for these images afford him an interpretation of life, and by reflecting on these processes he trains himself for life.

It is not only the agreeable and friendly images that he experiences as something universally intelligible: the serious, the troubled, the sad, the gloomy, the sudden restraints, the tricks of accident, anxious expectations, in short, the whole divine comedy of life, including the inferno, also pass before him, not like mere shadows on a wall—for he lives and suffers with these scenes—and yet not without the fleeting sensation of illusion. And perhaps many will, like myself, recall how amid the dangers and terrors of dreams they have occasionally said to themselves in self-encouragement, and not without success: "It is a dream! I will dream on!" I have likewise heard of people who were able to continue one and the same dream for three and even more successive nights—facts which indicate clearly how our innermost being, our common ground, experiences dreams with profound delight and a joyous necessity.

This joyous necessity of the dream experience has been embodied by the Greeks in their Apollo: Apollo, the god of all plastic energies, is at the same time the soothsaying god. He, who (as the etymology of the name indicates) is the "shining one," the deity of light, is also ruler over the beautiful illusion of the inner world of fantasy. The higher truth, the perfection of these states in contrast to the incompletely intelligible everyday world, this deep consciousness of nature, healing and helping in sleep and dreams, is at the same time the symbolical analogue of the soothsaying faculty and of the arts generally, which make life possible and worth living. But we must also include in our image of Apollo that delicate boundary which the dream image must not overstep lest it have a pathological effect (in which case mere appearance would deceive us as if it were crude reality). We must keep in mind that measured restraint, that freedom from the wilder emotions, that calm of the sculptor god. His eye must be "sunlike," as befits his origin; even when it is angry and distempered it is still hallowed by beautiful illusion. And so, in one sense, we might apply to Apollo the words of Schopenhauer when he speaks of the man wrapped in the veil of *māyā* (*Welt als Wille und Vorstellung,* I, p. 416): "Just as in a stormy sea that, unbounded in all directions, raises and drops mountainous waves, howling, a sailor sits in a boat and trusts in his frail bark: so in the midst of a world of torments the individual human being sits quietly, supported by and trusting in the *principium individuationis.*" In fact, we might say of Apollo that in him the unshaken faith in this *principium* and the calm repose of the man wrapped up in it receive their most sublime expression; and we might call Apollo himself the glorious divine image of the *principium individuationis,* through whose gestures and eyes all the joy and wisdom of "illusion," together with its beauty, speak to us.

In the same work Schopenhauer has depicted for us the tremendous *terror* which seizes man when he is suddenly dumfounded by the cognitive form of phenomena because the principle of sufficient reason, in some one of its manifestations, seems to suffer an exception. If we add to this terror the blissful ecstasy that wells from the innermost depths of man, indeed of nature, at this collapse of the *principium individuationis,* we steal a glimpse into the nature of the *Dionysian,* which is brought home to us most intimately by the analogy of intoxication.

Either under the influence of the narcotic draught, of which the songs of all primitive men and peoples speak, or with the potent coming of spring that penetrates all nature with joy, these Dionysian emotions awake, and as they grow in intensity everything subjective vanishes into complete self-forgetfulness. In the German Middle Ages, too, singing and dancing crowds, ever increasing in number, whirled themselves from place to place under this same Dionysian impulse. In these dancers of St. John and St. Vitus, we rediscover the Bacchic choruses of the Greeks, with their prehistory in Asia Minor, as far back as Babylon and the orgiastic Sacaea. There are some who, from obtuseness or lack of experience, turn away from such phenomena as from "folk-diseases," with the contempt or pity born of the consciousness of their own "healthy-mindedness." But of course such poor wretches have no idea how corpselike and ghostly their so-called "healthy-mindedness" looks when the glowing life of the Dionysian revelers roars past them.

Under the charm of the Dionysian not only is the union between man and man reaffirmed, but nature which has become alienated, hostile, or subjugated, celebrates once more her reconciliation with her lost son, man. Freely, earth proffers her gifts, and peacefully the beasts of prey of the rocks and desert approach. The chariot of Dionysus is covered with flowers and garlands; panthers and tigers walk under its yoke. Transform Beethoven's "Hymn to Joy" into a painting; let your imagination conceive the multitudes bowing to the dust, awestruck—then you will approach the Dionysian. Now the slave is a free man; now all the rigid, hostile barriers that necessity, caprice, or "impudent convention" have fixed between man and man are broken. Now, with the gospel of universal harmony, each one feels himself not only united, reconciled, and fused with his neighbor, but as one with him, as if the veil of *māyā* had been torn aside and were now merely fluttering in tatters before the mysterious primordial unity.

In song and in dance man expresses himself as a member of a higher community; he has forgotten how to walk and speak and is on the way toward flying into the air, dancing. His very gestures express enchantment. Just as the animals now talk, and the earth yields milk and honey, supernatural sounds emanate from him, too: he feels himself a god, he himself now walks about enchanted, in ecstasy, like the gods he saw walking in his dreams. He is no longer an artist, he has become a work of art: in these paroxysms of intoxication the artistic power of all nature reveals itself to the highest gratification of the primordial unity. The noblest clay, the most costly marble, man, is here kneaded and cut, and to the sound of the chisel strokes of the Dionysian world-artist rings out the cry of the Eleusinian mysteries: "Do you prostrate yourselves, millions? Do you sense your Maker, world?"

2

Thus far we have considered the Apollinian and its opposite, the Dionysian, as artistic energies which burst forth from nature herself, *without the mediation of the human artist*—energies in which nature's art impulses are satisfied in the most immediate and direct way—first the image world of dreams, whose completeness is not dependent upon the intellectual attitude or the artistic culture of any single being; and then as intoxicated reality, which likewise does not heed the single unit, but even seeks to destroy the individual and redeem him by a mystic feeling of oneness. With reference to these immediate art-states of nature, every artist is an "imitator," that is to say, either an Apollinian artist in dreams, or a Dionysian artist in ecstasies, or finally—as for example in Greek tragedy—at once artist in both dreams and ecstasies; so we may perhaps picture him sinking down in his Dionysian intoxication and mystical self-abnegation, alone and apart from the singing revelers, and we may imagine how, through Apollinian dream-inspiration, his own state, i.e., his oneness with the inmost ground of the world, is revealed to him in a *symbolical dream image.*

So much for these general premises and contrasts. Let us now approach the *Greeks* in order to learn how highly these *art impulses of nature* were developed in them. Thus we shall be in a position to understand and appreciate more deeply that relation of the Greek artist to his archetypes which is, according to the Aristotelian expression, "the imitation of nature." In spite of all the dream literature and the numerous dream anecdotes of the Greeks, we can speak of their *dreams* only conjecturally, though with reasonable assurance. If we consider the incredibly precise and unerring plastic power of their eyes, together with their vivid, frank delight in colors, we can hardly refrain from assuming even for their dreams (to the shame of all those born later) a certain logic of line and contour, colors and groups, a certain pictorial sequence reminding us of their finest bas-relief whose perfection would certainly justify us, if a comparison were possible, in designating the dreaming Greeks as Homers and Homer as a dreaming Greek—in a deeper sense than that in which modern man, speaking of his dreams, ventures to compare himself with Shakespeare.

On the other hand, we need not conjecture regarding the immense gap which separates the *Dionysian Greek* from the Dionysian barbarian. From all quarters of the ancient world—to say nothing here of the modern—from Rome to Babylon, we can point to the existence of Dionysian festivals, types which bear, at best, the same relation to the Greek festivals which the bearded satyr, who borrowed his name and attributes from the goat, bears to Dionysus himself. In nearly every case these festivals centered in extravagant sexual licentiousness, whose waves overwhelmed all family life and its venerable traditions; the most savage natural instincts were unleashed, including even that horrible mixture of sensuality and cruelty which has always seemed to me to be the real "witches' brew." For some time, however, the Greeks were apparently perfectly insulated and guarded against the feverish excitements of these festivals, though knowledge of them must have come to Greece on all the routes of land and sea; for the figure of Apollo, rising full of pride, held out the Gorgon's head to this grotesquely uncouth Dionysian power—and really could not have countered any more dangerous force. It is in Doric art that this majestically rejecting attitude of Apollo is immortalized.

The opposition between Apollo and Dionysus became more hazardous and even impossible, when similar impulses finally burst forth from the deepest roots of the Hellenic nature and made a path for themselves: the Delphic god, by a seasonally effected reconciliation, now contented himself with taking the destructive weapons from the hands of his powerful antagonist. This reconciliation is the most important moment in the history of the Greek cult: wherever we turn we note the revolutions resulting from this event. The two antagonists were reconciled; the boundary lines to be observed henceforth by each were sharply defined, and there was to be a periodical exchange of gifts of esteem. At bottom, however, the chasm was not bridged over. But if we observe how, under the pressure of this treaty of peace, the Dionysian power revealed itself, we shall now recognize in the Dionysian orgies of the Greeks, as compared with the Babylonian Sacaea with their reversion of man to the tiger and the ape, the significance of festivals of world redemption and days of transfiguration. It is with them that nature for the first time attains her artistic jubilee; it is with them that the destruction of the *principium individuationis* for the first time becomes an artistic phenomenon.

The horrible "witches' brew" of sensuality and cruelty becomes ineffective; only the curious blending and duality in the emotions of the Dionysian revelers remind us—as medicines remind us of deadly poisons—of the phenomenon that pain begets joy, that ecstasy may wring sounds of agony from us. At the very climax of joy there sounds a cry of horror or a yearning lamentation for an irretrievable loss. In these Greek festivals, nature seems to reveal a sentimental trait; it is as if she were heaving a sigh at her dismemberment into individuals. The song and pantomime of such dually-minded revelers was something new and unheard of in the Homeric-Greek world; and the Dionysian *music* in particular excited awe and terror. If music, as it would seem, had been known previously as an Apollinian art, it was so, strictly speaking, only as the wave beat of rhythm, whose formative power was developed for the representation of Apollinian states. The music of Apollo was Doric architectonics in tones, but in tones that were merely suggestive, such as those of the cithara. The very element which forms the essence of Dionysian music (and hence of music in general) is carefully excluded as un-Apollinian—namely, the emotional power of the tone, the uniform flow of the melody, and the utterly incomparable world of harmony. In the Dionysian dithyramb man is incited to the greatest exaltation of all his symbolic faculties; something never before experienced struggles for utterance—the annihilation of the veil of *mâyâ*, oneness as the soul of the race and of nature itself. The essence of nature is now to be expressed symbolically; we need a new world of symbols; and the entire symbolism of the body is called into play, not the mere symbolism of the lips, face, and speech but the whole pantomime of dancing, forcing every member into rhythmic movement. Then the other symbolic powers suddenly press forward, particularly those of music, in rhythmics, dynamics, and harmony. To grasp this collective release of all the symbolic powers, man must have already attained that height of self-abnegation which seeks to express itself symbolically through all these powers—and so the dithyrambic votary of Dionysus is understood only by his peers. With what astonishment must the Apollinian Greek have beheld him! With an astonishment that was all the greater the more it was mingled with the shuddering suspicion that all this was actually not so very alien to him after all, in fact, that it was only his Apollinian consciousness which, like a veil, hid this Dionysian world from his vision.

FRIEDRICH NIETZSCHE

Attempt at a Self-Criticism *

Whatever may be at the bottom of this questionable book, it must have been an exceptionally significant and fascinating question, and deeply personal at that; the time in which it was written, in *spite* of which it was written, bears witness to that—the exciting time of the Franco-Prussian War of 1870/71. As the thunder of the battle of Wörth was rolling over Europe, the muser and riddle-friend who was to be the father of this book sat somewhere in an Alpine nook, very bemused and beriddled, hence very concerned and yet unconcerned, and wrote down his thoughts about the *Greeks*—the core of the strange and almost inaccessible book to which this belated preface (or postscript) shall now be added. A few weeks later—and he himself was to be found under the walls of Metz, still wedded to the question marks that he had placed after the alleged "cheerfulness" of the Greeks and of Greek art. Eventually, in that month of profoundest suspense when the peace treaty was being debated at Versailles, he, too, attained peace with himself and, slowly convalescing from an illness contracted at the front, completed the final draft of *The Birth of Tragedy out of the Spirit of Music.*—Out of music? Music and tragedy? Greeks and the music of tragedy? Greeks and the art form of pessimism? The best turned out, most beautiful, most envied type of humanity to date, those most apt to seduce us to life, the Greeks—how now? They of all people should have *needed* tragedy? Even more—art? For what—Greek art?

You will guess where the big question mark concerning the value of existence had thus been raised. Is pessimism *necessarily* a sign of decline, decay,

---

* Friedrich Nietzsche, *The Birth of Tragedy and The Case of Wagner*, translated by Walter Kaufmann (New York: Random House, 1967), pp. 17-27. (Footnotes omitted.)

168

degeneration, weary and weak instincts—as it once was in India and now is, to all appearances, among us, "modern" men and Europeans? Is there a pessimism of *strength*? An intellectual predilection for the hard, gruesome, evil, problematic aspect of existence, prompted by well-being, by overflowing health, by the *fullness* of existence? Is it perhaps possible to suffer precisely from overfullness? The sharp-eyed courage that tempts and attempts, that *craves* the frightful as the enemy, the worthy enemy, against whom one can test one's strength? From whom one can learn what it means "to be frightened"? What is the significance of the *tragic* myth among the Greeks of the best, the strongest, the most courageous period? And the tremendous phenomenon of the Dionysian—and, born from it, tragedy—what might they signify?—And again: that of which tragedy died, the Socratism of morality, the dialectics, frugality, and cheerfulness of the theoretical man—how now? might not this very Socratism be a sign of decline, of weariness, of infection, of the anarchical dissolution of the instincts? And the "Greek cheerfulness" of the later Greeks—merely the afterglow of the sunset? The Epicureans' resolve *against* pessimism—a mere precaution of the afflicted? And science itself, our science—indeed, what is the significance of all science, viewed as a symptom of life? For what—worse yet, *whence*—all science? How now? Is the resolve to be so scientific about everything perhaps a kind of fear of, an escape from, pessimism? A subtle last resort against—*truth*? And, morally speaking, a sort of cowardice and falseness? Amorally speaking, a ruse? O Socrates, Socrates, was that perhaps *your* secret? O enigmatic ironist, was that perhaps your—irony?

2

What I then got hold of, something frightful and dangerous, a problem with horns but not necessarily a bull, in any case a *new* problem—today I should say that it was *the problem of science itself*, science considered for the first time as problematic, as questionable. But the book in which my youthful courage and suspicion found an outlet—what an *impossible* book had to result from a task so uncongenial to youth! Constructed from a lot of immature, overgreen personal experiences, all of them close to the limits of communication, presented in the context of *art*—for the problem of science cannot be recognized in the context of science—a book perhaps for artists who also have an analytic and retrospective penchant (in other words, an exceptional type of artist for whom one might have to look far and wide and really would not care to look); a book full of psychological innovations and artists' secrets, with an artist's metaphysics in the background; a youthful work full of the intrepid mood of youth, the moodiness of youth, independent, defiantly self-reliant even where it seems to bow before an authority and personal reverence; in sum, a first book, also in every bad sense of that label. In spite of the problem which seems congenial to old age, the book is marked by every defect of youth, with its "length in excess" and its "storm and stress." On the other hand, considering its success (especially with the great artist to whom it addressed itself as in a dialogue, Richard Wagner), it is a *proven* book, I mean one that in any case satisfied "the best minds of the time." In view of that, it really ought to be treated with some consideration and taciturnity. Still, I do not want to suppress entirely how disagreeable it now seems to me, how strange it appears now, after sixteen years—before a much older, a hundred times more demanding, but by no means colder eye which has not become a stranger to the task which this audacious book dared to tackle for the first time: *to look at science in the perspective of the artist, but at art in that of life.*

3

To say it once more: today I find it an impossible book: I consider it badly written, ponderous, embarrassing, image-mad and image-confused, sentimental, in places saccharine to the point of effeminacy, uneven in tempo, without the will to logical cleanliness, very convinced and therefore disdainful of proof, mistrustful even of the *propriety* of proof, a book for initiates, "music" for those dedicated to music, those who are closely related to begin with on the basis of common and rare aesthetic experiences, "music" meant as a sign of recognition for close relatives *in artibus*—an arrogant and rhapsodic book that sought to exclude right from the beginning the *profanum vulgus* of "the educated" even more than "the mass" or "folk." Still, the effect of the book proved and proves that it had a knack for seeking out fellow-rhapsodizers and for luring them on to new secret paths and dancing places. What found expression here was anyway—this was admitted with as much curiosity as antipathy—a *strange* voice, the disciple of a still "unknown God," one who concealed himself for the time being under the scholar's hood, under the gravity and dialectical ill humor of the German, even under the bad manners of the Wagnerian. Here was a spirit with strange, still nameless needs, a memory bursting with questions, experiences, concealed things after which the name of Dionysus was added as one more question mark. What spoke here—as was admitted, not without suspicion—was something like a mystical, almost maenadic soul that stammered with difficulty, a feat of the will, as in a strange tongue, almost undecided whether it should communicate or conceal itself. It should have *sung*, this "new soul"—and not spoken! What I had to say then—too bad that I did not dare say it as a poet: perhaps I had the ability. Or at least as a philologist: after all, even today practically everything in this field remains to be discovered and dug up by philologists! Above all, the problem that there *is* a problem here—and that the Greeks, as long as we lack an answer to the question "what is Dionysian?" remain as totally uncomprehended and unimaginable as ever.

4

Indeed, what is Dionysian?—This book contains an answer: one "who knows" is talking, the initiate and disciple of his god. *Now* I should perhaps speak more cautiously and less eloquently about such a difficult psychological question as that concerning the origin of tragedy among the Greeks. The question of the Greek's relation to pain, his degree of sensitivity, is basic: did this relation remain constant? Or did it change radically? The question is whether his ever stronger *craving for beauty*, for festivals, pleasures, new cults was rooted in some deficiency, privation, melancholy, pain? Supposing that this were true—and Pericles (or Thucydides) suggests as much in the great funeral oration—how should we then have to explain the origin of the opposite craving, which developed earlier in time, the *craving for the ugly;* the good, severe will of the older Greeks to pessimism, to the tragic myth, to the image of everything underlying existence that is frightful, evil, a riddle, destructive, fatal? What, then, would be the origin of tragedy? Perhaps *joy*, strength, overflowing health, overgreat fullness? And what, then, is the significance, physiologically speaking, of that madness out of which tragic and comic art developed—the Dionysian madness? How now? Is madness perhaps not necessarily the symptom of degeneration, decline, and the final stage of culture? Are there perhaps—a question for psychiatrists—neuroses of *health?* of the youth and youthfulness of a people? Where does that synthesis of god and billy goat in the satyr point? What experience of himself, what urge compelled the Greek to conceive the Dionysian enthusiast and primeval man as a satyr? And regarding the origin of the tragic chorus: did those centuries when the Greek body flourished and the Greek soul foamed over with health perhaps know endemic ecstasies? Visions and hallucinations shared by entire communities or assemblies at a cult? How now? Should the Greeks, precisely in the abundance of their youth, have had the will to the tragic and have been pessimists? Should it have been madness, to use one of Plato's phrases, that brought the greatest blessings upon Greece? On the other hand, conversely, could it be that the Greeks became more and more optimistic, superficial, and histrionic precisely in the period of dissolution and weakness—more and more ardent for logic and logicizing the world and thus more "cheerful" and "scientific"? How now? Could it be possible that, in spite of all "modern ideas" and the prejudices of a democratic taste, the triumph of *optimism*, the gradual prevalence of *rationality*, practical and theoretical *utilitarianism*, no less than democracy itself which developed at the same time, might all have been symptoms of a decline of strength, of impending old age, and of physiological weariness? These, and not pessimism? Was Epicurus an optimist—precisely because he was *afflicted?*

It is apparent that it was a whole cluster of grave questions with which this book burdened itself. Let us add the gravest question of all. What, seen in the perspective of *life*, *is* the significance of morality?

5

Already in the preface addressed to Richard Wagner, art, and *not* morality, is presented as the truly *metaphysical* activity of man. In the book itself the suggestive sentence is repeated several times, that the existence of the world is *jus-*

tified only as an aesthetic phenomenon. Indeed, the whole book knows only an artistic meaning and crypto-meaning behind all events—a "god," if you please, but certainly only an entirely reckless and amoral artist-god who wants to experience, whether he is building or destroying, in the good and in the bad, his own joy and glory—one who, creating worlds, frees himself from the *distress* of fullness and *overfullness* and from the *affliction* of the contradictions compressed in his soul. The world—at every moment the *attained* salvation of God, as the eternally changing, eternally new vision of the most deeply afflicted, discordant, and contradictory being who can find salvation only in *appearance:* you can call this whole artists' metaphysics arbitrary, idle, fantastic; what matters is that it betrays a spirit who will one day fight at any risk whatever the *moral* interpretation and significance of existence. Here, perhaps for the first time, a pessimism "beyond good and evil" is suggested. Here that "perversity of mind" gains speech and formulation against which Schopenhauer never wearies of hurling in advance his most irate curses and thunderbolts: a philosophy that dares to move, to demote, morality into the realm of appearance—and not merely among "appearances" or phenomena (in the sense assigned to these words by Idealistic philosophers), but among "deceptions," as semblance, delusion, error, interpretation, contrivance, art.

Perhaps the depth of this *antimoral* propensity is best inferred from the careful and hostile silence with which Christianity is treated throughout the whole book—Christianity as the most prodigal elaboration of the moral theme to which humanity has ever been subjected. In truth, nothing could be more opposed to the purely aesthetic interpretation and justification of the world which are taught in this book than the Christian teaching, which is, and wants to be, *only* moral and which relegates art, *every* art, to the realm of *lies;* with its absolute standards, beginning with the truthfulness of God, it negates, judges, and damns art. Behind this mode of thought and valuation, which must be hostile to art if it is at all genuine, I never failed to sense a *hostility to life*—a furious, vengeful antipathy to life itself: for all of life is based on semblance, art, deception, points of view, and the necessity of perspectives and error. Christianity was from the beginning, essentially and fundamentally, life's nausea and disgust with life, merely concealed behind, masked by, dressed up as, faith in "another" or "better" life. Hatred of "the world," condemnations of the passions, fear of beauty and sensuality, a beyond invented the better to slander this life, at bottom a craving for the nothing, for the end, for respite, for "the sabbath of sabbaths"—all this always struck me, no less than the unconditional will of Christianity to recognize *only* moral values, as the most dangerous and uncanny form of all possible forms of a "will to decline"—at the very least a sign of abysmal sickness, weariness, discouragement, exhaustion, and the impoverishment of life. For, confronted with morality (especially Christian, or unconditional, morality), life *must* continually and inevitably be in the wrong, because life *is* something essentially amoral—and eventually, crushed by the weight of contempt and the eternal No, life *must* then be felt to be unworthy of desire and altogether worthless. Morality itself—how now?

might not morality be "a will to negate life," a secret instinct of annihilation, a principle of decay, diminution, and slander—the beginning of the end? Hence, the danger of dangers?

It was *against* morality that my instinct turned with this questionable book, long ago; it was an instinct that aligned itself with life and that discovered for itself a fundamentally opposite doctrine and valuation of life—purely artistic and *anti-Christian*. What to call it? As a philologist and man of words I baptized it, not without taking some liberty—for who could claim to know the rightful name of the Antichrist?—in the name of a Greek god: I called it Dionysian.

6

It is clear what task I first dared to touch with this book? How I regret now that in those days I still lacked the courage (or immodesty?) to permit myself in every way an individual language of my own for such individual views and hazards—and that instead I tried laboriously to express by means of Schopenhauerian and Kantian formulas strange and new valuations which were basically at odds with Kant's and Schopenhauer's spirit and taste! What, after all, did Schopenhauer think of tragedy?

"That which bestows on everything tragic its peculiar elevating force"— he says in *The World as Will and Representation*, volume II, p. 495—"is the discovery that the world, that life, can never give real satisfaction and hence is *not worthy* of our affection: this constitutes the tragic spirit—it leads to *resignation*."

How differently Dionysus spoke to me! How far removed I was from all this resignationism!—But there is something far worse in this book, something I now regret still more than that I obscured and spoiled Dionysian premonitions with Schopenhauerian formulations: namely, that I *spoiled* the grandiose *Greek problem*, as it had arisen before my eyes, by introducing the most modern problems! That I appended hopes where there was no ground for hope, where everything pointed all too plainly to an end! That on the basis of the latest German music I began to rave about "the German spirit" as if that were in the process even then of discovering and finding itself again— at a time when the German spirit, which not long before had still had the will to dominate Europe and the strength to lead Europe, was just making its testament and *abdicating* forever, making its transition, under the pompous pretense of founding a *Reich*, to a leveling mediocrity, democracy, and "modern ideas"!

Indeed, meanwhile I have learned to consider this "German spirit" with a sufficient lack of hope or mercy; also, contemporary *German music*, which is romanticism through and through and most un-Greek of all possible art forms—moreover, a first-rate poison for the nerves, doubly dangerous among a people who love drink and who honor lack of clarity as a virtue, for it has the double quality of a narcotic that both intoxicates and spreads a *fog*.

To be sure, apart from all the hasty hopes and faulty applications to the present with which I spoiled my first book, there still remains the great Dionysian question mark I raised—regarding music as well: what would a music have to be like that would no longer be of romantic origin, like German music—but *Dionysian*?

7

But, my dear sir, what in the world is romantic if *your* book isn't? Can deep hatred against "the Now," against "reality" and "modern ideas" be pushed further than you pushed it in your artists' metaphysics? believing sooner in the Nothing, sooner in the devil than in "the Now"? Is it not a deep bass of wrath and the lust for destruction that we hear humming underneath all of your contrapuntal vocal art and seduction of the ear, a furious resolve against everything that is "now," a will that is not too far removed from practical nihilism and seems to say: "sooner let nothing be true than that *you* should be right, than that *your* truth should be proved right!"

Listen yourself, my dear pessimist and art-deifier, but with open ears, to a single passage chosen from your book—to the not ineloquent dragon-slayer passage which may have an insidious pied-piper sound for young ears and hearts. How now? Isn't this the typical creed of the romantic of 1830, masked by the pessimism of 1850? Even the usual romantic finale is sounded—break, breakdown, return and collapse before an old faith, before *the* old God. How now? Is your pessimists' book not itself a piece of anti-Hellenism and romanticism? Is it not itself something "equally intoxicating and befogging," in any case a narcotic, even a piece of music, *German* music? But listen:

"Let us imagine a coming generation with such intrepidity of vision, with such a heroic penchant for the tremendous; let us imagine the bold stride of these dragon-slayers, the proud audacity with which they turn their back on all the weakling's doctrines of optimism in order to 'live resolutely' in wholeness and fullness: *would it not be necessary* for the tragic man of such a culture, in view of his self-education for seriousness and terror, to desire a new art, the *art of metaphysical comfort,* to desire tragedy as his own proper Helen, and to exclaim with Faust:

> Should not my longing overleap the distance
> And draw the fairest form into existence?"

"Would it not be *necessary*?"—No, thrice no! O you young romantics: it would *not* be necessary! But it is highly probable that it will *end* that way, that *you* end that way—namely, "comforted," as it is written, in spite of all self-education for seriousness and terror, "comforted metaphysically"—in sum, as romantics end, as *Christians*.

No! You ought to learn the art of *this-worldly* comfort first; you ought to learn to laugh, my young friends, if you are hell-bent on remaining pessimists. Then perhaps, as laughers, you may some day dispatch all metaphysical comforts to the devil—metaphysics in front. Or, to say it in the language of that Dionysian monster who bears the name of Zarathustra:

"Raise up your hearts, my brothers, high, higher! And don't forget your legs! Raise up your legs, too, good dancers; and still better: stand on your heads!

"This crown of the laugher, the rose-wreath crown: I crown myself with this crown; I myself pronounced holy my laughter. I did not find anyone else today strong enough for that.

"Zarathustra, the dancer; Zarathustra, the light one who beckons with his wings, preparing for a flight, beckoning to all birds, ready and heady, blissfully lightheaded;

"Zarathustra, the soothsayer; Zarathustra, the sooth-laugher; not impatient; not unconditional; one who loves leaps and side-leaps: I crown myself with this crown.

"This crown of the laugher, the rose-wreath crown: to you, my brothers, I throw this crown. Laughter I have pronounced holy: you higher men, *learn—* to laugh!"

Thus Spoke Zarathustra, Part IV.

LEO TOLSTOY

TOLSTOY'S THEORY OF ART is important for two major reasons. One is that he offers a theory deeply pervaded by the Russian impulse toward unification and communication. Far more important, however, he offers the strongest account available of a view of art that is held by many people—that art succeeds when it arouses and transmits emotion, when it brings people together and enriches their common humanity.

LEO TOLSTOY

---

*What Is Art?**

The activity of art is based on the fact that a man receiving through his sense of hearing or sight another man's expression of feeling, is capable of experiencing the emotion which moved the man who expressed it. To take the simplest example: one man laughs and another, who hears, becomes merry; or a man weeps and another, who hears, feels sorrow. A man is excited or irritated, and another man, seeing him, is brought to a similar state of mind. By his movements or by the sounds of his voice a man expresses courage and determination or sadness and calmness, and this state of mind passes on to others. A man suffers, manifesting his sufferings by groans and spasms, and thus suffering transmits itself to other people; a man expresses his feelings of admiration, devotion, fear, respect, or love to certain objects, persons, or phenomena, and others are infected by the same feelings of admiration, devotion, fear, respect, or love to the same objects, persons, or phenomena.

And it is on this capacity of man to receive another man's expression of feeling, and to experience those feelings himself, that the activity of art is based.

If a man infects another or others directly, immediately, by his appearance or by the sounds he gives vent to at the very time he experiences the feeling; if he causes another man to yawn when he himself cannot help yawning, or to laugh or cry when he himself is obliged to laugh or cry, or to suffer when he himself is suffering—that does not amount to art.

Art begins when one person, with the object of joining another or others to himself in one and the same feeling, expresses that feeling by certain

---

* Leo Tolstoy, *What Is Art?*, translated by Louise and Aylmer Maude (London: Oxford University Press, 1930), pp. 171-173, 275-277.

external indications. To take the simplest example: a boy having experienced, let us say, fear on encountering a wolf, relates that encounter; and in order to evoke in others the feeling he has experienced, describes himself, his condition before the encounter, the surroundings, the wood, his own light-headedness, and then the wolf's appearance, its movements, the distance between himself and the wolf, and so forth. All this, if only the boy when telling the story, again experiences the feelings he had lived through, and infects the hearers and compels them to feel what he had experienced—is art. Even if the boy had not seen a wolf but had frequently been afraid of one, and if, wishing to evoke in others the fear he had felt, he invented an encounter with a wolf and recounted it so as to make his hearers share the feelings he experienced when he feared the wolf, that also would be art. And just in the same way it is art if a man, having experienced either the fear of suffering or the attraction of enjoyment (whether in reality or in imagination), expresses these feelings on canvas or in marble so that others are infected by them. And it is also art if a man feels or imagines to himself feelings of delight, gladness, sorrow, despair, courage, or despondency and the transition from one to another of these feelings, and expresses them by sounds so that the hearers are infected by them and experience them as they were experienced by the composer.

The feelings with which the artist infects others may be most various—very strong or very weak, very important or very significant, very bad or very good: feelings of love of one's country, self-devotion and submission to fate or to God expressed in a drama, raptures of lovers described in a novel, feelings of voluptuousness expressed in a picture, courage expressed in a triumphal march, merriment evoked by a dance, humour evoked by a funny story, the feeling of quietness transmitted by an evening landscape or by a lullaby, or the feeling of admiration evoked by a beautiful arabesque—it is all art.

If only the spectators or auditors are infected by the feelings which the author has felt, it is art.

To evoke in oneself a feeling one has once experienced and, having evoked it in oneself then by means of movements, lines, colours, sounds, or forms expressed in words, so to transmit that feeling that others experience the same feeling—this is the activity of art.

Art is a human activity consisting in this, that one man consciously, by means of certain external signs, hands on to others feelings he has lived through, and that others are infected by these feelings and also experience them. . . .

If a man is infected by the author's condition of soul, if he feels this emotion and this union with others, then the object which has effected this is art; but if there be no such infection, if there be not this union with the author and with others who are moved by the same work—then it is not art. And not only is infection a sure sign of art, but the degree of infectiousness is also the sole measure of excellence in art.

The stronger the infection the better is the art, as art, speaking now apart from its subject-matter—that is, not considering the quality of the feelings it transmits.

And the degree of the infectiousness of art depends on three conditions:—

(1) On the greater or lesser individuality of the feeling transmitted; (2) on the greater or lesser clearness with which the feeling is transmitted; (3) on the sincerity of the artist, that is, on the greater or lesser force with which the artist himself feels the emotion he transmits.

The more individual the feeling transmitted the more strongly does it act on the recipient; the more individual the state of the soul into which he is transferred the more pleasure does the recipient obtain and therefore the more readily and strongly does he join in it.

The clearness of expression assists infection because the recipient who mingles in consciousness with the author is the better satisfied the more clearly the feeling is transmitted which as it seems to him he has long known and felt and for which he has only now found expression.

But most of all is the degree of infectiousness of art increased by the degree of sincerity in the artist. As soon as the spectator, hearer, or reader, feels that the artist is infected by his own production and writes, sings, or plays, for himself and not merely to act on others, this mental condition of the artist infects the recipient; and, contrariwise, as soon as the spectator, reader, or hearer, feels that the author is not writing, singing, or playing, for his own satisfaction—does not himself feel what he wishes to express—but is doing it for him, the recipient, resistance immediately springs up and the most individual and the newest feelings and the cleverest technique not only fail to produce any infection but actually repel.

I have mentioned three conditions of contagion in art, but they may all be summed up into one, the last, sincerity, that is, that the artist should be impelled by an inner need to express his feeling. That condition includes the first; for if the artist is sincere he will express the feeling as he experienced it. And as each man is different from everyone else, his feeling will be individual for everyone else; and the more individual it is—the more the artist has drawn it from the depths of his nature—the more sympathetic and sincere will it be. And this same sincerity will impel the artist to find a clear expression of the feeling which he wishes to transmit.

Therefore this third condition—sincerity—is the most important of the three. It is always complied with in peasant art, and this explains why such art always acts so powerfully; but it is a condition almost entirely absent from our upper-class art, which is continually produced by artists actuated by personal aims of covetousness or vanity.

Such are the three conditions which divide art from its counterfeits, and which also decide the quality of every work of art considered apart from its subject-matter.

The absence of any one of these conditions excludes a work from the category of art and relegates it to that of art's counterfeits. If the work does not transmit the artist's peculiarity of feeling and is therefore not individual, if it is unintelligibly expressed, or if it has not proceeded from the author's inner need for expression—it is not a work of art. If all these conditions are present, even in the smallest degree, then the work, even if a weak one, is yet a work of art.

The presence in various degrees of these three conditions: individuality, clearness, and sincerity, decides the merit of a work of art, as art, apart from subject-matter. All works of art take rank of merit according to the degree in which they fulfill the first, the second, and the third of these conditions. In one the individuality of the feeling transmitted may predominate; in another, clearness of expression; in a third, sincerity; while a fourth may have sincerity and individuality but be deficient in clearness; a fifth, individuality and clearness, but less sincerity; and so forth, in all possible degrees and combinations.

Thus is art divided from what is not art, and thus is the quality of art, as art, decided, independently of its subject-matter, that is to say, apart from whether the feelings it transmits are good or bad.

II

Recent Systematic Theories

CLIVE BELL

BELL'S THEORY OF SIGNIFICANT FORM is among the more prominent examples of early twentieth-century theories derived from Kant, sharing in the assumption that art can intrinsically be neither cognitive nor moral, that the value of art lies in form alone. Bell's statement of significant form is exemplary in its purity, if obscure in what it portends.

CLIVE BELL

*Art**

The starting-point for all systems of aesthetics must be the personal experience of a peculiar emotion. The objects that provoke this emotion we call works of art. All sensitive people agree that there is a peculiar emotion provoked by works of art. I do not mean, of course, that all works provoke the same emotion. On the contrary, every work produces a different emotion. But all these emotions are recognisably the same in kind; so far, at any rate, the best opinion is on my side. That there is a particular kind of emotion provoked by works of visual art, and that this emotion is provoked by every kind of visual art, by pictures, sculptures, buildings, pots, carvings, textiles, &c., &c., is not disputed, I think, by anyone capable of feeling it. This emotion is called the aesthetic emotion; and if we can discover some quality common and peculiar to all the objects that provoke it, we shall have solved what I take to be the central problem of aesthetics. We shall have discovered the essential quality in a work of art, the quality that distinguishes works of art from all other classes of objects.

For either all works of visual art have some common quality, or when we speak of "works of art" we gibber. Everyone speaks of "art," making a mental classification by which he distinguishes the class "works of art" from all other classes. What is the justification of this classification? What is the quality common and peculiar to all members of this class? Whatever it be, no doubt it is often found in company with other qualities; but they are adventitious—it is essential. There must be some one quality without which a work of art cannot exist; possessing which, in the least degree, no work is altogether worthless.

* Clive Bell, *Art* (New York: Putnam, Capricorn, 1958), pp. 416-421.

What is this quality? What quality is shared by all objects that provoke our aesthetic emotions? What quality is common to Sta. Sophia and the windows at Chartres, Mexican sculpture, a Persian bowl, Chinese carpets, Giotto's frescoes at Padua, and the masterpieces of Poussin, Piero della Francesca, and Cézanne? Only one answer seems possible—significant form. In each, lines and colours combined in a particular way, certain forms and relations of forms, stir our aesthetic emotions. These relations and combinations of lines and colours, these aesthetically moving forms, I call "Significant Form"; and "Significant Form" is the one quality common to all works of visual art.

At this point it may be objected that I am making aesthetics a purely subjective business, since my only data are personal experiences of a particular emotion. It will be said that the objects that provoke this emotion vary with each individual, and that therefore a system of aesthetics can have no objective validity. It must be replied that any system of aesthetics which pretends to be based on some objective truth is so palpably ridiculous as not to be worth discussing. We have no other means of recognising a work of art than our feeling for it. The objects that provoke aesthetic emotion vary with each individual. Aesthetic judgments are, as the saying goes, matters of taste; and about tastes, as everyone is proud to admit, there is no disputing. A good critic may be able to make me see in a picture that had left me cold things that I had overlooked, till at last, receiving the aesthetic emotion, I recognise it as a work of art. To be continually pointing out those parts, the sum, or rather the combination, of which unite to produce significant form, is the function of criticism. But it is useless for a critic to tell me that something is a work of art; he must make me feel it for myself. This he can do only by making me see; he must get at my emotions through my eyes. Unless he can make me see something that moves me, he cannot force my emotions. I have no right to consider anything a work of art to which I cannot react emotionally; and I have no right to look for the essential quality in anything that I have not *felt* to be a work of art. The critic can affect my aesthetic theories only by affecting my aesthetic experience. All systems of aesthetics must be based on personal experience—that is to say, they must be subjective.

Yet, though all aesthetic theories must be based on aesthetic judgments, and ultimately all aesthetic judgments must be matters of personal taste, it would be rash to assert that no theory of aesthetics can have general validity. For, though A, B, C, D are the works that move me, and A, D, E, F the works that move you, it may well be that x is the only quality believed by either of us to be common to all the works in his list. We may all agree about aesthetics, and yet differ about particular works of art. We may differ as to the presence or absence of the quality x. My immediate object will be to show that significant form is the only quality common and peculiar to all the works of visual art that move me; and I will ask those whose aesthetic experience does not tally with mine to see whether this quality is not also, in their judgment, common to all works that move them, and whether they can discover any other quality of which the same can be said.

Also at this point a query arises, irrelevant indeed, but hardly to be suppressed: "Why are we so profoundly moved by forms related in a particular way?" The question is extremely interesting, but irrelevant to aesthetics. In pure aesthetics we have only to consider our emotion and its object: for the purposes of aesthetics we have no right, neither is there any necessity, to pry behind the object into the state of mind of him who made it. Later, I shall attempt to answer the question; for by so doing I may be able to develop my theory of the relation of art to life. I shall not, however, be under the delusion that I am rounding off my theory of aesthetics. For a discussion of aesthetics, it need be agreed only that forms arranged and combined according to certain unknown and mysterious laws do move us in a particular way, and that it is the business of an artist so to combine and arrange them that they shall move us. These moving combinations and arrangements I have called, for the sake of convenience and for a reason that will appear later, "Significant Form."

A third interruption has to be met.

"Are you forgetting about colour?" someone inquires. Certainly not; my term "significant form" included combinations of lines and of colours. The distinction between form and colour is an unreal one; you cannot conceive a colourless line or a colourless space; neither can you conceive a formless relation of colours. In a black and white drawing the spaces are all white and all are bounded by black lines; in most oil paintings the spaces are multi-coloured and so are the boundaries; you cannot imagine a boundary line without any content, or a content without a boundary line. Therefore, when I speak of significant form, I mean a combination of lines and colours (counting white and black as colours) that moves me aesthetically.

Some people may be surprised at my not having called this "beauty." Of course, to those who define beauty as "combinations of lines and colours that provoke aesthetic emotion," I willingly concede the right of substituting their word for mine. But most of us, however strict we may be, are apt to apply the epithet "beautiful" to objects that do not provoke that peculiar emotion produced by works of art. Everyone, I suspect, has called a butterfly or a flower beautiful. Does anyone feel the same kind of emotion for a butterfly or a flower that he feels for a cathedral or a picture? Surely, it is not what I call an aesthetic emotion that most of us feel, generally, for natural beauty. I shall suggest, later, that some people may, occasionally, see in nature what we see in art, and feel for her an aesthetic emotion; but I am satisfied that, as a rule, most people feel a very different kind of emotion for birds and flowers and the wings of butterflies from that which they feel for pictures, pots, temples and statues. Why these beautiful things do not move us as works of art move us is another, and not an aesthetic, question. For our immediate purpose we have to discover only what quality is common to objects that do move us as works of art. In the last part of this chapter, when I try to answer the question—"Why are we so profoundly moved by some combinations of lines and colours?" I shall hope to offer an acceptable explanation of why we are less profoundly moved by others.

Since we call a quality that does not raise the characteristic aesthetic emotion "Beauty," it would be misleading to call by the same name the quality that does. To make "beauty" the object of the aesthetic emotion, we must give to the word an over-strict and unfamiliar definition. Everyone sometimes uses "beauty" in an unaesthetic sense; most people habitually do so. To everyone, except perhaps here and there an occasional aesthete, the commonest sense of the word is unaesthetic. Of its grosser abuse, patent in our chatter about "beautiful huntin'" and "beautiful shootin'," I need not take account; it would be open to the precious to reply that they never do so abuse it. Besides, here there is no danger of confusion between the aesthetic and the non-aesthetic use; but when we speak of a beautiful woman there is. When an ordinary man speaks of a beautiful woman he certainly does not mean only that she moves him aesthetically; but when an artist calls a withered old hag beautiful he may sometimes mean what he means when he calls a battered torso beautiful. The ordinary man, if he be also a man of taste, will call the battered torso beautiful, but he will not call a withered hag beautiful because, in the matter of women, it is not to the aesthetic quality that the hag may possess, but to some other quality that he assigns the epithet. Indeed, most of us never dream of going for aesthetic emotions to human beings, from whom we ask something very different. This "something," when we find it in a young woman, we are apt to call it "beauty." We live in a nice age. With the man-in-the-street "beautiful" is more often than not synonymous with "desirable"; the word does not necessarily connote any aesthetic reaction whatever, and I am tempted to believe that in the minds of many the sexual flavour of the word is stronger than the aesthetic. I have noticed a consistency in those to whom the most beautiful thing in the world is a beautiful woman, and the next most beautiful thing a picture of one. The confusion between aesthetic and sensual beauty is not in their case so great as might be supposed. Perhaps there is none; for perhaps they have never had an aesthetic emotion to confuse with their other emotions. The art that they call "beautiful" is generally closely related to the women. A beautiful picture is a photograph of a pretty girl; beautiful music, the music that provokes emotions similar to those provoked by young ladies in musical farces; and beautiful poetry, the poetry that recalls the same emotions felt, twenty years earlier, for the rector's daughter. Clearly the word "beauty" is used to connote the objects of quite distinguishable emotions, and that is a reason for not employing a term which would land me inevitably in confusions and misunderstandings with my readers.

On the other hand, with those who judge it more exact to call these combinations and arrangements of form that provoke our aesthetic emotions, not "significant form," but "significant relations of form," and then try to make the best of two worlds, the aesthetic and the metaphysical, by calling these relations "rhythm," I have no quarrel whatever. Having made it clear that by "significant form" I mean arrangements and combinations that move us in a particular way, I willingly join hands with those who prefer to give a different name to the same thing.

The hypothesis that significant form is the essential quality in a work of art has at least one merit denied to many more famous and more striking—it does help to explain things. We are all familiar with pictures that interest us and excite our admiration, but do not move us as works of art. To this class belongs what I call "Descriptive Painting"—that is, painting in which forms are used not as objects of emotion, but as means of suggesting emotion or conveying information. Portraits of psychological and historical value, topographical works, pictures that tell stories and suggest situations, illustrations of all sorts, belong to this class. That we all recognise the distinction is clear, for who has not said that such and such a drawing was excellent as illustration, but as a work of art worthless? Of course many descriptive pictures possess, amongst other qualities, formal significance, and are therefore works of art: but many more do not. They interest us; they may move us too in a hundred different ways, but they do not move us aesthetically. According to my hypothesis they are not works of art. They leave untouched our aesthetic emotions because it is not their forms but the ideas or information suggested or conveyed by their forms that affect us.

R. G. COLLINGWOOD

COLLINGWOOD'S *PRINCIPLES OF ART* is among the better known works in philosophy of art of the twentieth century. Published in the 1930s, it has been widely read by artists and art historians. Certain aspects of Collingwood's position seem extreme, particularly his suggestion that art exists in the imagination, not in its embodiment. Nevertheless, his discussion of the distinction between art and craft is important, for it poses questions of how works of art differ from other things. Such questions are often quite pressing both within art itself—with respect to found works, for example—and within many theories of art. The "thingliness" of the work of art is very important for Heidegger, for example. The fundamental question Collingwood raises here is what makes art different from craft, *poiēsis* from *technē*.

R. G. COLLINGWOOD

---

*Principles of Art**

Art and Craft

§ 1. THE MEANING OF CRAFT. The first sense of the word 'art' to be distinguished from art proper is the obsolete sense in which it means what in this book I shall call craft. This is what *ars* means in ancient Latin, and what techne means in Greek: the power to produce a preconceived result by means of consciously controlled and directed action. In order to take the first step towards a sound aesthetic, it is necessary to disentangle the notion of craft from that of art proper..In order to do this, again, we must first enumerate the chief characteristics of craft.

(1) Craft always involves a distinction between means and end, each clearly conceived as something distinct from the other but related to it. The term 'means' is loosely applied to things that are used in order to reach the end, such as tools, machines, or fuel. Strictly, it applies not to the things but to the actions concerned with them: manipulating the tools, tending the machines, or burning the fuel. These actions (as implied by the literal sense of the word 'means') are passed through or traversed in order to reach the end, and are left behind when the end is reached. This may serve to distinguish the idea of means from two other ideas with which it is sometimes confused: that of part, and that of material. The relation of part to whole is like that of means to end, in that the part is indispensable to the whole, is what it is because of its relation to the whole, and may exist by itself before the whole comes into existence; but when the whole exists the part exists too, whereas,

---

* R. G. Collingwood, *The Principles of Art* (London: Oxford University Press, 1938), pp. 15-17, 20-25, 109-111, 121-123, 306-308. (Some footnotes omitted).

when the end exists, the means have ceased to exist. As for the idea of material, we shall return to that in (4) below.

(2) It involves a distinction between planning and execution. The result to be obtained is preconceived or thought out before being arrived at. The craftsman knows what he wants to make before he makes it. This foreknowledge is absolutely indispensable to craft: if something, for example stainless steel, is made without such foreknowledge, the making of it is not a case of craft but an accident. Moreover, this foreknowledge is not vague but precise. If a person sets out to make a table, but conceives the table only vaguely, as somewhere between two by four feet and three by six, and between two and three feet high, and so forth, he is no craftsman.

(3) Means and end are related in one way in the process of planning; in the opposite way in the process of execution. In planning the end is prior to the means. The end is thought out first, and afterwards the means are thought out. In execution the means come first, and the end is reached through them.

(4) There is a distinction between raw material and finished product or artifact. A craft is always exercised upon something, and aims at the transformation of this into something different. That upon which it works begins as raw material and ends as finished product. The raw material is found ready made before the special work of the craft begins.

(5) There is a distinction between form and matter. The matter is what is identical in the raw material and the finished product; the form is what is different, what the exercise of the craft changes. To describe the raw material as raw is not to imply that it is formless, but only that it has not yet the form which it is to acquire through 'transformation' into finished product.

(6) There is a hierarchical relation between various crafts, one supplying what another needs, one using what another provides. There are three kinds of hierarchy: of materials, of means, and of parts. *(a)* The raw material of one craft is the finished product of another. Thus the silviculturist propagates trees and looks after them as they grow, in order to provide raw material for the felling-men who transform them into logs; these are raw material for the saw-mill which transforms them into planks; and these, after a further process of selection and seasoning, become raw material for a joiner. *(b)* In the hierarchy of means, one craft supplies another with tools. Thus the timber-merchant supplies pit-props to the miner; the miner supplies coal to the blacksmith; the blacksmith supplies horseshoes to the farmer; and so on. *(c)* In the hierarchy of parts, a complex operation like the manufacture of a motorcar is parcelled out among a number of trades: one firm makes the engine, another the gears, another the chassis, another the tyres, another the electrical equipment, and so on; the final assembling is not strictly the manufacture of the car but only the bringing together of these parts. In one or more of these ways every craft has a hierarchical character; either as hierarchically related to other crafts, or as itself consisting of various heterogeneous operations hierarchically related among themselves.

Without claiming that these features together exhaust the notion of craft, or that each of them separately is peculiar to it, we may claim with tolerable confidence that where most of them are absent from a certain activity that activity is not a craft, and, if it is called by that name, is so called either by mistake or in a vague and inaccurate way. . . .

§ 3. BREAK-DOWN OF THE THEORY. (1) The first characteristic of craft is the distinction between means and end. Is this present in works of art? According to the technical theory, yes. A poem is means to the production of a certain state of mind in the audience, as a horseshoe is means to the production of a certain state of mind in the man whose horse is shod. And the poem in its turn will be an end to which other things are means. In the case of the horseshoe, this stage of the analysis is easy: we can enumerate lighting the forge, cutting a piece of iron off a bar, heating it, and so on. What is there analogous to these processes in the case of a poem? The poet may get paper and pen, fill the pen, sit down and square his elbows; but these actions are preparatory not to composition (which may go on in the poet's head) but to writing. Suppose the poem is a short one, and composed without the use of any writing materials; what are the means by which the poet composes it? I can think of no answer, unless comic answers are wanted, such as "using a rhyming dictionary," "pounding his foot on the floor or wagging his head or hand to mark the metre," or "getting drunk." If one looks at the matter seriously, one sees that the only factors in the situation are the poet, the poetic labour of his mind, and the poem. And if any supporter of the technical theory says "Right: then the poetic labour is the means, the poem the end," we shall ask him to find a blacksmith who can make a horseshoe by sheer labour, without forge, anvil, hammer, or tongs. It is because nothing corresponding to these exists in the case of the poem that the poem is not an end to which there are means.

Conversely, is a poem means to the production of a certain state of mind in an audience? Suppose a poet had read his verses to an audience, hoping that they would produce a certain result; and suppose the result were different; would that in itself prove the poem a bad one? It is a difficult question; some would say yes, others no. But if poetry were obviously a craft, the answer would be a prompt and unhesitating yes. The advocate of the technical theory must do a good deal of toe-chopping before he can get his facts to fit his theory at this point.

So far, the prospects of the technical theory are not too bright. Let us proceed.

(2) The distinction between planning and executing certainly exists in some works of art, namely those which are also works of craft or artifacts; for there is, of course, an overlap between these two things, as may be seen by the example of a building or a jar, which is made to order for the satisfaction of a specific demand, to serve a useful purpose, but may none the less be a work of art. But suppose a poet were making up verses as he walked; suddenly finding a line in his head, and then another, and then dissatisfied with them and

altering them until he had got them to his liking: what is the plan which he is executing? He may have had a vague idea that if he went for a walk he would be able to compose poetry; but what were, so to speak, the measurements and specifications of the poem he planned to compose? He may, no doubt, have been hoping to compose a sonnet on a particular subject specified by the editor of a review; but the point is that he may not, and that he is none the less a poet for composing without having any definite plan in his head. Or suppose a sculptor were not making a Madonna and child, three feet high, in Hoptonwood stone, guaranteed to placate the chancellor of the diocese and obtain a faculty for placing it in the vacant niche over a certain church door; but were simply playing about with clay, and found the clay under his fingers turning into a little dancing man: is this not a work of art because it was done without being planned in advance?

All this is very familiar. There would be no need to insist upon it, but that the technical theory of art relies on our forgetting it. While we are thinking of it, let us note the importance of not over-emphasizing it. Art as such does not imply the distinction between planning and execution. But *(a)* this is a merely negative characteristic, not a positive one. We must not erect the absence of plan into a positive force and call it inspiration, or the unconscious, or the like. *(b)* It is a permissible characteristic of art, not a compulsory one. If unplanned works of art are possible, it does not follow that no planned work is a work of art. That is the logical fallacy[1] that underlies one, or some, of the various things called romanticism. It may very well be true that the only works of art which can be made altogether without a plan are trifling ones, and that the greatest and most serious ones always contain an element of planning and therefore an element of craft. But that would not justify the technical theory of art.

(3) If neither means and end nor planning and execution can be distinguished in art proper, there obviously can be no reversal of order as between means and end, in planning and execution respectively.

(4) We next come to the distinction between raw material and finished product. Does this exist in art proper? If so, a poem is made out of certain raw material. What is the raw material out of which Ben Jonson made *Queene and Huntresse, chaste, and faire?* Words, perhaps. Well, what words? A smith makes a horseshoe not out of all the iron there is, but out of a certain piece of iron, cut off a certain bar that he keeps in the corner of the smithy. If Ben Jonson did anything at all like that, he said: "I want to make a nice little hymn to open Act v, Scene vi of *Cynthia's Revels.* Here is the English language, or as much of it as I know; I will use *thy* five times, *to* four times, *and, bright, excellently,* and *goddesse* three times each, and so on." He did nothing like this. The words which occur in the poem were never before his mind as a whole in an order different from that of the poem, out of which he shuffled them till the poem, as we have it, appeared. I do not deny that by sorting out the words, or the vowel sounds, or the consonant sounds, in a poem like this, we can make interesting and (I believe) important discoveries about the way in which Ben

Jonson's mind worked when he made the poem; and I am willing to allow that the technical theory of art is doing good service if it leads people to explore these matters; but if it can only express what it is trying to do by calling these words or sounds the materials out of which the poem is made, it is talking nonsense.

But perhaps there is a raw material of another kind: a feeling or emotion, for example, which is present to the poet's mind at the commencement of his labour, and which that labour converts into the poem. "Aus meinem grossen Schmerzen mach' ich die kleinen Lieder," said Heine; and he was doubtless right; the poet's labour can be justly described as converting emotions into poems. But this conversion is a very different kind of thing from the conversion of iron into horseshoes. If the two kinds of conversion were the same, a blacksmith could make horseshoes out of his desire to pay the rent. The something more, over and above that desire, which he must have in order to make horseshoes out of it, is the iron which is their raw material. In the poet's case that something more does not exist.

(5) In every work of art there is something which, in some sense of the word, may be called form. There is, to be rather more precise, something in the nature of rhythm, pattern, organization, design, or structure. But it does not follow that there is a distinction between form and matter. Where that distinction does exist, namely, in artifacts, the matter was there in the shape of raw material before the form was imposed upon it, and the form was there in the shape of a preconceived plan before being imposed upon the matter; and as the two coexist in the finished product we can see how the matter might have accepted a different form, or the form have been imposed upon a different matter. None of these statements applies to a work of art. Something was no doubt there before a poem came into being; there was, for example, a confused excitement in the poet's mind; but, as we have seen, this was not the raw material of the poem. There was also, no doubt, the impulse to write; but this impulse was not the form of the unwritten poem. And when the poem is written, there is nothing in it of which we can say, "this is a matter which might have taken on a different form," or "this is a form which might have been realized in a different matter."

When people have spoken of matter and form in connexion with art, or of that strange hybrid distinction, form and content, they have in fact been doing one of two things, or both confusedly at once. Either they have been assimilating a work of art to an artifact, and the artist's work to the craftsman's; or else they have been using these terms in a vaguely metaphorical way as means of referring to distinctions which really do exist in art, but are of a different kind. There is always in art a distinction between what is expressed and that which expresses it; there is a distinction between the initial impulse to write or paint or compose and the finished poem or picture or music; there is a distinction between an emotional element in the artist's experience and what may be called an intellectual element. All these deserve investigation; but none of them is a case of the distinction between form and matter.

(6) Finally, there is in art nothing which resembles the hierarchy of crafts, each dictating ends to the one below it, and providing either means or raw materials or parts to the one above. When a poet writes verses for a musician to set, these verses are not means to the musician's end, for they are incorporated in the song which is the musician's finished product, and it is characteristic of means, as we saw, to be left behind. But neither are they raw materials. The musician does not transform them into music; he sets them to music; and if the music which he writes for them had a raw material (which it has not), that raw material could not consist of verses. What happens is rather that the poet and musician collaborate to produce a work of art which owes something to each of them; and this is true even if in the poet's case there was no intention of collaborating. . . .

Art Proper: (1) As Expression

§ 2. EXPRESSING EMOTION AND AROUSING EMOTION. Our first question is this. Since the artist proper has something to do with emotion, and what he does with it is not to arouse it, what is it that he does? It will be remembered that the kind of answer we expect to this question is an answer derived from what we all know and all habitually say; nothing original or recondite, but something entirely commonplace.

Nothing could be more entirely commonplace than to say he expresses them. The idea is familiar to every artist, and to every one else who has any acquaintance with the arts. To state it is not to state a philosophical theory or definition of art; it is to state a fact or supposed fact about which, when we have sufficiently identified it, we shall have later to theorize philosophically. For the present it does not matter whether the fact that is alleged, when it is said that the artist expresses emotion, is really a fact or only supposed to be one. Whichever it is, we have to identify it, that is, to decide what it is that people are saying when they use the phrase. Later on, we shall have to see whether it will fit into a coherent theory.

They are referring to a situation, real or supposed, of a definite kind. When a man is said to express emotion, what is being said about him comes to this. At first, he is conscious of having an emotion, but not conscious of what this emotion is. All he is conscious of is a perturbation or excitement, which he feels going on within him, but of whose nature he is ignorant. While in this state, all he can say about his emotion is: "I feel . . . I don't know what I feel." From this helpless and oppressed condition he extricates himself by doing something which we call expressing himself. This is an activity which has something to do with the thing we call language: he expresses himself by speaking. It has also something to do with consciousness: the emotion expressed is an emotion of whose nature the person who feels it is no longer unconscious. It has also something to do with the way in which he feels the emotion. As unexpressed, he feels it in what we have called a helpless and oppressed way; as expressed, he feels it in a way from which this sense of oppression has vanished. His mind is somehow lightened and eased.

This lightening of emotions which is somehow connected with the expression of them has a certain resemblance to the 'catharsis' by which emotions are earthed through being discharged into a make-believe situation; but the two things are not the same. Suppose the emotion is one of anger. If it is effectively earthed, for example by fancying oneself kicking some one down stairs, it is thereafter no longer present in the mind as anger at all: we have worked it off and are rid of it. If it is expressed, for example by putting it into hot and bitter words, it does not disappear from the mind; we remain angry; but instead of the sense of oppression which accompanies an emotion of anger not yet recognized as such, we have that sense of alleviation which comes when we are conscious of our own emotion as anger, instead of being conscious of it only as an unidentified perturbation. This is what we refer to when we say that it "does us good" to express our emotions.

The expression of an emotion by speech may be addressed to some one; but if so it is not done with the intention of arousing a like emotion in him. If there is any effect which we wish to produce in the hearer, it is only the effect which we call making him understand how we feel. But, as we have already seen, this is just the effect which expressing our emotions has on ourselves. It makes us, as well as the people to whom we talk, understand how we feel. A person arousing emotion sets out to affect his audience in a way in which he himself is not necessarily affected. He and his audience stand in quite different relations to the act, very much as physician and patient stand in quite different relations towards a drug administered by the one and taken by the other. A person expressing emotion, on the contrary, is treating himself and his audience in the same kind of way; he is making his emotions clear to his audience, and that is what he is doing to himself.

It follows from this that the expression of emotion, simply as expression, is not addressed to any particular audience. It is addressed primarily to the speaker himself, and secondarily to any one who can understand. Here again, the speaker's attitude towards his audience is quite unlike that of a person desiring to arouse in his audience a certain emotion. If that is what he wishes to do, he must know the audience he is addressing. He must know what type of stimulus will produce the desired kind of reaction in people of that particular sort; and he must adapt his language to his audience in the sense of making sure that it contains stimuli appropriate to their peculiarities. If what he wishes to do is to express his emotions intelligibly, he has to express them in such a way as to be intelligible to himself; his audience is then in the position of persons who overhear him doing this. Thus the stimulus-and-reaction terminology has no applicability to the situation.

The means-and-end, or technique, terminology too is inapplicable. Until a man has expressed his emotion, he does not yet know what emotion it is. The act of expressing it is therefore an exploration of his own emotions. He is trying to find out what these emotions are. There is certainly here a directed process: an effort, that is, directed upon a certain end; but the end is not something foreseen and preconceived, to which appropriate means can be thought out in the light of our knowledge of its special character. Expression is an activity of which there can be no technique. . . .

§ 7. EXPRESSING EMOTION AND BETRAYING EMOTION. Finally, the expressing of emotion must not be confused with what may be called the betraying of it, that is, exhibiting symptoms of it. When it is said that the artist in the proper sense of that word is a person who expresses his emotions, this does not mean that if he is afraid he turns pale and stammers; if he is angry he turns red and bellows; and so forth. These things are no doubt called expressions; but just as we distinguish proper and improper senses of the word 'art', so we must distinguish proper and improper senses of the word 'expression', and in the context of a discussion about art this sense of expression is an improper sense. The characteristic mark of expression proper is lucidity or intelligibility; a person who expresses something thereby becomes conscious of what it is that he is expressing, and enables others to become conscious of it in himself and in them. Turning pale and stammering is a natural accompaniment of fear, but a person who in addition to being afraid also turns pale and stammers does not thereby become conscious of the precise quality of his emotion. About that he is as much in the dark as he would be if (were that possible) he could feel fear without also exhibiting these symptoms of it.

Confusion between these two senses of the word 'expression' may easily lead to false critical estimates, and so to false aesthetic theory. It is sometimes thought a merit in an actress that when she is acting a pathetic scene she can work herself up to such an extent as to weep real tears. There may be some ground for that opinion if acting is not an art but a craft, and if the actress's object in that scene is to produce grief in her audience; and even then the conclusion would follow only it it were true that grief cannot be produced in the audience unless symptoms of grief are exhibited by the performer. And no doubt this is how most people think of the actor's work. But if his business is not amusement but art, the object at which he is aiming is not to produce a preconceived emotional effect on his audience but by means of a system of expressions, or language, composed partly of speech and partly of gesture, to explore his own emotions: to discover emotions in himself of which he was unaware, and, by permitting the audience to witness the discovery, enable them to make a similar discovery about themselves. In that case it is not her ability to weep real tears that would mark out a good actress; it is her ability to make it clear to herself and her audience what the tears are about.

This applies to every kind of art. The artist never rants. A person who writes or paints or the like in order to blow off steam, using the traditional materials of art as means for exhibiting the symptoms of emotion, may deserve praise as an exhibitionist, but loses for the moment all claim to the title of artist. Exhibitionists have their uses; they may serve as an amusement, or they may be doing magic. The second category will contain, for example, those young men who, learning in the torment of their own bodies and minds what war is like, have stammered their indignation in verses, and published them in the hope of infecting others and causing them to abolish it. But these verses have nothing to do with poetry. . . .

The Artist and the Community

§ 3. THE BODILY 'WORK OF ART' . . . We get, therefore, this result. Every imaginative experience is a sensuous experience raised to the imaginative level by an act of consciousness; or, every imaginative experience is a sensuous experience together with consciousness of the same. Now the aesthetic experience is an imaginative experience. It is wholly and entirely imaginative; it contains no elements that are not imaginative, and the only power which can generate it is the power of the experient's consciousness. But it is not generated out of nothing. Being an imaginative experience, it presupposes a corresponding sensuous experience; where to say that it presupposes this does not mean that it arises subsequently to this, but that it is generated by the act which converts this into it. The sensuous experience need not exist by itself first. It may come into being under the very eyes, so to speak, of consciousness, so that it no sooner comes into being than it is transmuted into imagination. Nevertheless, there is always a distinction between what transmutes (consciousness), what is transmuted (sensation), and what it is transmuted into (imagination).

The transmuted or sensuous element in the aesthetic experience is the so-called outward element: in the case under examination, the artist's psycho-physical activity of painting; his visual sensation of the colours and shapes of his subject, his felt gestures as he manipulates his brush, the seen shapes of paint patches that these gestures leave on his canvass: in short, the total sensuous (or rather, sensuous-emotional) experience of a man at work before his easel. Unless this sensuous experience were actually present, there would be nothing out of which consciousness could generate the aesthetic experience which is "externalized" or "recorded" or "expressed" by the painted picture. But this sensuous experience, although it is actually present, is never present by itself. Every element in it comes into existence under the eyes of the painter's consciousness; or rather, this happens in so far as he is a good painter; it is only bad painters who paint without knowing what they are doing; and every element in it is therefore converted into imaginative experience at birth. Nevertheless, reflection distinguishes between the imaginative experience and the sensuous experience out of which it is thus made, and discovers that "nihil est in imaginatione quod non fuerit in sensu."

What of the case where a man looks at the subject without painting? He, too, has an aesthetic experience in so far as his impressions are transmuted into ideas by the activity of his imagination. But our artist was right to claim that there is far less in that experience than in the experience of a man who has painted the subject; for the sensuous elements involved in merely looking, even where looking is accompanied by a smile of pleasure, gestures, and so forth, are necessarily much scantier and poorer, and also much less highly organized in their totality, than the sensuous elements involved in painting. If you want to get more out of an experience, you must put more into it. The painter puts a great deal more into his experience of the subject than a man who merely looks at it; he puts into it, in addition, the whole consciously performed activity of painting it; what he gets out of it, therefore, is proportionately more. And this increment is an essential part of what he "externalizes" or "records" in his picture: he records there not the experience of looking at the subject without painting it, but the far richer and in some ways very different experience of looking at it and painting it together.

NOTE

1. It is an example of what I have elsewhere called the fallacy of precarious margins. Because art and craft overlap, the essence of art is sought not in the positive characteristics of all art, but in the characteristics of those works of art which are not works of craft. Thus the only things which are allowed to be works of art are those marginal examples which lie outside the overlap of art and craft. This is a precarious margin because further study may at any moment reveal the characteristics of craft in some of these examples. See *Essay on Philosophical Method.*

JOHN DEWEY

JOHN DEWEY IS THE MAJOR FIGURE of the classical period of American philosophy, a period that includes William James, George Herbert Mead, and Charles Sanders Peirce. Most of the members of this group have waned in influence and status through the twentieth century, and are largely unknown in Europe and the rest of the world, their work having been supplanted in the United States by language-based forms of analytic philosophy. Part of the decline may have been due to impoverished interpretations of Dewey's instrumentalism or pragmatism, as if Dewey maintained that knowledge had only practical implications.

An additional factor is that there appears to be lacking in Dewey's work a systematic metaphysics and epistemology: He was dubious about the possibility of a systematic theory that would capture the force of his central insight—that all human activities, including science and metaphysics, are to be evaluated and tested by their function in human experience. Recent Continental philosophers, particularly Heidegger and Foucault, but including most writers interested in hermeneutic forms of interpretation and epistemology, share Dewey's conviction that knowledge and thought, science and art, are conditioned by human history and are to be evaluated by a human future.

Dewey may have declined to offer an explicit metaphysical theory, but there is in his writings a systematic theory of experience. For Dewey, experience is not a human state or frame of mind, but is the field of lived human activity. Sometimes he characterizes the dimensions of that field as doing and undergoing, sometimes as means and ends, but he always emphasizes that experience is both relational and consummatory. Inquiry is largely concerned with means-ends relations, but all experience has consummatory qualities. Art is the unification in experience of those means that lead to consummatory ends. Where experience is most thoroughly unified and complete, there we find art. Like Nietzsche, Dewey takes art to be the model for the highest forms of human achievement.

Art as Experience*

THE LIVE CREATURE

By one of the ironic perversities that often attend the course of affairs, the existence of the works of art upon which formation of an esthetic theory depends has become an obstruction to theory about them. For one reason, these works are products that exist externally and physically. In common conception, the work of art is often identified with the building, book, painting, or statue in its existence apart from human experience. Since the actual work of art is what the product does with and in experience, the result is not favorable to understanding. In addition, the very perfection of some of these products, the prestige they possess because of a long history of unquestioned admiration, creates conventions that get in the way of fresh insight. When an art product once attains classic status, it somehow becomes isolated from the human conditions under which it was brought into being and from the human consequences it engenders in actual life-experience.

When artistic objects are separated from both conditions of origin and operation in experience, a wall is built around them that renders almost opaque their general significance, with which esthetic theory deals. Art is remitted to a separate realm, where it is cut off from that association with the materials and aims of every other form of human effort, undergoing, and achievement. A primary task is thus imposed upon one who undertakes to write upon the philosophy of the fine arts. This task is to restore continuity

* John Dewey, *Art as Experience* (New York: Putnam, 1934), pp. 1, 35-37, 47-48, 82-85, 106-109, 194-200, 272-275. (Footnote and chapter numbers omitted.)

between the refined and intensified forms of experience that are works of art and the everyday events, doings, and sufferings that are universally recognized to constitute experience. . . .

HAVING AN EXPERIENCE

Experience occurs continuously, because the interaction of live creature and environing conditions is involved in the very process of living. Under conditions of resistance and conflict, aspects and elements of the self and the world that are implicated in this interaction qualify experience with emotions and ideas so that conscious intent emerges. Oftentimes, however, the experience had is inchoate. Things are experienced but not in such a way that they are composed into *an* experience. There is distraction and dispersion; what we observe and what we think, what we desire and what we get, are at odds with each other. We put our hands to the plow and turn back; we start and then we stop, not because the experience has reached the end for the sake of which it was initiated but because of extraneous interruptions or of inner lethargy.

In contrast with such experience, we have *an* experience when the material experienced runs its course to fulfillment. Then and then only is it integrated within and demarcated in the general stream of experience from other experiences. A piece of work is finished in a way that is satisfactory; a problem receives its solution; a game is played through; a situation, whether that of eating a meal, playing a game of chess, carrying on a conversation, writing a book, or taking part in a political campaign, is so rounded out that its close is a consummation and not a cessation. Such an experience is a whole and carries with it its own individualizing quality and self-sufficiency. It is *an* experience.

Philosophers, even empirical philosophers, have spoken for the most part of experience at large. Idiomatic speech, however, refers to experiences each of which is singular, having its own beginning and end. For life is no uniform uninterrupted march or flow. It is a thing of histories, each with its own plot, its own inception and movement toward its close, each having its own particular rhythmic movement; each with its own unrepeated quality pervading it throughout. A flight of stairs, mechanical as it is, proceeds by individualized steps, not by undifferentiated progression, and an inclined plane is at least marked off from other things by abrupt discreteness.

Experience in this vital sense is defined by those situations and episodes that we spontaneously refer to as being "real experiences"; those things of which we say in recalling them, "that *was* an experience." It may have been something of tremendous importance—a quarrel with one who was once an intimate, a catastrophe finally averted by a hair's breadth. Or it may have been something that in comparison was slight—and which perhaps because of its very slightness illustrates all the better what is to be an experience. There is that meal in a Paris restaurant of which one says "that *was* an experience." It stands out as an enduring memorial of what food may be. Then there is that storm one went through in crossing the Atlantic—the storm that seemed in its fury, as it was experienced, to sum up in itself all that a storm can be, complete in itself, standing out because marked out from what went before and what came after.

In such experiences, every successive part flows freely, without seam and without unfilled blanks, into what ensues. At the same time there is no sacrifice of the self-identity of the parts. A river, as distinct from a pond, flows. But its flow gives a definiteness and interest to its successive portions greater than exist in the homogenous portions of a pond. In an experience, flow is from something to something. As one part leads into another and as one part carries on what went before, each gains distinctness in itself. The enduring whole is diversified by successive phases that are emphases of its varied colors.

Because of continuous merging, there are no holes, mechanical junctions, and dead centers when we have *an* experience. There are pauses, places of rest, but they punctuate and define the quality of movement. They sum up what has been undergone and prevent its dissipation and idle evaporation. Continued acceleration is breathless and prevents parts from gaining distinction. In a work of art, different acts, episodes, occurrences melt and fuse into unity, and yet do not disappear and lose their own character as they do so— just as in a genial conversation there is a continuous interchange and blending, and yet each speaker not only retains his own character but manifests it more clearly than is his wont.

An experience has a unity that gives it its name, *that* meal, that storm, that rupture of friendship. The existence of this unity is constituted by a single *quality* that pervades the entire experience in spite of the variation of its constituent parts. This unity is neither emotional, practical, nor intellectual, for these terms name distinctions that reflection can make within it. In discourse *about* an experience, we must make use of these adjectives of interpretation. In going over an experience in mind *after* its occurrence, we may find that one property rather than another was sufficiently dominant so that it characterizes the experience as a whole. There are absorbing inquiries and speculations which a scientific man and philosopher will recall as "experiences" in the emphatic sense. In final import they are intellectual. But in their actual occurrence they were emotional as well; they were purposive and volitional. Yet the experience was not a sum of these different characters; they were lost in it as distinctive traits. No thinker can ply his occupation save as he is lured and rewarded by total integral experiences that are intrinsically worth while. Without them he would never know what it is really to think and would be completely at a loss in distinguishing real thought from the spurious article. Thinking goes on in trains of ideas, but the ideas form a train only because they are much more than what an analytic psychology calls ideas. They are phases, emotionally and practically distinguished, of a developing underlying quality; they are its moving variations, not separate and independent like Locke's and Hume's so-called ideas and impressions, but are subtle shadings of a pervading and developing hue. . . .

Art denotes a process of doing or making. This is as true of fine as of technological art. Art involves molding of clay, chipping of marble, casting of bronze, laying on of pigments, construction of buildings, singing of songs, playing of instruments, enacting rôles on the stage, going through rhythmic movements in the dance. Every art does something with some physical material, the body or something outside the body, with or without the use of intervening tools, and with a view to production of something visible, audible, or tangible. So marked is the active or "doing" phase of art, that the dictionaries usually define it in terms of skilled action, ability in execution. The Oxford Dictionary illustrates by a quotation from John Stuart Mill: "Art is an endeavor after perfection in execution" while Matthew Arnold calls it "pure and flawless workmanship."

The word "esthetic" refers, as we have already noted, to experience as appreciative, perceiving, and enjoying. It denotes the consumer's rather than the producer's standpoint. It is Gusto, taste; and, as with cooking, overt skillful action is on the side of the cook who prepares, while taste is on the side of the consumer, as in gardening there is a distinction between the gardener who plants and tills and the householder who enjoys the finished product.

These very illustrations, however, as well as the relation that exists in having an experience between doing and undergoing, indicate that the distinction between esthetic and artistic cannot be pressed so far as to become a separation. Perfection in execution cannot be measured or defined in terms of execution; it implies those who perceive and enjoy the product that is executed. The cook prepares food for the consumer and the measure of the value of what is prepared is found in consumption. Mere perfection in execution, judged in its own terms in isolation, can probably be attained better by a machine than by human art. By itself, it is at most technique, and there are great artists who are not in the first ranks as technicians (witness Cézanne), just as there are great performers on the piano who are not great esthetically, and as Sargent is not a great painter.

Craftsmanship to be artistic in the final sense must be "loving"; it must care deeply for the subject matter upon which skill is exercised. A sculptor comes to mind whose busts are marvelously exact. It might be difficult to tell in the presence of a photograph of one of them and of a photograph of the original which was of the person himself. For virtuosity they are remarkable. But one doubts whether the maker of the busts had an experience of his own that he was concerned to have those share who look at his products. To be truly artistic, a work must also be esthetic—that is, framed for enjoyed receptive perception. Constant observation is, of course, necessary for the maker while he is producing. But if his perception is not also esthetic in nature, it is a colorless and cold recognition of what has been done, used as a stimulus to the next step in a process that is essentially mechanical.

In short, art, in its form, unites the very same relation of doing and undergoing, outgoing and incoming energy, that makes an experience to be an experience. Because of elimination of all that does not contribute to mutual organization of the factors of both action and reception into one another, and because of selection of just the aspects and traits that contribute to their interpenetration of each other, the product is a work of esthetic art. Man whittles, carves, sings, dances, gestures, molds, draws and paints. The doing or making is artistic when the perceived result is of such a nature that *its* qualities *as perceived* have controlled the question of production. The act of producing that is directed by intent to produce something that is enjoyed in the immediate experience of perceiving has qualities that a spontaneous or uncontrolled activity does not have. The artist embodies in himself the attitude of the perceiver while he works. . . .

THE EXPRESSIVE OBJECT

Expression, like construction, signifies both an action and its result. The last chapter considered it as an act. We are now concerned with the product, the object that is expressive, that says something to us. If the two meanings are separated, the object is viewed in isolation from the operation which produced it, and therefore apart from individuality of vision, since the act proceeds from an individual live creature. Theories which seize upon "expression," as if it denoted simply the object, always insist to the uttermost that the object of art is purely representative of other objects already in existence. They ignore the individual contribution which makes the object something new. They dwell upon its "universal" character, and upon its meaning—an ambiguous term, as we shall see. On the other hand, isolation of the act of expressing from the expressiveness possessed by the object leads to the notion that expression is merely a process of discharging personal emotion—the conception criticized in the last chapter.

The juice expressed by the wine press is what it is because of a prior act, and it is something new and distinctive. It does not merely represent other things. Yet it has something in common with other objects and it is made to appeal to other persons than the one who produced it. A poem and picture present material passed through the alembic of personal experience. They have no precedents in existence or in universal being. But, nonetheless, their material came from the public world and so has qualities in common with the material of other experiences, while the product awakens in other persons new perceptions of the meanings of the common world. The oppositions of individual and universal, of subjective and objective, of freedom and order, in which philosophers have reveled, have no place in the work of art. Expression as personal act and as objective result are organically connected with each other.

It is not necessary, therefore, to go into these metaphysical questions. We may approach the matter directly. What does it mean to say that a work of art is representative, since it must be representative in some sense if it is expressive? To say in general that a work of art is or is not representative is meaningless. For the word has many meanings. An affirmation of representative quality may be false in one sense and true in another. If literal reproduction is signified by "representative" then the work of art is not of that nature, for such a view ignores the uniqueness of the work due to the personal medium through which scenes and events have passed. Matisse said that the camera was a great boon to painters, since it relieved them from any apparent necessity of copying objects. But representation may also mean that the work of art tells something to those who enjoy it about the nature of their own experience of the world: that it presents the world in a new experience which they undergo.

A similar ambiguity attends the question of meaning in a work of art. Words are symbols which represent objects and actions in the sense of standing for them; in that sense they have meaning. A signboard has meaning when it says so many miles to such and such a place, with an arrow pointing the direction. But meaning in these two cases has a purely external reference; it stands for something by pointing to it. Meaning does not belong to the word and signboard of its own intrinsic right. They have meaning in the sense in which an algebraic formula or a cipher code has it. But there are other meanings that present themselves directly as possessions of objects which are experienced. Here there is no need for a code or convention of interpretation; the meaning is as inherent in immediate experience as is that of a flower garden. Denial of meaning to a work of art thus has two radically different significations. It may signify that a work of art has not the kind of meaning that belongs to signs and symbols in mathematics—a contention that is just. Or it may signify that the work of art is without meaning as nonsense is without it. The work of art certainly does not have that which is had by flags when used to signal another ship. But it does have that possessed by flags when they are used to decorate the deck of a ship for a dance.

Since there are presumably none who intend to assert that works of art are without meaning in the sense of being senseless, it might seem as if they simply intended to exclude external meaning, meaning that resides outside the work of art itself. Unfortunately, however, the case is not so simple. The denial of meaning to art usually rests upon the assumption that the kind of value (and meaning) that a work of art possesses is so unique that it is without community or connection with the contents of other modes of experience than the esthetic. It is, in short, another way of upholding what I have called the esoteric idea of fine art. The conception implied in the treatment of esthetic experience set forth in the previous chapters is, indeed, that the work of art has a unique *quality*, but that it is that of clarifying and concentrating meanings contained in scattered and weakened ways in the material of other experiences.

The problem in hand may be approached by drawing a distinction between expression and statement. Science states meanings; art expresses them. It is possible that this remark will itself illustrate the difference I have in mind better than will any amount of explanatory comment. Yet I venture upon some degree of amplification. The instance of a signboard may help. It directs one's course to a place, say a city. It does not in any way supply experience of that city even in a vicarious way. What it does do is to set forth some of the conditions that must be fulfilled in order to procure that experience. What holds in this instance may be generalized. Statement sets forth the conditions under which an experience of an object or situation may be had. It is a good, that is, effective, statement in the degree in which these conditions are stated in such a way that they can be used as *directions* by which one may arrive at the experience. It is a bad statement, confused and false, if it sets forth these conditions in such a way that when they are used as directions, they mislead or take one to the object in a wasteful way.

"Science" signifies just that mode of statement that is most helpful as direction. To take the old standard case—which science today seems bent upon modifying—the statement that water is H_2O is primarily a statement of the conditions under which water comes into existence. But it is also for those who understand it a direction for producing pure water and for testing anything that is likely to be taken for water. It is a "better" statement than popular and pre-scientific ones just because in stating the conditions for the existence of water comprehensively and exactly, it sets them forth in a way that gives direction concerning generation of water. Such, however, is the newness of scientific statement and its present prestige (due ultimately to its directive efficacy) that scientific statement is often thought to possess more than a signboard function and to disclose or be "expressive" of the inner nature of things. If it did, it would come into competition with art, and we should have to take sides and decide which of the two promulgates the more genuine revelation.

The poetic as distinct from the prosaic, esthetic art as distinct from scientific, expression as distinct from statement, does something different from leading to an experience. It constitutes one. A traveler who follows the statement or direction of a signboard finds himself in the city that has been pointed towards. He then may *have* in his own experience some of the meaning which the city possesses. We may have it to such an extent that the city has expressed itself to him—as Tintern Abbey expressed itself to Wordsworth in and through his poem. The city might, indeed, be trying to express itself in a celebration attended with pageantry and all other resources that would render its history and spirit perceptible. Then there is, if the visitor has himself the experience that permits him to participate, an expressive object, as different from the statements of a gazetteer, however full and correct they might be, as Wordsworth's poem is different from the account of Tintern Abbey given by an antiquarian. The poem, or painting, does not operate in the dimension of correct descriptive statement but in that of experience itself. Poetry and prose, literal photograph and painting, operate in different media to distinct ends. Prose is set forth in propositions. The logic of poetry is superpropositional even when it uses what are, grammatically speaking, propositions. The latter have intent; art is an immediate realization of intent. . . .

SUBSTANCE AND FORM

Because objects of art are expressive, they are a language. Rather they are many languages. For each art has its own medium and that medium is especially fitted for one kind of communication. Each medium says something that cannot be uttered as well or as completely in any other tongue. The needs of daily life have given superior practical importance to one mode of communication, that of speech. This fact has unfortunately given rise to a popular impression that the meanings expressed in architecture, sculpture, painting, and music can be translated into words with little if any loss. In fact, each art speaks an idiom that conveys what cannot be said in another language and yet remains the same.

Language exists only when it is listened to as well as spoken. The hearer is an indispensable partner. The work of art is complete only as it works in the experience of others than the one who created it. Thus language involves what logicians call a triadic relation. There is the speaker, the thing said, and the one spoken to. The external object, the product of art, is the connecting link between artist and audience. Even when the artist works in solitude all three terms are present. The work is there in progress, and the artist has to become vicariously the receiving audience. He can speak only as his work appeals to him as one spoken to through what he perceives. He observes and understands as a third person might note and interpret. Matisse is reported to have said: "When a painting is finished, it is like a new-born child. The artist himself must have time for understanding it." It must be lived with as a child is lived with, if we are to grasp the meaning of his being.

All language, whatever its medium, involves *what* is said and *how* it is said, or substance and form. The great question concerning substance and form is: Does matter come first ready-made, and search for a discovery of form in which to embody it come afterwards? Or is the whole creative effort of the artist an endeavor to form material so that it will be in actuality the authentic substance of a work of art? The question goes far and deep. The answer given it determines the issue of many other controverted points in esthetic criticism. Is there one esthetic value belonging to sense materials and another to a form that renders them expressive? Are all subjects fit for esthetic treatment or only a few which are set aside for that end by their intrinsically superior character? Is "beauty" another name for form descending from without, as a transcendent essence, upon material, or is it a name for the esthetic quality that appears whenever *material is formed* in a way that renders it adequately expressive? Is form, in its esthetic sense, something that uniquely marks off as esthetic from the beginning a certain realm of objects, or is it the abstract name for what emerges whenever an experience attains complete development?

All of these questions have been implicit in the discussions of the three previous chapters, and by implication have been answered. If an art product is taken to be one of *self*-expression and the self is regarded as something complete and self-contained in isolation, then of course substance and form fall apart. That in which a self-revelation is clothed, is, by the underlying assumption, external to the things expressed. The externality persists no matter which of the two is regarded as form and which as substance. It is also clear that if there be *no* self-expression, no free play of individuality, the product will of necessity be but an instance of a species; it will lack the freshness and originality found only in things that are individual on their own account. Here is a point from which the relation of form and substance may be approached.

The *material* out of which a work of art is composed belongs to the common world rather than to the self, and yet there is self-expression in art because the self assimilates that material in a distinctive way to reissue it into the public world in a form that builds a new object. This new object may have as its consequence similar reconstructions, recreations, of old and common material on the part of those who perceive it, and thus in time come to be established as part of the acknowledged world—as "universal." The material expressed cannot be private; that is the state of the mad-house. But the *manner* of saying it is individual, and, if the product is to be a work of art, induplicable. Identity of mode of production defines the work of a machine, the esthetic counterpart of which is the academic. The quality of a work of *art* is *sui generis* because the manner in which general material is rendered transforms it into a substance that is fresh and vital.

What is true of the producer is true of the perceiver. He may perceive academically, looking for identities with which he already is familiar; or learnedly, pedantically, looking for material to fit into a history or article he wishes to write, or sentimentally for illustrations of some theme emotionally dear. But if he perceives esthetically, he will create an experience of which the intrinsic subject matter, the substance, is new. An English critic, Mr. A. C. Bradley, has said that "poetry being poems, we are to think of a poem as it actually exists; and an actual poem is a succession of experiences—sounds, images, thought—through which we pass when we read a poem. . . . A poem exists in unnumberable degrees." And it also true that it exists in unnumberable qualities or kinds, no two readers having exactly the same experience, according to the "forms," or manners of response brought to it. A new poem is created by every one who reads poetically—not that its *raw* material is original for, after all, we live in the same old world, but that every individual brings with him, when he exercises his individuality, a way of seeing and feeling that in its interaction with old material creates something new, something previously not existing in experience.

A work of art no matter how old and classic is actually, not just potentially, a work of art only when it lives in some individualized experience. As a piece of parchment, of marble, of canvas, it remains (subject to the ravages of time) self-identical throughout the ages. But as a work of art, it is recreated every time it is esthetically experienced. No one doubts this fact in the rendering of a musical score; no one supposes that the lines and dots on paper are more than the recorded means of evoking the work of art. But what is true of it is equally true of the Parthenon as a building. It is absurd to ask what an artist "really" meant by his product; he himself would find different meanings in it at different days and hours and in different stages of his own development. If he could be articulate, he would say "I meant just *that*, and *that* means whatever you or any one can honestly, that is in virtue of your own vital experience, get out of it." Any other idea makes the boasted "universality" of the work of art a synonym for monotonous identity. The Parthenon, or whatever, is universal because it can continuously inspire new personal realizations in experience.

It is simply an impossibility that any one today should experience the Parthenon as the devout Athenian contemporary citizen experienced it, any more than the religious statuary of the twelfth century can mean, esthetically, even to a good Catholic today just what it meant to the worshippers of the old period. The "works" that fail to become *new* are not those which are universal but those which are "dated." The enduring art-product may have been, and probably was, called forth by something occasional, something having its own date and place. But *what* was evoked is a substance so formed that it can enter into the experiences of others and enable them to have more intense and more fully rounded out experiences of their own.

This is what it is to have form. It marks a way of envisaging, of feeling, and of presenting experienced matter so that it most readily and effectively becomes material for the construction of adequate experience on the part of those less gifted than the original creator. Hence there can be no distinction drawn, save in reflection, between form and substance. The work itself *is* matter formed into esthetic substance. The critic, the theorist, as a reflective student of the art product, however, not only may but must draw a distinction between them. Any skilled observer of a pugilist or a golf-player will, I suppose, institute distinctions between *what* is done and *how* it is done—between the knockout and the manner of the delivery of a blow; between the ball driven so many yards to such and such a line and the way the drive was executed. The artist, the one engaged in doing, will effect a similar distinction when he is interested in correcting an habitual error, or learning how better to secure a given effect. Yet the act itself is exactly *what* it is because of *how* it is done. In the act there is no distinction, but perfect integration of manner and content, form and substance. . . .

The undefined pervasive quality of an experience is that which binds together all the defined elements, the objects of which we are focally aware, making them a whole. The best evidence that such is the case is our constant sense of things as belonging or not belonging, of relevancy, a sense which is immediate. It cannot be a product of reflection, even though it requires reflection to find out whether some particular consideration is pertinent to what we are doing or thinking. For unless the sense were immediate, we should have no guide to our reflection. The sense of an extensive and underlying whole is the context of every experience and it is the essence of sanity. For the mad, the insane, thing to us is that which is torn from the common context and which stands alone and isolated, as anything must which occurs in a world totally different from ours. Without an indeterminate and undetermined setting, the material of any experience is incoherent.

A work of art elicits and accentuates this quality of being a whole and of belonging to the larger, all-inclusive, whole which is the universe in which we live. This fact, I think, is the explanation of that feeling of exquisite intelligibility and clarity we have in the presence of an object that is experienced with esthetic intensity. It explains also the religious feeling that accompanies intense esthetic perception. We are, as it were, introduced into a world beyond this world which is nevertheless the deeper reality of the world in which we live in our ordinary experiences. We are carried out beyond ourselves to find ourselves. I can see no psychological ground for such properties of an experience save that, somehow, the work of art operates to deepen and to raise to great clarity that sense of an enveloping undefined whole that accompanies every normal experience. This whole is then felt as an expansion of ourselves. For only one frustrated in a particular object of desire upon which he had staked himself, like Macbeth, finds that life is a tale told by an idiot, full of sound and fury, signifying nothing. Where egotism is not made the measure of reality and value, we are citizens of this vast world beyond ourselves, and any intense realization of its presence with and in us brings a peculiarly satisfying sense of unity in itself and with ourselves. . . .

The Common Substance of the Arts

. . . Every work of art has a particular medium by which, among other things, the qualitative pervasive whole is carried. In every experience we touch the world through some particular tentacle; we carry on our intercourse with it, it comes home to us, through a specialized organ. The entire organism with all its charge of the past and varied resources operates through a particular medium, that of eye, as it interacts with eye, ear, and touch. The fine arts lay hold of this fact and push it to its maximum of significance. In any ordinary visual perception, we see by means of light; we distinguish by means of reflected and refracted colors: that is a truism. But in ordinary perceptions, this medium of color is mixed, adulterated. While we see, we also hear; we feel pressures, and heat or cold. In a painting, color renders the scene without these alloys and impurities. They are part of the dross that is squeezed out and left behind in an act of intensified expression. The medium becomes color alone, and since color alone must now carry the qualities of movement, touch, sound, etc., that are present physically on their own account in ordinary vision, the expressiveness and energy of color are enhanced.

Photographs to primitive folk have, so it is said, a fearful magical quality. It is uncanny that solid and living things should be thus presented. There is evidence that when pictures of any kind first made their appearance, magical power was imputed to them. Their power of representation could come only from a supernatural source. To one who is not rendered callous by common contact with pictorial representations there is still something miraculous in the power of a contracted, flat, uniform thing to depict the wide and diversified universe of animate and inanimate things: it is possibly for this reason that popularly "art" tends to denote painting, and "artist" one who paints. Primitive man also imputed to sounds when used as words the power to control supernaturally the acts and secrets of men and to command, provided the right word was there, the forces of nature. The power of mere sounds to express in literature all events and objects is equally marvelous.

Such facts as these seem to me to suggest the role and significance of media for art. At first sight, it seems a fact not worth recording that every art has a medium of its own. Why put it down in black and white that painting cannot exist without color, music without sound, architecture without stone and wood, statuary without marble and bronze, literature without words, dancing without the living body? The answer has, I believe, been indicated. In every experience, there is the pervading underlying qualitative whole that corresponds to and manifests the whole organization of activities which constitute the mysterious human frame. But in every experience, this complex, this differentiated and recording, mechanism operates through special structures that take the lead, not in dispersed diffusion through all organs at once—save in panic when, as we truly say, one has lost one's *head*. "Medium" in fine art denotes the fact that this specialization and individualization of a particular organ of experience is carried to the point wherein all its possibilities are exploited. The eye or ear that is centrally active does not lose its specific character and its special fitness as the bearer of an experience that it uniquely makes possible. In art, the seeing or hearing that is dispersed and mixed in ordinary perceptions is concentrated until the peculiar office of the special medium operates with full energy, free from distraction.

"Medium" signifies first of all an intermediary. The import of the word "means" is the same. They are the middle, the intervening, things through which something now remote is brought to pass. Yet not all means are media. There are two kinds of means. One kind is external to that which is accomplished; the other kind is taken up into the consequences produced and remains immanent in them. There are ends which are merely welcome cessations and there are ends that are fulfillments of what went before. The toil of a laborer is too often only an antecedent to the wage he receives, as consumption of gasoline is merely a means to transportation. The means cease to act when the "end" is reached; one would be glad, as a rule, to get the result without having to employ the means. They are but a scaffolding.

Such external or *mere* means, as we properly term them, are usually of such a sort that others can be substituted for them; the particular ones employed are determined by some extraneous consideration, like cheapness. But the moment we say "media," we refer to means that are incorporated in the outcome. Even bricks and mortar become a part of the house they are employed to build; they are not mere means to its erection. Colors *are* the painting; tones are the music. A picture painted with water colors has a quality different from that painted with oil. Esthetic effects belong intrinsically to their medium; when another medium is substituted, we have a stunt rather than an object of art. Even when substitution is practiced with the utmost virtuosity or for any reason outside the kind of end desired, the product is mechanical or a tawdry sham—like boards painted to resemble stone in the construction of a cathedral, for stone is integral not just physically, but to the esthetic effect.

The difference between external and intrinsic operations runs through all the affairs of life. One student studies to pass an examination, to get promotion. To another, the means, the activity of learning, is completely one with what results from it. The consequence, instruction, illumination, is one with the process. Sometimes we journey to get somewhere else because we have business at the latter point and would gladly, were it possible, cut out the traveling. At other times we journey for the delight of moving about and seeing what we see. Means and end coalesce. If we run over in mind a number of such cases we quickly see that all the cases in which means and ends are external to one another are non-esthetic. This externality may even be regarded as a definition of the non-esthetic.

Being "good" for the sake of avoiding penalty, whether it be going to jail or to hell, makes conduct unlovely. It is as anesthetic as is going to the dentist's chair so as to avoid a lasting injury. When the Greeks identified the good and beautiful in actions, they revealed, in their feeling of grace and proportion in right conduct, a perception of fusion of means and ends. The adventures of a pirate have at least a romantic attraction lacking in the painful acquisitions of him who stays within the law merely because he thinks it pays better in the end to do so. A large part of popular revulsion against utilitarianism in moral theory is because of its exaggeration of sheer calculation. "Decorum" and "propriety" which once had a favorable, because esthetic, meaning are taking on a disparaging signification because they are understood to denote a primness or smugness assumed because of desire for an external end. In all ranges of experience, externality of means defines the mechanical. Much of what is termed spiritual is also unesthetic. But the unesthetic quality is because the things denoted by the word also exemplify separation of means and end; the "ideal" is so cut off from the realities, by which alone it can be striven for, that it is vapid. The "spiritual" gets a local habitation and achieves the solidity of form required for esthetic quality only when it is embodied in a sense of actual things. Even angels have to be provided in imagination with bodies and wings.

I have referred more than once to the esthetic quality that may inhere in scientific work. To the layman the material of the scientist is usually forbidding. To the inquirer there exists a fulfilling and consummatory quality, for conclusions sum up and perfect the conditions that lead up to them. Moreover, they have at times an elegant and even austere form. It is said that Clark Maxwell once introduced a symbol in order to make a physical equation symmetrical, and that it was only later that experimental results gave the symbol its meaning. I suppose that it is also true that if business men were the mere money-grubbers they are often supposed to be by the unsympathetic outsider, business would be much less attractive than it is. In practice, it may take on the properties of a game, and even when it is socially harmful it must have an esthetic quality to those whom it captivates.

Means are, then, media when they are not just preparatory or preliminary. As a medium, color is a go-between for the values weak and dispersed in ordinary experiences and the new concentrated perception occasioned by a painting. A phonographic disk is a vehicle of an effect and nothing more. The music which issues from it is also a vehicle but is something more; it is a vehicle which becomes one with what it carries; it coalesces with what it conveys. Physically, a brush and the movement of the hand in applying color to canvas are external to a painting. Not so artistically. Brush-strokes are an integral part of the esthetic effect of a painting when it is perceived. Some philosophers have put forth the idea that esthetic effect or beauty is a kind of ethereal essence which, in accommodation to flesh, is compelled to use external sensuous material as a vehicle. The doctrine implies that were not the soul imprisoned in the body, pictures would exist without colors, music without sounds, and literature without words. Except, however, for critics who tell us how they feel without telling or knowing in terms of media used *why* they feel as they do, and except for persons who identify gush with appreciation, media and esthetic effect are completely fused.

Sensitivity to a medium as a medium is the very heart of all artistic creation and esthetic perception. Such sensitiveness does not lug in extraneous material. When, for example, paintings are looked at as illustrations of historical scenes, of literature, of familiar scenes, they are not perceived in terms of their media. Or, when they are looked at simply with reference to the technic employed in making them what they are, they are not esthetically perceived. For here, too, means, are separated from ends. Analysis of the former becomes a substitute for enjoyment of the latter. It is true that artists seem themselves often to approach a work of art from an exclusively technical standpoint—and the outcome is at least refreshing after having had a dose of what is regarded as "appreciation." But in reality, for the most part, they so feel the whole that it is not necessary to dwell upon the end, the whole, in words, and so they are freed to consider how the latter is produced. . . .

THE CHALLENGE TO PHILOSOPHY

Esthetic experience is imaginative. This fact, in connection with a false idea of the nature of imagination, has obscured the larger fact that all *conscious* experience has of necessity some degree of imaginative quality. For while the roots of every experience are found in the interaction of a live creature with its environment, that experience becomes conscious, a matter of perception, only when meanings enter it that are derived from prior experiences. Imagination is the only gateway through which these meanings can find their way into a present interaction; or rather, as we have just seen, the conscious adjustment of the new and the old *is* imagination. Interaction of a living being with an environment is found in vegetative and animal life. But the experience enacted is human and conscious only as that which is given here and now is extended by meanings and values drawn from what is absent in fact and present only imaginatively.

There is always a gap between the here and now of direct interaction and the past interactions whose funded result constitutes the meanings with which we grasp and understand what is now occurring. Because of this gap, all conscious perception involves a risk; it is a venture into the unknown, for as it assimilates the present to the past it also brings about some reconstruction of that past. When past and present fit exactly into one another, when there is only recurrence, complete uniformity, the resulting experience is routine and mechanical; it does not come to consciousness in perception. The inertia of habit overrides adaption of the meaning of the here and now with that of experiences, without which there is no consciousness, the imaginative phase of experience.

Mind, that is the body of organized meanings by means of which events of the present have significance for us, does not always enter into the activities and undergoings that are going on here and now. Sometimes it is baffled and arrested. Then the stream of meanings aroused into activity by the present contact remain aloof. Then it forms the matter of reverie, of dream; ideas are floating, not anchored to any existence as its property, its possession of meanings. Emotions that are equally loose and floating cling to these ideas. The pleasure they afford is the reason why they are entertained and are allowed to occupy the scene; they are attached to existence only in a way that, as long as sanity abides, is felt to be only fanciful and unreal.

In every work of art, however, these meanings are actually embodied in a material which thereby becomes the medium for their expression. This fact constitutes the peculiarity of all experience that is definitely esthetic. Its imaginative quality dominates, because meanings and values that are wider and deeper than the particular here and now in which they are anchored are realized by way of *expressions* although not by way of an object that is physically efficacious in relation to other objects. Not even a useful object is produced except by the intervention of imagination. Some existent material was perceived in the light of relations and possibilities not hitherto realized when the steam engine was invented. But when the imagined possibilities were embodied in a new assemblage of natural materials, the steam engine took its place in nature as an object that has the same physical effects as those belonging to any other physical object. Steam did the physical work and produced the consequences that attend any expanding gas under definite physical conditions. The sole difference is that the conditions under which it operates have been arranged by human contrivance.

The work of art, however, unlike the machine, is not only the outcome of imagination, but operates imaginatively rather than in the realm of physical existences. What it does is to concentrate and enlarge an immediate experience. The formed matter of esthetic experience directly *expresses*, in other words, the meanings that are imaginatively evoked; it does not, like the material brought into new relations in a machine, merely provide *means* by which purposes over and beyond the existence of the object may be executed. And yet the meanings imaginatively summoned, assembled, and integrated are embodied in material existence that here and now interacts with the self. The work of art is thus a challenge to the performance of a like act of evocation and organization, through imagination, on the part of the one who experiences it. It is not just a stimulus to and means of an overt course of action.

This fact constitutes the uniqueness of esthetic experience, and this uniqueness is in turn a challenge to thought. It is particularly a challenge to that systematic thought called philosophy. For esthetic experience is experience in its integrity. Had not the term "pure" been so often abused in philosophic literature, had it not been so often employed to suggest that there is something alloyed, impure, in the very nature of experience and to denote something beyond experience, we might say that esthetic experience is pure experience. For it is experience freed from the forces that impede and confuse its development as experience; freed, that is, from factors that subordinate an experience as it is directly had to something beyond itself. To esthetic experience, then, the philosopher must go to understand what experience is.

For this reason, while the theory of esthetics put forth by a philosopher is incidentally a test of the capacity of its author to have the experience that is the subject-matter of his analysis, it is also much more than that. It is a test of the capacity of the system he puts forth to grasp the nature of experience itself. There is no test that so surely reveals the one-sidedness of a philosophy as its treatment of art and esthetic experience. Imaginative vision is the power that unifies all the constituents of the matter of a work of art, making a whole out of them in all their variety. Yet all the elements of our being that are displayed in special emphases and partial realizations in other experiences are merged in esthetic experience. And they are so completely merged in the immediate wholeness of the experience that each is submerged;—it does not present itself in consciousness as a distinct element.

Yet philosophies of esthetics have often set out from one factor that plays a part in the constitution of experience, and have attempted to interpret or "explain" the esthetic experience by a single element; in terms of sense, emotion, reason, of activity; imagination itself is viewed not as that which holds all other elements in solution but as a special faculty. The philosophies of esthetics are many and diverse. It is impossible to give even a résumé of them in a chapter. But criticism has a clew that, if it is followed, furnishes a sure guide through the labyrinth. We can ask what element, in the formation of experience, each system has taken as central and characteristic. If we start from this point, we find that theories fall of themselves into certain types, and that the particular strand of experience that is offered reveals, when it is placed in contrast with esthetic experience itself, the weakness of the theory. For it is shown that the system in question has superimposed some preconceived idea upon experience instead of encouraging or even allowing esthetic experience to tell its own tale.

SUSANNE LANGER

IN THE MIDDLE OF THE CENTURY, Susanne Langer developed a remarkable and influential theory of art, suggesting that an enriched theory of symbols could explain the nature of expression in art. In her earlier work, *Philosophy in a New Key*, Langer develops a theory of music as a presentational symbol, contrasting such a symbol with the discursive symbols of language and propositional thought. In her later work, especially *Feeling and Form*, she broadens the theory to the other arts, developing the notion of art as a symbol of the forms of feeling.

The most striking feature of Langer's theory, making it fascinating if implausible, is her suggestion that art symbolizes forms of feeling and that there is a close parallel between the different arts and the fundamental forms of feeling. Langer's theory offers an explanation as no other theory can of why we have the arts we do: Each art expresses a particular form of feeling, and the forms of feeling can be given a definite taxonomy.

SUSANNE LANGER

Feeling and Form*

THE SYMBOL OF FEELING

. . . The tonal structures we call "music" bear a close logical similarity to the forms of human feeling—forms of growth and of attenuation, flowing and slowing, conflict and resolution, speed, arrest, terrific excitement, calm, or subtle activation and dreamy lapses—not joy and sorrow perhaps, but the poignancy of either and both—the greatness and brevity and eternal passing of everything vitally felt. Such is the pattern, or logical form, of sentience; and the pattern of music is that same form worked out in pure, measured sound and silence. Music is a tonal analogue of emotive life.

Such formal analogy, or congruence of logical structures, is the prime requisite for the relation between a symbol and whatever it is to mean. The symbol and the object symbolized must have some common logical form.

But purely on the basis of formal analogy, there would be no telling which of two congruent structures was the symbol and which the meaning, since the relation of congruence, or formal likeness, is symmetrical, i.e. it works both ways. (If John looks so much like James that you can't tell him from James, then you can't tell James from John, either.) There must be a motive for choosing, as between two entities or two systems, one to be the symbol of the other. Usually the decisive reason is that one is easier to perceive and handle than the other. Now sounds are much easier to produce, combine, perceive, and identify, than feelings. Forms of sentience occur only

---

* Susanne K. Langer, *Feeling and Form: A Theory of Art* (New York: Scribner, 1953), pp. 27-32, 46-48, 72, 73, 87-89, 98-101, 102-103, 109-111, 125-126. (Footnotes omitted.)

222

in the course of nature, but musical forms may be invented and intoned at will. Their general patterns may be reincarnated again and again by repeated performance. The effect is actually never quite the same even though the physical repetition may be exact, as in recorded music, because the exact degree of one's familiarity with a passage affects the experience of it, and this factor can never be made permanent. Yet within a fairly wide range such variations are, happily, unimportant. To some musical forms even much less subtle changes are not really disturbing, for instance certain differences of instrumentation and even, within limits, of pitch or tempo. To others, they are fatal. But in the main, sound is a negotiable medium, capable of voluntary composition and repetition, whereas feeling is not; this trait recommends tonal structures for symbolic purposes.

Furthermore, a symbol is used to articulate ideas of something we wish to think about, and until we have a fairly adequate symbolism we cannot think about it. So *interest* always plays a major part in making one thing, or realm of things, the meaning of something else, the symbol or system of symbols.

Sound, as a sheer sensory factor in experience, may be soothing or exciting, pleasing or torturing; but so are the factors of taste, smell, and touch. Selecting and exploiting such somatic influences is self-indulgence, a very different thing from art. An enlightened society usually has some means, public or private, to support its artists, because their work is regarded as a spiritual triumph and a claim to greatness for the whole tribe. But mere epicures would hardly achieve such fame. Even chefs, perfumers, and upholsterers, who produce the means of sensory pleasure for others, are not rated as the torchbearers of culture and inspired creators. Only their own advertisements bestow such titles on them. If music, patterned sound, had no other office than to stimulate and soothe our nerves, pleasing our ears as well-combined foods please our palates, it might be highly popular, but never culturally important. Its historic development would be too trivial a subject to engage many people in its lifelong study, though a few desperate Ph.D. theses might be wrung from its anecdotal past under the rubric of "social history." And music conservatories would be properly rated exactly like cooking schools.

Our interest in music arises from its intimate relation to the all-important life of feeling, whatever that relation may be. After much debate on current theories, the conclusion reached in *Philosophy in a New Key* is that the function of music is not stimulation of feeling, but expression of it; and furthermore, not the symptomatic expression of feelings that beset the composer but a symbolic expression of the forms of sentience as he understands them. It bespeaks his imagination of feelings rather than his own emotional state, and expresses what he *knows about* the so-called "inner life"; and this may exceed his personal case, because music is a symbolic form to him through which he may learn as well as utter ideas of human sensibility.

There are many difficulties involved in the assumption that music is a symbol, because we are so deeply impressed with the paragon of symbolic form, namely language, that we naturally carry its characteristics over into our conceptions and expectations of any other mode. Yet music is not a kind of language. Its significance is really something different from what is traditionally and properly called "meaning." Perhaps the logicians and positivistic philosophers who have objected to the term "implicit meaning," on the ground that "meaning" properly so-called is always explicable, definable, and translatable, are prompted by a perfectly rational desire to keep so difficult a term free from any further entanglements and sources of confusion; and if this can be done without barring the concept itself which I have designated as "implicit meaning," it certainly seems the part of wisdom to accept their strictures.

Probably the readiest way to understand the precise nature of musical symbolization is to consider the characteristics of language and then, by comparison and contrast, note the different structure of music, and the consequent differences and similarities between the respective functions of those two logical forms. Because the prime purpose of language is discourse, the conceptual framework that has developed under its influence is known as "discursive reason." Usually, when one speaks of "reason" at all, one tacitly assumes its discursive pattern. But in a broader sense any appreciation of form, any awareness of patterns in experience, is "reason"; and discourse with all its refinements (e.g. mathematical symbolism, which is an extension of language) is only one possible pattern. For practical communication, scientific knowledge, and philosophical thought it is the only instrument we have. But on just that account there are whole domains of experience that philosophers deem "ineffable." If those domains appear to anyone the most important, that person is naturally inclined to condemn philosophy and science as barren and false. To such an evaluation one is entitled; not, however, to the claim of a better way to philosophical truth through instinct, intuition, feeling, or what have you. Intuition is the basic process of all understanding, just as operative in discursive thought as in clear sense perception and immediate judgment; there will be more to say about that presently. But it is no substitute for discursive logic in the making of any theory, contingent or transcendental.

The difference between discursive and non-discursive logical forms, their respective advantages and limitations, and their consequent symbolic uses have already been discussed in the previous book, but because the theory, there developed, of music as a symbolic form is our starting point here for a whole philosophy of art, the underlying semantic principles should perhaps be explicitly recalled first.

In language, which is the most amazing symbolic system humanity has invented, separate words are assigned to separately conceived items in experience on a basis of simple, one-to-one correlation. A word that is not composite (made of two or more independently meaningful vocables, such as "omni-potent," "com-posite") may be assigned to mean any object *taken as one.* We may even, by fiat, take a word like "omnipotent," and regarding it as one, assign it a connotation that is not composite, for instance by naming a race horse "Omnipotent." Thus Praisegod Barbon ("Barebones") was an indivisible being although his name is a composite word. He had a brother called "If-Christ-had-not-come-into-the-world-thou-wouldst-have-been-damned." The simple correlation between a name and its bearer held here between a whole sentence taken as one word and an object to which it was arbitrarily assigned. Any symbol that names something is "taken as one"; so is the object. A "crowd" is a lot of people, but *taken as a lot,* i.e. as one crowd.

So long as we correlate symbols and concepts in this simple fashion we are free to pair them as we like. A word or mark used arbitrarily to denote or connote something may be called an associative symbol, for its meaning depends entirely on association. As soon, however, as words taken to denote different things are used in combination, something is expressed by the way they are combined. The whole complex is a symbol, because the combination of words brings their connotations irresistibly together in a complex, too, and this complex of ideas is analogous to the word-complex. To anyone who knows the meanings of all the constituent words in the name of Praisegod's brother, the name is likely to sound absurd, because it is a sentence. The concepts associated with the words form a complex concept, the parts of which are related in a pattern analogous to the word-pattern. Word-meanings and grammatical forms, or rules for word-using, may be freely assigned; but once they are accepted, propositions emerge automatically as the meanings of sentences. One may say that the elements of propositions are *named* by words, but propositions themselves are *articulated* by sentences.

A complex symbol such as a sentence, or a map (whose outlines correspond formally to the vastly greater outlines of a country), or a graph (analogous, perhaps, to invisible conditions, the rise and fall of prices, the progress of an epidemic) is an *articulate form.* Its characteristic symbolic function is what I call *logical expression.* It expresses relations; and it may "mean"—connote or denote—any complex of elements that is of the same articulate form as the symbol, the form which the symbol "expresses."

Music, like language, is an articulate form. Its parts not only fuse together to yield a greater entity, but in so doing they maintain some degree of separate existence, and the sensuous character of each element is affected by its function in the complex whole. This means that the greater entity we call a composition is not merely produced by mixture, like a new color made by mixing paints, but is *articulated,* i.e. its internal structure is given to our perception.

Why, then, is it not a *language* of feeling, as it has often been called? Because its elements are not words—independent associative symbols with a reference fixed by convention. Only as an articulate form is it found to fit anything; and since there is no meaning assigned to any of its parts, it lacks one of the basic characteristics of language—fixed association, and therewith a single, unequivocal reference. We are always free to fill its subtle articulate forms with any meaning that fits them; that is, it may convey an idea of anything conceivable in its logical image. So, although we do receive it as a significant form, and comprehend the processes of life and sentience through its audible, dynamic pattern, it is not a language, because it has no vocabulary.

Perhaps, in the same spirit of strict nomenclature, one really should not refer to its content as "meaning," either. Just as music is only loosely and inexactly called a language, so its symbolic function is only loosely called meaning, because the factor of conventional reference is missing from it. In *Philosophy in a New Key* music was called an "unconsummated" symbol. But meaning, in the usual sense recognized in semantics, includes the condition of conventional reference, or consummation of the symbolic relationship. Music has *import,* and this import is the pattern of sentience—the pattern of life itself, as it is felt and directly known.

Let us therefore call the significance of music its "vital import" instead of "meaning," using "vital" not as a vague laudatory term, but as a qualifying adjective restricting the relevance of "import" to the dynamism of subjective experience.

So much, then, for the theory of music; music is "significant form," and its significance is that of a symbol, a highly articulated sensuous object, which by virtue of its dynamic structure can express the forms of vital experience which language is peculiarly unfit to convey. Feeling, life, motion and emotion constitute its import.

Here, in rough outline, is the special theory of music which may, I believe, be generalized to yield a theory of art as such. The basic concept is the articulate but non-discursive form of having import without conventional reference, and therefore presenting itself not as a symbol in the ordinary sense, but as a "significant form," in which the factor of significance is not logically discriminated, but is felt as a quality rather than recognized as a function. If this basic concept be applicable to all products of what we call "the arts," i.e. if all works of art may be regarded as significant forms in exactly the same sense as musical works, then all the essential propositions in the theory of music may be extended to the other arts, for they all define or elucidate the nature of the symbol and its import. . . .

SEMBLANCE

. . . What is "created" in a work of art? More than people generally realize when they speak of "being creative," or refer to the characters in a novel as the author's "creations." More than a delightful combination of sensory elements; far more than any reflection or "interpretation" of objects, people, events—the figments that artists *use* in their demiurgic work, and that have made some aestheticians refer to such work as "re-creation" rather than genuine creation. But an object that already exists—a vase of flowers, a living person—cannot be re-created. It would have to be destroyed to be re-created. Besides, a picture is neither a person nor a vase of flowers. It is an image, created for the first time out of things that are not imaginal, but quite realistic—canvas or paper, and paints or carbon or ink.

It is natural enough, perhaps, for naive reflection to center first of all round the relationship between an image and its object; and equally natural to treat a picture, statue, or a graphic description as an imitation of reality. The surprising thing is that long after art theory had passed the naive stage, and every serious thinker realized that imitation was neither the aim nor the measure of artistic creation, the traffic of the image with its model kept its central place among philosophical problems of art. It has figured as the question of form and content, of interpretation, of idealization, of belief and make-believe, and of impression and expression. Yet the idea of copying nature is not even applicable to all the arts. What does a building copy? On what given object does one model a melody?

A problem that will not die after philosophers have condemned it as irrelevant has still a gadfly mission in the intellectual world. Its significance merely is bigger, in fact, than any of its formulations. So here: the philosophical issue that is usually conceived in terms of image and object is really concerned with the nature of images as such and their essential difference from actualities. The difference is functional; consequently real objects, functioning in a way that is normal for images, may assume a purely imaginal status. That is why the character of an illusion may cling to works of art that do not represent anything. Imitation of other things is not the essential power of images, though it is a very important one by virtue of which the whole problem of fact and fiction originally came into the compass of our philosophical thought. But the true power of the image lies in the fact that it is an abstraction, a symbol, the bearer of an idea.

How can a work of art that does not represent anything—a building, a pot, a patterned textile—be called an image? It becomes an image when it presents itself purely to our vision, i.e. as a sheer visual form instead of a locally and practically related object. If we receive it as a completely visual thing, we abstract its appearance from its material existence. What we see in this way becomes simply a thing of vision—a form, an image. It detaches itself from its actual setting and acquires a different context.

An image in this sense, something that exists only for perception, abstracted from the physical and causal order, is the artist's creation. The image presented on a canvas is not a new "thing" among the things in the studio. The canvas was there, the paints were there; the painter has not added to them. Some excellent critics, and painters too, speak of his "arranging" forms and colors, and regard the resultant work primarily as an "arrangement." Whistler seems to have thought in these terms about his paintings. But even the forms are not phenomena in the order of actual things, as spots on a tablecloth are; the forms in a design—no matter how abstract—have a *life* that does not belong to mere spots. Something arises from the process of arranging colors on a surface, something that is created, not just gathered and set in a new order: that is the image. It emerges suddenly from the disposition of the pigments, and with its advent the very existence of the canvas and of the paint "arranged" on it seems to be abrogated; those actual objects become difficult to perceive in their own right. A new appearance has superseded their natural aspect.

An image is, indeed, a purely virtual "object." Its importance lies in the fact that we do not use it to guide us to something tangible and practical, but treat it as a complete entity with only visual attributes and relations. It has no others; its visible character is its entire being. . . .

VIRTUAL SPACE

. . . When the spatial experience of everyday life is refined by the precision and artifice of science, space becomes a coordinate in mathematical functions. It is never an entity. How, then, can it be "organized," "shaped," or "articulated"? We meet all these terms in the most serious literature of aesthetics.

The answer is, I think, that the space in which we live and act is not what is treated in art at all. The harmoniously organized space in a picture is not experiential space, known by sight and touch, by free motion and restraint, far and near sounds, voices lost or re-echoed. It is an entirely visual affair; for touch and hearing and muscular action it does not exist. For them there is a flat canvas, relatively small, or a cool blank wall, where for the eye there is deep space full of shapes. This purely visual space is an illusion, for our sensory experiences do not agree on it in their report. Pictorial space is not only organized by means of color (including black and white and the gamut of grays between them), it is created; without the organizing shapes it is simply not there. Like the space "behind" the surface of a mirror, it is what the physicists call "virtual space"—an intangible image.

This virtual space is the primary illusion of all plastic art. Every element of design, every use of color and semblance of shape, serves to produce and support and develop the picture space that exists for vision alone. Being only visual, this space has no continuity with the space in which we live; it is limited by the frame, or by surrounding blanks, or incongruous other things that cut it off. Yet its limits cannot even be said to *divide* it from practical space; for a boundary that divides things always connects them as well, and between the picture space and any other space there is no connection. The created virtual space is entirely self-contained and independent. . . .

Everything that is relevant and artistically valid in a picture must be visual; and everything visual serves architectonic purposes. Where in practical life we employ other faculties than sight to complete our fragmentary visual experiences—for instance memory, recorded measurements, beliefs about the physical constitution of things, knowledge of their relations in space even when they are behind us or blocked by other things—in the virtual space of a picture there are no such supporting data. Everything that is given at all is given to vision; therefore we must have *visual substitutes* for the things that are normally known by touch, movement or inference. That is why a direct copy of what we see is not enough. The copy of things seen would need the same supplementation from non-visual sources that the original perception demanded. The visual substitutes for the non-visible ingredients in space experience make the great difference between photographic rendering and creative rendering; the latter is necessarily a departure from direct imitation, because it is a construction of spatial entities out of color alone (perhaps only varying shades of one color), by all sorts of devices in order to present at once, with complete authority, the primary illusion of a perfectly visible and perfectly intelligible total space. . . .

The Modes of Virtual Space

. . . In the realm of sculpture the role of illusion seems less important than in painting, where a flat surface "creates" a three-dimensional space that is obviously virtual. Sculpture is actually three-dimensional; in what sense does it "create" space for the eye? This is probably the question which led Hildebrand to say that the sculptor's task was to present a three-dimensional object in the two-dimensional picture plane of "perceptual space." But the answer, though it satisfies and, in fact, aptly completes his theory, lacks the confirmation of direct experience and artistic intuition. Sculptors themselves rarely think in terms of pictures, and of ideal planes of vision staggered one behind the other to define deep space (except in perfectly flat relief with rectangular cuts, or even mere graven lines, which is really pictorial art, substituting the graving tool for a pencil). Sculpture, even when it is wedded to a background as in true relief, is essentially *volume,* not *scene.*

The volume, however, is not a cubic measure, like the space in a box. It is more than the bulk of the figure; it is a space made visible, and is more than the area which the figure actually occupies. The tangible form has a complement of empty space that it absolutely commands, that is given with it and only with it, and is, in fact, part of the sculptural volume. The figure itself seems to have a sort of continuity with the emptiness around it, however much its solid masses may assert themselves as such. The void enfolds it, and the enfolding space has vital form as a continuation of the figure.

The source of this illusion (for empty space, unenclosed, has actually no visible parts or shape) is the fundamental principle of sculptural volume: the semblance of organism. In the literature of sculpture, more than anywhere else, one meets with reference to "inevitable form," "necessary form," and "inviolable form." But what do these expressions mean? What, in nature, makes forms "inevitable," "necessary," "inviolable"? Nothing but *vital function.* Living organisms maintain themselves, resist change, strive to restore their structure when it has been forcibly interfered with. All other patterns are kaleidoscopic and casual; but organisms, performing characteristic functions, *must* have certain general forms, or perish. For them there is a norm of organic structure according to which, inevitably, they build themselves up, deriving matter from their chance environment; and their parts are built to carry on this process as it becomes more complex, so the parts have shapes necessary to their respective functions; yet the most specialized activities are supported at every moment by the process which they serve, the life of the whole. It is the functional whole that is inviolable. Break this, and all the subordinate activities cease, the constituent parts disintegrate, and "living form" has disappeared.

No other kind of form is actually "necessary," for necessity presupposes a measure in teleological terms, and nothing but life exhibits any telos. Only life, once put in motion, achieves certain forms inevitably, as long as it goes on at all: the acorn becomes an oak, however stunted or varied, the sparrow's egg a sparrow, the maggot a fly. Other accretions of matter may have *usual* forms, but do not strive to achieve them, nor maintain themselves in them. A crystal broken in half yields simply two pieces of crystal. A creature broken in half either dies, i.e. disintegrates, or repairs one part, or both parts, to function again as a whole. It may even break just because the new wholes are preformed, the repair all but made, so the break is its dynamic pattern.

There is nothing actually organic about a work of sculpture. Even carved wood is dead matter. Only its form is the form of life, and the space it makes visible is vitalized as it would be by organic activity at its center. It is *virtual kinetic volume*, created by—and with—the semblance of living form. . . .

Architecture creates the semblance of that World which is the counterpart of a Self. It is a total environment made visible. Where the Self is collective, as in a tribe, its World is communal; for personal Selfhood, it is the home. And as the actual environment of a being is a system of functional relations, so a virtual "environment," the created space of architecture, is a symbol of functional existence. This does not mean, however, that *signs* of important activities—hooks for implements, convenient benches, well-planned doors—play any part in its significance. In that false assumption lies the error of "functionalism"—lies not very deep, but perhaps as deep as the theory itself goes. Symbolic expression is something miles removed from provident planning or good arrangement. It does not suggest things to do, but embodies the feeling, the rhythm, the passion or sobriety, frivolity or fear with which any things at all are done. That is the image of life which is created in buildings; it is the visible semblance of an "ethnic domain," the symbol of humanity to be found in the strength and interplay of forms.

Because we are organisms, all our actions develop in organic fashion, and our feelings as well as our physical acts have an essentially metabolic pattern. Systole, diastole; making, unmaking; crescendo, diminuendo. Sustaining, sometimes, but never for indefinite lengths; life, death.

Similarly, the human environment, which is the counterpart of any human life, holds the imprint of a functional pattern; it is the complementary organic form. Therefore any building that can create the illusion of an ethnic world, a "place" articulated by the imprint of human life, must seem organic, like a living form. "Organization" is the watchword of architecture. In reading the works of great architects with a philosophical bent—Louis Sullivan for instance, or his pupil Frank Lloyd Wright, or Le Corbusier—one is fairly haunted by the concepts of organic growth, organic structure, life, nature, vital function, vital feeling, and an indefinite number of other notions that are biological rather than mechanical. None of these terms applies to the actual materials or the geographic space required by a building. "Life" and "organism" and "growth" have no relevance to real estate or builders' supplies. They refer to virtual space, the created domain of human relations and activities. The place which a house occupies on the face of the earth—that is to say, its location in actual space—remains the same place if the house burns up or is wrecked and removed. But the place created by the architect is an illusion, begotten by the visible expression of a feeling, sometimes called an "atmosphere." This kind of place disappears if the house is destroyed, or changes radically if the building undergoes any violent alteration. The alteration need not even be very radical or extensive. Top-heavy added dormers, gingerbread porches, and other excrescences are very spectacular diseases; bad coloring and confused interior furnishing, though mild by comparison, may be enough to destroy the architectural illusion of an ethnic totality, or virtual "place."

The proposition here advanced, that the primary illusion of plastic art, *virtual space,* appears in architecture as *envisagement of an ethnic domain,* has some interesting consequences. In the first place, it frees the conception of architecture from all bondage to special factors of construction, even the elementary ones of pier, lintel, and arch. The importance of such ancient devices is beyond dispute; yet even they may yield to new technical resources, and the creation that takes shape without their benefit may nonetheless be pure and unquestionable architecture. In the second place, it gives a new and forceful meaning to a principle insistently maintained by the great architects of our day—that architecture proceeds from the inside to the outside of a building, so that the façade is never a thing separately conceived, but like the skin or carapace of a living creature is the outer limit of a vital system, its protection against the world and at the same time its point of contact and interaction with the world. A building may be entirely enclosed by a solid, masking wall, like a Renaissance palace or a Turkish harem, where life lies open only to the court within; or it may have practically no shell at all, being divided from its surroundings only by glass and movable shades, curtains, and screens. Its virtual domain may include terraces and gardens, or rows of sphinxes, or a great rectangular pool. Sea and sky may fill the intervals between its columns and be gathered to its space. In the third place, this conception offers a criterion of what things belong to architecture, as essentials, as variables (like roofs or rooms convertible for summer and winter), or as auxiliaries. Furnishings belong to architecture just in so far as they take part in creating the ethnic domain. Pictures, treated by "interior decorators" as embellishments of a room may remain dissociated from it or even hostile. Yet a great picture *has a right to a room,* and a space frankly consecrated to it *is* an ethnic domain of a special sort, its function thus assigned. Many practical arrangements, on the other hand, have no architectural significance, though they be "built into" the house: steam or hot water heat, shutters in flues, etc. They affect the utility of the building, but not its semblance—not even its functional semblance. They are material factors, but not architectural elements. . . .

Let us return to the primary illusion of the plastic arts, *virtual space* in its several modes. The fact that these modes are just so many ways of creating space relates them as definitely as it distinguishes them, and suggests good reasons why diverse minds find expression, respectively, through the diverse basic abstractions giving rise to the great forms, and yet have a far greater affinity for forms of plastic art other than their own than for arts which do not create virtual space at all; to speak in specific instances, why a painter is likely to be a competent judge of architecture, sculpture, textile design, jewelry, pottery, or any other visual space creation, but is no more likely than any layman (and, of course, no less likely either) to have a special understanding of music or literature. Indeed, he is apt to judge some other arts, such as ballet or theater, entirely from the standpoint of plastic form, which is not paramount in their realms at all.

The deep divisions among the arts are those that set apart their very worlds, namely the differences in what the various arts create, or differences of primary illusion. Many people—artists, critics, and philosophers—are averse to any serious study of these divisions, because they feel that somehow art is one, and the unity is more real than the multiplicity which, they insist, can be only specious, due to material differences, purely technical, at the most skin-deep. Yet such a hasty rejection of a problem usually bespeaks fear of it rather than a firm conviction of its unimportance. I also believe that art is essentially one, that the symbolic function is the same in every kind of artistic expression, all kinds are equally great, and their logic is all of a piece, the logic of non-discursive form (which governs literary as well as all other created form). But the way to establish these articles of faith as reasonable propositions is not just to say them emphatically and often and deprecate evidence to the contrary; it is, rather, to examine the differences, and trace the distinctions among the arts as far as they can be followed. They go deeper than, offhand, one would suppose. But there is a definite level at which no more distinctions can be made; everything one can say of any single art can be said of any other as well. *There lies the unity.* All the divisions end at that depth, which is the philosophical foundation of art theory. . . .

THE IMAGE OF TIME

. . . The elements of music are moving forms of sound; but in their motion nothing is removed. The realm in which tonal entities move is a realm of pure *duration*. Like its elements, however, this duration is not an actual phenomenon. It is not a period—ten minutes or a half hour, some fraction of a day—but is something radically different from the time in which our public and practical life proceeds. It is completely incommensurable with the progress of common affairs. Musical duration is an image of what might be termed "lived" or "experienced" time—the passage of life that we feel as expectations become "now," and "now" turns into unalterable fact. Such passage is measurable only in terms of sensibilities, tensions, and emotions; and it has not merely a different measure, but an altogether different structure from practical or scientific time.

The semblance of this vital, experiential time is the primary illusion of music. All music creates an order of virtual time, in which its sonorous forms move in relation to each other—always and only to each other, for nothing else exists there. Virtual time is as separate from the sequence of actual happenings as virtual space from actual space. In the first place, it is entirely perceptible, through the agency of a single sense—hearing. There is no supplementing of one sort of experience by another. This alone makes it something quite different from our "common-sense" version of time, which is even more composite, heterogeneous, and fragmentary than our similar sense of space. Inward tensions and outward changes, heartbeats and clocks, daylight and routines and weariness furnish various incoherent temporal data, which we coordinate for practical purposes by letting the clock predominate. But music spreads out time for our direct and complete apprehension, by letting our hearing monopolize it—organize, fill, and shape it, all alone. It creates an image of time measured by the motion of forms that seem to give it substance, yet a substance that consists entirely of sound, so it is transitoriness itself. *Music makes time audible, and its form and continuity sensible.*

This theory of music is surprisingly corroborated by the observations of Basil de Selincourt in a short, little-known, but significant essay entitled "Music and Duration," which I have come across quite recently, and found remarkable on several counts, especially for the fact that the author distinguished, clearly and explicitly, between the actual and the virtual, with respect to both space and time. His words, written thirty years ago, may well be quoted here:

"Music is one of the forms of duration; it suspends ordinary time, and offers itself as an ideal substitute and equivalent. Nothing is more metaphorical or more forced in music than a suggestion that time is passing while we listen to it, that the development of the themes follows the action in time of some person or persons embodied in them, or that we ourselves change as we listen. . . . The space of which the painter makes use is a translated space, within which all objects are at rest, and though flies may walk about on his canvas, their steps do not measure the distance from one tone to another. . . . The Time of music is similarly an ideal time, and if we are less directly aware of it, the reason is that our life and consciousness are more closely conditioned by time than by space. . . . The ideal and the real spatial relations declare their different natures in the simplicity of the contrast which we perceive between them. Music, on the other hand, demands the absorption of the whole of our time-consciousness; our own continuity must be lost in that of the sound to which we listen. . . . Our very life is measured by rhythm: by our breathing, by our heartbeats. These are all irrelevant, their meaning is in abeyance, so long as time is music.

". . . If we are 'out of time' in listening to music, our state is best explained by the simple consideration that it is as difficult to be in two times at once as in two places. Music uses time as an element of expression; duration is its essence. The beginning and the end of a musical composition are only one if the music has possessed itself of the interval between them and wholly filled it."

The second radical divergence of virtual time from actual lies in its very structure, its logical pattern, which is not the one-dimensional order we assume for practical purposes (including all historical and scientific purposes). The virtual time created in music is an image of time in a different mode, i.e. appearing to have different terms and relations. . . .

The Musical Matrix

. . . What, then, is the essence of *all* music? The creation of virtual time, and its complete determination by the movement of audible forms. The devices for establishing this primary illusion of time are many; the recognition of related tones (fundamental and overtones, and by derivation our entire harmonic system) is the most powerful structural principle that has ever been employed, if artistic power be judged by the range and expressiveness of the structures to which the principle gives rise; but other musical traditions have used other devices. The drum has been used with wonderful effect to enthrall the ear, to push away, as it were, the world of practical time, and create a new time image in sound. In our own music the drum is a subsidiary element, but there are records of African music in which its constructive power is paramount. The voice, in such performances, serves essentially to contrast with the steady tone of the drum—to wander and rise and fall where the purely rhythmic element goes on like Fate. The effect is neither melody nor harmony, yet it is music: it has motion and autonomous form, and anyone familiar with many works of that sort would probably feel their structure and mood almost from the opening beat.

Another ruling principle of music has been the intonation of speech. If chant, in its oldest sense, has a protomusical line, that line is not constructed harmonically, like Schenker's *Urlinie*, but rests on some other principle. Yet choric chant, no matter what its poetic content, is essentially music. It creates a dynamic form, purely sonorous movement, that metes out its own audible Time even to a person who cannot understand the words, though that person inevitably misses some of the richness of the musical texture. But this is a subject for future discussion. The point at issue here is merely that music is more universal than any one artistic tradition, and the difference between music and noise is not the absence of this or that constructive principle, but of any commanding form whatever. Even noise may happen to furnish musical phenomena; hammers on anvils, rotary saws, dripping faucets are very apt to do so; but real music comes into being only when someone seizes on the motif and uses it, either as a form to be developed, or as an element to be assimilated to a greater form.

The essence of all composition—tonal or atonal, vocal or instrumental, even purely percussive, if you will—is the semblance of *organic* movement, the illusion of an indivisible whole. Vital organization is the frame of all feeling, because feeling exists only in living organisms; and the logic of all symbols that can express feeling is the logic of organic processes. The most characteristic principle of vital activity is rhythm. All life is rhythmic; under difficult circumstances, its rhythms may become very complex, but when they are really lost life cannot long endure. This rhythmic character of organism permeates music, because music is a symbolic presentation of the highest organic response, the emotional life of human beings. A succession of emotions that have no reference to each other do not constitute an "emotional life," any more than a discontinuous and independent functioning or organs collected under one skin would be a physical "life." The great office of music is to organize our conception of feeling into more than an occasional awareness of emotional storm, i.e. to give us an insight into what may truly be called the "life of feeling," or subjective unity of experience; and this it does by the same principle that organizes physical existence into a biological design—rhythm.

NELSON GOODMAN

GOODMAN'S *LANGUAGES OF ART* created a stir when it was published twenty years ago. A good part of the reaction was due to Goodman's status in the profession as a rigorous nominalist who nevertheless developed a theory in which art functions symbolically and cognitively. Goodman proposes a broadened theory of reference, complete with syntax and semantics, in which works of art refer, sometimes by representation, sometimes by exemplification and expression.

Goodman cannot be accused of attempting to interpret works of art as propositional, for there are important ways in which they are syntactically and semantically unique, even if there is no simple way in which they can be distinguished from other symbolic modes. But Goodman does claim that art is as cognitive as science. Even emotions function cognitively in art. At the same time, Goodman claims cognitive authority for art and weakens the unique cognitive authority of science.

The selections here are drawn from a paper in which many of Goodman's ideas are presented briefly and from the closing sections of *Languages of Art* where Goodman forcefully presents his cognitive theory of art.

NELSON GOODMAN

When Is Art?*

1. The Pure in Art

If attempts to answer the question "What is art?" characteristically end in frustration and confusion, perhaps—as so often in philosophy—the question is the wrong one. A reconception of the problem, together with application of some results of a study of the theory of symbols, may help to clarify such moot matters as the role of symbolism in art and the status as art of the 'found object' and so-called 'conceptual art.'

One remarkable view of the relation of symbols to works of art is illustrated in an incident bitingly reported by Mary McCarthy.[1]

> Seven years ago, when I taught in a progressive college, I had a pretty girl student in one of my classes who wanted to be a short-story writer. She was not studying with me, but she knew that I sometimes wrote short stories, and one day, breathless and glowing, she came up to me in the hall, to tell me that she had just written a story that her writing teacher, a Mr. Converse, was terribly excited about. "He thinks it's wonderful" she said, "and he's going to help me fix it up for publication."
>
> I asked what the story was about; the girl was a rather simple being who loved clothes and dates. Her answer had a deprecating tone. It was about a girl (herself) and some sailors she had met on the train. But then her face, which had looked perturbed for a moment, gladdened.
>
> "Mr. Converse is going over it with me and we're going to put in the symbols."

* Nelson Goodman, *Ways of World-Making* (Indianapolis: Hackett, 1978), pp. 57-70.

Today the bright-cyed art student will more likely be told, with equal subtlety, to keep out the symbols: but the underlying assumption is the same: that symbols, whether enhancements or distractions, are extrinsic to the work itself. A kindred notion seems to be reflected in what we take to be symbolic art. We think first of such works as Bosch's *Garden of Delight* or Goya's *Caprichos* or the Unicorn tapestries or Dali's drooping watches, and then perhaps of religious paintings, the more mystical the better. What is remarkable here is less the association of the symbolic with the esoteric or unearthly than the classification of works as symbolic upon the basis of their having symbols as their subject matter—that is, upon the basis of their depicting rather than of being symbols. This leaves as nonsymbolic art not only works that depict nothing but also portraits, still-lifes, and landscapes where the subjects are rendered in a straightforward way without arcane allusions and do not themselves stand as symbols.

On the other hand, when we choose works for classification as nonsymbolic, as art without symbols, we confine ourselves to works without subjects, for example, to purely abstract or decorative or formal paintings or buildings or musical compositions. Works that represent anything, no matter what and no matter how prosaically, are excluded; for to represent is surely to refer, to stand for, to symbolize. Every representational work is a symbol; and art without symbols is restricted to art without subject.

That representational works are symbolic according to one usage and nonsymbolic according to another matters little so long as we do not confuse the two usages. What matters very much, though, according to many contemporary artists and critics, is to isolate the work of art as such from whatever it symbolizes or refers to in any way. Let me set forth in quotation marks, since I am offering it for consideration without now expressing any opinion of it, a composite statement of a currently much advocated program or policy or point of view:

> What a picture symbolizes is external to it, and extraneous to the picture as a work of art. Its subject if it has one, its references—subtle or obvious—by means of symbols from some more or less well-recognized vocabulary, have nothing to do with its aesthetic or artistic significance or character. Whatever a picture refers to or stands for in any way, overt or occult, lies outside it. What really counts is not any such relationship to something else, not what the picture symbolizes, but what it is in itself—what its own intrinsic qualities are. Moreover, the more a picture focuses attention on what it symbolizes, the more we are distracted from its own properties. Accordingly, any symbolization by a picture is not only irrelevant but disturbing. Really pure art shuns all symbolization, refers to nothing, and is to be taken for just what it is, for its inherent character, not for anything it is associated with by some such remote relation as symbolization.

Such a manifesto packs punch. The counsel to concentrate on the intrinsic rather than the extrinsic, the insistence that a work of art is what it is rather than what it symbolizes, and the conclusion that pure art dispenses with external reference of all kinds have the solid sound of straight thinking, and promise to extricate art from smothering thickets of interpretation and commentary.

2. A Dilemma

But a dilemma confronts us here. If we accept this doctrine of the formalist or purist, we seem to be saying that the content of such works as the *Garden of Delight* and the *Caprichos* doesn't really matter and might better be left out. If we reject the doctrine, we seem to be holding that what counts is not just what a work is but lots of things it isn't. In the one case we seem to be advocating lobotomy on many great works; in the other we seem to be condoning impurity in art, emphasizing the extraneous.

The best course, I think, is to recognize the purist position as all right and all wrong. But how can that be? Let's begin by agreeing that what is extraneous is extraneous. But is what a symbol symbolizes always external to it? Certainly not for symbols of all kinds. Consider the symbols:

(a) "this string of words," which stands for itself;
(b) "word," which applies to itself among other words;
(c) "short," which applies to itself and some other words and many other things; and
(d) "having seven syllables," which has seven syllables.

Obviously what some symbols symbolize does not lie entirely outside the symbols. These cases cited are, of course, quite special ones, and the analogues among pictures—that is, pictures that are pictures of themselves or include themselves in what they depict can perhaps be set aside as too rare and idiosyncratic to carry any weight. Let's agree for the present that what a work represents, except in a few cases like these, is external to it and extraneous.

Does this mean that any work that represents nothing meets the purist's demands? Not at all. In the first place, some surely symbolic works such as Bosch's paintings of weird monsters, or the tapestry of a unicorn, represent nothing; for there are no such monsters or demons or unicorns anywhere but in such pictures or in verbal descriptions. To say that the tapestry 'represents a unicorn' amounts only to saying that it is a unicorn-picture, not that there is any animal, or anything at all that it portrays.[2] These works, even though there is nothing they represent, hardly satisfy the purist. Perhaps, though, this is just another philosopher's quibble; and I won't press the point. Let's agree that such pictures, though they represent nothing, are representational in character, hence symbolic and so not 'pure'. All the same, we must note in passing that their being representational involves no representation of anything outside them, so that the purist's objection to them cannot be on that ground. His case will have to be modified in one way or another, with some sacrifice of simplicity and force.

In the second place, not only representational works are symbolic. An abstract painting that represents nothing and is not representational at all may express, and so symbolize, a feeling or other quality, or an emotion or idea.[3] Just because expression is a way of symbolizing something outside the painting—which does not itself sense, feel or think—the purist rejects abstract expressionist as well as representational works.

For a work to be an instance of 'pure' art, of art without symbols, it must on this view neither represent nor express nor even be representational or expressive. But is that enough? Granted, such a work does not stand for anything outside it; all it has are its own properties. But of course if we put it that way, all the properties any picture or anything else has—even such a property as that of representing a given person—are properties of the picture, not properties outside it.

The predictable response is that the important distinction among the several properties a work may have lies between its internal or intrinsic, and its external or extrinsic properties; that while all are indeed its own properties, some of them obviously relate the picture to other things; and that a nonrepresentational, nonexpressive work has only internal properties.

This plainly doesn't work; for under any even faintly plausible classification of properties into internal and external, any picture or anything else has properties of both kinds. That a picture is in the Metropolitan Museum, that it was painted in Duluth, that it is younger than Methuselah, would hardly be called internal properties. Getting rid of representation and expression does not give us something free of such external or extraneous properties.

Furthermore, the very distinction between internal and external properties is a notoriously muddled one. Presumably the colors and shapes in a picture must be considered internal; but if an external property is one that relates the picture or object to something else, then colors and shapes obviously must be counted as external; for the color or shape of an object not only may be shared by other objects but also relates the object to others having the same or different colors or shapes.

Sometimes, the terms "internal" and "intrinsic" are dropped in favor of "formal." But the formal in this context cannot be a matter of shape alone. It must include color, and if color, what else? Texture? Size? Material? Of course, we may at will enumerate properties that are to be called formal; but the 'at will' gives the case away. The rationale, the justification, evaporates. The properties left out as nonformal can no longer be characterized as all and only those that relate the picture to something outside it. So we are still faced with the question what if any *principle* is involved—the question how the properties that matter in a nonrepresentational, nonexpressive painting are distinguished from the rest.

I think there is an answer to the question; but to approach it, we'll have to drop all this high-sounding talk of art and philosophy, and come down to earth with a thud.

3. Samples

Consider again an ordinary swatch of textile in a tailor's or upholsterer's sample book. It is unlikely to be a work of art or to picture or express anything. It's simply a sample—a simple sample. But what is it a sample of? Texture, color, weave, thickness, fiber content . . . ; the whole point of this sample, we are tempted to say, is that it was cut from a bolt and has all the same properties as the rest of the material. But that would be too hasty.

Let me tell you two stories—or one story with two parts. Mrs. Mary Tricias studied such a sample book, made her selection, and ordered from her favorite textile shop enough material for her overstuffed chair and sofa—insisting that it be exactly like the sample. When the bundle came she opened it eagerly and was dismayed when several hundred 2" x 3" pieces with zigzag edges exactly like the sample fluttered to the floor. When she called the shop, protesting loudly, the proprietor replied, injured and weary, "But Mrs. Tricias, you said the material must be exactly like the sample. When it arrived from the factory yesterday, I kept my assistants here half the night cutting it up to match the sample."

This incident was nearly forgotten some months later, when Mrs. Tricias, having sewed the pieces together and covered her furniture, decided to have a party. She went to the local bakery, selected a chocolate cupcake from those on display and ordered enough for fifty guests, to be delivered two weeks later. Just as the guests were beginning to arrive, a truck drove up with a single huge cake. The lady running the bakeshop was utterly discouraged by the complaint. "But Mrs. Tricias, you have no idea how much trouble we went to. My husband runs the textile shop and he warned me that your order would have to be in one piece."

The moral of this story is not simply that you can't win, but that a sample is a sample of some of its properties but not others. The swatch is a sample of texture, color, etc. but not of size or shape. The cupcake is a sample of color, texture, size, and shape, but still not of all its properties. Mrs. Tricias would have complained even more loudly if what was delivered to her was like the sample in having been baked on that same day two weeks earlier.

Now in general which of its properties is a sample a sample of? Not all its properties; for then the sample would be a sample of nothing but itself. And not its 'formal' or 'internal' or, indeed, any one specifiable set of properties. The kind of property sampled differs from case to case: the cupcake but not the swatch is a sample of size and shape; a specimen of ore may be a sample of what was mined at a given time and place. Moreover, the sampled properties vary widely with context and circumstance. Although the swatch is normally a sample of its texture, etc. but not of its shape or size, if I show it to you in answer to the question "What is an upholsterer's sample?" it then functions not as a sample of the material but as a sample of an upholsterer's sample, so that its size and shape are now among the properties it is a sample of.

In sum, the point is that a sample is a sample of—or *exemplifies*—only some of its properties, and that the properties to which it bears this relationship of exemplification[4] vary with circumstances and can only be distinguished as those properties that it serves, under the given circumstances, as a sample of. Being a sample of or exemplifying is a relationship something like that of being a friend; my friends are not distinguished by any single identifiable property or cluster of properties, but only by standing, for a period of time, in the relationship of friendship with me.

The implications for our problem concerning works of art may now be apparent. The properties that count in a purist painting are those that the picture makes manifest, selects, focuses upon, exhibits, heightens in our consciousness—those that it shows forth—in short, those properties that it does not merely possess but *exemplifies*, stands as a sample of.

If I am right about this, then even the purist's purest painting symbolizes. It exemplifies certain of its properties. But to exemplify is surely to symbolize—exemplification no less than representation or expression is a form of reference. A work of art, however free of representation and expression, is still a symbol even though what it symbolizes be not things or people or feelings but certain patterns of shape, color, texture that it shows forth.

What, then, of the purist's initial pronouncement that I said facetiously is all right and all wrong? It is all right in saying that what is extraneous is extraneous, in pointing out that what a picture represents often matters very little, in arguing that neither representation nor expression is required of a work, and in stressing the importance of so-called intrinsic or internal or 'formal' properties. But the statement is all wrong in assuming that representation and expression are the only symbolic functions that paintings may perform, in supposing that what a symbol symbolizes is always outside it, and in insisting that what counts in a painting is the mere possession rather than the exemplification of certain properties.

Whoever looks for art without symbols, then, will find none—if all the ways that works symbolize are taken into account. Art without representation or expression or exemplification—yes; art without all three—*no*.

To point out that purist art consists simply in the avoidance of certain kinds of symbolization is not to condemn it but only to uncover the fallacy in the usual manifestos advocating purist art to the exclusion of all other kinds. I am not debating the relative virtues of different schools or types or ways of painting. What seems to me more important is that recognition of the symbolic function of even purist painting gives us a clue to the perennial problem of when we do and when we don't have a work of art.

The literature on aesthetics is lettered with desperate attempts to answer the question "What is art?" This question, often hopelessly confused with the question "What is good art?," is acute in the case of found art—the stone picked out of the driveway and exhibited in a museum—and is further aggravated by the promotion of so-called environmental and conceptual art. Is a smashed automobile fender in an art gallery a work of art? What of something that is not even an object, and not exhibited in any gallery or museum—for example, the digging and filling-in of a hole in Central Park as prescribed by Oldenburg? If these are works of art, then are all stones in the driveway and all objects and occurrences works of art? If not, what distinguishes what is from what is not a work of art? That an artist calls it a work of art? That it is exhibited in a museum or gallery? No such answer carries any conviction.

As I remarked at the outset, part of the trouble lies in asking the wrong question—in failing to recognize that a thing may function as a work of art at some times and not at others. In crucial cases, the real question is not "What objects are (permanently) works of art?" but "When is an object a work of art?"—or more briefly, as in my title, "When is art?"

My answer is that just as an object may be a symbol—for instance, a sample—at certain times and under certain circumstances and not at others, so an object may be a work of art at some times and not at others. Indeed, just by virtue of functioning as a symbol in a certain way does an object become, while so functioning, a work of art. The stone is normally no work of art while in the driveway, but may be so when on display in an art museum. In the driveway, it usually performs no symbolic function. In the art museum, it exemplifies certain of its properties—e.g., properties of shape, color, texture. The hole-digging and filling functions as a work insofar as our attention is directed to it as an exemplifying symbol. On the other hand, a Rembrandt painting may cease to function as a work of art when used to replace a broken window or as a blanket.

Now, of course, to function as a symbol in some way or other is not in itself to function as a work of art. Our swatch, when serving as a sample, does not then and thereby become a work of art. Things function as works of art only when their symbolic functioning has certain characteristics. Our stone in a museum of geology takes on symbolic functions as a sample of the stones of a given period, origin, or composition, but it is not then functioning as a work of art.

The question just what characteristics distinguish or are indicative of the symbolizing that constitutes functioning as a work of art calls for careful study in the light of a general theory of symbols. That is more than I can undertake here, but I venture the tentative thought that there are five symptoms of the aesthetic:[5] (1) syntactic density, where the finest differences in certain respects constitute a difference between symbols—for example, an ungraduated mercury thermometer as contrasted with an electronic digital-read-out instrument; (2) semantic density, where symbols are provided for things distinguished by the finest differences in certain respects—for example, not only the ungraduated thermometer again but also ordinary English, though it is not syntactically dense; (3) relative repleteness, where comparatively many aspects of a symbol are significant—for example, a single-line drawing of a mountain by Hokusai where every feature of shape, line, thickness, etc. counts, in contrast with perhaps the same line as a chart of daily stockmarket averages, where all that counts is the height of the line above the base; (4)

exemplification, where a symbol, whether or not it denotes, symbolizes by serving as a sample of properties it literally or metaphorically possesses; and finally (5) multiple and complex reference, where a symbol performs several integrated and interacting referential functions,[6] some direct and some mediated through other symbols.

These symptoms provide no definition, much less a full-blooded description or a celebration. Presence or absence of one or more of them does not qualify or disqualify anything as aesthetic; nor does the extent to which these features are present measure the extent to which an object or experience is aesthetic.[7] Symptoms, after all, are but clues; the patient may have the symptoms without the disease, or the disease without the symptoms. And even for these five symptoms to come somewhere near being disjunctively necessary and conjunctively (as a syndrome) sufficient might well call for some redrawing of the vague and vagrant borderlines of the aesthetic. Still, notice that these properties tend to focus attention on the symbol rather than, or at least along with, what it refers to. Where we can never determine precisely just which symbol of a system we have or whether we have the same one on a second occasion, where the referent is so elusive that properly fitting a symbol to it requires endless care, where more rather than fewer features of the symbol count, where the symbol is an instance of properties it symbolizes and may perform many inter-related simple and complex referential functions, we cannot merely look through the symbol to what it refers to as we do in obeying traffic lights or reading scientific texts, but must attend constantly to the symbol itself as in seeing paintings or reading poetry. This emphasis upon the nontransparency of a work of art, upon the primacy of the work over what it refers to, far from involving denial or disregard of symbolic functions, derives from certain characteristics of a work as a symbol.[8]

Quite apart from specifying the particular characteristics differentiating aesthetic from other symbolization, the answer to the question "When is art?" thus seems to me clearly to be in terms of symbolic function. Perhaps to say that an object is art when and only when it so functions is to overstate the case or to speak elliptically. The Rembrandt painting remains a work of art, as it remains a painting, while functioning only as a blanket; and the stone from the driveway may not strictly become art by functioning as art.[9] Similarly, a chair remains a chair even if never sat on, and a packing case remains a packing case even if never used except for sitting on. To say what art does is not to say what art is; but I submit that the former is the matter of primary and peculiar concern. The further question of defining stable property in terms of ephemeral function—the what in terms of the when—is not confined to the arts but is quite general, and is the same for defining chairs as for defining objects of art. The parade of instant and inadequate answers is also much the same: that whether an object is art—or a chair—depends upon intent or upon whether it sometimes or usually or always or exclusively functions as such. Because all this tends to obscure more special and significant questions concerning art, I have turned my attention from what art is to what art does.

A salient feature of symbolization, I have urged, is that it may come and go. An object may symbolize different things at different times, and nothing at other times. An inert or purely utilitarian object may come to function as art, and a work of art may come to function as an inert or purely utilitarian object. Perhaps, rather than art being long and life short, both are transient.

The bearing that this inquiry into the nature of works of art has upon the overall undertaking of this book should by now have become quite clear. How an object or event functions as a work explains how, through certain modes of reference, what so functions may contribute to a vision of—and to the making of—a world.

NOTES

1. "Settling the Colonel's Hash," *Harper's Magazine,* 1954; reprinted in *On the Contrary* (Farrar, Straus and Cudahy, 1961), p. 225.

2. See further "On Likeness of Meaning" (1949) and "On Some Differences about Meaning" (1953), *Problems and Projects* (Indianapolis: Hackett, 1972), pp. 221-238; also *Languages of Art (LA),* pp. 21-26.

3. Motion, for instance, as well as emotion may be expressed in a black and white picture. Also see the discussion of expression in *LA,* pp. 85-95.

4. For further discussion of exemplification, see *LA,* pp. 52-67.

5. See *LA,* pp. 252-255 and the earlier passages there alluded to. The fifth symptom has been added above as the result of conversations with Professors Paul Hernadi and Alan Nagel of the University of Iowa.

6. This excludes ordinary ambiguity, where a term has two or more quite independent denotations at quite different times and in quite different contexts.

7. That poetry, for example, which is not syntactically dense, is less art or less likely to be art than painting that exhibits all four symptoms thus does not at all follow. Some aesthetic symbols may have fewer of the symptoms than some nonaesthetic symbols. This is sometimes misunderstood.

8. This is another version of the dictum that the purist is all right and all wrong.

9. Just as what is not red may look or be said to be red *at certain times,* so what is not art may function as or be said to be art at certain times. That an object functions as art at a given time, that it has the status of art at that time, and that it is art at that time may all be taken as saying the same thing—so long as we take none of these as ascribing to the object any stable status.

Languages of Art*

ART AND THE UNDERSTANDING

The Question of Merit

Folklore has it that the good picture is pretty. At the next higher level, "pretty" is replaced by "beautiful," since the best pictures are often obviously not pretty. But again, many of them are in the most obvious sense ugly. If the beautiful excludes the ugly, beauty is no measure of aesthetic merit; but if the beautiful may be ugly, then "beauty" becomes only an alternative and misleading word for aesthetic merit.

Little more light is shed by the dictum that while science is judged by its truth, art is judged by the satisfaction it gives. Many of the objections urged earlier against satisfaction, yielded or anticipated, as a distinguishing feature of the aesthetic weigh also against satisfaction as a criterion of aesthetic merit: satisfaction cannot be identified with pleasure, and positing a special aesthetic feeling begs the question. We are left with the unhelpful formula that what is aesthetically good is aesthetically satisfactory. The question is what makes a work good or satisfactory.

Being satisfactory is in general relative to function and purpose. A good furnace heats the house to the required temperature evenly, economically, quietly, and safely. A good scientific theory accounts for the relevant facts clearly and simply. We have seen that works of art or their instances perform one or more among certain referential functions: representation, descrip-

---

* Nelson Goodman, from "Art and the Understanding," last chapter of *Languages of Art*, 2nd ed. (Indianapolis: Hackett, 1976), pp. 255-264.

tion, exemplification, expression. The question what constitutes effective symbolization of any of these kinds raises in turn the question what purpose such symbolization serves.

An answer sometimes given is that exercise of the symbolizing faculties beyond immediate need has the more remote practical purpose of developing our abilities and techniques to cope with future contingencies. Aesthetic experience becomes a gymnasium workout, pictures and symphonies the barbells and punching bags we use in strengthening our intellectual muscles. Art equips us for survival, conquest, and gain. And it channels surplus energy away from destructive outlets. It makes the scientist more acute, the merchant more astute, and clears the streets of juvenile delinquents. Art, long derided as the idle amusement of the guiltily leisure class, is acclaimed as a universal servant of mankind. This is a comforting view for those who must reconcile aesthetic inclinations with a conviction that all value reduces to practical utility.

More lighthearted and perhaps more simpleminded is the almost opposite answer: that symbolization is an irrepressible propensity of man, that he goes on symbolizing beyond immediate necessity just for the joy of it or because he cannot stop. In aesthetic experience, he is a puppy cavorting or a well-digger who digs doggedly on after finding enough water. Art is not practical but playful or compulsive. Dogs bark because they are canine, men symbolize because they are human; and dogs go on barking and men go on symbolizing when there is no practical need just because they cannot stop and because it is such fun.

A third answer, bypassing the issue over practicality versus fun, points to communication as the purpose of symbolizing. Man is a social animal, communication is a requisite for social intercourse, and symbols are media of communication. Works of art are messages conveying facts, thoughts, and feelings; and their study belongs to the omnivorous new growth called 'communications theory'. Art depends upon and helps sustain society—exists because, and helps ensure, that no man is an island.

Each of these explanations—in terms of gymnastics, play, or conversation—distends and distorts a partial truth. Exercise of the symbolizing skills *may* somewhat improve practical proficiency; the cryptographic character of symbol invention and interpretation *does* give them the fascination of a game; and symbols *are* indispensable to communication. But the lawyer or admiral improving his professional competence by hours in museums, the cavorting puppy, the neurotic well-digger, and the woman on the telephone do not, separately or together, give the whole picture. What all three miss is that the drive is curiosity and the aim enlightenment. Use of symbols beyond immediate need is for the sake of understanding, not practice; what compels is the urge to know, what delights is discovery, and communication is secondary to the apprehension and formulation of what is to be communicated. The primary purpose is cognition in and for itself; the practicality, pleasure, compulsion, and communicative utility all depend upon this.

Symbolization, then, is to be judged fundamentally by how well it serves the cognitive purpose: by the delicacy of its discriminations and the aptness of its allusions; by the way it works in grasping, exploring, and informing the world; by how it analyzes, sorts, orders, and organizes; by how it participates in the making, manipulation, retention, and transformation of knowledge. Considerations of simplicity and subtlety, power and precision, scope and selectivity, familiarity and freshness, are all relevant and often contend with one another; their weighting is relative to our interests, our information, and our inquiry.

So much for the cognitive efficacy of symbolization in general, but what of aesthetic excellence in particular? Distinguishing between the aesthetic and the meritorious cuts both ways. If excellence is not required of the aesthetic, neither is the excellence appropriate to aesthetic objects confined to them. Rather, the general excellence just sketched becomes aesthetic when exhibited by aesthetic objects; that is, aesthetic merit is such excellence in any symbolic functioning that, by its particular constellation of attributes, qualifies as aesthetic. This subsumption of aesthetic under cognitive excellence calls for one more reminder that the cognitive, while contrasted with both the practical and the passive, does not exclude the sensory or the emotive, that what we know through art is felt in our bones and nerves and muscles as well as grasped by our minds, that all the sensitivity and responsiveness of the organism participates in the invention and interpretation of symbols.

The problem of ugliness dissolves; for pleasure and prettiness neither define nor measure either the aesthetic experience or the work of art. The pleasantness or unpleasantness of a symbol does not determine its general cognitive efficacy or its specifically aesthetic merit. *Macbeth* and the Goya *Witches' Sabbath* no more call for apology than do *Pygmalion* and the Botticelli *Venus*.

The dynamics of taste, often embarrassing to those who seek inflexible standards of immutable excellence, also become readily understandable. After a time and for a time, the finest painting may pall and the greatest music madden. A work may be successively offensive, fascinating, comfortable, and boring. These are the vicissitudes of the vehicles and instruments of knowledge. We focus upon frontiers; the peak of interest in a symbol tends to occur at the time of revelation, somewhere midway in the passage from the obscure to the obvious. But there is endurance and renewal, too. Discoveries become available knowledge only when preserved in accessible form; the trenchant and laden symbol does not become worthless when it becomes familiar, but is incorporated in the base for further exploration. And where there is density in the symbol system, familiarity is never complete and final; another look may always disclose significant new subtleties. Moreover, what we read from and learn through a symbol varies with what we bring to it. Not only do we discover the world through our symbols but we understand and reappraise our symbols progressively in the light of our growing experience. Both the dynamics and the durability of aesthetic value are natural consequences of its cognitive character.

Like considerations explain the relevance to aesthetic merit of experience remote from the work. What a Manet or Monet or Cézanne does to our subsequent seeing of the world is as pertinent to their appraisal as is any direct confrontation. How our lookings at pictures and our listenings to music[1] inform what we encounter later and elsewhere is integral to them as cognitive. The absurd and awkward myth of the insularity of aesthetic experience can be scrapped.

The role of theme and variation—common in architecture and other arts as well as in music—also becomes intelligible. Establishment and modification of motifs, abstraction and elaboration of patterns, differentiation and interrelation of modes of transformation, all are processes of constructive search; and the measures applicable are not those of passive enjoyment but those of cognitive efficacy: delicacy of discrimination, power of integration, and justice of proportion between recognition and discovery. Indeed, one typical way of advancing knowledge is by progressive variation upon a theme. Among modern composers, theme and variation along with all recognizable pattern is sometimes scorned, and maximum unpredictability is the declared aim; but, as C. I. Lewis pointed out,[2] complete irregularity is inconceivable—if no sequence is ever repeated in a given composition, that fact in itself constitutes a notable regularity.

Aesthetic merit, however, has by no means been my main concern in this book, and I am somewhat uncomfortable about having arrived at an incipient definition of what is often confusingly called 'beauty'. Excessive concentration on the question of excellence has been responsible, I think, for constriction and distortion of aesthetic inquiry.[3] To say that a work of art is good or even to say how good it is does not after all provide much information, does not tell us whether the work is evocative, robust, vibrant, or exquisitely designed, and still less what are its salient specific qualities of color, shape, or sound. Moreover, works of art are not race-horses, and picking a winner is not the primary goal. Rather than judgments of particular characteristics being mere means toward an ultimate appraisal, judgments of aesthetic value are often means toward discovering such characteristics. If a connoisseur tells me that one of two Cycladic idols that seem to me almost indistinguishable is much finer than the other, this inspires me to look for and may help me find the significant differences between the two. Estimates of excellence are among the minor aids to insight. Judging the excellence of works of art or the goodness of people is not the best way of understanding them. And a criterion of aesthetic merit is no more the major aim of aesthetics than a criterion of virtue is the major aim of psychology.

In short, conceiving of aesthetic experience as a form of understanding results both in resolving and in devaluing the question of aesthetic value.

7. Art and the Understanding

In saying that aesthetic experience is cognitive experience distinguished by the dominance of certain symbolic characteristics and judged by standards of cognitive efficacy, have I overlooked the sharpest contrast: that in science, unlike art, the ultimate test is truth? Do not the two domains differ most drastically in that truth means all for the one, nothing for the other?

Despite rife doctrine, truth by itself matters very little in science. We can generate volumes of dependable truths at will so long as we are unconcerned with their importance; the multiplication tables are inexhaustible, and empirical truths abound. Scientific hypotheses, however true, are worthless unless they meet minimal demands of scope or specificity imposed by our inquiry, unless they effect some telling analysis or synthesis, unless they raise or answer significant questions. Truth is not enough; it is at most a necessary condition. But even this concedes too much; the noblest scientific laws are seldom quite true. Minor discrepancies are overridden in the interest of breadth or power or simplicity.[4] Science denies its data as the statesman denies his constituents—within the limits of prudence.

Yet neither is truth one among competing criteria involved in the rating of scientific hypothesis. Given any assemblage of evidence, countless alternative hypothesis conform to it. We cannot choose among them on grounds of truth; for we have no direct access to their truth. Rather, we judge them by such features as their simplicity and strength. These criteria are not supplemental to truth but applied hopefully as a means for arriving at the nearest approximation to truth that is compatible with our other interests.

Does this leave us with the cardinal residual difference that truth—though not enough, not necessary, and not a touchstone for choosing among hypotheses—is nevertheless a consideration relevant in science but not in art? Even so meek a formulation suggests too strong a contrast. Truth of a hypothesis after all is a matter of fit—fit with a body of theory, and fit of hypothesis and theory to the data at hand and the facts to be encountered. And as Philipp Frank liked to remind us, goodness of fit takes a two-way adjustment—of theory to facts and of facts to theory—with the double aim of comfort and a new look. But such fitness, such aptness in conforming to and reforming our knowledge and our world, is equally relevant for the aesthetic symbol. Truth and its aesthetic counterpart amount to appropriateness under different names. If we speak of hypotheses but not of works of art as true, that is because we reserve the terms "true" and "false" for symbols in sentential form. I do not say this difference is negligible, but it is specific rather than generic, a difference in field of application rather than in formula, and marks no schism between the scientific and the aesthetic.

None of this is directed toward obliterating the distinction between art and science. Declarations of indissoluble unity—whether of the sciences, the arts, the arts and sciences together, or of mankind—tend anyway to focus attention upon the differences. What I am stressing is that the affinities here are deeper, and the significant differentia other, than is often supposed. The difference between art and science is not that between feeling and fact, intuition and inference, delight and deliberation, synthesis and analysis, sensation and cerebration, concreteness and abstraction, passion and action, mediacy and immediacy, or truth and beauty, but rather a difference in domination of certain specific characteristics of symbols.

NOTES

1. Music can inform perception not only of other sounds but also of the rhythms and patterns of what we see. Such cross-transference of structural properties seems to me a basic and important aspect of learning, not merely a matter for novel experimentation by composers, dancers, and painters.

2. *Mind and the World Order* (New York: Charles Scribner's Sons, 1929), p. 385.

3. Cf. my "Merit as Means" in *Art and Philosophy*, ed. S. Hook (New York: New York University Press, 1966), pp. 56-57.

4. See my "Science and Simplicity" in *Philosophy of Science Today*, ed. S. Morgenbesser (New York: Basic Books, Inc., 1967), pp. 68-78.

MARTIN HEIDEGGER

HEIDEGGER SEEMS DESTINED to become the most prominent philosopher of the Continental tradition in the twentieth century. His major work, *Being and Time*, defines what he calls the "ontological difference"—the difference between Being and beings—and approaches it from within the context of human experience. *Dasein* is that being whose nature is to question Being. The questioning addresses the nature and conditions of being human and of being able to question at all. The answer is that beings can "be" only if there is a place where human being meets Being, a place where beings come into presence. In his later work, Heidegger refers to this meeting place in a variety of ways: Framework, Appropriation, Clearing. If there is presence, there must be conditions for that presence. But every interrogation of these conditions is simultaneously a revealing and a concealing, since interrogation is dependent on finite human conditions.

In this context, Heidegger's view of art, especially poetry, is very important, since the mutual concealing-unconcealing that he takes to be truth—*alētheia*—is in his view nullified in propositional and representational thought. Art, however, can reveal without pretending to total unconcealment. Art takes us into the Clearing in which the conditions of thought and being can be interrogated in new ways, in which things are "let be."

Many questions are relevant to understanding Heidegger. But the question for art may be whether his understanding of truth in art imposes too narrow a view on the wealth of variety in works and forms of art. Derrida discusses some of these issues in "Restitutions." A related question is whether Heidegger overemphasizes poetry, whether any art can be regarded as superior to other arts in fundamental ways.

MARTIN HEIDEGGER

*The Origin of the Work of Art**

Origin here means that from and by which something is what it is and as it is. What something is, as it is, we call its essence or nature. The origin of something is the source of its nature. The question concerning the origin of the work of art asks about the source of its nature. On the usual view, the work arises out of and by means of the activity of the artist. But by what and whence is the artist what he is? By the work; for to say that the work does credit to the master means that it is the work that first lets the artist emerge as a master of his art. The artist is the origin of the work. The work is the origin of the artist. Neither is without the other. Nevertheless, neither is the sole support of the other. In themselves and in their interrelations artist and work *are* each of them by virtue of a third thing which is prior to both, namely that which also gives artist and work of art their names—art.

As necessarily as the artist is the origin of the work in a different way than the work is the origin of the artist, so it is equally certain that, in a still different way, art is the origin of both artist and work. But can art be an origin at all? Where and how does art occur? Art—this is nothing more than a word to which nothing real any longer corresponds. It may pass for a collective idea under which we find a place for that which alone is real in art: works and artists. Even if the word art were taken to signify more than a collective notion, what is meant by the word could exist only on the basis of the actuality of works and artists. Or is the converse the case? Do works and artists exist only because art exists as their origin?

---

* Martin Heidegger, *Poetry, Language, Thought,* translated by Albert Hofstadter (New York: Harper and Row, 1975), pp. 17-20, 32-65, 71-75. (Greek accents have been added.)

Whatever the decision may be, the question of the origin of the work of art becomes a question about the nature of art. Since the question whether and how art in general exists must still remain open, we shall attempt to discover the nature of art in the place where art undoubtedly prevails in a real way. Art is present in the art work. But what and how is a work of art?

What art is should be inferable from the work. What the work of art is we can come to know only from the nature of art. Anyone can easily see that we are moving in a circle. Ordinary understanding demands that this circle be avoided because it violates logic. What art is can be gathered from a comparative examination of actual art works. But how are we to be certain that we are indeed basing such an examination on art works if we do not know beforehand what art is? And the nature of art can no more be arrived at by a derivation from higher concepts than by a collection of characteristics of actual art works. For such a derivation, too, already has in view the characteristics that must suffice to establish that what we take in advance to be an art work is one in fact. But selecting works from among given objects, and deriving concepts from principles, are equally impossible here, and where these procedures are practiced they are a self-deception.

Thus we are compelled to follow the circle. This is neither a makeshift nor a defect. To enter upon this path is the strength of thought, to continue on it is the feast of thought, assuming that thinking is a craft. Not only is the main step from work to art a circle like the step from art to work, but every separate step that we attempt circles in this circle.

In order to discover the nature of the art that really prevails in the work, let us go to the actual work and ask the work what and how it is.

Works of art are familiar to everyone. Architectural and sculptural works can be seen installed in public places, in churches, and in dwellings. Art works of the most diverse periods and peoples are housed in collections and exhibitions. If we consider the works in their untouched actuality and do not deceive ourselves, the result is that the works are as naturally present as are things. The picture hangs on the wall like a rifle or a hat. A painting, e.g., the one by Van Gogh that represents a pair of peasant shoes, travels from one exhibition to another. Works of art are shipped like coal from the Ruhr and logs from the Black Forest. During the First World War Hölderlin's hymns were packed in the soldier's knapsack together with cleaning gear. Beethoven's quartets lie in the storerooms of the publishing house like potatoes in a cellar.

All works have this thingly character. What would they be without it? But perhaps this rather crude and external view of the work is objectionable to us. Shippers or charwomen in museums may operate with such conceptions of the work of art. We, however, have to take works as they are encountered by those who experience and enjoy them. But even the much-vaunted aesthetic experience cannot get around the thingly aspect of the art work. There is something stony in a work of architecture, wooden in a carving, colored in a painting, spoken in a linguistic work, sonorous in a musical composition. The thingly element is so irremovably present in the art work that we are compelled rather to say conversely that the architectural work is in stone, the carving is in wood, the painting in color, the linguistic work in speech, the musical composition in sound. "Obviously," it will be replied. No doubt. But what is this self-evident thingly element in the work of art?

Presumably it becomes superfluous and confusing to inquire into this feature, since the art work is something else over and above the thingly element. This something else in the work constitutes its artistic nature. The art work is, to be sure, a thing that is made, but it says something other than the mere thing itself is, *allo agoreuei.* The work makes public something other than itself; it manifests something other; it is an allegory. In the work of art something other is brought together with the thing that is made. To bring together is, in Greek, *sumballein.* The work is a symbol.

Allegory and symbol provide the conceptual frame within whose channel of vision the art work has for a long time been characterized. But this one element in a work that manifests another, this one element that joins with another, is the thingly feature in the art work. It seems almost as though the thingly element in the art work is like the substructure into and upon which the other, authentic element is built. And is it not this thingly feature in the work that the artist really makes by his handicraft?

Our aim is to arrive at the immediate and full reality of the work of art, for only in this way shall we discover real art also within it. Hence we must first bring to view the thingly element of the work. To this end it is necessary that we should know with sufficient clarity what a thing is. Only then can we say whether the art work is a thing, but a thing to which something else adheres; only then can we decide whether the work is at bottom something else and not a thing at all.

Thing and Work

. . . That the thingness of the thing is particularly difficult to express and only seldom expressible is infallibly documented by the history of its interpretation indicated above. This history coincides with the destiny in accordance with which Western thought has hitherto thought the Being of beings. However, not only do we now establish this point; at the same time we discover a clue in this history. Is it an accident that in the interpretation of the thing the view that takes matter and form as guide attains to special dominance? This definition of the thing derives from an interpretation of the equipmental being of equipment. And equipment, having come into being through human making, is particularly familiar to human thinking. At the same time, this familiar being has a peculiar intermediate position between thing and work. We shall follow this clue and search first for the equipmental character of equipment. Perhaps this will suggest something to us about the thingly character of the thing and the workly character of the work. We must only avoid making thing and work prematurely into subspecies of equipment. We are disregarding the possibility, however, that differences relating to the history of Being may yet also be present in the way equipment *is*.

But what path leads to the equipmental quality of equipment? How shall we discover what a piece of equipment truly is? The procedure necessary at present must plainly avoid any attempts that again immediately entail the encroachments of the usual interpretations. We are most easily insured against this if we simply describe some equipment without any philosophical theory.

We choose as example a common sort of equipment—a pair of peasant shoes. We do not even need to exhibit actual pieces of this sort of useful article in order to describe them. Everyone is acquainted with them. But since it is a matter here of direct description, it may be well to facilitate the visual realization of them. For this purpose a pictorial representation suffices. We shall choose a well-known painting by Van Gogh, who painted such shoes several times. But what is there to see here? Everyone knows what shoes consist of. If they are not wooden or bast shoes, there will be leather soles and uppers, joined together by thread and nails. Such gear serves to clothe the feet. Depending on the use to which the shoes are to be put, whether for work in the field or for dancing, matter and form will differ.

Such statements, no doubt correct, only explicate what we already know. The equipmental quality of equipment consists in its usefulness. But what about this usefulness itself? In conceiving it, do we already conceive along with it the equipmental character of equipment? In order to succeed in doing this, must we not look out for useful equipment in its use? The peasant woman wears her shoes in the field. Only here are they what they are. They are all the more genuinely so, the less the peasant woman thinks about the shoes while she is at work, or looks at them at all, or is even aware of them. She stands and walks in them. That is how shoes actually serve. It is in this process of the use of equipment that we must actually encounter the character of equipment.

As long as we only imagine a pair of shoes in general, or simply look at the empty, unused shoes as they merely stand there in the picture, we shall never discover what the equipmental being of the equipment in truth is. From Van Gogh's painting we cannot even tell where these shoes stand. There is nothing surrounding this pair of peasant shoes in or to which they might belong—only an undefined space. There are not even clods of soil from the field or the field-path sticking to them, which would at least hint at their use. A pair of peasant shoes and nothing more. And yet—

From the dark opening of the worn insides of the shoes the toilsome tread of the worker stares forth. In the stiffly rugged heaviness of the shoes there is the accumulated tenacity of her slow trudge through the far-spreading and ever-uniform furrows of the field swept by a raw wind. On the leather lie the dampness and richness of the soil. Under the soles slides the loneliness of the field-path as evening falls. In the shoes vibrates the silent call of the earth, its quiet gift of the ripening grain and its unexplained self-refusal in the fallow desolation of the wintry field. This equipment is pervaded by uncomplaining anxiety as to the certainty of bread, the wordless joy of having once more withstood want, the trembling before the impending childbed and shivering at the surrounding menace of death. This equipment belongs to the *earth*, and it is protected in the *world* of the peasant woman. From out of this protected belonging the equipment itself rises to its resting-within-itself.

But perhaps it is only in the picture that we notice all this about the shoes. The peasant woman, on the other hand, simply wears them. If only this simple wearing were so simple. When she takes off her shoes late in the evening, in deep but healthy fatigue, and reaches out for them again in the still dim dawn, or passes them by on the day of rest, she knows all this without noticing or reflecting. The equipmental quality of the equipment consists indeed in its usefulness. But this usefulness itself rests in the abundance of an essential being of the equipment. We call it reliability. By virtue of this reliability the peasant woman is made privy to the silent call of the earth; by virtue of the reliability of the equipment she is sure of her world. World and earth exist for her, and for those who are with her in her mode of being, only thus—in the equipment. We say "only" and therewith fall into error; for the reliability of the equipment first gives to the simple world its security and assures to the earth the freedom of its steady thrust.

The equipmental being of equipment, reliability, keeps gathered within itself all things according to their manner and extent. The usefulness of equipment is nevertheless only the essential consequence of reliability. The former vibrates in the latter and would be nothing without it. A single piece of equipment is worn out and used up; but at the same time the use itself also falls into disuse, wears away, and becomes usual. Thus equipmentality wastes away, sinks into mere stuff. In such wasting, reliability vanishes. This dwindling, however, to which use-things owe their boringly obtrusive usualness, is only one more testimony to the original nature of equipmental being. The worn-out usualness of the equipment then obtrudes itself as the sole mode of being, apparently peculiar to it exclusively. Only blank usefulness now remains visible. It awakens the impression that the origin of equipment lies in a mere fabricating that impresses a form upon some matter. Nevertheless, in its genuinely equipmental being, equipment stems from a more distant source. Matter and form and their distinction have a deeper origin.

The repose of equipment resting within itself consists in its reliability. Only in this reliability do we discern what equipment in truth is. But we still know nothing of what we first sought: the thing's thingly character. And we know nothing at all of what we really and solely seek: the workly character of the work in the sense of the work of art.

Or have we already learned something unwittingly, in passing so to speak, about the work-being of the work?

The equipmental quality of equipment was discovered. But how? Not by a description and explanation of a pair of shoes actually present; not by a report about the process of making shoes; and also not by the observation of the actual use of shoes occurring here and there; but only by bringing ourselves before Van Gogh's painting. This painting spoke. In the vicinity of the work we were suddenly somewhere else than we usually tend to be.

The art work let us know what shoes are in truth. It would be the worst self-deception to think that our description, as a subjective action, had first depicted everything thus and then projected it into the painting. If anything is questionable here, it is rather that we experienced too little in the neighborhood of the work and that we expressed the experience too crudely and too literally. But above all, the work did not, as it might seem at first, serve merely for a better visualizing of what a piece of equipment is. Rather, the equipmentality of equipment first genuinely arrives at its appearance through the work and only in the work.

What happens here? What is at work in the work? Van Gogh's painting is the disclosure of what the equipment, the pair of peasant shoes, *is* in truth. This entity emerges into the unconcealedness of its being. The Greeks called the unconcealedness of beings *alētheia.* We say "truth" and think little enough in using this word. If there occurs in the work a disclosure of a particular being, disclosing what and how it is, then there is here an occurring, a happening of truth at work.

In the work of art the truth of an entity has set itself to work. "To set" means here: to bring to a stand. Some particular entity, a pair of peasant shoes, comes in the work to stand in the light of its being. The being of the being comes into the steadiness of its shining.

The nature of art would then be this: the truth of beings setting itself to work. But until now art presumably has had to do with the beautiful and beauty, and not with truth. The arts that produce such works are called the beautiful or fine arts, in contrast with the applied or industrial arts that manufacture equipment. In fine art the art itself is not beautiful, but is called so because it produces the beautiful. Truth, in contrast, belongs to logic. Beauty, however, is reserved for aesthetics.

But perhaps the proposition that art is truth setting itself to work intends to revive the fortunately obsolete view that art is an imitation and depiction of reality? The reproduction of what exists requires, to be sure, agreement with the actual being, adaptation to it; the Middle Ages called it *adaequatio;* Aristotle already spoke of *homoiosis.* Agreement with what *is* has long been taken to be the essence of truth. But then, is it our opinion that this painting by Van Gogh depicts a pair of actually existing peasant shoes, and is a work of art because it does so successfully? Is it our opinion that the painting draws a likeness from something actual and transposes it into a product of artistic—production? By no means.

The work, therefore, is not the reproduction of some particular entity that happens to be present at any given time; it is, on the contrary, the reproduction of the thing's general essence. But then where and how is this general essence, so that art works are able to agree with it? With what nature of what thing should a Greek temple agree? Who could maintain the impossible view that the Idea of Temple is represented in the building? And yet, truth is set to work in such a work, if it is a work. Or let us think of Hölderlin's hymn, "The

Rhine." What is pregiven to the poet, and how is it given, so that it can then be regiven in the poem? And if in the case of this hymn and similar poems the idea of a copy-relation between something already actual and the art work clearly fails, the view that the work is a copy is confirmed in the best possible way by a work of the kind presented in C. F. Meyer's poem "Roman Fountain."

Roman Fountain

The jet ascends and falling fills
The marble basin circling round;
This, veiling itself over, spills
Into a second basin's ground.
The second in such plenty lives,
Its bubbling flood a third invests,
And each at once receives and gives
And streams and rests.

This is neither a poetic painting of a fountain actually present nor a reproduction of the general essence of a Roman fountain. Yet truth is put into the work. What truth is happening in the work? Can truth happen at all and thus be historical? Yet truth, people say, is something timeless and supertemporal.

We seek the reality of the art work in order to find there the art prevailing within it. The thingly substructure is what proved to be the most immediate reality in the work. But to comprehend this thingly feature the traditional thing-concepts are not adequate; for they themselves fail to grasp the nature of the thing. The currently predominant thing-concept, thing as formed matter, is not even derived from the nature of the thing but from the nature of equipment. It also turned out that equipmental being generally has long since occupied a peculiar preeminence in the interpretation of beings. This preeminence of equipmentality, which however did not actually come to mind, suggested that we pose the question of equipment anew while avoiding the current interpretations.

We allowed a work to tell us what equipment is. By this means, almost clandestinely, it came to light what is at work in the work: the disclosure of the particular being in its being, the happening of truth. If, however, the reality of the work can be defined solely by means of what is at work in the work, then what about our intention to seek out the real art work in its reality? As long as we supposed that the reality of the work lay primarily in its thingly substructure we were going astray. We are now confronted by a remarkable result of our considerations—if it still deserves to be called a result at all. Two points become clear:

First: the dominant thing-concepts are inadequate as means of grasping the thingly aspect of the work.

Second: what we tried to treat as the most immediate reality of the work, its thingly substructure, does not belong to the work in that way at all.

As soon as we look for such a thingly substructure in the work, we have unwittingly taken the work as equipment, to which we then also ascribe a superstructure supposed to contain its artistic quality. But the work is not a piece of equipment that is fitted out in addition with an aesthetic value that adheres to it. The work is no more anything of the kind than the bare thing is a piece of equipment that merely lacks the specific equipmental characteristics of usefulness and being made.

Our formulation of the question of the work has been shaken because we asked, not about the work but half about a thing and half about equipment. Still, this formulation of the question was not first developed by us. It is the formulation native to aesthetics. The way in which aesthetics views the art work from the outset is dominated by the traditional interpretation of all beings. But the shaking of this accustomed formulation is not the essential point. What matters is a first opening of our vision to the fact that what is workly in the work, equipmental in equipment, and thingly in the thing comes closer to us only when we think the Being of beings. To this end it is necessary beforehand that the barriers of our preconceptions fall away and that the current pseudo concepts be set aside. That is why we had to take this detour. But it brings us directly to a road that may lead to a determination of the thingly feature in the work. The thingly feature in the work should not be denied; but if it belongs admittedly to the work-being of the work, it must be conceived by way of the work's workly nature. If this is so, then the road toward the determination of the thingly reality of the work leads not from thing to work but from work to thing.

The art work opens up in its own way the Being of beings. This opening up, i.e., this deconcealing, i.e., the truth of beings, happens in the work. In the art work, the truth of what is has set itself to work. Art is truth setting itself to work. What is truth itself, that it sometimes comes to pass as art? What is this setting-itself-to-work?

The Work and Truth

The origin of the art work is art. But what is art? Art is real in the art work. Hence we first seek the reality of the work. In what does it consist? Art works universally display a thingly character, albeit in a wholly distinct way. The attempt to interpret this thing-character of the work with the aid of the usual thing-concepts failed—not only because these concepts do not lay hold of the thingly feature, but because, in raising the question of its thingly substructure, we force the work into a preconceived framework by which we obstruct our own access to the work-being of the work. Nothing can be discovered about the thingly aspect of the work so long as the pure self-subsistence of the work has not distinctly displayed itself.

Yet is the work ever in itself accessible? To gain access to the work, it would be necessary to remove it from all relations to something other than itself, in order to let it stand on its own for itself alone. But the artist's most peculiar intention already aims in this direction. The work is to be released by him to its pure self-subsistence. It is precisely in great art—and only such art is under consideration here—that the artist remains inconsequential as compared with the work, almost like a passageway that destroys itself in the creative process for the work to emerge.

Well, then, the works themselves stand and hang in collections and exhibitions. But are they here in themselves as the works they themselves are, or are they not rather here as objects of the art industry? Works are made available for public and private art appreciation. Official agencies assume the care and maintenance of works. Connoisseurs and critics busy themselves with them. Art dealers supply the market. Art-historical study makes the works the objects of a science. Yet in all this busy activity do we encounter the work itself?

The Aegina sculptures in the Munich collection, Sophocles' *Antigone* in the best critical edition, are, as the works they are, torn out of their own native sphere. However high their quality and power of impression, however good their state of preservation, however certain their interpretation, placing them in a collection has withdrawn them from their own world. But even when we make an effort to cancel or avoid such displacement of works—when, for instance, we visit the temple in Paestum at its own site or the Bamberg cathedral on its own square—the world of the work that stands there has perished.

World-withdrawal and world-decay can never be undone. The works are no longer the same as they once were. It is they themselves, to be sure, that we encounter there, but they themselves are gone by. As bygone works they stand over against us in the realm of tradition and conservation. Henceforth they remain merely such objects. Their standing before us is still indeed a consequence of, but no longer the same as, their former self-subsistence. This self-subsistence has fled from them. The whole art industry, even if carried to the extreme and exercised in every way for the sake of works themselves, extends only to the object-being of the works. But this does not constitute their work-being.

But does the work still remain a work if it stands outside all relations? Is is not essential for the work to stand in relations? Yes, of course—except that it remains to ask in what relations it stands.

Where does a work belong? The work belongs, as work, uniquely within the realm that is opened up by itself. For the work-being of the work is present in, and only in, such opening up. We said that in the work there was a happening of truth at work. The reference to Van Gogh's picture tried to point to this happening. With regard to it there arose the question as to what truth is and how truth can happen.

We now ask the question of truth with a view to the work. But in order to become more familiar with what the question involves, it is necessary to make visible once more the happening of truth in the work. For this attempt let us deliberately select a work that cannot be ranked as representational art.

A building, a Greek temple, portrays nothing. It simply stands there in the middle of the rock-cleft valley. The building encloses the figure of the god, and in this concealment lets it stand out into the holy precinct through the open portico. By means of the temple, the god is present in the temple. This presence of the god is in itself the extension and delimitation of the precinct as a holy precinct. The temple and its precinct, however, do not fade away into the indefinite. It is the temple-work that first fits together and at the same time gathers around itself the unity of those paths and relations in which birth and death, disaster and blessing, victory and disgrace, endurance and decline acquire the shape of destiny for human being. The all-governing expanse of this open relational context is the world of this historical people. Only from and in this expanse does the nation first return to itself for the fulfillment of its vocation.

Standing there, the building rests on the rocky ground. This resting of the work draws up out of the rock the mystery of that rock's clumsy yet spontaneous support. Standing there, the building holds its ground against the storm raging above it and so first makes the storm itself manifest in its violence. The luster and gleam of the stone, though itself apparently glowing only by the grace of the sun, yet first brings to light the light of the day, the breadth of the sky, the darkness of the night. The temple's firm towering makes visible the invisible space of air. The steadfastness of the work contrasts with the surge of the surf, and its own repose brings out the raging of the sea. Tree and grass, eagle and bull, snake and cricket first enter into their distinctive shapes and thus come to appear as what they are. The Greeks early called this emerging and rising in itself and in all things *phusis*. It clears and illuminates, also, that on which and in which man bases his dwelling. We call this ground the *earth*. What this word says is not to be associated with the idea of a mass of matter deposited somewhere, or with the merely astronomical idea of a planet. Earth is that whence the arising brings back and shelters everything that arises without violation. In the things that arise, earth is present as the sheltering agent.

The temple-work, standing there, opens up a world and at the same time sets this world back again on earth, which itself only thus emerges as native ground. But men and animals, plants and things, are never present and familiar as unchangeable objects, only to represent incidentally also a fitting environment for the temple, which one fine day is added to what is already there. We shall get closer to what *is*, rather, if we think of all this in reverse order, assuming of course that we have, to begin with, an eye for how differently everything then faces us. Mere reversing, done for its own sake, reveals nothing.

The temple, in its standing there, first gives to things their look and to men their outlook on themselves. This view remains open as long as the work is a work, as long as the god has not fled from it. It is the same with the sculpture of the god, votive offering of the victor in the athletic games. It is not a portrait whose purpose is to make it easier to realize how the god looks;

rather, it is a work that lets the god himself be present and thus *is* the god himself. The same holds for the linguistic work. In the tragedy nothing is staged or displayed theatrically, but the battle of the new gods against the old is being fought. The linguistic work, originating in the speech of the people, does not refer to this battle; it transforms the people's saying so that now every living word fights the battle and puts up for decision what is holy and what unholy, what great and what small, what brave and what cowardly, what lofty and what flighty, what master and what slave (cf. Heraclitus, Fragment 53).

In what, then, does the work-being of the work consist? Keeping steadily in view the points just crudely enough indicated, two essential features of the work may for the moment be brought out more distinctly. We set out here, from the long familiar foreground of the work's being, the thingly character which gives support to our customary attitude toward the work.

When a work is brought into a collection or placed in an exhibition we say also that it is "set up." But this setting up differs essentially from setting up in the sense of erecting a building, raising a statue, presenting a tragedy at a holy festival. Such setting up is erecting in the sense of dedication and praise. Here "setting up" no longer means a bare placing. To dedicate means to consecrate, in the sense that in setting up the work the holy is opened up as holy and the god is invoked into the openness of his presence. Praise belongs to dedication as doing honor to the dignity and splendor of the god. Dignity and splendor are not properties beside and behind which the god, too, stands as something distinct, but it is rather in the dignity, in the splendor that the god is present. In the reflected glory of this splendor there glows, i.e., there lightens itself, what we called the word. To e-rect means: to open the right in the sense of a guiding measure, a form in which what belongs to the nature of being gives guidance. But why is the setting up of a work an erecting that consecrates and praises? Because the work, in its work-being, demands it. How is it that the work comes to demand such a setting up? Because it itself, in its own work-being, is something that sets up. What does the work, as work, set up? Towering up within itself, the work opens up a *world* and keeps it abidingly in force.

To be a work means to set up a world. But what is it to be a world? The answer was hinted at when we referred to the temple. On the path we must follow here, the nature of world can only be indicated. What is more, this indication limits itself to warding off anything that might at first distort our view of the world's nature.

The world is not the mere collection of the countable or uncountable, familiar and unfamiliar things that are just there. But neither is it a merely imagined framework added by our representation to the sum of such given things. The *world worlds,* and is more fully in being than the tangible and perceptible realm in which we believe ourselves to be at home. World is never an object that stands before us and can be seen. World is the ever-nonobjective to which we are subject as long as the paths of birth and death, blessing and curse keep us transported into Being. Wherever those decisions of our history that relate to our very being are made, are taken up and abandoned by us, go unrecognized and are rediscovered by new inquiry, there the world worlds. A stone is worldless. Plant and animal likewise have no world; but they belong to the covert throng of a surrounding into which they are linked. The peasant woman, on the other hand, has a world because she dwells in the overtness of beings, of the things that are. Her equipment, in its reliability, gives to this world a necessity and nearness of its own. By the opening up of a world, all things gain their lingering and hastening, their remoteness and nearness, their scope and limits. In a world's worlding is gathered that spaciousness out of which the protective grace of the gods is granted or withheld. Even this doom of the god remaining absent is a way in which world worlds.

A work, by being a work, makes space for that spaciousness. "To make space for" means here especially to liberate the Open and to establish it in its structure. This in-stalling occurs through the erecting mentioned earlier. The work as work sets up a world. The work holds open the Open of the world. But the setting up of a world is only the first essential feature in the work-being of a work to be referred to here. Starting again from the foreground of the work, we shall attempt to make clear in the same way the second essential feature that belongs with the first.

When a work is created, brought forth out of this or that work-material—stone, wood, metal, color, language, tone—we say also that it is made, set forth out of it. But just as the work requires a setting up in the sense of a con-secrating-praising erection, because the work's work-being consists in the set-ting up of a world, so a setting forth is needed because the work-being of the work itself has the character of setting forth. The work as work, in its pres-encing, is a setting forth, a making. But what does the work set forth? We come to know about this only when we explore what comes to the fore and is customarily spoken of as the making or production of works.

To work-being there belongs the setting up of a world. Thinking of it within this perspective, what is the nature of that in the work which is usually called the work material? Because it is determined by usefulness and service-ability, equipment takes into its service that of which it consists: the matter. In fabricating equipment—e.g., an ax—stone is used, and used up. It disappears into usefulness. The material is all the better and more suitable the less it resists perishing in the equipmental being of the equipment. By contrast the temple-work, in setting up a world, does not cause the material to disappear, but rather causes it to come forth for the very first time and to come into the Open of the work's world. The rock comes to bear and rest and so first becomes rock; metals come to glitter and shimmer, colors to glow, tones to sing, the word to speak. All this comes forth as the work sets itself back into the massiveness and heaviness of stone, into the firmness and pliancy of wood, into the hardness and luster of metal, into the lighting and darkening of color, into the clang of tone, and into the naming power of the word.

That into which the work sets itself back and which it causes to come forth in this setting back of itself we called the earth. Earth is that which comes forth and shelters. Earth, self-dependent, is effortless and untiring. Upon the earth and in it, historical man grounds his dwelling in the world. In setting up a world, the work sets forth the earth. This setting forth must be thought here in the strict sense of the word. The work moves the earth itself into the Open of a world and keeps it there. *The work lets the earth be an earth.*

But why must this setting forth of the earth happen in such a way that the work sets itself back into it? What is the earth that it attains to the unconcealed in just such a manner? A stone presses downward and manifests its heaviness. But while this heaviness exerts an opposing pressure upon us it denies us any penetration into it. If we attempt such a penetration by breaking open the rock, it still does not display in its fragments anything inward that has been disclosed. The stone has instantly withdrawn again into the same dull pressure and bulk of its fragments. If we try to lay hold of the stone's heaviness in another way, by placing the stone on a balance, we merely bring the heaviness into the form of a calculated weight. This perhaps very precise determination of the stone remains a number, but the weight's burden has escaped us. Color shines and wants only to shine. When we analyze it in rational terms by measuring its wavelengths, it is gone. It shows itself only when it remains undisclosed and unexplained. Earth thus shatters every attempt to penetrate into it. It causes every merely calculating importunity upon it to turn into a destruction. This destruction may herald itself under the appearance of mastery and of progress in the form of the technical-scientific objectivation of nature, but this mastery nevertheless remains an impotence of will. The earth appears openly cleared as itself only when it is perceived and preserved as that which is by nature undisclosable, that which shrinks from every disclosure and constantly keeps itself closed up. All things of earth, and the earth itself as a whole, flow together into a reciprocal accord. But this confluence is not a blurring of their outlines. Here there flows the stream, restful within itself, of the setting of bounds, which delimits everything present within its presence. Thus in each of the self-secluding things there is the same not-knowing-of-one-another. The earth is essentially self-secluding. To set forth the earth means to bring it into the Open as the self-secluding.

This setting forth of the earth is achieved by the work as it sets itself back into the earth. The self-seclusion of earth, however, is not a uniform, inflexible staying under cover, but unfolds itself in an inexhaustible variety of simple modes and shapes. To be sure, the sculptor uses stone just as the mason uses it, in his own way. But he does not use it up. That happens in a certain way only where the work miscarries. To be sure, the painter also uses pigment, but in such a way that color is not used up but rather only now comes to shine forth. To be sure, the poet also uses the word—not, however, like ordinary speakers and writers who have to use them up, but rather in such a way that the word only now becomes and remains truly a word.

Nowhere in the work is there any trace of a work-material. It even remains doubtful whether, in the essential definition of equipment, what the equipment consists of is properly described in its equipmental nature as matter.

The setting up of a world and the setting forth of earth are two essential features in the work-being of the work. They belong together, however, in the unity of work-being. This is the unity we seek when we ponder the self-subsistence of the work and try to express in words this closed, unitary repose of self-support.

But in the essential features just mentioned, if our account has any validity at all, we have indicated in the work rather a happening and in no sense a repose, for what is rest if not the opposite of motion? It is at any rate not an opposite that excludes motion from itself, but rather includes it. Only what is in motion can rest. The mode of rest varies with the kind of motion. In motion as the mere displacement of a body, rest is, to be sure, only the limiting case of motion. Where rest includes motion, there can exist a repose which is an inner concentration of motion, hence a highest state of agitation, assuming that the mode of motion requires such a rest. Now the repose of the work that rests in itself is of this sort. We shall come nearer to this repose if we can succeed in grasping the state of movement of the happening in work-being in its full unity. We ask: What relation do the setting up of a world and the setting forth of the earth exhibit in the work itself?

The world is the self-disclosing openness of the broad paths of the simple and essential decisions in the destiny of an historical people. The earth is the spontaneous forthcoming of that which is continually self-secluding and to that extent sheltering and concealing. World and earth are essentially different from one another and yet are never separated. The world grounds itself on the earth, and earth juts through world. But the relation between world and earth does not wither away into the empty unity of opposites unconcerned with one another. The world, in resting upon the earth, strives to surmount it. As self-opening it cannot endure anything closed. The earth, however, as sheltering and concealing, tends always to draw the world into itself and keep it there.

The opposition of world and earth is a striving. But we would surely all too easily falsify its nature if we were to confound striving with discord and dispute, and thus see it only as disorder and destruction. In essential striving, rather, the opponents raise each other into the self-assertion of their natures. Self-assertion of nature, however, is never a rigid insistence upon some contingent state, but surrender to the concealed originality of the source of one's own being. In the struggle, each opponent carries the other beyond itself. Thus the striving becomes even more intense as striving, and more authentically what it is. The more the struggle overdoes itself on its own part, the more inflexibly do the opponents let themselves go into the intimacy of simple belonging to one another. The earth cannot dispense with the Open of the world if it itself is to appear as earth in the liberated surge of its self-seclusion. The world, again, cannot soar out of the earth's sight if, as the governing breadth and path of all essential destiny, it is to ground itself on a resolute foundation.

In setting up a world and setting forth the earth, the work is an instigating of this striving. This does not happen so that the work should at the same time settle and put an end to the conflict in an insipid agreement, but so that the strife may remain a strife. Setting up a world and setting forth the earth, the work accomplishes this striving. The work-being of the work consists in the fighting of the battle between world and earth. It is because the struggle arrives at its high point in the simplicity of intimacy that the unity of the work comes about in the fighting of the battle. The fighting of the battle is the continually self-overreaching gathering of the work's agitation. The repose of the work that rests in itself thus has its presencing in the intimacy of striving.

From this repose of the work we can now first see what is at work in the work. Until now it was a merely provisional assertion that in an art work the truth is set to work. In what way does truth happen in the work-being of the work, i.e., now, how does truth happen in the fighting of the battle between world and earth? What is truth?

How slight and stunted our knowledge of the nature of truth is, is shown by the laxity we permit ourselves in using this basic word. By truth is usually meant this or that particular truth. That means: something true. A cognition articulated in a proposition can be of this sort. However, we call not only a proposition true, but also a thing, true gold in contrast with sham gold. True here means genuine, real gold. What does the expression "real" mean here? To us it is what is in truth. The true is what corresponds to the real, and the real is what is in truth. The circle has closed again.

What does "in truth" mean? Truth is the essence of the true. What do we have in mind when speaking of essence? Usually it is thought to be those features held in common by everything that is true. The essence is discovered in the generic and universal concept, which represents the one feature that holds indifferently for many things. This indifferent essence (essentiality in the sense of *essentia*) is, however, only the inessential essence. What does the essential essence of something consist in? Presumably it lies in what the entity *is* in truth. The true essential nature of a thing is determined by way of its true being, by way of the truth of the given being. But we are now seeking not the truth of essential nature but the essential nature of truth. There thus appears a curious tangle. Is it only a curiosity or even merely the empty sophistry of a conceptual game, or is it—an abyss?

Truth means the nature of the true. We think this nature in recollecting the Greek word *alētheia*, the unconcealedness of beings. But is this enough to define the nature of truth? Are we not passing off a mere change of word usage—unconcealedness instead of truth—as a characterization of fact? Certainly we do not get beyond an interchange of names as long as we do not come to know what must have happened in order to be compelled to tell the *nature* of truth in the word "unconcealedness."

Does this require a revival of Greek philosophy? Not at all. A revival, even if such an impossibility were possible, would be of no help to us; for the hidden history of Greek philosophy consists from its beginning in this, that it does not remain in conformity with the nature of truth that flashes out in the word *alētheia*, and has to misdirect its knowing and its speaking about the nature of truth more and more into the discussion of a derivative nature of truth. The nature of truth as *alêtheia* was not thought out in the thinking of the Greeks nor since then, and least of all in the philosophy that followed after. Unconcealedness is, for thought, the most concealed thing in Greek existence, although from early times it determines the presence of everything present.

Yet why should we not be satisfied with the nature of truth that has by now been familiar to us for centuries? Truth means today and has long meant the agreement or conformity of knowledge with fact. However, the fact must show itself to be fact if knowledge and the proposition that forms and expresses knowledge are to be able to conform to the fact; otherwise the fact cannot become binding on the proposition. How can fact show itself if it cannot itself stand forth out of concealedness, if it does not itself stand in the unconcealed? A proposition is true by conforming to the unconcealed, to what is true. Propositional truth is always, and always exclusively, this correctness. The critical concepts of truth which, since Descartes, start out from truth as certainty, are merely variations of the definition of truth as correctness. This nature of truth which is familiar to us—correctness in representation—stands and falls with truth as unconcealedness of beings.

If here and elsewhere we conceive of truth as unconcealedness, we are not merely taking refuge in a more literal translation of a Greek word. We are reminding ourselves of what, unexperienced and unthought, underlies our familiar and therefore outworn nature of truth in the sense of correctness. We do, of course, occasionally take the trouble to concede that naturally, in order to understand and verify the correctness (truth) of a proposition one really should go back to something that is already evident, and that this presupposition is indeed unavoidable. As long as we talk and believe in this way, we always understand truth merely as correctness, which of course still requires a further presupposition, that we ourselves just happen to make, heaven knows how or why.

But it is not we who presuppose the unconcealedness of beings; rather, the unconcealedness of beings (Being) puts us into such a condition of being that in our representation we always remain installed within and in attendance upon unconcealedness. Not only must that in *conformity* with which a cognition orders itself be already in some way unconcealed. The entire *realm* in which this "conforming to something" goes on must already occur as a whole in the unconcealed; and this holds equally of that *for* which the conformity of a proposition to fact becomes manifest. With all our correct representations we would get nowhere, we could not even presuppose that there already is manifest something to which we can conform ourselves, unless the unconcealedness of beings had already exposed us to, placed us in that lighted realm in which every being stands for us and from which it withdraws.

But how does this take place? How does truth happen as this unconcealedness? First, however, we must say more clearly what this unconcealedness itself is.

Things are, and human beings, gifts, and sacrifices are, animals and plants are, equipment and works are. That which is, the particular being, stands in Being. Through Being there passes a veiled destiny that is ordained between the godly and the countergodly. There is much in being that man cannot master. There is but little that comes to be known. What is known remains inexact, what is mastered insecure. What is, is never of our making or even merely the product of our minds, as it might all too easily seem. When we contemplate this whole as one, then we apprehend, so it appears, all that is—though we grasp it crudely enough.

And yet—beyond what is, not away from it but before it, there is still something else that happens. In the midst of beings as a whole an open place occurs. There is a clearing, a lighting. Thought of in reference to what is, to beings, this clearing is in a greater degree than are beings. This open center is therefore not surrounded by what is; rather, the lighting center itself encircles all that is, like the Nothing which we scarcely know.

That which is can only be, as a being, if it stands within and stands out within what is lighted in this clearing. Only this clearing grants and guarantees to us humans a passage to those beings that we ourselves are not, and access to the being that we ourselves are. Thanks to this clearing, beings are unconcealed in certain changing degrees. And yet a being can be *concealed*, too, only within the sphere of what is lighted. Each being we encounter and which encounters us keeps to this curious opposition of presence in that it always withholds itself at the same time in a concealedness. The clearing in which beings stand is in itself at the same time concealment. Concealment, however, prevails in the midst of beings in a twofold way.

Beings refuse themselves to us down to that one and seemingly least feature which we touch upon most readily when we can say no more of beings than that they are. Concealment as refusal is not simply and only the limit of knowledge in any given circumstance, but the beginning of the clearing of what is lighted. But concealment, though of another sort, to be sure, at the same time also occurs within what is lighted. One being places itself in front of another being, the one helps to hide the other, the former obscures the latter, a few obstruct many, one denies all. Here concealment is not simple refusal. Rather, a being appears, but it presents itself as other than it is.

This concealment is dissembling. If one being did not simulate another, we could not make mistakes or act mistakenly in regard to beings; we could not go astray and transgress, and especially could never overreach ourselves. That a being should be able to deceive as semblance is the condition for our being able to be deceived, not conversely.

Concealment can be a refusal or merely a dissembling. We are never fully certain whether it is the one or the other. Concealment conceals and dissembles itself. This means: the open place in the midst of beings, the clearing, is never a rigid stage with a permanently raised curtain on which the play of beings runs its course. Rather, the clearing happens only as this double concealment. The unconcealedness of beings—this is never a merely existent state, but a happening. Unconcealedness (truth) is neither an attribute of factual things in the sense of beings, nor one of propositions.

We believe we are at home in the immediate circle of beings. That which is, is familiar, reliable, ordinary. Nevertheless, the clearing is pervaded by a constant concealment in the double form of refusal and dissembling. At bottom, the ordinary is not ordinary; it is extra-ordinary, uncanny. The nature of truth, that is, of unconcealedness, is dominated throughout by a denial. Yet this denial is not a defect or a fault, as though truth were an unalloyed unconcealedness that has rid itself of everything concealed. If truth could accomplish this, it would no longer be itself. *This denial, in the form of a double concealment, belongs to the nature of truth as unconcealedness.* Truth, in its nature, is un-truth. We put the matter this way in order to serve notice, with a possibly surprising trenchancy, that denial in the manner of concealment belongs to unconcealedness as clearing. The proposition, "the nature of truth is untruth," is not, however, intended to state that truth is at bottom falsehood. Nor does it mean that truth is never itself but, viewed dialectically, is always also its opposite.

Truth occurs precisely as itself in that the concealing denial, as refusal, provides its constant source to all clearing, and yet, as dissembling, it metes out to all clearing the indefeasible severity of error. Concealing denial is intended to denote that opposition in the nature of truth which subsists between clearing, or lighting, and concealing. It is the opposition of the primal conflict. The nature of truth is, in itself, the primal conflict in which that open center is won within which what is, stands, and from which it sets itself back into itself.

This Open happens in the midst of beings. It exhibits an essential feature which we have already mentioned. To the Open there belong a world and the earth. But the world is not simply the Open that corresponds to clearing, and the earth is not simply the Closed that corresponds to concealment. Rather, the world is the clearing of the paths of the essential guiding directions with which all decision complies. Every decision, however, bases itself on something not mastered, something concealed, confusing; else it would never be a decision. The earth is not simply the Closed but rather that which rises up as self-closing. World and earth are always intrinsically and essentially in conflict, belligerent by nature. Only as such do they enter into the conflict of clearing and concealing.

Earth juts through the world and world grounds itself on the earth only so far as truth happens as the primal conflict between clearing and concealing. But how does truth happen? We answer: it happens in a few essential ways. One of these ways in which truth happens is the work-being of the work. Setting up a world and setting forth the earth, the work is the fighting of the battle in which the unconcealedness of beings as a whole, or truth, is won.

Truth happens in the temple's standing where it is. This does not mean that something is correctly represented and rendered here, but that what is as a whole is brought into unconcealedness and held therein. To hold *(halten)* originally means to tend, keep, take care *(hüten)*. Truth happens in Van Gogh's painting. This does not mean that something is correctly portrayed, but rather that in the revelation of the equipmental being of the shoes, that which is as a whole—world and earth in their counterplay—attains to unconcealedness.

Thus in the work it is truth, not only something true, that is at work. The picture that shows the peasant shoes, the poem that says the Roman fountain, do not just make manifest what this isolated being as such is—if indeed they manifest anything at all; rather, they make unconcealedness as such happen in regard to what is as a whole. The more simply and authentically the shoes are engrossed in their nature, the more plainly and purely the fountain is engrossed in its nature—the more directly and engagingly do all beings attain to a greater degree of being along with them. That is how self-concealing being is illuminated. Light of this kind joins its shining to and into the work. This shining, joined in the work, is the beautiful. *Beauty is one way in which truth occurs as unconcealedness.*

We now, indeed, grasp the nature of truth more clearly in certain respects. What is at work in the work may accordingly have become more clear. But the work's now visible work-being still does not tell us anything about the work's closest and most obtrusive reality, about the thingly aspect of the work. Indeed it almost seems as though, in pursuing the exclusive aim of grasping the work's independence as purely as possible, we had completely overlooked the one thing, that a work is always a work, which means that it is something worked out, brought about, effected. If there is anything that distinguishes the work as work, it is that the work has been created. Since the work is created, and creation requires a medium out of which and in which it creates, the thingly element, too, enters into the work. This is incontestable. Still the question remains: how does being created belong to the work? This can be elucidated only if two points are cleared up:

1. What do being created and creation mean here in distinction from making and being made?

2. What is the inmost nature of work itself, from which alone can be gauged how far createdness belongs to the work and how far it determines the work-being of the work?

Creation is here always thought of in reference to the work. To the nature of the work there belongs the happening of truth. From the outset we define the nature of creating by its relation to the nature of truth as the unconcealedness of beings. The pertinence of createdness to the work can be elucidated only by way of a more fundamental clarification of the nature of truth. The question of truth and its nature returns again.

We must raise that question once more, if the proposition that truth is at work in the work is not to remain a mere assertion.

We must now first ask in a more essential way: how does the impulse toward such a thing as a work lie in the nature of truth? Of what nature is truth, that it can be set into work, or even under certain conditions must be set into work, in order to be *as* truth? But we defined the setting-into-a-work of truth as the nature of art. Hence our last question becomes:

What is truth, that it can happen as, or even must happen as, art? How is it that art exists at all?

Truth and Art

Art is the origin of the art work and of the artist. Origin is the source of the nature in which the being of an entity is present. What is art? We seek its nature in the actual work. The actual reality of the work has been defined by that which is at work in the work, by the happening of truth. This happening we think of as the fighting of the conflict between world and earth. Repose occurs in the concentrated agitation of this conflict. The independence or self-composure of the work is grounded here.

In the work, the happening of truth is at work. But what is thus at work, is so *in* the work. This means that the actual work is here already presupposed as the bearer of this happening. At once the problem of the thingly feature of the given work confronts us again. One thing thus finally becomes clear; however zealously we inquire into the work's self-sufficiency, we shall still fail to find its actuality as long as we do not also agree to take the work as something worked, effected. To take it thus lies closest at hand, for in the word "work" we hear what is worked. The workly character of the work consists in its having been created by the artist. It may seem curious that this most obvious and all-clarifying definition of the work is mentioned only now.

The work's createdness, however, can obviously be grasped only in terms of the process of creation. Thus, constrained by the facts, we must consent after all to go into the activity of the artist in order to arrive at the origin of the work of art. The attempt to define the work-being of the work purely in terms of the work itself proves to be unfeasible.

In turning away now from the work to examine the nature of the creative process, we should like nevertheless to keep in mind what was said first of the picture of the peasant shoes and later of the Greek temple.

We think of creation as a bringing forth. But the making of equipment, too, is a bringing forth. Handicraft—a remarkable play of language—does not, to be sure, create works, not even when we contrast, as we must, the handmade with the factory product. But what is it that distinguishes bringing forth as creation from bringing forth in the mode of making? It is as difficult to track down the essential features of the creation of works and the making of equipment as it is easy to distinguish verbally between the two modes of bringing forth. Going along with first appearances we find the same procedure in the activity of potter and sculptor, of joiner and painter. The creation of a work requires craftsmanship. Great artists prize craftsmanship most highly. They are the first to call for its painstaking cultivation, based on complete mastery. They above all others constantly strive to educate themselves ever anew in thorough craftsmanship. It has often enough been pointed out that the Greeks, who knew quite a bit about works of art, use the same word *technē* for the craft and art and call the craftsman and the artist by the same name: *technitēs*.

It thus seems advisable to define the nature of creative work in terms of its craft aspect. But reference to the linguistic usage of the Greeks, with their experience of the fact, must give us pause. However usual and convincing the reference may be to the Greek practice of naming craft and art by the same name, *technē*, it nevertheless remains oblique and superficial; for *technē* signifies neither craft nor art, and not at all the technical in our present-day sense; it never means a kind of practical performance.

The word *technē* denotes rather a mode of knowing. To know means to have seen, in the widest sense of seeing, which means to apprehend what is present, as such. For Greek thought the nature of knowing consists in *alētheia*, that is, in the uncovering of beings. It supports and guides all comportment toward beings. *Technē*, as knowledge experienced in the Greek manner, is a bringing forth of beings in that it *brings forth* present beings as such beings *out of* concealedness and specifically *into* the unconcealedness of their appearance; *technē* never signifies the action of making.

The artist is a *technitēs* not because he is also a craftsman, but because both the setting forth of works and the setting forth of equipment occur in a bringing forth and presenting that causes being in the first place to come forward and be present in assuming an appearance. Yet all this happens in the midst of the being that grows out of its own accord, *phusis*. Calling art *technē* does not at all imply that the artist's action is seen in the light of craft. What looks like craft in the creation of a work is of a different sort. This doing is determined and pervaded by the nature of creation, and indeed remains contained within that creating.

What then, if not craft, is to guide our thinking about the nature of creation? What else than a view of what is to be created: the work? Although it becomes actual only as the creative act is performed, and thus depends for its reality upon this act, the nature of creation is determined by the nature of the work. Even though the work's createdness has a relation to creation, nevertheless both createdness and creation must be defined in terms of the work-being of the work. And now it can no longer seem strange that we first and at length dealt with the work alone, to bring its createdness into view only at the end. If createdness belongs to the work as essentially as the word "work" makes it sound, then we must try to understand even more essentially what so far could be defined as the work-being of the work.

In the light of the definition of the work we have reached at this point, according to which the happening of truth is at work in the work, we are able to characterize creation as follows: to create is to cause something to emerge as a thing that has been brought forth. The work's becoming a work is a way in which truth becomes and happens. It all rests on the nature of truth. But what is truth, that it has to happen in such a thing as something created? How does truth have an impulse toward a work grounded in its very nature?

Is this intelligible in terms of the nature of truth as thus far elucidated?

Truth is un-truth, insofar as there belongs to it the reservoir of the not-yet-uncovered, the un-uncovered, in the sense of concealment. In unconcealedness, as truth, there occurs also the other "un-" of a double restraint or refusal. Truth occurs as such in the opposition of clearing and double concealing. Truth is the primal conflict in which, always in some particular way, the Open is won within which everything stands and from which everything withholds itself that shows itself and withdraws itself as a being. Whenever and however this conflict breaks out and happens, the opponents, lighting or clearing and concealing, move apart because of it. Thus the Open of the place of conflict is won. The openness of this Open, that is, truth, can be what it is, namely, *this* openness, only if and as long as it establishes itself within its Open. Hence there must always be some being in this Open, something that is, in which the openness takes its stand and attains its constancy. In taking possession thus of the Open, the openness holds open the Open and sustains it. Setting and taking possession are here everywhere drawn from the Greek sense of *thesis,* which means a setting up in the unconcealed.

In referring to this self-establishing of openness in the Open, thinking touches on a sphere that cannot yet be explicated here. Only this much should be noted, that if the nature of the unconcealedness of beings belongs in any way to Being itself (cf. *Being and Time,* § 44[1]), then Being, by way of its own nature, lets the place of openness (the lighting-clearing of the There) happen, and introduces it as a place of the sort in which each being emerges or arises in its own way.

Truth happens only by establishing itself in the conflict and sphere opened up by the truth itself. Because truth is the opposition of clearing and concealing, there belongs to it what is here to be called establishing. But truth does not exist in itself beforehand, somewhere among the stars, only later to descend elsewhere among beings. This is impossible for the reason alone that it is after all only the openness of beings that first affords the possibility of a somewhere and of a place filled by present beings. Clearing of openness and establishment in the Open belong together. They are the same single nature of the happening of truth. This happening is historical in many ways.

One essential way in which truth establishes itself in the beings it has opened up is truth setting itself into work. Another way in which truth occurs is the act that founds a political state. Still another way in which truth comes to shine forth is the nearness of that which is not simply a being, but the being that is most of all. Still another way in which truth grounds itself is the essential sacrifice. Still another way in which truth becomes is the thinker's questioning, which, as the thinking of Being, names Being in its question-worthiness. By contrast, science is not an original happening of truth, but always the cultivation of a domain of truth already opened, specifically by apprehending and confirming that which shows itself to be possibly and necessarily correct within that field. When and insofar as a science passes beyond correctness and goes on to a truth, which means that it arrives at the essential disclosure of what is as such, it is philosophy.

Because it is in the nature of truth to establish itself within that which is, in order thus first to become truth, therefore the impulse toward the work lies in the nature of truth as one of truth's distinctive possibilities by which it can itself occur as being in the midst of beings.

The establishing of truth in the work is the bringing forth of a being such as never was before and will never come to be again. The bringing forth places this being in the Open in such a way that what is to be brought forth first clears the openness of the Open into which it comes forth. Where this bringing forth expressly brings the openness of beings, or truth, that which is brought forth is a work. Creation is such a bringing forth. As such a bringing, it is rather a receiving and an incorporating of a relation to unconcealed-ness. What, accordingly, does the createdness consist in? It may be elucidated by two essential determinations.

Truth establishes itself in the work. Truth is present only as the conflict between lighting and concealing in the opposition of world and earth. Truth wills to be established in the work as this conflict of world and earth. The con-flict is not to be resolved in a being brought forth for the purpose, nor is it to be merely housed there; the conflict, on the contrary, is started by it. This being must therefore contain within itself the essential traits of the conflict. In the strife the unity of world and earth is won. As a world opens itself, it sub-mits to the decision of an historical humanity the question of victory and defeat, blessing and curse, mastery and slavery. The dawning world brings out what is as yet undecided and measureless, and thus discloses the hidden necessity of measure and decisiveness.

But as a world opens itself the earth comes to rise up. It stands forth as that which bears all, as that which is sheltered in its own law and always wrapped up in itself. World demands its decisiveness and its measure and lets beings attain to the Open of their paths. Earth, bearing and jutting, strives to keep itself closed and to entrust everything to its law. The conflict is not a rift *(Riss)* as a mere cleft is ripped open; rather, it is the intimacy with which opponents belong to each other. This rift carries the opponents into the source of their unity by virtue of their common ground. It is a basic design, an outline sketch, that draws the basic features of the rise of the lighting of beings. This rift does not let the opponents break apart; it brings the opposi-tion of measure and boundary into their common outline.

Truth establishes itself as a strife within a being that is to be brought forth only in such a way that the conflict opens up in this being, that is, this being is itself brought into the rift-design. The rift-design is the drawing together, into a unity, of sketch and basic design, breach and outline. Truth establishes itself in a being in such a way, indeed, that this being itself occupies the Open of truth. This occupying, however, can happen only if what is to be brought forth, the rift, entrusts itself to the self-secluding factor that juts up in the Open. The rift must set itself back into the heavy weight of stone, the dumb hardness of wood, the dark glow of colors. As the earth takes the rift back into itself, the rift is set forth into the Open and thus placed, that is, set, within that which towers up into the Open as self-closing and sheltering.

The strife that is brought into the rift and thus set back into the earth and thus fixed in place is *figure, shape, Gestalt.* Createdness of the work means: truth's being fixed in place in the figure. Figure is the structure in whose shape the rift composes and submits itself. This composed rift is the fitting or joining of the shining of truth. What is here called figure, *Gestalt,* is always to be thought in terms of the particular placing *(Stellen)* and framing or framework *(Ge-stell)* as which the work occurs when it sets itself up and sets itself forth.

In the creation of a work, the conflict, as rift, must be set back into the earth, and the earth itself must be set forth and used as the self-closing factor. This use, however, does not use up or misuse the earth as matter, but rather sets it free to be nothing but itself. This use of the earth is a working with it that, to be sure, looks like the employment of matter in handicraft. Hence the appearance that artistic creation is also an activity of handicraft. It never is. But it is at all times a use of the earth in the fixing in place of truth in the figure. In contrast, the making of equipment is never directly the effecting of the happening of truth. The production of equipment is finished when a material has been so formed as to be ready for use. For equipment to be ready means that it is dismissed beyond itself, to be used up in serviceability.

Not so when a work is created. This becomes clear in the light of the second characteristic, which may be introduced here.

The readiness of equipment and the createdness of the work agree in this, that in each case something is produced. But in contrast to all other modes of production, the work is distinguished by being created so that its createdness is part of the created work. But does not this hold true for everything brought forth, indeed for anything that has in any way come to be? Everything brought forth surely has this endowment of having been brought forth, if it has any endowment at all. Certainly. But in the work, createdness is expressly created into the created being, so that it stands out from it, from the being thus brought forth, in an expressly particular way. If this is how matters stand, then we must also be able to discover and experience the createdness explicitly in the work.

The emergence of createdness from the work does not mean that the work is to give the impression of having been made by a great artist. The point is not that the created being be certified as the performance of a capable person, so that the producer is thereby brought to public notice. It is not the "N. N. fecit" that is to be made known. Rather, the simple "factum est" is to be held forth into the Open by the work: namely this, that unconcealedness of what is has happened here, and that as this happening it happens here for the first time; or, that such a work *is* at all rather than is not. The thrust that the work as this work is, and the uninterruptedness of this plain thrust, constitute the steadfastness of the work's self-subsistence. Precisely where the artist and the process and the circumstances of the genesis of the work remain unknown, this thrust, this *"that* it is" of createdness, emerges into view most purely from the work. . . .

The reality of the work has become not only clearer for us in the light of its work-being, but also essentially richer. The preservers of a work belong to its createdness with an essentiality equal to that of the creators. But it is the work that makes the creators possible in their nature, and that by its own nature is in need of preservers. If art is the origin of the work, this means that art lets those who naturally belong together at work, the creator and the preserver, originate, each in his own nature. What, however, is art itself that we call it rightly an origin?

In the work, the happening of truth is at work and, indeed, at work according to the manner of a work. Accordingly the nature of art was defined to begin with as the setting-into-work of truth. Yet this definition is intentionally ambiguous. It says on the one hand: art is the fixing in place of a self-establishing truth in the figure. This happens in creation as the bringing forth of the unconcealedness of what is. Setting-into-work, however, also means: the bringing of work-being into movement and happening. This happens as preservation. Thus art is: the creative preserving of truth in the work. *Art then is the becoming and happening of truth.* Does truth, then, arise out of nothing? It does indeed if by nothing is meant the mere not of that which is, and if we here think of that which is an object present in the ordinary way, which thereafter comes to light and is challenged by the existence of the work as only presumptively a true being. Truth is never gathered from objects that are present and ordinary. Rather, the opening up of the Open, and the clearing of what is, happens only as the openness is projected, sketched out, that makes its advent in thrownness.[2]

Truth, as the clearing and concealing of what is, happens in being composed, as a poet composes a poem. *All art,* as the letting happen of the advent of the truth of what is, is, as such, *essentially poetry.* The nature of art, on which both the art work and the artist depend, is the setting-itself-into-work of truth. It is due to art's poetic nature that, in the midst of what is, art breaks open an open place, in whose openness everything is other than usual. By virtue of the projected sketch set into the work of the unconcealedness of what is, which casts itself toward us, everything ordinary and hitherto existing becomes an unbeing. This unbeing has lost the capacity to give and keep being as measure. The curious fact here is that the work in no way affects hitherto existing entities by causal connections. The working of the work does not consist in the taking effect of a cause. It lies in a change, happening from out of the work, of the unconcealedness of what is, and this means, of Being.

Poetry, however, is not an aimless imagining of whimsicalities and not a flight of mere notions and fancies into the realm of the unreal. What poetry, as illuminating projection, unfolds of unconcealedness and projects ahead into the design of the figure, is the Open which poetry lets happen, and indeed in such a way that only now, in the midst of beings, the Open brings beings to shine and ring out. If we fix our vision on the nature of the work and its connection with the happening of the truth of what is, it becomes questionable whether the nature of poetry, and this means at the same time the nature of projection, can be adequately thought of in terms of the power of imagination.

The nature of poetry, which has now been ascertained very broadly—but not on that account vaguely, may here be kept firmly in mind as something worthy of questioning, something that still has to be thought through.

If all art is in essence poetry, then the arts of architecture, painting, sculpture, and music must be traced back to poesy. That is pure arbitrariness. It certainly is, as long as we mean that those arts are varieties of the art of language, if it is permissible to characterize poesy by that easily misinterpretable title. But poesy is only one mode of the lighting projection of truth, i.e., of poetic composition in this wider sense. Nevertheless, the linguistic work, the poem in the narrower sense, has a privileged position in the domain of the arts.

To see this, only the right concept of language is needed. In the current view, language is held to be a kind of communication. It serves for verbal exchange and agreement, and in general for communicating. But language is not only and not primarily an audible and written expression of what is to be communicated. It not only puts forth in words and statements what is overtly or covertly intended to be communicated; language alone brings what is, as something that is, into the Open for the first time. Where there is no language, as in the being of stone, plant, and animal, there is also no openness of what is, and consequently no openness either of that which is not and of the empty.

Language, by naming beings for the first time, first brings beings to word and to appearance. Only this naming nominates beings *to* their being *from out* of their being. Such saying is a projecting of the clearing, in which announcement is made of what it is that beings come into the Open *as*. Projecting is the release of a throw by which unconcealedness submits and infuses itself into what is as such. This projective announcement forthwith becomes a renunciation of all the dim confusion in which what is veils and withdraws itself.

Projective saying is poetry: the saying of world and earth, the saying of the arena of their conflict and thus of the place of all nearness and remoteness of the gods. Poetry is the saying of the unconcealedness of what is. Actual language at any given moment is the happening of this saying, in which a people's world historically arises for it and the earth is preserved as that which remains closed. Projective saying is saying which, in preparing the sayable, simultaneously brings the unsayable as such into a world. In such saying, the concepts of an historical people's nature, i.e., of its belonging to world history, are formed for that folk, before it.

Poetry is thought of here in so broad a sense and at the same time in such intimate unity of being with language and word, that we must leave open whether art, in all its modes from architecture to poesy, exhausts the nature of poetry.

Language itself is poetry in the essential sense. But since language is the happening in which for man beings first disclose themselves to him each time as beings, poesy—or poetry in the narrower sense—is the most original form of poetry in the essential sense. Language is not poetry because it is the primal poesy; rather, poesy takes place in language because language preserves the original nature of poetry. Building and plastic creation, on the other hand, always happen already, and happen only, in the Open of saying and naming. It is the Open that pervades and guides them. But for this very reason they remain their own ways and modes in which truth orders itself into work. They are an ever special poetizing within the clearing of what is, which has already happened unnoticed in language.

Art, as the setting-into-work of truth, is poetry. Not only the creation of the work is poetic, but equally poetic, though in its own way, is the preserving of the work; for a work is in actual effect as a work only when we remove ourselves from our commonplace routine and move into what is disclosed by the work, so as to bring our own nature itself to take a stand in the truth of what is.

NOTES

1. Martin Heidegger, *Being and Time*, translated by John Macquarrie and Edward Robinson (New York: Harper & Row, 1962).—TR

2. Thrownness, *Geworfenheit*, is understood in *Being and Time* as an existential characteristic of *Dasein*, human being, its thatness, its "that it is," and it refers to the facticity of human being's being handed over to itself, its being on its own responsibility; as long as human being is what it is, it is thrown, cast, "im Wurf." Projection, *Entwurf*, on the other hand, is a second existential character of human being, referring to its driving forward toward its own possibility of being. It takes the form of understanding, which the author speaks of as the mode of being of human being in which human being *is* in its possibilities *as* possibilities. It is not the mere having of a preconceived plan, but is the projecting of possibility in human being that occurs antecedently to all plans and makes planning possible. Human being is both thrown and projected; it is thrown project, factical directedness toward possibilities of being.—TR

MAURICE MERLEAU-PONTY

MERLEAU-PONTY IS REGARDED by many as the major French philosopher in the phenomenological tradition. His importance is due to his detailed development of figure-ground relationships as a basis for understanding thought and action—based finally on his theory of perception—and to his development of the notion of ambiguity. This is his way of expressing the principle that being and experience cannot be entirely determinate, for that would be incompatible with knowledge as well as action.

The following selection is remarkable for its development of Merleau-Ponty's view of vision, not simply as a contingent feature of human experience, but as a fundamental human or natural condition. Painting, for Merleau-Ponty, is the embodiment of vision, and vision is a condition of being human. We may wonder whether Merleau-Ponty's theory can be generalized to other arts, whether each art is to be associated with an authoritative mode of perception. We must also question whether painting can stand in so intimate a relationship to vision as Merleau-Ponty requires.

MAURICE MERLEAU-PONTY

Eye and Mind *

1

. . . Scientific thinking, a thinking which looks on from above, and thinks of the object-in-general, must return to the "there is" which underlies it; to the site, the soil of the sensible and opened world such as it is in our life and for our body—not that possible body which we may legitimately think of as an information machine but that actual body I call mine, this sentinel standing quietly at the command of my words and my acts. Further, *associated bodies* must be brought forward along with my body—the "others," not merely as my congeners, as the zoologist says, but the others who haunt me and whom I haunt; the "others" along *with* whom I haunt a single, present, and actual Being as no animal ever haunted those beings of his own species, locale, or habitat. In this primordial historicity, science's agile and improvisatory thought will learn to ground itself upon things themselves and upon itself, and will once more become philosophy. . . .

But art, especially painting, draws upon this fabric of brute meaning which activism [or operationalism—*Trans.*] would prefer to ignore. Art and only art does so in full innocence. From the writer and the philosopher, in contrast, we want opinions and advice. We will not allow them to hold the world suspended. We want them to take a stand; they cannot waive the responsibilities of men who speak. Music, at the other extreme, is too far

---

* Maurice Merleau-Ponty, *The Primacy of Perception*, translated by Carleton Dallery, edited by James M. Edie (Evanston, Ill.: Northwestern University Press, 1964), pp. 160-169, 178-190. (Footnotes omitted.)

beyond the world and the designatable to depict anything but certain outlines of Being—its ebb and flow, its growth, its upheavals, its turbulence.

Only the painter is entitled to look at everything without being obliged to appraise what he sees. For the painter, we might say, the watchwords of knowledge and action lose their meaning and force. Political regimes which denounce "degenerate" painting rarely destroy paintings. They hide them, and one senses here an element of "one never knows" amounting almost to a recognition. The reproach of escapism is seldom aimed at the painter; we do not hold it against Cézanne that he lived hidden away at Estaque during the war of 1870. And we recall with respect his "C'est effrayant, la vie," even when the lowliest student, ever since Nietzsche, would flatly reject philosophy if it did not teach how to live fully [à être de grands vivants]. It is as if in the painter's calling there were some urgency above all other claims on him. Strong or frail in life, he is incontestably sovereign in his own rumination of the world. With no other technique than what his eyes and hands discover in seeing and painting, he persists in drawing from this world, with its din of history's glories and scandals, *canvases* which will hardly add to the angers or the hopes of man—and no one complains.

What, then, is this secret science which he has or which he seeks? That dimension which lets Van Gogh say he must go "further on"? What is this fundamental of painting, perhaps of all culture?

2

THE PAINTER "takes his body with him," says Valéry. Indeed we cannot imagine how a *mind* could paint. It is by lending his body to the world that the artist changes the world into paintings. To understand these transubstantiations we must go back to the working, actual body—not the body as a chunk of space or a bundle of functions but that body which is an intertwining of vision and movement.

I have only to see something to know how to reach it and deal with it, even if I do not know how this happens in the nervous machine. My mobile body makes a difference in the visible world, being a part of it; that is why I can steer it through the visible. Conversely, it is just as true that vision is attached to movement. We see only what we look at. What would vision be without eye movement? And how could the movement of the eyes bring things together if the movement were blind? If it were only a reflex? If it did not have its antennae, its clairvoyance? If vision were not prefigured in it?

In principle all my changes of place figure in a corner of my landscape; they are recorded on the map of the visible. Everything I see is in principle within my reach, at least within reach of my sight, and is marked upon the map of the "I can." Each of the two maps is complete. The visible world and the world of my motor projects are each total parts of the same Being.

This extraordinary overlapping, which we never think about sufficiently, forbids us to conceive of vision as an operation of thought that would set up before the mind a picture or a representation of the world, a world of immanence and of ideality. Immersed in the visible by his body, itself visible, the see-er does not appropriate what he sees; he merely approaches it by looking, he opens himself to the world. And on its side, this world of which he is a part is not *in itself,* or matter. My movement is not a decision made by the mind, an absolute doing which would decree, from the depths of a subjective retreat, some change of place miraculously executed in extended space. It is the natural consequence and the maturation of my vision. I say of a thing that it is moved; but my body moves itself, my movement deploys itself. It is not ignorant of itself; it is not blind for itself; it radiates from a self. . . .

The enigma is that my body simultaneously sees and is seen. That which looks at all things can also look at itself and recognize, in what it sees, the "other side" of its power of looking. It sees itself seeing; it touches itself touching; it is visible and sensitive for itself. It is not a self through transparence, like thought, which only thinks its object by assimilating it, by constituting it, by transforming it into thought. It is a self through confusion, narcissism, through inherence of the one who sees in that which he sees, and through inherence of sensing in the sensed—a self, therefore, that is caught up in things, that has a front and a back, a past and a future. . . .

This initial paradox cannot but produce others. Visible and mobile, my body is a thing among things; it is caught in the fabric of the world, and its cohesion is that of a thing. But because it moves itself and sees, it holds things in a circle around itself. Things are an annex or prolongation of itself; they are incrusted into its flesh, they are part of its full definition; the world is made of the same stuff as the body. This way of turning things around *[ces renverse-ments],* these antinomies, are different ways of saying that vision happens among, or is caught in, things—in that place where something visible undertakes to see, becomes visible for itself by virtue of the sight of things; in that place where there persists, like the mother water in crystal, the undividedness *[l'indivision]* of the sensing and the sensed.

This interiority no more precedes the material arrangement of the human body than it results from it. What if our eyes were made in such a way as to prevent our seeing any part of our body, or if some baneful arrangement of the body were to let us move our hands over things, while preventing us from touching our own body? Or what if, like certain animals, we had lateral eyes with no cross blending of visual fields? Such a body would not reflect itself; it would be an almost adamantine body, not really flesh, not really the body of a human being. There would be no humanity.

But humanity is not produced as the effect of our articulations or by the way our eyes are implanted in us (still less by the existence of mirrors which could make our entire body visible to us). These contingencies and others like them, without which mankind would not exist, do not by simple summation bring it about that there *is* a single man.

The body's animation is not the assemblage or juxtaposition of its parts. Nor is it a question of a mind or spirit coming down from somewhere else into an automaton; this would still suppose that the body itself is without an inside and without a "self." There is a human body when, between the seeing and the seen, between touching and the touched, between one eye and the other, between hand and hand a blending of some sort takes place—when the spark is lit between sensing and sensible, lighting the fire that will not stop burning until some accident of the body will undo what no accident would have sufficed to do. . . .

Once this strange system of exchanges is given, we find before us all the problems of painting. These exchanges illustrate the enigma of the body, and this enigma justifies them. Since things and my body are made of the same stuff, vision must somehow take place in them; their manifest visibility must be repeated in the body by a secret visibility. "Nature is on the inside," says Cézanne. Quality, light, color, depth, which are there before us, are there only because they awaken an echo in our body and because the body welcomes them.

Things have an internal equivalent in me; they arouse in me a carnal formula of their presence. Why shouldn't these [correspondences] in their turn give rise to some [external] visible shape in which anyone else would recognize those motifs which support his own inspection of the world? Thus there appears a "visible" of the second power, a carnal essence or icon of the first. It is not a faded copy, a *trompe-l'oeil*, or another *thing*. The animals painted on the walls of Lascaux are not there in the same way as the fissures and limestone formations. But they are not *elsewhere*. Pushed forward here, held back there, held up by the wall's mass they use so adroitly, they spread around the wall without ever breaking from their elusive moorings in it. I would be at great pains to say *where* is the painting I am looking at. For I do not look at it as I do at a thing; I do not fix it in its place. My gaze wanders in it as in the halos of Being. It is more accurate to say that I see according to it, or with it, than that I *see it*.

The word "image" is in bad repute because we have thoughtlessly believed that a design was a tracing, a copy, a second thing, and that the mental image was such a design, belonging among our private bric-a-brac. But if in fact it is nothing of the kind, then neither the design nor the painting belongs to the in-itself any more than the image does. They are the inside of the outside and the outside of the inside, which the duplicity of feeling *[le sentir]* makes possible and without which we would never understand the quasi presence and immanent visibility which make up the whole problem of the imaginary. The picture and the actor's mimicry are not devices to be borrowed from the real world in order to signify prosaic things which are absent. For the imaginary is much nearer to, and much farther away from, the actual— nearer because it is in my body as a diagram of the life of the actual, with all its pulp and carnal obverse *[son envers charnel]* exposed to view for the first time. In this sense, Giacometti says energetically, "What interests me in all paintings is resemblance—that is, what is resemblance for me: something which makes me discover more of the world." And the imaginary is much farther away from the actual because the painting is an analogue or likeness only according to the body; because it does *not* present the *mind* with an occasion to rethink the constitutive relations of things; because, rather, it offers to our *sight* *[regard]*, so that it might join with them, the inward traces of vision, and because it offers to vision its inward tapestries, the imaginary texture of the real.

Shall we say, then, that we look out from the inside, that there is a third eye which sees the paintings and even the mental images, as we used to speak of a third ear which grasped messages from the outside through the noises they caused inside us? But how would this help us when the real problem is to understand how it happens that our fleshly eyes are already much more than receptors for light rays, colors, and lines? They are computers of the world, which have the gift of the visible as it was once said that the inspired man had the gift of tongues. Of course this gift is earned by exercise; it is not in a few months, or in solitude, that a painter comes into full possession of his vision. But that is not the question; precocious or belated, spontaneous or cultivated in museums, his vision in any event learns only by seeing and learns only from itself. The eye sees the world, sees what inadequacies *[manques]* keep the world from being a painting, sees what keeps a painting from being itself, sees—on the palette—the colors awaited by the painting, and sees, once it is done, the painting that answers to all these inadequacies just as it sees the paintings of others as other answers to other inadequacies.

It is no more possible to make a restrictive inventory of the visible than it is to catalogue the possible usages of a language or even its vocabulary and devices. The eye is an instrument that moves itself, a means which invents its own ends; it is *that which* has been moved by some impact of the world, which it then restores to the visible through the offices of an agile hand.

In whatever civilization it is born, from whatever beliefs, motives, or thoughts, no matter what ceremonies surround it—and even when it appears devoted to something else—from Lascaux to our time, pure or impure, figurative or not, painting celebrates no other enigma but that of visibility.

What we have just said amounts to a truism. The painter's world is a visible world, nothing but visible: a world almost demented because it is complete when it is yet only partial. Painting awakens and carries to its highest pitch a delirium which is vision itself, for to see is *to have at a distance;* painting spreads this strange possession to all aspects of Being, which must in some fashion become visible in order to enter into the work of art. When, apropos of Italian painting, the young Berenson spoke of an evocation of tactile values, he could hardly have been more mistaken; painting evokes nothing, least of all the tactile. What it does is much different, almost the inverse. It gives visible existence to what profane vision believes to be invisible; thanks to it we do not need a "muscular sense" in order to possess the voluminosity of the world. This voracious vision, reaching beyond the "visual givens," opens upon a texture of Being of which the discrete sensorial messages are only the punctuations or the caesurae. The eye lives in this texture as a man lives in his house.

Let us remain within the visible in the narrow and prosaic sense. The painter, whatever he is, *while he is painting* practices a magical theory of vision. He is obliged to admit that objects before him pass into him or else that, according to Malebranche's sarcastic dilemma, the mind goes out through the eyes to wander among objects; for the painter never ceases adjusting his clairvoyance to them. (It makes no difference if he does not paint from "nature"; he paints, in any case, because he has seen, because the world has at least once emblazoned in him the ciphers of the visible.) He must affirm, as one philosopher has said, that vision is a mirror or concentration of the universe or that, in another's words, the *idios kosmos* opens by virtue of vision upon a *koinos kosmos;* in short, that the same thing is both out there in the world and here in the heart of vision—the same or, if one prefers, a *similar* thing, but according to an efficacious similarity which is the parent, the genesis, the metamorphosis of Being in his vision. It is the mountain itself which from out there makes itself seen by the painter; it is the mountain that he interrogates with his gaze.

What exactly does he ask of it? To unveil the means, visible and not otherwise, by which it makes itself a mountain before our eyes. Light, lighting, shadows, reflections, color, all the objects of his quest are not altogether real objects; like ghosts, they have only visual existence. In fact they exist only at the threshold of profane vision; they are not seen by everyone. The painter's gaze asks them what they do to suddenly cause something to be and to be *this* thing, what they do to compose this worldly talisman and to make us see the visible.

We see that the hand pointing to us in *The Nightwatch* is truly there only when we see that its shadow on the captain's body presents it simultaneously in profile. The spatiality of the captain lies at the meeting place of two lines of sight which are incompossible and yet together. Everyone with eyes has at some time or other witnessed this play of shadows, or something like it, and has been made by it to see a space and the things included therein. But it works in us without us; it hides itself in making the object visible. To see the object, it is necessary *not* to see the play of shadows and light around it. The visible in the profane sense forgets its premises; it rests upon a total visibility which is to be re-created and which liberates the phantoms captive in it. The moderns, as we know, have liberated many others; they have added many a blank note *[note sourde]* to the official gamut of our means of seeing. But the interrogation of painting in any case looks toward this secret and feverish genesis of things in our body.

And so it is not a question asked of someone who doesn't know by someone who does—the schoolmaster's question. The question comes from one who does not know, and it is addressed to a vision, a seeing, which knows everything and which we do not make, for it makes itself in us. Max Ernst (with the surrealists) says rightly, "Just as the role of the poet since [Rimbaud's] famous *Lettre du voyant* consists in writing under the dictation of what is being thought, of what articulates itself in him, the role of the painter is to grasp and project what is seen in him." The painter lives in fascination. The actions most proper to him—those gestures, those paths which he alone can trace and which will be revelations to others (because the others do not lack what he lacks or in the same way)—to him they seem to emanate from the things themselves, like the patterns of the constellations.

Inevitably the roles between him and the visible are reversed. That is why so many painters have said that things look at them. As André Marchand says, after Klee: "In a forest, I have felt many times over that it was not I who looked at the forest. Some days I felt that the trees were looking at me, were speaking to me. . . . I was there, listening. . . . I think that the painter must be penetrated by the universe and not want to penetrate it. . . . I expect to be inwardly submerged, buried. Perhaps I paint to break out."

We speak of "inspiration," and the word should be taken literally. There really is inspiration and expiration of Being, action and passion so slightly discernible that it becomes impossible to distinguish between what sees and what is seen, what paints and what is painted.

It can be said that a human is born at the instant when something that was only virtually visible, inside the mother's body, becomes at one and the same time visible for itself and for us. The painter's vision is a continued birth.

In paintings themselves we would seek a figured philosophy of vision—its iconography, perhaps. It is no accident, for example, that frequently in Dutch paintings (as in many others) an empty interior is "digested" by the "round eye of the mirror." This prehuman way of seeing things is the painter's way. More completely than lights, shadows, and reflections, the mirror image anticipates, within things, the labor of vision. Like all other technical objects, such as signs and tools, the mirror arises upon the open circuit [that goes] from seeing body to visible body. Every technique is a "technique of the body." A technique outlines and amplifies the metaphysical structure of our flesh. The mirror appears because I am seeing-visible *[voyant-visible]*, because there is a reflexivity of the sensible; the mirror translates and reproduces that reflexivity. My outside completes itself in and through the sensible. Everything I have that is most secret goes into this *visage*, this face, this flat and closed entity about which my reflection in the water has already made me puzzle. Schilder observes that, smoking a pipe before a mirror, I feel the sleek, burning surface of the wood not only where my fingers are but also in those ghostlike fingers, those merely visible fingers inside the mirror. The mirror's ghost lies outside my body, and by the same token my own body's "invisibility" can invest the other bodies I see. Hence my body can assume segments derived from the body of another, just as my substance passes into them; man is mirror for man. The mirror itself is the instrument of a universal magic that changes things into a spectacle, spectacles into things, myself into another, and another into myself. Artists have often mused upon mirrors because beneath this "mechanical trick," they recognized, just as they did in the case of the trick of perspective, the metamorphosis of seeing and seen which defines both our flesh and the painter's vocation. This explains why they have so often liked to draw themselves in the act of painting (they still do—witness Matisse's drawings), adding to what *they* saw then, what *things* say of them. It is as if they were claiming that there is a total or absolute vision, outside of which there is nothing and which closed itself over them. Where in the realm of the understanding can we place these occult operations, together with the potions and idols they concoct? What can we call them? Consider, as Sartre did in *Nausea*, the smile of a long-dead king which continues to exist and to reproduce itself *[de se produire et de se reproduire]* on the surface of a canvas. It is too little to say that it is there as an image or essence; it is there as itself, as that which was always most alive about it, even now as I look at the painting. The "world's instant" that Cézanne wanted to paint, an instant long since passed away, is still thrown at us by his paintings. His Mount Saint Victor is made and remade from one end of the world to the other in a way that is different from, but no less energetic than, that of the hard rock above Aix. Essence and existence, imaginary and real, visible and invisible—a painting mixes up all our categories in laying out its oneiric universe of canal essences, of effective likenesses, of mute meanings. . . .

4

THE ENTIRE MODERN HISTORY of painting, with its efforts to detach itself from illusionism and to acquire its own dimensions, has a metaphysical significance. This is not something to be demonstrated. Not for reasons drawn from the limits of objectivity in history and from the inevitable plurality of interpretations, which would prevent the linking of a philosophy and an event; the metaphysics we have in mind is not a body of detached ideas *[idées séparées]* for which inductive justifications could be sought in the experiential realm. There are, in the flesh of contingency, a structure of the event and a virtue peculiar to the scenario. These do not prevent the plurality of interpretations but in fact are the deepest reasons for this plurality. They make the event into a durable theme of historical life and have a right to philosophical status. In a sense everything that could have been said and that will be said about the French Revolution has always been and is henceforth within it, in that wave which arched itself out of a roil of discrete facts, with its froth of the past and its crest of the future. And it is always by looking more deeply into *how it came about* that we give and will go on giving new representations of it. As for the history of art works, if they are great, the sense we give to them later on has issued from them. It is the work itself that has opened the field from which it appears in another light. It changes *itself* and *becomes* what follows; the interminable reinterpretations to which it is *legitimately* susceptible change it only in itself. And if the historian unearths beneath its manifest content the surplus and thickness of meaning, the texture which held the promise of a long history, this active manner of being, then, this possibility he unveils in the work, this monogram he finds there—all are grounds for a philosophical meditation. But such a labor demands a long familiarity with history. We lack everything for its execution, both the competence and the place. Just the same, since the power or the fecundity of art works exceeds every positive causal or filial relation, there is nothing wrong with letting a layman, speaking from his memory of a few paintings and books, tell us how painting enters into his reflections; how painting deposits in him a feeling of profound discordance, a feeling of mutation within the relations of man and Being. Such feelings arise in him when he holds a universe of classical thought, en bloc, up against the explorations [recherches] of modern painting. This is a sort of history by contact, perhaps, never extending beyond the limits of one person, owing everything nevertheless to his frequentation of others. . . .

"I believe Cézanne was seeking depth all his life," says Giacometti. Says Robert Delaunay, "Depth is the new inspiration." Four centuries after the "solutions" of the Renaissance and three centuries after Descartes, depth is still new, and it insists on being sought, not "once in a lifetime" but all through life. It cannot be merely a question of an unmysterious interval, as seen from an airplane, between these trees nearby and those farther away. Nor is it a matter of the way things are conjured away, one by another, as we see happen so vividly in a perspective drawing. These two views are very explicit and raise no problems. The enigma, though, lies in their bond, in what is between them. The enigma consists in the fact that I see things, each one in its place, precisely because they eclipse one another, and that they are rivals before my sight precisely because each one is in its own place. Their exteriority is known in their envelopment and their mutual dependence in their autonomy. Once depth is understood in this way, we can no longer call it a third dimension. In the first place, if it were a dimension, it would be the *first* one; there are forms and definite planes only if it is stipulated how far from me their different parts are. But a *first* dimension that contains all the others is no longer a dimension, at least, in the ordinary sense of a *certain relationship* according to which we make measurements. Depth thus understood is, rather, the experience of the reversibility of dimensions, of a global "locality"—everything in the same place at the same time, a locality from which height, width, and depth are abstracted, of a voluminosity we express in a word when we say that a thing is *there*. In search of depth Cézanne seeks this deflagration of Being, and it is all in the modes of space, in form as much as anything. Cézanne knows already what cubism will repeat: that the external form, the envelope, is secondary and derived, that it is not that which causes a thing to take form, that this shell of space must be shattered, this fruit bowl broken— and what is there to paint, then? Cubes, spheres, and cones (as he said once)? Pure forms which have the solidity of what could be defined by an internal law of construction, forms which all together, as traces or slices of the thing, let it appear between them like a face in the reeds? This would be to put Being's solidity on one side and its variety on the other. Cézanne made an experiment of this kind in his middle period. He opted for the solid, for space—and came to find that inside this space, a box or container too large for them, the things began to move, color against color; they began to modulate in instability. Thus we must seek space and its content *as* together. The problem is generalized; it is no longer that of distance, of life, of form; it is also, and equally, the problem of color.

Color is the "place where our brain and the universe meet," he says in that admirable idiom of the artisan of Being which Klee liked to cite. It is for the benefit of color that we must break up the form-spectacle. Thus the question is not of colors, "simulacra of the colors of nature." The question, rather, concerns the dimension of color, that dimension which creates identities, differences, a texture, a materiality, a something—creates them from itself, for itself. . . .

Yet (and this must be emphasized) there is no one master key of the visible, and color alone is no closer to being such a key than space is. The return to color has the merit of getting somewhat nearer to "the heart of things," but this heart is beyond the color envelope just as it is beyond the space envelope. The *Portrait of Vallier* sets white spaces between the colors which take on the function of giving shape to, and setting off, a being more general than the yellow-being or green-being or blue-being. Also in the water colors of Cézanne's last years, for example, space (which had been taken to be evidence itself and of which it was believed that the question of *where* was not to be asked) radiates around planes that cannot be assigned to any place at all: "a superimposing of transparent surfaces," "a flowing movement of planes of color which overlap, which advance and retreat."

Obviously it is not a matter of adding one more dimension to those of the flat canvas, of organizing an illusion or an objectless perception whose perfection consists in simulating an empirical vision to the maximum degree. Pictorial depth (as well as painted height and width) comes "I know not whence" to alight upon, and take root in, the sustaining support. The painter's vision is not a view upon the *outside*, a merely "physical-optical" relation with the world. The world no longer stands before him through representation; rather, it is the painter to whom the things of the world give birth by a sort of concentration or coming-to-itself of the visible. Ultimately the painting relates to nothing at all among experienced things unless it is first of all "autofigurative." It is a spectacle of something only by being a "spectacle of nothing," by breaking the "skin of things" to show how the things become things, how the world becomes world. Apollinaire said that in a poem there are phrases which do not appear to have been *created*, which seem to have *formed themselves*. And Henri Michaux said that sometimes Klee's colors seem to have been born slowly upon the canvas, to have emanated from some primordial ground, "exhaled at the right place" like a patina or a mold. Art is not construction, artifice, meticulous relationship to a space and a world existing outside. It is truly the "inarticulate cry," as Hermes Trismegistus said, "which seemed to be the voice of the light." And once it is present it awakens powers dormant in ordinary vision, a secret of preexistence. When through the water's thickness I see the tiling at the bottom of a pool, I do not see it *despite* the water and the reflections there; I see it through them and because of them. If there were no distortions, no ripples of sunlight, if it were without this flesh that I saw the geometry of the tiles, then I would cease to see it *as* it is and where it is—which is to say, beyond any identical, specific place. I cannot say that the water itself—the aqueous power, the sirupy and shimmering element—is *in* space; all this is not somewhere else either, but it is not in the pool. It inhabits it, it materializes itself there, yet it is not contained there; and if I raise my eyes toward the screen of cypresses where the web of reflections is playing, I cannot gainsay the fact that the water visits it, too, or at least sends into it, upon it, its active and living essence. This internal animation, the radiation of the visible is what the painter seeks under the name of depth, of space, of color.

Anyone who thinks about the matter finds it astonishing that very often a good painter can also make good drawings or good sculpture. Since neither the means of expression nor the creative gestures are comparable, this fact [of competence in several media] is proof that there is a system of equivalences, a Logos of lines, of lighting, of colors, of reliefs, of masses—a conceptless presentation of universal Being. The effort of modern painting has been directed not so much toward choosing between line and color, or even between the figuration of things and the creation of signs, as it has been toward multiplying the systems of equivalences, toward severing their adherence to the envelope of things. This effort might force us to create new materials or new means of expression, but it could well be realized at times by the reexamination and reinvestment of those which existed already.

There has been, for example, a prosaic conception of the line as a positive attribute and a property of the object in itself. Thus, it is the outer contour of the apple or the border between the plowed field and the meadow, considered as present in the world, such that, guided by points taken from the real world, the pencil or brush would only have to pass over them. But this line has been contested by all modern painting, and probably by all painting, as we are led to think by da Vinci's comment in his *Treatise on Painting*: "The secret of the art of drawing is to discover in each object the particular way in which a certain flexuous line, which is, so to speak, its generating axis, is directed through its whole extent. . . ." Both Ravaisson and Bergson sensed something important in this, without daring to decipher the oracle all the way. Bergson scarcely looked for the "sinuous outline" *[serpentement]* outside living beings, and he rather timidly advanced the idea that the undulating line "could be no one of the visible lines of the figure," that it is "no more here than there," and yet "gives the key to the whole." He was on the threshold of that gripping discovery, already familiar to the painters, that there are no lines visible in themselves, that neither the contour of the apple nor the border between field and meadow is in *this* place or that, that they are always on the near or the far side of the point we look at. They are always between or behind whatever we fix our eyes upon; they are indicated, implicated, and even very imperiously demanded by the things, but they themselves are not things. They were supposed to circumscribe the apple or the meadow, but the apple and the meadow "form themselves" from themselves, and come into the visible as if they had come from a pre-spatial world behind the scenes.

Yet this contestation of the prosaic line is far from ruling out all lines in painting, as the impressionists may have thought. It is simply a matter of freeing the line, of revivifying its constituting power; and we are not faced with a contradiction when we see it reappear and triumph in painters like Klee or Matisse, who more than anyone believed in color. For henceforth, as Klee said, the line no longer imitates the visible; it "renders visible"; it is the blueprint of a genesis of things. Perhaps no one before Klee had "let a line muse." The beginning of the line's path establishes or installs a certain level or mode of the linear, a certain manner for the line to be and to make itself a line, "to go line." Relative to it, every subsequent inflection will have a diacritical value, will be another aspect of the line's relationship to itself, will form an adventure, a history, a meaning of the line—all this according as it slants more or less, more or less rapidly, more or less subtly. Making its way in space, it nevertheless corrodes prosaic space and the *partes extra partes;* it develops a way of extending itself actively into that space which sub-tends the spatiality of a thing quite as much as that of a man or an apple tree. This is so simply because, as Klee said, to give the generating axis of a man the painter "would have to have a network of lines so entangled that it could no longer be a question of a truly elementary representation."

In view of this situation two alternatives are open, and it makes little difference which one is chosen. First, the painter may, like Klee, decide to hold rigorously to the principle of the genesis of the visible, the principle of fundamental, indirect, or—as Klee used to say—absolute painting, and then leave it up to the *title* to designate by its prosaic name the entity thus constituted, in order to leave the painting free to function more purely as a painting. Or alternatively he may choose with Matisse (in his drawings) to put into a single line both the prosaic definition *[signalement]* of the entity and the hidden *[sourde]* operation which composes in it such softness or inertia and such force as are required to constitute it as *nude,* as *face,* as *flower.*

There is a painting by Klee of two holly leaves, done in the most figurative manner. At first glance the leaves are thoroughly indecipherable, and they remain to the end monstrous, unbelievable, ghostly, *on account of their exactness [à force d'exactitude].* And Matisse's women (let us keep in mind his contemporaries' sarcasm) were not immediately women; they became women. It is Matisse who taught us to see their contours not in a "physical-optical" way but rather as structural filaments *[des nervures],* as the axes of a corporeal system of activity and passivity. Figurative or not, the line is no longer a thing or an imitation of a thing. It is a certain disequilibrium kept up within the indifference of the white paper; it is a certain process of gouging within the in-itself, a certain constitutive emptiness—an emptiness which, as Moore's statues show decisively, upholds the pretended positivity of the things. The line is no longer the apparition of an entity upon a vacant background, as it was in classical geometry. It is, as in modern geometries, the restriction, segrega-tion, or modulation of a pre-given spatiality.

Just as it has created the latent line, painting has made itself a movement without displacement, a movement by vibration or radiation. And well it should, since, as we say, painting is an art of space and since it comes about upon a canvas or sheet of paper and so lacks the wherewithal to devise things that actually move. But the immobile canvas could suggest a change of place in the same way that a shooting star's track on my retina suggests a transition, a motion not contained in it. The painting itself would offer to my eyes almost the same thing offered them by real movements: a series of appropriately mixed, instantaneous glimpses along with, if a living thing is involved, attitudes unstably suspended between a before and an after—in short, the outsides of a change of place which the spectator would read from the imprint it leaves. Here Rodin's well-known remark reveals its full weight: the instantaneous glimpses, the unstable attitudes, petrify the movement, as is shown by so many photographs in which an athlete-in-motion is forever frozen. We could not thaw him out by multiplying the glimpses. Marey's photographs, the cubists' analyses, Duchamp's *La Mariée* do not move; they give a Zenonian reverie on movement. We see a rigid body as if it were a piece of armor going through its motions; it is here and it is there, magically, but it does not *go* from here to there. Cinema portrays movement, but *how*? Is it, as we are inclined to believe, by copying more closely the changes of place? We may presume not, since slow-motion shows a body floating among objects like an alga but not moving *itself*.

Movement is given, says Rodin, by an image in which the arms, the legs, the trunk, and the head are each taken at a different instant, an image which therefore portrays the body in an attitude which it never at any instant really held and which imposes fictive linkages between the parts, as if this mutual confrontation of incompossibles could, and could alone, cause transition and duration to arise in bronze and on canvas. The only successful instantaneous glimpses of movement are those which approach this paradoxical arrange-ment—when, for example, a walking man is taken at the moment when both his feet are touching the ground; for then we almost have the temporal ubiq-uity of the body which brings it about that the man *bestrides* space. The picture makes movement visible by its internal discordance. Each member's position, precisely by virtue of its incompatibility with the others' (according to the body's logic), is otherwise dated or is not "in time" with the others; and since all of them remain visibly within the unity of a body, it is the body which comes to bestride them [*la durée*]. Its movement is something premeditated between legs, trunk, arms, and head in some virtual "control center," and it breaks forth only with a subsequent change of place. When a horse is photographed at that instant when he is completely off the ground, with his legs almost folded under him—an instant, therefore, when he must be moving— why does he look as if he were leaping in place? Then why do Géricault's horses really *run* on canvas, in a posture impossible for a real horse at the gallop? It is just that the horses in *Epsom Derby* bring me to see the body's grip upon the soil and that, according to a logic of body and world I know well, these "grips" upon space are also ways of taking hold of time *[la durée].* Rodin said very wisely, "It is the artist who is truthful, while the photograph is mendacious; for, in reality, time never stops cold." The photograph keeps open the instants which the onrush of time closes up forthwith; it destroys the overtaking, the overlapping, the "metamorphosis" [Rodin] of time. But this is what painting, in contrast, makes visible, because the horses have in them that "leaving here, going there," because they have a foot in each instant. Painting searches not for the outside of movement but for its secret ciphers, of which there are some still more subtle than those of which Rodin spoke. All flesh, and even that of the world, radiates beyond itself. But whether or not one is, depending on the times and the "school," attached more to manifest movement or to the monumental, the art of painting is never altogether outside time, because it is always within the carnal *[dans le charnel].*

Now perhaps we have a better sense of what is meant by that little verb "to see." Vision is not a certain mode of thought or presence to self; it is the means given me for being absent from myself, for being present at the fission of Being from the inside—the fission at whose termination, and not before, I come back to myself.

Painters always knew this. Da Vinci invoked a "pictorial science" which does not speak with words (and still less with numbers) but with *oeuvres* which exist in the visible just as natural things do and which nevertheless communicate through those things "to all the generations of the universe." This silent science, says Rilke (apropos of Rodin), brings into the *oeuvre* the forms of things "whose seal has not been broken"; it comes from the eye as the "window of the soul." "The eye . . . through which the beauty of the universe is revealed to our contemplation is of such excellence that whoever should resign himself to losing it would deprive himself of the knowledge of all the works of nature, the sight of which makes the soul live happily in its body's prison, thanks to the eyes which show him the infinite variety of creation: whoever loses them abandons his soul in a dark prison where all hope of once more seeing the sun, the light of the universe, must vanish." The eye accomplishes the prodigious work of opening the soul to what is not soul—the joyous realm of things and their god, the sun.

A Cartesian can believe that the existing world is not visible, that the only light is that of the mind, and that all vision takes place in God. A painter cannot grant that our openness to the world is illusory or indirect, that what we see is not the world itself, or that the mind has to do only with its thoughts or with another mind. He accepts with all its difficulties the myth of the windows of the soul; it must be that what has no place is subjected to a body—even more, that what has no place be initiated *by* the body to all the others and to nature. We must take literally what vision teaches us: namely, that through it we come in contact with the sun and the stars, that we are everywhere all at once, and that even our power to imagine ourselves elsewhere—"I am in Petersburg in my bed, in Paris, my eyes see the sun"—or to intend *[viser]* real beings wherever they are, borrows from vision and employs means we owe to it. Vision alone makes us learn that beings that are different, "exterior," foreign to one another, are yet absolutely *together,* are "simultaneity"; this is a mystery psychologists handle the way a child handles explosives. Robert Delaunay says succinctly, "The railroad track is the image of succession which comes closest to the parallel: the parity of the rails." The rails converge and do not converge; they converge *in order to* remain equidistant down below. The world is in accordance with my perspective *in order to* be independent of me, is for me *in order to be* without me, and to be the world. The "visual quale" gives me, and alone gives me, the presence of what is not me, of what *is* simply and fully. It does so because, like texture, it is the concretion of a universal visibility, of a unique space which separates and reunites, which sustains every cohesion (and even that of past and future, since there would be no such cohesion if they were not essentially relevant to the same space). Every visual something, as individual as it is, functions also as a dimension, because it gives itself as the result of a dehiscence of Being. What this ultimately means is that the proper essence *[le propre]* of the visible is to have a layer *[doublure]* of invisibility in the strict sense, which it makes present as a certain absence. "In their time, our bygone antipodes, the impressionists, were perfectly right in making their abode with the castaways and the undergrowth of daily life. As for us, our heart throbs to bring us closer to the depths. . . . These oddities will become . . . realities . . . because instead of being held to the diversely intense restoration of the visible, they will annex to it the proper share *[la part]* of the invisible, occultly apperceived." There is that which reaches the eye directly *[de face],* the frontal properties of the visible; but there is also that which reaches it from below—the profound postural latency where the body raises itself to see—and that which reaches vision from above like the phenomena of flight, of swimming, of movement, where it participates no longer in the heaviness of origins but in free accomplishments. Through it, then, the painter touches the two extremities. In the immemorial depth of the visible, something moved, caught fire, and engulfed his body; everything he paints is in answer to this incitement, and his hand is "nothing but the instrument of a distant will." Vision encounters, as at a crossroads, all the aspects of Being. "[A] certain fire pretends to be alive; it awakens. Working its way along the hand as conductor, it reaches the support and engulfs it; then a leaping spark closes the circle it was to trace, coming back to the eye, and beyond."

There is no break at all in this circuit; it is impossible to say that nature ends here and that man or expression starts here. It is, therefore, mute Being which itself comes to show forth its own meaning. Herein lies the reason why the dilemma between figurative and nonfigurative art is badly posed; it is true and uncontradictory that no grape was ever what it is in the most figurative painting and that no painting, no matter how abstract, can get away from Being, that even Caravaggio's grape is the grape itself. This precession of what is upon what one sees and makes seen, of what one sees and makes seen upon what is—this is vision itself. And to give the ontological formula of painting we hardly need to force the painter's own words, Klee's words written at the age of thirty-seven and ultimately inscribed on his tomb: "I cannot be caught in immanence."

5

BECAUSE DEPTH, color, form, line, movement, contour, physiognomy are all branches of Being and because each one can sway all the rest, there are no separated, distinct "problems" in painting, no really opposed paths, no partial "solutions," no cumulative progress, no irretrievable options. There is nothing to prevent a painter from going back to one of the devices he has shied away from—making it, of course, speak differently. Rouault's contours are not those of Ingres. Light is the "old sultana," says Georges Limbour, "whose charms withered away at the beginning of this century." Expelled first by the painters of materials *[les peintres de le matière],* it reappears finally in Dubuffet as a certain texture of matter. One is never immune to this kind of turning back or to the least expected convergences; some of Rodin's fragments are almost statues by Germain Richier *because they were both sculptors*—that is to say, enmeshed in a single, identical network of Being. For the same reason nothing is ever finally acquired and possessed for good.

In "working over" a favorite problem, even if it is just the problem of velvet or wool, the true painter unknowingly upsets the givens of all the other problems. His quest is total even where it looks partial. Just when he has reached proficiency in some area, he finds that he has reopened another one where everything he said before must be said again in a different way. The upshot is that what he has found he does not yet have. It remains to be sought out; the discovery itself calls forth still further quests. The idea of a universal painting, of a totalization of painting, of a fully and definitively achieved painting is an idea bereft of sense. For painters the world will always be yet to be painted, even if it lasts millions of years . . . it will end without having been conquered in painting.

Panofsky shows that the "problems" of painting which magnetize its history are often solved obliquely, not in the course of inquiries instigated to solve them but, on the contrary, at some point when the painters, having reached an impasse, apparently forget those problems and permit themselves to be attracted by other things. Then suddenly, altogether off guard, they turn up the old problems and surmount the obstacle. This unhearing *[sourde]* historicity, advancing through the labyrinth by detours, transgression, slow encroachments and sudden drives, does not imply that the painter does not know what he wants. It does imply that what he wants is beyond the means and goals at hand and commands from afar all our *useful* activity.

We are so fascinated by the classical idea of intellectual adequation that painting's mute "thinking" sometimes leaves us with the impression of a vain swirl of significations, a paralyzed or miscarried utterance. Suppose, then, that one answers that no thought ever detaches itself completely from a sustaining support; that the only privilege of speaking-thought is to have rendered its own support manageable; that the figurations of literature and philosophy are no more settled than those of painting and are no more capable of being accumulated into a stable treasure; that even science learns to recognize a zone of the "fundamental," peopled with dense, open, rent *[déchirés]* beings of which an exhaustive treatment is out of the question—like the cyberneticians' "aesthetic information" or mathematical-physical "groups of operations"; that, in the end, we are never in a position to take stock of everything objectively or to think of progress in itself; and that the whole of human history is, in a certain sense, stationary. *What*, says the understanding, like [Stendhal's] Lamiel, *is it only that?*

Is this the highest point of reason, to realize that the soil beneath our feet is shifting, to pompously name "interrogation" what is only a persistent state of stupor, to call "research" or "quest" what is only trudging in a circle, to call "Being" that which never fully *is*?

But this disappointment issues from that spurious fantasy which claims for itself a positivity capable of making up for its own emptiness. It is the regret of not being everything, and a rather groundless regret at that. For if we cannot establish a hierarchy of civilizations or speak of progress—neither in painting nor in anything else that matters—it is not because some fate holds us back; it is, rather, because the very first painting in some sense went to the farthest reach of the future. If no painting comes to be *the* painting, if no work is ever absolutely completed and done with, still each creation changes, alters, enlightens, deepens, confirms, exalts, re-creates, or creates in advance all the others. If creations are not a possession, it is not only that, like all things, they pass away; it is also that they have almost all their life still before them.

STEPHEN DAVID ROSS

ONE MAY SAY art is important because it enriches our surroundings and our experience. Such enrichment is the manifestation of inexhaustibility by contrast. Both of these notions, inexhaustibility and contrast, express ideas of enrichment and multiplicity. They are defined in this selection in terms of a systematic ontology. It may be useful to give a very brief summary of the principles and categories of the ordinal theory.

To be is to be an order of constituents and to be located as a constituent in many orders. This multiple locatedness is equivalent with inexhaustibility, with the proviso that there is no all-encompassing order. Every order has an integrity in a given location—its unitariness in that location—and a scope composed of its sphere of relations in that location. Integrities and scopes vary with location, but an order may possess a gross integrity over many locations. It then may be said to prevail over those locations. Where its integrity varies, an order may be said to be deviant over those locations. Finally, where certain constituents of an order are settled in relation to each other, we may say they are actualities in that location; where they comprise alternatives, we may say they are possibilities in that location. Contrasts are an interplay of prevalence and devia·ce, but always involve variations in integrity and scope, possibilities and actualities. Where the similarities and differences among the constituents of a contrast are heightened, relative to typical experience, we have intensity of contrast. Where contrasts become reflexive, rising to contrasts of contrasts inexhaustibly, we have deeper and more profound contrasts. Art manifests inexhaustibility by contrast, by intensification and enrichment, thereby attaining profound significance, that of opening worlds for us to inhabit, worlds revelatory of our lives and experiences.

The selections here include a discussion of interpretation and criticism, especially of an intermodal form of criticism I call "illustrement."

STEPHEN DAVID ROSS

A Theory of Art:
Inexhaustibility by Contrast*

INTRODUCTION

. . . The theory to be developed here, then, is that aesthetic and artistic values—
they are of the same species—are intense contrasts. Contrasts are conjunctions, unifications, syntheses, of dissimilar, opposing constituents. Intensity is
attained where the opposition is stronger or where the unification is exceptional. The most important feature of contrast is its capacity to produce level
upon level of complex contrast upon contrast. In this respect it is very like
romantic irony, which admits of irony upon irony, and the theory of romantic
irony is an incomplete theory of contrast founded upon the central contrast of
artist and audience.

The notion of intensity of contrast may appear to be a matter of degree:
greater unification of disparate elements, a greater range of variation within a
common synthesis. In this sense, artistic value would also be a matter of
degree, and the greater the intensity of contrast, the greater the value. Now I
can understand the notion of greater and lesser *intensity of feeling*, though I
think it would be very difficult to explain. But many intensely felt works of art
are sentimental and trite, many great works are cold and restricted in the
feelings they engender. I do not share the common view that works of art
arouse in us immediately the question of how good they are, how much better

* Stephen David Ross, *A Theory of Art: Inexhaustibility by Contrast* (Albany: State University of
New York Press, 1982), pp. 5-7, 90-98, 152-153, 195-196, 198-203, 206-207, 209-210, 214-222.
(Chapter numbers omitted.)

and worse than others. I do not believe that evaluation, estimation, and appraisal are defining elements of aesthetic judgment. The fundamental question of artistic value, I believe, is not *how much value a work has,* but what its characteristics are, not *how much* intensity of contrast there is, but *how* a work achieves its intensity of contrast.

Fundamentally, artistic value is grounded in *incomparability*. Yet while works of art are incomparable in many respects, especially those respects which define their value, they are indefinitely comparable in other respects. The theory of contrast makes both of these features clear. Contrasts are dependent on similarities and differences, on relations as well as sovereignty. Works of art and natural objects are comparable *because* they are contrasting, as are any and all of their constituents. Nevertheless, the complexity of contrasts also engenders uniqueness and singularity, since there are contrasts in every work that can be shared with no other works or objects. The terms of contrasts are relational and common; the contrasts achieved are frequently incomparable and unique, are always singular in some important respects.

In addition, intensity is not a matter of degree. Particular contrasts are not more intense than others, for there could be no scale of measurement. They are rather intense in the ways they are: conjunctions mated with departures, similarities with dissimilarities, unification with plurality. How then are works of art judged better than others? Most of the time, I suggest, they are not so comparable except in a particular respect. Some paintings are more balanced, more serene, more harmonious, than others, better perhaps in that respect—but not overall, in all respects. I think it is a fundamental error pervasive throughout the history of art to suppose that artistic value forces a scale of measurement upon us. Works of art are comparable as are all things, but artistic values are not. Intensity of contrast is not a matter of degree but of kind.

The central difficulty has been mentioned for a theory in which artistic value is founded on richness and complexity, ascending to higher and higher levels upon levels of opposition and relation: how it is able to deal with important works of sublime simplicity, how it is able to explain movements toward purification as in minimalist painting. Two answers will be given: First, mentioned above, perfection is a primary mode of contrast, one of its three fundamental dimensions. This means that every fine work of art and natural beauty is appreciated for its perfection in some respects in contrast with works and objects that lack such perfections. This is obviously insufficient to do full justice to minimalism, however, for salient perfection is frequently a minor quality of minimalist works. The second answer is given by the capacity of contrasts to engender complexity by aggregation through time. Purity and simplicity can only be in certain respects, frequently heightening the rich intensity of contrasts in other respects, at other levels. Here the capacity of contrasts to enter rich and complex aggregates is essential again. Here also, history and tradition are essential components of complex contrasts, providing a background against which minimalist works inhabit more complex contrasts in proportion to their purity and simplicity. This solution has the further advantage of acknowledging that the history and traditions of art are primary features of intense and compelling contrasts, part of the essential values of art, rather than accidental features of time and development as in theories which emphasize purely sensuous pleasures. The capacity of works of art to absorb traditions and subsequent events into themselves requires an ordinal theory for explanation, since in such a theory the identity (or integrity) of an order is a function of some of its constituents and is variable with the location of the order in question.

There are many theories of art: significant form, expression, objectified pleasure, and so forth. Most of them can be classified as theories of rightness or richness or as a synthesis of the two, usually from one side or the other. All, I will argue, are incomplete theories of contrast, even where no contrasts are explicitly indicated. The reason for this is that what they propose is not aesthetically valuable unless it involves intensity of contrast, however covertly assumed. Far more important, all such theories are insufficiently general, and in two senses. There are arts and works of art which are neglected in the theory proposed. There are also important features of relevant works which are not included within the theory proposed—for example, the contrast of colors in a theory of forms, random and aleatory elements in a theory of expression, terrible and fearsome elements in theories of harmonious beauty and pleasure, and so forth. In fact, I will argue, no single relationship can define artistic value, only a relationship built upon level upon level of complex oppositions, similarities and differences. Complexity is the foundation of the ordinal theory, which is why that theory can provide an adequate basis for a theory of art. Art is built upon complexity and inexhaustibility even in its simplest and purest works. Only the theory of contrast as delineated here can explain this feature of art: that the simplest works are sometimes pregnant with the most sublime, profound, and complex qualities. . . .

THE THEORY OF CONTRAST

. . . Why is such intensity of contrast a supreme value? A number of answers may be given, ranging from lived experience to ordinality itself. Intensity of contrast may be regarded as a product of a free act of mind, lying in the act of creation itself, the production of a work to be in the fullest ordinal sense, filled with inexhaustible diversities and similarities. Of course, all the modes of judgment can b. employed in intensity of contrast. Nevertheless, the free play of constructive judgment is the creation of works simply to be, dependent only on the contrast of what they are with what they are not and what they might be.

Being, in an ordinal theory, is functional and relational: what an order is is its function within and relevance to other orders. To be, then, is in contrast with all the locations and functions of an order. Alternatively, being is ordinality and inexhaustibility. Both assertion and action seek to simplify ordinality, to escape inexhaustibility, to establish conditions for truth and control. Only art dwells in the richness of ordinality and its inexhaustibility, seeking to enhance orders with novel possibilities, to engender new integrities, to create new intense contrasts. Science and politics certainly enrich experience and produce novel and intense contrasts. Art, however, revels in these contrasts, maximizes relevant possibilities, heightens variations and oppositions.

Science seeks an understanding grounded in actuality and integrity, though it can attain it only because of novel possibilities and the openness of its own scopic constituents. It emphasizes prevalence and actuality, while it indirectly exhibits deviance and possibility. Action seeks control over orders in experience through the transformation of possibilities into actualities, deviances into prevalences. It emphasizes the complementarity of the ordinal categories, but it exhibits as a specter the relevance of uncontrolled possibilities, deviances, and scopes. Only art revels in and manifests the inexhaustibility of orders, emphasizing the relevance of novel possibilities and deviances amidst the prevalence and actualities of orders in human experience.

Art is the manifestation of inexhaustibility, achieved through intensity of contrast. Reciprocally, it is the creation of intense contrasts, thereby manifesting inexhaustibility. In both cases, inexhaustibility must be understood in the full sense of ordinality: the complementary relationship of determinateness and indeterminateness. Inexhaustibility is not pure indeterminateness, pure freedom, unrestrictedness. Nothing can be unconditioned. This principle is expressed by the complementary of the ordinal categories: prevalence and deviance, integrity and scope, actuality and possibility. In each pair, one member may be regarded as expressive of determinateness, the other of indeterminateness—in a particular respect. In addition, each pair is dependent on ordinal location, and what is prevalent in one location is deviant in another and conversely; what is a constituent of the integrity of an order in one location is a constituent of its scope in another and conversely; what is a possibility in one location is an actuality in another and conversely. This functional complementarity is essential to the notion of ordinal inexhaustibility, and it is maintained throughout all the ordinal categories.

Every order is inexhaustible. The ordinal theory asserts this principle and thereby testifies to inexhaustibility. Science and morality confront inexhaustibility in every judgment: every theory is inexhaustible and is faced by inadequacies generated by the inexhaustibility of other orders. Action is faced with possibilities of failure at every turn. Both confront inexhaustibility; both can succeed in their judgmental terms only because of inexhaustibility—that which enables them to invent new judgments and to pursue new forms of query. But both are constrained by external validating conditions. Art, however, revels in inexhaustibility, creating new forms to enhance the openness of orders. Art is not unconditioned, for it could not then be anything at all. But it is an inexhaustible play of contrasts upon each other, an inexhaustible enhancement of orders in experience.

Inexhaustibility is expressed by all the ordinal categories. Art, then, is inexhaustible through the interplay of possibilities and actualities, integrities and scopes, as well as prevalences and deviances. I have emphasized the latter for a fundamental reason: that inexhaustibility is of *orders*, and requires an emphasis not only on integrities but on gross integrities over many different locations. This interplay of gross integrities over constituent integrities, seen as a form of contrast, is precisely prevalence amidst deviance. Nevertheless, the corresponding contrasts among integrities and scopes, possibilities and actualities, must be understood to be included in the contrast of prevalence and deviance. The sovereignty of a work of art, grounded in the first instance in its integrity and prevalence, has direct implications for its constituent actualities and possibilities, on the ways in which possibilities are constitutive of its prevalence. The interplay of possibilities and actualities, which I have identified with the *worldiness* of art, is a direct expression of its inexhaustibility. Possibilities are such a direct expression of inexhaustibility. But they can be such only in a close and therefore contrasting relation to the integral prevalence of the work of art. Art manifests inexhaustibility through all the ordinal categories, an inexhaustibility inherent in the inexhaustibility of judgment and query, but which I am interpreting as an interplay of prevalence and deviance, related to the other categories through the nature of ordinality.

Intensity of contrast, then, has a metaphysical foundation in ordinality and inexhaustibility, but also manifests such inexhaustibility in the free play of judgment and query. This is a most supreme value. As a consequence, we appreciate the exhibition of pregnancy and promise, novelty and transformation, the excitement of intense contrast. These intense contrasts are savored because they are extraordinary and remarkable. It is not our appreciation that makes them extraordinary.

This leads me, in concluding this chapter, to a conception of art toward which I take a very qualified position—that works of art are expressive of emotion and produce particularly vital and intense emotional experiences. The theory of intensity of contrast entails that works of art need not be emotional to be effective and important. Rather, art is created for human response, but no particular mode of response alone is appropriate. This is a consequence of ordinal inexhaustibility. Intensity of contrast is defined relative to human perspectives, human orders. Yet such orders are inexhaustible individually in their constituents and integrities and inexhaustible as well collectively. There is no particular sphere of experience—emotional, intellectual, immediate, or otherwise—that can determine the value of art, for art both revels in and is the revelation of inexhaustibility through contrast. All the modes of judgment in response, all the forms of articulation and query, are the natural fulfillment of art and aesthetic value.

Aesthetic value is intensity of contrast, but relative to any kind, any sphere of experience: individual, social, or cultural, emotional or intellectual.

Intensity is available for feeling, as is any constituent of experience, but is neither a form of feeling nor accessible only through certain kinds of feeling. The power of art is to enrich our surroundings, our lives, with novel forms and creations, enjoying inexhaustibility and enhancing it. We appreciate such achievements in all the ways we can, and in all the ways we can invent, therefore in no particular ways. This openness of art to novelty and inexhaustibility is what differentiates it from science and from practical affairs. Art is not in this way different from philosophy, which also manifests and revels in inexhaustibility. The difference here lies not in intensity of contrast or ordinality, but in how they are manifested, a difference that is as likely to be diminished in certain works of art and philosophy as it is to be augmented.

Art is construction, and its value lies in the distinctiveness of its works. Such a distinctiveness is a contrast—a contrast among the constituents of the work and relative to the traits of experiences in which it is to be assimilated. The distinctive, remarkable character of a great work of art is a double contrast—relative to its constituents and relative to some spheres of human experience. Yet the distinctiveness of works of art is an achievement that manifests inexhaustibility: that is what intensity of contrast exhibits. The sovereignty of the work—its prevailing integrity—is manifested in inexhaustible ways and with inexhaustible contrasting relations. Such achievements arouse in us the most sublime of emotions, as we bask in their glory. But it is their glory and achievement which we admire, and we respond to them in all ways we can find by which we can express our admiration of them, ways which are themselves inexhaustible.

CONTRASTS AND AESTHETIC VALUE: DIMENSIONS AND GENERAL TYPES

The theory of art and aesthetic value developed in this essay may be summarized in three brief principles: (1) *aesthetic value is intensity of contrast;* (2) *intensity of contrast manifests inexhaustibility;* (3) *art is the methodic construction of intense contrasts.* I have developed the theory of contrast in connection with an ordinal metaphysics and have argued that only an ordinal theory can provide a satisfactory basis for the theory of contrast and for methodic construction. I have also traced some of the elements of judgment and query in relation to ordinality, although a more complete analysis of art in relation to constructive judgment and query is required, and will be developed throughout the ensuing discussion, but primarily in connection with interpretation and criticism in Chapter 6. What is needed first is a detailed development of the notion of intensity of contrast in relation to art and works of art and to aesthetic value in nature. The purpose of this chapter and the next is to develop a rudimentary taxonomy of contrasts relevant to aesthetic value.

This will be accomplished by discriminating three dimensions of contrast—perfection, invention, and celebration—and five gen_ral types of contrast—traditionary, intramedial, intermedial, intermodal, and intersubjective—plus a type of contrast derived from fundamental ordinal considerations—integral and scopic contrasts. The three dimensions are inherent in all contrasts, in and out of art. They are dimensional in the two senses that they all apply to every intense contrast and that they must be understood together, in interaction, producing further contrasts among contrasts. In this sense, the three dimensions manifest the most general sense of what intense contrast is, and are to be understood in terms of the fundamental categories of the theory of orders.

The three dimensions of aesthetic value are perfection, invention, and celebration. They may be interpreted straightforwardly in terms of the ordinal categories: perfection as an emphasis on prevalence amidst deviance among relevant subaltern orders, invention as deviance among established prevalences, celebration as the sovereign interplay of all the categories in lived experience. Yet the principle that art manifests inexhaustibility, that aesthetic value is such a manifestation, suggests a very different triad of dimensions of aesthetic value, given directly by the pairs of ordinal categories: integrity with scope, prevalence with deviance, possibility with actuality. Integral-scopic contrasts are fundamental to art and aesthetic value. Indeed, I consider them so important, so essential to artistic inexhaustibility, that I place them in a class by themselves. The interplay of prevalence and deviance is the foundation of the notion of contrast, and cannot be regarded as simply one among other dimensions. Rather, all the dimensions of aesthetic value must be interpretable in terms of the interplay of prevalence and deviance. The contrast of possibilities and actualities is a more difficult matter. Rather than regarding this contrast as a dimension of aesthetic value, I view it as inherent in all contrasts: the interplay between the actual properties of works of art and their contrasts in relation to the possibilities engendered for them throughout different orders in human experience. Art revels in possibilities and in the related contrasts of prevalence and deviance, integrity and scope.

Another reason for emphasizing the dimensions of perfection, invention, and celebration is based on the established traditions of art. Perfection, invention, and celebration seem to me to express the powers assigned most commonly to works of art. Nevertheless, the apparent arbitrariness of this classification supports the general principle that the inexhaustibility of orders and of art entails that every classification of contrasts will be arbitrary in part, and that other classificatory systems would serve as well, to certain well-defined purposes, though any valid system, I claim, can be interpreted in terms of the ordinal categories.

The five major types of contrast are very general but are not dimensional: they are relevant to all intense contrasts, to all works of art and artistic value, but one or another may in a particular case be of quite minor importance. Nevertheless, they express certain fundamental features of works of art: that such works are constructed at a time and place, in the context of established traditions; that they are comprised of materials which have become typical over the history of art; that construction is only one of the modes of judgment, while every mode of judgment is pervasive throughout judgment; finally, that every construction inhabits a public world containing diverse persons who interpret and judge works of art in different ways due to their different circumstances. The dimensions of aesthetic value pertain to intensity of contrast; the general types of contrast pertain to constructive judgment and by extension to aesthetic value in natural objects. Finally, integral and scopic contrasts manifest the ordinal inexhaustibility of works of art and intense contrasts which is a central feature of our experience of art. Nevertheless, the grounding of integral and scopic contrasts in the theory of orders suggests that they are not relevant to aesthetic value alone, but are inherent in ordinality generally. . . .

The Dimensions of Artistic Value

The three dimensions of artistic value are perfection, invention, and celebration. Each comprises an inexhaustible family of contrasts; yet each may be viewed as a contrast in itself: perfection with mediocrity; invention with repetition; celebration with ordinariness. Each is a feature of the fundamental aesthetic contrast: what is noteworthy in contrast with what does not merit attention. Aesthetic value belongs to beings which are extraordinary in contrast with what is not—in terms not of a *reason, end,* or *result,* but of *how* and *in which respects* they are so. A work of art is worthy of our attention, not in terms of its effects but in what it is. It is created to be given attention, and if successful, the attention is justified. The question a work of art poses for us is "to what shall we attend, and in what manner?"

It follows that each of the three dimensions expresses not a measure or degree, but a type of incomparability. The sovereignty of the work of art is expressed through all the dimensions of value. A work is not more perfect, or perfect in more ways, than other works, not more inventive or more celebrative, but perfect in the ways it is perfect, original in just the respects it is original—including how perfect are its inventions and how original are its perfections—and finally, celebrative as it is celebrative. All these dimensions are comprised of contrasts, inexhaustibly and profoundly, so that relations are central to art as to all orders. However, the dimensions also express a work's sovereignty, how *it* is perfect, for example, while the relevant contrasts express its manifold relevance and significance. Put another way, perfection, invention, and celebration express sovereign traits of a work of art, its incomparability; but the constituents of sovereignty and incomparability are relational and manifold, ordinal and inexhaustible, not holistic, ineffable, and unanalyzable. The pervasiveness of relationality throughout contrasts entails, I will show, that sovereignty can be expressed by no particular forms of contrast, but lies in complex interactions among contrasts, especially in the contribution of all the major forms of contrast to integral and scopic contrasts which involve variations in the identity and prevalence of individual works and orders.

Perfection, invention, and celebration are "dimensions" and not "types." All are relevant to every work of art and to every candidate for artistic value, with different emphases. Each is comprised of contrasts; together, in higher levels of contrast, they define the forms of artistic value relevant to any individual work. Where one or another is largely absent, artistic value is greatly diminished. The first two dimensions closely interact, since a superior work is perfect in respects original to it, while its inventions are realized perfectly. Nevertheless, perfection and originality are not simply holistic qualities of a work of art, but include subtle properties of details and recessive features of works which may be largely repetitive on the whole. Invention is important even where works are largely repetitive—as in early Russian iconic art—but in the small rather than as gross properties of the work. Celebration is a function of both perfection and invention. It both is heightened by their presence and contributes to their intensity. Where important inventions and perfections are conjoined with great celebration, the work becomes celebrative of itself. We travel thousands of miles to visit a museum or to witness a performance. When the celebrative dimension of art is diminished, works molder in libraries and museums. When their celebrative possibilities cease to be effective, works become mere artifacts, of historical importance only, lacking artistic vitality.[1] Artistic value is defined by the three dimensions together, in complex interaction, weakened where any of the three is diminished unless enhanced in compensating ways by the others at higher levels of contrast. . . .

CONTRASTS AND AESTHETIC VALUE: SPECIFIC KINDS OF CONTRAST

The three dimensions and five general types of contrast represent fundamental and pervasive characteristics of art. The three dimensions are essential features of aesthetic value: the five general types express pervasive features of constructive judgment. In addition, there are integral and scopic contrasts which express the metaphysical conditions of ordinality and inexhaustibility. Wherever there is art, there is an inexhaustible variety of contrasts involving perfection, invention, and celebration, as well as contrasts based on artistic mediums and traditions, diverse audiences, different interpretations and conceptions, and a plurality of modes of judgment. Wherever we find aesthetic value—for example, in natural events—we find contrasts involving perfection, rarity, and memorability, but also contrasts based on the ways in such found objects function celebratively in human experience: relative to established traditions and expectations, to diverse audiences and their different responses, in terms of materials and composition. All contrasts can be uniquely intense where methodically created. The most striking difference, however, between constructed and found works resides in intersubjective contrasts, for the prominence of the artist-audience contrast in art makes the absence of the artist for found objects the basis of particularity intense appearance-reality contrast.

These nine general types of contrast, with modifications, are therefore pervasive throughout art and natural orders, wherever aesthetic value is to be found. This pervasiveness and generality may obscure the intensity of the contrasts which fall under them. This is an important feature of generality, and produces an important type of contrast. It reflects an important characteristic of all aesthetic contrasts. General types of contrast are pervasive throughout experience in just those ways that obscure their contrast precisely because their generality is at the expense of diversity and detail. Very specific types of contrast, however, resonate throughout works of art and natural events at every general level and throughout virtually every other specific type of contrast. This is a consequence of the nature of contrasts, of inexhaustibly complex levels of contrast, and of the richness of works of art. The most specific artistic elements engender relevant contrasts by further contrast over all the general types and among other specific types of contrast. This phenomenon is an essential feature of the richness of works of art and the powers they have for us. . . .

CRITICISM, INTERPRETATION, ILLUSTREMENT

In order for a work of art to maintain its vitality, it must be complex in both its integrity and its scope. Greatness in art depends on an enduring richness within the integrity of the work that sustains a remarkable, inexhaustible range of possibilities for the enhancement of its scope in subsequent experience. Great works enrich our lives in myriad ways, providing extraordinarily different significations for different audiences. In addition, different world views and cultural expectations provide different conceptions of art within which a given work has varied integrities as well as scopes. Every location establishes a different integrity for a work of art, some widely varied because of major changes in life and experience. If greatness in art is enduring intensity of contrast, endurance is a function of the capacity of a work to adapt to new developments by absorbing them into its range of contrasts. A work of art is multifarious both in what it is and in what it makes possible, varying with the conditions of life and art. Such a multiplicity is required by the inexhaustibility of orders made manifest in art.

We are led to the inevitable and important function of interpretation for the arts—of delineating determinate orders within which a work possesses intense contrasts. The inexhaustibility of contrasts in art must be complemented by the specification of integrities if inexhaustibility is to be anything but indeterminateness and if works of art are to possess sovereignty and incomparability. The theory of orders may be expected to provide a foundation for settling some of the controversies concerning the functions of criticism—especially, whether criticism may be descriptive as well as interpretive; whether the arts require critical analysis; or whether, instead, criticism is merely a parasitic activity feeding off great works, providing fulfillment only for minds incapable of creative thought. The answer to these questions given by the theories of contrast and ordinality, in brief, is that the inexhaustibility manifested in art *demands* interpretation and criticism, inexhaustibly and multifariously. Criticism—especially in that form which I call "illustrement"—is the judgmental fulfillment of art as art is the manifestation of ordinal inexhaustibility.

Description

. . . A work of art may be described as any order may be described—by stating true propositions about it, a sufficient number to satisfy our desire for completeness, though ordinality entails that no description of any order can be complete or univalent without qualification. Assertive judgment is that mode in which accuracy is the predominant goal—an accuracy realized in propositions and subject to the constraints of evidence and the logical conditions of discourse. Wherever there is an appeal to logical conditions, information, and evidence such that a meaningful question is expected to have a single, univalent answer, we are functioning in the assertive mode of judgment.

If science is loosely identified with systematic and inventive assertive judgment—it is that mode of query in which assertive judgment is predominant—then description of a work of art can be given by the science of art. There may, of course, be descriptions drawn from everyday experience which fall under no known science. These may always be improved, rendered more effective and precise, by scientific development. Nevertheless, there are many sciences which can describe works of art: behavioral, social, and physical. A work may be described in terms of its physical materials. It may be weighed, its volume measured, its dimensions charted, its various outlines and profiles reproduced and delimited. A work or a performance may be studied like any physical object or event. A work may also be described in terms of the psychophysical responses of a given individual or group of individuals. The various emotional responses of an observer may be charted by instruments measuring his blood pressure, heartbeat, brain waves, and the like. If such descriptions seem somehow irrelevant, we may simply examine the physical properties of works of art. A musical or theatrical performance may be described in terms of the events taking place on the stage. Every such description will be limited and relative, for ordinality entails the incompleteness of every assertive account relative to the inexhaustibility of orders. Nevertheless, descriptions of works of art may be entirely adequate for the purposes to which they are put, if such ends are defined carefully enough. . . .

To many sensitive critics and observers, what I have called description is of no aesthetic relevance. While there are true descriptions of a work of art, they are held irrelevant to its artistic qualities. The ordinal theory entails that every such description is limited and incomplete: there is no ideal description, complete in every way, to which all other true descriptions approximate. Nevertheless, it is untenable to hold that what can be truly described is irrelevant to a work of art, since the components of contrasts as well as works can be delineated accurately. I have suggested what I take to be the kernel of truth in this view that description is irrelevant to aesthetic value. It is founded on the inexhaustibility of orders and the manifestation of such inexhaustibility in art. The inherent limitations of description relative to ordinality are a mortal weakness relative to the values of art.

A description can at best delineate the properties of a work of art relative to a given interpretation—that is, relative to one of its integrities. If every order had a single gross integrity, defining its place in a world order, then an ideal description would provide all the information that could be provided about any of them. But orders are inexhaustible, and every order has multiple integrities. Possibilities as well as actualities, scopes as well as integrities, deviances as well as prevalences, are present in every order, making every description inadequate in fundamental respects, exhibitive of the indeterminateness inherent in every ordinal condition. It follows that only a given integrity can be described relative to a given superaltern order, and only those possibilities relevant to the superaltern order can be delimited. The superaltern order provides both the conditions that establish validation for any judgment—including description—and the intrinsic limitations of every such determination. Insofar as artistic inventiveness provides novel integrities for works of art, novel possibilities and spheres of application, insofar as changing conditions introduce novel perspectives with novel integrities, assertive judgment will inevitably fail relative to those perspectives. Insofar as the contrasts pertinent to works of art are multifarious, multivalent, and inexhaustible, insofar as such works continually demand from us new and important interpretations, description can provide information of only limited relevance. The multiplicity of contrasts relative to any fine work relegates description to a subordinate, highly circumscribed role, heavily dependent on locating conditions defined by other modes of judgment and changing conditions of experience. The truer the description, the more publicly available, the more definite its confirmational conditions, the more definite are its artistic limitations. A poor work of art, lacking multiple richnesses, might seem to encourage a univalent interpretation and thereby a satisfactory description. But even here, the work has multiple integrities, though they may not represent to us forceful values. It has the changing integrities given by the changing face of art itself, due to the contributions of novel masterpieces. Art revels in the plurality of contrasts and possibilities relevant to created works, rendering every description, however detailed and accurate, a limited, almost useless expression of the values of such works and a clear manifestation of the limitations of assertive judgment relative to ordinal inexhaustibility.

Inexhaustibility has both a positive and a negative side. The limitations of description relative to inexhaustibility can be reformulated in a more positive way. Description is relative to integrities: the inexhaustibility of orders and their integrities entails that description too is inexhaustible. There are inexhaustibly many descriptions, related in many ways but also distinct in ways that are important in other respects. This inexhaustibility is expressed by the multiplicity of sciences, irreducible to any supreme science, but also constantly growing and developing sciences produced by new questions and points of view. It is expressed also in the multiplicity of modes of judgment, irreducible to any supreme mode of judgment, so that assertive judgment alone is incomplete, requiring supplementation by the other modes of judgment, and requiring supplementation inexhaustibly by other descriptions, relative to other locating perspectives. Description is inexhaustible in the two major senses indicated and, confronted with the inexhaustibility manifested by contrast in art, almost always appears irrelevant to art. The most accurate and truthful description of a work of art cannot fundamentally express its inexhaustibility, which requires the supplementation of inexhaustibly other descriptions and modes of query. Works of art call for inexhaustibly many and diverse descriptions—drawn from all the spheres of assertive judgment as well as inexhaustibly many methodic approaches and modes of query. Art, like being, calls upon the inexhaustible resources of human thought for its illumination.

Criticism

. . . What is commonly called "criticism" is frequently associated with evaluation in terms of consequences and effects. Works are criticized for being morally confused or reprehensible, vague in their solutions to the problems of life. By comparison, science provides solutions to its problems. But a scientific textbook is often evaluated as an act in terms of its success in communicating the principles and facts of the science to students. Art is often judged similarly as successful communication of an idea—thus an act to be apprehended in terms of its effectiveness and success. Artists are sometimes expected to have a complete moral vision, and their works are criticized for betraying moral confusion—even where situations are confused and afford only partial understanding. If art is not to be dogmatic, nevertheless it is to be enlightened and humane. Art is often thought a great teacher, and it can wield great influence. Such influence is not aesthetic, but active and moral. . . .

. . . The statement that a work of art is excellently or poorly constructed is primarily an act, seeking to influence an audience and to estimate the effects of the work upon them. *Calling* a work "excellent"—as against responding to it as such in an indefinite variety of ways—is an attempt at communication and influence, seeking to persuade, to affect sensibilities, to direct activities. It is essentially an act—though like all judgments, it may be located within any of the modes. The judgment that a work is well made or poorly constructed is not typically a true or false report about responses and reactions, nor even about the structural characteristics of the work, but is a deed performed to attain specific effects—to lead someone to attend to the work or to refrain, to manipulate taste, or to manifest the reviewer's sensibilities.

Suppose a sensitive, educated person reads a book of poems and finds them flawed. What is the function of his *saying* that the poems are weak?—educative, manipulative, predictive at best. An insensitive student may be taught how to read poetry more critically. A philistine may have his sensibilities challenged. A reader may have his responses articulated. What, however, of another reader who finds the poems excellent—for good or ill, justified or not? The criticism is irrelevant to his responses except to engender antipathy and controversy. At best, evaluative criticism offers prospects of effective intersubjective contrasts, but in severely truncated form. What of the poems themselves: are they good or bad? They may be good in some respects, poor in others; good in some contexts, poor in others; good for some audiences, poor for others. There is no single set of criteria, no overarching perspective, for which a work of art is unqualifiedly good or bad. Some of the contrasts comprising the poems' values may be intense only in certain perspectives; other contrasts may be irrelevant in those perspectives. Criticism as assessment sacrifices the multifarious and intense contrasts of a work to a particular end, and cannot therefore portray an adequate portion of the range of values relevant to any complex work of art.

Criticism is largely active judgment directed toward influence and persuasion. In this form, it has no specifically aesthetic function. Even worse, it frequently though inadvertently defines a work as an active judgment, the artist as a social agent. Now works of art do have consequences and play roles in social and political affairs. Were there a single, supreme political order, then art would have its role to play there with all other social instruments. We may even entertain the principle that constructive judgments are to be avoided when their moral effects are undesirable. This is what Plato tells us,—and nearly all theories of a supreme polity reach the same conclusion. If the moral and political order of judgments is more important, then art must be subordinated to moral considerations.

Ordinality, however, suggests that constructive judgments have their own values. The conclusion is that there is no supreme utopian state, no political and moral order supreme in all respects, no perfect balance of all relevant considerations. Art emphasizes plurality within and among moral orders, invention within action as well as science. Marxists may forswear bourgeois art, but it is the inventiveness and plurality of the arts they condemn. From their point of view, art is to be original only within circumscribed limits. Art pursued for its own sake is too free—and, from a moral point of view, that may be so. Yet there is no comprehensive order of experience within which all the models of judgment may be assigned a univalent function. Art manifests inexhaustibility by contrast; evaluative criticism must locate a work in a particular context of social and individual experience to reach its verdicts, necessarily diminishing the work's range of inexhaustibility. Moral and political judgments cannot tolerate inexhaustibility, and find it a constant challenge to overcome, frustrated by the omnipresence of failure in human experience. . . .

Interpretation

We may now consider constructive judgments in response to a work of art—what I call "interpretation." Setting aside the effects and consequences of a critical work, we may find it noteworthy itself in its intensity of contrast. A critical work is constructed, and can itself be a work of art or approach one. My concern now is with elucidating the connection between a fine work of art and a superior work of interpretation, the latter noteworthy in its own right yet also illuminating the work with which it deals. This relationship of illumination seems to undermine the sovereignty of the critical work, and such works are often denied the sovereignty, the incomparability of masterpieces of art. Yet it is essential to avoid conceiving a constructive judgment so that it is an active judgment in disguise, interpreting it entirely in terms of its utility.

A constructive judgment in response to a work of art is the creation of another work which articulates the first, which fulfills some artistic possibilities for it in further judgment by contrast. Insofar as the second work profoundly realizes possibilities belonging to the first, it illuminates it, promoting new and higher levels of contrast. Works in intense contrast illuminate and illustrate each other. A contrast among a variety of orders is exhibitive of each of their integrities in a particular location.

It is tempting but misleading to say that we have here a reconstruction of the original work: we would expect too great a similarity. Our concern is not with reconstruction, but with *construction in contrast.* The two works may have little in common—as a modern dance may be choreographed in response to the story of Oedipus, lacking all language and poetic devices, yet enhancing the original work and its human implications. We might regard a constructive judgment in response to a work of art as a *comment* upon it except for the connotations of assertion and discourse. The point is that a work may be illuminated more by another work, illuminated more in particular ways, than by a faithful description or by an active appraisal. Assertion and action provide illumination, but so does construction: by intensity of contrast. I have in mind here Keats' *Upon Looking in to Chapman's Homer* and Nietzsche's *Birth of Tragedy* as well as Racine's *Phèdre* and Anouilh's *Antigone.* Any work created in response to another work is a constructive judgment which may illuminate it through contrasts. Artistic works can be profoundly revealing of qualities of other works through irony and emphasis, by omission and augmentation, even by mere relevance. We need not restrict ourselves to works of art. The writings of Hume and Berkeley are more illuminating of parts of Locke's *Essay* than any commentaries. And they would be so without mentioning Locke by name or taking up his particular claims polemically.

What is required is that the contrasts which are part of the integrity of the interpretive work include the integrity of the original as a constituent (always a *particular* integrity). More precisely still, the interpretive work establishes an order within which the original is given an integrity and in which this integrity and certain features of its scope are articulated by contrast. Such a relationship need not interfere with the sovereignty of the work except where there is implied comparison with the original. This is the difference between interpretive critical works, which illuminate by contrast, and interpretive artistic works, which also illuminate by contrast, but through their own sovereignty. Where a great artist is influenced by another, his work manifests important judgments relevant to the other's work. It is natural for us to say that the second artist interprets the work of the first in his own creations. Because of this, influence studies have a fundamental artistic significance, not merely that of historical reflection. In a like manner, the common style or genre of several artists is revealed through the work of each of them, and each is enhanced by the comparison. This is fundamental in traditionary contrasts. Mozart, Haydn, and Beethoven provide the clearest and most illuminating "comment" or judgment upon the classical style and upon each other's work. Artists who work in the same time and culture reflect constructive judgments upon each other's works, sometimes by rejection and selectivity, sometimes by influence and a common attack on similar problems. Where inexhaustibility is manifested by construction, the created work is art. Critical works do not manifest inexhaustibility individually, through their own sovereignty, but only in the aggregate. That is why they are not as such art. . . .

Illustrement

There is no single and best way to articulate a work of art, but different ways valid relative to different circumstances and modes of judgment. It is appropriate to respond to works of art by assertive, active, or constructive judgments—description, criticism, or interpretation. It is also valid to regard works of art in relation to general theories or in their role in a cosmic or pervasive human order. And it is valid as well to respond to assertive or active judgments by works of art. The interpretation of the modes of judgment is of central importance as is the inexhaustibility of ordinality.

Illustrement is therefore not the *right* or *best* way to articulate a work of art. It is simply one of the forms of articulation, of profound intermodality. It is not even the only or best way to *explain* a work of art: all of the modes of articulative query are forms of explanation, of knowledge, relative to different standards and expectations. Illustrement coordinates the various modes of judgment within a methodically inventive enterprise: it is therefore a mode of query which articulates a work of art emphasizing none of the modes of judgment in particular, employing them all to its particular purposes. It is the rational fulfillment of intensity of contrast by means of all known modes of judgment and query together. The question I will now address is whether illustrement is itself a novel mode of judgment—in effect establishing a novel mode of validation distinct from those appropriate to the modes of judgment discussed above. The question is intelligible only if we grant the possibility of novel modes of judgment and query, novel forms of validation. Inexhaustibility and functionality are the central conditions on which this possibility is based, establishing diverse modes which function pervasively throughout judgment and query.

I have identified criticism with assessment, with active judgment. But clearly the finest works of literary criticism are illustrive and multimodal.² It is necessary here to introduce some distinctions. Illustrement is a mode of articulation, but so are description, criticism, and interpretation. Illustrement is a mode of query, but so in general are description, criticism, interpretation, and philosophy of art. Illustrement is the illumination of a work of art through further judgment—methodic, inventive, and interrogative—in which no mode of judgment in particular predominates.

Articulation is judgment for the sake of further judgment, establishing and ramifying spheres of continuing judgment. Query is methodic, inventive, and interrogative judgment concerned predominantly with validation. Science, ethics, art, and philosophy are the major forms of query. The principle of the interpenetration of the modes of judgment entails that every mode of query is intermodal, for every mode of judgment may be regarded as applicable to any particular judgment. Nevertheless, there is an important distinction for query relative to the pervasiveness and plurality of the modes of judgment. Every judgment is located in all the modes of judgment at once, but disjunctively or plurally. A statement is an assertion but may be regarded as an act. The two modes of validation here are relatively independent (except from the standpoint of pragmatic theories which make active judgment primary or psychological theories which would explain everything said in terms of aims and consequences). The modality of the judgment is not transformed by interpenetration and interrelation, but is essentially disjunctive. Query may be carried on predominantly within a single mode of judgment, methodically and interrogatively, inventively and validly. Where other modes of judgment are introduced, they do not affect the character of the query or the predominant mode of judgment. Description, interpretation, and criticism are methodic and inventive ways of articulating works of art and are modes of query. But in each the emphasis on a particular mode of judgment is predominant when not exclusive, and a single mode of validation is also predominant.

Alternatively, query may be typically and insistently intermodal. My particular concern here is with distinguishing illustrement from description, criticism, interpretation, and the theory of art. The latter are either unimodal or disjunctively multimodal (except for the last, which emphasizes generality, syndetic judgment). Illustrement is methodic, inventive, deliberative intermodal query relative to works of art. There is description, but in the service of evaluation and interpretation. There is a concern for the larger issues of art in relation to individual works. There is implicit evaluation based on both interpretation and description. There is interpretation to establish the integrity of the work relative to an accurate understanding of its effects. There is a deliberate and methodic enterprise in which a work of art is illuminated or revealed—illustred—in several modes of judgment conjunctively. None of the modes is predominant, though one may be emphasized, and an amalgam of all the modes is established.

Illustrement is query in which the variety of modes of judgment is employed to illustre a work of art—to reveal its nature, heighten its intensity, transform our understanding, improve our sensibilities. The best works of illustrement transform our perceptions of art by employing all the modes of judgment, none in particular. Illustrement is the manifestation through query of the powers of a work of art—and, through controlled and inventive judgment, actualization of the powers of art in general relative to the nature of life and experience. Illustrement respects the powers of art, intensity of contrast, in relation to both art and judgment, leading to still more complex contrasts produced by the synthetic powers of the mind. Illustrement both illuminates intense contrasts and produces higher contrasts. It thereby fulfills the inexhaustibility of art in its own inexhaustibility, bringing all the powers of judgment to bear upon the inexhaustible richnesses of art. Art manifests inexhaustibility; illustrement needs the complete rational powers of the mind to fulfill that manifestation.

A brief review of the dimensions and general types of contrast may be useful in the context of illustrement. We clearly value works of art for their excellences and perfections, their achievements and triumphs: but in illustrement, we describe and evaluate such perfections, place them in a general context of a theory of art, and establish interpretations which exhibit such perfections by contrast. Analogously, every work of art is valued for its originality and invention, however subtle and restricted, manifested in illustrement by all the modes of judgment. Perfection and invention are particularly manifested by illustrive perfection and invention, a reason why illustrement is no less a mode of query than art itself. The celebrativeness of great works is perhaps more difficult to describe, except in terms of social expectations and responses, but is interpreted by contrasts and evaluated implicitly. Here the power of contrasts to produce intensity through synthesis at higher levels is very important, for the celebrativeness of art is enhanced by the celebrative power of illustrement. The greater the power of the works they inspire, the greater the celebrative power of masterpieces of art. The orders created in illustrement, to the extent that they are sovereign and compelling in their own terms, engender effective and intense integral and scopic contrasts, manifesting the inexhaustibility of orders directly through the inexhaustibility of art.

More interesting, perhaps, are the general types of contrast, for they are relevant to some of the central controversies in the theory of criticism. Traditionary contrasts are relevant not only to stylistic and historical readings, but to the entire conception of *intertextuality*, where a work's relations to other works, earlier and later, are primary determinants of its identity and value.[3] Yet such traditionary contrasts are only one of the major kinds of contrast. The importance of the medium and its relation to some domains of application and meaning are closely related to intramedial and intermodal contrasts, while relations among different arts are pertinent to intermedial contrasts. Variations among readings and interpretations, including differences between artist and audience, are included within intersubjective contrasts, leading to various integrated and scopic contrasts that are relative to the multifarious identities of works of art, their radical context-sensitivity and variability.[4]

It is essential to emphasize that all these contrasts are available to judgment and articulation, in all the modes, that even integral-scopic contrasts may be described, evaluated, and interpreted. More important still, since variability of identity is a central type of contrast relevant to works of art, it is absorbed into the work's identity and character, part of it, a constituent of its integrity. This may be the central reply to unrestricted relativism: not any and all readings may be assimilated to the public integrity of a work of art, though aberrant and idiosyncratic readings are part of the scopic vitality of important works and contribute to their influence in human experience. Works of art are inexhaustible and multifarious in their integrities and possibilities, and illustrement of such works may take an inexhaustible number of forms. Nevertheless, the constraints on illustrement defined by intermodality of judgment and the theory of contrast establish important and determinate criteria for illustrative validation.

How is the validation of illustrement to be established? In reading the best works of criticism, do we expect them to meet the criteria of validation of each of the modes of articulation separately—description, criticism, interpretation, theory—or do we expect a novel mode of validation? There are three possibilities: (a) Illustrement might be a conjunction of all the modes of query in relation to art, illustring a work and its value, but ultimately attaining validation only relative to modes of judgment taken singly. Here we may regard illustrement as methodically intermodal, yet successful only relative to each mode taken individually. A given work of illustrement would thus be a satisfactory or true description, a convincing critical appraisal, a compelling interpretation, and a revelation of artistic principles in application. It would be each of them singly and many of them only in sum. (b) Illustrement may be an amalgam of the modes of judgment which attains a mode of validation comprised of each of the others in some aggregate: accurate where necessary, convincing in its evaluation, compelling in interpretation, and systematically effective. It must meet all the criteria of the different modes of judgment, but in different ratios and emphases, based perhaps on a certain sum or balance of all the separate modes of validation. (c) By conjunction and the establishment of unique methods of judgment and query, illustrement may attain a novel mode of validation comprised of all the modes of judgment and query, but reducible to none of them in particular nor to any aggregate sum.

I do not believe that alternative (a) is persuasive. We have description, criticism, and interpretation, but we also have methods for the analysis of works of art which are far more complex and illuminating. However, establishing which of alternatives (b) and (c) applies to illustrement in its more complex forms may be impossible at this time. No field today is more in flux and more critical of its fundamental tenets than the theory of reading—interpretation and illustrement. Some literary criticism is merely multimodal. Some is more complex and functions within all the modes of judgment together, providing a form of validation involving all the different modes. Nevertheless, it is far from clear whether illustrement has evolved and established a novel and intermodal species of validation unique to the reading and understanding of works of art. In fact, there is a continuing conservative tendency to reject the uniqueness of illustrive judgment, dividing intermodal articulation into its component modes. An alternative tendency has been to reject the uniqueness of illustrement relative to art, seeking a uniform theory of interpretation and analysis appropriate to all language codes or texts. The latter development may be the outcome of an intuition that interpretation is effectively based on a unique mode of judgment and query. Nevertheless, it appears that illustrive works are sometimes based on conception of validation appropriate to (b) and sometimes to (c)—when not to (a)—and that the issue of whether illustrement is a novel mode of query is as yet an open question.

There is an important reason why it may remain an open question indefinitely, a reason rooted in inexhaustibility and contrast. In order to establish a plausible case for the uniqueness of illustrement as a mode of query, it would be necessary to define a unique and clear method of illustrive validation. Yet all the modes of judgment and query are relevant to criticism and interpretation, and no particular synthesis or composite is primary. There is, then, a continual contrasting tension between alternatives (b) and (c) relative to every work of art and illustrive interpretation, leaving open the inexhaustible possibility of further contrasts and types of interpretation. Alternatively, there is an indefinite variety of kinds of illustrement, with different modes of validation relevant to them, so that no one particular mode of illustrive validation can be the maximal fulfillment of aesthetic value.

This brief discussion indicates clearly that illustrement is not a *superior* mode of articulation and query relative to individual works of art, and that it certainly is not the only appropriate mode. Moreover, there is no systematic basis for determining whether illustrement establishes a novel coordination among the modes of query in the articulation of works of art or whether it establishes a hybrid aggregate of the various modes of judgment producing only aggregative validation. Every mode of judgment is pervasive through experience and judgment—a consideration against viewing illustrement as a fundamental mode of judgment. Therefore, every mode of judgment, including hybrid modes engendered through query, is appropriate to works of art. Query is methodic and inventive interrogative judgment, and works of art may be queried in any, in all, or in a few of modes of judgment, separately or in the aggregate. Nevertheless, I will argue that we may generalize illustrement so that it manifests the rational fulfillment of articulative query.

It is appropriate here to return to the principle that a fine work of art is a created order of intense contrasts. Value is found within a work through response to these contrasts—whether conscious or unconscious, explicit or implicit, in discourse, action, or further construction. A work of art succeeds if it engenders articulative responses to its contrasts in some mode of judgment. A momentary aesthetic experience may be poignant and intensely effective. Though never repeated, it may be remembered. Some works have effects in their own time, or upon a small audience, and pass from the scene. Yet they are not failures for their small term if their articulative impact has been significant. It is a remarkable thing to be deeply moved by a work of art or to sense that one is in the presence of an exceptional creation—though the emotion may pass never to be recaptured, and even if what was once exceptional later becomes trite. Some works have an impact for a certain age or walk of life, their constrasts having significance for a particular audience.

Fashions come and go in the arts, especially romances and adventures. As life changes, and our surroundings are transformed, fashionable works of art change also. What was fascinating to readers of two hundred years ago is no longer fascinating; today there are new idols. In contrast with such fashionable works, there are others which endure in their remarkable qualities, fascinating to all ages, all generations, and at all times—and for varied reasons.

Such works are often not *more* intense emotionally than are other, less successful works. They are often less affecting, and may be less immediately satisfying. They may be very complex, requiring profound study. Or they may be very subtle, appealing to rarified sensibilities. Their distinguishing characteristic is their endurance as remarkable for nearly all human beings who gain access to them. These works I have called "great"—the monuments of art: but such an epithet is meant more to describe their endurance than to capture specific qualities inherent in their construction.

Illustrement is faced with a complex task: to gain understanding of the significant contrasts found within important works of art and to estimate their enduring greatness. The latter judgment is so corrupted by expectations concerning the future of mankind and the need to manipulate taste that it can seldom be defended. Human life might change to the point where the most important works of our time would be meaningless, devoid of relevant comparisons. It is more important to know what within works of art may be found valuable than to predict whether human beings in some distant future will understand those contrasts. It is more important to define taste and to educate it than to foretell enduring aesthetic values. And finally, it is more important to add new works to the store than merely to enjoy the old—especially where old and new are illustred by contrast. All of these normative judgments are active and moral, and are subservient to that mode of validation. Nevertheless, in the same terms, it is more valuable to emphasize that constructive judgment is a distinct mode than to regard all works of art as a result of deeds and actions—though they are such and may be evaluated as such.

Interpretation and illustrement are of paramount importance to the arts. The greatness of a work resides in its enduring value for mankind. But its service to art and to humanity resides not so much in enjoyment as in further articulation. Here I must emphasize again that personal responses are judgments and may be articulations, though often of minimal scope. Response in terms of new works is the most sublime realization of possibilities in art.

The basis of art is pluralistic: creations within the arts show us that the world is not one but continually new and inexhaustible. We must respond to even the greatest works with other works, perhaps lesser ones, but which contrast with and thus illustre the greatness of the works of the past. Here personal responses—in one's conversations, works, and fantasies—are to be regarded as creative interpretations, though of modest ramifications. Science seems to tell us that knowledge might reach completion. And even morals would appear to afford a remarkable degree of systematization. Both are but appearances. Nevertheless, it is the arts which communicate to us unmistakably that greatness is never at an end and that artistic values reside in further judgments, especially novel creations, inexhaustibly.

NOTES

1. This is surely what Dewey means in the opening paragraphs of *Art as Experience* (New York: Minton, Balch, 1934, p. 3) when he claims that

> When artistic objects are separated from both conditions of origin and operation in experience, a wall is built around them that renders almost opaque their general significance, with which esthetic theory deals. Art is remitted to a separate realm, where it is cut off from that association with the materials and aims of every other form of human effect, undergoing, and achievement.
>
> In common conception, the work of art is often identified with the building, book, painting, or statue in its existence apart from human experience. Since the actual work of art is what the product does with and in experience, the result is not favorable to understanding.

Nevertheless, it is the work which is celebrative, not the activities of artist or audience. In addition, celebration is one of three dimensions of artistic value, and can be neither wholly absent from any work which was ever part of lived experience nor made the sole basis of artistic value. Celebration is a function of lived experience, but is not to be traced simply to the living of experience, as Dewey sometimes seems to suggest.

2. For an informal presentation of this view, see Morris Weitz, *Hamlet and the Philosophy of Literary Criticism* (Chicago: University of Chicago Press, 1964). Weitz finds elements of description, explanation, evaluation, and poetics in literary criticism, but offers no systematic theory of how they function in relation.

3. See the works of Julia Kristeva and Harold Bloom, in particular: "Influence, as I conceive it, means that there are *no* texts, but only relationships *between* texts. These relationships depend upon a critical act, a misreading or misprision, that one poet performs upon another, and that does not differ in kind from the necessary critical acts performed by every strong reader upon every text he encounters. The influence-relation governs reading as it governs writing, and reading is therefore a miswriting just as writing is a misreading. As literary history lengthens, all poetry necessarily becomes

verse-criticism, just as all criticism becomes prose-poetry." (Harold Bloom, *A Map of Misreading* [New York: Oxford University Press, 1975] p. 3.) This view is a confused and limited harbinger of the theory of illustrement, limited by its emphasis on traditionary contrasts and confused altogether by the notion of *mis*reading and *mis*writing.

4. The fundamental and inalienable *difference* between the perspectives of author and reader is the foundation of Hans-Georg Gadamer's *fusion of horizons* (*Truth and Method* [New York: Seabury, 1975]). Gadamer's is perhaps the most effective and constructive theory founded on intersubjective contrasts, though it is greatly weakened by its emphasis on fusion and on historical time. The contrasts which are essential to art and interpretation are, as the theory of contrast indicates, inexhaustibly diverse, not simply a function of artist-audience variability.

III

Interpretation and Criticism

STEPHEN PEPPER

STEPHEN PEPPER SEEMS a relatively minor figure among the giants of the classical American tradition, yet he deserves a wider audience for certain of his contributions. I refer particularly to his theory of world hypotheses, that there are discernible forms of metaphysical expression, each of which can be sustained as a general hypothesis for the interpretation of our experience.

Pepper wrote several books on art. The selection here is too short to offer an adequate view of his theory, but it does capture quite incisively an important conception of interpretation, stated succinctly and quite powerfully by Pepper, that within the field of lived experience, works of art define the conditions for their interpretation. It follows that a determinate interpretation can be given for works that achieve this definition, that interpretation can be a science. Pepper's view of science is sophisticated and complex, demonstrating that the science of interpretation of works of art may be no simpler than the analogous science of the interpretation of historical events.

STEPHEN PEPPER

The Work of Art *

Think of yourself entering a gallery of an art museum. Suppose your eye catches a picture at the end of the room which attracts your attention and arouses your incipient admiration. Do you stop at the doorway and there relish the experience? No, pleasant as the picture is at that distance, it would be tantalizing to be kept there at a distance. The very consummatory structure of the situation draws you into the room to a position neither too near nor too far, where the colors and shapes are to be seen at their best. If there is a glass over the picture, you will move so that all glare is eliminated. In short, in a consummatory field of activity a person is drawn to the optimum condition of consummatory response with respect to the object—and, when the object is a work of art, specifically with respect to the stimulating aesthetic vehicle. And all positions or conditions less than the optimum are by the dynamics of the field rejected as less good than the optimum to which the dynamics of the field draws the spectator.

And similarly with music. We seek a location neither too near nor too far, where the sounds come at a consummatory optimum. To hear good music in the distance is to be drawn towards it where it can be heard best. The Pied Piper in the fable drew the children after him by means of this principle. They followed him because to stay behind as he moved forward was to drop out of the area of optimum reception. And our manipulation of the volume and the tone of a phonograph has the same significance.

We may call this the consummatory principle. It is the tendency to make the most of the consummatory field. The dynamics of the field draws the agent to the optimum area of satisfaction.

* Stephen Pepper, *The Work of Art* (Bloomington, Ind.: Indiana University Press, 1955), pp. 50-59.

Now, if we have grasped the principle, we see that it is a selective system like an appetitive drive. In fact, it is the terminal phase of a positive desire. For the structure of a purposive act motivated by an appetitive drive like hunger is such as to draw an organism as quickly as possible to the consummatory field where the drive can attain quiescence. Acts are selected as right or wrong in proportion as they conduce or fail to conduce to the attainment of the consummatory field. But, having attained that field, then (barring the pressure of a practical emergency) the principle of action changes to that of maximizing satisfaction in the field. Acts are selected as right or wrong in proportion as they increase or decrease the available satisfaction, in proportion as they approach to or recede from areas of optimum reception. That the principle of selection changes within the consummatory field from what it was in the approach to this field can be seen by the fact that outside the field the quicker the activity is over the better, whereas within the field the longer the period of activity the better. The trend for the optimum of stimulation within the field has the effect of holding the organism there as long as possible. This is, of course, just a more detailed description of the well-recognized contrast between practical achievement and aesthetic contemplation. For practical achievement, the rule of the shortest path holds—the speedier the better. But for aesthetic enjoyment, the longer the better.

The point for us to note, however, is that the consummatory principle, which seeks to intensify and draw out enjoyment, is a selective principle. This point is often missed. Even in the very simple examples we have just offered the selective operation of the consummatory field emerges. The structure of the field causes a person who moves from a more to a less favorable position within the field to consider his movement an error and to correct it to a better position. And so from better to better positions the person moves until he finds the optimum position which actually has been operating all the time as the norm for the correctness and incorrectness of every move of the spectator within the field. It is a natural norm determined by the structure of the specific consummatory field and is described in declarative sentences just as a physicist might describe a magnetic field.

The dynamics of this selective system, like that of a purposive structure relating means and end, is such that the impulse for the optimum is the same as that which motivates the error in the approach to the optimum. Just as the drive which charges the anticipation of the end is the very one that charges the incorrect choice of a means so that in the very dynamics of the system the means acknowledges its incorrectness by virtue of the end; so here the consummatory principle by which the organism seeks to maximize its enjoyment in the consummatory field determines both the optimum point and the points of lesser receptivity. In this way a movement into a less favorable position is acknowledged as an error by the same dynamics that leads the organism to correct its error and feel its way towards the optimum.

Let us note, too, that the point of optimum receptivity is not known to the organism ahead of his responses in the consummatory field, unless he had previous experience and remembers. Where is the best point to see a picture, or to listen to a piano? One has to move around in the consummatory area and find out. Nevertheless, that point is settled by the very structure of the field. It is a dispositional property of the situation. For the organism moving about in the field it is the ideal and norm of correctness of all his actions in the field. It is the place where he *ought* to be. And this is a declarative statement concerning the structure of the field!

Now, I think you can see where all these preliminaries are heading. They point to the statement that the object of criticism is the terminal area of optimum receptivity for the vehicle of a work of art.

For consider what is sought in the fullness of contemplation of a picture like Breughel's *Winter*. To stand before it in the most favorable position under a favorable light is a beginning. But to perceive all the relevant details and to gather them up in successive discriminations and fundings of the content of the picture are parts of the same process. The balance and tensions of the forms, the linear design, the drama of the represented scene, and the attendant emotions are all in the consummatory field of the picture as truly as the point of most favorable visibility. The discriminative mind is drawn to find these in the consummatory field of this picture as compellingly as the body is attracted from the door at the end of the gallery to the optimum position a few feet in front of the picture. The search for his optimum consummatory area will be tentative and accompanied by many incorrect responses, just as a naive perceiver's search for the optimum position of visibility would be. The incorrect responses are the mistaking of irrelevant for relevant details in the object of criticism.

If I have made my point, there is no need to argue further about the basic issue of this discussion. For if the object of criticism is the optimum area of appreciation of the relevant characters stimulated by the vehicle of a work of art, then this is a matter of description and any description a writer gives of it will be true or false. If a writer describes his response to a work as though this were authoritative and yet leaves out many relevant features or inserts some irrelevant ones, he is making a false judgment which the consummatory field of the work will itself in time correct through the later discriminations of this same man, or of some other man more discriminating than he. If some spectator fails to reach the optimum point of visibility for a picture, the point is still there in the consummatory field, drawing any interested person to reach it who enters the field and stays there long enough. So also with the object of criticism as the optimum area of aesthetic contemplation.

For the point I am making is that an aesthetic judgment about a work of art, in at least one significant and common sense of the term, is a judgment about the capacity of the work for giving satisfaction to a discriminating perceiver, and that this is a judgment which is at once true or false and evaluative. When a critic says Breughel's *Winter* is "good" he is affirming a high degree of satisfaction to be obtained in the optimum perception of the work. He is not requesting anyone to agree with him, though he does expect other men as discriminating as he himself to confirm the truth of his judgment. The reason for this expectation is that the judgment refers to the norm of a selective system—namely, that system which operates in the consummatory field for the maximizing of satisfaction under the control of an enduring vehicle. For it is, of course, the facts of the situation that justify the prediction. For when a person is attracted to an object in the consummatory field, he does tend to adjust his behavior in the direction of the optimum response in respect to the controlling vehicle. In this operation of the selective system, the errors are predicted along with the successive approaches to complete appreciation.

When a critic states that Breughel's *Winter* is beautiful, he is accordingly referring to a consummatory field and the operation of a selective system within that field. He is referring to an area of optimum receptivity and to the content of response obtainable in that area. He may describe this content of the relevant characters of the fully appreciated picture in great detail. These characters will include emotions and feelings as well as colors, lines, and representational meanings. He is asserting in declarative terms that this is the response a person will get if he maximizes the relevant satisfactions in this consummatory area. His statement is of the "if-then" form and recognizes that most persons entering this consummatory field will have many inadequate perceptions of the picture on their way towards an optimum response. The ordinary way of expressing the discrepancy between the inadequate perceptions and the optimum response is that these perceptions are not what they ought to be, for they ought to be the perception of the optimum response. In making this normative statement the critic is not commanding other people to make their perceptions conform to his. On the contrary, he is showing these people the ultimate perception they themselves are trying to attain by their entrance into the consummatory field and by their attraction to this object. The critic is like the helpful guide who shows you just where you can get the best view of the object. Perhaps the object is a waterfall and you have to climb a thousand feet to the finest view of it. But the critic is not commanding you to climb. He is telling you a fact about your consummatory field, and if your drive is strong enough from your interest in the falls, it is a safe prediction you will find that observation point. You would, in fact, find it for yourself if your interest persisted, but if you follow the directions of the experienced guide it will save you some trouble and pains.

Now obviously this is not the end. It is only the beginning of the story of responsible aesthetic criticism. There are many things that need to be straightened out and amplified. Just what, in concrete detail, is the object of criticism? What, more precisely, constitutes relevancy? May there not be a considerable variance in the optimum response? May there not be alternative objects of criticism in response to a single aesthetic vehicle? Is the object of criticism ever exhaustively attained? Isn't it an extrapolated ideal towards which men's perceptions approach? To most of these questions I would with various qualifications give an affirmative answer.

But the big point to see is that in our description of the process of aesthetic criticism all such questions are open to intelligent treatment. They are questions of fact to be settled in terms of the evidence concerning the factual relations among the aesthetic vehicle, the successive perceptions of it, and the process of approaching aesthetic maximization in the object of criticism.

E. D. HIRSCH, JR.

THE FUNDAMENTAL PROBLEM OF INTERPRETATION, given the diversity and richness of works of art, is the problem of norms. How can we establish the authority of a given interpretation of a text or work, which is situated in so many different historical and social contexts? Hirsch's response is that we cannot suppose that the work itself has authority. If we demand interpretive norms, the only alternative is to let the author determine the meaning of the work. Hirsch offers a theory of the "meaning" of a work contrasted with the "significance" of a work to an audience.

E. D. HIRSCH, JR.

Validity in Interpretation *

A. Banishment of the Author

It is a task for the historian of culture to explain why there has been in the past four decades a heavy and largely victorious assault on the sensible belief that a text means what its author meant. In the earliest and most decisive wave of the attack (launched by Eliot, Pound, and their associates) the battleground was literary: the proposition that textual meaning is independent of the author's control was associated with the literary doctrine that the best poetry is impersonal, objective, and autonomous; that it leads an afterlife of its own, totally cut off from the life of its author.[1] This programmatic notion of what poetry should be became subtly identified with a notion of what all poetry and indeed all forms of literature necessarily must be. It was not simply desirable that literature should detach itself from the subjective realm of the author's personal thoughts and feelings; it was, rather, an indubitable fact that all written language remains independent of that subjective realm. At a slightly later period, and for different reasons, this same notion of semantic autonomy was advanced by Heidegger and his followers.[2] The idea also has been advocated by writers who believe with Jung that individual expressions may quite unwittingly express archetypal, communal meanings. In some branches of linguistics, particularly in so-called information theory, the semantic autonomy of language has been a working assumption. The theory has found another home in the work of non-Jungians who have interested themselves (as Eliot did earlier) in symbolism, though Cassirer, whose name is sometimes invoked

---

* E. D. Hirsch, Jr., from "In Defense of the Author," Chapter 1 of *Validity in Interpretation* (New Haven, Conn.: Yale University Press, 1967), pp. 1-23.

by such writers, did not believe in the semantic autonomy of language.[3] As I said, it is the job of the cultural historian to explain why this doctrine should have gained currency in recent times, but it is the theorist's job to determine how far the theory of semantic autonomy deserves acceptance.

Literary scholars have often contended that the theory of authorial irrelevance was entirely beneficial to literary criticism and scholarship because it shifted the focus of discussion from the author to his work. Made confident by the theory, the modern critic has faithfully and closely examined the text to ferret out its independent meaning instead of its supposed significance to the author's life. That this shift toward exegesis has been desirable most critics would agree, whether or not they adhere to the theory of semantic autonomy. But the theory accompanied the exegetical movement for historical not logical reasons, since no logical necessity compels a critic to banish an author in order to analyze his text. Nevertheless, through its historical association with close exegesis, the theory has liberated much subtlety and intelligence. Unfortunately, it has also frequently encouraged willful arbitrariness and extravagance in academic criticism and has been one very important cause of the prevailing skepticism which calls into doubt the possibility of objectively valid interpretation. These disadvantages would be tolerable, of course, if the theory were true. In intellectual affairs skepticism is preferable to illusion.

The disadvantages of the theory could not have been easily predicted in the exciting days when the old order of academic criticism was being overthrown. At that time such naïvetés as the positivistic biases of literary history, the casting about for influences and other causal patterns, and the postromantic fascination with the habits, feelings, and experiences surrounding the act of composition were very justly brought under attack. It became increasingly obvious that the theoretical foundations of the old criticism were weak and inadequate. It cannot be said, therefore, that the theory of authorial irrelevance was inferior to the theories or quasi-theories it replaced, nor can it be doubted that the immediate effect of banishing the author was wholly beneficial and invigorating. Now, at a distance of several decades, the difficulties that attend the theory of semantic autonomy have clearly emerged and are responsible for that uneasiness which persists in the academies, although the theory has long been victorious.

That this state of academic skepticism and disarray results largely from the theory of authorial irrelevance is, I think, a fact of our recent intellectual history. For, once the author had been ruthlessly banished as the determiner of his text's meaning, it very gradually appeared that no adequate principle existed for judging the validity of an interpretation. By an inner necessity the study of "what a text says" became the study of what it says to an individual critic. It became fashionable to talk about a critic's "reading" of a text, and this word began to appear in the titles of scholarly works. The word seemed to imply that if the author had been banished, the critic still remained, and his new, original, urbane, ingenious, or relevant "reading" carried its own interest.

What had not been noticed in the earliest enthusiasm for going back to "what the text says" was that the text had to represent *somebody's* meaning—if not the author's, then the critic's. It is true that a theory was erected under which the meaning of the text was equated with everything it could plausibly be taken to mean. . . . The theory of semantic autonomy forced itself into such unsatisfactory, ad hoc formulations because in its zeal to banish the author it ignored the fact that meaning is an affair of consciousness not of words. Almost any word sequence can, under the conventions of language, legitimately represent more than one complex of meaning.[4] A word sequence means nothing in particular until somebody either means something by it or understands something from it. There is no magic land of meanings outside human consciousness. Whenever meaning is connected to words, a person is making the connection, and the particular meanings he lends to them are never the only legitimate ones under the norms and conventions of his language.

One proof that the conventions of language can sponsor different meanings from the same sequence of words resides in the fact that interpreters can and do disagree. When these disagreements occur, how are they to be resolved? Under the theory of semantic autonomy they cannot be resolved, since the meaning is not what the author meant, but "what the poem means to different sensitive readers."[5] One interpretation is as valid as another, so long as it is "sensitive" or "plausible." Yet the teacher of literature who adheres to Eliot's theory is also by profession the preserver of a heritage and the conveyor of knowledge. On what ground does he claim that his "reading" is more valid than that of any pupil? On no very firm ground. This impasse is a principal cause of the loss of bearings sometimes felt though not often confessed by academic critics.

One ad hoc theory that has been advanced to circumvent this chaotic democracy of "readings" deserves special mention here because it involves the problem of value, a problem that preoccupies some modern literary theorists. The most valid reading of a text is the "best" reading.[6] But even if we assumed that a critic did not have access to the divine criteria by which he could determine the best reading, he would still be left with two equally compelling normative ideals—the best meaning and the author's meaning. Moreover, if the best meaning were not the author's then it would have to be the critic's—in which case the critic would be the author of the best meaning. Whenever meaning is attached to a sequence of words it is impossible to escape an author.

Thus, when critics deliberately banished the original author, they themselves usurped his place, and this led unerringly to some of our present-day theoretical confusions. Where before there had been but one author, there now arose a multiplicity of them, each carrying as much authority as the next. To banish the original author as the determiner of meaning was to reject the only compelling normative principle that could lend validity to an interpretation. On the other hand, it might be the case that there does not really exist a viable normative ideal that governs the interpretation of texts. This would follow if any of the various arguments brought against the author were to hold. For if the meaning of a text is not the author's, then no interpretation can possibly correspond to *the* meaning of the text, since the text can have no determinate or determinable meaning. If a theorist wants to save the ideal of validity he has to save the author as well, and, in the present-day context, his first task will be to show that the prevailing arguments against the author are questionable and vulnerable.

B. *"The Meaning of a Text Changes–Even for the Author"*

A doctrine widely accepted at the present time is that the meaning of a text changes.[7] According to the radical historicistic view, textual meaning changes from era to era; according to the psychologistic view, it changes from reading to reading. Since the putative changes of meaning experienced by the author himself must be limited to a rather brief historical span, only the psychologistic view need concern us here. Of course, if any theory of semantic mutability were true, it would legitimately banish the author's meaning as a normative principle in interpretation, for if textual meaning could change in any respect there could be no principle for distinguishing a valid interpretation from a false one. But that is yet another problem that will be dealt with in a suitable place.[8] Here I need not discuss the general (and insoluble) normative problems that would be raised by a meaning which could change, but only the conditions that have caused critics to accuse authors of such fickleness.

Everyone who has written knows that his opinion of his own work changes and that his responses to his own text vary from reading to reading. Frequently an author may realize that he no longer agrees with his earlier meaning or expression and will revise his text. Our problem, of course, has nothing to do with revision or even with the fact that an author may explain his meaning differently at different times, since the authors are sometimes inept explainers of their meanings, as Plato observed. Even the puzzling case of the author who no longer understands his own text at all is irrelevant to our problem, since his predicament is due to the fact that an author, like anyone else, can forget what he meant. We all know that sometimes a person remembers correctly and sometimes not, and that sometimes a person recognizes his mistakes of memory and corrects them. None of this has any theoretical interest whatever.

When critics assert that the author's understanding of his text changes, they refer to the experience that everybody has when he rereads his own work. His response to it is different. This is a phenomenon that certainly does have theoretical importance—though not of the sort sometimes allotted to it. The phenomenon of changing authorial responses is important because it illustrates the difference between textual meaning and what is loosely termed a "response" to the text.

Probably the most extreme examples of this phenomenon are cases of authorial self-repudiation, such as Arnold's public attack on his masterpiece, *Empedocles on Etna*, or Schelling's rejection of all the philosophy he had written before 1809. In these cases there cannot be the slightest doubt that the author's later response to his work was quite different from his original response. Instead of seeming beautiful, profound, or brilliant, the work seemed misguided, trivial, and false, and its meaning was no longer one that the author wished to convey. However, these examples do not show that the meaning of the work had changed, but precisely the opposite. If the work's meaning had changed (instead of the author himself and his attitudes), then the author would not have needed to repudiate his meaning and could have spared himself the discomfort of a public recantation. No doubt the *significance* of the work to the author had changed a great deal, but its meaning had not changed at all.

This is the crux of the matter in all those cases of authorial mutability with which I am familiar. It is not the meaning of the text which changes, but its significance to the author. This distinction is too often ignored. *Meaning* is that which is represented by a text; it is what the author meant by his use of a particular sign sequence; it is what the signs represent. *Significance,* on the other hand, names a relationship between that meaning and a person, or a conception, or a situation, or indeed anything imaginable. Authors, who like everyone else change their attitudes, feelings, opinions, and value criteria in the course of time, will obviously in the course of time tend to view their own work in different contexts. Clearly what changes for them is not the meanings of the work, but rather their relationship to that meaning. Significance always implies a relationship, and one constant, unchanging pole of that relationship is what the text means. Failure to consider this simple and essential distinction has been the source of enormous confusion in hermeneutic theory.

If we really believed that the meaning of a text had changed for its author, there could be only one way that we could know it: he would have to tell us. How else could we know that his understanding had changed—understanding being a silent and private phenomenon? Even if an author reported that his understanding of his meaning had changed, we should not be put off by the implausibility of the statement but should follow out its implications in a spirit of calm inquiry. The author would have to report something like this: "By these words I meant so and so, but now I observe that I really meant something different," or, "By these words I meant so and so, but I insist that from now on they shall mean something different." Such an event is unlikely because authors who feel this way usually undertake a revision of their text in order to convey their new meaning more effectively. Nevertheless, it is an event that *could* occur, and its very possibility shows once again that the same sequence of linguistic signs can represent more than one complex of meaning.

Yet, even though the author has indeed changed his mind about the meaning he wants to convey by his words, he has not managed to change his earlier meaning. This is very easily proved by his own report. He could report a change in his understanding only if he were able to compare his earlier construction of his meaning with his later construction. That is the only way he could know that there is a difference: he holds both meanings before his mind and rejects the earlier one. But his earlier meaning is not thereby changed in any way. Such a report from an author would simply force a choice on the interpreter, who would have to decide which of the author's two meanings he is going to concern himself with. He would have to decide which "text" he wanted to interpret at the moment. The critic is destined to fall into puzzlement if he confuses one text with the other or if he assumes that the author's will is entirely irrelevant to his task.

This example is, as I said, quite improbable. I do not know of a single instance where an author has been so eccentric as to report without any intention to deceive that he now means by his text what he did not mean. (Deliberate lies are, of course, another matter; they have no more theoretical interest than failures of memory.) I was forced into this improbable example by the improbability of the original thesis, namely that an author's meaning changes for himself. What the example showed on the contrary was that an author's original meaning *cannot* change—even for himself, though it can certainly be repudiated. When critics speak of changes in meaning, they are usually referring to changes in significance. Such changes are, of course, predictable and inevitable, and since the primary object of criticism, as distinct from interpretation, is significance, I shall have more to say about this distinction later. For the moment, enough has been said to show that the author's revaluation of his text's significance does not change its meaning and, further, that arguments which rely on such examples are not effective weapons for attacking either the stability or the normative authority of the author's original meaning.

C. "It Does Not Matter What an Author Means—Only What His Text Says"

As I pointed out in section A, this central tenet in the doctrine of semantic autonomy is crucial to the problem of validity. If the tenet were true, then any reading of a text would be "valid," since any reading would correspond to what the text "says"—for that reader. It is useless to introduce normative concepts like "sensitive," "plausible," "rich," and "interesting," since what the text "says" might not, after all, be any of those things. Validity of interpretation is not the same as inventiveness of interpretation. Validity implies the correspondence of an interpretation to a meaning which is represented by the text, and none of the above criteria for discriminating among interpretations would apply to a text which is dull, simple, insensitive, implausible, or uninteresting. Such a text might not be worth interpreting, but a criterion of validity which cannot cope with such a text is not worth crediting.

The proponents of semantic autonomy in England and America can almost always be relied on to point to the example of T. S. Eliot, who more than once refused to comment on the meanings of his own texts. Eliot's refusals were based on his view that the author has no control over the words he has loosed upon the world and no special privileges as an interpreter of them. It would have been quite inconsistent with this view if Eliot had complained when someone misinterpreted his writings, and, so far as I know, Eliot with stoical consistency never did complain. But Eliot never went so far as to assert that he did not mean anything in particular by his writings. Presumably he did mean something by them, and it is a permissible task to attempt to discover what he meant. Such a task has a determinate object and therefore could be accomplished correctly or incorrectly. However, the task of finding out what a text says has no determinate object, since the text can say different things to different readers. One reading is as valid or invalid as another. However, the decisive objection to the theory of semantic autonomy is not that it inconveniently fails to provide an adequate criterion of validity. The decisive objection must be sought within the theory itself and in the faultiness of the arguments used to support it.

One now-famous argument is based on the distinction between a mere intention to do something and the concrete accomplishment of that intention. The author's desire to communicate a particular meaning is not necessarily the same as his success in doing so. Since his actual performance is presented in his text, any special attempt to divine his intention would falsely equate his private wish with his public accomplishment. Textual meaning is a public affair. The wide dissemination of this argument and its acceptance as an axiom of recent literary criticism can be traced to the influence of a vigorous essay, "The Intentional Fallacy," written by W. K. Wimsatt and Monroe Beardsley and first published in 1946.[9] The critic of the arguments in that essay is faced with the problem of distinguishing between the essay itself and the popular use that has been made of it, for what is widely taken for granted as established truth was not argued and could not have been successfully argued in the essay. Although Wimsatt and Beardsley carefully distinguished between three types of intentional evidence, acknowledging that two of them are proper and admissible, their careful distinctions and qualifications have now vanished in the popular version which consists in the false and facile dogma that what an author intended is irrelevant to the meaning of his text.

The best way to indicate what is fallacious in this popular version is to discuss first the dimension in which it is perfectly valid—evaluation. It would be absurd to evaluate the stylistic felicity of a text without distinguishing between the author's intention to convey a meaning and, on the other hand, his effectiveness in conveying it. It would be similarly absurd to judge the profundity of a treatise on morality without distinguishing between the author's intention to be profound and his success in being so. Evaluation is constantly distinguishing between intention and accomplishment. Take this example: A poet intends in a four-line poem to convey a sense of desolation, but what he manages to convey to some readers is a sense that the sea is wet, to others that twilight is approaching. Obviously his intention to convey desolation is not identical with his stylistic effectiveness in doing so, and the anti-intentionalists quite justly point this out. But the intentional fallacy is properly applicable *only* to artistic success and to other normative criteria like profundity, consistency, and so on. The anti-intentionalist quite properly defends the right and duty of the critic to judge freely on his own criteria and to expose discrepancies between wish and deed. However, the intentional fallacy has no proper application whatever to verbal meaning. In the above example the only universally valid meaning of the poem is the sense of desolation. If the critic has not understood that point, he will not even reach an accurate judgment—namely, that the meaning was ineptly expressed and perhaps was not worth expressing in the first place.

Beneath the so-called intentional fallacy and, more generally, the doctrine of semantic autonomy lies an assumption which if true would at least render plausible the view that the meaning of a text is independent of the author's intention. I refer to the concept of a public consensus. If a poet intended his poem to convey desolation, and if to every competent reader his poem conveyed only a sense that twilight is approaching, then such public unanimity would make a very strong case (in this particular instance) for the practical irrelevance of the author's intention. But when has such unanimity occurred? If it existed generally, there would not be any problems of interpretation.

The myth of the public consensus has been decisive in gaining wide acceptance for the doctrine that the author's intention is irrelevant to what the text says. That myth permits the confident belief that the "saying" of the text is a public fact firmly governed by public norms. But if this public meaning exists, why is it that we, who are the public, disagree? Is there one group of us that constitutes the true public, while the rest are heretics and outsiders? By what standard is it judged that a correct insight into public norms is lacking in all those readers who are (except for the text at hand) competent readers of texts? The idea of a public meaning sponsored not by the author's intention but by a public consensus is based upon a fundamental error of observation and logic. It is an empirical fact that the consensus does not exist, and it is a logical error to erect a stable normative concept (i.e. *the* public meaning) out of an unstable descriptive one. The public meaning of a text is nothing more or less than those meanings which the public happens to construe from the text. Any meanings which two or more members of the public construe is ipso facto within the public norms that govern language and its interpretation. Vox populi: vox populi.

If a text means what it says, then it means nothing in particular. Its saying has no determinate existence but must be the saying of the author or a reader. The text does not exist even as a sequence of words until it is construed; until then, it is merely a sequence of signs. For sometimes words can have homonyms (just as, by analogy, entire texts can), and sometimes the same word can be quite a different word. For example, when we read in Wordsworth's *Intimations Ode* the phrase "most worthy to be blessed," are we to understand "most" as a superlative or merely an intensifier like "very"? Even on this primitive level, signs can be variously construed, and until they are construed the text "says" nothing at all.

D. "The Author's Meaning is Inaccessible"

Since we are all different from the author, we cannot reproduce his intended meaning in ourselves, and even if by some accident we could, we still would not be certain that we had done so. Why concern ourselves, therefore, with an inherently impossible task when we can better employ our energies in useful occupations such as making the text relevant to our present concerns or judging its conformity to high standards of excellence? The goal of reproducing an inaccessible and private past is to be dismissed as a futile enterprise. Of course, it is essential to understand some of the public facts of language and history in order not to miss allusions or mistake the contemporary senses of words, but these preliminary tasks remain squarely in the public domain and do not concern a private world beyond the reach of written language.

Before touching on the key issue in this argument—namely, that the author's intended meaning cannot be known—I would like to make an observation about the subsidiary argument respecting the public and private dimensions of textual meaning. According to this argument, it would be a mistake to confuse a public fact—namely, language—with a private fact—namely, the author's mind. But I have never encountered an interpretation that inferred truly private meanings from a text. An interpreter might, of course, infer meanings which according to our judgment could not possibly under any circumstances be implied by the author's words, but in that case, we would reject the interpretation not because it is private but because it is probably wrong. That meaning, we say, cannot be implied by those words. If our skepticism were shared by all readers of the interpretation, then it would be reasonable to say that the interpretation is private. However, it is a rare interpretation that does not have at least a few adherents, and if it has any at all, then the meaning is not private; it is at worst improbable.

Whenever an interpretation manages to convince another person, that in itself proves beyond doubt that the author's words *can* publicly imply such a meaning. Since the interpreted meaning *was* conveyed to another person, indeed to at least two other persons, the only significant interpretive question is, "Did the author really intend that public meaning by his words?" To object that such a meaning is highly personal and ought not to have been intended is a legitimate aesthetic or moral judgment, but is irrelevant to the question of meaning. That meaning—if the author did mean it—has proved itself to be public, and if the interpreter manages to do his job convincingly, the meaning can become available to a very large public. It is simply a self-contradiction for a member of the public to say, "Yes, I see that the author did mean that, but it is a private not a public meaning."

The impulse that underlies this self-contradictory sort of argument is a sound insight that deserves to be couched in terms more suitable than "public" and "private." The issue is first of all a moral and aesthetic one. It is proper to demand of authors that they show consideration for their readers, that they use their linguistic inheritance with some regard for the generality of men and not just for a chosen few. Yet many new usages are bound to elude the generality of men until readers become habituated to them. The risk of resorting to semi-private implications—available at first only to a few—is very often worth taking, particularly if the new usage does finally become widely understood. The language expands by virtue of such risky innovations. However, the soundest objection to so-called private meanings does not relate to moral and aesthetic judgment but to the practice of interpretation. Those interpreters who look for personal implications in such formalized utterances as poems very often disregard genre conventions and limitations of which the author was very well aware. When an author composes a poem, he usually intends it as an utterance whose implications are not obscurely autobiographical. There may be exceptions to this rule of thumb, and poetic kinds are too various to warrant any unqualified generalizations about the conventions of poetry and the intentions of authors, but too many interpreters in the past have sought autobiographical meanings where none were meant. Such interpreters have been insensitive to the proprieties observed by the author and to his intentions. The fallacy in such interpretations is not that the inferred meanings are private, but that they are probably not the author's meanings. Whether a meaning is autobiographical is a neutral and by itself irrelevant issue in interpretation. The only thing that counts is whether the interpretation is probably right.

The genuine distinction between public and private meaning resides in the first part of the argument, where it is asserted that the author's intended meaning cannot be known. Since we cannot get inside the author's head, it is useless to fret about an intention that cannot be observed, and equally useless to try to reproduce a private meaning experience that cannot be reproduced. Now the assertion that the author's meaning cannot be reproduced presupposes the same psychologistic theory of meaning which underlies the notion that an author's meaning changes even for himself. Not even the author can reproduce his original meaning because nothing can bring back his original meaning experience. But as I suggested, the irreproducibility of meaning experiences is not the same as the irreproducibility of meaning. The psychologistic identification of textual meaning with a meaning experience is inadmissible. Meaning experiences *are* private, but they are not meanings.

The most important argument to consider here is the one which states that the author's intended meaning cannot be *certainly* known. This argument cannot be successfully met because it is self-evidently true. I can never know another person's intended meaning with certainty because I cannot get inside his head to compare the meaning he intends with the meaning I understand, and only by such direct comparison could I be certain that his meaning and my own are identical. But this obvious fact should not be allowed to sanction the overly hasty conclusion that the author's intended meaning is inaccessible and is therefore a useless object of interpretation. It is a logical mistake to confuse the impossibility of certainty in understanding with the impossibility of understanding. It is a similar, though more subtle, mistake to identify knowledge with certainty. A good many disciplines do not pretend to certainty, and the more sophisticated the methodology of the discipline, the less likely that its goal will be defined as certainty of knowledge. Since genuine certainty in interpretation is impossible, the aim of the discipline must be to reach a consensus, on the basis of what is known, that correct understanding has *probably* been achieved. The issue is not whether certainty is accessible to the interpreter but whether the author's intended meaning is accessible to him. Is correct understanding possible? That is the question raised by the thesis under examination.

Most of us would answer that the author's meaning is only partially accessible to an interpreter. We cannot know all the meanings the author entertained when he wrote down his text, as we infer from two familiar kinds of evidence. Whenever I speak I am usually attending to ("have in mind") meanings that are outside my subject of discourse. Furthermore, I am always aware that the meanings I can convey through discourse are more limited than the meanings I can entertain. I cannot, for example, adequately convey through words many of my visual perceptions—though these perceptions are meanings, which is to say, objects of consciousness. It is altogether likely that no text can ever convey all the meanings an author had in mind as he wrote.

But this obvious fact is not decisive. Why should anyone with common sense wish to equate an author's textual meaning with all the meanings he happened to entertain when he wrote? Some of these he had no intention of conveying by his words. Any author knows that written verbal utterances can convey only verbal meanings—that is to say, meanings which can be conveyed to others by the words he uses. The interpretation of texts is concerned exclusively with sharable meanings, and not everything I am thinking of when I write can be shared with others by means of my words. Conversely, many of my sharable meanings are meanings which I am not directly thinking of at all. They are so-called unconscious meanings. It betrays a totally inadequate conception of verbal meaning to equate it with what the author "has in mind." The only question that can relevantly be at issue is whether the *verbal* meaning which an author intends is accessible to the interpreter of his text.

Most authors believe in the accessibility of their verbal meaning, for otherwise most of them would not write. However, no one could unanswerably defend this universal faith. Neither the author nor the interpreter can ever be certain that communication has occurred or that it can occur. But again, certainty is not the point at issue. It is far more likely that an author and an interpreter can entertain identical meanings than that they cannot. The faith that speakers have in the possibility of communication has been built up in the very process of learning a language, particularly in those instances when the actions of the interpreter have confirmed to the author that he has been understood. These primitive confirmations are the foundation for our faith in far less primitive modes of communication. The inaccessibility of verbal meaning is a doctrine that experience suggests to be false, though neither experience nor argument can prove its falsity. But since the skeptical doctrine of inaccessibility is highly improbable, it should be rejected as a working assumption of interpretation.

Of course, it is quite reasonable to take a skeptical position that is less sweeping than the thesis under examination: certain texts might, because of their character or age, represent authorial meanings which are now inaccessible. No one would, I think, deny the reasonable form of skepticism. However, similar versions of such skepticism are far less acceptable, particularly in those theories which deny the accessibility of the author's meaning whenever the text descends from an earlier cultural era or whenever the text happens to be literary. These views are endemic respectively to radical historicism and to the theory that literary texts are ontologically distinct from nonliterary ones. Both of these theories are challenged in subsequent chapters. However, even if these theories were acceptable, they could not uphold the thesis that an author's verbal meaning is inaccessible, for that is an empirical generalization which neither theory nor experience can decisively confirm or deny. Nevertheless, with a high degree of probability, that generalization is false, and it is impossible and quite unnecessary to go beyond this conclusion.

E. "The Author Often Does Not Know What He Means"

Ever since Plato's Socrates talked to the poets and asked them with quite unsatisfactory results to explain "some of the most elaborate passages in their own writings," it has been a commonplace that an author often does not really know what he means.[10] Kant insisted that not even Plato knew what he meant, and that he, Kant, could understand some of Plato's writings better than Plato did himself.[11] Such examples of authorial ignorance are, no doubt, among the most damaging weapons in the attack on the author. If it can be shown (as it apparently can) that in some cases the author does not really know what he means, then it seems to follow that the author's meaning cannot constitute a general principle or norm for determining the meaning of a text, and it is precisely such a general normative principle that is required in defining the concept of validity.

Not all cases of authorial ignorance are of the same type. Plato, for instance, no doubt knew very well what he meant by his theory of Ideas, but it may have been, as Kant believed, that the theory of Ideas had different and more general implications than those Plato enunciated in his dialogues. Though Kant called this a case of understanding the author better than the author understood himself, his phrasing was inexact, for it was not Plato's meaning that Kant understood better than Plato, but rather the subject matter that Plato was attempting to analyze. The notion that Kant's understanding of the Ideas was superior to Plato's implies that there is a subject matter to which Plato's meaning was inadequate. If we do not make this distinction between subject matter and meaning, we have no basis for judging that Kant's understanding is better than Plato's.[12] Kant's statement would have been more precise if he had said that he understood Plato's meaning better than Plato. If we do not make and preserve the distinction between a man's meaning and his subject matter, we cannot distinguish between true and false, better and worse meanings.

This example illustrates one of the two main types of authorial ignorance. It has greatest importance in those genres of writing that aspire to tell the truth about a particular subject matter. The other principal type of authorial ignorance pertains not to the subject matter but to the author's meaning itself, and can be illustrated whenever casual conversation is subjected to stylistic analysis:

> "Did you know that those last two sentences of yours had parallel constructions which emphasized their similarity of meaning?"
> "No! How clever of me! I suppose I really did want to emphasize the similarity, though I wasn't aware of that, and I had no idea I was using rhetorical devices to do it."

What this example illustrates is that there are usually components of an author's intended meaning that he is not conscious of. It is precisely here, where an interpreter makes these intended but unconscious meanings explicit, that he can rightfully claim to understand the author better than the author himself. But here again a clarification is required. The interpreter's right to such a claim exists only when he carefully avoids confusing meaning with subject matter, as in the example of Plato and Kant. The interpreter may believe that he is drawing out implications that are "necessary" accompaniments to the author's meaning, but such necessary accompaniments are rarely unavoidable components of someone's *meaning*. They become necessary associations, only within a given *subject matter*.[13] For example, although the concept "two" necessarily implies a whole array of concepts including those of succession, integer, set, and so on, these may not be implied in a given usage of the word, since that usage could be inadequate or misconceived with respect to the subject matter in which "two" falls. Only within that subject matter does there subsist necessity of implication. Thus, by claiming to perceive implications of which the author was not conscious, we may sometimes distort and falsify the meaning of which he was conscious, which is not "better understanding" but simply misunderstanding of the author's meaning.

But let us assume that such misunderstanding has been avoided and that the interpreter really has made explicit certain aspects of an author's undoubted meaning of which the author was unconscious—as in stylistic analysis of casual conversation. The further question then arises: How can an author mean something he did not mean? The answer to that question is simple. It is not possible to mean what one does not mean, though it is very possible to mean what one is not conscious of meaning. That is the entire issue in the argument based on authorial ignorance. That a man may not be conscious of all that he means is no more remarkable than that he may not be conscious of all that he does. There is a difference between meaning and consciousness of meaning, and since meaning is an affair of consciousness, one can say more precisely that there is a difference between consciousness and self-consciousness. Indeed, when an author's meaning is complicated, he cannot possibly at a given moment be paying attention to all its complexities. But the distinction between attended and unattended meanings is not the same as the distinction between what an author means and what he does not mean. No example of the author's ignorance with respect to his meaning could legitimately show that his intended meaning and the meaning of his text are two different things.

Other varieties of authorial ignorance are therefore of little theoretical interest. When Plato observed that poets could not *explain* what they meant, he intimated that poets were ineffectual, weak-minded, and vague—particularly with respect to their "most elaborate passages." But he would not have contended that a vague, uncertain, cloudy, and pretentious meaning is not a meaning, or that it is not the poet's meaning.[14] Even when a poet declares that his poem means whatever it is taken to mean (as in the case of some modern writers who believe in the current theory of public meaning and authorial irrelevance), then, no doubt, his poem may not mean anything in particular. Yet even in such a limiting case it is still the author who "determines" the meaning.

One final illustration of authorial ignorance, a favorite among literary critics, is based on an examination of an author's early drafts, which often indicate that what the author apparently intended when he began writing is frequently quite different from what his final work means. Such examples show how considerations of style, genre, and local texture may play a larger part in his final meaning than that played by his original intention, but these interesting observations have hardly any theoretical significance. If a poet in his first draft means something different than he means in his last, it does not imply that somebody other than the poet is doing the meaning. If the poet capitalizes on a local effect which he had not originally intended, so much the better if it makes a better poem. All this surely does not imply that an author does not mean what he means, or that his text does not mean what he intends to convey.

If there is a single moral to the analyses of this chapter, it is that meaning is an affair of consciousness and not of physical signs or things. Consciousness is, in turn, an affair of persons, and in textual interpretation the persons involved are an author and a reader. The meanings that are actualized by the reader are either shared with the author or belong to the reader alone. While this statement of the issue may affront our deeply ingrained sense that language carries its own autonomous meanings, it in no way calls into question the power of language. On the contrary, it takes for granted that all meaning communicated by texts is to some extent language-bound, that no textual meaning can transcend the meaning possibilities and the control of the language in which it is expressed. What been denied here is that linguistic signs can somehow speak their own meaning—a mystical idea that has never been persuasively defended.

NOTES

1. The classic statement is in T. S. Eliot, "Tradition and the Individual Talent," *Selected Essays* (New York, 1932).

2. See, for example, Martin Heidegger, *Unterwegs zur Sprache* (Pfullingen, 1959).

3. See Ernst Cassirer, *The Philosophy of Symbolic Forms:* Vol. 1, *Language,* trans. R. Manheim (New Haven, 1953), particularly pp. 69, 178, 213, 249-50, and passim.

4. The random example that I use later in the book is the sentence: "I am going to town today." Different senses can be lent to the sentence by the simple device of placing a strong emphasis on any of the different words.

5. The phrase is from T. S. Eliot, *On Poetry and Poets* (New York, 1957), p. 126.

6. It would be invidious to name any individual critics as the begetter of this widespread and imprecise notion. By the "best" reading, of course, some critics mean the most valid reading, but the idea of bestness is widely used to embrace indiscriminately both the idea of validity and of such aesthetic values as richness, inclusiveness, tension, or complexity—as though validity and aesthetic excellence must somehow be identical.

7. See René Wellek and Austin Warren, *Theory of Literature* (New York, 1948), Chap. 12.

8. Verbal meaning can be the same for different interpreters by virtue of the fact that verbal meaning has the character of a type. A type covers a range of actualizations (one example would be a phoneme) and yet in each actualization remains (like a phoneme) the identical type.

9. *Sewanee Review,* 54 (1946). Reprinted in William K. Wimsatt, Jr., *The Verbal Icon: Studies in the Meaning of Poetry* (Lexington, Ky., 1954).

10. Plato, *Apology,* 22b-c.

11. Immanuel Kant, *Critique of Pure Reason,* trans. N. K. Smith (London, 1933), A 314, B 370, p. 310: "I shall not engage here in any literary enquiry into the meaning which this illustrious author attached to the expression. I need only remark that it is by no means unusual upon comparing the thoughts which an author has expressed in regard to his subject, whether in ordinary conversation or in writing, to find that we understand him better than he has understood himself."

12. The distinction between meaning and subject matter . . . is one foundation for my objections to Gadamer's identification of meaning with *Sache.* . . .

13. This distinction was not observed in the interesting essay by O. Bollknow, "Was heisst es einen Verfasser zu verstehen besser als er sich selber verstanden hat?" in *Das Verstehen, Drei Aufsätz zur Theorie des Geisteswissenschaften* (Mainz, 1949).

14. Or at least that of the muse who temporarily possesses him—the muse being, in those unseemly cases, the real author.

HANS-GEORG GADAMER

GADAMER'S THEORY MAY BE the most thorough, positive theory of interpretation that has emerged from the Continental phenomenological tradition. The fundamental assumption of this tradition, which underlies its
hermeneutical epistemology, is that understanding is always from within a
lived, human context, both individual and social. There is no standard outside
interpretation against which to measure its accuracy. We interpret documents
and works from within our own lived historical context while taking the
author's context into account.

Gadamer studied with Heidegger and views himself as Heideggerian.
His theory, however, is far more positive than Heidegger's, far more a theory
of how we can understand works that emerge from conditions that are strange
to us. Gadamer suggests that essential to such interpretation is an acknowledgment of the conditions underlying our own perspectives—he calls them
"prejudgments" or "prejudices." The second requirement is that a fusion of
the different horizons of author and audience be possible, based on overt
understanding of their prejudgments. Fundamental is the notion of a fusion
of perspectives or surrounding worlds, a presupposed unity of language and
thought, realized through conversation, questioning and answering.

The selections here include Gadamer's criticism of Kant's theory of
taste as offering no explanation of the importance of art while Kant's theory
of genius cannot be reconciled adequately with his theory of taste. The other
passages present important features of Gadamer's hermeneutic theory.

HANS-GEORG GADAMER

Truth and Method *

Kant's Doctrine of Taste and Genius

(i) THE TRANSCENDENTAL QUALITY OF TASTE. Kant himself was surprised to find, in the process of investigating the foundations of taste, an a priori element which went beyond empirical universality.[1] This insight gave birth to the *Critique of Judgment*. It is no longer a mere critique of taste in the sense in which taste is the object of critical judgment by an observer. It is a critique of critique; that is, it is concerned with the status of this kind of critical attitude in matters of taste. It is no longer a mere question of empirical principles which are supposed to justify a widespread and dominant taste such as, for example, the favourite problem of the origins of differences in taste, but it is concerned with a genuine a priori that, in itself, would be a total justification of the possibility of criticism.

Clearly the value of the beautiful cannot be derived and proved from a universal principle. No one supposes that questions of taste can be decided by argument and proof. Still, it is equally clear that good taste will never be a truly empirical universal, so that the appeal to the prevailing taste misses the real nature of taste. We saw that it lies in its nature not to submit blindly to popular values and to chosen models and simply imitate them. In the area of aesthetic taste the model and pattern certainly has its proper function but, as Kant rightly says, not for imitation, but for following.[2] The model and example encourages taste to go its own way, but it does not do the latter's job for it. 'For taste must be an original faculty'.[3]

---

* Hans-Georg Gadamer, *Truth and Method* (New York: Seabury, 1975), pp. 39-42, 46-51, 84-89, 108-114, 235-240, 333-341. (Some changes have been made in punctuation and spelling.)

On the other hand our outline of the history of the concept has shown clearly enough that in taste it is not particular preference that decides, in the case of an aesthetic judgment, but a supra-empirical norm is operative. We shall be able to see that Kant's grounding of aesthetics on the judgment of taste does justice to both aspects of the phenomenon, its empirical non-universality and its a priori claim to universality. But the price that he pays for this legitimation of criticism in the area of taste is that he denies that taste has any significance as knowledge. It is a subjective principle to which he reduces sensus communis. In it nothing is known of the objects which are judged as beautiful, but it is stated only that a priori there is a feeling of pleasure connected with them in the subjective consciousness. As we know, Kant sees this feeling as based on the finality that the representation of the object possesses for our faculty of knowledge. It is a free play of imagination and understanding, a subjective relationship that is altogether appropriate to knowledge and that exhibits the reason for the pleasure in the object. This appropriate, subjective relationship in fact, is in its idea the same for all, i.e., it is universally communicable and thus grounds the claim that the judgment of taste possesses universality.

This is the principle that Kant discovers in aesthetic judgment. It is its own law. Inasmuch, it is an a priori effect of the beautiful which stands halfway between a mere sensuous and empirical agreement in matters of taste and a rationalistic universal observance of a rule. Admittedly, if one takes its relationship to Lebensgefühl (lit. 'feeling of life') as its only basis, one can no longer call taste a cognitio sensitive. In it no knowledge of the object is imparted, but nor is it simply a question of a subjective reaction, as produced by what is pleasant to the senses. Taste is 'reflective'.

When Kant thus calls taste the true sensus communis,[4] he is no longer considering the great moral and political tradition of the concept of sensus communis that we outlined above. Rather, he sees this idea as comprising two elements: first, the universality of taste inasmuch as it is the result of the free play of all our cognitive powers and is not limited to a specific area like an external sense, secondly the communal quality of taste, inasmuch as, according to Kant, it abstracts from all such subjective, private conditions as attractiveness and emotion. Thus the universality of this 'sense' is negatively determined in both its aspects by that from which something is abstracted, and not positively by what grounds communicability and creates community.

Yet it is true for Kant the old connection between taste and society remains valid. But the 'culture of taste' is treated only as an appendage in 'The Methodology of Taste'.[5] There the humaniora, as represented by the Greek model, is the sociability appropriate to humanity, and the cultivation of moral feeling is the way in which genuine taste is able to assume a definite unchangeable form.[6] Thus the definiteness of the contents of taste is not part of its transcendental function. Kant is interested only insofar as there is a special principle of aesthetic judgment, and that is why he is interested only in the pure judgment of taste.

It accords with his transcendental design that in analysing taste one can take examples of aesthetic pleasure as well from natural beauty, as from the decorative and from artistic representation. The type of object, the idea of which pleases, does not affect the essence of the aesthetic judgment. The critique of aesthetic judgment does not seek to be a philosophy of art—however much art is an object of this judgment. The concept of the 'pure aesthetic judgment of taste' is a methodological abstraction which bears no relation to the difference between nature and art. Thus it is necessary to make a more exact examination of Kant's aesthetics and relate them to the interpretations made of them in the philosophy of art, especially in relation to the idea of genius. . . .

(iv) THE CONCERN FOR THE BEAUTIFUL IN NATURE AND IN ART. When Kant raises the question of the interest that is taken in the beautiful not empirically, but a priori, this question of the interest in the beautiful as opposed to the fundamental statement of the absence of interest in aesthetic pleasure raises a new problem and completes the transition from the standpoint of taste to the standpoint of genius. It is the same doctrine that is developed in connection with both phenomena. It is important, in establishing foundations, to free the 'critique of taste' from sensualistic and rationalistic prejudices. It is quite in order that here the question of the type of object being aesthetically judged (and thus the whole question of the relation between the beauty of nature and that of art) is not asked by Kant. But this dimension of the question is necessarily opened up if one thinks the standpoint of taste through—which involves going beyond it.[7] The interesting significance of the beautiful is the really operative problem in the Kantian aesthetic. It is different for nature and art, and the comparison between the naturally and the artistically beautiful brings the problem to a head.

Here we find Kant himself.[8] As we would expect, it is not for the sake of art that Kant goes beyond 'disinterested pleasure' and enquires into the interest in the beautiful. From the doctrine of the ideal of beauty we had derived one advantage of art as against natural beauty: the advantage of being a more direct expression of the moral. Kant, on the contrary, emphasises primarily (§ 42) the advantage of natural over artistic beauty. It is not only for the pure aesthetic judgment that natural beauty has an advantage, namely to make it clear that the beautiful depends on the consonance of the thing represented with our cognitive faculty. This is so clearly the case with natural beauty because it possesses no significance of content, and thus manifests the judgment of taste in its unintellectualised purity.

But it does not have only this methodological advantage; according to Kant it also has one of content, and he obviously thinks a great deal of this point of his doctrine. Beautiful nature is able to arouse an immediate interest, namely a moral one. Finding the beautiful forms of nature beautiful points beyond itself to the thought "that nature has produced that beauty." Where this thought arouses interest we have cultivation of the moral sensibility. While

Kant, instructed by Rousseau, refuses to argue back from the refinement of taste for the beautiful in general to moral sensibility, the sense of the beauty of nature is for Kant a special case. That nature is beautiful arouses interest only in someone who "has already developed his interest in the morally good." Hence the interest in natural beauty is "related to the moral sphere." By observing the unintentional consonance of nature with our pleasure, which is independent of any interest, i.e., the wonderful finality of nature for us, it points to us as to the ultimate goal of creation, to our 'moral destiny'.

Here the rejection of perfection-aesthetics fits beautifully with the moral significance of natural beauty. Precisely because in nature we find no ends in themselves and yet find beauty, i.e., a conformity with the goal of our pleasures, nature gives us a 'sign' that we are in fact the ultimate end, the final goal of creation. The dissolution of ancient cosmological thought, which assigned man his place in the total structure of being and to each existent its goal of perfection, gives the world, which ceases to be beautiful as a structure of absolute ends, the new beauty of finality for us. It becomes 'nature', whose innocence consists in the fact that it knows nothing of man and of his social vices. Nevertheless it has something to say to us. In the light of the idea of an intelligible destiny for mankind, nature, as beautiful, finds a language that brings it to us.

Naturally the significance of art also depends on the fact that it speaks to us, that it confronts man with himself in his morally determined existence. But the products of art exist only in order to address us in this way—natural objects, however, do not exist to address us in this way. This is the significant interest of the naturally beautiful, that it is still able to make us conscious of our moral purpose. Art cannot communicate to us this self-discovery of man in unintentional reality. That man can encounter himself in art is not the confirmation of himself by another.

That is right, as far as it goes. The conclusiveness of Kant's argument is impressive, but he does not employ the appropriate criteria for the phenomenon of art. One can make a counterargument. The advantage that natural beauty has over artistic beauty is only the other side of natural beauty's lack of specific expressive power. Thus, contrariwise, one can see the advantage of art over natural beauty in the fact that the language of art is a demanding language which does not offer itself freely and vaguely for interpretation according to one's mood, but speaks to us in a significant and definite way. And the wonderful and mysterious thing about art is that this definiteness is by no means a fetter for our mind, but in fact opens up the area in which freedom operates in the play of our mental faculties. Kant is right when he says[9] that art must be able "to be looked at as nature," i.e., please without betraying the constraint of rules. We do not consider the intentional agreement of what is represented with reality we know, we do not look to see what it resembles, we do not measure its claim to significance by a criterion that we already know well, but on the contrary this criterion, the 'idea' becomes, in an unlimited way, 'aesthetically expanded'.[10]

Kant's definition of art as the 'beautiful representation of a thing'[11] takes account of this inasmuch as even the ugly is beautiful in its representation through art. Nevertheless, the actual nature of art emerges badly from the contrast with natural beauty. If the idea of a thing were presented only in a beautiful way, that would be a representation according to the rules, and would fulfil only the minimum requirement of all beauty. But for Kant art is more than the 'beautiful representation of an object': it is the presentation of aesthetic ideas, i.e., of something that lies beyond all concepts. The concept of the genius seeks to formulate this insight of Kant's.

It cannot be denied that the doctrine of aesthetic ideas, through whose representation the artist infinitely expands the given concept and encourages the free play of the mental faculties, has something unsatisfactory about it for a modern reader. It looks as if these ideas were being connected to the already dominant concept like the attributes of a deity to its form. The traditional superiority of the rational concept over the inexponible aesthetic representation is so strong that even with Kant there arises the false appearance of the concept preceding the aesthetic idea, where it is not at all the understanding, but the imagination that is chief among the faculties involved.[12] The aesthetician will find enough other statements in the light of which it is difficult for Kant to hold on to his leading insight into the incomprehensibility of the beautiful while at the same time preserving its compelling quality, without involuntarily claiming the superiority of the idea.

But the basic lines of his thinking are free from these faults and are of an impressive logicality, which reaches its climax in the function of the concept of genius in the account of the basis of art. Even without going into a more detailed interpretation of this "capacity to represent aesthetic ideas," it may be indicated that Kant here is not deflected from his concern with transcendental philosophy and pushed into the cul-de-sac of a psychology of artistic creation. Rather, the irrationality of genius brings out an element of productive creation, shown both in creator and recipient, namely that there is no other way of laying hold of the meaning of a work of art than in the unique form of the work and in the mystery of its impression which can never be fully expressed by any language. Hence the concept of the genius corresponds to what Kant sees as the crucial thing about aesthetic taste, namely the playful facility of one's mental powers, the expansion of vitality which comes from the harmony between imagination and understanding, and invites one to linger before the beautiful. Genius is a manifestation of this vivifying spirit for, as opposed to the pedant's rigid adherence to rules, genius shows the free sweep of invention and thus an originality which creates new models.

(v) THE RELATION BETWEEN TASTE AND GENIUS. In this situation the question arises of how Kant sees the mutual relation between taste and genius. Kant preserves for taste its privileged position, inasmuch as the works of art that are the art of genius stand under the guiding aspect of beauty. One may find the subsequent improvements to the invention of genius that are required by taste regrettable, but taste is the necessary discipline that genius needs. Thus, in cases of conflict, Kant considers that taste should prevail. But this is not an important question for, basically, taste has common ground with genius. The art of genius is to make the free play of the mental faculties communicable. This is achieved by the aesthetic ideas that it invents. But communicability of a state of mind, of pleasure, was characteristic of the aesthetic pleasure of taste. It is a faculty of judgment, i.e., a reflective taste, but what it reflects about is that state of mind which is the stimulation of the cognitive powers, which is given by both natural and artistic beauty. Thus the systematic significance of the concept of genius is limited to the particular case of the artistically beautiful, whereas the concept of taste is universal.

That Kant makes the concept of genius serve his transcendental concern completely and does not slip into empirical psychology is clearly shown by his limiting the concept of genius to artistic creation. If he withholds this name from the great inventors and investigators in the spheres of science and technology,[13] this is, seen in terms of empirical psychology, quite unfair. Wherever one must "come upon something" that cannot be found through learning and methodical work alone, i.e., wherever there is inventio, where something is due to inspiration and not to methodical calculation, the important thing is ingenium, genius. And yet Kant's intention is correct: only the work of art is naturally so determined that it can be created only by genius. It is only with the artist that the 'invention'—the work—remains, according to its very nature, related to the spirit—the spirit that creates as well as the one that judges and enjoys. Only there can inventions not be imitated, and hence it is right when Kant speaks (only here) of genius—from a transcendental point of view—and defines art as the art of genius. All other achievements and inventions of genius, however much genius there may be in the invention, are not determined in their essence by it.

I maintain that for Kant the concept of genius was really only a complement to what was of interest to him 'for transcendental reasons' in aesthetic judgment. We should not forget that the second part of the *Critique of Judgment* is concerned only with nature (and with its being judged by concepts of finality) and not at all with art. Thus for the systematic intention of the whole, the application of aesthetic judgment to the beautiful and sublime in nature is more important than the transcendental foundation of art. The "finality of nature for our cognitive faculties" which, as we have seen, is possible only in the case of natural beauty (and not of art) has, as the transcendental principle of aesthetic judgment, at the same time the function of preparing the understanding for applying the concept of finality to nature.[14] Thus the critique of taste, i.e. aesthetics, is a preparation for teleology. It is Kant's philosophical intention to legitimate teleology, whose constitutive claim in the knowledge of nature had been destroyed by the *Critique of Pure Reason*, as a principle of judgment—an intention which brings the whole of his philosophy to a systematic conclusion. Judgment provides the bridge between understanding and reason. The intelligible towards which taste points, the supersensible substrate in man, contains at the same time the mediation between concepts of nature and concepts of freedom.[15] This is the systematic significance that the problem of natural beauty has for Kant: it grounds the central position of teleology. It alone, not art, can assist the legitimation of the concept of finality for the judgment of nature. For this systematic reason alone the "pure" judgment of taste provides the essential basis of the third *Critique*.

But even within the critique of aesthetic judgment there is no question of the position of genius ousting that of taste. One has only to look at how Kant describes the genius; the genius is a favourite of nature—just as natural beauty is looked on as a favour of nature. We must be able to look at art as if it were nature. Through genius, nature gives art its rules. In all these phrases[16] the concept of nature is the uncontested criterion.

Thus what the concept of genius achieves is only to place the products of art aesthetically on the same level as natural beauty. Art also is looked at aesthetically, i.e., it also is a case for reflective judgment. What is intentionally produced, and hence purposive, is not to be related to an idea, but seeks to please in being simply judged—just like natural beauty. "Art is art created by genius" means that for artistic beauty also there is no other principle of judgment, no criterion of concept and knowledge than that of its finality for the feeling of freedom in the play of our cognitive faculties. Beauty in nature or art[17] has the same a priori principle, which lies entirely within subjectivity. The autonomy of aesthetic judgment does not mean that there is an autonomous sphere of validity for beautiful objects. Kant's transcendental reflection on the a priori of judgment justifies the claim of the aesthetic judgment, but basically it does not permit a philosophical aesthetics in the sense of a philosophy of art (Kant himself says that no doctrine or metaphysics here corresponded to the critique). . . .[18]

Critique of the Abstraction of Aesthetic Consciousness

. . . How can the nature of artistic pleasure and the difference between what a craftsman has made and an artist has created be understood without the concept of genius?

How can even the perfection of a work of art, its being finished, be conceived? Whatever else is made or produced takes the criterion of its perfection from its purpose, i.e., is determined by the use that is to be made of it. The work is finished if it answers to the purpose for which it is intended.[19] How is one, then, to understand the criterion for the perfection of a work of art? However rationally and soberly one may consider artistic 'production', much that we call works of art is not intended to be used, and none derives the measure of its completion from such a purpose. Does not, then, the work's existence appear to be the breaking-off of a formative process which actually points beyond it? Perhaps it is not at all completable in itself?

Paul Valéry, in fact, thought this was the case. But he did not work out the consequence that followed for someone who encounters a work of art and endeavours to understand it. If it is true that a work of art is not, in itself, completable, what is the criterion for correct reception and understanding? A chance and random breaking-off of a formative process cannot contain anything binding.[20] From this, then, it follows that what he makes of what he finds must be left to the recipient. One way of understanding a work of art is then no less legitimate than another. There is no criterion of an appropriate reaction. Not only that the artist himself does not possess one—the aesthetics of genius would agree here. Rather, every encounter with the work has the rank and the justification of a new production. This seems to me an untenable hermeneutic nihilism. If Valéry sometimes drew these conclusions for his work[21] in order to avoid the myth of the unconscious production of genius, he has, in my view, become entangled in it, for now he transfers to reader and interpreter the authority of absolute creation which he himself no longer desires to exert. But genius in understanding is, in fact, of no more help than genius in creation.

The same difficulty arises if one starts from the idea of the aesthetic experience instead of from the idea of the genius. On this subject the fundamental essay by George von Lukács, 'Die Subjekt-Objekt Beziehung in der Ästhetik'[22] revealed the problem. He ascribes to the aesthetic sphere a Heraclitean structure, by which he means that the unity of the aesthetic object is not something that is actually given. The work of art is only a form, a mere modal point in the possible variety of aesthetic experiences in which only the aesthetic object is present. As is evident, absolute discontinuity, i.e., the disintegration of the unity of the aesthetic object into the multiplicity of experiences, is the necessary consequence of an aesthetics of experience. Following Lukács' ideas, Oskar Becker has stated outright that "in terms of time the work exists only in a moment [i.e., now]; it is 'now' this work and now it is this work no longer"![23] Actually, that is logical. Basing aesthetics on experience leads to an absolute series of points, which annihilates both the unity of the work of art and the identity of the artist with himself, and the identity of the man understanding or enjoying the work of art.[24]

Kierkegaard seems to me to have shown the untenability of this position, in that he recognised the destructive consequence of subjectivism and was the first to describe the self-destruction of aesthetic immediacy. His theory of the aesthetic stage of existence is developed from the standpoint of the moralist who has seen how desperate and untenable is existence in pure immediacy and discontinuity. Hence his criticism of the aesthetic consciousness is of fundamental importance because he shows the inner contradictions of aesthetic existence, so that it is forced to go beyond itself. In that the aesthetic stage of existence proves itself untenable, it is recognised that even the phenomenon of art imposes a task on existence; namely, despite the demands of the absorbing presence of the particular aesthetic impression, of achieving that continuity of self-understanding which alone can support human existence.[25] If one still wanted to attempt a definition of aesthetic existence which constituted it outside the hermeneutic continuity of human existence, the point of Kierkegaard's criticism would, in my view, have been missed. Even if it may be admitted that in the aesthetic phenomenon there appear limits to the historical self-understanding of existence that correspond to the limit set up by that part of nature that, posited in the mind as its condition, is projected into the mental sphere in many different forms—myth, dream—as the unconscious preformation of conscious life, we still have no point of view which would allow us to see, from outside, what limits and conditions us from itself and ourselves, as beings that are limited and conditioned in this way. Even that which is closed to our understanding is experienced by ourselves as something limiting and thus belongs to the continuity of self-understanding in which human existence moves. The recognition of the "impermanence of the beautiful and the adventurousness of the artist" (Hinfälligkeit des Schönen und der Abenteuerlichkeit des Künstlers) is thus, in fact, not the description of a mode of being outside the "hermeneutic phenomenology of existence," but is rather the formulation of the need of preserving, in spite of this discontinuity of aesthetic being and aesthetic experience, the hermeneutic continuity which constitutes our being.[26]

The pantheon of art is not a timeless presence which offers itself to pure aesthetic consciousness but the assembled achievements of the human mind as it has realised itself historically. Aesthetic experience also is a mode of self-understanding. But all self-understanding takes place in relation to something else that is understood and includes the unity and sameness of this other. Inasmuch as we encounter the work of art in the world and a world in the individual work of art, this does not remain a strange universe into which we are magically transported for a time. Rather, we learn to understand ourselves in it, and that means that we preserve the discontinuity of the experience in the continuity of our existence. Therefore it is necessary to adopt an attitude to the beautiful and to art that does not lay claim to immediacy, but corresponds to the historical reality of man. The appeal to immediacy, to the genius of the moment, to the significance of the 'experience', cannot withstand the claim of human existence to continuity and unity of self-understanding. The experience of art must not be side-tracked into the uncommittedness of the aesthetic awareness.

This negative insight, expressed positively, means that art is knowledge and the experience of the work of art is a sharing of this knowledge.

This raises the question of how one can do justice to the truth of aesthetic experience and overcome the radical subjectivisation of the aesthetic that began with Kant's *Critique of Aesthetic Judgment*. We have shown that it was a methodological abstraction corresponding to a quite particular transcendental task of laying foundations which led Kant to relate aesthetic judgment entirely to the condition of the subject. If, however, this aesthetic abstraction was subsequently understood as a content and was changed into the demand to understand art purely aesthetically, we can now see how this demand for abstraction ends in an indissoluble contradiction with the true experience of art.

Is there to be no knowledge in art? Does not the experience of art contain a claim to truth which is certainly different from that of science, but equally certainly is not inferior to it? And is not the task of aesthetics precisely to provide a basis for the fact that artistic experience is a mode of knowledge of a unique kind, certainly different from that sensory knowledge which provides science with the data from which it constructs the knowledge of nature, and certainly different from all moral rational knowledge and indeed from all conceptual knowledge, but still knowledge, i.e., the transmission of truth?

This can hardly be recognised if, with Kant, one measures the truth of knowledge by the scientific concept of knowledge and the scientific concept of reality. It is necessary to take the idea of experience more broadly than Kant did, so that the experience of the work of art can be understood as experience. For this we can appeal to Hegel's fine lectures on aesthetics. Here the truth that lies in every artistic experience is recognised and at the same time mediated with historical consciousness. Hence aesthetics becomes a history of world-views, i.e., a history of truth, as it is seen in the mirror of art. It is also a fundamental recognition of the task that I formulated of justifying the knowledge of truth in the experience of art itself.

The concept of world-view, which first appears in Hegel in the *Phänomenologie des Geistes*[27] as a term for Kant's and Fichte's postulatory amplification of the basic moral experience to a moral world order, acquires only in aesthetics its proper significance. It is the multiplicity and the possible change of world-views that has given to the concept of world-view its familiar ring.[28] But the history of art is the chief example of this, because this historical multiplicity cannot be resolved into the unity of a progress towards true art. It is true that Hegel was able to recognise the truth of art only by letting the inclusive knowledge of philosophy surpass it and by constructing the history of world-views, like world history and the history of philosophy, from the developed self-consciousness of the present. But this cannot be seen simply as mistaken, in that the sphere of the subjective mind is far exceeded. This move beyond it remains a lasting element of truth in Hegelian thought. Certainly, inasmuch as it makes the truth of the concept all powerful, which resolves all experience within itself, Hegel's philosophy at the same time disavows the way of truth that it has recognised in the experience of art. If we want to justify this in its own right, then we must realise fully what 'truth' here means. It is in the human sciences as a whole that an answer to this question must be found. For they do not seek to surpass, but to understand the variety of experiences—aesthetic, historical, religious or political consciousness—but that means that they anticipate truth in them. We shall have to go into the relationship between Hegel and the self-understanding of the human sciences represented by the 'historical school' and the way in which they differ as to what makes it possible to understand properly what truth means in the human sciences. At any rate, we shall not be able to do justice to the problem of art from the point of view of aesthetic consciousness, but only within this wider framework.

We made only one step in this direction in seeking to correct the self-interpretation of the aesthetic consciousness and in retrieving the question of the truth of art, of which the aesthetic experience is a testimony. Thus our concern is to see the experience of art in such a way that it is understood as experience. The experience of art is not to be falsified by being turned into a possession of aesthetic culture and hence neutralised in its proper claim. We shall see that this involves a far-reaching hermeneutical consequence, inasmuch as all encounter with the language of art is an encounter with a still unfinished process and is itself part of this process. This is what must be emphasised against the aesthetic consciousness and its neutralisation of the truth question.

If speculative idealism sought to overcome the aesthetic subjectivism and agnosticism, based on Kant, by elevating itself to the standpoint of infinite knowledge, then, as we have seen, this gnostic self-redemption of finitude involved making art a part of philosophy. Instead of this we shall have to hold firmly to the standpoint of finiteness. The productive thing about Heidegger's criticism of modern subjectivism seems to me that his temporal interpretation of being has opened up new possibilities. Interpretation of being from the horizon of time does not mean, as it is constantly misunderstood to mean, that There-being is radically temporal, so that it can no longer be considered as everlasting or eternal, but that it can be understood only in relation to its own time and future. If this were the meaning it would not be a critique and an overcoming of subjectivism, but an 'existentialist' radicalisation of it, which one could easily foresee would have a collectivist future. The philosophical question, however, which is involved here, is directed precisely at this subjectivism itself. The latter is driven to its final point only in order to question it. The philosophical question asks what is the being of self-understanding? With this question it totally transcends the horizon of this self-understanding. In removing time as its hidden ground, it does not preach blind commitment out of nihilistic despair, but opens itself to a hitherto concealed experience, transcending thinking from the position of subjectivity, an experience that Heidegger calls 'being'.

In order to do justice to the experience of art we began with the criticism of the aesthetic consciousness. The experience of art acknowledges that it cannot present the perfect truth of what it experiences in terms of final knowledge. Here there is no absolute progress and no final exhaustion of what lies in a work of art. The experience of art knows this of itself. At the same time it is necessary not simply to accept what the aesthetic consciousness considers to be its experience. For it considers it, as we say, in the final analysis as the discontinuity of experiences. But we have found this to be unacceptable.

We do not, then, ask the experience of art to tell us how it thinks of itself, but what it is in truth and what its truth is, even if it does not know what it is and cannot say what it knows—just so Heidegger has asked what metaphysics is, in contrast to what it thinks itself to be. In the experience of art we see a genuine experience induced by the work, which does not leave him who has it unchanged, and we enquire into the mode of being of that which is experienced in this way. So we hope to understand better what kind of truth it is that encounters us there.

We shall see that this opens up the dimension in which, in the 'understanding' with which the human sciences are concerned, the question of truth is raised in a new way. . . .

The Temporality of the Aesthetic

What kind of contemporaneity is this? What kind of temporality belongs to aesthetic being? This contemporaneity and presentness of aesthetic being is called, in general, its timelessness. But this timelessness has to be thought of together with the temporality to which it essentially belongs. Timelessness is primarily only a dialectical feature which arises out of temporality and in contrast with it. Even if one speaks of two kinds of temporality, a historical and a supra-historical one, as does Sedlmayr, for example, following Baader and with reference to Bollnow, in an effort to determine the temporality of the work of art,[29] one cannot move beyond a dialectical tension between the two. The supra-historical 'sacred' time, in which the 'present' is not the fleeting movement but the fullness of time, is described from the point of view of existential temporality. The inadequacy of this kind of antithesis emerges when one inevitably discovers that 'true time' projects into historical-existential 'appearance time'. This kind of projection would obviously have the character of an epiphany, but this means that for the experiencing consciousness it is without continuity.

This involves again all the difficulties of the aesthetic awareness, which we pointed out above. For it is precisely continuity that every understanding of time has to achieve, even when it is a question of the temporality of a work of art. Here the misunderstanding of Heidegger's ontological exposition of the time horizon avenges itself. Instead of holding on to the methodological significance of the existential analytic of There-being, people treat this existential, historical temporality of There-being, determined by care and the movement towards death, i.e., radical finiteness, as one among many possible ways of understanding existence, and it is forgotten that it is the mode of being of understanding itself which is here revealed as temporality. The withdrawal of the proper temporality of the work of art as 'sacred time' from transient historical time remains, in fact, a mere mirroring of the human and finite experience of art. Only a biblical theology of time, starting not from the standpoint of human self-understanding, but from divine revelation, would be able to speak of a 'sacred time' and theologically justify the analogy between the timelessness of the work of art and this 'sacred time'. Without this kind of theological justification, to speak of 'sacred time' obscures the real problem, which does not lie in the atemporality of the work of art but in its temporality. Thus we take up our question again: what kind of temporality is this?[30]

We started from the position that the work of art is play, i.e., that its actual being cannot be detached from its representation and that in the representation the unity and identity of a structure emerge. To be dependent on self-representation is part of its nature. This means that however much it may be changed and distorted in the representation, it still remains itself. This constitutes the validity of every representation, that it contains a relation to the structure itself and submits itself to the criterion of its correctness. Even the extreme of a wholly distorting representation confirms this. It becomes known as a distortion inasmuch as the representation is intended and appreciated as the representation of the structure. The representation has, in an indissoluble, indelible way the character of the repetition. Repetition does not mean here that something is repeated in the literal sense, i.e., can be reduced to something original. Rather, every repetition is equally an original of the work.

We know this kind of highly puzzling time structure from festivals.[31] It is in the nature, at least of periodic festivals, to be repeated. We call that the return of the festival. But the returning festival is neither another, nor the mere remembrance of the one that was originally celebrated. The originally sacral character of all festivals obviously excludes the kind of distinction that we know in the time-experience of the present; memory and expectation. The time-experience of the festival is rather its celebration, a present time sui generis.

The temporal character of celebration is difficult to grasp on the basis of the customary chronological experience of succession. If the return of the festival is related to the usual experience of time and its dimensions, it appears as historical temporality. The festival changes from one time to the next. For there are always other things going on at the same time. Nevertheless it would still remain, under this historical aspect, one and the same festival that undergoes this kind of change. It was originally of a certain nature and was celebrated in this way, then different, and then different again.

However, this aspect does not cover the time character of the festival that comes from its being celebrated. For the essence of the festival its historical connections are secondary. As a festival it is not an identity, in the manner of an historical event, but neither is it determined by its origin so that there was once the 'real' festival—as distinct from the way in which it came later to be celebrated. From the start it belonged to it that it should be regularly celebrated. Thus it is its own original essence always to be something different (even when celebrated in exactly the same way). An entity that exists only by always being something different is temporal in a more radical sense than everything that belongs to history. It has its being only in becoming and in return.[32]

A festival exists only in being celebrated. This is not to say that it is of a subjective character and has its being only in the subjectivity of those celebrating it. Rather the festival is celebrated because it is there. The same is true of drama—it must be represented for the spectator, and yet its being is by no means just the point of intersection of the experiences that the spectators have. Rather the contrary is true, that the being of the spectator is determined by his being there present. To be present does not mean simply to be in the presence of something else that is there at the same time. To be present means to share. If someone was present at something, he knows all about how it really was. It is only in a derived sense that presence at something means also a kind of subjective attitude, that of attention to something. Thus to watch something is a genuine mode of sharing. Perhaps we may remind the reader of the idea of sacral communion which lies behind the original Greek idea of theoria. Theoros means someone who takes part in a mission to a festival. Such a person has no other qualification and function than to be there. Thus the theoros is a spectator in the literal sense of the word, who shares in the solemn act through his presence at it and in this way acquires his sacred quality: for example, of inviolability.

In the same way, Greek metaphysics still conceives the nature of theoria and of nous as pure presence to what is truly real,[33] and also the capacity to be able to act theoretically is defined for us by the fact that in attending to something it is possible to forget one's own purposes.[34] But theoria is not to be conceived primarily as an attitude of subjectivity, as a self-determination of the subjective consciousness, but in terms of what it is contemplating. Theoria is a true sharing, not something active, but something passive (pathos), namely being totally involved in and carried away by what one sees. It is from this point that people have tried recently to explain the religious background of the Greek idea of reason.[35]

We started by saying that the true being of the spectator, who is part of the play of art, cannot be adequately understood in terms of subjectivity, as an attitude of the aesthetic consciousness. But this does not mean that the nature of the spectator cannot be described in terms of being present at something, in the way that we pointed out. To be present, as a subjective act of a human attitude, has the character of being outside oneself. Even Plato, in his *Phaedrus*, makes the mistake of judging the ecstasy of being outside oneself from the point of view of rational reasonableness and of seeing it as the mere negation of being within oneself, i.e., as a kind of madness. In fact, being outside oneself is the positive possibility of being wholly with something else. This kind of being present is a self-forgetfulness, and it is the nature of the spectator to give himself in self-forgetfulness to what he is watching. Self-forgetfulness here is anything but a primitive condition, for it arises from the attention to the object, which is the positive act of the spectator.[36]

Obviously there is an important difference between a spectator who gives himself entirely to the play of art, and someone who merely gapes at something out of curiosity. It is also characteristic of curiosity that it is as if drawn away by what it looks at, that it forgets itself entirely in it, and cannot tear itself away from it. But the important thing about an object of curiosity is that it is basically of no concern to the spectator, it has no meaning for him.

There is nothing in it which he would really be able to come back to and which would focus his attention. For it is the formal quality of novelty, i.e., abstract difference, which makes up the charm of what one looks at. This is seen in the fact that its dialectical complement is becoming bored and jaded. Whereas that which presents itself to the spectator as the play of art does not simply exhaust itself in the ecstatic emotion of the moment, but has a claim to permanence and the permanence of a claim.

The word 'claim' does not occur here by accident. In the type of theological reflection which started with Kierkegaard and which we call 'dialectical theology' this idea has made possible a theological explanation of what is meant by Kierkegaard's notion of simultaneity. A claim is something lasting. Its justification (or pretended justification) is the first thing. Because a claim continues, it can be affirmed at any time. A claim exists against someone and must therefore be asserted against him; but the concept of a claim also contains the idea that it is not itself a fixed demand, the fulfillment of which is agreed by both sides, but is, rather, the ground for such. A claim is the legal basis for an unspecified demand. If it is to be answered in such a way as to be settled, then it must first take the form of a demand when it is made. It belongs to the permanence of a claim that it is concretised into a demand.

The application to lutheran theology is that the claim of the call to faith persists since the proclamation of the gospel and is made afresh in preaching. The words of the sermon perform this total mediation which otherwise is the work of the religious rite, say, of the mass. We shall see that the word is called also in other ways to mediate contemporaneity, and that therefore in the problem of hermeneutics it has the chief place.

At any rate 'contemporaneity' forms part of the being of the work of art. It constitutes the nature of 'being present'. It is not the simultaneity of the aesthetic consciousness, for that simultaneity refers to the coexistence and the equal validity of different aesthetic objects of experience in the one consciousness. Contemporaneity, however, here means that a single thing that presents itself to us achieves in its presentation full presentness, however remote its origin may be. Thus contemporaneity is not a mode of givenness in consciousness, but a task for consciousness and an achievement that is required of it. It consists in holding on to the object in such a way that it becomes contemporaneous, but this means that all mediation is dissolved in total presentness.

This idea of contemporaneity comes, as we know, from Kierkegaard, who gave to it a particular theological emphasis.[37] Contemporaneity, for Kierkegaard, does not mean existing at the same time, but is a formulation of the believer's task of so totally combining one's own presence and the redeeming act of Christ, that the latter is experienced as something present (not as something in the past) and is taken seriously as such. Against this the simultaneity of the aesthetic consciousness depends on the concealment of the task that contemporaneity sets.

Hence contemporaneity is something that is found especially in the religious act, and in the sermon. The sense of being present is here the genuine sharing in the redemptive action itself. No one can doubt that the aesthetic differentiation, e.g., of a 'beautiful' ceremony or of a 'good' sermon is, in view of the appeal that is made to us, misplaced. Now I maintain that the same thing is basically true for the experience of art. Here also mediation must be conceived as total. Neither the separate life of the creating artist—his biography—nor that of the performer who acts a work, nor that of the spectator who is watching the play, has any separate legitimacy in the face of the being of the work of art.

What unfolds before one is for every one so lifted out of the continuing progression of the world and so self-enclosed as to make an independent circle of meaning that no one is motivated to go beyond it to another future and reality. The spectator is set at an absolute distance which makes any practical, purposive share in it impossible. But the distance is, in the literal sense, aesthetic distance, for it is the distance from seeing that makes possible the proper and comprehensive sharing in what is represented before one. Thus to the ecstatic self-forgetfulness of the spectator there corresponds his continuity with himself. Precisely that in which he loses himself as a spectator requires his own continuity. It is the truth of his own world, the religious and moral world in which he lives, which presents itself to him and in which he recognises himself. Just as the parousia, absolute presence, describes the ontological mode of aesthetic being, and a work of art is the same wherever it becomes such a presence, so the absolute moment in which a spectator stands is at once self-forgetfulness and reconciliation with self. That which detaches him from everything also gives him back the whole of his being.

The dependence of aesthetic being on representation does not mean any deficiency, any lack of autonomous determination of meaning. It belongs to its essence. The spectator is an essential element of the kind of play that we call aesthetic. Let us remember here the famous definition of tragedy which we find in Aristotle's *Poetics*. There the attitude of the spectator is expressly included in the definition. . . .

FOUNDATIONS OF A THEORY OF HERMENEUTICAL EXPERIENCE

The Hermeneutic Circle and the Problem of Prejudices

(i) HEIDEGGER'S DISCLOSURE OF THE FORE-STRUCTURE OF UNDERSTANDING. Heidegger went into the problems of historical hermeneutics and criticism only in order to develop from it, for the purposes of ontology, the fore-structure of understanding.[38] Contrariwise, our question is how hermeneutics, once freed from the ontological obstructions of the scientific concept of objectivity, can do justice to the historicality of understanding. The way in which hermeneutics has traditionally understood itself is based on its character as art or technique.[39] This is true even of Dilthey's extension of hermeneutics to become an organon of the human sciences. It may be asked whether there is such a thing as this art or technique of understanding—we shall come back to the point. But at any rate we may enquire into the consequences that Heidegger's fundamental derivation of the circular structure of understanding from the temporality of There-being has for the hermeneutics of the human sciences. These consequences do not need to be such that a theory is applied to practice and the latter now be performed differently, i.e., in a way that is technically correct. They could also consist in a correction (and purification of inadequate manners) of the way in which constantly exercised understanding understands itself—a procedure that would benefit the art of understanding at most only indirectly.

Hence we shall examine once more Heidegger's description of the hermeneutical circle in order to use, for our own purpose, the new fundamental significance acquired here by the circular structure. Heidegger writes: "It is not to be reduced to the level of a vicious circle, or even of a circle which is merely tolerated. In the circle is hidden a positive possibility of the most primordial kind of knowing. To be sure, we genuinely take hold of this possibility only when, in our interpretation, we have understood that our first, last and constant task is never to allow our fore-having, fore-sight, and fore-conception to be presented to us by fancies and popular conceptions, but rather to make the scientific theme secure by working out these fore-structures in terms of the things themselves." (*Being and Time*, p. 153)

What Heidegger works out here is not primarily a demand on the practice of understanding, but is a description of the way in which interpretation through understanding is achieved. The point of Heidegger's hermeneutical thinking is not so much to prove that there is a circle as to show that this circle possesses an ontologically positive significance. The description as such will be obvious to every interpreter who knows what he is about.[40] All correct interpretation must be on guard against arbitrary fancies and the limitations imposed by imperceptible habits of thought and direct its gaze 'on the things themselves' (which, in the case of the literary critic, are meaningful texts, which themselves are again concerned with objects). It is clear that to let the object take over in this way is not a matter for the interpreter of a single decision, but is "the first, last and constant task." For it is necessary to keep one's gaze fixed on the thing throughout all the distractions that the interpreter will constantly experience in the process and which originate in himself. A person who is trying to understand a text is always performing an act of projecting. He projects before himself a meaning for the text as a whole as soon as some initial meaning emerges in the text. Again, the latter emerges only because he is reading the text with particular expectations in regard to a certain meaning. The working out of this fore-project, which is constantly revised in terms of what emerges as he penetrates into the meaning, is understanding what is there.

This description is, of course, a rough abbreviation of the whole. The process that Heidegger describes is that every revision of the fore-project is capable of projecting before itself a new project of meaning, that rival projects can emerge side by side until it becomes clearer what the unity of meaning is, that interpretation begins with fore-conceptions that are replaced by more suitable ones. This constant process of new projection is the movement of understanding and interpretation. A person who is trying to understand is exposed to distraction from fore-meanings that are not borne out by the things themselves. The working-out of appropriate projects, anticipatory in nature, to be confirmed 'by the things' themselves, is the constant task of understanding. The only 'objectivity' here is the confirmation of a fore-meaning in its being worked out. The only thing that characterises the arbitrariness of inappropriate fore-meanings is that they come to nothing in the working-out. But understanding achieves its full potentiality only when the fore-meanings that it uses are not arbitrary. Thus it is quite right for the interpreter not to approach the text directly, relying solely on the fore-meaning at once available to him, but rather to examine explicitly the legitimacy, i.e., the origin and validity, of the fore-meanings present within him.

This fundamental requirement must be seen as the radicalisation of a procedure that in fact we exercise whenever we understand anything. Every text presents the task of not simply employing unexamined our own linguistic usage—or in the case of a foreign language the usage that we are familiar with from writers or from daily intercourse. We regard our task as rather that of deriving our understanding of the text from the linguistic usage of the time of the author. The question is, of course, to what extent this general requirement can be fulfilled. In the field of semantics, in particular, we are confronted with the problem of the unconscious nature of our own use of language. How do we discover that there is a difference between our own customary usage and that of the text?

I think we must say that it is generally the experience of being pulled up short by the text. Either it does not yield any meaning or its meaning is not compatible with what we had expected. It is this that makes us take account of possible difference in usage. It is a general presupposition that can be questioned only in particular cases that someone who speaks the same language as I do uses the words in the sense familiar to me. The same thing is true in the case of a foreign language, i.e., that we all think we have a normal knowledge of it and assume this normal usage when we are reading a text.

What is true of the fore-meaning of usage, however, is equally true of the fore-meanings with regard to content with which we read texts, and which make up our fore-understanding. Here too we may ask how we can break the spell of our own fore-meanings. . . . What another person tells me, whether in conversation, letter, book or whatever, is generally thought automatically to be his own and not my opinion; and it is this that I am to take note of without necessarily having to share it. But this presupposition is not something that makes understanding easier, but harder, in that the fore-meanings that determine my own understanding can go entirely unnoticed. If they give rise to misunderstandings, how can misunderstandings of a text be

recognised at all if there is nothing else to contradict? How can a text be protected from misunderstanding from the start?

If we examine the situation more closely, however, we find that meanings cannot be understood in an arbitrary way. Just as we cannot continually
misunderstand the use of a word without its affecting the meaning of the
whole, so we cannot hold blindly to our own fore-meaning of the thing if we
would understand the meaning of another. Of course this does not mean
that when we listen to someone or read a book we must forget all our fore-
meanings concerning the content, and all our own ideas. All that is asked is
that we remain open to the meaning of the other person or of the text. But
this openness always includes our placing the other meaning in a relation
with the whole of our own meanings or ourselves in a relation to it. Now it is
the case that meanings represent a fluid variety of possibilities (when compared with the agreement presented by a language and a vocabulary), but it is
still not the case that within this variety of what can be thought, i.e., of what a
reader can find meaningful and hence expect to find, everything is possible,
and if a person fails to hear what the other person is really saying, he will not
be able to place correctly what he has misunderstood within the range of his
own various expectations of meaning. Thus there is a criterion here also. The
hermeneutical task becomes automatically a questioning of things and is
always in part determined by this. This places hermeneutical work on a firm
basis. If a person is trying to understand something, he will not be able to rely
from the start on his own chance previous ideas, missing as logically and
stubbornly as possible the actual meaning of the text until the latter becomes
so persistently audible that it breaks through the imagined understanding of
it. Rather, a person trying to understand a text is prepared for it to tell him
something. That is why a hermeneutically trained mind must be, from the
start, sensitive to the text's quality of newness. But this kind of sensitivity
involves neither 'neutrality' in the matter of the object nor the extinction of
one's self, but the conscious assimilation of one's own fore-meanings and
prejudices. The important thing is to be aware of one's own bias, so that the
text may present itself in all its newness and thus be able to assert its own truth
against one's own fore-meanings.

When Heidegger showed that what we call the "reading of what is there"
is the fore-structure of understanding, this was, phenomenologically, completely correct. He also showed by an example the task that arises from this. In
Being and Time he gave a concrete example, in the question of being, of the
general statement that was, for him, a hermeneutical problem.[41] In order to
explain the hermeneutical situation of the question of being in regard to
fore-having, fore-sight and fore-conception, he critically applied his question,
directed at metaphysics, to important turning-points in the history of metaphysics. Here he was actually doing simply what the historical, hermeneutical
consciousness requires in every case. Methodologically conscious understanding will be concerned not merely to form anticipatory ideas, but to make
them conscious, so as to check them and thus acquire right understanding

from the things themselves. This is what Heidegger means when he talks about 'securing' our scientific theme by deriving our fore-having, fore-sight and fore-conceptions from the things themselves.

It is not, then, at all a case of safeguarding ourselves against the tradition that speaks out of the text but, on the contrary, to keep everything away that could hinder us in understanding it in terms of the thing. It is the tyranny of hidden prejudices that makes us deaf to the language that speaks to us in tradition. Heidegger's demonstration that the concept of consciousness in Descartes and of spirit in Hegel is still influenced by Greek substance-ontology, which sees being in terms of what is present and actual, undoubtedly goes beyond the self-understanding of modern metaphysics, yet not in an arbitrary, willful way, but on the basis of a fore-having that in fact makes this tradition intelligible by revealing the ontological premises of the concept of subjectivity. On the other hand, Heidegger discovers in Kant's critique of 'dogmatic' metaphysics the idea of a metaphysics of the finite which is a challenge to his own ontological scheme. Thus he 'secures' the scientific theme by framing it within the understanding of tradition and so putting it, in a sense, at risk. This is the concrete form of the historical consciousness that is involved in understanding.

This recognition that all understanding inevitably involves some prejudice gives the hermeneutical problem its real thrust. By the light of this insight it appears that historicism, despite its critique of rationalism and of natural law philosophy, is based on the modern enlightenment and unknowingly shares its prejudices. And there is one prejudice of the enlightenment that is essential to it: the fundamental prejudice of the enlightenment is the prejudice against prejudice itself, which deprives tradition of its power.

Historical analysis shows that it is not until the enlightenment that the concept of prejudice acquires the negative aspect we are familiar with. Actually 'prejudice' means a judgment that is given before all the elements that determine a situation have been finally examined. In German legal terminology a 'prejudice' is a provisional legal verdict before the final verdict is reached. For someone involved in a legal dispute, this kind of judgment against him affects his chances adversely. Accordingly, the French préjudice, as well as the Latin praejudicium, means simply 'adverse effect', 'disadvantage', 'harm'. But this negative sense is only a consecutive one. The negative consequence depends precisely on the positive validity, the value of the provisional decision as a prejudgment, which is that of any precedent.

Thus 'prejudice' certainly does not mean a false judgment, but it is part of the idea that it can have a positive and a negative value. This is due clearly to the influence of the Latin praejudicium. There are such things as préjugés légitimes. This seems a long way from our current use of the word. The German Vorurteil, like English 'prejudice' and even more than the French préjugé, seems to have become limited in its meaning, through the enlightenment and its critique of religion, and have the sense simply of an 'unfounded judgment'.[42] It is only its having a basis, a methodological justification (and not the fact that it may be actually correct) that gives a judgment its dignity. The lack of such a basis does not mean, for the enlightenment, that there might be other kinds of certainty, but rather that the judgment does not have any foundation in the facts themselves, i.e., that it is 'unfounded'. This is a conclusion only in the spirit of rationalism. It is the reason for the discrediting of prejudices and the claim by scientific knowledge completely to exclude them.

Modern science, in adopting this principle, is following the rule of Cartesian doubt of accepting nothing as certain which can in any way be doubted, and the idea of the method that adheres to this requirement. In our introductory observations we have already pointed out how difficult it is to harmonise the historical knowledge that helps to shape our historical consciousness with this ideal and how difficult it is, for that reason, for the modern concept of method to grasp its true nature. This is the place to turn these negative statements into positive ones. The concept of the 'prejudice' is where we can make a beginning. . . .

The Hermeneutical Priority of the Question

(ii) THE LOGIC OF QUESTION AND ANSWER. Thus we come back to the point that the hermeneutic phenomenon also contains within itself the original meaning of conversation and the structure of question and answer. For an historical text to be made the object of interpretation means that it asks a question of the interpreter. Thus interpretation always involves a relation to the question that is asked of the interpreter. To understand a text means to understand this question. But this takes place, as we showed, by our achieving the hermeneutical horizon. We now recognise this as the horizon of the question within which the sense of the text is determined.

Thus a person who seeks to understand must question what lies behind what is said. He must understand it as an answer to a question. If we go back behind what is said, then we inevitably ask questions beyond what is said. We understand the sense of the text only by acquiring the horizon of the question that, as such, necessarily includes other possible answers. Thus the meaning of a sentence is relative to the question to which it is a reply, i.e., it necessarily goes beyond what is said in it. The logic of the human sciences is, then, as appears from what we have said, a logic of the question.

Despite Plato we are not very ready for such a logic. Almost the only person I find a link with here is R. G. Collingwood. In a brilliant and cogent critique of the 'realist' Oxford school he developed the idea of a logic of question and answer, but unfortunately never developed it systematically.[43] He clearly saw what was missing in naive hermeneutics founded on the prevailing philosophical critique. In particular the practice that Collingwood found in English universities of discussing 'statements', though perhaps a good training of intelligence, obviously failed to take account of the historicality that is part of all understanding. Collingwood argues thus: We can understand a text only when we have understood the question to which it is an answer. But since this question can be derived solely from the text and accordingly the appropriateness of the reply is the methodological presupposition for the reconstruction of the question, any criticism of this reply from some other quarter is pure mock-fighting. It is like the understanding of works of art. A work of art can be understood only if we assume its adequacy as an expression of the artistic idea. Here also we have to discover the question which it answers, if we are to understand it as an answer. This is, in fact, an axiom of all hermeneutics which we described above as the 'fore-conception of completion'.[44]

This is, for Collingwood, the nerve of all historical knowledge. The historical method requires that the logic of question and answer be applied to historical tradition. We shall understand historical events only if we reconstruct the question to which the historical actions of the persons concerned were the answer. As an example Collingwood cites the Battle of Trafalgar and Nelson's plan on which it was based. The example is intended to show that the course of the battle helps us to understand Nelson's real plan, because it was successfully carried out. The plan of his opponent, however, because it failed, cannot be reconstructed from the events. Thus understanding the course of the battle and understanding the plan that Nelson carried out in it are one and the same process.[45]

In fact we cannot avoid the discovery that the logic of question and answer has to reconstruct two different questions that have also two different answers: the question of meaning in the course of a great event and the question of whether this event went according to plan. Clearly, the two questions coincide only when the plan coincides with the course of events. But this is a presupposition that, as men involved in history, we cannot maintain as a methodological principle when concerned with a historical tradition which deals with such men. Tolstoy's celebrated description of the council of war before the battle, in which all the strategic possibilities are calculated and all the plans considered, thoroughly and perceptively, while the general sits there and sleeps, but in the night before the battle goes round all the sentry-posts, is obviously a more accurate account of what we call history. Kutusov gets nearer to the reality and the forces that determine it than the strategists of the war council. The conclusion to be drawn from this example is that the interpreter of history always runs the risk of hypostasizing the sequence of events when he sees their significance as that intended by actors and planners.[46]

This is a legitimate undertaking only if Hegel's conditions hold good, i.e., that the philosophy of history is made party to the plans of the world spirit and on the basis of this esoteric knowledge is able to mark out certain individuals as of world-historical importance, there being a real co-ordination between their particular ideas and the world-historical meaning of events. But it is impossible to derive a hermeneutical principle for the knowledge of history from these cases that are characterised by the coming together of the subjective and objective in history. In regard to historical tradition Hegel's theory has, clearly, only a limited truth. The infinite web of motivations that constitutes history only occasionally and for a short period acquires in a single individual the clarity of what has been planned. Thus what Hegel describes as an outstanding case rests on the general basis of the disproportion that exists between the subjective thoughts of an individual and the meaning of the whole course of history. As a rule we experience the course of events as something that continually changes our plans and expectations. Someone who tries to stick to his plans discovers precisely how powerless his reason is. There are odd occasions when everything happens, as it were, of its own accord, i.e., events seem to be automatically in accord with our plans and wishes. On these occasions we can say that everything is going according to plan. But to apply this experience to the whole of history is to undertake a great extrapolation that entirely contradicts our experience.

The use that Collingwood makes of the logic of question and answer in hermeneutical theory is now made ambiguous by this extrapolation. Our understanding of written tradition as such is not of a kind that we can simply presuppose that the meaning that we discover in it agrees with that which its author intended. Just as the events of history do not in general manifest any agreement with the subjective ideas of the person who stands and acts within history, so the sense of a text in general reaches far beyond what its author originally intended. But the task of understanding is concerned in the first place with the meaning of the text itself.

This is clearly what Collingwood had in mind when he denied that there is any difference between the historical question and the philosophical question to which the text is supposed to be an answer. Nevertheless, we must hold on to the point that the question that we are concerned to reconstruct has to do not with the mental experiences of the author, but simply with the meaning of the text itself. Thus it must be possible, if we have understood the meaning of a sentence, i.e., have reconstructed the question to which it is really the answer, to enquire also about the questioner and his meaning, to which the text is, perhaps, only the imagined answer. Collingwood is wrong when he finds it methodologically unsound to differentiate between the question to which the text is imagined to be an answer and the question to which it really is an answer. He is right only insofar as the understanding of a text does not generally involve such a distinction, if we are concerned with the object of which the text speaks. The reconstruction of the ideas of an author is a quite different task.

We shall have to ask what are the conditions that apply to this different task. For it is undoubtedly true that, compared with the genuine hermeneutical experience that understands the meaning of the text, the reconstruction of what the author really had in mind is a limited undertaking. It is the seduction of historicism to see in this kind of reduction a scientific virtue and regard understanding as a kind of reconstruction which in effect repeats the process of how the text came into being. Hence it follows the ideal familiar to us from our knowledge of nature, where we understand a process only when we are able to reproduce it artificially.

I have shown [elsewhere] how questionable is Vico's statement that this ideal finds its purest fulfillment in history, because it is there that man encounters his own human historical reality. I have asserted, against this, that every historian and literary critic must reckon with the fundamental non-definitiveness of the horizon in which his understanding moves. Historical tradition can be understood only by being considered in its further determinations resulting from the progress of events. Similarly, the literary critic, who is dealing with poetic or philosophical texts, knows that they are inexhaustible. In both cases it is the progress of events that brings out new aspects of meaning in historical material. Through being re-actualised in understanding, the texts are drawn into a genuine process in exactly the same way as are the events themselves through their continuance. This is what we described as the effective-historical element within the hermeneutical experience. Every actualisation in understanding can be regarded as an historical potentiality of what is understood. It is part of the historical finiteness of our being that we are aware that after us others will understand in a different way. And yet it is a fact equally well established that it remains the same work, the fullness of whose meaning is proved in the changing process of understanding, just as it is the same history whose meaning is constantly being further determined. The hermeneutical reduction to the author's meaning is just as inappropriate as the reduction of historical events to the intentions of their protagonists.

We cannot however, simply take the reconstruction of the question to which a given text is an answer simply as an achievement of historical method. The first thing is the question that the text presents us with, our response to the word handed down to us, so that its understanding must already include the work of historical self-mediation of present and tradition. Thus the relation of question and answer is, in fact, reversed. The voice that speaks to us from the past—be it text, work, trace—itself poses a question and places our meaning in openness. In order to answer this question, we, of whom the question is asked, must ourselves begin to ask questions. We must attempt to reconstruct the question to which the transmitted text is the answer. But we shall not be able to do this without going beyond the historical horizon it presents us with. The reconstruction of the question to which the text is presumed to be the answer takes place itself within a process of questioning through which we seek the answer to the question that the text asks us. A reconstructed question can never stand within its original horizon: for the historical horizon that is outlined in the reconstruction is not a truly comprehensive one. It is, rather, included within the horizon that embraces us as the questioners who have responded to the word that has been handed down.

Hence it is a hermeneutical necessity always to go beyond mere reconstruction. We cannot avoid thinking about that which was unquestionably accepted, and hence not thought about, by an author, and bringing it into the openness of the question. This is not to open the door to arbitrariness in interpretation, but to reveal what always takes place. The understanding of the word of the tradition always requires that the reconstructed question be set within the openness of its questionableness, i.e., that it merge with the question that tradition is for us. If the 'historical' question emerges by itself, this means that it no longer raises itself as a question. It results from the coming to an end of understanding—a wrong turning at which we get stuck. It is part of real understanding, however, that we regain the concepts of an historical past in such a way that they also include our own comprehension of them. I earlier called this 'the fusing of horizons'. We can say, with Collingwood, that we understand only when we understand the question to which something is the answer, and it is true that what is understood in this way does not remain detached in its meaning from our own meaning. Rather, the reconstruction of the question, from which the meaning of a text is to be understood as an answer, passes into our own questioning. For the text must be understood as an answer to a real question.

The close relation that exists between question and understanding is what gives the hermeneutic experience its true dimension. However much a person seeking understanding may leave open the truth of what is said, however much he may turn away from the immediate meaning of the object and consider, rather, its deeper significance, and take the latter not as true, but merely as meaningful, so that the possibility of its truth remains unsettled, this is the real and basic nature of a question, namely to make things indeterminate. Questions always bring out the undetermined possibilities of a thing. That is why there cannot be an understanding of the questionableness of an object that turns away from real questions, in the same way that there can be the understanding of a meaning that turns away from meaning. To understand the questionableness of something is always to question it. There can be no testing or potential attitude to questioning, for questioning is not the positing, but the testing of possibilities. Here the nature of questioning indicates what is demonstrated by the operation of the Platonic dialogue. A person who thinks must ask himself questions. Even when a person says that at such and such a point a question might arise, this is already a real questioning that simply masks itself, out of either caution or politeness.

This is the reason that all understanding is always more than the mere recreation of someone else's meaning. Asking it opens up possibilities of meaning and thus what is meaningful passes into one's own thinking on the subject. Questions that we do not ourselves ask, such as those that we regard as out of date or pointless, are understood in a curious fashion. We understand how certain questions came to be asked in particular historical circumstances. Understanding such questions means, then, understanding the particular presuppositions whose demise makes the question no longer relevant. An example is perpetual motion. The horizon of meaning of such questions is only apparently still open. They are no longer understood as questions. For what we understand, in such cases, is precisely that there is no question.

To understand a question means to ask it. To understand an opinion is to understand it as the answer to a question.

The logic of question and answer that Collingwood elaborated does away with talk of the permanent problem that underlay the relation of the "Oxford realists" to the classics of philosophy, and hence with the problem of the history of problems developed by neokantianism. History of problems would be truly history only if it acknowledged the identity of the problem as a pure abstraction and permitted itself a transformation into questioning. There is no such thing, in fact, as a point outside history from which the identity of a problem can be conceived within the vicissitudes of the various attempts to solve it. It is true that all understanding of the texts of philosophy requires the recognition of the knowledge that they contain. Without this we would understand nothing at all. But this does not mean that we in any way step outside the historical conditions in which we find ourselves and in which we understand. The problem that we recognise is not in fact simply the same if it is to be understood in a genuine question. We can regard it as the same only because of our historical shortsightedness. The standpoint that is beyond any standpoint, a standpoint from which we could conceive its true identity, is a pure illusion.

We can understand the reason for this now. The concept of the problem is clearly the formulation of an abstraction, namely the detachment of the content of the question from the question that in fact first reveals it. It refers to the abstract schema to which real and really motivated questions can be reduced and under which they can be subsumed. This kind of 'problem' has fallen out of the motivated context of questioning, from which it receives the clarity of its sense. Hence it is insoluble, like every question that has no clear unambiguous sense, because it is not properly motivated and asked.

This confirms also the origin of the concept of the problem. It does not belong in the sphere of those "honestly motivated refutations"[47] in which the truth of the object is advanced, but in the sphere of dialectic as a weapon to amaze or make a fool of one's opponent. In Aristotle, the word problema refers to those questions that appear as open alternatives because there is evidence for both views and we think that they cannot be decided by reasons, since the questions involved are too great.[48] Hence problems are not real questions that present themselves and hence acquire the pattern of their answer from the genesis of their meaning, but are alternatives that can only be accepted as themselves and thus can only be treated in a dialectical way. This dialectical sense of the 'problem' has its place in rhetoric, not in philosophy. It is part of the concept that there can be no clear decision on the basis of reasons. That is why Kant sees the rise of the concept of the problem as limited to the dialectic of pure reason. Problems are 'tasks that emerge entirely from its own womb', i.e., products of reason itself, the complete solution of which it cannot hope to achieve.[49] It is interesting that in the nineteenth century, with the collapse of the direct tradition of philosophical questioning and the rise of historicism, the concept of the problem acquires a universal validity—a sign of the fact that the direct relation to the questions of philosophy no longer exists. It is typical of the embarrassment of the philosophical consciousness that when faced with historicism, it took flight into the abstraction of the concept of the problem and saw no problem about the manner in which problems actually 'exist'. The history of problems in neokantianism is a bastard of historicism. The critique of the concept of the problem that is conducted with the means of a logic of question and answer must destroy the illusion that there are problems as there are stars in the sky.[50] Reflection on the hermeneutical experience transforms problems back to questions that arise and that derive their sense from their motivation.

The dialectic of question and answer, that was disclosed in the structure of the hermeneutical experience, now permits us to state in more detail the type of consciousness that effective-historical consciousness is. For the dialectic of question and answer that we demonstrated makes understanding appear as a reciprocal relationship of the same kind as conversation. It is true that a text does not speak to us in the same way as does another person. We, who are attempting to understand, must ourselves make it speak. But we found that this kind of understanding, "making the text speak," is not an arbitrary procedure that we undertake on our own initiative but that, as a question, it is related to the answer that is expected in the text. The anticipation of an answer itself presumes that the person asking is part of the tradition and regards himself as addressed by it. This is the truth of the effective-historical consciousness. It is the historically experienced consciousness that, by renouncing the chimera of perfect enlightenment, is open to the experience of history. We described its realisation as the fusion of the horizons of understanding, which is what mediates between the text and its interpreter.

The guiding idea of the following discussion is that the fusion of the horizons that takes place in understanding is the proper achievement of language. Admittedly, the nature of language is one of the most mysterious questions that exist for man to ponder on. Language is so uncannily near to our thinking and when it functions it is so little an object that it seems to conceal its own being from us. In our analysis of the thinking of the human sciences, however, we came so close to this universal mystery of language that is prior to everything else, that we can entrust ourselves to the object that we are investigating to guide us safely in the quest. In other words we are seeking to approach the mystery of language from the conversation that we ourselves are.

If we seek to examine the hermeneutical phenomenon according to the model of the conversation between two persons, the chief thing that these apparently so different situations have in common—the understanding of a text and the understanding that occurs in conversation—is that both are concerned with an object that is placed before them. Just as one person seeks to reach agreement with his partner concerning an object, so the interpreter understands the object of which the text speaks. This understanding of the object must take place in a linguistic form; not that the understanding is subsequently put into words, but in the way in which the understanding comes about—whether in the case of a text or a conversation with another person who presents us with the object—lies the coming-into-language of the thing itself. Thus we shall first consider the structure of conversation proper, in order to bring out the specific character of that other form of conversation that is the understanding of texts. Whereas up to now we have emphasised the constitutive significance of the question for the hermeneutical phenomenon, in terms of the conversation, we must now demonstrate the linguistic nature of conversation, which is the basis of the question, as an element of hermeneutics.

Our first point is that language, in which something comes to be language, is not a possession at the disposal of one or the other of the interlocutors. Every conversation presupposes a common language, or, it creates a common language. Something is placed in the centre, as the Greeks said, which the partners to the dialogue both share, and concerning which they can exchange ideas with one another. Hence agreement concerning the object, which it is the purpose of the conversation to bring about, necessarily means that a common language must first be worked out in the conversation. This is not an external matter of simply adjusting our tools, nor is it even right to say that the partners adapt themselves to one another but, rather, in the successful conversation they both come under the influence of the truth of the object and are thus bound to one another in a new community. To reach an understanding with one's partner in a dialogue is not merely a matter of total self-expression and the successful assertion of one's own point of view, but a transformation into a communion, in which we do not remain what we were.[51]

NOTES

1. Cf. Paul Menzer, *Kants Ästhetik in ihrer Entwicklung*, 1952.

2. *Kritik der Urteilskraft*, 1799, p. 139, cf. p. 200 (Meredith pp. 77, 169, 171, 179, 181).

3. *Ibid.* § 17 (p. 54; Meredith p. 75).

4. *Ibid.* § 20ff. (p. 64; Meredith p. 82ff.).

5. *Ibid.* § 60.

6. *Ibid.* p. 264 (§ 60 Meredith p. 227). Nevertheless, despite his critique of the English philosophy of moral feeling, he could not fail to see that this phenomenon of moral feeling is related to the aesthetic. In any case, when he says that pleasure in the beauty of nature is 'related to the moral', he is also able to say that moral feeling, this effect of practical judgment, is *a priori* a delight (*Ibid.*, p. 169; Meredith § 42, p. 159).

7. Rudolf Odebrecht (in *Form und Geist, Der Aufstieg des dialektischen Gedankens in Kants Ästhetik*, Berlin, 1930) recognised these connections.

8. Schiller rightly felt this when he wrote: "If one has learned to admire the writer only as a great thinker, one will rejoice to discover here a trace of his heart." *Über naive und sentimentalische Dichtung, Werke*, ed. Güntter and Witkowski, Leipzig, 1910 ff., part 17, p. 480.

9. *Kritik der Urteilskraft*, 1799, 3rd ed., p. 179f. (§ 45, Meredith p. 166f.).

10. *Ibid.* p. 194 (§ 49 Meredith p. 177).

11. *Ibid.* p. 188 (Meredith p. 172, § 48).

12. *Ibid.* p. 161 (§ 35 Meredith p. 143) "Where imagination in its freedom arouses the understanding"; also p. 194: "thus the imagination is creative here and sets in motion the faculty of intellectual ideas (reason)." (§ 49 Meredith p. 177).

13. *Ibid.* pp. 183f. (§ 47 Meredith, pp. 169ff.).

14. *Ibid.* p. li (§ vii).

15. *Ibid.* p. lv ff. (§ ix; Meredith p. 38ff.).

16. *Ibid.* p. 181 (§§ 45-6; Meredith pp. 166-168).

17. Kant characteristically prefers 'or' to 'and'.

18. *Ibid.* p. x or lii. (Meredith Preface p. 7 and § viii, p. 36).

19. Cf. Plato's remark on the superior knowledge of the user over the producer, *Republic* x, 601c.

20. It was my interest in this question that guided me in my Goethe studies. Cf. *Vom geistigen Lauf des Menschen*, 1949; also my lecture "Zur Fragwürdigkeit des ästhetischen Bewusstseins," Venice, 1958 (*Rivista di Estetica*, III–A III pp. 374-383).

21. *Variété* III, Commentaires de Charmes: "My verses have whatever meaning is given them," "Mes vers ont le sens qu'on leur prête."

22. In *Logos* VII 1917-18. Valéry compares the work of art with a chemical catalyst (*loc. cit.*, p. 83).

23. Oskar Becker, "Die Hinfälligkeit des Schönen und die Abenteuerlichkeit des Künstler," *Husserl-Festschrift*, 1928, p. 51.

24. Already in K. P. Moritz we read "The work has already reached its highest goal in its formation, in its coming to be" (*Von der bildenden Nachahmung des Schönen*, 1788).

25. Cf. Hans Sedlmayr, "Kierkegaard über Picasso" in *Wort und Wahrheit* 5, p. 356ff.

26. The brilliant ideas of Oskar Becker on 'paraontology' seem to me to regard the 'hermeneutic phenomenology' of Heidegger too much as a statement of content and too little as one of methodology. In content the outcoming of this paraontology, which Oskar Becker himself attempts, logically thinking his way through the problems, comes back to the very point which Heidegger had fixed methodologically. The quarrel over 'nature' is repeated here, in which Schelling was deflated by the methodological consequence of Fichte's theory of science. If the attempt at paraontology is to acknowledge its complementary character, then it must transcend itself in the direction of something that includes both, a dialectic statement of the actual dimension of the question of being, which Heidegger has raised and which Becker does not appear to

recognise as such when he points out the 'hyperontological' dimension of the aesthetic problem in order thus to determine ontologically the *subjectivity* of the artistic genius (see further his essay "Künstler und Philosoph" in *Konkrete Vernunft, Festschrift für Erich Rothacker.*

27. Ed Hoffmeister, p. 424ff.

28. The word *Weltanschauung* (cf A. Gätze, *Euphorion*, 1924) at first retains the relationship to the *mundus sensibilis*, even in Hegel, inasmuch as it is art, to the ideas of which the main world-views belong (*Aesthetik*, II 131). But since according to Hegel the definiteness of a world-view is for the artist a thing of the past, the variety and relativity of world-view has become the concern of reflection and interiority.

29. Hans Sedlmayr, *Kunst und Wahrheit*, 1958, p. 140ff.

30. For the following, compare the fine analyses by R. and G. Koebner, *Vom Schönen und seiner Wahrheit*, 1957, which I came across only when my own work was completed. Cf. the review in the *Philosophische Rundschau* 7, p. 79.

31. Walter F. Otto and Karl Kerényi have noted the importance of the festival for the history of religions and anthropology (cf. Karl Kerényi, *Vom Wesen des Festes*, Paideuma, 1938).

32. Aristotle refers to the characteristic mode of being of the *apeiron;* for instance in his discussion of the mode of being of the day, the games, and hence the festival—a discussion that does not forget Anaximander. (Physics III, 6, 206 a 20). Had Anaximander already sought to define the fact that the *apeiron* never came to an end in relation to such pure time phenomena? Did he perhaps intend more than can be conceived in the Aristotelian ideas of becoming and being? For the image of the day recurs in another connection with a special function: in Plato's *Parmenides* (131b) Socrates seeks to demonstrate the relation of the idea to things in terms of the presence of the day, which exists for all. Here by means of the nature of the day, there is demonstrated not what exists only as it passes away, but the unsharable presence and *parousia* of something that remains the same, despite the fact that the day is everywhere different. When the early thinkers thought of being, i.e., presence, did that which was presence for them appear in the light of a sacral communion in which the divine shows itself? The *parousia* of the divine is still for Aristotle the most real being, *energeia* (Met XIII, 7) which is limited by no *dunamei*. The character of this time cannot be grasped in terms of the usual experience of succession. The dimensions of time and the experience of these dimensions cause us to see the return of the festival only as something historical: the one and the same thing changes from time to time. But in fact a festival is not one and the same thing; it exists by being always something different. An entity that exists only in always being something else is temporal in a radical sense: it has its being in becoming. Cf on the ontological character of the 'while' *(Weile)* M. Heidegger, *Holzwege, p.* 322ff.

33. Cf. my essay "Zur Vorgeschichte der Metaphysik" on the relationship between *'Zein'* and *'Denken'* in Parmenides (*Anteile*, 1949).

34. Cf. what was said above on . . . about culture, formation *(Bildung)*.

35. Cf. Gerhard Krüger, *Einsicht und Leidenschaft. Das Wesen des platonischen Denkens,* first edition (1940). The Introduction in particular contains important

insights. Since then a published lecture by Krüger (*Grundfragen der Philosophie*, 1958) has made his systematic intentions even clearer. Perhaps we may make a few observations on what he says. His criticism of modern thinking and its emancipation from all connections with 'ontic truth' seems to me without foundation. That modern science, however constructively it may proceed, has never abandoned and never can abandon its fundamental connection with experiment, modern philosophy has never been able to forget. One only has to think of Kant's question of how a pure natural science is possible. But one is also very unfair to speculative idealism if one understands it in the onesided way that Krüger does. Its construction of the totality of all determinants of thought is by no means the thinking out of some random view of the world, but desires to bring into thinking the absolute *a posteriori* character of experiment. This is the exact sense of transcendental reflection. The example of Hegel can teach us that even the renewal of classical conceptual realism can be attempted by its aid. Krüger's view of modern thought is based entirely on the desperate extremism of Nietzsche. However, the perspectivism of the latter's 'will-to-power' is not in agreement with idealistic philosophy but, on the contrary, has grown up on the soil which nineteenth century historicism had prepared after the collapse of idealist philosophy. Hence I am not able to give the same value as Krüger to Dilthey's theory of knowledge in the human sciences. Rather, the important thing, in my view, is to correct the philosophical interpretation of the modern human sciences, which even in Dilthey proves to be too dominated by the onesided methodological thinking of the exact natural sciences. I certainly agree with Krüger when he appeals to the experience of life and the experience of the artist. But the continuing validity of these for our thinking seems to me to show that the contrast between classical thought and modern thought, in Krüger's oversimplified formulation, is itself a modern construction.

If we are reflecting on the experience of art—as opposed to the subjectivisation of philosophical aesthetics—we are not concerned simply with a question of aesthetics, but with an adequate self-interpretation of modern thought in general, which has more in it than the modern concept of method recognises.

36. E. Fink has tried to clarify the meaning of man's being outside himself in enthusiasm by making a distinction which is obviously inspired by Plato's *Phaedrus*. But whereas there the counter-ideal of pure rationality makes the distinction that between good and bad madness, Fink lacks a corresponding criterion when he contrasts 'purely human rapture' with that enthusiasm by which man is in God. For ultimately 'purely human rapture' is also a being away from oneself and an involvement with something else which man is not able to achieve of himself, but which comes over him, and thus seems indistinguishable from enthusiasm. That there is a kind of rapture which it is in man's power to induce and that enthusiasm is the experience of a superior power which simply overwhelms us: these distinctions of control over oneself and of being overwhelmed are themselves conceived in terms of power and therefore do not do justice to the interrelation of being outside oneself and being involved with something, which is the case in every form of rapture and enthusiasm. The forms of 'purely human rapture' described by Fink are themselves, if only they are not narcissistically and psychologically misinterpreted, modes of 'finite self-transcendence of finiteness' (cf. Eugen Fink, *Vom Wesen des Enthusiasmus*, esp. pp. 22-25).

37. Kierkegaard, *Philosophical Fragments*, ch. 4, and elsewhere.

38. Heidegger, *Being and Time*, p. 312ff.

39. Cf. Schleiermacher's *Hermeneutik* (ed. H. Kimmerle in *Abhandlungen der Heidelberger Akademie,* 1959, 2nd *Abhandlung*), which is explicitly committed to the old ideal of technique (p. 127, note): "I . . . hate it when theory does not go beyond nature and the bases of art, whose object it is."

40. Cf. E. Staiger's description, which is in accord with that of Heidegger, in *Die Kunst der Interpretation*, p. 11ff. I do not however, agree that the work of a literary critic begins only "when we are in the situation of a contemporary reader." This is something we never are, and yet we are capable of understanding, although we can never achieve a definite 'personal or temporal identity' with, the author. Cf. also Appendix IV, pp. 456-57 above.

41. *Being and Time*, pp. 312ff.

42. Cf. Leo Strauss, *Die Religionskritik Spinozas*, p. 163: "The word 'prejudice' is the most suitable expression for the great aim of the enlightenment, the desire for free, untrammeled verification; the *Vorurteil* is the unambiguous polemical correlate of the very ambiguous word 'freedom'."

43. Cf. Collingwood's *Autobiography* which, at my suggestion, was published in German translation as *Denken*, p. 30ff., as well as the unpublished dissertation of Joachim Finkeldei, *Grund und Wesen des Fragens,* Heidelberg 1954. A similar position is adopted by Croce (who influenced Collingwood) in his *Logic* where he understands every definition as an answer to a question and hence historical (*Logic as Science of the Pure Concept,* tr. Ainsley, London, 1917).

44. Cf. . . . . my critique of Guardini in the *Philosophische Rundschau* 2, pp. 82-92, where I said: "All criticism of literature is always the self-criticism of interpretation."

45. Collingwood, *An Autobiography*, Galaxy ed., Oxford, 1970, p. 70.

46. There are some good observations on this subject in Erich Seeberg's "Zum Problem der pneumatischen Exegese" in the *Sellin-Festschrift*, p. 127ff.

47. Plato, *Ep* VII, 344b.

48. Aristotle, *Topics*, I, 11.

49. *Critique of Pure Reason* A 321ff.

50. Nicolai Hartmann, in his essay, "Der philosophische Gedanke und seine Geschichte," in the *Abhandlungen der preussischen Akademie der Wissenschaften,* 1936, 5, rightly pointed out that the important thing is to realise once more in our own minds what the great thinkers realised. But when, in order to hold something fixed against the inroads of historicism, he distinguished between the constancy of what the 'real problems are concerned with' and the changing nature of the way in which they have to be both asked and answered, he failed to see that neither 'change', nor 'constancy', the antithesis of 'problem' and 'system', nor the criterion of 'achievements' is in agreement with the character of philosophy as knowledge. When he wrote that

'only when the individual makes his own the enormous intellectual experience of the centuries, and his own experience is based on what he has recognised and what has been well-tried, can that knowledge be sure of its own further progress' (p. 18), he interpreted the 'systematic acquaintance with the problems' according to the model of a process of knowledge that does not at all measure up to the complicated reticulation of tradition and history, which we have seen in hermeneutical consciousness.

51. Cf. my "Was ist Wahrheit?", *Zeitwende* 28, 1957, pp. 226-237.

Paul Ricoeur

If Gadamer may be regarded as seeking to provide a positive theory of understanding and interpretation from within the shadow of Heidegger's work, Ricoeur is his French counterpart. Ricoeur is also prominent for his efforts to reconcile his essentially Continental, hermeneutic position with the major trends in Anglo-American semantic theory.

One of Ricoeur's major concerns is with the nature of symbolism, especially in psychoanalysis and religion, but including as well metaphor and other figuration. His position, Heideggerean at heart, is that symbols reveal to us characteristics of reality that cannot be expressed in more semantically pure propositional and representational forms.

PAUL RICOEUR

The Problem of Double Meaning as Hermeneutic Problem and as Semantic Problem*

This presentation is intended to be interdisciplinary in scope. I will attempt to study several ways of approaching a single problem, symbolism, and to reflect upon the signification of the diversity of these approaches. I like to grant philosophy the role of arbitrator, and I have previously attempted to arbitrate the conflict of several hermeneutics in modern culture: the hermeneutics which demystifies and the hermeneutics which recovers meaning.[1] This is not the problem that I intend to take up again here; rather, I wish to consider a different problem, occasioned by a different kind of split. The approaches to symbolism which I propose to bring face to face represent different *strategic levels*. I will consider two and even a third strategic level and will take hermeneutics as a single strategic level, that of *texts*. This level will be confronted with the semantics of linguists, but this semantics itself includes two different strategic levels. First is the level of *lexical* semantics, which is often called simply "semantics" (for example, by Stephen Ullmann or P. Guiraud). It is maintained at the level of words or, rather, as Ullmann proposes, of names, of the process of nomination or denomination. But before our eyes a *structural* semantics is being constituted as well, characterized, among other things, by a change of level and a change of unit, by the passage from molar

---

* Paul Ricoeur, *The Conflict of Interpretations* translated by Kathleen McLaughlin (Evanston, Ill.: Northwestern University Press, 1974), pp. 62-78.

units of communication, such as words and *a fortiori* texts, to molecular units, considered to be the basic structures of signification.

I propose to examine what becomes of our problem of symbolism when it is transferred from one level of consideration to the other. Certain problems which I had the opportunity to discuss under the title "Structure and Hermeneutics" will turn up again, but perhaps under more favorable conditions; for the risk of conflict that occurs at the same level between a *philosophy* of interpretation and a structural *science* can be averted by a method which places at different levels of realization the meaning effects being considered.

Broadly speaking, I want to show that the change of scale of the problem causes the appearance of the atomic *constitution* which alone permits a scientific treatment of the problem; the path of *analysis*, the decomposition into smaller units, is the very path of science, as one sees in the use of the analytic process in automatic translation. In turn, I would also like to show that the reduction to simple elements sanctions the elimination of a fundamental function of symbolism which can appear only at the higher level of *manifestation* and which places symbolism in relation with reality, with experience, with the world, with existence (I am intentionally leaving the choice open among these terms). In short, I would like to establish that the way of analysis and the way of synthesis do not coincide, are not equivalent: by way of analysis one discovers the *elements* of signification, which no longer have any relation to the things said; by way of synthesis is revealed the function of signification, which is to *say* and finally to *"show."*

I. The Hermeneutic Level

In order to carry out our inquiry, it is important to be sure that it is the same problem which is treated on three different levels. This problem I have termed the problem of *multiple meaning*. By this I designate a certain meaning effect, according to which one expression, of variable dimensions, while signifying one thing at the same time signifies *another* thing without ceasing to signify the first. In the proper sense of the word, it is the allegorical function of language *(all-ēgoreō:* "while saying one thing to say another thing").

What defines hermeneutics, at least in relation to the other strategic levels which we are going to consider, is first of all the length of sequences with which it works and which I call texts. It was first in the exegesis of biblical texts and then secular ones that the idea of a hermeneutics, conceived as a science of the rules of exegesis, was constituted. Here the notion of text has a precise and limited meaning. Dilthey, in his great article "Die Entstehung der Hermeneutik," said: "We call exegesis or interpretation the art of comprehending vital manifestations fixed in a durable fashion"; and again: "The art of comprehending gravitates around the interpretation of human testimonies preserved by writing"; and yet again: "We call exegesis, interpretation, the art of comprehending the written manifestations of life." Now, in addition to a certain length in relation to the minimal sequences with which the linguist likes to work, the text includes the internal organization of a work, a *Zusammenhang*, an internal connection. The first achievement of modern hermeneutics was to posit as a rule that one proceed from the whole to the part and the details, to treat, for example, a biblical pericope as a linking or—to use Schleiermacher's terms—as the relationship between an internal form and an external form.

For the interpreter, it is the text which has a multiple meaning; the problem of multiple meaning is posed for him only if what is being considered is a whole in which events, persons, institutions, and natural or historical realities are articulated. It is an entire "economy," an entire signifying whole, which lends itself to the transfer of meaning from the historical to the spiritual level. In the entire mediaeval tradition of the multiple meanings of Scripture, it is through great wholes that the quadruple meaning is articulated.[2]

Today this problem of multiple meaning is no longer simply the problem of exegesis in the biblical or even in the secular sense of the word; it is rather an interdisciplinary problem, which I wish to consider first on a single strategic level, on a homogeneous plane—that of the text. The phenomenology of religion, after the fashion of van der Leeuw and, to a certain extent, after the fashion of Eliade, Freudian and Jungian psychoanalysis (I am not distinguishing between them here), literary criticism ("New" or not), allows us to generalize the notion of text to signifying wholes of a different degree of complexity than that of sentences. I will consider here only one example, sufficiently removed from biblical exegesis so as to give an idea of the fullness of the hermeneutic field. The dream is treated by Freud as a *narration,* which can be extremely brief but which always has an internal multiplicity; according to Freud, it is a question of substituting for this narration, unintelligible at the first hearing, a more meaningful text, which would be to the first as the latent is to the patent. There is thus a vast area of double meaning, whose internal connections clearly set forth the diversity of hermeneutics.

Now, what causes the diversity of these various hermeneutics? For one thing, they reflect differences in technique: psychological decipherment is one thing, biblical exegesis is another. The difference here depends on the internal rules of interpretation; it is an epistemological difference. But these differences of technique in turn refer back to different intents concerning the function of interpretation: it is one thing to use hermeneutics as a weapon of suspicion against the "mystification" of false consciousness; it is another thing to use it as a preparation for a better understanding of what once made sense, of what once was said.

Now, the very possibility of divergent and rival hermeneutics—on the level of technique and on the level of intent—is related to a fundamental condition which, to my mind, characterizes the entire strategic level of the various hermeneutics, and it is this fundamental condition which now holds our attention. It consists in the following: that symbolics is the means of expressing an extralinguistic reality. This is of the greatest importance for the subsequent confrontation; anticipating an expression which will take on its precise meaning only on another strategic level, I will say that in hermeneutics there is no closed system of the universe of signs. While linguistics moves inside the enclosure of a self-sufficient universe and encounters only intrasignificant relations—relations of mutual interpretation between signs (to use the vocabulary of Charles Sanders Peirce)—hermeneutics is ruled by the open state of the universe of signs.

My aim is to show that this rule of the open state is connected to the very scale on which interpretation, understood as exegesis, operates and that the closing of the linguistic universe is accomplished only by a change of scale and by the consideration of small signifying units.

What do we mean here by "open state"? In each hermeneutic discipline, interpretation is at the hinge between linguistics and nonlinguistics, between language and lived experience (of whatever kind). What causes the specific character of various hermeneutics is precisely that this *grip* of language on being and of being on language takes place according to different modes. Thus, dream symbolism can in no way be a simple play of meanings, referring back and forth among themselves; it is the milieu of expression where desire is uttered. For my part, I have proposed the notion of a semantics of desire in order to designate this interweaving of two kinds of relations: relations of force, expressed in a dynamics, and relations of meaning, expressed in an exegesis of meaning. Symbolism occurs because what is symbolizable is found initially in nonlinguistic reality, which Freud terms instinct, considered in its affective and representative agents. It is these emissaries and their derivatives that are revealed and hidden in the meaning effects we call symptoms, dreams, myths, ideals, illusions. Far from moving in a closed linguistic circle, we are ceaselessly at the juncture of the erotic and the semantic. The power of the symbol is due to the fact that double meaning is the mode in which the very ruse of desire is expressed.

The same thing is true at the other end of the hermeneutic scale: if there is some sense in speaking of a hermeneutics of the sacred, it lies in the degree to which the double meaning of a text which, for example, in telling me about the Exodus, opens onto a certain state of wandering which is lived existentially as a movement from captivity to deliverance. Under the summons of a word which gives what it ordains, the double meaning aims here at deciphering an existential movement, a certain ontological condition of man, by means of the surplus of meaning attached to the event which, in its literalness, is situated in the observable historical world. Here, double meaning is the means of detecting a condition of being.

In this way, symbolism, taken at the level of manifestation in texts, marks the breakthrough of language toward something other than itself—what I call its *opening*. This breakthrough is *saying*; and saying is showing. Rival hermeneutics conflict not over the structure of double meaning but over the mode of its opening, over the finality of showing. This is the strength and the weakness of hermeneutics; its weakness because, taking language at the moment when it escapes from its enclosure, it takes it at the moment when it also escapes a scientific treatment, which can begin only by postulating the closed system of the signifying universe. All other weaknesses flow from this one, and first and foremost the conspicuous weakness of delivering hermeneutics over to the warfare of rival philosophical projects. But this weakness is also its strength, because the place where language escapes from itself and escapes us is also the place where language comes to itself, the place where language is *saying*. Whether I understand the relation of showing-hiding as a psychoanalyst or as a phenomenologist of religion (and I think that today these two possibilities must be assumed together), the understanding is in each case like a force which *discovers*, which manifests, which brings to light, a force which language utilizes and becomes itself. Then language becomes *silent* before what it says.

I will venture to summarize this in a few words: the sole philosophical interest in symbolism is that it reveals, by its structure of double meaning, the equivocalness of being: "Being speaks in many ways." Symbolism's *raison d'être* is to open the multiplicity of meaning to the equivocalness of being.

The remainder of this investigation aims at discovering why this grip on being is related to the scale of discourse which we have called the text and which is realized as dream or hymn. This is something we do not know yet but will learn through comparisons with other approaches to the problem of double meaning, where the change of scale will be marked at once by progress toward scientific rigor and by the disappearance of this ontological function of language which we have called *saying*.

II. Lexical Semantics

The first change of scale is the one which makes us consider *lexical units*. Part of the Saussurean heritage is on this level, but only part of it. Indeed, we shall later consider the work that begins with the application of phonological analysis to semantics and which, to do this, requires a much more radical change of scale, since the lexemes, as they are called, are still on the level of the manifestation of discourse, as were the large units we considered earlier. Nevertheless, a certain kind of description and even a certain explanation of symbolism can be carried out at this first level.

First, a description. The problem of multiple meaning can in fact be limited in lexical semantics to polysemy, that is, to the possibility for a name (I am adopting S. Ullmann's terminology)[3] to have more than one meaning. It is possible to describe this meaning effect in the Saussurean terms of "signifier" and "signified" (Ullmann's "name" and "sense"). Thus, the relation to the thing is already excluded, although Ullmann does not make a final choice between the illustration in Ogden Richard's "basic triangle"—symbol-referent-reference—and the Saussurean analysis into two levels. (Later we will see why: the closed system of the linguistic universe is not yet complete at this level.)

We will continue the description in Saussurean terms, distinguishing a "synchronic" definition and a "diachronic" definition of double meaning. The synchronic definition: in a given state of language, the same word has several meanings; strictly speaking, polysemy is a synchronic concept. In diachrony, multiple meaning is called a change of meaning, a transfer of meaning. Of course, the two approaches must be combined in order to take a global view of the problem of polysemy at the lexical level; for in polysemy, changes of meaning are considered in their synchronic dimension, that is to say, the old and the new are contemporaneous in the same system. Moreover, these changes of meaning are to be taken as guides in disentangling the synchronic skein. A semantic change, in turn, always appears as an alteration in a preceding system; if one does not know the place of a meaning in a system state, one has no notion of the nature of the change which affects the value of this meaning.

Finally, we can extend the description of polysemy further along Saussurean lines by considering the sign no longer as the internal relation between a signifier and a signified, between a name and a meaning (this was necessary in order to formally define polysemy), but in its relation to other signs. This recalls the principle of the *Course in General Linguistics;*[4] treat signs as differences within a system. What becomes of polysemy if we place it in this perspective, which is that of structural linguistics? Some light is shed initially on what can be called the functional character of polysemy. But this is only an initial clarification, for we remain on the level of language *[la langue]*, while the symbol is a function of speaking *[la parole]*, that is, an expression in discourse. But, as Godel has shown in the *Sources manuscrites du "Cours de linguistique générale,"*[5] as soon as one considers the "mechanism of language," one remains in an intermediate position between system and execution. It is at the level of the mechanism of language that the rule of ordered polysemy, which is that of ordinary language, is discovered. This phenomenon of ordered or limited polysemy is at the crossroads of two processes: the first originates in the sign, considered as "accumulative intention." Left to itself, it is a process of expansion which continues to the point of a surplus charge of meaning (overload), as we see in certain words which, because they signify too many things, cease to signify anything, or in certain traditional symbols which have taken on so many contradictory values that they tend to neutralize one another (the fire that burns and warms, the water that both quenches thirst and drowns). In contrast, there is also a process of limitation exercised by the rest of the semantic field and first of all by the structuring of certain organized fields, like those studied by Jost Trier, the author of the theory of semantic fields. Here we are still on Saussurean ground, for a sign does not have, or is not, a fixed signification but a value in opposition to other values; it results from the relation between an identity and a difference. This regulating, which arises from the conflict between the semantic expansion of signs and the limiting action of the field, is similar in its effects to the organization of a phonological system, although it differs profoundly from the latter in its mechanism. In fact, the difference between the organization of a semantic field and that of a phonological system is considerable. Far from having a merely differential, and hence oppositional, function, the values are also cumulative; and this makes polysemy one of the prime problems in semantics, perhaps the central one. Here we touch upon what is specific to the semantic level and what allows the phenomenon of double meaning. Urban has remarked that what makes language an instrument of knowledge is precisely the fact that a sign can indicate one thing without ceasing to indicate another thing and thus that, in order to have an expressive value in regard to the second, it must be constituted as a sign of the first. And he added this: "The 'accumulated intention' of words is the fruitful source of ambiguity, but it is also the source of that analogous predication through which alone the symbolic power of language comes into being."[6]

Urban's penetrating remark gives us a glimpse of what could be called the functionality of polysemy. What appeared to us at the level of texts as a particular sector of discourse, namely, the sector of plurivocity, now seems to us to be grounded in a general property of lexical units, namely, to function as accumulators of meaning, as a switch operating between the old and the new. It is in this way that double meaning can take on an expressive function with regard to realities signified in an indirect manner. But how does this occur?

Here again Saussure can guide us by means of his distinction between two axes of speech [langage] function (actually, here he is no longer speaking of language [langue] as a system of signs at a given moment but of the mechanism of language or discourse, which goes along with speaking [la parole]). In the spoken chain, he remarked, signs are in a double relation: in a syntagmatic relation, which links opposing signs in a relation in praesentia, and in an associative relation, which compares signs which are similar and thus have the capacity to be substituted for one another, but compares them only in a relation in absentia. This distinction, as we know, has been revived by Roman Jakobson,[7] who formulates it in similar terms: the "concatenation relation" and the "selection relation." This distinction is of great importance for the investigation of the problem of semantics in general and of symbolism in particular. Indeed, it is the combined play of these two axes—concatenation and selection—that makes up the relation between syntax and semantics.

Now, with Jakobson, we have assured a linguistic status not only for semantics but for symbolism as well. The axis of substitutions is in fact the axis of similarities, while the axis of concatenations is the axis of contiguities. It is thus possible to make correspond to the Saussurean distinction a distinction formerly confined to rhetoric, the distinction between metaphor and metonymy; or, rather, it is possible to assign to the polarity of metaphor and metonymy the more general functional sense of a polarity between two processes and to speak of the metaphoric process and the metonymic process.

Here we touch a root of the same process of symbolization which earlier we reached directly as an effect of the text. Here we grasp its mechanism in what we can now call an effect of context. Let us look once more at the functioning of ordered polysemy, which we considered earlier with field theory at the level of language. Then it was a question of limited polysemy; ordered polysemy is properly a meaning effect produced in discourse. When I speak, I realize only a part of the potential signified; the rest is erased by the total signification of the sentence, which operates as the unit of speaking. But the rest of the semantic possibilities are not canceled; they float around the words as possibilities not completely eliminated. The context thus plays the role of filter; when a single dimension of meaning passes through by means of the play of affinities and reinforcements of all analogous dimensions of other lexical terms, a meaning effect is created which can attain perfect univocity, as in technical languages. It is in this way that we make univocal statements with multivocal words by means of this sorting or screening action of the context. It happens, however, that a sentence is constructed so that it does not succeed in reducing the potential meaning to a monosemic usage but maintains or even creates a rivalry among several ranges of meaning. Discourse can, by various means, realize *ambiguity,* which thus appears as the combination of a lexical fact—polysemy—and a contextual fact—the possibility allowed to several distinct or even opposed values of a single name to be realized in the same sequence.

Let us take our bearings at the end of this second part. What have we gained by transposing in this way onto the lexical level problems encountered on the hermeneutic level? What have we gained, and what have we lost?

We have certainly gained a more precise knowledge of symbolism: it now appears to us to be a meaning effect, observable on the level of discourse but constructed on the base of a more elementary function of signs. This function was in turn traced back to the existence of an axis of language other than the linear axis, along which are found the successive and contiguous series arising from syntax. Semantics and, in particular, the problems of polysemy and metaphor assumed their rightful place in linguistics. By receiving a determined linguistic status, the process considered receives a functional value. Polysemy is thus not in itself a pathological phenomenon, nor is symbolism an ornament of language; polysemy and symbolism are part of the constitution and the functioning of *all* language.

Such are the achievements in the area of description and function, but the inclusion of our problem on the linguistic level has another side as well: semantics can indeed be included in linguistics, but at what price? At the price of keeping the analysis within the enclosure of the linguistic universe. This we have not made apparent, but we see it clearly if we include some traits of Jakobson's analysis omitted in the previous account. In order to justify the intrinsically linguistic character of semantics, Jakobson compares Saussure's views on associative relations (in his terms, the axis of substitutions) to the views of Charles Sanders Peirce on the remarkable power of signs to be mutually interpreted. This is a notion of interpretation that has nothing in common with exegesis: every sign, according to Peirce, requires, in addition to two protagonists, an interpretant. The function of the interpretant is filled by another sign or group of signs which develops the meaning of the first sign and which can be substituted for the sign being considered. This notion of an interpretant, in Peirce's sense, joins the Saussurean notion of a substitutive group, but at the same time it reveals the place of this notion inside an intralinguistic play of relations. Every sign, we say, can be translated by another sign in which it is developed more fully; this includes definitions, equational predications, circumlocutions, predicative relations, and symbols. But by saying this, what have we done? We have resolved a semantical problem by means of the metalinguistic function, that is, according to another of Jakobson's studies, which deals with the multiple functions included in communication, by means of a function that relates a sequence of discourse to the code and not to the referent. That this is the case is evident in the fact that when Jakobson advocates the structural analysis of the metaphoric process (which, we will remember, has been assimilated to the group of operations which utilize resemblances on the axis of substitutions), it is as a metalinguistic operation that he develops his analysis of the metaphoric process. It is insofar as the signs intersignify among themselves that they enter into relations of substitution and so make the metaphoric process possible. In this way, semantics and its problem of multiple meaning remain inside the closed system of language. It is not by chance that the linguist here invokes the logician: "Symbolic logic," notes Jakobson, "has not ceased to remind us that linguistic meanings constituted by the system of analytic relations of one expression to other expressions does not presuppose the presence of things."[8] There is no better way of stating that a more rigorous treatment of the problem of double meaning has been paid for by abandoning its aim toward things. At the end of part I, we said that the philosophical import of symbolism is that in symbolism the equivocalness of being is conveyed by means of the multivocity of our signs. We now know that the science of this multivocity—the science of linguistics—requires that we remain within the enclosure of the universe of signs. Does this not indicate a particular relation between the *philosophy* of language and the *science* of language, between hermeneutics as philosophy and semantics as science?

This is an articulation we will specify by a new change of scale—to structural semantics as it is practiced not only in applied linguistics (for example, in automatic translation) but also in theoretical linguistics, in all the work that is today included under the heading of structural semantics.

III. Structural Semantics

Three methodological choices, according to Greimas,[9] direct structural semantics. From the outset this discipline adopts the axiom of the closed state of the linguistic universe. By virtue of this axiom, semantics is governed by the metalinguistic operations of translating one order of signs into another order of signs. But while in Jakobson the relation between the structures of the language object and those constituted by metalanguage is unclear, here the hierarchical levels of language are very clearly articulated. First, there is the language object, then the language in which the elementary structures of the preceding level are described, next the language in which the operant concepts of this description are elaborated, and finally the language in which we state axioms and define the preceding levels. By means of this clear view of the hierarchical levels of language within the enclosure of linguistics, the postulate of this science is better illustrated, namely, that the structures built on the metalinguistic level are the same as the structures which are immanent in language. The second postulate or methodological choice concerns the change of strategic level of the analysis; one takes as a reference not words (lexemes) but underlying structures, constituted wholly for the needs of analysis.

I can give here only a minimal idea of this enterprise; it is a question of working with a new unit of value, the seme, which is always found in a relation of binary opposition of the type long-short, breadth-depth, etc., but at a more basic level than lexical units. No seme, no semic category, even if its denomination is borrowed from ordinary language, is identical to a lexeme appearing in discourse. We are no longer dealing with object terms but with relations of conjunction and disjunction: disjunction into two semes (for example, masculine-feminine), conjunction under a single trait (for example, gender). Semic analysis consists in establishing for a group of lexemes the hierarchical tree of conjunctions and disjunctions which constitute it entirely. We can see the advantage of this analysis for applied linguistics: binary relations can be calculated in a system of base 1 (0,1), and the conjunctions-disjunctions lend themselves to processing by machines of a cybernetic type (open circuit, closed circuit).

But this analysis benefits theory as well, for semes are units of meaning constructed from their relational structures alone. The ideal is to reconstruct the whole lexical level from a much smaller number of these elementary structures of meaning. If it were successful—this is not a superhuman endeavor—the object terms would be defined wholly, in an exhaustive analysis, as a collection of semes containing only conjunctions-disjunctions and hierarchies of relations—in short, as semic systems.

The third postulate is that the units which we know as lexemes in descriptive linguistics and which we employ as words in discourse belong to the level of the *manifestation of discourse* and not to the level of *immanence*.

Words—to use ordinary language—have a mode of presence other than the mode of existence of these structures. This point is of the greatest importance for our investigation, for what we considered as multiple meaning and as symbolic function is a "meaning effect" which is manifested in discourse but whose principle is situated at a different level.

The entire effort of structural semantics will be to reconstruct, bit by bit, the relations that allow us to account for these meaning effects, following an increasing complexity. I will retain here only two points of this reconstruction. First, it is possible to take up once more, with an unequaled degree of precision and rigor, the problem of multiple meaning, taken as a lexical property, and the problem of symbolic function in units greater than words, let us say, in sentences. Structural semantics attempts to account for the semantic richness of words by means of a highly original method which consists in matching the variants of meaning to classes of contexts. The variants of meaning can then be analyzed in a fixed nucleus, which is common to all the contexts, and in contextual variables. If we place this analysis inside the framework of operational language, by reducing lexemes to a collection of semes, we can then define the variable meaning effects of a word as derivatives of semes—or of sememes—arising from the conjunction of a semic nucleus and of one or several contextual semes, which are themselves semic classes corresponding to contextual classes.

What was necessarily imprecise in our preceding analysis, namely, the notion of semantic possibility, now takes on a precise analytic character. We can transcribe every meaning effect into formulas containing only conjunctions, disjunctions, and hierarchical relations and can thus localize precisely the contextual variable which brings about the meaning effect. Likewise we can account, with a much greater degree of precision and rigor, for the role played by the context, which we first described in rather vague terms as a screening action or as the play of affinities between certain dimensions of meaning of the various words in a sentence. We can now speak of a sorting among contextual variables; to employ Greimas's example, in "The dog barks," the contextual variable "animal" common to "dog" and to "barks" allows us to eliminate the meanings of the word "dog" that would refer not to an animal but to a thing[10] and, likewise, the meanings of the word "barks" that might, for example, apply to a man. The sorting action of the context thus consists in a reinforcement of semes on the basis of reiteration.

As we see in this analysis of contextual function, we find once more the same problems we dealt with in the second part, but they are now approached with a precision that an analytical instrument alone can provide. The theory of context is, in this respect, quite striking; by making the stability of the meaning in a sentence depend on the reiteration of the same semes, we can rigorously define what can be termed the isotopy of a discourse, that is, its elaboration at a homogeneous level of meaning; we can say that "The dog barks" is a statement about an animal.

It is starting from this concept of the isotopy of discourse that the problem of symbolism can also be studied with the same analytical methods. What happens in the case of an equivocal or plurivocal discourse? The following: the isotopy of discourse is not assured by the context; rather, the context, instead of filtering a series of isotopic sememes, allows the development of several semantic series belonging to discordant isotopies.

It seems to me that the conquest of this deliberately and radically analytic level allows us to better understand the relations between the three strategic levels which we have successively occupied. We worked first as exegetes with vast units of discourse, with texts, then as lexical semanticians with the meaning of words, i.e., with names, and then as structural semanticians with semic constellations. Our change of level has not been in vain; it marks an increase in rigor and, if I may say so, in scientific method. We have progressively approached the Leibnizian ideal of a universal characteristic. It would be false to say that we have eliminated symbolism; rather, it has ceased to be an enigma, a fascinating and possibly mystifying reality, to the extent that it invites a twofold explanation. It is first of all situated in relation to multiple meaning, which is a question of lexemes and thus of language. In this respect, symbolism in itself possesses nothing remarkable; all words used in ordinary language have more than one meaning. Bachelard's "fire" is no more extraordinary in this respect than any word in the dictionary. Thus the illusion that the symbol must be an enigma at the level of words vanishes; instead, the possibility of symbolism is rooted in a function common to all words, in a universal function of language, namely, the ability of lexemes to develop contextual variations. But symbolism is related to discourse in another way as well: it is in discourse and nowhere else that equivocalness exists. Discourse thus constitutes a particular meaning effect: planned ambiguity is the work of certain contexts and, we can now say, of texts, which construct a certain isotopy in order to suggest another isotopy. The transfer of meaning, the metaphor (in the etymological sense of the word), appears again, but this time as a change of isotopy, as the play of multiple, concurrent, superimposed isotopies. The notion of isotopy has thus allowed us to assign the place of metaphor in language with greater precision than did the notion of the axis of substitutions, borrowed by Jakobson from Saussure.

But then, I ask you, does the philosopher not find his stake in the question at the end of this journey? Can he not legitimately ask why in certain cases discourse cultivates ambiguity? The philosopher's question can be made more precise: ambiguity, to do what? Or rather, to *say what*? We are brought back to the essential point here: the closed state of the linguistic universe. To the extent that we delved into the density of language, moved away from its level of manifestation, and progressed toward sublexical units of meaning—to this very extent we realized the closed state of language. The units of meaning elicited by structural analysis signify nothing; they are only combinatory possibilities. They say nothing; they conjoin and disjoin.

There are, then, two ways of accounting for symbolism: by means of what constitutes it and by means of what it attempts to say. What constitutes it demands a structural analysis, and this structural analysis dissipates the "marvel" of symbolism. That is its function and, I would venture to say, its mission; symbolism works with the resources of all language, which in themselves have no mystery.

As for what symbolism attempts to say, this cannot be taught by a structural linguistics; in the coming and going between analysis and synthesis, the going is not the same as the coming. On the return path a problematic emerges which analysis has progressively eliminated. Ruyer has termed it "expressivity," not in the sense of expressing emotion, that is, in the sense in which the speaker expressed himself, but in the sense in which language expresses something, says something. The emergence of expressivity is conveyed by the heterogeneity between the level of discourse, or level of manifestation, and the level of language, or level of immanence, which alone is accessible to analysis. Lexemes do not exist only for the analysis of semic constellations but also for the synthesis of units of meaning which are understood immediately.

It is perhaps the emergence of expressivity which constitutes the marvel of language. Greimas puts it very well: "There is perhaps a mystery of language, and this is a question for philosophy; there is no mystery in language." I think we too can say that there is no mystery in language; the most poetic, the most "sacred," symbolism works with the same semic variables as the most banal word in the dictionary. But there is a mystery *of* language, namely, that language speaks, says something, says something about being. If there is an enigma of symbolism, it resides wholly on the level of manifestation, where the equivocalness of being is spoken in the equivocalness of discourse.

Is not philosophy's task then to ceaselessly reopen, toward the being which is expressed, this discourse which linguistics, due to its method, never ceases to confine within the closed universe of signs and within the purely internal play of their mutual relations?

NOTES

1. See *La Symbolique du mal* (Paris: Aubier, 1960). English translation by Emerson Buchanan, *The Symbolism of Evil* (Boston: Beacon Press, 1969).

2. H. de Lubac, *L'Exégèse médiévale: Les quatre sens de l'Ecriture,* 4 vols. (Paris, 1953-65).

3. Stephen Ullmann, *The Principles of Semantics* (New York: Philosophical Library, 1957).

4. Ferdinand de Saussure, *Course in General Linguistics,* trans. Wade Baskin (New York: Philosophical Library, 1959).

5. Robert Godel, *Sources manuscrites du "Cours de linguistique générale" de Ferdinand de Saussure* (Geneva and Paris: Droz-Minard, 1957).

6. Ullmann, *Principles of Semantics*, p. 117.

7. Roman Jakobson, *Essais de linguistique générale* (Paris: Editions de Minuit, 1963), chap. 2.

8. *Ibid.*, p. 42.

9. A. J. Greimas, *La Sémantique structurelle* (Paris: Larousse, 1966).

10. [Here, Ricoeur's example is an idiomatic usage of the French word *chien* in the expression *le chien du fusil,* "the hammer of a gun."—TRANS.]

JACQUES DERRIDA

In "Tympan" (Introduction to *Margins of Philosophy*, trans. Alan Bass [Chicago: University of Chicago Press, 1982]), Derrida suggests that philosophy has always attempted to think, to control, its limit. Although he is speaking of Hegel, this brief characterization expresses what may be Derrida's own lifelong project: to think of philosophy thinking its limit so as to extricate it from the dream that it might be able to define itself.

Derrida has become famous for the idea of deconstruction, which may be interpreted here as a project directed at texts that hope to set their limits for themselves, opening and criticizing them precisely at the point at which this project collapses. In his earlier works, Derrida took writing to be the figure of the movement in language that escaped from the possibility of rational closure. He called "logocentrism" the view that truth might be said in language as if without disturbance at the limits of language. The idea of closure in the limits of language should be read in relation to the sublime in Kant and the selection from Gadamer.

The selections here show Derrida working on the themes of limit and truth in relation to art, although the themes of language and writing continue to circulate around the thought of truth in painting. The opening selection is the introduction to *The Truth in Painting*, "Passe-Partout" ("master-skeleton key" or "frame with a removable back"), another figure of opening and closure. In it, Derrida asks us to think of the idea of idiom in painting. The first of the two longer selections is from "Parergon," to be understood as "outside" or at the very limit of the work, which Derrida pursues through a reading of the *Critique of Judgment*, partly in relation to Kant's own view of limits, partly in relation to the frame of the painting, ornamentation, and the limits of a human body. The explicit theme is that the work requires its limits, its frame, to be a work, yet the frame, the *parergon*, is treated (by Kant and others) as extraneous. The entire discussion is concerned with what can be meant by calling something "extraneous," given that it performs its task with a certain necessity. The third selection from *The Truth in Painting* is from "Restitutions," a reading of a few passages from *The Origin of the Work of Art* out of a "secret correspondence" between Heidegger and Meyer Schapiro on the truth of Van Gogh's painting(s) of (a pair of) shoes. Heidegger claims the shoes to be a peasant woman's, open to the call of the earth. Schapiro claims that they are Van Gogh's own shoes. What kind of truth, Derrida asks, demands that the shoes be restored to their owner? He takes the laces, the pairing, the correspondence, all as figures of limit and closure, in relation to an inquiry into truth in art and truth in general.

Finally, the last selection is one of Derrida's most provocative. He and Peter Eisenman were to collaborate on an architectural project in Paris. The entire collaboration ended with this letter Derrida sent to Eisenman. It asks some of the most enigmatic and deepest questions that might be asked about any art. Even if we think that Derrida on the whole is playing with Eisenman, how can we ignore the questions he asks him? Especially, what of glass? It is probably not extraneous that Derrida wrote a work called *Glas* (Paris: Editions Galilee, 1974); trans. John P. Leavey, Jr. and Richard Rand (Lincoln: University of Nebraska Press, 1986). In French, *"glas"* means funeral bell. What in art of death? What in architecture of glass?

JACQUES DERRIDA

*The Truth in Painting**

PASSE-PARTOUT

1

Someone, not me, comes and says the words: "I am interested in the idiom in painting."

You get the picture: the speaker is impassive, he remained motionless for the duration of his sentence, careful to refrain from any gesture. At the point where you were perhaps expecting it, near the head and around certain words, for example "in painting," he did not imitate the double horns of quotation marks, he did not depict a form of writing with his fingers in the air. He merely comes and announces to you: "I am interested in the idiom in painting."

As he comes and has just come *[vient de venir]*, the frame is missing, the edges of any context open out wide. You are not completely in the dark, but what does he mean exactly?

Does he mean that he is interested in the idiom "in painting," in the idiom itself, for its own sake, "in painting" (an expression that is in itself strongly idiomatic; but what is an idiom?)?

That he is interested in the idiomatic expression itself, in the words "in painting"? Interested in words in painting or in the words "in painting"? Or in the words "'in painting'"?

---

* Jacques Derrida, *The Truth in Painting*, trans. Geoff Bennington and Ian McLeod (Chicago: University of Chicago Press, 1987), pp. 1-13, 21-22, 57-64, 124-27, 135-36, 140-41, 258-59, 276-77, 312, 318, 332-34, 363-66, 376. (Illustrations and notes omitted.)

That he is interested in the idiom in painting, i.e., in what pertains to the idiom, the idiomatic trait or style (that which is singular, proper, inimitable) in the domain of painting, or else—another possible translation—in the singularity or the irreducible specificity of pictorial art, of that "language" which painting is supposed to be, etc.?

Which makes, if you count them well, at least four hypotheses; but each one divides again, is grafted and contaminated by all the others, and you would never be finished translating them.

Nor will I.

And if you were to bide your time awhile here in these pages, you would discover that I cannot dominate the situation, or translate it, or describe it. I cannot report what is going on in it, or narrate it or depict it, or pronounce it or mimic it, or offer it up to be read or formalized without remainder. I would always have to renew, reproduce, and reintroduce into the formalizing economy of my tale—overloaded each time with some supplement—the very indecision which I was trying to reduce. At the end of the line it would be just as if I had just said: "I am interested in the idiom in painting."

And should I now write it several times, loading the text with quotation marks, with quotation marks within quotation marks, with italics, with square brackets, with pictographed gestures, even if I were to multiply the refinements of punctuation in all the codes, I wager that at the end the initial residue would return. It would have set in train a divided Prime Mover.

And I leave you now with someone who comes and says the words, it is not I: "I am interested in the idiom in painting."

2

The Truth in Painting is signed Cézanne. It is a saying of Cézanne's.

Resounding in the title of a book, it sounds, then, like a due.

So, to render it to Cézanne; and first of all to Damisch, who cites it before me, I shall acknowledge the debt. I must do that. In order that the trait should return to its rightful owner.

But the truth in painting was always something owed.

Cézanne had promised to pay up: "I OWE YOU THE TRUTH IN PAINTING AND I WILL TELL IT TO YOU" (to Emile Bernard, 23 October 1905).

A strange utterance. The speaker is a painter. He is speaking, or rather writing, for this is a letter and this "bon mot" is more easily written than spoken. He is writing, in a language which shows nothing. He causes nothing to be seen, describes nothing, and represents even less. The sentence in no way operates in the mode of the statement/assertion *[constat]*, it says nothing that exists outside the event which it constitutes but it commits the signatory with an utterance which the theorists of speech acts would here call "performative," more precisely with that sort of performative which they call "promise." For the moment I am borrowing from them only some convenient approximations, which are really only the names of problems, without knowing if there really are any such things as pure "constatives" and "performatives."

What does Cézanne do? He writes what he could say, but with a saying that does not assert anything. The "I owe you" itself, which could include a descriptive reference (I say, I know, I see that I owe you) is tied to an *acknowledgment* of debt which commits as much as it describes: it subscribes to.

Cézanne's promise, the promise made by the one whose signature is linked to a certain type of event in the history of painting and which binds more than one person after him, is a singular promise. Its performance does not promise, literally, to *say* in the constative sense, but again to *"do."* It promises another "performative," and the content of the promise is determined, like its form, by the possibility of that other. Performative supplementarity is thus open to infinity. With no descriptive or "constative" reference, the promise makes an event (it "does something" in uttering) provided that this possibility is assured by a certain conventional framing, in other words a context marked by performative fiction. Henceforth the promise does not make an event as does any "speech act": as a supplement to the act which it is or constitutes, it "produces" a singular event which depends on the performative structure of the utterance—a promise. But by way of another supplement, the object of this promise, that which is promised by the promise, is another performative, a "saying" which might well be—we do not yet know this—a "painting" which neither says nor describes anything, etc.

One of the conditions for the performance of such an event, for the unchaining of its chain, would, according to the classical theorists of speech acts, be that Cézanne should mean to say something and that one should be able to understand it. This condition would be part of the fiction, in other words of the set of conventional protocols, at the moment when someone such as Emile Bernard sets about opening a letter.

Let us suppose that I wrote this book in order to find out whether that condition could ever be fulfilled, whether there was even any sense in defining it—which remains to be seen.

Does speech-act theory have its counterpart in painting? Does it know its way around painting?

Since it always, and necessarily, has recourse to the values of intention, truth, and sincerity, an absolute protocol must immediately stick at this first question: what must truth be in order to be *owed [due]*, even be *rendered [rendue]*? In painting? And if it consisted, in painting, of *rendering*, what would one mean when one promised to render it itself as a due or a sum rendered *[un rendu]*?

What does it mean, to render?

What about restriction? And in painting?

Let us open the letter, after Emile Bernard. So "the truth in painting" would be a characteristic trait of Cézanne.

He supposedly signed it as one signs a shaft of wit. How can this be recognized?

First of all by this: that the event, the doubly uncertain double event contracts, and makes a contract with itself only at the instant when the singularity of the trait divides in order to link itself to the play, the chance, and the economy of a language. If there existed, in full purity, any (quantity of) idiom or dialect, one ought to be able to recognize them, at work, in this trait of Cézanne. They alone would be capable of providing so powerful an economic formalization in the elliptical savings of a natural language, and of saying so many things in so few words, as long as there still remain remainders *(leipsomena)*, to exceed and overflow the ellipse in its reserve, to set the economy going by exposing it to its chance.

Let us suppose that I have ventured this book, in its four movements, for the interest—or the grace—of these remainders.

Remains—the untranslatable.

Not that the idiom "of the truth in painting" is simply untranslatable, I mean the idiom of the locution, for the quotation marks are not enough to assure us of it: it could be a matter of the idiom of truth in painting, of that to which this strange locution seems to be able to refer and which can already be understood in a multitude of ways. Untranslatable: this locution is not absolutely so. In another language, given enough space, time, and endurance, it might be possible for long discourses to propose laborious approaches to it. But untranslatable it remains in its economic performance, in the ellipsis of its trait, the word by word, the word for word, or the trait for trait in which it contracts: as many words, signs, letters, the same quantity or the same expense for the same semantic content, with the same revenue of surplus value. That is what interests me, this "interest," when I say: "I am interested in the idiom of truth in painting."

You can always try to translate.

As for the meaning, for which of its pertinent features *[traits]* should one account in a translation which would no longer have an eye to pedagogical expense? There are at least four of them, supposing, *concesso non dato*, that the unity of each one remains unbroachable.

1. That which pertains to *[a trait à]* the thing itself. By reason of the power ascribed to painting (the power of direct reproduction or restitution, adequation or transparency, etc.), "the truth in painting," in the French language which is not a painting, could mean and be understood as: truth itself restored, in person, without mediation, makeup, mask, or veil. In other words the true truth or the truth of the truth, restituted in its power of restitution, truth looking sufficiently like itself to escape any misprision, any illusion; and even any representation—but sufficiently divided already to resemble, produce, or engender itself twice over, in accordance with the two genitives: truth of truth and truth of truth.

2. That which pertains, therefore, to adequate *representation,* in the order of fiction or in the *relief* of its effigy. In the French language, if such a one exists and is not a painting, "the truth in painting" could mean and be understood as: the truth faithfully represented, trait for trait, in its portrait. And this can go

from reflection to allegory. The truth, then, is no longer itself in that which represents it in painting, it is merely its double, however good a likeness it is and precisely other by reason of the likeness. Truth of truth still, with the two genitives, but this time the value of adequation has *pushed aside* that of unveiling. The painting of the truth can be adequate to its model, in representing it, but it does not manifest it *itself*, in presenting it. But since the model here is truth, i.e., that value of presentation or representation, of unveiling or adequation, Cézanne's stroke *[trait]* opens up the abyss. (Heidegger in *The Origin of the Work of Art* names the "stroke" *[Riss]* which not only opens above the gulf but also holds together the opposite edges of it.) If we are to understand Cézanne's sentence, the truth (presentation *or* representation, unveiling *or* adequation) must be rendered "in painting" either by presentation or by representation, according to the two models of truth. Truth, the painter's model, must be rendered in painting according to the two models of truth. Henceforth, the abyssal expression "truth of the truth," which will have made it be said that the truth is the nontruth, can be crossed with itself according to all sort of chiasmi, according as one determines the model as presentation or as representation. Presentation of the representation, presentation of the presentation, representation of the representation, representation of the presentation. Have I counted them correctly? That makes at least four possibilities.

3. That which pertains to the *picturality*, in the "proper" sense, of the presentation or of the representation. Truth could be presented or represented quite otherwise, according to other modes. Here it is done *in painting*: and not in discourse (as is commonly the case), in literature, poetry, theater; nor is it done in the time of music or in other spaces (architecture or sculpture). Thus we retain here that which is proper to an art, the art of the signatory, of Cézanne the painter. That which is proper to an art and an art understood in the proper sense this time, in the expression "in painting." We did not do this in the two previous cases: "painting" was there to figure the presentation or representation of a model, which happened to be the truth. But this troping figuration was valid for the logic of any other art of presentation or representation. In the French language, if there is one that is one and if it is not a painting, "the truth in painting" could mean and be understood as: the truth, as shown, presented or represented in the field of the pictural properly speaking, in the pictural, properly pictural mode, even if this mode is tropological with respect to truth itself. To understand the expression "truth in painting" in this way, no doubt one has to move away a little from the greater force of usage (assuming that there are any rigorous criteria for evaluating it), while nevertheless maintaining grammatical and syntactical and even semantic normality. But that's what an idiom is, if there is any such thing. It does not merely fix the economic propriety of a "focus," but regulates the possibility of play, of divergences, of the equivocal—a whole economy, precisely, of the trait. This economy parasitizes itself.

4. That which pertains to truth in the order of painting, then, and *on the subject of* painting, not only as regards the pictorial presentation or represen-

tation of truth. The parasitizing of the expression "in painting" by itself allows it to harbor a new sense: the truth as regards painting, that which is *true on* that art which is called pictural. If one now defines that art by its truth-value, in one sense or the other, one will understand here the true on the true. In the French language, if there is one that is one and which is not painting, and if nonetheless it can open its system up to its own parasitism, "the truth in painting" can mean and be understood as: truth in the domain of painting and on the subject of it, *in painting,* as in the saying "to be knowledgeable in painting." I owe you the truth on painting and I will tell it to you, and as painting ought to be the truth, I owe you the truth about the truth and I will tell it to you. In letting itself be parasitized, the system of language as a system of the idiom has perhaps parasitized the system of painting; more precisely, it will have shown up, by analogy, the essential parasitizing which opens every system to its outside and divides the unity of the line *[trait]* which purports to mark its edges. This partition of the edge is perhaps what is inscribed and occurs everywhere *[se passe partout]* in this book; and the protocol-frame is endlessly multiplied in it, from *lemmata* to *parerga,* from *exergues* to *cartouches.* Starting with the idiom of the *passe-partout.* One is always tempted by this faith in the idiom: it supposedly says only one thing, properly speaking, and says it only in linking form and meaning too strictly to lend itself to translation. But if the idiom were this, were it what it is thought it must be, it would not be that, but it would lose all strength and would not make a language. It would be deprived of that which in it plays with truth-effects. If the phrase "the truth in painting" has the force of "truth" and in its play opens onto the abyss, then perhaps what is at stake in painting is truth, and in truth what is at stake (that idiom) is the abyss.

Cézanne's trait is easily freed from an immediate context. Is it even necessary to know that it was signed by a painter? Its force even depends on this capacity to play with the determinations of the context without making itself indeterminate. No doubt the trait acts as a passe-partout. It circulates very quickly among its possibilities. With disconcerting agility it displaces its accents or its hidden punctuation, it potentializes and formalizes and economizes on enormous discourses, it multiplies the dealings and transactions, the contraband and graft and parasitizing among them. But it only *acts as* a passe-partout, this is only an appearance: it does not mean everything and anything. And besides, like every passe-partout (in the strictest sense!), it must formally, i.e., by its forms, answer to a finite system of constraints.

What does a passe-partout do? What does it cause to be done or shown?

3

The painter does not promise to *paint* these four truths in painting, to render what he owes. Literally, at least, he commits himself to *saying* them: "I owe you the truth in painting and I will tell it to you." If we understand him literally, he swears an oath to *speak;* he does not only speak, he promises to do so, he commits himself to speak. He swears an oath to say, by speech, the truth in painting, and the four truths in painting. The act of speech—the promise—gives itself out as true, or in any case truthful and sincere, and it veritably does promise to say truly the truth. In painting, don't forget.

But must we take a painter literally, once he starts to speak? Coming from a Cézanne, "I will tell it to you" can be understood figuratively: he could have promised to tell the truth, in painting, to tell these four truths according to the pictorial metaphor of discourse or as a discourse silently working the space of painting. And since he promises to tell them "in painting," one does not even need to know of the signatory, for this hypothesis, that he is a painter.

This connection *[trait]* between the letter, discourse, painting is perhaps all that happens in or all that threads its way through *The Truth in Painting*.

The signatory promises, it seems, to "say" in painting, by painting, the truth and even, if you like, the truth in painting. "I owe you the truth in painting" can easily be understood as: "I must render the truth to you in painting," in the form of painting and by acting as a painter myself. We have not got to the end of this *speech act* promising perhaps a *painting act*. With this verbal promise, this performative which does not describe anything, Cézanne *does* something, as much as and more than he says. But in doing so, he promises that he will *say* the truth in painting. What he does is to commit himself to say something. But that saying could well be a doing, or a discursive doing, another performative saying, producing a truth which was not already there, or a pictorial doing which, by reason of some occupancy of painting by speech, would have the value of saying. In the performance of this performative promising another performative saying nothing that will be *there,* the allegory of truth in painting is far from offering itself completely naked on a canvas.

Thus one dreams of a painting without truth, which, without debt and running the risk of no longer saying anything to anyone [of not interesting anyone: *ne plus rien dire à personne*–TRANS.], would still not give up painting. And this "without," for example in the phrase "without debt" or "without truth," forms one of the lightweight imports of this book.

What happens everywhere where these supplements of unchained performatives interlace their simulacra and the most serious quality of their literality? What happens in a game so perverse but also so necessary? One wonders what is left of it when the idiom-effect joins the party, the trait scarcely leaving the initiative to the so-called signatory of the promise. Did Cézanne *promise, truly* promise, promise to *say*, to say *the truth,* to say *in painting* the truth *in painting*?

And me?

4

I write four times here, *around* painting.

The first time I am occupied with folding the great philosophical question of the tradition ("What is art?" "the beautiful?" "representation?" "the origin of the work of art?" etc.) on to the insistent atopics of the *parergon:* neither work *(ergon)* nor outside the work *[hors d'oeuvre]*, neither inside nor outside, neither above nor below, it disconcerts any opposition but does not remain indeterminate and it *gives rise* to the work. It is no longer merely around the work. That which it puts in place—the instances of the frame, the title, the signature, the legend, etc.—does not stop disturbing the *internal* order of discourse on painting, its works, its commerce, its evaluations, its surplus-values, its speculation, its law, and its hierarchies. On what conditions, if it's even possible, can one exceed, dismantle, or displace the heritage of the great philosophies of art which still dominate this whole problematic, above all those of Kant, Hegel, and, in another respect, that of Heidegger? These prolegomena of *The Truth in Painting,* themselves the *parergon* of this book, are ringed together by a circle.

The second time, more attentive to the ring *[cerne]* itself, I attempt to decrypt or unseal a singular contract, the one that can link the phonic trait to the so-called *graphic* trait, even prior to the existence of the word (e.g., GL, or TR, or + R). Invisible and inaudible, this contract follows other paths, through different point-changes: it has to do with the letter and the proper name *in painting*, with narration, technical reproduction, ideology, the phoneme, the biographeme, and politics, among other things and still in painting. The opportunity will be given by *The Journey of the Drawing* by Valerio Adami.

The third time, putting in question again the trait as a signature, whether this signature passes via the proper name known as *patronymic* or via the idiom of the draftsman sometimes called *ductus,* I explore in its logical consistency the system of *duction* (production, reproduction, induction, reduction, etc.). This amounts to treating the trait, its unity and divisibility, otherwise, and it goes without saying that this has to do with the initial, as in "someone's initials," and with repetition and number, the model and paradigm, the series, the date, the event (the time, the chance, the throw, the turn), above all with genealogy and remainders, in the work of mourning: *in painting. Cartouches* gives its name—proper and common, masculine and feminine—to the opportunity furnished by *The Pocket Size Tlingit Coffin,* by Gérard Titus-Carmel.

The fourth time, I interweave all these threads through a polylogue of n + 1 voices, which happens to be that of a woman. What happens (and of what? and of whom?) wherever shoelaces are presented? Present themselves and disappear *(da/fort),* pass over and under, inside and outside, from left to right and vice versa? And what happens with (does without) shoelaces when they are more or less undone? What takes place when they are unlaced in painting? One looks for the revenue (return on investment) or the ghost *[revenant],* that which has just come back *[vient de revenir],* in these steps without steps, in these shoes of which nothing assures us that they make a pair. Thus the question of the *interlace [l'entrelacs]* and the *disparate* resounds. To whom and to what do the "shoes of Van Gogh" return in their truth of painting? What is a desire of *restitution* if it pertains to *[a trait à]* the truth in painting? The opportunity here was given by a sort of duel between Heidegger and Schapiro. A third party (more than a third party, nothing *less* than witnesses) feigned death while the two of them fenced, for the sake of giving back *[rendre]* these shoes, properly, honestly, and lawfully, to their true addressee.

Four times, then, *around* painting, to turn merely around it, in the neighboring regions which one authorizes oneself to enter, that's the whole story, to recognize and contain, like the surrounds of the work of art, or at most its outskirts: frame, title, signature, museum, archive, reproduction, discourse, market, in short: everywhere where one legislates on *the right to painting* by marking the limit, with a slash marking an opposition *[d'un trait d'opposition]* which one would like to be indivisible. Four times around color, too, which is thought to be extraneous to the trait, as if chromatic difference did not count. Now a *parergon* and some *cartouches* leave no assurance as to the right of such an approach. We have to approach things otherwise.

The common feature *[trait]* of these four times is perhaps the trait. Insofar as it is never common, nor even one, with and without itself. Its divisibility founds text, traces and remains.

Discourses on painting are perhaps destined to reproduce the limit which constitutes them, whatever they do and whatever they say: there is for them an inside and an outside of the work as soon as there is work. A series of oppositions comes in the train of this one, which, incidentally, is not necessarily primary (for it belongs to a system whose edging itself reintroduces the problem). And there the trait is always determined as an opposition-slash.

But what happens *before* the difference becomes opposition in the trait, or *without* its doing so? And what if there were not even a *becoming* here? For *becoming* has perhaps always had as its concept this determination of difference as opposition.

So the question would no longer be "What is a trait?" or "What does a trait become?" or "What pertains to such a trait?" but "How does the trait treat itself? Does it contract in its retreat?" A trait never appears, never itself, because it marks the difference between the forms or the contents of the appearing. A trait never appears, never itself, never for a first time. It begins by retrac(t)ing *[se retirer]*. I follow here the logical succession of what I long ago called, before getting around to the turn of painting, the *broaching [entame]* of the origin: that which opens, with a trace, without initiating anything.

One space remains to be broached in order to give place to the truth in painting. Neither inside nor outside, it spaces itself without letting itself be framed but it does not stand outside the frame. It works the frame, makes it work, lets it work, gives it work to do (let, make, and give will be my most misunderstood words in this book). The trait is attracted and retrac(t)ed there by itself, attracts and dispenses with itself there *[il s'y attire et s'y passe, de lui-même]*. It is situated. It situates between the visible edging and the phantom in the center, from which we *fascinate*. I propose to use this word intransitively, as one would say "we hallucinate," "I salivate," "you expire," "she has a hard-on," or "the boat lies at anchor" *[le bâteau mouille]*. *Between* the outside and the inside, between the external and the internal edge-line, the framer and the framed, the figure and the ground, form and content, signifier and signified, and *so on* for any two-faced opposition. The trait thus divides in this place where it takes place. The emblem for this *topos* seems undiscoverable; I shall borrow it from the nomenclature of framing: the *passe-partout*.

The passe-partout which here creates an event must not pass for a master key. You will not be able to pass it from hand to hand like a convenient instrument, a short treatise, a viaticum or even an organon or pocket canon, in short a transcendental pass, a password to open all doors, decipher all texts and keep their chains under surveillance. If you rushed to understand it in this way, I would have to issue a warning *[avertissement]*: this forward *[avertissement]* is not a passe-partout.

I write right on the passe-partout well known to picture-framers. And in order to broach it, right on this supposedly virgin surface, generally cut out of a square of cardboard and open in its "middle" to let the work appear. The latter can, moreover, be replaced by another which thus slides into the passe-partout as an "example." To that extent, the passe-partout remains a structure with a movable base; but although it lets something appear, it does not form a frame in the strict sense, rather a frame within the frame. Without ceasing (that goes without saying) to space itself out, it plays its card or its cardboard *between* the frame, in what is properly speaking its internal edge, and the external edge of what it gives us to see, lets or makes appear in its empty enclosure: the picture, the painting, the figure, the form, the system of strokes *[traits]* and of colors.

What appears, then, and generally under glass, only appears to do without the passe-partout on which it banks *[fait fonds]*.

This would be almost the place for a preface or a foreward, *between*, on the one hand, the cover that bears the names (author and publisher) and the titles (work and series or field), the copyright, the fly leaf, and, on the other hand, the first word of the book, here the first line of *Lemmata*, with which one ought to "begin."

Passe-partout, the word and the thing, has other uses, but what would be the point of listing them? They can be found easily *[ils se trouvent tout seuls]*. And if I were to put them all in a table *[tableau: also "picture"—*Trans.*]*, there would always be one that would play among the others, one taken out of the series in order to surround it, with yet one more turn.

Passe-partout nevertheless cannot be written in the plural, by reason of grammatical law. This derives from its idiomatic makeup and the grammatical invariability of the adverb. But it can be understood in the plural: "Curiosities of all sorts, plaster casts, molds, sketches, copies, passe-partout containing engravings" (Théophile Gautier). In a word, it is written in the singular but the law of its agreements may require the plural.

The internal edges of a passe-partout are often beveled.

PARERGON

. . . If, therefore, one were to broach lessons on art or aesthetics by a question of this type ("What is art?" "What is the origin of art or of works of art?" "What is the meaning of art?" "What does art mean?" etc.), the form of the question would already provide an answer. Art would be predetermined or precomprehended in it. A conceptual opposition which has traditionally served to comprehend art would already, always, be at work there: for example the opposition between meaning, as inner content, and form. Under the apparent diversity of the historical forms of art, the concepts of art or the words which seem to translate "art" in Greek, Latin, the Germanic languages, etc. (but the closure of this list is already problematic), one would be seeking a one-and-naked meaning *[un sens un et nu]* which would inform from the inside, like a content, while distinguishing itself from the forms which it informs. In order to think art in general, one thus accredits a series of oppositions (meaning/form, inside/outside, content/container, signified/signifier, represented/representer, etc.) which, precisely, structure the traditional interpretation of works of art. One makes of art in general an object in which one claims to distinguish an inner meaning, the invariant, and a multiplicity of external variations *through* which, as through so many veils, one would try to see or restore the true, full, originary meaning: one, naked. Or again, in an analogous gesture, by asking what art *means* (to say), one submits the mark "art" to a very determined regime of interpretation which has supervened in history: it consists, in its *tautology* without reserve, in interrogating the *vouloir-dire* of every work of so-called art, even if its form is not that of saying. In this way one wonders what a plastic or musical work means (to say), submitting all productions to the authority of speech and the "discursive" arts

such that by accelerating the rhythm a little one would go on to this collusion: between the question ("What is art?" "What is the origin of the work of art?" "What is the meaning of art or of the history of art?") and the hierarchical classification of the arts. When a philosopher repeats this question without transforming it, without destroying it in its form, its question-form, its onto-interrogative structure, he has already subjected the whole of *space* to the discursive arts, to voice and the *logos*. . . .

So, as an example among examples, the clothing on statues *(Gewänder an Statuen)* would have the function of a *parergon* and an ornament. This means *(das heisst),* as Kant makes clear, that which is not internal or intrinsic *(innerlich),* as an integral part *(als Bestandstück),* to the total representation of the object *(in die ganze Vorstellung des Gegenstandes)* but which belongs to it only in an extrinsic way *(nur äusserlich)* as a surplus, an addition, an adjunct *(als Zuthat),* a supplement.

Hors-d'oeuvres, then, the clothes of statues, which both decorate and
veil their nudity. Hors-d'oeuvres stuck onto the edging of the work nonetheless, and to the edging of the represented body to the extent that—such is the
argument—they supposedly do not belong to the whole of the representation. What is represented in the representation would be the naked and natural body; the representative essence of the statue would be related to this,
and the only beautiful thing in the statue would be that representation; it
alone would be essentially, purely, and intrinsically beautiful, "the proper
object of a pure judgment of taste."

This delimitation of the center and the integrity of the representation, of
its inside and its outside, might already seem strange. One wonders, too,
where to have clothing commence. Where does a *parergon* begin and end.
Would any garment be a *parergon*. G-strings and the like. What to do with
absolutely transparent veils. And how to transpose the statement to painting. For example, Cranach's Lucretia holds only a light band of transparent
veil in front of her sex: where is the *parergon*? Should one regard as a *parergon*
the dagger which is not part of her naked and natural body and whose point
she holds turned toward herself, touching her skin (in that case only the point
of the *parergon* would touch her body, in the middle of a triangle formed by
her two breasts and her navel)? A *parergon*, the necklace that she wears around
her neck? The question of the representative and objectivizing essence, of
its outside and its inside, of the criteria engaged in this delimitation, of the
value of naturalness which is presupposed in it, and, secondarily or primarily,
of the place of the human body or of its privilege in this whole problematic. If
any *parergon* is only added on by virtue of an internal lack in the system to
which it is added (as was verified in *Religion*), what is it that is lacking in the
representation of the body so that the garment should come and supplement
it? And what would art have to do with this? What would it give to be seen?
Cause to be seen? Let us see? Let us cause to be seen? Or let itself be shown?

We are only at the beginning of our astonishment at this paragraph.
(*Parergon* also means the exceptional, the strange, the extraordinary.) I have
torn the "garment" a little too hastily from the middle of a series of three
examples, of three parerga which are no less strange. Each in itself, first of all,
and then in their association. The example immediately following is that of the
columns around sumptuous buildings (*Säulengänge um Prachtgebäude*). These
columns are also, then, supplementary *parerga*. After the garment, the column? Why would the column be external to the building? Where does the criterion, the critical organ, the organum of discernment come from here? It is
no less obscure than in the previous case. It even presents an extra difficulty:
the *parergon* is added this time to a work which *does not represent anything* and
which is itself already *added to* nature. We think we know what properly
belongs or does not belong to the human body, what is detached or not
detached from it—even though the parergon is precisely an ill-detachable
detachment. But in a work of architecture, the *Vorstellung*, the representation is not structurally representational or else is so only through detours

complicated enough, no doubt, to disconcert anyone who tried to discern, in a critical manner, the inside from the outside, the integral part and the detachable part. So as not to add to these complications, I shall leave to one side, provisionally, the case of columns in the form of the human body, those that support or represent the support of a window (and does a window form part of the inside of a building or not? And what about the window of a building in a painting?), and which can be naked or clothed, can represent a man or a woman, a distinction to which Kant makes no reference.

With this example of the columns is announced the whole problematic of inscription in a milieu, of the marking out of the work in a field of which it is always difficult to decide if it is natural or artificial and, in this latter case, if it is *parergon* or *ergon*. For not every milieu, even if it is contiguous with the work, constitutes a *parergon* in the Kantian sense. The natural site chosen for the erection of a temple is obviously not a *parergon*. Nor is an artificial site: neither the crossroads, nor the church, nor the museum, nor the other works around one or other. But the garment or the column is. Why? It is not because they are detached but on the contrary because they are more difficult to detach and above all because without them, without their quasi-detachment, the lack on the inside of the work would appear; or (which amounts to the same thing for a lack) would not appear. What constitutes them as *parerga* is not simply their exteriority as a surplus, it is the internal structural link which rivets them to the lack in the interior of the *ergon*. And this lack would be constitutive of the very unity of the *ergon*. Without this lack, the *ergon* would have no need of a *parergon*. The *ergon*'s lack is the lack of a *parergon*, of the garment or the column which nevertheless remains exterior to it. How to give *energeia* its due?

Can one attach the third example to this series of examples, to the question that they pose? It is in fact the first of the examples, and I have proceeded in reverse. In appearance it is difficult to associate it with the other two. It is to do with the frames for paintings *(Einfassungen der Gemälde)*. The frame: a *parergon* like the others. The series might seem surprising. How can one assimilate the function of a frame to that of a garment on (in, around, or up against) a statue, and to that of columns around a building? And what about a frame framing a painting representing a building surrounded by columns in clothed human form? What is incomprehensible about the edge, about the *à-bord* appears not only at the internal limit, the one that passes between the frame and the painting, the clothing and the body, the column and the building, but also at the external limit. *Parerga* have a thickness, a surface which separates them not only (as Kant would have it) from the integral inside, from the body proper of the *ergon*, but also from the outside, from the wall on which the painting is hung, from the space in which statue or column is erected, then, step by step, from the whole field of historical, economic, political inscription in which the drive to signature is produced (an analogous problem, as we shall see further on). No "theory," no "practice," no "theoretical practice" can intervene effectively in this field if it does not weigh up and bear on the frame, which is the decisive structure of what is at stake, at the invisible limit to (between) the interiority of meaning (put under shelter by the whole hermeneuticist, semioticist, phenomenologicalist, and formalist tradition) *and* (to) all the empiricisms of the extrinsic which, incapable of either seeing or reading, miss the question completely.

The *parergon* stands out *[se détache]* both from the *ergon* (the work) and from the milieu, it stands out first of all like a figure on a ground. But it does not stand out in the same way as the work. The latter also stands out against a ground. But the parergonal frame stands out against two grounds *[fonds]*, but with respect to each of those two grounds, it merges *[se fond]* into the other. With respect to the work which can serve as a ground for it, it merges into the wall, and then, gradually, into the general text. With respect to the background which the general text is, it merges into the work which stands out against the general background. There is always a form on a ground, but the *parergon* is a form which has as its traditional determination not that it stands out but that it disappears, buries itself, effaces itself, melts away at the moment it deploys its greatest energy. The frame is in no case a background in the way that the milieu or the work can be, but neither is its thickness as margin a figure. Or at least it is a figure which comes away of its own accord *[s'enlève d'elle-même]*.

What would Kant have said about a frame framing a painting representing a building surrounded by columns (examples of this are numerous), columns in the form of clothed human bodies (the frescoes on the vault of the Sistine Chapel—what is its frame?—whose represented, painted object is a sculpted volume itself representing, for example to the right of Jonah, naked children forming a column which supports a ceiling, etc. Same implication around the Persian Sibyl or around Zachariah holding a book in his hand, or around Jeremiah, or the Libyan Sibyl; it is difficult to say whether the children-columns are clothed or unclothed: they are *bearing* clothes), the whole frame being placed on the easel of a painter who is himself represented by another painting.

It may appear that I am taking unfair advantage by persisting with two or three possibly fortuitous examples from a secondary subchapter; and that it would be better to go to less marginal places in the work, nearer to the center and the heart of the matter *[le fond]*. To be sure. The objection presupposes that one already knows what is the center or the heart of the third *Critique*, that one has already located its frame and the limit of its field. But nothing seems more difficult to determine. The *Critique* presents itself as a work *(ergon)* with several sides, and as such it ought to allow itself to be centered and framed, to have its ground delimited by being marked out, with a frame, against a general background. But this frame is problematical. I do not know what is essential and what is accessory in a work. And above all I do not know what this thing is, that is neither essential nor accessory, neither proper nor improper, and that Kant calls *parergon*, for example the frame. Where does the frame take place. Does it take place. Where does it begin. Where does it end.

What is its internal limit. Its external limit. And its surface between the two limits. I do not know whether the passage in the third *Critique* where the *parergon* is defined is itself a *parergon*. Before deciding what is parergonal in a text which poses the question of the *parergon*, one has to know what a *parergon* is—at least, if there is any such thing.

To the impatient objector, if s/he insists on seeing the thing itself at last: the whole analytic of aesthetic judgment forever assumes that one can distinguish rigorously between the intrinsic and the extrinsic. Aesthetic judgment *must* properly bear upon intrinsic beauty, not on finery and surrounds. Hence one must know—this is a fundamental presupposition, presupposing what is fundamental—how to determine the intrinsic—what is framed—and know what one is excluding as frame *and* outside-the-frame. We are thus *already* at the unlocatable center of the problem. And when Kant replies to our question "What is a frame?" by saying: it's a *parergon*, a hybrid of outside and inside, but a hybrid which is not a mixture or a half-measure, an outside which is called to the inside of the inside in order to constitute it as an inside; and when he gives as examples of the *parergon*, alongside the frame, clothing and column, we ask to see, we say to ourselves that there are "great difficulties" here, and that the choice of examples, and their association, is not self-evident.

The more so because, according to the logic of the supplement, the parergon is divided in two. At the limit between work and absence of work, it divides in two. And this division gives rise to a sort of pathology of the *parergon*, the forms of which must be named and classified, just as *Religion* recognized four types of parergonal misdeeds or detriments. Kant is in the process of determining "the proper object of the pure judgment of taste." But he does not simply exclude from it the parergon as such and in general. Only in certain conditions. The criterion of exclusion is here a formality.

What must we understand by formality?

The *parergon* (frame, garment, column) can augment the pleasure of taste *(Wohlgefallen des Geschmacks)*, contribute to the proper and intrinsically aesthetic representation if it intervenes *by its form (durch seine Form)* and only by its form. If it has a "beautiful form," it forms part of the judgment of taste properly speaking or in any case intervenes directly in it. This is, if you like, the normal *parergon*. But if on the other hand it is not beautiful, purely beautiful, i.e., of a formal beauty, it lapses into *adornment (Schmuck)* and harms the beauty of the work, it does it wrong and causes it detriment *(Abbruch)*. This is analogous to the detriment or damage *(Nachteil)* of *Religion*.

Now the example of this degradation of the simple *parergon* into a seductive adornment is again a frame, this time the gilded frame *(goldene Rahmen)*, the gilding of the frame done in order to recommend the painting to our attention by its attraction *(Reiz)*. What is bad, external to the pure object of taste, is thus what seduces by an attraction; and the example of what leads astray by its force of attraction is a color, the gilding, in as much as it is non-form, content, or sensory matter. The deterioration of the *parergon*, the per-

version, the adornment, is the attraction of sensory matter. As design, organization of lines, forming of angles, the frame is not at all an adornment and
one cannot do without it. But in its purity, it ought to remain colorless,
deprived of all empirical sensory materiality. . . .

What is the colossal?

By opposition to works of art and to finite and finalized things of nature,
"raw nature" can offer or present the "prodigious," the *Ungeheuer* (the enormous, the immense, the excessive, the astonishing, the unheard-of, sometimes the monstrous). "Prodigious" things become sublime objects only if
they remain foreign both to fear and to seduction, to "attraction." An object
is "prodigious" when, by its size *(Grösse)*, it annihilates and reduces to nothing
(vernichtet) the end which constitutes its concept. The prodigious exceeds the
final limit, and puts an end to it. It overflows its end and its concept. *Prodigious,* or monstrous—let us pay close attention to this—is the characteristic of
an *object,* and of an object in its relation to its end and to its concept. The *colossal,* which is not the prodigious, nor the monstrous, qualifies the "mere presentation" *(blosse Darstellung)* of a concept. But not just any concept: the mere
presentation of a concept which is "almost too large for any presentation" *(der
für alle Darstellung beinahe zu gross ist).* A concept can be too big, *almost too* big
for presentation.

Colossal (kolossalisch) thus qualifies the presentation, the putting on stage
or into presence, the catching-sight, rather, of some thing, but of something
which is not a thing, since it is a concept. And the presentation of this concept
inasmuch as it is not presentable. Nor simply unpresentable: *almost unpresentable.* And by reason of its size: it is "almost too large." This concept is
announced and then eludes presentation on the stage. One would say, by
reason of its almost excessive size, that it was obscene.

How can the category of the "almost too" be arrested? The pure and
simple "too" would bring the colossal down: it would render presentation
impossible. The "without too" or the "not too," the "enough" would have
the same effect. How are we to think, in the presence of a presentation, the
standing-there-upright *(Darstellen)* of an excess of size which remains merely
almost excessive, at the *barely* crossed edge of a limiting line *[trait]?* And which
is incised, so to speak, in excess?

The *almost too* thus forms the singular originality, without edging or
simple overspill, of the colossal. Although it has an essential relation to
approximation, to the approaching movement of the approach *(beinahe zu
gross),* although it names the indecision of the approach, the concept of the
"almost-too," as a concept, has nothing of an empirical approximation about
it. It did not slip from Kant's pen. (I shall risk here the definition of the
philosophos kolossos, who is not the "great philosopher": he's the one who calculates almost too well the approaches to the "almost too" in his text.) The
almost too retains a certain categorical fixity. It is repeated regularly, and each
time associated with "big." Kant adds, in fact, immediately afterward, that

the presentation of a concept becomes difficult, in its "goal," when the intuition of the object is "almost too great" for our "power of apprehension" *(Auffassungsvermögen)*. It "becomes difficult" *(erschwert wird)*, progressively, by continuous approximation. But where, then, do we cut off ? Where are we to delimit the trait of the *almost too?*

The "power of apprehension" seems to give the measure here. Let us not rush toward what would, by the slant of the metaphor, of (schematic or symbolic) hypotyposis, immediately put the *Auffassen* in our hands or under our noses. This problematic is necessary, and would lead just as well to the famous paragraph 59 of the third *Critique* as to the Hegelian treatment of the "Fassen" as a dead metaphor. I shall provisionally skirt around it, using other trajectories ("White Mythology" in *Margins,* and "Economimesis") to authorize this avoidance.

The "almost-too-large" of the colossal (if we were in a hurry, we'd translate this as: of the phallus which doubles the corpse; but never be in a hurry when it's a matter of erection, let the thing happen) is thus determined, if one can still say so, in its relative indetermination, as almost too large with regard, if one could still say so, to the grasp, to apprehension, to our power of apprehension. (I shall not abuse the word *apprehension:* at the limits of apprehension, the colossal is almost frightening, it worries by its relative indetermination: What's coming? What's going to happen? etc. But it must not cause fear, says Kant.)

The hold of apprehension is not that of comprehension. In this problematic, the question is always that of knowing if one can take hold of (apprehend or comprehend, which is not the same thing), how can we set about taking hold *[comment s'y prendre pour prendre]*, and to what limits prehension can and must extend. How to deal with *[s'y prendre avec]* the *colossal?* Why is it almost too large for our *Auffassung,* for our apprehension, and decidedly too large for our *Zusammenfassung,* our comprehension? A little earlier *[Un peu plus haut]* in the same chapter, Kant had distinguished two powers of the imagination. When it relates intuitively to a *quantum* in order to use it as a measure or as a numerical unit of measure, it has at its disposal the *apprehensio (Auffassung)* or the *comprehensio aesthetica (Zusammenfassung).* The former can go to infinity, the latter has difficulty following and becomes harder and harder according as the apprehension progresses. It quickly attains its maximum: the fundamental aesthetic measure for the evaluation of magnitudes.

So what about the -prehend with respect to the colossal? Why does Kant call *colossal,* without apparent reference to the colossus, the presentation of a concept (of a *Begriff* whose *Begreifen* itself would not go without a taking hold and a taking sight of)? What is the presentation of a concept, if it may be sometimes colossal and, as such, unequal to the concept which, even while remaining too large for its own presentation, nonetheless never leaves off presenting itself, colossally? Finally, what would the sublime have to do with *[aurait à voir avec]* all these inadequations? . . .

What is the question, then? The question that Kant does not pose and yet which we can pose from inside his discourse. And if we can pose it from inside his discourse, this is because without being posed there, it is not without posing itself there. Questions can also be parergonal. Here it is.

Let us try to consider magnitude anew. This name translates the absolutely large, not absolute largeness (since this "large" is alien to and incommensurable with dimension), nor the large absolute (since one might be tempted to invert or permutate the two attributes and transform one or other into a substantive), but the absolutely large, an incorrect syntax to designate a value which is neither absolutely nominalizable (the largeness of the large) nor a mere modification of the noun (the large *as* largeness). It is because it is absolutely large that this large is no longer of the order or at the orders of largeness as dimension. It is larger than largeness, neither large nor largeness, but absolutely large. So what is the question? Here it is.

Why can magnitude, which is not a quantity, and not a comparable quantity in the order of phenomena, let itself be represented under the category of quantity rather than some other category? What does it have in common or analogous with that category even when it is incomparable with it? In other words, why call magnitude or "absolutely large" that which is no longer a quantity? Why this reference, still, to a cise in space? Then, another question, still the same, if phenomenalization is to be admitted, why would the sublime be the absolutely large and not the absolutely small? Why would the absolute excess of dimension, or rather of quantity, be schematized on the side of largeness and not of smallness? Why this valorization of the large which thus still intervenes in a comparison between incomparables? To be sure, the absolutely large is not compared with anything, not with any phenomenal dimension in any case, but it is *preferred* to the absolutely small. In short, why is the sublime large and not small? Why is the large (absolutely) sublime and not the small (absolutely)? Kant posits the fact of this preference, of this pleasure taken in the larger or of the greater pleasure taken in the large, of this economy which quasi-tautologically makes the more worth more than the less and the absolutely large more than the absolutely small, since the schema of preference (the more) leads into it as an analytical consequence. If indeed one asks oneself, as I have just done, why preference should go to the largest, one forgets naïvely that the more and hence largeness are inscribed in the movement and in the very concept of preference. So we have to displace the question: *Why should there be a preference?* And more strictly, why, if in phenomenality the excess of quantity is to announce itself, and likewise the movement beyond comparison, why should it do so on the side of the large and not the small, the largest and not the smallest, the less large or the absolutely small?

Kant posits that the preference can only be subjective but the very tautology of the proposition dispenses him from questioning it. If no mathematics can as such justify a preference, an advantage, a superiority, a privilege

(Vorzug), it must be that an aesthetic judgment is implied in it, and a subjective measure coming to found reflective judgments. An object, even if it were to be indifferent to us in its existence, still pleases us by its mere largeness, even if one considers it as without form *(formlos)*, and this feeling is universally communicable. The relation to this largeness is not mathematical, nor is the "respect" which it inspires, and no more is the "contempt" aroused by "what we call simply small." Kant does not ask himself why this should go without saying, naturally toward the largest and the highest. The question is all the more inevitable because the nonphenomenal infinity of the idea must always be presented in intuition. Now everything that is "presented" in intuition and therefore "represented" aesthetically, every phenomenon is also a *quantum*. But what decides that, in this *quantum*, the more is worth more than the less, and the large more or better than the small? The agency of decision or "preference" can as such be neither phenomenal nor noumenal, neither sensible nor intelligible. . . .

This primary (subjective, sensory, immediate, living) measure proceeds from the body. And it takes the body as its primary object. We must now verify this. *It is the body which erects itself as a measure.* It provides the measuring and measured unit of measure: of the smallest and the largest possible, of the minimum and the maximum, and likewise of the passage from the one to the other.

The body, I was saying. The body of man, as is understood and goes without saying. It is *starting from* it that the erection of the largest is preferred.

Everything is measured here on the scale of *[à la taille de]* the body. Of man. It is to this fundamental measurer *(Grundmass)* that the colossal must be related, its excess of cise, its insufficient cise, the almost and the almost too much which holds it or raises or lowers it between two measures.

We have just glimpsed it: for the aesthetic evaluation to give rise to a mathematical measure, the intervention of the imagination is indispensable. The imagination takes hold of *(aufnimmt)* a sensory quantum in order to make an empirical estimation of it. Now the imagination, being intermediate between sensibility and understanding, is capable of *two operations.* And we rediscover here the two edges, the two faces of the trait, of the limit or of the cise. Imagination is the cise because it has two cises. The cise always has two cises: it de-limits. It has the cise of what it delimits and the cise of what it de-limits, of what it limits and of what is liberated in it of its limits. Two operations of the imagination, then, which are both *prehensions.* Apprehension *(apprehensio, Auffassung)* can go to the infinite *without difficulty.* The other operation, comprehension *(comprehensio, Zusammenfassung)* cannot follow, it is finite, subjected to the *intuitus derivatus* and to the sensory. It arrives very quickly at a maximum, which is then set up as a fundamental measure. This maximum of comprehension is "the fundamental measure, aesthetically the largest, of the evaluation of size." And if apprehension extends beyond this maximum, it lets go in comprehension what it gains in apprehension. Whence this apparently paradoxical conclusion: the right place, the ideal *topos* for the experience of the sublime, for the inadequation of presentation to the unpresentable, will be a median place, an average place of the body which would provide an aesthetic maximum without losing itself in the mathematical infinite. Things must come to a relationship of body to body: the "sublime" body (the one that provokes the feeling of the sublime) must be far enough away for the maximum size to appear and remain sensible, but close enough to be seen and "comprehended," not to lose itself in the mathematical indefinite. Regulated, measured dis-tance *[é-loignement] between* a too-close and a too-far.

RESTITUTIONS

—Why always say of painting that it renders, that it restitutes?

—to discharge a more or less ghostly debt, restitute the shoes, render them to their rightful owner; if it's a matter of knowing from where they *return*, from the city (Schapiro) or the fields (Heidegger), like rats, which I suddenly have an idea they look like (then who is these rats' Rat Man?), unless it is rather that they look like snares *[pièges à lacets]* lying in wait for the stroller in the middle of the museum (will s/he be able to avoid being in too much of a hurry and catching his/her feet in them?); if it's a question of knowing what revenue is still produced by their out-of-service dereliction, what surplus value is unleashed by the annulment of their use value: *outside* the picture, inside the *picture*, and, third, as a picture, or to put it very equivocally, *in their painting truth;* if it's a question of knowing what ghost's step *[quel pas de revenant]*, city dweller or peasant, still comes to haunt them ("the ghost of my other I," the other I of Vincent the signatory, as Schapiro suggests quoting Knut Hamsun—but Heidegger also does this, elsewhere); if it's a question of knowing whether the shoes in question are haunted by some ghost or are ghosting/returning *[la revenance]* itself (but then what are, who are in truth, and whose and what's, these things?). In short, what does it all come down to *[ça revient à quoi]*? To whom? To whom and to what are we to restitute, to reattach, to readjust precisely

—to what shoe size exactly, made to measure, adequately

—and where from? How? If at least it's a question of knowing, returning will be from long range *[d'une longue portée]*.

What I'm saying is that there will have been a correspondence between Meyer Schapiro and Martin Heidegger.

One of them says in 1935: that pair comes back to/belongs to/amounts to the peasant, and even the peasant woman

—what makes him so sure that they are a *pair of* shoes? What is a pair?

—I don't know yet. In any case, Heidegger has no doubt about it; it's a pair-of-peasant-shoes *(ein Paar Bauernschuhe)*. And *ça revient*, this indissociable whole, this paired thing, from the fields and to the peasant, man or even woman. Thus Heidegger does not answer one question, he is sure of the thing before any other question. So it seems. The other one, not agreeing at all, says after mature reflection, thirty-three years later, exhibiting the juridical exhibits (but without asking himself any questions beyond this and without asking any other question): no, there's been an error and a projection, if not deception and perjury, *ça revient*, this pair, from the city

—what makes him so sure that it's a *pair of* shoes? . . .

—So Schapiro, insouciant, lays a trap for Heidegger. He already suspects the "error," "projection," "imagination" in Heidegger's text pointed
out to him by his friend and colleague Goldstein. The hearing having begun
thus, he writes to Professor Heidegger (that's what he calls him when speaking
of the colleague and correspondent, and simply Heidegger for the famous
thinker, author of *The Origin of the Work of Art*): which picture exactly were you
referring to? The "kind" reply from Professor H. ("In reply to my question,
Professor Heidegger has kindly written me that the picture to which he
referred is one that he saw in a show at Amsterdam in March 1930. This is
clearly de la Faille's no. 255.") closes on its author like a trap. You can hear the
noise: clear. It's clear, "clearly," understood, the case has been heard, de la
Faille 255, that can't come down/back to peasanthood: "They are the shoes of
the artist, by that time a man of the town and city." Hearing over, sentence
decided: all that's required is to complete or refine the account of this trial
which, all in all, was rapidly expedited. The professor is caught. Schapiro,
confirmed in his suspicion, can now reconstitute one of the possible mechanisms of the mistake, a mistake which is itself in the service of an instinctual
and political pathos (the rural, peasant "ideology"): a sort of resoling carried
out with the aid of the sole from another picture seen at the same exhibition
in 1930. That was the first mistake, the first trap, before the one set for the
professor by Schapiro to make up the pair and leave him no chance. This by
way of reply to the question put to me a moment ago: all the causes of this
trial will have been traps (as if figured in advance by the apparent stake of the
debate: to whom is the trap due?), pitfalls or, if you prefer, snares *[des lacets]*,
traps with laces. *Old Boots with Laces*, this is the title given by the large catalog
of the Tuileries exhibition (1971-72) (collection of the Vincent Van Gogh
National Museum in Amsterdam) to the picture which Professor Schapiro
claims to identify on the basis of Professor Heidegger's unwary reply, and
which he reproduces under the title *Old Shoes*. I do not yet know how much is
due to Van Gogh in the choice of this title. But as a certain essential indeterminacy forms part of our problem which is also the problem of the title and
the discourse produced (for example by the author) *on the subject* of the picture, it is perhaps right to leave the thing some suspense. The authors of the
catalog I just quoted took the de la Faille into account, the same de la Faille
which is Schapiro's authority ("The titles given by Vincent in his correspondence, and commonly adopted, have been made more specific when they
were not sufficiently explicit, whence some differences compared with either
the titles usual in the past, or those of the new Catalogue Raisonné by J. Baart
de la Faille . . ."). Whether named by Van Gogh or not, in a title or a letter,
these laces (for tightening or slackening the grip, more or less strictly, on the
bearing or borne subject) sketch out the very form of the trap. As fascinating
as they are (by that very fact) negligible for the two professors who make not
the slightest allusion to them. That's one of the causes: the lace. A thing

whose name is, in French, also the name of a trap [*le lacet*: "snare"]. It does not only stand for what passes through the eyelets of shoes or corsets. Our voices, in this very place— . . .

   b. The "same truth," that "presented" by the picture, is not for Heidegger "peasant" truth, a truth the essential content of which would depend on the attribution (however imprudent) of the shoes to peasantry. The "peasant" characteristic remains secondary here. The "same truth" could be "presented" by any shoe painting, or even by any experience of shoes and even of any "product" in general: the truth being that of a being-product coming back from "further away" than the matter-form couple, further away even than a "distinction between the two." This truth is due to a "more distant origin." It is not the truth of a *relationship* (of adequation or attribution) between such-and-such a product and such-and-such an owner, user, holder, bearer/wearer-borne. The belonging of the product "shoes" does not relate to a given *subjectum,* or even to a given world. What is said of belonging to the world and the earth is valid for the town and for the fields. Not indifferently, but equally.
   Thus Schapiro is mistaken about the primary function of the pictorial reference. He also gets wrong a Heideggerian argument which should ruin in advance his own restitution of the shoes to Van Gogh: art as "putting to work of truth" is neither an "imitation," nor a "description" copying the "real," nor a "reproduction," whether it represents a singular thing or a general essence. For the whole of Schapiro's case, on the other hand, calls on real shoes: the picture is supposed to imitate them, represent them, reproduce them. Their belonging has then to be determined as a belonging to a real or supposedly real subject, to an individual whose extremities, outside the picture, should not remain bare [*déchaussées*; also, "loose" (of teeth)] for long . . .

   —That's the whole dissymmetry, the innocent outbidding of this correspondence. One claim is more naïve, more excessive, if one can say that, than the other. One attribution exceeds the other. Imagine an auctioneer who is both an expert and a buyer, pushing up the bidding in the empty room. Bidding for secondhand, more or less unmatched shoes on a framed canvas. On the one hand, Schapiro's attribution remains in the aesthetics of representation, and even of the most empiricist kind: either short of (precritical), or going beyond (excessive), the movement carried out by *The Origin* in the passage just translated. But on his side, by saying *"Bauernschuhe"* without asking himself any questions about this, Heidegger falls short of his discourse on the truth in painting, and is even more naïve than Schapiro. Excessive to the extent of talking about peasants' shoes even before any question of "representation," and already in the order of a "presentative" truth. The fact is that the step backwards from a truth of adequation to a truth of unveiling, whatever its necessity and its "critical" force, can also leave one practically disarmed in the face of the ingenuous, the precritical, the dogmatic, in the face of any "preinvestment" (be it "fantasmatic," "ideological," etc., or whatever name you call it). There's a law here. This is perhaps one of the secrets of this correspondence, of its dissymmetry or its excessive symmetry: in the contract of truth ("I owe you the truth in painting"), between truth as adequation (of a representation, here an attributive one, on Schapiro's side) and the truth of unveiled presence (Heidegger's side). For the moment let us leave this truth contract, between the two truths. (What is *doing* the *contracting* there has to do with a *trait (Riss)* and an attraction *[attrait] (Zug)* of the work, with a *Gezüge*, which will draw us much further into Heidegger's text.) The truth of the shoes as things due (the object of the subject) constrains this correspondence and we ought (supposing one ever has to ought) to reexamine its terms later. One of the innumerable difficulties in reading *The Origin* and especially this passage, is that of grasping the furtive moment when a certain line is crossed, and of grasping too the step with which it is crossed. . . .

Shoes are used. *Das Zeugsein des Zeuges besteht in seiner Dienlichkeit,* "the being-product of the product resides in its usefulness," that's "what we know already."

—But when it comes to the usefulness proper to the shoes, Heidegger lets equivocality lie and in truth will never lift it, even when he claims to be recalling it in its most banal obviousness. He has said first of all that shoes *are used* to shoe the foot, to clothe it, to cover it *(dient zur Fussbekleidung)*. Referred to a given part of the body which is exposed (especially in its undersides) and which it is a matter of protecting, hiding (but why?), binding if not adorning (Heidegger is interested in this garment only by virtue of its *usefulness,* and in its usefulness only by virtue of walking and working, which will not be without its consequences), the shoe is not yet, in this first phase, posited as an instrument. Only as a *useful* garment. On the other hand, in the following paragraph, the peasant woman appears on the scene, and utilization is referred to the step, to walking, to upright station, and to work, in short, to feet in movement. As though a shoe without movement or contact with the ground, touching (in short) only the feet, lost its meaning and *all* usefulness. That isn't a contradiction, but by not insisting on the garment or at least on the garment outside work, on adornment, the postiche, on travesty or display investiture, on uses *other than* walking, or on using what is useless, one can be immobilized before two limits that are at least virtual. First, that of not understanding how the uselessness which will soon be in question can be "useful" (uselessness of the empty shoes, more or less loosened, out of step *[hors de marche];* and the picture itself out of use, taken out like the shoes it exhibits, the out-of-use here showing both out-of-use and use, the suspended use of the shoes "in" the suspended (hung) picture, and vice versa). Second, the so-called process of fetishization of the produced *and* the worked, of the shoes and the painting, cannot be *thematically* questioned in its already coded problematical zones (coded if only for the sake of criticizing them): the "sexual" and the "economic." *This* is where I would situate the stake of the pair, of the parity or the pairedness of the shoes. A pair of shoes is more easily treated as a *utility* than a single shoe or two shoes which aren't a pair. The pair inhibits at least, if it does not prevent, the "fetishizing" movement; it rivets things to use, to "normal" use; it shoes better and makes things walk according to the law. It is perhaps in order to exclude the question of a certain uselessness or of a so-called perverse usage, that Heidegger and Schapiro denied themselves the slightest doubt as to the parity or pairedness of these two shoes. They bound them together in order to bind them to the law of normal usage. They *bound*, chained, repressed the diabolical, that which would be diabolical about a duplicity without parity, a double without a pair. They ligatured a worrying dismemberment in order to limit it. This was a condition of their doing justice to the truth they thought they owed in painting. What would they have done, try to imagine it, with two shoes for the same foot, or with a shoe even more solitary than these two here? Would they have been able to produce the same discourse taking as their example certain shoes by Adami (especially that woman's shoe, you can't tell whether it's on or off, the heel remaining—though apparently uncovered—veiled by a stocking or rather by what, between stocking and shoe, like another undie, a supplementary undergarment in this striptease . . .) or Miró's *Nature morte au vieux soulier* (1973)? Or that (dead?) woman's shoe that Magritte entitles *La Lune*? Or *The Shoe* by Lindner? When you assure yourself of the thing as of a pair, when you forget that detachment also goes from one shoe to the other and divides the pair, you repress all these questions, you force them back into order. . . .

—This is an investigation that smells of the police. This reasoning around a pair of stolen or hijacked shoes is all the more understandable as coming from a private detective, a Dupin who wants finally to return the thing, to give back the shoes

—*the* shoe, perhaps, the double of the shoe which has made a pair for itself, the double's shoe. The spectral analysis of the internal separation of a pair, as I was proposing a moment ago, in five points, if—

—from a Dupin who wants to give the thing back to the rightful owner, to do homage with this restitution (adjusted to the shoe size of the princess), letting himself be trapped in turn, the more easily, I was saying, because this police discourse is fussing around nothing, all in all, remainders of nothing, vestiges, traces with neither presence nor absence on a soil without ground or on a foundered subsoil. *Fort, Da*: the shoe size plays with the comma.

—Elsewhere it's been written that it *can* always *not* arrive at its destination, it can always not *return* to port [*au port*, to a wearing]. That's what the condition of *revenance* is like. In "The Purveyor of Truth," replace the literal "letter" by a "shoe" and you will read: "This is what loses and risks, without guarantee of return, the restance of anything whatsoever: a shoe does not always arrive at its destination, and once that belongs to its structure, one can say that it never truly arrives there, that when it does arrive, its possibility-of-not-arriving torments it with an internal drift." One can fit this statement to the divisibility of a pair. No more than a letter, a pair is not indivisible.

—That's why, not speaking merely as a policeman but above all about police discourse, I did not say, like Heidegger, *they are* peasant shoes, but against him: *nothing proves that they are peasant shoes* (Schapiro's only incontestable proposition, in my view); and I did not say, like Schapiro, they are the shoes of a city dweller and even of Van Gogh, but against him: nothing proves or can prove that "they are the shoes of the artist, by that time a man of the town and city." Each time you read "they are clearly . . . ," "this is clearly . . . ," "are evidently . . . ," it does not signify that it is clear or evident, very much the contrary, but that it is necessary to deny the intrinsic obscurity of the thing, its essential crypt, and that it's necessary to make us believe that it is clear quite simply because the proof will always be lacking. "Clearly" and "evidently" bear first of all on the restitution of the shoes to Van Gogh, on the *ownership* of the shoes which supposedly revert *[reviendraient]* to him as his sole property (they are less prone to be fetishized as the thing of the other, something other, something else, for being old, familiar, worn, shaped to the foot, stained). I underline: "They are *clearly* pictures of the artist's *own* shoes, not the shoes of a peasant . . ." "*'a pair of old shoes'* which are *evidently* his *own*. . . ." Further on, "clearly" ensures the identification, this time, of a picture on the basis of a letter from Heidegger which made a surprising trajectory. We could speak of it as a prolonged diversion. "In reply to my question, Professor Heidegger has kindly written me that the picture to which he referred is one that he saw in a show at Amsterdam in March 1930. This is clearly de la Faille's no. 255. . . ." Why is this clear? Nothing is said about that. Is it because the catalog of this exhibition excluded any other possibility? Then why not say so? In that case the whole of the improbable and laborious demonstration that precedes would have been superfluous. And into the bargain, even if, setting out from Heidegger's reference (in his letter) to his reference (in his text) as identical to the reference (in his visit to the exhibition of 1930), even if these references were superimposable and left no doubt as to *this* picture (De la Faille no. 255), it would still be necessary to prove (1) that all peasantliness (if something of the sort existed in the matter of such shoes) was excluded from it, and (2) that these shoes were those of Van Gogh. But what we have said about the preceding paragraph ruins all possibility of proof in this regard.

His certainty seems all the more peremptory in its precision because immediately after having identified *the* picture, Schapiro has to evoke the possibility of a contamination between certain traits belonging to two paintings in Heidegger's reference: "There was also exhibited at the same time a painting with three pairs of shoes (6 no. 250), and it is possible that the exposed sole of a shoe in this picture inspired the reference to the sole in the philosopher's account. But from neither of these pictures, nor from any of the others, could one properly say that a painting of shoes by Van Gogh expresses the being or essence of a peasant woman's shoes and her relation to nature and work. They are the shoes of the artist, by that time a man of the town and city.". . . Identification (in all the senses of this word, and they are numerous), attribution, reappropriation: desire no longer has any limit. *First moment,* first demand: Schapiro considers the picture to be a "copy" and ignores an elementary structural law in inferring relations of property in the "reality" external to the painting, in the alleged model of the copy: not only, he says, does it not come back to peasant or peasant woman (and this is to jump too quickly, concluding from the improbable to the excluded) but they come back to a man, to a man who is a painter, to a painter who is the signatory of the painting, proprietor of his signature as much as of his shoes, which here *come back to the same (thing)*. *Second moment,* second demand: since this is not enough for a perfect restitution, the *real* wearer-holder-proprietor-signatory (so many accumulated values, so much augmented capital, for these meanings are added onto, not confused with, one another) of the *painted* shoes must be more defined, the shoe size must be more rigorous and the thing more securely fitted. The man to whom you're returning his goods must also be "man of the town and city." And this must, at a given moment ("by that time"), fix him in his essence, for, otherwise, why wouldn't he have played the peasant while living in the city? As if Van Gogh could not be from town *and* country, as if he could not keep in himself something of the peasant (or keep with him some peasant shoes: what exactly is that?) once he had become provisionally a city dweller! As if he could not paint peasant shoes while wearing town shoes! As if he could not paint, with his brushes, in bare feet! As if one painted shoes with one's shoes! For that is the third demand and the *third moment*: thus defined, the *real* proprietor, etc., of the *painted* shoes (an epithet which retains or produces the whole ambiguity of the relation between model and image) must be situated substantially in time and space. Once you've thought you could identify the picture that Heidegger meant, once you've attributed its subject (certain determinate shoes) to the subject (wearer, holder, proprietor, signatory artist, man, city dweller), it is still necessary that the painter, present *in a certain city on a certain date*, should have been unable to paint anything other than town shoes, the nearest ones *(Da!)* possible. Shoes painted *starting out from* shoes worn, which therefore *do not start out*, or at least don't go far, and are already back. Where? There. Where is there? There, look, here, here right now.

—And yet. Just like Heidegger, whom he quotes with irony on this point, Schapiro rules out the possibility that there might be the slightest "projection" on his own side. Sure of having scientifically determined the content and the origin of the painting (town shoes as the personal object of the painter), Schapiro has an easy time denouncing Heidegger's identificatory projection: Heidegger has annexed the shoes to his social landscape and hypercathected them with his "heavy pathos of the native and the countryman." He has done the very thing he was guarding against: he has "imagined everything and projected it into the painting.". . .

—You would say, then, that Schapiro, Heidegger, and a few others, when in front of the picture, very reasonably had a bet on the pair? That they gambled on the pair? And that they did so—(no) more bets—in order to avoid the risks of betting? Which they did not succeed in doing, since you have to reckon with the wager of the unconscious or the unconscious of the wager, if you prefer. Still (no) more bets. With the result that the trap always works in the interlace, or else causes to work/walk, lets walk, or paralyzes. (No) more bets, no bet, a betting step [pas de pari]. They bet on the pair, on comparison, on a wager that limits the risks of the *absolute* wager, which limits *itself* and *tightens itself* to the point of self-strangulation. To the point of tying itself so as not to absolve itself. For the cunning twist stems from the fact that the *absolute* bet must never exclude the disparate or *absolute* unevenness [l'impair]. So they bet, for good or ill, against the possibility of betting. We'll call *disparate* that which opens up the *fort: da* of shoe size, the play of dis/appearing, to the possibility of dis-pairing. To have tricked fate [Avoir fait marcher le destin; also, literally, to have made it walk or work], and to have provoked someone to make an impossible bet: that is what remains of Van Gogh's coup, the genius of his unevenness [son impair; also, "his blunder"].

JACQUES DERRIDA

Letter to Peter Eisenman *

My dear Peter,

I am simultaneously sending this letter, with the cassette that accompanies it, to Hillis, who must talk with us over the course of the anticipated meeting. As he must also moderate and enliven it, but for other reasons as well, Hillis is therefore, along with you, the first addressee of these questions. He understands better that any other the labyrinth, as we all know. And what I am going to say to you will probably reverberate in a sort of labyrinth. I am entrusting to the recording of the voice or the letter that which is not yet visible to me and cannot guide my steps toward an end/exist, that can barely guide them toward an "issue." I am not even sure myself whether what I am sending you holds up. But that is perhaps by design, and it is of this I plan to speak to you. In any case, I very much regret the necessity of depriving myself of this meeting with you, the two of you, all of you.

But now, do not worry, I am not going to argue with you. And I am not going to abuse my absence, not even to tell you that you perhaps believe in it, absence, too much. This reference to absence is perhaps one of the things (because there are others) that has most troubled me in your discourse on architecture, and if that were my first question you could perhaps profit from my absence to speak about it a little, about absence in general, about the role that this word "absence" will have been able to play at least in what you believed you could *say* if not *do* with your architecture. One could multiply

---

* Jacques Derrida, "A Letter to Peter Eisenman," in *Assemblage* (12), pp. 7-13. (Some changes have been made in spelling.)

examples, but I am limiting myself to what you say about the presence of an absence in *Moving Arrows Eros and Other Errors*, which concerns Romeo's chateau, "a palimpsest and a quarry," etc. This discourse on absence or the presence of an absence perplexes me not only because it bypasses so many tricks, complications, traps that the philosopher, especially if he is a bit of a dialectician, knows only too well and fears to find you caught up in again, but also because it has authorized many religious interpretations, not to mention vaguely judeo-transcendental ideologizations, of your work. I suspect a little that you liked and encouraged these interpretations even as you discreetly denied it with a smile, which would make a misunderstanding a little more or a little less than a misunderstanding. My question has to do not only with absence or the presence of absence, but with God. Voila, if I did not come it is not just because I am tired and overworked, held up in Paris, but precisely to have the opportunity to ask you directly a question about God that I would never have dared to do in Irvine if I had been present in person; instead, I am glad that this question comes to you by way of this voice, that is to say, on tape. The same question brings up others, a whole group of closely related questions. For example, at the risk of shocking you: Whether it has to do with houses, museums, or the laboratories of research universities, what distinguishes your architectural space from that of the temple, indeed of the synagogue (by this word I mean a Greek word used for a Jewish concept)? Where will the break, the rupture have been in this respect, if there is one, if there was one, for you and for other architects of this period with whom you feel yourself associated? I remain very perplexed about this subject and if I had been there I would have been a difficult interlocutor. If you were to construct a place of worship, Buddhist, for example, or a cathedral, a mosque, a synagogue (hypotheses that you are not obliged to accept), what would be your primary concern today? I will make allusion shortly to Libeskind's project in Berlin for a Jewish Museum. We spoke about this the other morning in New York, but let us leave that behind for the moment.

Naturally, this question concerns also your interpretation of *chora* in "our" "work," if one can say in quotations our work "in common." I am not sure that you have detheologized and deontologized *chora* in as radical a way as I would have wished (*chora* is neither the void, as you suggest sometimes, nor absence, nor invisibility, nor certainly the contrary from which there are, and this is what interests me, a large number of consequences). It is true that for me it was easier, in a certain way. I did not have anything to "do" with it and would not have been able to do anything with it, that is, for the city of Paris, for La Villette, the little city; you see what I mean (and the whole difference is perhaps between us). But I would like you to say something to our friends in Irvine, while speaking to them of the difference between our respective relations to discourse, on the one hand, and to the operation of architecture, to its putting into action, on the other hand. Profit from my absence in order to speak freely. But don't just say whatever, because as everything is being recorded today, and memory, always the same, not being at all the same, I will know all that you will have said publicly. I had the feeling, and I believe that you said it somewhere, that you have judged me to be too reserved, in our "choral work," a little bit absent, entrenched in discourse, without obliging you to change, to change place, without disturbing you enough. It is doubtless true that there would be a great deal to say about this subject, which is complicated because it is that of the place *(chora)* and of displacement itself. If I had come, I would have spoken perhaps of my own displacement in the course of "choral work" but here it is you who must speak. Therefore tell me whether *after Choral Work* (as you yourself said in Irvine in the spring) your work took, in effect, a new direction and engaged itself in other paths. What has happened? What for you is this period? this history? How does one determine the boundaries of it or put rhythm into it? When did we begin to work together, had we never done so, on this *Choral Work* that is not yet constructed but that one sees and reads everywhere? When will we stop?

This all brings me directly to the next question. It also concerns a certain absence. Not my absence today in Irvine where I would have so much liked to see you again along with other friends, even more so since I was one of those who had wished for and prepared this meeting (and I must ask you to forgive me and to make others forgive me); but absence like the shadowed sound of the voice—you see what I mean by this. What relations (new or archi-ancient, in any case different) does architecture, particularly yours, carry on, must it carry on, with the voice, the capacity of voice, but also therefore with telephonic machines of all sorts that structure and transform our experience of space every day? The question of the nearly immediate telephonic address, certainly *nearly* immediate, and I underline, but also the question of telephonic archivation, as is the case right here, with the spacing of time that telephonic archivation at once supposes and structures. If one can imagine a whole labyrinthlike history of architecture, guided by the entwined thread of this question, where would one be today and tomorrow, and you?

This question of history, as the history of spacing, like the spacing of time and voice, does not separate itself from the history of visibility (immediately mediate), that is to say, from all history of architecture; it is so great that I will not even dare to touch upon it, but will "address" this question, as you say in English, through economy and through metonymy, under the form of a single word, glass *(glas, glass)*.

What is there of glass in your work? What do you say about it? What do you do with it? How does one talk about it? In optical terms or in tactile terms? Regarding tactility, it would be good if, continuing what we were saying the other morning in New York, you would speak to our friends of the erotic tricks, of the calls of desire, do I dare say, of the sex appeal of the architectural forms about which you think, with which you work, to which you give yourself up. Whether its directions are new or not, does this seduction come as supplement, into the bargain, as precisely the "subsidy/bonus of seduction" or "subsidy/bonus of pleasure"? Or is it essential? Isn't the subsidy/bonus essential, at least? But, then, what would the subsidy/bonus *itself* be? Subsidy/Bonus? For the author of *Moving Arrows Eros and Other Errors*, what is the relation between subsidy/bonus and the rest in the calculations and the negotiations of the architect? As my American students sometimes disarmingly ask me, Could you elaborate on that? I return now to my question, after this long parenthesis on your desire, my question about glass that is not perhaps so far off. What terms do we use to speak about glass? Technical and material terms? Economic terms? The terms of urbanism? The terms of social relations? The terms of transparency and immediacy, of love or of police, of the border that is perhaps erased between the public and the private, etc.? "Glass" is an old word, and am I wrong if I believe that you are interested in glass, that you perhaps even like it? Does it only have to do with new materials that resemble glass but are no longer it, and so on? Before letting you speak about glass, I bring up a text by Benjamin, *Erfahrung und Armut*, which I'm sure you know (it also concerns architecture and was published in 1933, which is not just any date, in Germany or elsewhere). From it I extract at the outset only the following, on which our friends will certainly like to hear you comment.

> But Scheerbart—to return to him—most values that his people, and according to their model, his fellow citizens, live in apartments that correspond to their rank: in houses of moving and slippery glass, such as those that Loos and Le Corbusier have since erected. It is not for nothing that glass is such a hard and smooth material upon which nothing attaches itself. Also a cold and concise material. Things made of glass have no 'aura' *[Die Dinge aus Glas haben keine 'Aura']*. In general, glass is the enemy of secrecy. It is also the enemy of possession. The great poet Andre Gide once said, 'Each thing that I wish to possess becomes opaque for me.'

(Here we return to the question of desire and glass, of the desire of glass: I have elsewhere tried to follow this experience of desire as the experience of glass in Blanchot, especially in *La Folie du jour* and in *L'Arrêt de mort*.)

> Do people such as Scheerbart dream of glass masonry *[Glasbauten]* in order to have recognized a new poverty *[Bekenner einer neuen Armut]*? But perhaps a comparison here will reveal more than the theory. Upon entering a room of the eighties, and despite the 'comfortable intimacy' *['Gemütlichkeit']* that perhaps reigns there, the strongest impression will be, 'You have nothing to look for here.' You have nothing to look for here because there is no ground here upon which the inhabitant would not have already left his trace: by knickknacks on shelves, by doilies on the armchair, by the sheer curtains at the windows, or by the fire screen in front of the fireplace. A beautiful word from Brecht here helps us go far, farther: 'Erase your traces!' *[Verwisch die Spuren!]*, so says the refrain of the first poem in *Anthologie pour les habitants des villes*. . . . Scheerbart and his glass and the Bauhaus and its steel have opened the way: they have created spaces in which it is difficult to leave traces. 'After all that has been said,' declares Scheerbart twenty years later, 'we can easily speak of a "culture of glass" *["Glaskultur"]*. The new environ-

ment of glass will completely change man. And the only thing left to hope for now is that the new glass culture will not encounter too many opponents.'

What do you think, Peter, of these propositions? Would you be an "opponent," a supporter? Or, as I suppose, but perhaps wrongly, neither one nor the other? In any case, could you say something about it and why?

Benjamin's text speaks, as you have seen, of a "new poverty" (homonym if not synonym for a new expression, a new French concept, to designate a wandering group of poor people, indeed, of the "homeless," which is irreducible to categorizations, classifications, and former localizations of marginality or of the social ladder: the low income, the proletariat as a class, the unemployed, etc.). And the new poverty, the one about which Benjamin speaks, and none other, should be "our" future, already our present. From this fascinating text that is politically ambiguous and that must not be too fragmented, I extract the following:

> Scheerbart is interested in the question of knowing what our telescopes, our airplanes, and our rockets do to men of the past in transforming them into completely new creatures, worthy of notice and affection. Furthermore, these creatures already speak in an entirely new language. And what is Decisive *[das Entscheidende]* in this language is the tendency toward the Arbitrary Construct *[zum willkürlichen Konstruktiven]*, a tendency that particularly resists the organic. It is through this tendency that the language of these men, or rather of Scheerbart's people, cannot be confused with any other; because these people object to this principle of humanism that calls for the correspondence with humans. Even up to their proper names. . . . Poverty of experience *[Erfahrungsarmut]*: one must not understand by this that these men desire a 'New Experience.' No, they want to liberate themselves from experience, they want a world in which they can make their poverty be recognized—the exterior and eventually also the interior—in such a pure and distinct way that something decent comes of it. And they are not always ignorant and inexperienced. One can say the opposite: they have consumed *[gefressen]* all of that, 'culture' and 'man' until they are satiated and tired. . . . We have become impoverished. We have abandoned one piece after another of the heritage of humanity and often we should have wagered it to Mont-de-Piété [the Mount of Piety] for a hundredth of its value, in order to receive as an advance the few coins of the 'Present' *[des 'Aktuellen']*. In the door stands economic crisis, behind her a shadow, the war to come. Today, to attach oneself to something has become the business of the small number of the powerful, and God knows whether they are not more human than the majority; for the most part more barbarous, but not in the good sense *[nicht auf die gute Art]*. The others, however, must settle in once again and with Little. They relate it to the men who created the Fundamentally New *[das von Grund auf Neue zu ihrer Sache gemacht]*, and who founded it upon understanding and self-denial. In its buildings *[Bauten]*, its paintings, and its histories, humanity prepares itself to outlive *[überleben]*, if necessary, culture. And most important, humanity does this while laughing. Perhaps this laughter here and there sounds barbarous. Good

(Gut). Therefore let he who is an individual *[der Einzelne]* occasionally give a little humanity to the mass, which one day will return it to him with interest. (trans. Ph. Beck and B. Stiegler)

What do you think of this text, Peter, in particular of a poverty that *should* not cause another one to be forgotten? What do you think of these two barbarities that must not be confused and as much as possible—is it possible?—must not be allowed to contaminate each other? What do you think of what Benjamin called the "present" and of his "few coins"? What, for you, would be "good" barbarity in architecture and elsewhere? And the "present"? I know that there is a present that you do not want, but what best breaks (today? tomorrow?) with this present? And you who want to abstract architecture in proportion to man, in proportion even to his scale, how do you understand this "destructive," in Benjamin's sense, discourse in the mouth of "these people [who] object to this principle of humanism that calls for [architecture's] correspondence with humans. Even up to their proper names."?

Therefore, Peter, I would like, and your listeners in Irvine, I imagine, will perhaps like, to hear you speak about the relations between architecture today and poverty. All poverties, the one about which Benjamin speaks and the other; between architecture and capital (the equivalent today of the "economic crisis" occurring in 1930 *"in der Tur,"* in the "opening of the door"); between architecture and war (the equivalent today of the "shadow" and of what "comes" with it); the scandals surrounding social housing, "housing" in general (not without recalling what we have both said, which is a little too complicated for a letter, of the habitable and the inhabitable in architecture), and the "homeless," "homelessness" today in the United States and elsewhere.

This letter is already too long. I shall speed up a little to link schematically other questions or requests to the preceding ones. I cited this text by Benjamin, among other reasons, to lead you to ruin and to destruction. As you know, what he says about "aura" destroyed by glass (and by technology in general) is articulated in a difficult discourse on "destruction." In the *Trauerspiel* (and certainly elsewhere but I don't remember where anymore), Benjamin talks about the ruin, especially about the "baroque cult of the ruin," "the most noble matter of baroque creation." In the photocopied pages I am sending you, Benjamin declares that for the baroque "the ancient inheritance is comparable, in each one of its components, to the elements from which is concocted the new totality. No, they build it. Because the achieved vision of this new thing is that: the ruin. . . . The work [of art] confirms itself as ruin. In the allegoric edifice of the *Trauerspiel,* these ruined forms of the salvaged work of art clearly have always already come unfastened." I will say nothing about Benjamin's concept of the ruin, which is also the concept of a certain mourning in affirmation, indeed the salvation of the work of art; I will, however, use this as a pretext to ask you the following.

First, is there a relationship between your writing of the palimpsest, your architectural experience of memory (in *Choral Work,* for example, but also everywhere else), and "something" like the ruin that is no longer a thing? In what way would you say, and would you say it, is your calculation, reckoning, of memory not baroque in this Benjaminian sense, despite some appearances? Second, if all architecture is finished, if therefore it carries within itself the traces of its future destruction, the already past future, future perfect, of its ruin, according to methods that are each time original, if it is haunted, indeed signed, by the spectral silhouette of this ruin, at work even in the pedestal of its stone, in its metal or its glass, what would again bring the architecture of "the period" (just yesterday, today, tomorrow; use whatever words you want, modern, postmodern, post-postmodern, or amodern, etc.) back to the ruin, to the experience of "its own" ruin? In the past, great architectural inventions constituted their essential destructability, even their fragility, as a resistance to destruction or as a monumentalization of the ruin itself (the baroque according to Benjamin, right?). Is a new image of the ruin to come already sketching itself in the design of the architecture that we would like to recognize as the architecture of our present, of our future, if one can still say that, in the design of your architecture, in the past future, the future perfect, of its memory, so that it already draws and calculates itself, so that it already leaves its future trace in your projects? Taking into account what we were saying previously about Man (and God), will we again be able to speak of "the memory of man," as we say in French, for this architecture? In relation to the ruin, to fragility, to destructibility, in other words, to the future, could you return to what we were talking about the other morning in New York, about excess and "weakness"? Every time that excess presents itself (it never presents itself except above and beyond ontological oppositions), for my part, I hesitate to use words of force or of weakness. But it is certainly inevitable as soon as there is announcement. This is nothing more than a pretext so that *you* talk about it, Hillis and you.

Finally, from fragility I turn to ashes, for me the other name or the surname for the essence (not the essential) of the step, of the trace, of writing, the place without place of deconstruction. There where deconstruction inscribes itself. (In "Feu la cendre"—excuse my reference to something that dates from nearly twenty years ago—this conception of ashes, as the trace itself, was principally reserved for, or rather entrusted to, the "burn everything" and to the "holocaust.") To return to our problem and to hear again the fragile words of "fragility," of "ashes," of "absence," or "invisibility," of "Jewish" or not "Jewish" architectural space, what do you think of the Berlin Museum Competition, about which we also spoke the other morning in New York? In particular, what do you think of the words of Libeskind, the "winner" of the "competition," as printed in a recently published interview with him in the newsletter of the architecture school at Columbia? Here I must content myself with quoting:

> And in turn the void materializes itself in the space outside as something that has been ruined, or rather as the solid remainder of an independent structure,

which is a voided void. Then there is a fragmentation and a splintering, marking the lack of coherence of the museum as a whole, showing that it has come undone in order to become accessible, functionally and intellectually. . . . It's conceived as a museum for all Berliners, for all citizens. Not only those of the present, but those of the future and the past who must find their heritage and hope in this particular form, which is to transcend passive involvement and become participation. With its special emphasis on housing the Jewish Museum, it is an attempt to give a voice to a common fate—to the contradictions of the ordered and disordered, the chosen and the not chosen, the vocal and the silent. In that sense, the particular urban condition of Lindenstrasse, of this area of the city, becomes the spiritual site, the nexus, where Berlin's precarious destiny is mirrored. It is fractured and displaced, but also transformed and transgressed. The past fatality of the German Jewish cultural relation to Berlin is enacted now in the realm of the invisible. It is this invisibility which I have tried to bring to visibility. So the new extension is conceived as an emblem, where the invisible, the void, makes itself apparent as such. . . . It's not a collage or a collision or a dialectic simply, but a new type of organization which is really organized around a void, around what is not visible. And what is not visible is the collection of this Jewish Museum, which is reducible to archival material, since the physicality of it has disappeared. The problem of the Jewish Museum is taken as the problem of Jewish culture itself—let's put it this way, as the problem of an avant-garde of humanity, an avant-garde that has been incinerated in its own history, in the Holocaust. In this sense, I believe this scheme joins architecture to questions that are now relevant to all humanity. What I've tried to say is that the Jewish history of Berlin is not separable from the history of modernity, from the destiny of this incineration of history; they are bound together. But bound not through any obvious forms, but rather through a negativity; through an absence of meaning and an absence of artifacts. Absence, therefore, serves as a way of binding in depth, and in a totally different manner, the shared hopes of people. It is a conception that is absolutely opposed to reducing the museum to a detached memorial.

Once again void, absence, negativity, in Libeskind as in you. I leave you alone to deal with these words, dear Peter, dear Hillis; I will tell you what I think some other time, but I suggested what I think at the beginning. Once again I have spoken too much and naturally I abuse my absence. I admit it as a sign of love. Forgive me, Hillis and you, and ask our friends, your listeners, to forgive me for not being there to speak with them and to listen to you.

Affectionately,
Jacques

P.S. 1. This tape was recorded and this transcription finished when I read, at the end of an interview (in the special edition of the Spanish magazine *Arquitectura* devoted to "Deconstruction" [270]—it's the title of the introduction), the following lines from you that were already anticipating my questions: "I never talk about deconstruction. Other people use that word because they are not architects. It is very difficult to talk about architecture in terms of deconstruction, because we are not talking about ruins or fragments. The term is too metaphorical and too literal for architecture. Deconstruction is dealing with architecture as a metaphor, and we are dealing with architecture as a reality. . . . I believe poststructuralism is basically what I mean by postmodernism. In other words, postmodernism is poststructuralism in the widest sense of the word." I certainly believe that I would *not* subscribe to *any* one of these statements, to *any* one of these 7 sentences, neither to 1 nor to 2 nor to 3 nor to 4 nor to 5 nor to 6 nor to 7. But I cannot explain it here and I, truly, never talk much *about* deconstruction. Not spontaneously. If you wish, you could display 1, 2, 3, 4, 5, 6, 7 before the listeners and try to convince them by refuting the contrary propositions or you could let this postscript fall to the side.

P.S. 2. I was certainly forgetting the fundamental question. In other words, the question of foundation, of what you do at the foundation of the foundation or at the foundation of the foundation in your architectural design. Let's talk fundamentally about Earth itself. I have questioned you in a noncircuitous fashion about God and Man. I was thinking about the Sky and the Earth. What does architecture, and primarily yours, have to see and do with *experience*, that is to say, with the voyage that makes its way outside of Earth? Then, if we don't give up architecture, and I believe that we are not giving it up, what are the effects on "design" itself of terrestrial architecture, of this possibility? Of this definite possibility from now on of leaving the terrestrial soil? Will we say that the architecture of a rocket and of astronomy in general (already announced by literature, at least, and long before becoming "effective"), that they dispense with foundations and thus of "standing up," of *the* "standing up," of the *vertical* stance of man, of the building in general? Or do these architectures (of rockets and astronomy in general) recalculate foundations and does the calculation remain a terrestrial *difference*, something which I somewhat doubt? What would be an architecture that, without holding, without standing upright, vertically, would not fall again into ruin? How do all these possibilities and even questions (those of holding up, holding together, standing or not) record themselves, if you think that they do? What traces do they leave in what you would build right now in Spain, in Japan, in Ohio, in Berlin, in Paris, and, tomorrow, I hope, in Irvine?

MICHEL FOUCAULT

ONE OF THE MOST IMPORTANT of recent Continental writers, Foucault is best known for his analysis of the relations among knowledge, power, and discourse—the ways in which the language we use to describe social phenomena (madness, sexuality, punishment, art, . . .) plays a pervasive political role and is effectively an instrument of domination. There is, Foucault argues, no politically neutral form of expression or understanding. The main selection here is one of his rare applications of his theory to visual art. It is accompanied by a brief selection in which he explains his methods and aims. "Las Meninas" is the first chapter in *The Order of Things*, a work concerned with the relation between language and representation. Foucault takes *Las Meninas* to present us with the absent figure of representation, invisible in the painting, the sovereign subject, "Man," that makes representation possible.

MICHEL FOUCAULT

The Order of Things *

PREFACE

The fundamental codes of a culture—those governing its language, its schemas of perception, its exchanges, its techniques, its values, the hierarchy of its practices—establish for every man, from the very first, the empirical orders with which he will be dealing and within which he will be at home. At the other extremity of thought, there are the scientific theories or the philosophical interpretations which explain why order exists in general, what universal law it obeys, what principle can account for it, and why this particular order has been established and not some other. But between these two regions, so distant from one another, lies a domain which, even though its role is mainly an intermediary one, is nonetheless fundamental: it is more confused, more obscure, and probably less easy to analyze. It is here that a culture, imperceptibly deviating from the empirical orders prescribed for it by its primary codes, instituting an initial separation from them, causes them to lose their original transparency, relinquishes its immediate and invisible powers, frees itself sufficiently to discover that these orders are perhaps not the only possible ones or the best ones; this culture then finds itself faced with the stark fact that there exists, below the level of its spontaneous orders, things that are in themselves capable of being ordered, that belong to a certain unspoken order; the fact, in short, that order *exists*. As though emancipating itself to some extent from its linguistic, perceptual, and practical grids, the culture superimposed on them another kind of grid which neutralized them,

---

* Michel Foucault, *The Order of Things* (New York: Random House, 1970), pp. xx-xxii, 3-16.

which by this superimposition both revealed and excluded them at the same time, so that the culture, by this very process, came face to face with order in its primary state. It is on the basis of this newly perceived order that the codes of language, perception, and practice are criticized and rendered partially invalid. It is on the basis of this order, taken as a firm foundation, that general theories as to the ordering of things, and the interpretation that such an ordering involves, will be constructed. Thus, between the already "encoded" eye and reflexive knowledge there is a middle region which liberates order itself: it is here that it appears, according to the culture and the age in question, continuous and graduated or discontinuous and piecemeal, linked to space or constituted anew at each instant by the driving force of time, related to a series of variables or defined by separate systems of coherences, composed of resemblances which are either successive or corresponding, organized around increasing differences, etc. This middle region, then, in so far as it makes manifest the modes of being of order, can be posited as the most fundamental of all: anterior to words, perceptions, and gestures, which are then taken to be more or less exact, more or less happy, expressions of it (which is why this experience of order in its pure primary state always plays a critical role); more solid, more archaic, less dubious, always more "true" than the theories that attempt to give those expressions explicit form, exhaustive application, or philosophical foundation. Thus, in every culture, between the use of what one might call the ordering codes and reflections upon order itself, there is the pure experience of order and of its modes of being.

The present study is an attempt to analyse that experience. I am concerned to show its developments, since the sixteenth century, in the mainstream of a culture such as ours: in what way, as one traces—against the current, as it were—language as it has been spoken, natural creatures as they have been perceived and grouped together, and exchanges as they have been practised; in what way, then, our culture has made manifest the existence of order, and how, to the modalities of that order, the exchanges owed their laws, the living beings their constants, the words their sequence and their representative value; what modalities of order have been recognized, posited, linked with space and time, in order to create the positive basis of knowledge as we find it employed in grammar and philology, in natural history and biology, in the study of wealth and political economy. Quite obviously, such an analysis does not belong to the history of ideas or of science: it is rather an inquiry whose aim is to rediscover on what basis knowledge and theory became possible; within what space of order knowledge was constituted; on the basis of what historical *a priori*, and in the element of what positivity, ideas could appear, sciences be established, experience be reflected in philosophies, rationalities be formed, only, perhaps, to dissolve and vanish soon afterwards. I am not concerned, therefore, to describe the progress of knowledge towards an objectivity in which today's science can finally be recognized; what I am attempting to bring to light is the epistemological field, the *episteme* in which knowledge, envisaged apart from all criteria having reference to its rational value or to its objective forms, grounds its positivity and thereby manifests a history which is not that of its growing perfection, but rather that of its conditions of possibility; in this account, what should appear are those configurations within the *space* of knowledge which have given rise to the diverse forms of empirical science. Such an enterprise is not so much a history, in the traditional meaning of that word, as an "archaeology."[1]

LAS MENINAS

1. The painter is standing a little back from his canvas. He is glancing at his model; perhaps he is considering whether to add some finishing touch, though it is also possible that the first stroke has not yet been made. The arm holding the brush is bent to the left, towards the palette; it is motionless, for an instant, between canvas and paints. The skilled hand is suspended in mid-air, arrested in rapt attention on the painter's gaze; and the gaze, in return, waits upon the arrested gesture. Between the fine point of the brush and the steely gaze, the scene is about to yield up its volume.

But not without a subtle system of feints. By standing back a little, the painter has placed himself to one side of the painting on which he is working. That is, for the spectator at present observing him he is to the right of his canvas, while the latter, the canvas, takes up the whole of the extreme left. And the canvas has its back turned to that spectator: he can see nothing of it but the reverse side, together with the huge frame on which it is stretched. The painter, on the other hand, is perfectly visible in his full height; or at any rate, he is not masked by the tall canvas which may soon absorb him, when, taking a step towards it again, he returns to his task; he has no doubt just appeared, at this very instant, before the eyes of the spectator, emerging from what is virtually a sort of vast cage projected backwards by the surface he is painting. Now he can be seen, caught in a moment of stillness, at the neutral centre of this oscillation. His dark torso and bright face are half-way between the visible and the invisible: emerging from that canvas beyond our view, he moves into our gaze; but when, in a moment, he makes a step to the right, removing himself from our gaze, he will be standing exactly in front of the canvas he is painting; he will enter that region where his painting, neglected for an instant, will, for him, become visible once more, free of shadow and free of reticence. As though the painter could not at the same time be seen on the picture where he is represented and also see that upon which he is representing something. He rules at the threshold of those two incompatible visibilities.

The painter is looking, his face turned slightly and his head leaning towards one shoulder. He is staring at a point to which, even though it is invisible, we, the spectators, can easily assign an object, since it is we, ourselves, who are that point: our bodies, our faces, our eyes. The spectacle he is observing is thus doubly invisible: first, because it is not represented within the space of the painting, and, second, because it is situated precisely in that blind point, in that essential hiding-place into which our gaze disappears from ourselves at the moment of our actual looking. And yet, how could we fail to see that invisibility, there in front of our eyes, since it has its own perceptible equivalent, its sealed-in figure, in the painting itself? We could, in effect, guess what it is the painter is looking at if it were possible for us to glance for a moment at the canvas he is working on; but all we can see of that canvas is its texture, the horizontal and vertical bars of the stretcher, and the obliquely rising foot of the easel. The tall, monotonous rectangle occupying the whole left portion of the real picture, and representing the back of the canvas within the picture, reconstitutes in the form of a surface the invisibility in depth of what the artist is observing: that space in which we are, and which we are. From the eyes of the painter to what he is observing there runs a compelling line that we, the onlookers, have no power of evading: it runs through the real picture and emerges from its surface to join the place from which we see the painter observing us; this dotted line reaches out to us ineluctably, and links us to the representation of the picture.

In appearance, this locus is a simple one; a matter of pure reciprocity: we are looking at a picture in which the painter is in turn looking out at us. A mere confrontation, eyes catching one another's glance, direct looks super-imposing themselves upon one another as they cross. And yet this slender line of reciprocal visibility embraces a whole complex network of uncertainties, exchanges, and feints. The painter is turning his eyes towards us only in so far as we happen to occupy the same position as his subject. We, the spectators, are an additional factor. Though greeted by that gaze, we are also dismissed by it, replaced by that which was always there before we were: the model itself. But, inversely, the painter's gaze, addressed to the void confronting him out-side the picture, accepts as many models as there are spectators; in this precise but neutral place, the observer and the observed take part in a ceaseless exchange. No gaze is stable, or rather, in the neutral furrow of the gaze pierc-ing at a right angle through the canvas, subject and object, the spectator and the model, reverse their roles to infinity. And here the great canvas with its back to us on the extreme left of the picture exercises its second function: stubbornly invisible, it prevents the relation of these gazes from ever being dis-coverable or definitely established. The opaque fixity that it establishes on one side renders forever unstable the play of metamorphoses established in the centre between spectator and model. Because we can see only that reverse side, we do not know who we are, or what we are doing. Seen or seeing? The painter is observing a place which, from moment to moment, never ceases to change its content, its form, its face, its identity. But the attentive immobility of his eyes refers us back to another direction which they have often followed already, and which soon, there can be no doubt, they will take again: that of the motionless canvas upon which is being traced, has already been traced per-haps, for a long time and forever, a portrait that will never again be erased. So that the painter's sovereign gaze commands a virtual triangle whose outline defines this picture of a picture: at the top—the only visible corner—the painter's eyes; at one of the base angles, the invisible place occupied by the model; at the other base angle, the figure probably sketched out on the invis-ible surface of the canvas.

As soon as they place the spectator in the field of their gaze, the painter's eyes seize hold of him, force him to enter the picture, assign him a place at once privileged and inescapable, levy their luminous and visible tribute from him, and project it upon the inaccessible surface of the canvas within the picture. He sees his invisibility made visible to the painter and transposed into an image forever invisible to himself. A shock that is augmented and made more inevitable still by a marginal trap. At the extreme right, the picture is lit by a window represented in very sharp perspective; so sharp that we can see scarcely more than the embrasure; so that the flood of light streaming through it bathes at the same time, and with equal generosity, two neighboring spaces, overlapping but irreducible: the surface of the painting, together with the volume it represents (which is to say, the painter's studio, or the salon in which his easel is now set up), and, in front of that surface, the real volume occupied by the spectator (or again, the unreal site of the model). And as it passes through the room from right to left, this vast flood of golden light carries both the spectator towards the painter and the model towards the canvas; it is this light too, which, washing over the painter, makes him visible to the spectator and turns into golden lines, in the model's eyes, the frame of that enigmatic canvas on which his image, once transported there, is to be imprisoned. This extreme, partial, scarcely indicated window frees a whole flow of daylight which serves as the common locus of the representation. It balances the invisible canvas on the other side of the picture: just as that canvas, by turning its back to the spectators, folds itself in against the picture representing it, and forms, by the superimposition of its reverse and visible side upon the surface of the picture depicting it, the ground, inaccessible to us, on which there shimmers the Image *par excellence*, so does the window, a pure aperture, establish a space as manifest as the other is hidden; as much the common ground of painter, figures, models, and spectators, as the other is solitary (for no one is looking at it, not even the painter). From the right, there streams in through an invisible window the pure volume of a light that renders all representation visible; to the left extends the surface that conceals, on the other side of its all too visible woven texture, the representation it bears. The light, by flooding the scene (I mean the room as well as the canvas, the room represented on the canvas, and the room in which the canvas stands), envelops the figures and the spectators and carries them with it, under the painter's gaze, towards the place where his brush will represent them. But that place is concealed from us. We are observing ourselves being observed by the painter, and made visible to his eyes by the same light that enables us to see him. And just as we are about to apprehend ourselves, transcribed by his hand as though in a mirror, we find that we can in fact apprehend nothing of that mirror but its lustreless back. The other side of a psyche.

Now, as it happens, exactly opposite the spectators—ourselves—on the wall forming the far end of the room, Velázquez has represented a series of pictures; and we see that among all those hanging canvases there is one that shines with particular brightness. Its frame is wider and darker than those of the others; yet there is a fine white line around its inner edge diffusing over its whole surface a light whose source is not easy to determine; for it comes from nowhere, unless it be from a space within itself. In this strange light, two silhouettes are apparent, while above them, and a little behind them, is a heavy purple curtain. The other pictures reveal little more than a few paler patches buried in a darkness without depth. This particular one, on the other hand, opens onto a perspective of space in which recognizable forms recede from us in a light that belongs only to itself. Among all these elements intended to provide representations, while impending them, hiding them, concealing them because of their position or their distance from us, this is the only one that fulfills its function in all honesty and enables us to see what it is supposed to show. Despite its distance from us, despite the shadows all around it. But it isn't a picture: it is a mirror. It offers us at last that enchantment of the double that until now has been denied us, not only by the distant paintings but also by the light in the foreground with its ironic canvas.

Of all the representations represented in the picture this is the only one visible; but no one is looking at it. Upright beside his canvas, his attention entirely taken up by his model, the painter is unable to see this looking-glass shining so softly behind him. The other figures in the picture are also, for the most part, turned to face what must be taking place in front—towards the bright invisibility bordering the canvas, towards that balcony of light where their eyes can gaze at those who are gazing back at them, and not towards that dark recess which marks the far end of the room in which they are represented. There are, it is true, some heads turned away from us in profile: but not one of them is turned far enough to see, at the back of the room, that solitary mirror, that tiny glowing rectangle which is nothing other than visibility, yet without any gaze able to grasp it, to render it actual, and to enjoy the suddenly ripe fruit of the spectacle it offers.

It must be admitted that this indifference is equalled only by the mirror's own. It is reflecting nothing, in fact, of all that is there in the same space as itself: neither the painter with his back to it, nor the figures in the centre of the room. It is not the visible it reflects, in those bright depths. In Dutch painting it was traditional for mirrors to play a duplicating role: they repeated the original contents of the picture, only inside an unreal, modified, contracted, concave space. One saw in them the same things as one saw in the first instance in the painting, but decomposed and recomposed according to a different law. Here, the mirror is saying nothing that has already been said before. Yet its position is more or less completely central: its upper edge is exactly on an imaginary line running half-way between the top and the bottom of the painting, it hangs right in the middle of the far wall (or at least in the middle of the portion we can see); it ought, therefore, to be governed by the same lines of perspective as the picture itself; we might well expect the same studio, the same painter, the same canvas to be arranged within it according to an identical space; it could be the perfect duplication.

In fact, it shows us nothing of what is represented in the picture itself. Its motionless gaze extends out in front of the picture, into that necessarily invisible region which forms its exterior face, to apprehend the figures arranged in that space. Instead of surrounding visible objects, this mirror cuts straight through the whole field of the representation, ignoring all it might apprehend within that field, and restores visibility to that which resides outside all view. But the invisibility that it overcomes in this way is not the invisibility of what is hidden: it does not make its way around any obstacle, it is not distorting any perspective, it is addressing itself to what is invisible both because of the picture's structure and because of its existence as painting. What it is reflecting is that which all the figures within the painting are looking at so fixedly, or at least those who are looking straight ahead; it is therefore what the spectator would be able to see if the painting extended further forward, if its bottom edge were brought lower until it included the figures the painter is using as models. But it is also, since the picture does stop there, displaying only the painter and his studio, what is exterior to the picture, in so far as it is a picture—in other words, a rectangular fragment of lines and colours intended to represent something to the eyes of any possible spectator. At the far end of the room, ignored by all, the unexpected mirror holds in its glow the figures that the painter is looking at (the painter in his represented, objective reality, the reality of the painter at his work); but also the figures that are looking at the painter (in that material reality which the lines and the colours have laid out upon the canvas). These two groups of figures are both equally inaccessible, but in different ways: the first because of an effect of composition peculiar to the painting; the second because of the law that presides over the very existence of all pictures in general. Here, the action of representation consists in bringing one of these two forms of invisibility into the place of the other, in an unstable superimposition—and in rendering them both, at the same moment, at the other extremity of the picture—at that pole which is the very height of its representation: that of a reflected depth in the far recess of the painting's depth. The mirror provides a metathesis of visibility that affects both the space represented in the picture and its nature as representation; it allows us to see, in the centre of the canvas, what in the painting is of necessity doubly invisible.

A strangely literal, though inverted, application of the advice given, so it is said, to his pupil by the old Pachero when the former was working in his studio in Seville: "The image should stand out from the frame."

2. But perhaps it is time to give a name at last to that image which appears in the depths of the mirror, and which the painter is contemplating in front of the picture. Perhaps it would be better, once and for all, to determine the identities of all the figures presented or indicated here, so as to avoid embroiling ourselves forever in those vague, rather abstract designations, so constantly prone to misunderstanding and duplication, "the painter," "the characters," "the models," "the spectators," "the images." Rather than pursue to infinity a language inevitably inadequate to the visible fact, it would be better to say that Velázquez composed a picture; that in this picture he represented himself, in his studio or in a room of the Escurial, in the act of painting two figures whom the Infanta Margarita has come there to watch, together with an entourage of duennas, maids of honour, courtiers, and dwarfs; that we can

attribute names to this group of people with great precision: tradition recognizes that here we have Doña Maria Agustina Sarmiente, over there Nieto, in the foreground Nicolaso Pertusato, an Italian jester. We could then add that the two personages serving as models to the painter are not visible, at least directly; but that we can see them in a mirror; and that they are, without any doubt, King Philip IV and his wife, Mariana.

These proper names would form useful landmarks and avoid ambiguous designations; they would tell us in any case what the painter is looking at, and the majority of the characters in the picture along with him. But the relation of language to painting is an infinite relation. It is not that words are imperfect, or that, when confronted by the visible, they prove insuperably inadequate. Neither can be reduced to the other's terms: it is in vain that we say what we see; what we see never resides in what we say. And it is in vain that we attempt to show, by the use of images, metaphors, or similes, what we are saying; the space where they achieve their splendour is not that deployed by our eyes but that defined by the sequential elements of syntax. And the proper name, in this particular context, is merely an artifice: it gives us a finger to point with, in other words, to pass surreptitiously from the space where one speaks to the space where one looks; in other words, to fold one over the other as though they were equivalents. But if one wishes to keep the relation of language to vision open, if one wishes to treat their incompatibility as a starting-point for speech instead of as an obstacle to be avoided, so as to stay as close as possible to both, then one must erase those proper names and preserve the infinity of the task. It is perhaps through the medium of this grey, anonymous language, always over-meticulous and repetitive because too broad, that the painting may, little by little, release its illuminations.

We must therefore pretend not to know who is to be reflected in the depths of that mirror, and interrogate that reflection in its own terms.

First, it is the reverse of the great canvas represented on the left. The reverse, or rather the right side, since it displays in full face what the canvas, by its position, is hiding from us. Furthermore, it is both in opposition to the window and a reinforcement of it. Like the window, it provides a ground which is common to the painting and to what lies outside it. But the window operates by the continuous movement of an effusion which, flowing from right to left, unites the attentive figures, the painter, and the canvas, with the spectacle they are observing; whereas the mirror, on the other hand, by means of a violent, instantaneous movement, a movement of pure surprise, leaps out from the picture in order to reach that which is observed yet invisible in front of it, and then, at the far end of its fictitious depth, to render it visible yet indifferent to every gaze. The compelling tracer line, joining the reflection to that which it is reflecting, cuts perpendicularly through the lateral flood of light. Lastly—and this is the mirror's third function—it stands adjacent to a doorway which forms an opening, like the mirror itself, in the far wall of the room. This doorway too forms a bright and sharply defined rectangle whose soft light does not shine through into the room. It would be nothing but a gilded panel if it were not recessed out from the room by means of one leaf of a carved door, the curve of a curtain, and the shadows of several steps. Beyond the steps, a corridor begins; but instead of losing itself in obscurity, it is dissipated in a yellow dazzle where the light, without coming in, whirls around on itself in dynamic repose. Against this background, at once near and limitless, a man stands out in full-length silhouette; he is seen in profile; with one hand he is holding back the weight of a curtain; his feet are placed on different steps; one knee is bent. He may be about to enter the room; or he may be merely observing what is going on inside it, content to surprise those within without being seen himself. Like the mirror, his eyes are directed towards the other side of the scene; nor is anyone paying any more attention to him than to the mirror. We do not know where he has come from: it could be that by following uncertain corridors he has just made his way around the outside of the room in which these characters are collected and the painter is at work; perhaps he too, a short while ago, was there in the forefront of the scene, in the invisible region still being contemplated by all those eyes in the picture. Like the images perceived in the looking-glass, it is possible that he too is an emissary from that evident yet hidden space. Even so, there is a difference: he is there in flesh and blood; he has appeared from the outside, on the threshold of the area represented; he is indubitable—not a probable reflection but an irruption. The mirror, by making visible, beyond even the walls of the studio itself, what is happening in front of the picture, creates, in its sagittal dimension, an oscillation between the interior and the exterior. One foot only on the lower step, his body entirely in profile, the ambiguous visitor is coming in and going out at the same time, like a pendulum caught at the bottom of its swing. He repeats on the spot, but in the dark reality of his body, the instantaneous movement of those images flashing across the room, plunging into the mirror, being reflected there, and springing out from it again like visible, new, and identical species. Pale, minuscule, those silhouetted figures in the mirror are challenged by the tall, solid stature of the man appearing in the doorway.

But we must move down again from the back of the picture towards the front of the stage; we must leave that periphery whose volute we have just been following. Starting from the painter's gaze, which constitutes an off-centre centre to the left, we perceive first of all the back of the canvas, then the paintings hung on the wall, with the mirror in their centre, then the open doorway, then more pictures, of which, because of the sharpness of the perspective, we can see no more than the edges of the frames, and finally, at the extreme right, the window, or rather the groove in the wall from which the light is pouring. This spiral shell presents us with the entire cycle of representation: the gaze, the palette and brush, the canvas innocent of signs (these are the material tools of representation), the paintings, the reflections, the real man (the completed representation, but as it were freed from its illusory or truthful contents, which are juxtaposed to it); then the representation dissolves again: we can see only the frames, and the light that is flooding the pictures from outside, but that they, in return, must reconstitute in their own kind, as though it were coming from elsewhere, passing through their dark wooden frames. And we do, in fact, see this light on the painting, apparently welling out from the crack of the frame; and from there it moves over to touch the brow, the cheekbones, the eyes, the gaze of the painter, who is holding a palette in one hand and in the other a fine brush. . . And so the spiral is closed, or rather, by means of that light, is opened.

This opening is not, like the one in the back wall, made by pulling back a door; it is the whole breadth of the picture itself, and the looks that pass across it are not those of a distant visitor. The frieze that occupies the foreground and the middle ground of the picture represents—if we include the painter—eight characters. Five of these, their heads more or less bent, turned or inclined, are looking straight out at right angles to the surface of the picture. The centre of the group is occupied by the little Infanta, with her flared pink and grey dress. The princess is turning her head towards the right side of the picture, while her torso and the big panniers of her dress slant away slightly towards the left; but her gaze is directed absolutely straight towards the spectator standing in front of the painting. A vertical line dividing the canvas into two equal halves would pass between the child's eyes. Her face is a third of the total height of the picture above the lower frame. So that here, beyond all question, resides the principal theme of the composition; this is the very object of this painting. As though to prove this and to emphasize it even more, Velázquez has made use of a traditional visual device: beside the principal figure he has placed a secondary one, kneeling and looking in towards the central one. Like a donor in prayer, like an angel greeting the Virgin, a maid of honour on her knees is stretching out her hands towards the princess. Her face stands out in perfect profile against the background. It is at the same height as that of the child. This attendant is looking at the princess and only at the princess. A little to the right, there stands another maid of honour, also turned towards the Infanta, leaning slightly over her, but with her eyes clearly directed towards the front, towards the same spot already being gazed at by the painter and the princess. Lastly, two other groups made up of two figures each: one of these groups is further away; the other, made up of the two dwarfs, is right in the foreground. One character in each of these pairs is looking straight out, the other to the left or the right. Because of their positions and their size, these two groups correspond and themselves form a pair: behind, the courtiers (the woman, to the left, looks to the right); in front, the dwarfs (the boy, who is at the extreme right, looks in towards the centre of the picture). This group of characters, arranged in this manner, can be taken to constitute, according to the way one looks at the picture and the centre of reference chosen, two different figures. The first would be a large X: the top left-hand point of this X would be the painter's eyes; the top right-hand one, the male courtier's eyes; at the bottom left-hand corner there is the corner of the canvas represented with its back towards us (or, more exactly, the foot of the easel); at the bottom right-hand corner, the dwarf (his foot on the dog's back). Where these two lines intersect, at the centre of the X, are the eyes of the Infanta. The second figure would be more that of a vast curve, its two ends determined by the painter on the left and the male courtier on the right—both these extremities occurring high up in the picture and set back from its surface; the centre of the curve, much nearer to us, would coincide with the princess's face and the look her maid of honour is directing towards her. This curve describes a shallow hollow across the centre of the picture which at once contains and sets off the position of the mirror at the back.

There are thus two centres around which the picture may be organized, according to whether the fluttering attention of the spectator decides to settle in this place or in that. The princess is standing upright in the centre of a St. Andrew's cross, which is revolving around her with its eddies of courtiers, maids of honour, animals, and fools. But this pivoting movement is frozen. Frozen by a spectacle that would be absolutely invisible if those same characters, suddenly motionless, were not offering us, as though in the hollow of a goblet, the possibility of seeing in the depths of a mirror the unforeseen double of what they are observing. In depth, it is the princess who is superimposed on the mirror; vertically, it is the reflection that is superimposed on the face. But, because of the perspective, they are very close to one another. Moreover, from each of them there springs an ineluctable line: the line issuing from the mirror crosses the whole of the depth represented (and even more, since the mirror forms a hole in the back wall and brings a further space into being behind it); the other line is shorter: it comes from the child's eyes and crosses only the foreground. These two sagittal lines converge at a very sharp angle, and the point where they meet, springing out from the painted surface, occurs in front of the picture, more or less exactly at the spot from which we are observing it. It is an uncertain point because we cannot see it; yet it is an inevitable and perfectly defined point too, since it is determined by those two dominating figures and confirmed further by other, adjacent dotted lines which also have their origin inside the picture and emerge from it in a similar fashion.

What is there, then, we ask at last, in that place which is completely inaccessible because it is exterior to the picture, yet is prescribed by all the lines of its composition? What is the spectacle, what are the faces that are reflected first of all in the depths of the Infanta's eyes, then in the courtiers' and the painter's, and finally in the distant glow of the mirror? But the question immediately becomes a double one: the face reflected in the mirror is also the face that is contemplating it; what all the figures in the picture are looking at are the two figures to whose eyes they too present a scene to be observed. The entire picture is looking out at a scene for which it is itself a scene. A condition of pure reciprocity manifested by the observing and observed mirror, the two stages of which are uncoupled at the two lower corners of the picture: on the left the canvas with its back to us, by means of which the exterior point is made into pure spectacle; to the right the dog lying on the floor, the only element in the picture that is neither looking at anything nor moving, because it is not intended, with its deep reliefs and the light playing on its silky hair, to be anything but an object to be seen.

Our first glance at the painting told us what it is that creates this spectacle-as-observation. It is the two sovereigns. One can sense their presence already in the respectful gaze of the figures in the picture, in the astonishment of the child and the dwarfs. We recognize them, at the far end of the picture, in the two tiny silhouettes gleaming out from the looking-glass. In the midst of all those attentive faces, all those richly dressed bodies, they are the palest, the most unreal, the most compromised of all the painting's images: a movement, a little light, would be sufficient to eclipse them. Of all these figures represented before us, they are also the most ignored, since no one is paying the slightest attention to that reflection which has slipped into the room behind them all, silently occupying its unsuspected space; in so far as they are visible, they are the frailest and the most distant form of all reality. Inversely, in so far as they stand outside the picture and are therefore withdrawn from it in an essential invisibility, they provide the centre around which the entire representation is ordered: it is they who are being faced, it is towards them that everyone is turned, it is to their eyes that the princess is being presented in her holiday clothes; from the canvas with its back to us to the Infanta, and from the Infanta to the dwarf playing on the extreme right, there runs a curve (or again, the lower fork of the X opens) that orders the whole arrangement of the picture to their gaze and thus makes apparent the true centre of the composition, to which the Infanta's gaze and the image in the mirror are both finally subject.

In the realm of the anecdote, this centre is symbolically sovereign, since it is occupied by King Philip IV and his wife. But it is so above all because of the triple function it fulfils in relation to the picture. For in it there occurs an exact superimposition of the model's gaze as it is being painted, of the spectator's as he contemplates the painting, and of the painter's as he is composing his picture (not the one represented, but the one in front of us which we are discussing). These three "observing" functions come together in a point exterior to the picture: that is, an ideal point in relation to what is represented, but a perfectly real one too, since it is also the starting-point that makes the representation possible. Within that reality itself, it cannot not be invisible. And yet, that reality is projected within the picture—projected and diffracted in three forms which correspond to the three functions of that ideal and real point. They are: on the left, the painter with his palette in his hand (a self-portrait of Velázquez); to the right, the visitor, one foot on the step, ready to enter the room; he is taking in the scene from the back, but he can see the royal couple, who are the spectacle itself, from the front; and lastly, in the centre, the reflection of the king and the queen, richly dressed, motionless, in the attitude of patient models.

A reflection that shows us quite simply, and in shadow, what all those in the foreground are looking at. It restores, as if by magic, what is lacking in every gaze: in the painter's, the model, which his represented double is duplicating over there in the picture; in the king's, his portrait, which is being finished off on that slope of the canvas that he cannot perceive from where he stands; in that of the spectator, the real centre of the scene, whose place he himself has taken as though by usurpation. But perhaps this generosity on the part of the mirror is feigned; perhaps it is hiding as much as and even more than it reveals. That space where the king and his wife hold sway belongs equally well to the artist and to the spectator: in the depths of the mirror there could also appear—there ought to appear—the anonymous face of the passer-by and that of Velázquez. For the function of that reflection is to draw into the interior of the picture what is intimately foreign to it: the gaze which has organized it and the gaze for which it is displayed. But because they are present within the picture, to the right and to the left, the artist and the visitor cannot be given a place in the mirror: just as the king appears in the depths of the looking-glass precisely because he does not belong to the picture.

In the great volute that runs around the perimeter of the studio, from the gaze of the painter, with his motionless hand and palette, right round to the finished paintings, representation came into being, reached completion, only to dissolve once more into the light; the cycle was complete. The lines that run through the depth of the picture, on the other hand, are not complete; they all lack a segment of their trajectories. This gap is caused by the absence of the king—an absence that is an artifice on the part of the painter. But this artifice both conceals and indicates another vacancy which is, on the contrary, immediate: that of the painter and the spectator when they are looking at or composing the picture. It may be that, in this picture, as in all the representations of which it is, as it were, the manifest essence, the profound invisibility of what one sees is inseparable from the invisibility of the person seeing—despite all mirrors, reflections, imitations, and portraits. Around the scene are arranged all the signs and successive forms of representation; but the double relation of the representation to its model and to its sovereign, to its author as well as to the person to whom it is being offered, this relation is necessarily interrupted. It can never be present without some residuum, even in a representation that offers itself as a spectacle. In the depth that traverses the picture, hollowing it into a fictitious recess and projecting it forward in front of itself, it is not possible for the pure felicity of the image ever to present in a full light both the master who is representing and the sovereign who is being represented.

Perhaps there exists, in this painting by Velázquez, the representation as it were, of Classical representation, and the definition of the space it opens up to us. And, indeed, representation undertakes to represent itself here in all its elements, with its images, the eyes to which it is offered, the faces it makes visible, the gestures that call it into being. But there, in the midst of this dispersion which it is simultaneously grouping together and spreading out before us, indicated compellingly from every side, is an essential void: the necessary disappearance of that which is its foundation—of the person it resembles and the person in whose eyes it is only a resemblance. This very subject—which is the same—has been elided. And representation, freed finally from the relation that was impeding it, can offer itself as representation in its pure form.

NOTE

1. The problems of method raised by such an "archaeology" will be examined in a later work.

IV

Discussions

EDWARD BULLOUGH

AMONG THE MOST POPULAR views of aesthetic experience, so widespread that it has entered ordinary discourse on art, is Bullough's notion of "aesthetic distance." The metaphorical character of this notion of "distance" has aroused much criticism from philosophers, yet it is clear that Bullough has captured an important and common way in which artists and teachers think of art.

Bullough's notion owes an enormous debt to Kant, and the idea of distance may be viewed as a dramatic rendering of Kant's distinction between the purposeless delight of art and the interested pleasure we derive from successful practical affairs. The issue concerns the autonomy of art, and Bullough's notion of distance is no more capable of resolving that issue without difficulty than most other theories which strive to ensure the importance of art by separating it from the discursive and practical affairs of life. Nevertheless, there is an important phenomenon that is captured by the notion of distance, that a work of art is not to be regarded as a practical object even when made of ordinary materials, even when it is nothing but a found object.

EDWARD BULLOUGH

*'Psychical Distance' as a Factor in Art and as an Aesthetic Principle**

I

1. The conception of 'Distance' suggests, in connection with Art, certain trains of thought by no means devoid of interest or of speculative importance. Perhaps the most obvious suggestion is that of *actual spatial* distance, i.e. the distance of a work of Art from the spectator, or that of *represented spatial* distance, i.e. the distance represented within the work. Less obvious, more metaphorical, is the meaning of *temporal* distance. The first was noticed already by Aristotle in *Poetics;* the second has played a great part in the history of painting in the form of perspective; the distinction between these two kinds of distance assumes special importance theoretically in the differentiation between sculpture in the round, and relief-sculpture. Temporal distance, remoteness from us in point of time, though often a cause of misconceptions, has been declared to be a factor of considerable weight in our appreciation.

It is not, however, in any of these meanings that 'Distance' is put forward here, though it will be clear in the course of this essay that the above-mentioned kinds of distance are rather special forms of the conception of distance as advocated here, and derive whatever *aesthetic* qualities they may pos-

* Edward Bullough, "'Psychical Distance' as a Factor in Art and as an Aesthetic Principle," *British Journal of Psychology* (1912), pp. 87-98.

sess from Distance in its *general* connotation. This general connotation is 'Psychical Distance'.

A short illustration will explain what is meant by 'Psychical Distance'. Imagine a fog at sea: for most people it is an experience of acute unpleasantness. Apart from the physical annoyance and remoter forms of discomfort such as delays, it is apt to produce feelings of peculiar anxiety, fears of invisible dangers, strains of watching and listening for distant and unlocalised signals. The listless movements of the ship and her warning calls soon tell upon the nerves of the passengers; and that special, expectant, tacit anxiety and nervousness, always associated with this experience, make a fog the dreaded terror of the sea (all the more terrifying because of its very silence and gentleness) for the expert seafarer no less than for the ignorant landsman.

Nevertheless, a fog at sea can be a source of intense relish and enjoyment. Abstract from the experience of the sea fog, for the moment, its danger and practical unpleasantness, just as every one in the enjoyment of a mountain-climb disregards its physical labour and its danger (though, it is not denied, that these may incidentally enter into the enjoyment and enhance it); direct the attention to the features 'objectively' constituting the phenomenon—the veil surrounding you with an opaqueness as of transparent milk, blurring the outline of things and distorting their shapes into weird grotesqueness; observe the carrying-power of the air, producing the impression as if you could touch some far-off siren by merely putting out your hand and letting it lose itself behind the white wall; note the curious creamy smoothness of the water, hypocritically denying as it were any suggestion of danger; and, above all, the strange solitude and remoteness from the world, as it can be found only on the highest mountain-tops: and the experience may acquire, in its uncanny mingling of repose and terror, a flavour of such concentrated poignancy and delight as to contrast sharply with the blind and distempered anxiety of its other aspects. This contrast, often emerging with startling suddenness, is like a momentary switching on of some new current, or the passing ray of a brighter light, illuminating the outlook upon perhaps the most ordinary and familiar objects—an impression which we experience sometimes in instants of direct extremity, when our practical interest snaps like a wire from sheer overtension, and we watch the consummation of some impending catastrophe with the marvelling unconcern of a mere spectator.

It is a difference of outlook, due—if such a metaphor is permissible—to the insertion of Distance. This Distance appears to lie between our own self and its affections, using the latter term in its broadest sense as anything which affects our being, bodily or spiritually, e.g. as sensation, perception, emotional state or idea. Usually, though not always, it amounts to the same thing to say that the Distance lies between our own self and such objects as are the sources or vehicles of such affections.

Thus, in the fog, the transformation by Distance is produced in the first instance by putting the phenomenon, so to speak, out of gear with our practical, actual self; by allowing it to stand outside the context of our personal needs and ends—in short, by looking at it 'objectively', as it has often been called, by permitting only such reactions on our part as emphasise the 'objective' features of the experience, and by interpreting even our 'subjective' affections not as modes of *our* being but rather as characteristics of the phenomenon.

The working of Distance is, accordingly, not simple, but highly complex. It has a *negative*, inhibitory aspect—the cutting-out of the practical sides of things and of our practical attitude to them—and a *positive* side—the elaboration of the experience on the new basis created by the inhibitory action of Distance.

2. Consequently, this distanced view of things is not, and cannot be, our normal outlook. As a rule, experience constantly turns the same side towards us, namely, that which has the strongest practical force of appeal. We are not ordinarily aware of those aspects of things which do not touch us immediately and practically, nor are we generally conscious of impressions apart from our own self which is impressed. The sudden view of things from their reverse, usually unnoticed, side, comes upon us as a revelation, and such relevations are precisely those of Art. In this most general sense, Distance is a factor in all Art.

3. It is, for this very reason, also an aesthetic principle. The aesthetic contemplation and the aesthetic outlook have often been described as 'objective'. We speak of 'objective' artists as Shakespeare or Velásquez, of 'objective' works or art-forms as Homer's *Iliad* or the drama. It is a term constantly occurring in discussions and criticisms, though its sense, if pressed at all, becomes very questionable. For certain forms of Art, such as lyrical poetry, are said to be 'subjective'; Shelley, for example, would usually be considered a 'subjective' writer. On the other hand, no work of Art can be genuinely 'objective' in the sense in which this term might be applied to a work on history or to a scientific treatise; nor can it be 'subjective' in the ordinary acceptance of that term, as a personal feeling, a direct statement of a wish or belief, or a cry of passion is subjective. 'Objectivity' and 'subjectivity' are a pair of opposites which in their mutual exclusiveness when applied to Art soon lead to confusion.

Nor are they the only pair of opposites. Art has with equal vigour been declared alternately 'idealistic' and 'realistic', 'sensual' and 'spiritual', 'individualistic' and 'typical'. Between the defence of either terms of such antitheses most aesthetic theories have vacillated. It is one of the contentions of this essay that such opposites find their synthesis in the more fundamental conception of Distance.

Distance further provides the much needed criterion of the beautiful as distinct from the merely agreeable.

Again, it marks one of the most important steps in the process of artistic creation and serves as a distinguishing feature of what is commonly so loosely described as the 'artistic temperament'.

Finally, it may claim to be considered as one of the essential characteristics of the 'aesthetic consciousness', if I may describe by this term that special mental attitude towards, and outlook upon, experience, which finds its most pregnant expression in the various forms of Art.

II

Distance, as I said before, is obtained by separating the object and its appeal from one's own self, by putting it out of gear with practical needs and ends. Thereby the 'contemplation' of the object becomes alone possible. But it does not mean that the relation between the self and the object is broken to the extent of becoming 'impersonal'. Of the alternatives 'personal' and 'impersonal' the latter surely comes nearer to the truth; but here, as elsewhere, we meet the difficulty of having to express certain facts in terms coined for entirely different uses. To do so usually results in paradoxes, which are nowhere more inevitable than in discussions upon Art. 'Personal' and 'impersonal', 'subjective' and 'objective' are such terms, devised for purposes other than aesthetic speculation, and becoming loose and ambiguous as soon as applied outside the sphere of their special meanings. In giving preference therefore to the term 'impersonal' to describe the relation between the spectator and a work of Art, it is to be noticed that it is not impersonal in the sense in which we speak of the 'impersonal' character of Science, for instance. In order to obtain 'objectively valid' results, the scientist excludes the 'personal factor', i.e. his personal wishes as to the validity of his results, his predilection for any particular system to be proved or disproved by his research. It goes without saying that all experiments and investigations are undertaken out of a personal interest in the science, for the ultimate support of a definite assumption, and involve personal hopes of success; but this does not affect the 'dispassionate' attitude of the investigator, under pain of being accused of 'manufacturing his evidence'.

1. Distance does not imply an impersonal, purely intellectually interested relation of such a kind. On the contrary, it describes a *personal* relation, often highly emotionally coloured, but *of a peculiar character*. Its peculiarity lies in that the personal character of the relation has been, so to speak, filtered. It has been cleared of the practical, concrete nature of its appeal, without, however, thereby losing its original constitution. One of the best-known examples is to be found in our attitude towards the events and characters of the drama: they appeal to us like persons and incidents of normal experience, except that that side of their appeal, which would usually affect us in a directly personal manner, is held in abeyance. This difference, so well known as to be almost trivial, is generally explained by reference to the knowledge that the characters and situations are 'unreal', imaginary. In this sense Witasek[1] operating with Meinong's theory of *Annahmen,* has described the emotions involved in witnessing a drama as *Scheingefühle,* a term which has so frequently been misunderstood in discussions of his theories. But, as a matter

of fact, the 'assumption' upon which the imaginative emotional reaction is based is not necessarily the condition, but often the consequence, of Distance; that is to say, the converse of the reason usually stated would then be true: viz. that Distance, by changing our relation to the characters, renders them seemingly fictitious, not that the fictitiousness of the characters alters our feelings toward them. It is, of course, to be granted that the actual and admitted unreality of the dramatic action reinforces the effect of Distance. But surely the proverbial unsophisticated yokel, whose chivalrous interference in the play on behalf of the hapless heroine can only be prevented by impressing upon him that 'they are only pretending', is not the ideal type of theatrical audience. The proof of the seeming paradox that it is Distance which primarily gives to dramatic action the appearance of unreality and not vice versa, is the observation that the same filtration of our sentiments and the same seeming 'unreality' of *actual* men and things occur, when at times, by a sudden change of inward perspective, we are overcome by the feeling that 'all the world's a stage'.

2. This personal, but 'distanced' relation (as I will venture to call this nameless character of our view) directs attention to a strange fact which appears to be one of the fundamental paradoxes of Art: it is what I propose to call 'the antinomy of Distance'.

It will be readily admitted that a work of Art has the more chance of appealing to us the better it finds us prepared for its particular kind of appeal. Indeed, without some degree of predisposition on our part, it must necessarily remain incomprehensible, and to that extent, unappreciated. The success and intensity of its appeal would seem, therefore, to stand in direct proportion to the completeness with which it corresponds with our intellectual and emotional peculiarities and the idiosyncrasies of our experience. The absence of such a concordance between the characters of a work and of the spectator is, of course, the most general explanation for differences of 'tastes'.

At the same time, such a principle of concordance requires a qualification, which leads at once to the antinomy of Distance.

Suppose a man, who believes that he has cause to be jealous about his wife, witnesses a performance of *Othello*. He will the more perfectly appreciate the situation, conduct and character of Othello, the more exactly the feelings and experiences of Othello coincide with his own—at least he *ought* to on the above principle of concordance. In point of fact, he will probably do anything but appreciate the play. In reality, the concordance will merely render him acutely conscious of his own jealousy; by a sudden reversal of perspective he will no longer see Othello apparently betrayed by Desdemona, but himself in an analogous situation with his own wife. This reversal of perspective is the consequence of the loss of Distance.

If this be taken as a typical case, it follows that the qualification required is that the coincidence should be as complete as is compatible with maintaining Distance. The jealous spectator of *Othello* will indeed appreciate and enter into the play the more keenly, the greater the resemblance with his own experience—*provided* that he succeeds in keeping the Distance between the action of the play and his personal feelings: a very difficult performance in the circumstances. It is on account of the same difficulty that the expert and the professional critic make a bad audience, since their expertness and critical professionalism are *practical* activities, involving their concrete personality and constantly endangering their Distance. (It is, by the way, one of the reasons why Criticism is an art, for it requires the constant interchange from the practical to the distanced attitude and vice versa, which is characteristic of artists.)

The same qualification applies to the artist. He will prove artistically most effective in the formulation of an intensely *personal* experience, but he can formulate it artistically only on condition of a detachment from the experience *qua personal.* Hence the statement of so many artists that artistic formulation was to them a kind of catharsis, a means of ridding themselves of feelings and ideas the acuteness of which they felt almost as a kind of obsession. Hence, on the other hand, the failure of the average man to convey to others at all adequately the impression of an overwhelming joy or sorrow. His personal implication in the event renders it impossible for him to formulate and present it in such a way as to make others, like himself, feel all the meaning and fullness which it possesses for him.

What is therefore, both in appreciation and production, most desirable is the *utmost decrease of Distance without its disappearance.*

3. Closely related, in fact a presupposition to the 'antinomy', is the *variability* of Distance. Herein especially lies the advantage of Distance compared with such terms as 'objectivity' and 'detachment'. Neither of them implies a *personal* relation—indeed both actually preclude it; and the mere inflexibility and exclusiveness of their opposites render their application generally meaningless.

Distance, on the contrary, admits naturally of degrees, and differs not only according to the nature of the *object,* which may impose a greater or smaller degree of Distance, but varies also according to the *individual's capacity* for maintaining a greater or lesser degree. And here one may remark that not only do *persons differ from each other* in their habitual measure of Distance, but that the *same individual differs* in his ability to maintain it in the face of different objects and of different arts.

There exist, therefore, two different sets of conditions affecting the degree of Distance in any given case: those offered by the object and those realised by the subject. In their interplay they afford one of the most extensive explanations for varieties of aesthetic experience, since loss of Distance, whether due to the one or the other, means loss of aesthetic appreciation.

In short, Distance may be said *to be variable both according to the distancing-power of the individual, and according to the character of the object.*

There are two ways of losing Distance: either to 'under-distance' or to 'over-distance'. 'Under-distancing' is the commonest failing of the *subject,* an excess of Distance is a frequent failing of *Art,* especially in the past. Historically it looks almost as if Art had attempted to meet the deficiency of Distance on the part of the subject and had overshot the mark in this endeavour. It will be seen later that this is actually true, for it appears that over-distanced Art is specially designed for a class of appreciation which has difficulty to rise spontaneously to any degree of Distance. The consequence of a loss of Distance through one or other cause is familiar: the verdict in the case of under-distancing is that the work is "crudely naturalistic," "harrowing," "repulsive in its realism." An excess of Distance produces the impression of improbability, artificiality, emptiness or absurdity.

The individual tends, as I just stated, to under-distance rather than to lose Distance by over-distancing. *Theoretically* there is no limit to the decrease of Distance. In theory, therefore, not only the usual subjects of Art, but even the most personal affections, whether ideas, percepts or emotions, can be sufficiently distanced to be aesthetically appreciable. Especially artists are gifted in this direction to a remarkable extent. The average individual, on the contrary, very rapidly reaches his limit of decreasing Distance, his 'Distance-limit', i.e. that point at which Distance is lost and appreciation either disappears or changes its character.

In the *practice*, therefore, of the average person, a limit does exist which marks the minimum at which his appreciation can maintain itself in the aesthetic field, and this average minimum lies considerably higher than the Distance-limit of the artist. It is practically impossible to fix this average limit, in the absence of data, and on account of the wide fluctuations from person to person to which this limit is subject. But it is safe to infer that, in art practice, explicit references to organic affections, to the material existence of the body, especially to sexual matters, lie normally below the Distance-limit, and can be touched upon by Art only with special precautions. Allusions to social institutions of any degree of personal importance—in particular, allusions implying any doubt as to their validity—the questioning of some generally recognised ethical sanctions, references to topical subjects occupying public attention at the moment, and such like, are all dangerously near the average limit and may at any time fall below it, arousing, instead of aesthetic appreciation, concrete hostility or mere amusement.

This difference in the Distance-limit between artists and the public has been the source of much misunderstanding and injustice. Many an artist has seen his work condemned and himself ostracised for the sake of so-called 'immoralities' which to him were bona fide aesthetic objects. His power of distancing, nay, the necessity of distancing feelings, sensations, situations which for the average person are too intimately bound up with his concrete existence to be regarded in that light, have often quite unjustly earned for him accusations of cynicism, sensualism, morbidness or frivolity. The same misconception has arisen over many 'problem plays' and 'problem novels' in which the public have persisted in seeing nothing but a supposed 'problem' of the moment, whereas the author may have been—and often has demonstrably been—able to distance the subject-matter sufficiently to rise above its practical problematic import and to regard it simply as a dramatically and humanly interesting situation.

The variability of Distance in respect to Art, disregarding for the moment the subjective complication, appears both as a general feature in Art, and in the differences between the special arts.

It has been an old problem why the 'arts of the eye and of the ear' should have reached the practically exclusive predominance over arts of other senses. Attempts to raise 'culinary art' to the level of a Fine Art have failed in spite of all propaganda, as completely as the creation of scent or liqueur 'symphonies'. There is little doubt that, apart from other excellent reasons of a partly psycho-physical, partly technical nature, the actual, *spatial distance* separating objects of sight and hearing from the subject has contributed strongly to the development of this monopoly. In a similar manner *temporal remoteness* produces Distance, and objects removed from us in point of time are *ipso facto* distanced to an extent which was impossible for their contemporaries. Many pictures, plays and poems had, as a matter of fact, rather an expository or illustrative significance—as for instance much ecclesiastical Art—or the force of a direct practical appeal—as the invectives of many satires or comedies—which seem to us nowadays irreconcilable with their aesthetic claims. Such works have consequently profited greatly by lapse of time and have reached the level of Art only with the help of temporal distance, while others, on the contrary, often for the same reason have suffered a loss of Distance, through *over*-distancing.

Special mention must be made of a group of artistic conceptions which present excessive Distance in their form of appeal rather than in their actual presentation—a point illustrating the necessity of distinguishing between distancing an object and distancing the appeal of which it is the source. I mean here what is often rather loosely termed 'idealistic Art', that is, Art springing from abstract conceptions, expressing allegorical meanings, or illustrating general truths. Generalisations and abstractions suffer under this disadvantage that they have too much general applicability to invite a personal interest in them, and too little individual concreteness to prevent them applying to us in all their force. They appeal to everybody and therefore to none. An axiom of Euclid belongs to nobody, just because it compels everyone's assent; general conceptions like Patriotism, Friendship, Love, Hope, Life, Death, concern as much Dick, Tom and Harry as myself, and I, therefore, either feel unable to get into any kind of personal relation to them, or, if I do so, they become at once, emphatically and concretely, *my* Patriotism, *my* Friendship, *my* Love, *my* Hope, *my* Life and Death. By mere force of generalisation, a general truth or a universal ideal is so far distanced from myself that I fail to realise it concretely at all, or, when I do so, I can realise it only as part of my *practical actual being*, i.e. it falls below the Distance-limit altogether. 'Idealistic Art' suffers consequently under the peculiar difficulty that its excess of Distance turns generally into an *under*-distanced appeal—all the more easily, as it is the usual failing of the subject to *under*—rather than to over-distance.

The different special arts show at the present time very marked variations in the degree of Distance which they usually impose or require for their
appreciation. Unfortunately here again the absence of data makes itself felt
and indicates the necessity of conducting observations, possibly experiments,
so as to place these suggestions upon a securer basis. In one single art, viz. the
theatre, a small amount of information is available, from an unexpected source,
namely the proceedings of the censorship committee,[2] which on closer examination might be made to yield evidence of interest to the psychologist. In fact,
the whole censorship problem, as far as it does not turn upon purely economic questions, may be said to hinge upon Distance; if every member of the
public could be trusted to keep it, there would be no sense whatever in the
existence of a censor of plays. There is, of course, no doubt that, speaking generally, theatrical performances *eo ipso* run a special risk of a loss of Distance
owing to the material presentment[3] of its subject-matter. The physical presence of living human beings as vehicles of dramatic art is a difficulty which no
art has to face in the same way. A similar, in many ways even greater, risk confronts *dancing*: though attracting perhaps a less widely spread human interest,
its animal spirits are frequently quite unrelieved by any glimmer of spirituality
and consequently form a proportionately stronger lure to under-distancing. In
the higher forms of dancing technical execution of the most wearing kind
makes up a great deal for its intrinsic tendency towards a loss of Distance, and
as a popular performance, at least in southern Europe, it has retained much of
its ancient artistic glamour, producing a peculiarly subtle balancing of Distance between the pure delight of bodily movement and high technical accomplishment. In passing, it is interesting to observe (as bearing upon the development of Distance) that this art, once as much a fine art as music and
considered by the Greeks as a particularly valuable educational exercise,
should—except in sporadic cases—have fallen so low from the pedestal it once
occupied. Next to the theatre and dancing stands *sculpture*. Though not using
a *living* bodily medium, yet the human form in its full spatial materiality constitutes a similar threat to Distance. Our northern habits of dress and ignorance of the human body have enormously increased the difficulty of distancing Sculpture, in part through the gross misconceptions to which it is
exposed, in part owing to a complete lack of standards of bodily perfection,
and an inability to realise the distinction between sculptural form and bodily
shape, which is the only but fundamental point distinguishing a statue from a
cast taken from life. In *painting* it is apparently the form of its presentment
and the usual reduction in scale which would explain why this art can venture
to approach more closely than sculpture to the normal Distance-limit. . . .
Music and *architecture* have a curious position. These two most abstract of all
arts show a remarkable fluctuation in their Distances. Certain kinds of music,
especially 'pure' music, or 'classical' or 'heavy' music, appear for many people
over-distanced; light, 'catchy' tunes, on the contrary, easily reach that degree
of decreasing Distance below which they cease to be Art and become a pure
amusement. In spite of its strange abstractness which to many philosophers

has made it comparable to architecture and mathematics, music possesses a sensuous, frequently sensual, character: the undoubted physiological and muscular stimulus of its melodies and harmonies, no less than its rhythmic aspects, would seem to account for the occasional disappearance of Distance. To this might be added its strong tendency, especially in unmusical people, to stimulate trains of thought quite disconnected with itself, following channels of subjective inclinations—day-dreams of a more or less directly personal character. *Architecture* requires almost uniformly a very great Distance; that is to say, the majority of persons derive no aesthetic appreciation from architecture as such, apart from the incidental impression of its decorative features and its associations. The causes are numerous, but prominent among them are the confusion of building with architecture and the predominance of utilitarian purposes, which overshadow the architectural claims upon the attention.

4. That all art requires a Distance-limit beyond which, and a Distance within which only, aesthetic appreciation becomes possible, is the *psychological formulation of a general characteristic of Art,* viz. its *anti-realistic nature.* Though seemingly paradoxical, this applies as much to 'naturalistic' as to 'idealistic' Art. The difference commonly expressed by these epithets is at bottom merely the difference in the degree of Distance; and this produces, so far as 'naturalism' and 'idealism' in Art are not meaningless labels, the usual result that what appears obnoxiously 'naturalistic' to one person, may be 'idealistic' to another. To say that Art is anti-realistic simply insists upon the fact that Art is not nature, never pretends to be nature and strongly resists any confusion with nature. It emphasizes the *art-character* of Art: 'artistic' is synonymous with 'anti-realistic'; it explains even sometimes a very marked degree of artificiality.

NOTES

1. H. Witasek, "Zur psychologischen Analyse der aesthetischen Einfühlung," *Ztsch. f. Psychol. u. Physiol. der Sinnesorg.,* 1901, xxv, 1ff.; *Grundzüge der Aesthetik* (Leipzig, 1904).

2. Report from the Joint Select Committee of the House of Lords and the House of Commons on Stage Plays (Censorship), 1909.

3. I shall use the term 'presentment' to denote the manner of presenting, in distinction to 'presentation' as that which is presented.

ARTHUR DANTO

ONE OF THE IMPORTANT phenomena of twentieth-century art is that ordinary objects may be transmuted into art, simply by being displayed, unchanged in other respects. This has raised important and fundamental questions about the nature of art. Danto's systematic and detailed treatment of this issue is to be found throughout his recent writing, but especially in *Transfiguration of the Commonplace* (Cambridge, Massachusetts: Harvard University Press, 1981). The article included here has been widely reprinted, and has had considerable influence, especially upon George Dickie's institutional theory of art (George Dickie, *Art and the Aesthetic*, Ithaca, New York: Cornell University Press, 1974). Dickie defines a work of art as an artifact "which has had conferred upon it the status of candidate for appreciation by some person or persons acting on behalf of a certain social institution (the artworld)" (p. 34).

The notion of the "artworld" is introduced by Danto to acknowledge that what would be a work of art in one cultural context would not be a work in another. Danto also raises the important question of the relationship between art and its theory in determining whether something is a work of art.

ARTHUR DANTO

*The Artworld**

> Hamlet: Do you see nothing there?
> The Queen: Nothing at all; yet all that is I see.
>
> —Shakespeare, *Hamlet*, Act III, Scene IV

Hamlet and Socrates, though in praise and deprecation respectively, spoke of art as a mirror held up to nature. As with many disagreements in attitude, this one has a factual basis. Socrates saw mirrors as but reflecting what we can already see; so art, insofar as mirrorlike, yields idle accurate duplications of the appearances of things, and is of no cognitive benefit whatever. Hamlet, more acutely, recognized a remarkable feature of reflecting surfaces, namely that they show us what we could not otherwise perceive—our own face and form—and so art, insofar as it is mirrorlike, reveals us to ourselves, and is, even by socratic criteria, of some cognitive utility after all. As a philosopher, however, I find Socrates' discussion defective on other, perhaps less profound grounds than these. If a mirror-image of *o* is indeed an imitation of *o*, then, if art is imitation, mirror-images are art. But in fact mirroring objects no more is art than returning weapons to a madman is justice; and reference to mirrorings would be just the sly sort of counterinstance we would expect Socrates to bring forward in rebuttal of the theory he instead uses them to illustrate. If that theory requires us to class *these* as art, it thereby shows its inadequacy: "is an imitation" will not do as a sufficient condition for "is art." Yet, perhaps because artists *were* engaged in imitation, in Socrates' time and after, the insufficiency of the theory was not noticed until the invention of photography.

* Arthur Danto, "The Artworld," *Journal of Philosophy* (1964), pp. 571-584.

Once rejected as a sufficient condition, mimesis was quickly discarded as even a necessary one; and since the achievement of Kandinsky, mimetic features have been relegated to the periphery of critical concern, so much so that some works survive in spite of possessing those virtues, excellence in which was once celebrated as the essence of art, narrowly escaping demotion to mere illustrations.

It is, of course, indispensable in socratic discussion that all participants be masters of the concept up for analysis, since the aim is to match a real defining expression to a term in active use, and the test for adequacy presumably consists in showing that the former analyzes and applies to all and only those things of which the latter is true. The popular disclaimer notwithstanding, then, Socrates' auditors purportedly knew what art was as well as what they liked; and a theory of art, regarded here as a real definition of "Art," is accordingly not to be of great use in helping men to recognize instances of its application. Their antecedent ability to do this is precisely what the adequacy of the theory is to be tested against, the problem being only to make explicit what they already know. It is *our* use of the term that the theory allegedly means to capture, but we are supposedly able, in the words of a recent writer, "to separate those objects which are works of art from those which are not, because . . . we know how correctly to use the word 'art' and to apply the phrase 'work of art'." Theories, on this account, are somewhat like mirror-images on Socrates' account, showing forth what we already know, wordy reflections of the actual linguistic practice we are masters in.

But telling artworks from other things is not so simple a matter, even for native speakers, and these days one might not be aware he was on artistic terrain without an artistic theory to tell him so. And part of the reason for this lies in the fact that terrain is constituted artistic in virtue of artistic theories, so that one use of theories, in addition to helping us discriminate art from the rest, consists in making art possible. Glaucon and the others could hardly have known what was art and what not: otherwise they would never have been taken in by mirror-images.

I

Suppose one thinks of the discovery of a whole new class of artworks as something analogous to the discovery of a whole new class of facts anywhere, viz., as something for theoreticians to explain. In science, as elsewhere, we often accommodate new facts to old theories via auxiliary hypotheses, a pardonable enough conservatism when the theory in question is deemed too valuable to be jettisoned all at once. Now the Imitation Theory of Art (IT) is, if one but thinks it through, an exceedingly powerful theory, explaining a great many phenomena connected with the causation and evaluation of artworks, bringing a surprising unity into a complex domain. Moreover, it is a simple matter to shore it up against many purported counterinstances by such auxiliary hypotheses as that the artist who deviates from mimeticity is perverse, inept, or mad. Ineptitude, chicanery, or folly are, in fact, testable predications. Suppose, then, tests reveal that these hypotheses fail to hold, that the theory, now beyond repair, must be replaced. And a new theory is worked out, capturing what it can of the old theory's competence, together with the heretofore recalcitrant facts. One might, thinking along these lines, represent certain episodes in the history of art as not dissimilar to certain episodes in the history of science, where a conceptual revolution is being effected and where refusal to countenance certain facts, while in part due to prejudice, inertia, and self-interest, is due also to the fact that a well-established, or at least widely credited theory is being threatened in such a way that all coherence goes.

Some such episode transpired with the advent of post-impressionist paintings. In terms of the prevailing artistic theory (IT), it was impossible to accept these as art unless inept art: otherwise they could be discounted as hoaxes, self-advertisements, or the visual counterparts of madmen's ravings. So to get them accepted *as* art, on a footing with the *Transfiguration* (not to speak of a Landseer stag), required not so much a revolution in taste as a theoretical revision of rather considerable proportions, involving not only the artistic enfranchisement of these objects, but an emphasis upon newly significant features of accepted artworks, so that quite different accounts of their status as artworks would now have to be given. As a result of the new theory's acceptance, not only were post-impressionist paintings taken up as art, but numbers of objects (masks, weapons, etc.) were transferred from anthropological museums (and heterogeneous other places) to *musées des beaux arts,* though, as we would expect from the fact that a criterion for the acceptance of a new theory is that it account for whatever the older one did, nothing had to be transferred out of the *musée des beaux arts*—even if there were internal rearrangements as between storage rooms and exhibition space. Countless native speakers hung upon suburban mantelpieces innumerable replicas of paradigm cases for teaching the expression "work of art" that would have sent their Edwardian forebears into linguistic apoplexy.

To be sure, I distort by speaking of a theory: historically, there were several, all interestingly enough, more or less defined in terms of the IT. Art-historical complexities must yield before the exigencies of logical exposition, and I shall speak as though there were one replacing theory, partially compensating for historical falsity by choosing one which was actually enunciated. According to it, the artists in question were to be understood not as unsuccessfully imitating real forms but as successfully creating new ones, quite as real as the forms which the older art had been thought, in its best examples, to be creditably imitating. Art, after all, had long since been thought of as creative (Vasari says that God was the first artist), and the post-impressionists were to be explained as genuinely creative, aiming, in Roger Fry's words, "not at illusion but reality." This theory (RT) furnished a whole new mode of looking at painting, old and new. Indeed, one might almost interpret the crude drawing in Van Gogh and Cézanne, the dislocation of form from contour in Rouault and Dufy, the arbitrary use of color planes in Gauguin and the Fauves, as so many ways of drawing attention to the fact that these were *non-imitations*, specifically intended not to deceive. Logically, this would be roughly like printing "Not Legal Tender" across a brilliantly counterfeited dollar bill, the resulting object (counterfeit *cum* inscription) rendered incapable of deceiving anyone. It is not an illusory dollar bill, but then, just because it is non-illusory it does not automatically become a real dollar bill either. It rather occupies a freshly opened area between real objects and real facsimiles of real objects: it is a non-facsimile, if one requires a word, and a new contribution to the world. Thus, Van Gogh's *Potato Eaters*, as a consequence of certain unmistakable distortions, turns out to be a non-facsimile of real-life potato eaters; and inasmuch as these are not facsimiles of potato eaters, Van Gogh's picture, as a non-imitation, had as much right to be called a real object as did its putative subjects. By means of this theory (RT), artworks re-entered the thick of things from which socratic theory (IT) had sought to evict them: if no *more* real than what carpenters wrought, they were at least no *less* real. The Post-Impressionist won a victory in ontology.

It is in terms of RT that we must understand the artworks around us today. Thus Roy Lichtenstein paints comic-strip panels, though ten or twelve feet high. These are reasonably faithful projections onto a gigantesque scale of the homely frames from the daily tabloid, but it is precisely the scale that counts. A skilled engraver might incise *The Virgin and the Chancellor Rollin* on a pinhead, and it would be recognizable as such to the keen of sight, but an engraving of a Barnett Newman on a similar scale would be a blob, disappearing in the reduction. A *photograph* of a Lichtenstein is indiscernible from a photograph of a counterpart panel from *Steve Canyon;* but the photograph fails to capture the scale, and hence is as inaccurate a reproduction as a black-and-white engraving of Botticelli, scale being essential here as color there. Lichtensteins, then, are not imitations but *new entities*, as giant whelks would be. Jasper Johns, by contrast, paints objects with respect to which questions of scale are irrelevant. Yet his objects cannot be imitations, for they have the remarkable property that any intended copy of a member of this class of objects is automatically a member of the class itself, so that these objects are logically inimitable. Thus, a copy of a numeral just *is* that numeral: a painting of 3 is a 3 made of paint. Johns, in addition, paints targets, flags, and maps. Finally, in what I hope are not unwitting footnotes to Plato, two of our pioneers—Robert Rauschenberg and Claes Oldenburg— have made genuine beds.

Rauschenberg's bed hangs on a wall, and is streaked with some desultory housepaint. Oldenburg's bed is a rhomboid, narrower at one end than the other, with what one might speak of as a built-in perspective: ideal for small bedrooms. As beds, these sell at singularly inflated prices, but one *could* sleep in either of them: Rauschenberg has expressed the fear that someone might just climb into his bed and fall asleep. Imagine, now, a certain Testadura—a plain speaker and noted philistine—who is not aware that these are art, and who takes them to be reality simple and pure. He attributes the paintstreaks on Rauschenberg's bed to the slovenliness of the owner, and the bias in the Oldenburg bed to the ineptitude of the builder or the whimsy, perhaps, of whoever had it "custom-made." These would be mistakes, but mistakes of rather an odd kind, and not terribly different from that made by the stunned birds who pecked the sham grapes of Zeuxis. They mistook art for reality, and so has Testadura. But it was meant to *be* reality, according to RT. Can one have mistaken reality for reality? How shall we describe Testadura's error? What, after all, prevents Oldenburg's creation from being a misshapen bed? This is equivalent to asking what makes it art, and with this query we enter a domain of conceptual inquiry where native speakers are poor guides: *they* are lost themselves.

II

To mistake an artwork for a real object is no great feat when an artwork is the real object one mistakes it for. The problem is how to avoid such errors, or to remove them once they are made. The artwork is a bed, and not a bed-illusion; so there is nothing like the traumatic encounter against a flat surface that brought it home to the birds of Zeuxis that they had been duped. Except for the guard cautioning Testadura not to sleep on the artworks, he might never have discovered that this was an artwork and not a bed; and since, after all, one cannot discover that a bed is not a bed, how is Testadura to realize that he has made an error? A certain sort of explanation is required, for the error here is a curiously philosophical one, rather like, if we may assume as correct some well-known views of P. F. Strawson, mistaking a person for a material body when the truth is that a person *is* a material body in the sense that a whole class of predicates, sensibly applicable to material bodies, are sensibly, and by appeal to no different criteria, applicable to persons. So you cannot *discover* that a person is not a material body.

We begin by explaining, perhaps, that the paintstreaks are not to be explained away, that they are *part* of the object, so the object is not a mere bed with—as it happens—streaks of paint spilled over it, but a complex object fabricated out of a bed and some paintstreaks: a paint-bed. Similarly, a person is not a material body with—as it happens—some thoughts superadded, but is a complex entity made up of a body and some conscious states: a conscious-body. Persons, like artworks, must then be taken as irreducible to *parts* of themselves, and are in that sense primitive. Or, more accurately, the paintstreaks are not part of the real object—the bed—which happens to be part of the artwork, but are, *like* the bed, part of the artwork as such. And this might be generalized into a rough characterization of artworks that happen to contain real objects as parts of themselves: not every part of an artwork A is part of a real object R when R is part of A and can, moreover, be detached from A and seen *merely* as R. The mistake thus far will have been to mistake A for *part* of itself, namely R, even though it would not be incorrect to say that *A* is *R*, that the artwork is a bed. It is the "is" which requires clarification here.

There is an *is* that figures prominently in statements concerning art-works which is not the *is* of either identity or predication; nor is it the *is* of existence, of identification, or some special *is* made up to serve a philosophic end. Nevertheless, it is in common usage, and is readily mastered by children. It is the sense of *is* in accordance with which a child, shown a circle and a triangle and asked which is him and which his sister, will point to the triangle saying "That is me"; or, in response to my question, the person next to me points to the man in purple and says "That one is Lear"; or in the gallery I point, for my companion's benefit, to a spot in the painting before us and say "That white dab is Icarus." We do not mean, in these instances, that whatever is pointed to stands for, or represents, what it is said to be, for the *word* "Icarus" stands for or represents Icarus: yet I would not in the same sense of *is* point to the word and say "That is Icarus." The sentence "That *a* is *b*" is perfectly compatible with "That *a* is not *b*" when the first employs this sense of *is* and the second employs some other, though *a* and *b* are used nonambiguously throughout. Often, indeed, the truth of the first *requires* the truth of the second. The first, in fact, is incompatible with "That *a* is not *b*" only when the *is* is used nonambiguously throughout. For want of a word I shall designate this the *is of artistic identification;* in each case in which it is used, the *a* stands for some specific physical property of, or physical part of, an object; and, finally, it is a necessary condition for something to be an artwork that some part or property of it be designable by the subject of a sentence that employs this special *is*. It is an *is*, incidentally, which has near-relatives in marginal and mythical pronouncements. (Thus, one *is* Quetzalcoatl; those *are* the Pillars of Hercules.)

Let me illustrate. Two painters are asked to decorate the east and west walls of a science library with frescoes to be respectively called *Newton's First Law* and *Newton's Third Law*. These paintings, when finally unveiled, look, scale apart, as follows:

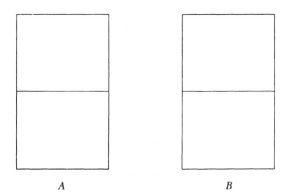

A   B

As objects I shall suppose the works to be indiscernible: a black, horizontal line on a white ground, equally large in each dimension and element. *B* explains his work as follows: a mass, pressing downward, is met by a mass pressing upward: the lower mass equally and oppositely to the upper one. *A* explains his work as follows: the line through the space is the path of an isolated particle. The path goes from edge to edge, to give the sense of its *going beyond*. If it ended or began within the space, the line would be curved: and it is parallel to the top and bottom edges, for if it were closer to one than to another, there would have to be a force accounting for it, and this is inconsistent with its being the path of an *isolated* particle.

   Much follows from these artistic identifications. To regard the middle line as an edge (mass meeting mass) imposes the need to identify the top and bottom half of the picture as rectangles, and as two distinct parts (not necessarily as two masses, for the line could be the edge of *one* mass jutting up— or down—into empty space). If it is an edge, we cannot thus take the entire area of the painting as a single space: it is rather composed of two forms, or one form and a non-form. We could take the entire area as a single space only by taking the middle horizontal as a *line* which is not an edge. But this almost requires a three-dimensional identification of the whole picture: the area can be a flat surface which the line is *above (Jet-flight)*, or *below (Submarine-path)*, or *on (Line)*, or *in (Fissure)*, or *through (Newton's First Law)*—though in this last case the area is not a flat surface but a transparent cross section of absolute space. We could make all these prepositional qualifications clear by imagining perpendicular cross sections to the picture plane. Then, depending upon the applicable prepositional clause, the area is (artistically) interrupted or not by the horizontal element. If we take the line as *through* space, the edges of the picture are not really the edges of the space: the space goes beyond the picture if the line itself does; and we are in the same space as the line is. As *B*, the edges of the picture can be *part* of the picture in case the masses go right to the edges, so that the edges of the picture are *their* edges. In that case, the vertices of the picture would be the vertices of the masses, except that the masses have four vertices more than the picture itself does: here four vertices would be part of the artwork which were not part of the real object. Again, the faces of the masses could be the face of the picture, and in looking at the picture, we are looking at these faces: but *space* has no face, and on the reading of *A* the work has to be read as faceless, and the face of the physical object would not be part of the artwork. Notice here how one artistic identification engenders another artistic identification, and how, consistently with a given identification, we are *required* to give others and *precluded* from still others: indeed, a given identification determines how many elements the work is to contain. These different identifications are incompatible with one another, or generally so, and each might be said to make a different artwork, even though each artwork contains the identical real object as part of itself—or at least parts of the identical real object as parts of itself. There are, of course, senseless identifications: no one could, I think, sensibly read the middle horizontal as *Love's*

Labour's Lost or *The Ascendency of St. Erasmus.* Finally, notice how acceptance of one identification rather than another is in effect to exchange one *world* for another. We could, indeed, enter a quiet poetic world by identifying the upper area with a clear and cloudless sky, reflected in the still surface of the water below, whiteness kept from whiteness only by the unreal boundary of the horizon.

And now Testadura, having hovered in the wings throughout this discussion, protests that *all he sees is paint;* a white painted oblong with a black line painted across it. And how right he really is: that is all he sees or that anybody can, we aesthetes included. So, if he asks us to show him what there is further to see, to demonstrate through pointing that this is an artwork *(Sea and Sky)*, we cannot comply, for he has overlooked nothing (and it would be absurd to suppose he had, that there was something tiny we could point to and he, peering closely, say "So it is! A work of art after all!"). We cannot help him until he has mastered the *is of artistic identification* and so *constitutes* it a work of art. If he cannot achieve this, he will never look upon artworks: he will be like a child who sees sticks as sticks.

But what about pure abstractions, say something that looks just like *A* but is entitled *No. 7*? The 10th Street abstractionist blankly insists that there is nothing here but white paint and black, and none of our literary identifications need apply. What then distinguishes him from Testadura, whose philistine utterances are indiscernible from his? And how can it be an artwork for him and not for Testadura, when they agree that there is nothing that does not meet the eye? The answer, unpopular as it is likely to be to purists of every variety, lies in the fact that this artist has returned to the physicality of paint through an atmosphere compounded of artistic theories and the history of recent and remote painting, elements of which he is trying to refine out of his own work; and as a consequence of this his work belongs in this atmosphere and is part of this history. He has achieved abstraction through rejection of artistic identifications, returning to the real world from which such identifications remove us (he thinks), somewhat in the mode of Ch'ing Yuan, who wrote:

> Before I had studied Zen for thirty years, I saw mountains as mountains and waters as waters. When I arrived at a more intimate knowledge, I came to the point where I saw that mountains are not mountains, and waters are not waters. But now that I have got the very substance I am at rest. For it is just that I see mountains once again as mountains, and waters once again as waters.

His identification of what he has made is logically dependent upon the theories and history he rejects. The difference between his utterance and Testadura's "This is black paint and white paint and nothing more" lies in the fact that he is still using the *is* of artistic identification, so that his use of "That black paint is black paint" is not a tautology. Testadura is not at that stage. To see something as art requires something the eye cannot decry—an atmosphere of artistic theory, a knowledge of the history of art: an artworld.

III

Mr. Andy Warhol, the Pop artist, displays facsimiles of Brillo cartons, piled high, in neat stacks, as in the stockroom of the supermarket. They happen to be of wood, painted to look like cardboard, and why not? To paraphrase the critic of the *Times*, if one may make the facsimile of a human being out of bronze, why not the facsimile of a Brillo carton out of plywood? The cost of these boxes happens to be 2×10^3 that of their homely counterparts in real life—a differential hardly ascribable to their advantage in durability. In fact the Brillo people might, at some slight increase of cost, make their boxes out of plywood without these becoming artworks, and Warhol might make *his* out of cardboard without their ceasing to be art. So we may forget questions of intrinsic value, and ask why the Brillo people cannot manufacture art and why Warhol cannot *but* make artworks. Well, his are made by hand, to be sure. Which is like an insane reversal of Picasso's strategy in pasting the label from a bottle of Suze onto a drawing, saying as it were that the academic artist, concerned with exact imitation, must always fall short of the real thing: so why not just *use* the real thing? The Pop artist laboriously reproduces machine-made objects by hand, e.g., painting the labels on coffee cans (one can hear the familiar commendation "Entirely made by hand" falling painfully out of the guide's vocabulary when confronted by these objects). But the difference cannot consist in craft: a man who carved pebbles out of stones and carefully constructed a work called *Gravel Pile* might invoke the labor theory of value to account for the price he demands; but the question is, What makes it art? And why need Warhol *make* these things anyway? Why not just scrawl his signature across one? Or crush one up and display it as *Crushed Brillo Box* ("A protest against mechanization . . .") or simply display a Brillo carton as *Uncrushed Brillo Box* ("A bold affirmation of the plastic authenticity of industrial . . .")? Is this man a kind of Midas, turning whatever he touches into the gold of pure art? And the whole world consisting of latent artworks waiting, like the bread and wine of reality, to be transfigured, through some dark mystery, into the indiscernible flesh and blood of the sacrament? Never mind that the Brillo box may not be good, much less great art. The impressive thing is that it is art at all. But if it is, why are not the indiscernible Brillo boxes that are in the stockroom? Or *has* the whole distinction between art and reality broken down?

Suppose a man collects objects (ready-mades), including a Brillo carton; we praise the exhibit for variety, ingenuity, what you will. Next he exhibits nothing but Brillo cartons, and we criticize it as dull, repetitive, self-plagiarizing—or (more profoundly) claim that he is obsessed by regularity and repetition, as in *Marienbad*. Or he piles them high, leaving a narrow path; we tread our way through the smooth opaque stacks and find it an unsettling experience, and write it up as the closing in of consumer products, confining us as prisoners: or we say he is a modern pyramid builder. True, we don't say these things about the stockboy. But then a stockroom is not an art gallery, and we cannot readily separate the Brillo cartons from the gallery they are in, any more than we can separate the Rauschenberg bed from the paint upon it. Outside the gallery, they are pasteboard cartons. But then, scoured clean of paint, Rauschenberg's bed is a bed, just what it was before it was transformed into art. But then if we think this matter through, we discover that the artist has failed, really and of necessity, to produce a mere real object. He has produced an artwork, his use of real Brillo cartons being but an expansion of the resources available to artists, a contribution to *artists' materials*, as oil paint was, or *tuche*.

What in the end makes the difference between a Brillo box and a work of art consisting of a Brillo Box is a certain theory of art. It is the theory that takes it up into the world of art, and keeps it from collapsing into the real object which it is (in a sense of *is* other than that of artistic identification). Of course, without the theory, one is unlikely to see it as art, and in order to see it as part of the artworld, one must have mastered a good deal of artistic theory as well as a considerable amount of the history of recent New York painting. It could not have been art fifty years ago. But then there could not have been, everything being equal, flight insurance in the Middle Ages, or Etruscan typewriter erasers. The world has to be ready for certain things, the artworld no less than the real one. It is the role of artistic theories, these days as always, to make the artworld, and art, possible. It would, I should think, never have occurred to the painters of Lascaux that they were producing *art* on those walls. Not unless there were neolithic aestheticians.

IV

The artworld stands to the real world in something like the relationship in which the City of God stands to the Earthly City. Certain objects, like certain individuals, enjoy the double citizenship, but there remains, the RT notwithstanding, a fundamental contrast between artworks and real objects. Perhaps this was already dimly sensed by the early framers of the IT who, inchoately realizing the nonreality of art, were perhaps limited only in supposing that the sole way objects had of being other than real is to be sham, so that artworks necessarily had to be imitations of real objects. This was too narrow. So Yeats saw in writing "Once out of nature I shall never take/My bodily form from any natural thing." It is but a matter of choice: and the Brillo box of the artworld may be just the Brillo box of the real one, separated and united by the *is* of artistic identification. But I should like to say some final words about the theories that make artworks possible, and their relationship to one another. In so doing, I shall beg some of the hardest philosophical questions I know.

I shall now think of pairs of predicates related to each other as "opposites," conceding straight off the vagueness of this *démodé* term. Contradictory predicates are not opposites, since one of each of them must apply to every object in the universe, and neither of a pair of opposites need apply to some objects in the universe. An object must first be of a certain kind before either of a pair of opposites applies to it, and then at most and at least one of the opposites must apply to it. So opposites are not contraries, for contraries may both be false of some objects in the universe, but opposites cannot both be false; for of some objects, neither of a pair of opposites *sensibly* applies, unless the object is of the right sort. Then, if the object is of the required kind, the opposites behave as contradictories. If F and non-F are opposites, an object o must be of a certain kind K before either of these sensibly applies; but if o is a member of K, then o either is F or non-F, to the exclusion of the other. The class of pairs of opposites that sensibly apply to the $(ô)Ko$ I shall designate as the class of *K-relevant predicates*. And a necessary condition for an object to be of a kind K is that at least one pair of K-relevant opposites be sensibly applicable to it. But, in fact, if an object is of kind K, at least and at most one of each K-relevant pair of opposites applies to it.

I am now interested in the K-relevant predicates for the class K of artworks. And let F and non-F be an opposite pair of such predicates. Now it might happen that, throughout an entire period of time, every artwork is non-F. But since nothing thus far is both an artwork and F, it might never occur to anyone that non-F is an artistically relevant predicate. The non-F-ness of artworks goes unmarked. By contrast, all works up to a given time might be G, it never occurring to anyone until that time that something might both be an artwork and non-G; indeed, it might have been thought that G was a *defining trait* of artworks when in fact something might first have to be an artwork before G is sensibly predicable of it—in which case non-G might also be predicable of artworks, and G itself then could not have been a defining trait of this class.

Let G be "is representational" and let F be "is expressionist." At a given time, these and their opposites are perhaps the only art-relevant predicates in critical use. Now letting '+' stand for a given predicate P and '−' for its opposite non-P, we may construct a style matrix more or less as follows:

F	G
+	+
+	−
−	+
−	−

The rows determine available styles, given the active critical vocabulary: representational expressionistic (e.g., Fauvism); representational nonexpressionistic (Ingres); nonrepresentational expressionistic (Abstract Expressionism); nonrepresentational nonexpressionist (hard-edge abstraction). Plainly, as we add art-relevant predicates, we increase the number of available styles at the rate of 2^n. It is, of course, not easy to see in advance which predicates are going to be added or replaced by their opposites, but suppose an artist determines that H shall henceforth be artistically relevant for his paintings. Then, in fact, both H and non-H become artistically relevant for *all* painting, and if his is the first and only painting that is H, every other painting in existence becomes non-H, and the entire community of paintings is enriched, together with a doubling of the available style opportunities. It is this retroactive enrichment of the entities in the artworld that makes it possible to discuss Raphael and De Kooning together, or Lichtenstein and Michelangelo. The greater the variety of artistically relevant predicates, the more complex the individual members of the artworld become; and the more one knows of the entire population of the artworld, the richer one's experience with any of its members.

In this regard, notice that, if there are m artistically relevant predicates, there is always a bottom row with m minuses. This row is apt to be occupied by purists. Having scoured their canvasses clear of what they regard as inessential, they credit themselves with having distilled out the essence of art. But this is just their fallacy: exactly as many artistically relevant predicates stand true of their square monochromes as stand true of any member of the Artworld, and they can *exist* as artworks only insofar as "impure" paintings exist. Strictly speaking, a black square by Reinhardt is artistically as rich as Titian's *Sacred and Profane Love*. This explains how less is more.

Fashion, as it happens, favors certain rows of the style matrix: museums, connoisseurs, and others are makeweights in the Artworld. To insist, or seek to, that all artists become representational, perhaps to gain entry into a specially prestigious exhibition, cuts the available style matrix in half: there are then $2^n/2$ ways of satisfying the requirement, and museums then can exhibit all these "approaches" to the topic they have set. But this is a matter of almost purely sociological interest: one row in the matrix is as legitimate as another. An artistic breakthrough consists, I suppose, in adding the possibility of a column to the matrix. Artists then, with greater or less alacrity, occupy the positions thus opened up: this is a remarkable feature of contemporary art, and for those unfamiliar with the matrix, it is hard, and perhaps impossible, to recognize certain positions as occupied by artworks. Nor would these things be artworks without the theories and the histories of the Artworld.

Brillo boxes enter the artworld with that same tonic incongruity the *commedia dell'arte* characters bring into *Ariadne auf Naxos*. Whatever is the artistically relevant predicate in virtue of which they gain their entry, the rest of the Artworld becomes that much the richer in having the opposite predicate available and applicable to its members. And, to return to the views of Hamlet with which we began this discussion, Brillo boxes may reveal us to ourselves as well as anything might: as a mirror held up to nature, they might serve to catch the conscience of our kings.

MIKHAIL MIKHAILOVICH BAKHTIN

AFTER AN UNFORTUNATE PERIOD of obscurity, due in no small part to his life and career in post-World War I Russia, Bakhtin has emerged as a major figure in contemporary discussions of literature and language. Particularly striking is his sense, expressed in the selections below, of the multiplicity of voices—he calls them "languages"—that inhabit the novelist's imagination and works. This theme of linguistic multiplicity is a major motif of what is called "postmodernism," and should be associated with the essays by Lyotard below and by Ricoeur, Derrida, and Foucault above.

MIKHAIL MIKHAILOVICH BAKHTIN

*Discourse in the Novel**

For the philosophy of language, for linguistics and for stylistics structured on their base, a whole series of phenomena have therefore remained almost entirely beyond the realm of consideration: these include the specific phenomena that are present in discourse and that are determined by its dialogic orientation, first, amid others' utterances inside a *single* language (the primordial dialogism of discourse), amid other "social languages" within a single *national* language and finally amid different national languages within the same *culture*, that is, the same socio-ideological conceptual horizon.[1]

In recent decades, it is true, these phenomena have begun to attract the attention of scholars in language and stylistics, but their fundamental and wide-ranging significance in all spheres of the life of discourse is still far from acknowledged.

The dialogic orientation of a word among other words (of all kinds and degrees of otherness) creates new and significant artistic potential in discourse, creates the potential for a distinctive art of prose, which has found its fullest and deepest expression in the novel.

We will focus our attention here on various forms and degrees of dialogic orientation in discourse, and on the special potential for a distinctive prose-art.

As treated by traditional stylistic thought, the word acknowledges only itself (that is, only its own context), its own object, its own direct expression and its own unitary and singular language. It acknowledges another word, one

* M. M. Bakhtin, "Discourse in the Novel," *The Dialogic Imagination*, ed. by Michael Holquist, trans. by Caryl Emerson and Michael Holquist (Austin: Univ. of Texas Press, 1981), pp. 275-300.

lying outside its own context, only as the neutral word of language, as the word of no one in particular, as simply the potential for speech. The direct word, as traditional stylistics understands it, encounters in its orientation toward the object only the resistance of the object itself (the impossibility of its being exhausted by a word, the impossibility of saying it all), but it does not encounter in its path toward the object the fundamental and richly varied opposition of another's word. No one hinders this word, no one argues with it.

But no living word relates to its object in a *singular* way: between the word and its object, between the word and the speaking subject, there exists an elastic environment of other, alien words about the same object, the same theme, and this is an environment that it is often difficult to penetrate. It is precisely in the process of living interaction with this specific environment that the word may be individualized and given stylistic shape.

Indeed, any concrete discourse (utterance) finds the object at which it was directed already as it were overlain with qualifications, open to dispute, charged with value, already enveloped in an obscuring mist—or, on the contrary, by the "light" of alien words that have already been spoken about it. It is entangled, shot through with shared thoughts, points of view, alien value judgments and accents. The word, directed toward its object, enters a dialogically agitated and tension-filled environment of alien words, value judgments and accents, weaves in and out of complex interrelationships, merges with some, recoils from others, intersects with yet a third group: and all this may crucially shape discourse, may leave a trace in all its semantic layers, may complicate its expression and influence its entire stylistic profile.

The living utterance, having taken meaning and shape at a particular historical moment in a socially specific environment, cannot fail to brush up against thousands of living dialogic threads, woven by socio-ideological consciousness around the given object of an utterance; it cannot fail to become an active participant in social dialogue. After all, the utterance arises out of this dialogue as a continuation of it and as a rejoinder to it—it does not approach the object from the sidelines.

The way in which the word conceptualizes its object is a complex act—all objects, open to dispute and overlain as they are with qualifications, are from one side highlighted while from the other side dimmed by heteroglot social opinion, by an alien word about them.[2] And into this complex play of light and shadow the word enters—it becomes saturated with this play, and must determine within it the boundaries of its own semantic and stylistic contours. The way in which the word conceives its object is complicated by a dialogic interaction within the object between various aspects of its socio-verbal intelligibility. And an artistic representation, an "image" of the object, may be penetrated by this dialogic play of verbal intentions that meet and are interwoven in it; such an image need not stifle these forces, but on the contrary may activate and organize them. If we imagine the *intention* of such a word, that is, its *directionality toward the object*, in the form of a ray of light, then the living and unrepeatable play of colors and light on the facets of the image that it constructs can be explained as the spectral dispersion of the ray-word, not within the object itself (as would be the case in the play of an image-as-trope, in poetic speech taken in the narrow sense, in an "autotelic word"), but rather as its spectral dispersion in an atmosphere filled with the alien words, value judgments and accents through which the ray passes on its way toward the object; the social atmosphere of the word, the atmosphere that surrounds the object, makes the facets of the image sparkle.

The word, breaking through to its own meaning and its own expression across an environment full of alien words and variously evaluating accents, harmonizing with some of the elements in this environment and striking a dissonance with others, is able, in this dialogized process, to shape its own stylistic profile and tone.

Such is the *image in artistic prose* and the image of *novelistic prose* in particular. In the atmosphere of the novel, the direct and unmediated intention of a word presents itself as something impermissably naive, something in fact impossible, for naiveté itself, under authentic novelistic conditions, takes on the nature of an internal polemic and is consequently dialogized (in, for example, the work of the Sentimentalists, in Chateaubriand and in Tolstoy). Such a dialogized image can occur in all the poetic genres as well, even in the lyric (to be sure, without setting the tone).[3] But such an image can fully unfold, achieve full complexity and depth and at the same time artistic closure, only under the conditions present in the genre of the novel.

In the poetic image narrowly conceived (in the image-as-trope), all activity—the dynamics of the image-as-word—is completely exhausted by the play between the word (with all its aspects) and the object (in all its aspects). The word plunges into the inexhaustible wealth and contradictory multiplicity of the object itself, with its "virginal," still "unuttered" nature; therefore it presumes nothing beyond the borders of its own context (except, of course, what can be found in the treasure-house of language itself). The word forgets that its object has its own history of contradictory acts of verbal recognition, as well as that heteroglossia that is always present in such acts of recognition.

For the writer of artistic prose, on the contrary, the object reveals first of all precisely the socially heteroglot multiplicity of its names, definitions and value judgments. Instead of the virginal fullness and inexhaustibility of the object itself, the prose writer confronts a multitude of routes, roads and paths that have been laid down in the object by social consciousness. Along with the internal contradictions inside the object itself, the prose writer witnesses as well the unfolding of social heteroglossia *surrounding* the object, the Tower-of-Babel mixing of languages that goes on around any object; the dialectics of the object are interwoven with the social dialogue surrounding it. For the prose writer, the object is a focal point for heteroglot voices among which his own voice must also sound; these voices create the background necessary for his own voice, outside of which his artistic prose nuances cannot be perceived, and without which they "do not sound."

The prose artist evaluates the social heteroglossia surrounding objects into an image that has finished contours, an image completely shot through with dialogized overtones; he creates artistically calculated nuances on all the fundamental voices and tones of this heteroglossia. But as we have already said, every extra-artistic prose discourse—in any of its forms, quotidian, rhetorical, scholarly—cannot fail to be oriented toward the "already uttered," the "already known," the "common opinion" and so forth. The dialogic orientation of discourse is a phenomenon that is, of course, a property of *any* discourse. It is the natural orientation of any living discourse. On all its various routes toward the object, in all its directions, the word encounters an alien word and cannot help encountering it in a living, tension-filled interaction. Only the mythical Adam, who approached a virginal and as yet verbally unqualified world with the first word, could really have escaped from start to finish this dialogic inter-orientation with the alien word that occurs in the object. Concrete historical human discourse does not have this privilege: it can deviate from such inter-orientation only on a conditional basis and only to a certain degree.

It is all the more remarkable that linguistics and the philosophy of discourse have been primarily oriented precisely toward this artificial, preconditioned status of the word, a word excised from dialogue and taken for the norm (although the primacy of dialogue over monologue is frequently proclaimed). Dialogue is studied merely as a compositional form in the structuring of speech, but the internal dialogism of the word (which occurs in a monologic utterance as well as in a rejoinder), the dialogism that penetrates its entire structure, all its semantic and expressive layers, is almost entirely ignored. But it is precisely this internal dialogism of the word, which does not assume any external compositional forms of dialogue, that cannot be isolated as an independent act, separate from the word's ability to form a concept *[koncipirovanie]* of its object—it is precisely this internal dialogism that has such enormous power to shape style. The internal dialogism of the word finds expression in a series of peculiar features in semantics, syntax and stylistics that have remained up to the present time completely unstudied by linguistics and stylistics (nor, what is more, have the peculiar semantic features of ordinary dialogue been studied).

The word is born in a dialogue as a living rejoinder within it; the word is shaped in dialogic interaction with an alien word that is already in the object. A word forms a concept of its own object in a dialogic way.

But this does not exhaust the internal dialogism of the word. It encounters an alien word not only in the object itself: every word is directed toward an *answer* and cannot escape the profound influence of the answering word that it anticipates.

The word in living conversation is directly, blatantly, oriented toward a future answer-word: it provokes an answer, anticipates it and structures itself in the answer's direction. Forming itself in an atmosphere of the already spoken, the word is at the same time determined by that which has not yet been said but which is needed and in fact anticipated by the answering word. Such is the situation in any living dialogue.

All rhetorical forms, monologic in their compositional structure, are oriented toward the listener and his answer. This orientation toward the listener is usually considered the basic constitutive feature of rhetorical discourse.[4] It is highly significant for rhetoric that this relationship toward the concrete listener, taking him into account, is a relationship that enters into the very internal construction of rhetorical discourse. This orientation toward an answer is open, blatant and concrete.

This open orientation toward the listener and his answer in everyday dialogue and in rhetorical forms has attracted the attention of linguists. But even where this has been the case, linguists have by and large gotten no further than the compositional forms by which the listener is taken into account; they have not sought influence springing from more profound meaning and style. They have taken into consideration only those aspects of style determined by demands for comprehensibility and clarity—that is, precisely those aspects that are deprived of any internal dialogism, that take the listener for a person who passively understands but not for one who actively answers and reacts.

The listener and his response are regularly taken into account when it comes to everyday dialogue and rhetoric, but every other sort of discourse as well is oriented toward an understanding that is "responsive"—although this orientation is not particularized in an independent act and is not compositionally marked. Responsive understanding is a fundamental force, one that participates in the formulation of discourse, and it is moreover an *active* understanding, one that discourse senses as resistance or support enriching the discourse.

Linguistics and the philosophy of language acknowledge only a passive understanding of discourse, and moreover this takes place by and large on the level of common language, that is, it is an understanding of an utterance's *neutral signification* and not its *actual meaning*.

The linguistic significance of a given utterance is understood against the background of language, while its actual meaning is understood against the background of other concrete utterances on the same theme, a background made up of contradictory opinions, points of view and value judgments—that is, precisely that background that, as we see, complicates the path of any word toward its object. Only now this contradictory environment of alien words is present to the speaker not in the object, but rather in the consciousness of the listener, as his apperceptive background, pregnant with responses and objections. And every utterance is oriented toward this apperceptive background of understanding, which is not a linguistic background but rather one composed of specific objects and emotional expressions. There occurs a new encounter between the utterance and an alien word, which makes itself felt as a new and unique influence on its style.

A passive understanding of linguistic meaning is no understanding at all, it is only the abstract aspect of meaning. But even a more concrete *passive* understanding of the meaning of the utterance, an understanding of the speaker's intention insofar as that understanding remains purely passive, purely receptive, contributes nothing new to the word under consideration, only mirroring it, seeking, at its most ambitious, merely the full reproduction of that which is already given in the word—even such an understanding never goes beyond the boundaries of the word's context and in no way enriches the word. Therefore, insofar as the speaker operates with such a passive understanding, nothing new can be introduced into his discourse; there can be no new aspects in his discourse relating to concrete objects and emotional expressions. Indeed the purely negative demands, such as could only emerge from a passive understanding (for instance, a need for greater clarity, more persuasiveness, more vividness and so forth), leave the speaker in his own personal context, within his own boundaries; such negative demands are completely immanent in the speaker's own discourse and do not go beyond his semantic or expressive self-sufficiency.

In the actual life of speech, every concrete act of understanding is active: it assimilates the word to be understood into its own conceptual system filled with specific objects and emotional expressions, and is indissolubly merged with the response, with a motivated agreement or disagreement. To some extent, primacy belongs to the response, as the activating principle: it creates the ground for understanding, it prepares the ground for an active and engaged understanding. Understanding comes to fruition only in the response. Understanding and response are dialectically merged and mutually condition each other; one is impossible without the other.

Thus an active understanding, one that assimilates the word under consideration into a new conceptual system, that of the one striving to understand, establishes a series of complex interrelationships, consonances and dissonances with the word and enriches it with new elements. It is precisely such an understanding that the speaker counts on. Therefore his orientation toward the listener is an orientation toward a specific conceptual horizon, toward the specific world of the listener; it introduces totally new elements into his discourse; it is in this way, after all, that various different points of view, conceptual horizons, systems for providing expressive accents, various social "languages" come to interact with one another. The speaker strives to get a reading on his own word, and on his own conceptual system that determines this word, within the alien conceptual system of the understanding receiver; he enters into dialogical relationships with certain aspects of this system. The speaker breaks through the alien conceptual horizon of the listener, constructs his own utterance on alien territory, against his, the listener's, apperceptive background.

This new form of internal dialogism of the word is different from that form determined by an encounter with an alien word within the object itself: here it is not the object that serves as the arena for the encounter, but rather the subjective belief system of the listener. Thus this dialogism bears a more subjective, psychological and (frequently) random character, sometimes crassly accommodating, sometimes provocatively polemical. Very often, especially in the rhetorical forms, this orientation toward the listener and the related internal dialogism of the word may simply overshadow the object: the strong point of any concrete listener becomes a self-sufficient focus of attention, and one that interferes with the word's creative work on its referent.

Although they differ in their essentials and give rise to varying stylistic effects in discourse, the dialogic relationship toward an alien word within the object and the relationship toward an alien word in the anticipated answer of the listener can, nevertheless, be very tightly interwoven with each other, becoming almost indistinguishable during stylistic analysis.

Thus, discourse in Tolstoy is characterized by a sharp internal dialogism, and this discourse is moreover dialogized in the belief system of the reader—whose peculiar semantic and expressive characteristics Tolstoy acutely senses—as well as in the object. These two lines of dialogization (having in most cases polemical overtones) are tightly interwoven in his style: even in the most "lyrical" expressions and the most "epic" descriptions, Tolstoy's discourse harmonizes and disharmonizes (more often disharmonizes) with various aspects of the heteroglot socio-verbal consciousness ensnaring the object, while at the same time polemically invading the reader's belief and evaluative system, striving to stun and destroy the apperceptive background of the reader's active understanding. In this respect Tolstoy is an heir of the eighteenth century, especially of Rousseau. This propagandizing impulse sometimes leads to a narrowing-down of heteroglot social consciousness (against which Tolstoy polemicizes) to the consciousness of his immediate contemporary, a contemporary of the day and not of the epoch; what follows from this is a radical concretization of dialogization (almost always undertaken in the service of a polemic). For this reason Tolstoy's dialogization, no matter how acutely we sense it in the expressive profile of his style, sometimes requires special historical or literary commentary: we are not sure with *what* precisely a given tone is in harmony or disharmony, for this dissonance or consonance has entered into the positive project of creating a style.[5] It is true that such extreme concreteness (which approaches at time the feuilleton) is present only in those secondary aspects, the overtones of internal dialogization in Tolstoy's discourse.

In those examples of the internal dialogization of discourse that we have chosen (the internal, as contrasted with the external, compositionally marked, dialogue) the relationship to the alien word, to an alien utterance enters into the positing of the style. Style organically contains within itself indices that reach outside itself, a correspondence of its own elements and the elements of an alien context. The internal politics of style (how the elements are put together) is determined by its external politics (its relationship to alien discourse). Discourse lives, as it were, on the boundary between its own context and another, alien, context.

In any actual dialogue the rejoinder also leads such a double life: it is structured and conceptualized in the context of the dialogue as a whole, which consists of its own utterances ("own" from the point of view of the speaker) and of alien utterances (those of the partner). One cannot excise the rejoinder from this combined context made up of one's own words and the words of another without losing its sense and tone. It is an organic part of a heteroglot unity.

The phenomenon of internal dialogization, as we have said, is present to a greater or lesser extent in all realms of the life of the word. But if in extra-artistic prose (everyday, rhetorical, scholarly) dialogization usually stands apart, crystallizes into a special kind of act of its own and runs its course in ordinary dialogue or in other, compositionally clearly marked forms for mixing and polemicizing with the discourse of another—then in *artistic* prose, and especially in the novel, this dialogization penetrates from within the very way in which the word conceives its object and its means for expressing itself, reformulating the semantics and syntactical structure of discourse. Here dialogic inter-orientation becomes, as it were, an event of discourse itself, animating from within and dramatizing discourse in all its aspects.

In the majority of poetic genres (poetic in the narrow sense), as we have said, the internal dialogization of discourse is not put to artistic use, it does not enter into the work's "aesthetic object," and is artificially extinguished in poetic discourse. In the novel, however, this internal dialogization becomes one of the most fundamental aspects of prose style and undergoes a specific artistic elaboration.

But internal dialogization can become such a crucial force for creating form only where individual differences and contradictions are enriched by social heteroglossia, where dialogic reverberations do not sound in the semantic heights of discourse (as happens in the rhetorical genres) but penetrate the deep strata of discourse, dialogize language itself and the world view a particular language has (the internal form of discourse)—where the dialogue of voices arises directly out of a social dialogue of "languages," where an alien utterance begins to sound like a socially alien language, where the orientation of the word among alien utterances changes into an orientation of a word among socially alien languages within the boundaries of one and the same national language. . . .

Language—like the living concrete environment in which the consciousness of the verbal artist lives—is never unitary. It is unitary only as an abstract grammatical system of normative forms, taken in isolation from the concrete, ideological conceptualizations that fill it, and in isolation from the uninterrupted process of historical becoming that is a characteristic of all living language. Actual social life and historical becoming create within an abstractly unitary national language a multitude of concrete worlds, a multitude of bounded verbal-ideological and social belief systems; within these various systems (identical in the abstract) are elements of language filled with various semantic and axiological content and each with its own different sound.

Literary language—both spoken and written—although it is unitary not only in its shared, abstract, linguistic markers but also in its forms for conceptualizing these abstract markers, is itself stratified and heteroglot in its aspect as an expressive system, that is, in the forms that carry its meanings.

This stratification is accomplished first of all by the specific organisms called *genres*. Certain features of language (lexicological, semantic, syntactic) will knit together with the intentional aim, and with the overall accentual system inherent in one or another genre: oratorical, publicistic, newspaper and journalistic genres, the genres of low literature (penny dreadfuls, for instance) or, finally, the various genres of high literature. Certain features of language take on the specific favor of a given genre: they knit together with specific points of view, specific approaches, forms of thinking, nuances and accents characteristic of the given genre.

In addition, there is interwoven with this generic stratification of language a *professional* stratification of language, in the broad sense of the term "professional": the language of the lawyer, the doctor, the businessman, the politician, the public education teacher and so forth, and these sometimes coincide with, and sometimes depart from, the stratification into genres. It goes without saying that these languages differ from each other not only in their vocabularies; they involve specific forms of manifesting intentions, forms for making conceptualization and evaluation concrete. And even the very language of the writer (the poet or novelist) can be taken as a professional jargon on a par with professional jargons.

What is important to us here is the intentional dimensions, that is, the denotative and expressive dimension of the "shared" language's stratification. It is in fact not the neutral linguistic components of language being stratified and differentiated, but rather a situation in which the intentional possibilities of language are being expropriated: these possibilities are realized in specific directions, filled with specific content, they are made concrete, particular, and are permeated with concrete value judgments; they knit together with specific objects and with the belief systems of certain genres of expression and points of view peculiar to particular professions. Within these points of view, that is, for the speakers of the language themselves, these generic languages and professional jargons are directly intentional—they denote and express directly and fully, and are capable of expressing themselves without mediation; but outside, that is, for those not participating in the given purview, these languages may be treated as objects, as typifactions, as local color. For such outsiders, the intentions premeating these languages become *things*, limited in their meaning and expression; they attract to, or excise from, such language a particular word—making it difficult for the word to be utilized in a directly intentional way, without any qualifications.

But the situation is far from exhausted by the generic and professional stratification of the common literary language. Although at its very core literary language is frequently socially homogeneous, as the oral and written language of a dominant social group, there is nevertheless always present, even here, a certain degree of social differentiation, a social stratification, that in other eras can become extremely acute. Social stratification may here and there coincide with generic and professional stratification, but in essence it is, of course, a thing completely autonomous and peculiar to itself.

Social stratification is also and primarily determined by differences between the forms used to convey meaning and between the expressive planes of various belief systems—that is, stratification expresses itself in typical differences in ways used to conceptualize and accentuate elements of language, and stratification may not violate the abstractly linguistic dialectological unity of the shared literary language.

What is more, all socially significant world views have the capacity to exploit the intentional possibilities of language through the medium of their specific concrete instancing. Various tendencies (artistic and otherwise), circles, journals, particular newspapers, even particular significant artistic works and individual persons are all capable of stratifying language, in proportion to their social significance; they are capable of attracting its words and forms into their orbit by means of their own characteristic intentions and accents, and in so doing to a certain extent alienating these words and forms from other tendencies, parties, artistic works and persons.

Every socially significant verbal performance has the ability—sometimes for a long period of time, and for a wide circle of persons—to infect with its own intention certain aspects of language that had been affected by its semantic and expressive impulse, imposing on them specific semantic nuances and specific axiological overtones; thus, it can create slogan-words, curse-words, praise-words and so forth.

In any given historical moment of verbal-ideological life, each generation at each social level has its own language; moreover, every age group has as a matter of fact its own language, its own vocabulary, its own particular accentual system that, in their turn, vary depending on social level, academic institution (the language of the cadet, the high school student, the trade school student are all different languages) and other stratifying factors. All this is brought about by socially typifying languages, no matter how narrow the social circle in which they are spoken. It is even possible to have a family jargon define the societal limits of a language, as, for instance, the jargon of the Irtenevs in Tolstoy, with its special vocabulary and unique accentual system.

And finally, at any given moment, languages of various epochs and periods of socio-ideological life cohabit with one another. Even languages of the day exist: one could say that today's and yesterday's socio-ideological and political "day" do not, in a certain sense, share the same language; every day represents another socio-ideological semantic "state of affairs," another vocabulary, another accentual system, with its own slogans, its own ways of assigning blame and praise. Poetry depersonalizes "days" in language, while prose, as we shall see, often deliberately intensifies difference between them, gives them embodied representation and dialogically opposes them to one another in unresolvable dialogues.

Thus at any given moment of its historical existence, language is heteroglot from top to bottom: it represents the co-existence of socio-ideological contradictions between the present and the past, between differing epochs of the past, between different socio-ideological groups in the present, between tendencies, schools, circles and so forth, all given a bodily form. These "languages" of heteroglossia intersect each other in a variety of ways, forming new socially typifying "languages."

Each of these "languages" of heteroglossia requires a methodology very different from the others; each is grounded in a completely different principle for marking differences and for establishing units (for some this principle is functional, in others it is the principle of theme and content, in yet others it is, properly speaking, a socio-dialectological principle). Therefore languages do not *exclude* each other, but rather intersect with each other in many different ways (the Ukrainian language, the language of the epic poem, of early Symbolism, of the student, of a particular generation of children, of the run-of-the-mill intellectual, of the Nietzschean and so on). It might even seem that the very word "language" loses all meaning in the process—for apparently there is no single plane on which all these "languages" might be juxtaposed to one another.

In actual fact, however, there does exist a common plane that methodologically justifies our juxtaposing them: all languages of heteroglossia, whatever the principle underlying them and making each unique, are specific points of view on the world, forms for conceptualizing the world in words, specific world views, each characterized by its own objects, meanings and values. As such they all may be juxtaposed to one another, mutually supplement one another, contradict one another and be interrelated dialogically. As such they encounter one another and co-exist in the consciousness of real people—first and foremost, in the creative consciousness of people who write novels. As such, these languages live a real life, they struggle and evolve in an environment of social heteroglossia. Therefore they are all able to enter into the unitary plane of the novel, which can unite in itself parodic stylizations of generic languages, various forms of stylizations and illustrations of professional and period-bound languages, the languages of particular generations, of social dialects and others (as occurs, for example, in the English comic novel). They may all be drawn in by the novelist for the orchestration of his themes and for the refracted (indirect) expression of his intentions and values.

This is why we constantly put forward the referential and expressive—that is, intentional—factors as the force that stratifies and differentiates the common literary language, and not the linguistic markers (lexical coloration, semantic overtones, etc.) of generic languages, professional jargons and so forth—markers that are, so to speak, the sclerotic deposits of an intentional process, signs left behind on the path of the real living project of an intention, of the particular way it imparts meaning to general linguistic norms. These external markers, linguistically observable and fixable, cannot in themselves be understood or studied without understanding the specific conceptualization they have been given by an intention.

Discourse lives, as it were, beyond itself, in a living impulse [*napravlennost'*] toward the object; if we detach ourselves completely from this impulse all we have left is the naked corpse of the word, from which we can learn nothing at all about the social situation or the fate of a given word in life. *To study the word as such, ignoring the impulse that reaches out beyond it, is just as senseless as to study psychological experience outside the context of that real life toward which it was directed and by which it is determined.* . . .

The language of the prose writer deploys itself according to degrees of greater or lesser proximity to the author and to his ultimate semantic instantiation: certain aspects of language directly and unmediatedly express (as in poetry) the semantic and expressive intentions of the author, others refract these intentions; the writer of prose does not meld completely with any of these words, but rather accents each of them in a particular way—humorously, ironically, parodically and so forth;[6] yet another group may stand even further from the author's ultimate semantic instantiation, still more thoroughly refracting his intentions; and there are, finally, those words that are completely denied any authorial intentions: the author does not express *himself* in them (as the author of the word)—rather, he *exhibits* them as a unique speech-thing, they function for him as something completely reified. Therefore the stratification of language—generic, professional, social in the narrow sense, that of particular world views, particular tendencies, particular individuals, the social speech diversity and language-diversity (dialects) of language—upon entering the novel all these strata establish their own special order within it, and become a unique artistic system orchestrating the intentional theme of the author.

Thus a prose writer can distance himself from the language of his own work, while at the same time distancing himself, in varying degrees, from the different layers and aspects of the work. He can make use of language without wholly giving himself up to it, he may treat it as semi-alien or completely alien to himself, while compelling language ultimately to serve all his own intentions. The author does not speak in a given language (from which he distances himself to a greater or lesser degree), but he speaks, as it were, *through* language, a language that has somehow more or less materialized, become objectivized, that he merely ventriloquates.

The prose writer as a novelist does not strip away the intentions of others from the heteroglot language of his works, he does not violate those socio-ideological cultural horizons (big and little worlds) that open up behind heteroglot languages—rather, he welcomes them into his work. The prose writer makes use of words that are already populated with the social intentions of others and compels them to serve his own new intentions, to serve a second master. Therefore the intentions of the prose writer are refracted, and refracted *at different angles,* depending on the degree to which the refracted, heteroglot languages he deals with are socio-ideologically alien, already embodied and already objectivized.

The orientation of the word amid the utterances and languages of others, and all the specific phenomena connected with this orientation, takes on *artistic* significance in novel style. Diversity of voices and heteroglossia enter the novel and organize themselves within it into a structured artistic system. This constitutes the distinguishing feature of the novel as a genre.

Any stylistics capable of dealing with the distinctiveness of the novel as a genre must be a *sociological stylistics*. The internal social dialogism of novelistic discourse requires the concrete social context of discourse to be exposed, to be revealed as the force that determines its entire stylistic structure, its "form" and its "content," determining it not from without, but from within; for indeed, social dialogue reverberates in all aspects of discourse, in those relating to "content" as well as the "formal" aspects themselves.

The development of the novel is a function of the deepening of dialogic essence, its increased scope and greater precision. Fewer and fewer neutral, hard elements ("rock bottom truths") remain that are not drawn into dialogue. Dialogue moves into the deepest molecular and, ultimately, subatomic levels.

Of course, even the poetic word is social, but poetic forms reflect lengthier social processes, i.e., those tendencies in social life requiring centuries to unfold. The novelistic word, however, registers with extreme subtlety the tiniest shifts and oscillations of the social atmosphere; it does so, moreover, while registering it as a whole, in all of its aspects.

When heteroglossia enters the novel it becomes subject to an artistic reworking. The social and historical voices populating language, all its words and all its forms, which provide language with its particular concrete conceptualizations, are organized in the novel into a structured stylistic system that expresses the differentiated socio-ideological position of the author amid the heteroglossia of his epoch.

NOTES

1. Linguistics acknowledges only a mechanical reciprocal influencing and intermixing of languages (that is, one that is unconscious and determined by social conditions) which is reflected in abstract linguistic elements (phonetic and morphological).

2. Highly significant in this respect is the struggle that must be undertaken in such movements as Rousseauism, Naturalism, Impressionism, Acmeism, Dadaism, Surrealism and analogous schools with the "qualified" nature of the object (a struggle occasioned by the idea of a return to primordial consciousness, to original consciousness, to the object itself in itself, to pure perception and so forth).

3. The Horatian lyric, Villon, Heine, Laforgue, Annenskij and others—despite the fact that these are extremely varied instances.

4. Cf. V. Vinogradov's book *On Artistic Prose*, the chapter "Rhetoric and Poetics," pp. 75ff., where definitions taken from the older rhetorics are introduced.

5. Cf. B. M. Eichenbaum's book *Lev Tolstoj*, book I (Leningrad, 1928), which contains much relevant material; for example, an explication of the topical context of "Family Happiness."

6. That is to say, the words are not his if we understand them as direct words, but they are his as things that are being transmitted ironically, exhibited and so forth, that is, as words that are understood from the distances appropriate to humor, irony, parody, etc.

PSYCHOLOGY AND ART: FREUD, JUNG, VYGOTSKY

THE FOLLOWING SECTION PRESENTS three psychologists whose theories are important for the understanding of art. Little needs to be said about Freud's importance, nor about the relevance of psychological and psychoanalytical theories to the understanding of art. Freud draws a parallel between daydreams and art, each having important functions in the lives of human agents. He offers a view in which the significance of art lies in its relationship to unconscious processes, in its role relative to censorship and repression in everyday and pathological experience. Such a view tends to make the importance of art obscure, and Jung replies with a far more universal view of the collective unconscious, of archetypes that inhabit the recesses of all human inner experience, expressed in myth and religion but also in art. Jung's criticism of Freud is that the significance of art cannot lie exclusively in personal psychological material, but must transcend the person to universal characteristics of humanity.

Lev Vygotsky, a Soviet psychologist from the first half of the twentieth century, is not as well known as Freud and Jung, but his view of how individuality and the inner life are derived from social experience has been received with enthusiasm by many cognitive and social psychologists, and has important implications for the understanding of art and the work of artists.

SIGMUND FREUD

*The Relation of the Poet to Day-Dreaming**

We laymen have always wondered greatly—like the cardinal who put the question to Ariosto—how that strange being, the poet, comes by his material. What makes him able to carry us with him in such a way and to arouse emotions in us of which we thought ourselves perhaps not even capable? Our interest in the problem is only stimulated by the circumstance that if we ask poets themselves they give us no explanation of the matter, or at least no satisfactory explanation. The knowledge that not even the clearest insight into the factors conditioning the choice of imaginative material, or into the nature of the ability to fashion that material, will ever make writers of us does not in any way detract from our interest.

If we could only find some activity in ourselves, or in people like ourselves, which was in any way akin to the writing of imaginative works! If we could do so, then examination of it would give us a hope of obtaining some insight into the creative powers of imaginative writers. And indeed, there is some prospect of achieving this—writers themselves always try to lessen the distance between their kind and ordinary human beings; they so often assure us that every man is at heart a poet, and that the last poet will not die until the last human being does.

We ought surely to look in the child for the first traces of imaginative activity. The child's best loved and most absorbing occupation is play. Perhaps

---

* Sigmund Freud, *Collected Papers*, Vol. 4 (article translated by I. F. Grant Duff) (New York: Basic Books), pp. 173-183 (complete). First published in *Neue Revue*, Vol. I, 1908; reprinted in *Sammlung*, Zweite Folge.

we may say that every child at play behaves like an imaginative writer, in that he creates a world of his own or, more truly, he rearranges the things of his world and orders it in a new way that pleases him better. It would be incorrect to think that he does not take this world seriously; on the contrary, he takes his play very seriously and expends a great deal of emotion on it. The opposite of play is not serious occupation but—reality. Notwithstanding the large affective cathexis of his play-world, the child distinguishes it perfectly from reality; only he likes to borrow the objects and circumstances that he imagines from the tangible and visible things of the real world. It is only this linking of it to reality that still distinguishes a child's 'play' from 'day-dreaming'.

Now the writer does the same as the child at play: he creates a world of phantasy which he takes very seriously; that is, he invests it with a great deal of affect, while separating it sharply from reality. Language has preserved this relationship between children's play and poetic creation. It designates certain kinds of imaginative creation, concerned with tangible objects and capable of representation, as 'plays'; the people who present them are called 'players'. The unreality of this poetical world of imagination, however, has very important consequences for literary technique, for many things which if they happened in real life could produce no pleasure can nevertheless give enjoyment in a play—many emotions which are essentially painful may become a source of enjoyment to the spectators and hearers of a poet's work.

There is another consideration relating to the contrast between reality and play on which we will dwell for a moment. Long after a child has grown up and stopped playing, after he has for decades attempted to grasp the realities of life with all seriousness, he may one day come to a state of mind in which the contrast between play and reality is again abrogated. The adult can remember with what intense seriousness he carried on his childish play; then by comparing his would-be serious occupations with his childhood's play, he manages to throw off the heavy burden of life and obtain the great pleasure of humour.

As they grow up, people cease to play, and appear to give up the pleasure they derived from play. But anyone who knows anything of the mental life of human beings is aware that hardly anything is more difficult to them than to give up a pleasure they have once tasted. Really we never can relinquish anything; we only exchange one thing for something else. When we appear to give something up, all we really do is to adopt a substitute. So when the human being grows up and ceases to play he only gives up the connection with real objects; instead of playing he then begins to create phantasy. He builds castles in the air and creates what are called day-dreams. I believe that the greater number of human beings create phantasies at times as long as they live. This is a fact which has been overlooked for a long time, and its importance has therefore not been properly appreciated.

The phantasies of human beings are less easy to observe than the play of children. Children do, it is true, play alone, or form with other children a closed world in their minds for the purposes of play; but a child does not conceal his play from adults, even though his playing is quite unconcerned with them. The adult, on the other hand, is ashamed of his day-dreams and conceals them from other people; he cherishes them as his most intimate possessions and as a rule he would rather confess all his misdeeds than tell his day-dreams. For this reason he may believe that he is the only person who makes up such phantasies, without having any idea that everybody else tells themselves stories of the same kind. Day-dreaming is a continuation of play, nevertheless, and the motives which lie behind these two activities contain a very good reason for this different behaviour in the child at play and in the day-dreaming adult.

The play of children is determined by their wishes—really by the child's *one* wish, which is to be grown-up, the wish that helps to 'bring him up'. He always plays at being grown-up; in play he imitates what is known to him of the lives of adults. Now he has no reason to conceal this wish. With the adult it is otherwise; on the one hand, he knows that he is expected not to play any longer or to day-dream, but to be making his way in a real world. On the other hand, some of the wishes from which his phantasies spring are such as have to be entirely hidden; therefore he is ashamed of his phantasies as being childish and as something prohibited.

If they are concealed with so much secretiveness, you will ask, how do we know so much about the human propensity to create phantasies? Now there is a certain class of human beings upon whom not a god, indeed, but a stern goddess—Necessity—has laid the task of giving an account of what they suffer and what they enjoy. These people are the neurotics; among other things they have to confess their phantasies to the physician to whom they go in the hope of recovering through mental treatment. This is our best source of knowledge, and we have later found good reason to suppose that our patients tell us about themselves nothing that we could not also hear from healthy people.

Let us try to learn some of the characteristics of day-dreaming. We can begin by saying that happy people never make phantasies, only unsatisfied ones. Unsatisfied wishes are the driving power behind phantasies; every separate phantasy contains the fulfilment of a wish, and improves on unsatisfactory reality. The impelling wishes vary according to the sex, character and circumstances of the creator; they may be easily divided, however, into two principal groups. Either they are ambitious wishes, serving to exalt the person creating them, or they are erotic. In young women erotic wishes dominate the phantasies almost exclusively, for their ambition is generally comprised in their erotic longings; in young men egoistic and ambitious wishes assert themselves plainly enough alongside their erotic desires. But we will not lay stress on the distinction between these two trends; we prefer to emphasize the fact that they are often united. In many altar-pieces the portrait of the donor is to be found in one corner of the picture; and in the greater number of ambitious day-dreams, too, we can discover a woman in some corner, for whom the dreamer performs all his heroic deeds and at whose feet all his triumphs are to be laid. Here you see we have strong enough motives for concealment; a well-brought-up woman is, indeed, credited with only a minimum of erotic desire, while a young man has to learn to suppress the overweening self-regard he acquires in the indulgent atmosphere surrounding his childhood, so that he may find his proper place in a society that is full of other persons making similar claims.

We must not imagine that the various products of this impulse towards phantasy, castles in the air or day-dreams, are stereotyped or unchangeable. On the contrary, they fit themselves into the changing impressions of life, alter with the vicissitudes of life; every deep new impression gives them what might be called a 'date-stamp'. The relation of phantasies to time is altogether of great importance. One may say that a phantasy at one and the same moment hovers between three periods of time—the three periods of our ideation. The activity of phantasy in the mind is linked up with some current impression, occasioned by some event in the present, which had the power to rouse an intense desire. From there it wanders back to the memory of an early experience, generally belonging to infancy, in which this wish was fulfilled. Then it creates for itself a situation which is to emerge in the future, representing the fulfilment of the wish—this is the day-dream or phantasy, which now carries in it traces both of the occasion which engendered it and of some past memory. So past, present and future are threaded, as it were, on the string of the wish that runs through them all.

A very ordinary example may serve to make my statement clearer. Take the case of a poor orphan lad, to whom you have given the address of some employer where he may perhaps get work. On the way there he falls into a day-dream suitable to the situation from which it springs. The content of the phantasy will be somewhat as follows: He is taken on and pleases his new employer, makes himself indispensable in the business, is taken into the family of the employer, and marries the charming daughter of the house. Then he comes to conduct the business first as a partner, and then as successor to his father-in-law. In this way the dreamer regains what he had in his happy childhood, the protecting house, his loving parents and the first objects of his affection. You will see from such an example how the wish employs some event in the present to plan a future on the pattern of the past.

Much more could be said about phantasies, but I will only allude as briefly as possible to certain points. If phantasies become over-luxuriant and over-powerful, the necessary conditions for an outbreak of neurosis or psychosis are constituted; phantasies are also the first preliminary stage in the mind of the symptoms of illness of which our patients complain. A broad by-path here branches off into pathology.

I cannot pass over the relation of phantasies to dreams. Our nocturnal dreams are nothing but such phantasies, as we can make clear by interpreting them.[1] Language, in its unrivalled wisdom, long ago decided the question of the essential nature of dreams by giving the name of 'day-dreams' to the airy creations of phantasy. If the meaning of our dreams usually remains obscure in spite of this clue, it is because of the circumstance that at night wishes of which we are ashamed also become active in us, wishes which we have to hide from ourselves, which were consequently repressed and pushed back into the unconscious. Such repressed wishes and their derivatives can therefore achieve expression only when almost completely disguised. When scientific work had succeeded in elucidating the distortion in dreams, it was no longer difficult to recognize that nocturnal dreams are fulfilments of desires in exactly the same way as day-dreams are—those phantasies with which we are all so familiar.

So much for day-dreaming; now for the poet! Shall we dare really to compare an imaginative writer with 'one who dreams in broad daylight', and his creations with day-dreams? Here, surely, a first distinction is forced upon us; we must distinguish between poets who, like the bygone creators of epics and tragedies, take over their material ready-made, and those who seem to create their material spontaneously. Let us keep to the latter, and let us also not choose for our comparison those writers who are most highly esteemed by critics. We will choose the less pretentious writers of romances, novels and stories, who are read all the same by the widest circles of men and women. There is one very marked characteristic in the productions of these writers which must strike us all: they all have a hero who is the centre of interest, for whom the author tries to win our sympathy by every possible means, and whom he places under the protection of a special providence. If at the end of one chapter the hero is left unconscious and bleeding from severe wounds, I am sure to find him at the beginning of the next being carefully tended and on the way to recovery; if the first volume ends in the hero being shipwrecked in a storm at sea, I am certain to hear at the beginning of the next of his hairbreadth escape—otherwise, indeed, the story could not continue. The feeling of security with which I follow the hero through his dangerous adventures is the same as that with which a real hero throws himself into the water to save a drowning man, or exposes himself to the fire of the enemy while storming a battery. It is this very feeling of being a hero which one of our best authors has well expressed in the famous phrase, *'Es kann dir nix g'schehen!'*[2] It seems to me, however, that this significant mark of invulnerability very clearly betrays—His Majesty the Ego, the hero of all day-dreams and all novels.

The same relationship is hinted at in yet other characteristics of these egocentric stories. When all the women in a novel invariably fall in love with the hero, this can hardly be looked upon as a description of reality, but it is easily understood as an essential constituent of a day-dream. The same thing holds good when the other people in the story are sharply divided into good and bad, with complete disregard of the manifold variety in the traits of real human beings; the 'good' ones are those who help the ego in its character of hero, while the 'bad' are his enemies and rivals.

We do not in any way fail to recognize that many imaginative productions have travelled far from the original naïve day-dream, but I cannot suppress the surmise that even the most extreme variations could be brought into relationship with this model by an uninterrupted series of transitions. It has struck me in many so-called psychological novels, too, that only one person—once again the hero—is described from within; the author dwells in his soul and looks upon the other people from outside. The psychological novel in general probably owes its peculiarities to the tendency of modern writers to split up their ego by self-observation into many component-egos, and in this way to personify the conflicting trends in their own mental life in many heroes. There are certain novels, which might be called 'excentric', that seem to stand in marked contradiction to the typical day-dream; in these the person introduced as the hero plays the least active part of anyone, and seems instead to let the actions and sufferings of other people pass him by like a spectator. Many of the later novels of Zola belong to this class. But I must say that the psychological analysis of people who are not writers, and who deviate in many things from the so-called norm, has shown us analogous variations in their day-dreams in which the ego contents itself with the role of spectator.

If our comparison of the imaginative writer with the day-dreamer, and of poetic production with the day-dream, is to be of any value, it must show itself fruitful in some way or other. Let us try, for instance, to examine the works of writers in reference to the idea propounded above, the relation of the phantasy to the wish that runs through it and to the three periods of time; and with its help let us study the connection between the life of the writer and his productions. Hitherto it has not been known what preliminary ideas would constitute an approach to this problem; very often this relation has been regarded as much simpler than it is; but the insight gained from phantasies leads us to expect the following state of things. Some actual experience which made a strong impression on the writer had stirred up a memory of an earlier experience, generally belonging to childhood, which then arouses a wish that finds a fulfilment in the work in question, and in which elements of the recent event and the old memory should be discernible.

Do not be alarmed at the complexity of this formula; I myself expect that in reality it will prove itself to be too schematic, but that possibly it may contain a first means of approach to the true state of affairs. From some attempts I have made I think that this way of approaching works of the imagination might not be unfruitful. You will not forget that the stress laid on the writer's memories of his childhood, which perhaps seems so strange, is ultimately derived from the hypothesis that imaginative creation, like day-dreaming, is a continuation of and substitute for the play of childhood.

We will not neglect to refer also to that class of imaginative work which must be recognized not as spontaneous production, but as a refashioning of ready-made material. Here, too, the writer retains a certain amount of independence, which can express itself in the choice of material and in changes in the material chosen, which are often considerable. As far as it goes, this material is derived from the racial treasure-house of myths, legends and fairy-tales. The study of these creations of racial psychology is in no way complete, but it seems extremely probable that myths, for example, are distorted vestiges of the wish-phantasies of whole nations—the age-long dreams of young humanity.

You will say that, although writers came first in the title of this paper, I have told you far less about them than about phantasy. I am aware of that, and will try to excuse myself by pointing to the present state of our knowledge. I could only throw out suggestions and bring up interesting points which arise from the study of phantasies, and which pass beyond them to the problem of the choice of literary material. We have not touched on the other problem at all, *i.e.*, what are the means which writers use to achieve those emotional reactions in us that are roused by their productions. But I would at least point out to you the path which leads from our discussion of day-dreams to the problems of the effect produced on us by imaginative works.

You will remember that we said the day-dreamer hid his phantasies carefully from other people because he had reason to be ashamed of them. I may now add that even if he were to communicate them to us, he would give us no pleasure by his disclosures. When we hear such phantasies they repel us, or at least leave us cold. But when a man of literary talent presents his plays, or relates what we take to be his personal day-dreams, we experience great pleasure arising probably from many sources. How the writer accomplishes this is his innermost secret; the essential *ars poetica* lies in the technique by which our feeling of repulsion is overcome, and this has certainly to do with those barriers erected between every individual being and all others. We can guess at two methods used in this technique. The writer softens the egotistical character of the day-dream by changes and disguises, and he bribes us by the offer of a purely formal, that is, aesthetic, pleasure in the presentation of his phantasies. The increment of pleasure which is offered us in order to release yet greater pleasure arising from deeper sources in the mind is called an 'incitement premium' or technically, 'fore-pleasure'. I am of opinion that all the aesthetic pleasure we gain from the works of imaginative writers is of the same type as this 'fore-pleasure', and that the true enjoyment of literature proceeds from the release of tensions in our minds. Perhaps much that brings about this result consists in the writer's putting us into a position in which we can enjoy our own day-dreams without reproach or shame. Here we reach a path leading into novel, interesting and complicated researches, but we also, at least for the present, arrive at the end of the present discussion.

NOTES

1. Cf. Freud, *Die Traumdeutung.*

2. Anzengruber. [The phrase means 'Nothing can happen to *me!*'—Trans.]

CARL GUSTAV JUNG

*Psychology and Literature**

It is obvious enough that psychology, being the study of psychic processes, can be brought to bear upon the study of literature, for the human psyche is the womb of all the sciences and arts. We may expect psychological research, on the one hand, to explain the formation of a work of art, and on the other to reveal the factors that make a person artistically creative. The psychologist is thus faced with two separate and distinct tasks, and must approach them in radically different ways.

In the case of the work of art we have to deal with a product of complicated psychic activities—but a product that is apparently intentional and consciously shaped. In the case of the artist we must deal with the psychic apparatus itself. In the first instance we must attempt the psychological analysis of a definitely circumscribed and concrete artistic achievement, while in the second we must analyse the living and creative human being as a unique personality. Although these two undertakings are closely related and even interdependent, neither of them can yield the explanations that are sought by the other. It is of course possible to draw inferences about the artist from the work of art, and *vice versa*, but these inferences are never conclusive. At best they are probable surmises or lucky guesses. A knowledge of Goethe's particular relation to his mother throws some light upon Faust's exclamation: "The mothers—mothers—how very strange it sounds!" But it does not enable us to see how the attachment to his mother could produce the *Faust* drama itself, however unmistakably we sense in the man Goethe a deep connection

* Carl Gustav Jung, "Psychology and Literature," translated by W. S. Dell and Cary F. Baynes, in *Modern Man in Search of a Soul* (New York: Harcourt Brace Jovanovich, 1955), pp. 208-223.

507

between the two. Nor are we more successful in reasoning in the reverse direction. There is nothing in *The Nibelungenring* that would enable us to recognize or definitely infer the fact that Wagner occasionally liked to wear womanish clothes, though hidden connections exist between the heroic masculine world of the Nibelungs and a certain pathological effeminacy in the man Wagner.

The present state of development of psychology does not allow us to establish those rigorous causal connections which we expect of a science. It is only in the realm of the psychophysiological instincts and reflexes that we can confidently operate with the idea of causality. From the point where psychic life begins—that is, at a level of greater complexity—the psychologist must content himself with more or less widely ranging descriptions of happenings and with the vivid portrayal of the warp and weft of the mind in all its amazing intricacy. In doing this, he must refrain from designating any one psychic process, taken by itself, as "necessary." Were this not the state of affairs, and could the psychologist be relied upon to uncover the causal connections within a work of art and in the process of artistic creation, he would leave the study of art no ground to stand on and would reduce it to a special branch of his own science. The psychologist, to be sure, may never abandon his claim to investigate and establish causal relations in complicated psychic events. To do so would be to deny psychology the right to exist. Yet he can never make good this claim in the fullest sense, because the creative aspect of life which finds its clearest expression in art baffles all attempts at rational formulation. Any reaction to stimulus may be causally explained; but the creative act, which is the absolute antithesis of mere reaction, will for ever elude the human understanding. It can only be described in its manifestations; it can be obscurely sensed, but never wholly grasped. Psychology and the study of art will always have to turn to one another for help, and the one will not invalidate the other. It is an important principle of psychology that psychic events are derivable. It is a principle in the study of art that a psychic product is something in and for itself—whether the work of art or the artist himself is in question. Both principles are valid in spite of their relativity.

The Work of Art

There is a fundamental difference of approach between the psychologist's examination of a literary work, and that of the literary critic. What is of decisive importance and value for the latter may be quite irrelevant for the former. Literary products of highly dubious merit are often of the greatest interest to the psychologist. For instance, the so-called "psychological novel" is by no means as rewarding for the psychologist as the literary-minded suppose. Considered as a whole such a novel explains itself. It has done its own work of psychological interpretation, and the psychologist can at most criticize or enlarge upon this. The important question as to how a particular author came to write a particular novel is of course left unanswered, but I wish to reserve this general problem for the second part of my essay.

The novels which are most fruitful for the psychologist are those in which the author has not already given a psychological interpretation of his characters, and which therefore leave room for analysis and explanation, or even invite it by their mode of presentation. Good examples of this kind of writing are the novels of Benoît, and English fiction in the manner of Rider Haggard, including the vein exploited by Conan Doyle which yields that most cherished article of mass-production, the detective story. Melville's *Moby Dick*, which I consider the greatest American novel, also comes within this class of writings. An exciting narrative that is apparently quite devoid of psychological exposition is just what interests the psychologist most of all. Such a tale is built upon a groundwork of implicit psychological assumptions, and, in the measure that the author is unconscious of them, they reveal themselves, pure and unalloyed, to the critical discernment. In the psychological novel, on the other hand, the author himself attempts to reshape his material so as to raise it from the level of crude contingency to that of psychological exposition and illumination—a procedure which all too often clouds the psychological significance of the work or hides it from view. It is precisely to novels of this sort that the layman goes for "psychology"; while it is novels of the other kind that challenge the psychologist, for he alone can give them deeper meaning.

I have been speaking in terms of the novel, but I am dealing with a psychological fact which is not restricted to this particular form of literary art. We meet with it in the works of the poets as well, and are confronted with it when we compare the first and second parts of the *Faust* drama. The love-tragedy of Gretchen explains itself; there is nothing that the psychologist can add to it that the poet has not already said in better words. The second part, on the other hand, calls for explanation. The prodigious richness of the imaginative material has so overtaxed the poet's formative powers that nothing is self-explanatory and every verse adds to the reader's need of an interpretation. The two parts of *Faust* illustrate by way of extremes this psychological distinction between works of literature.

In order to emphasize the distinction, I will call the one mode of artistic creation *psychological*, and the other *visionary*. The psychological mode deals with materials drawn from the realm of human consciousness—for instance, with the lessons of life, with emotional shocks, the experience of passion and the crises of human destiny in general—all of which go to make up the conscious life of man, and his feeling life in particular. This material is psychically assimilated by the poet, raised from the commonplace to the level of poetic experience, and given an expression which forces the reader to greater clarity and depth of human insight by bringing fully into his consciousness what he ordinarily evades and overlooks or senses only with a feeling of dull discomfort. The poet's work is an interpretation and illumination of the contents of consciousness, of the ineluctable experiences of human life with its eternally recurrent sorrow and joy. He leaves nothing over for the psychologist, unless, indeed, we expect the latter to expound the reasons for which Faust falls in love with Gretchen, or which drive Gretchen to murder her child! Such themes go to make up the lot of humankind; they repeat themselves millions of times and are responsible for the monotony of the police-court and of the penal code. No obscurity whatever surrounds them, for they fully explain themselves.

Countless literary works belong to this class: the many novels dealing with love, the environment, the family, crime and society, as well as didactic poetry, the larger number of lyrics, and the drama, both tragic and comic. Whatever its particular form may be, the psychological work of art always takes its materials from the vast realm of conscious human experience—from the vivid foreground of life, we might say. I have called this mode of artistic creation psychological because in its activity it nowhere transcends the bounds of psychological intelligibility. Everything that it embraces—the experience as well as its artistic expression—belongs to the realm of the understandable. Even the basic experiences themselves, though non-rational, have nothing strange about them; on the contrary, they are that which has been known from the beginning of time—passion and its fated outcome, man's subjection to the turns of destiny, eternal nature with its beauty and its horror.

The profound difference between the first and second parts of *Faust* marks the difference between the psychological and the visionary modes of artistic creation. The latter reverses all the conditions of the former. The experience that furnishes the material for artistic expression is no longer familiar. It is a strange something that derives its existence from the hinterland of man's mind—that suggests the abyss of time separating us from pre-human ages, or evokes a super-human world of contrasting light and darkness. It is a primordial experience which surpasses man's understanding, and to which he is therefore in danger of succumbing. The value and the force of the experience are given by its enormity. It arises from timeless depths; it is foreign and cold, many-sided, demonic and grotesque. A grimly ridiculous sample of the eternal chaos—a *crimen laesae majestatis humanae*, to use Nietzsche's words—it bursts asunder our human standards of value and of aesthetic form. The disturbing vision of monstrous and meaningless happenings that in every way exceed the grasp of human feeling and comprehension makes quite other demands upon the powers of the artist than do the experiences of the foreground of life. These never rend the curtain that veils the cosmos; they never transcend the bounds of the humanly possible, and for this reason are readily shaped to the demands of art, no matter how great a shock to the individual they may be. But the primordial experiences rend from top to bottom the curtain upon which is painted the picture of an ordered world, and allow a glimpse into the unfathomed abyss of what has not yet become. It is a vision of other worlds, or of the obscuration of the spirit, or of the beginning of things before the age of man, or of the unborn generations of the future? We cannot say that it is any or none of these.

Shaping—re-shaping—
The eternal spirit's eternal pastime.

We find such vision in *The Shepherd of Hermas,* in Dante, in the second part of *Faust,* in Nietzsche's Dionysian exuberance, in Wagner's *Nibelungenring,* in Spitteler's *Olympischer Frühling,* in the poetry of William Blake, in the *Ipnerotomachia* of the monk Francesco Colonna, and in Jacob Boehme's philosophic and poetic stammerings. In a more restricted and specific way, the primordial experience furnishes material for Rider Haggard in the fiction-cycle that turns upon *She,* and it does the same for Benoit, chiefly in *L'Atlantide,* for Kubin in *Die andere Seite,* for Meyrink in *Das grüne Gesicht*—a book whose importance we should not undervalue—for Goetz in *Das Reich ohne Raum,* and for Barlach in *Der tote Tag.* This list might be greatly extended.

In dealing with the psychological mode of artistic creation, we never need ask ourselves what the material consists of or what it means. But this question forces itself upon us as soon as we come to the visionary mode of creation. We are astonished, taken aback, confused, put on our guard or even disgusted—and we demand commentaries and explanations. We are reminded in nothing of everyday, human life, but rather of dreams, nighttime fears and the dark recesses of the mind that we sometimes sense with misgiving. The reading public for the most part repudiates this kind of writing—unless, indeed, it is coarsely sensational—and even the literary critic feels embarrassed by it. It is true that Dante and Wagner have smoothed the approach to it. The visionary experience is cloaked, in Dante's case, by the introduction of historical facts, and, in that of Wagner, by mythological events—so that history and mythology are sometimes taken to be the materials with which these poets worked. But with neither of them does the moving force and the deeper significance lie there. For both it is contained in the visionary experience. Rider Haggard, pardonably enough, is generally held to be a mere inventor of fiction. Yet even with him the story is primarily a means of giving expression to significant material. However much the tale may seem to overgrow the content, the latter outweighs the former in importance.

The obscurity as to the sources of the material in visionary creation is very strange, and the exact opposite of what we find in the psychological mode of creation. We are even led to suspect that this obscurity is not unintentional. We are naturally inclined to suppose—and Freudian psychology encourages us to do so—that some highly personal experience underlies this grotesque darkness. We hope thus to explain these strange glimpses of chaos and to understand why it sometimes seems as though the poet had intentionally concealed his basic experience from us. It is only a step from this way of looking at the matter to the statement that we are here dealing with a pathological and neurotic art—a step which is justified in so far as the material of the visionary creator shows certain traits that we find in the fantasies of the insane. The converse also is true; we often discover in the mental output of psychotic persons a wealth of meaning that we should expect rather from the works of a genius. The psychologist who follows Freud will of course be inclined to take the writings in question as a problem in pathology. On the assumption that an intimate, personal experience underlies what I call the "primordial vision"—an experience, that is to say, which cannot be accepted by the conscious outlook—he will try to account for the curious images of the vision by calling them cover-figures and by supposing that they represent an attempted concealment of the basic experience. This, according to his view, might be an experience in love which is morally or aesthetically incompatible with the personality as a whole or at least with certain fictions of the conscious mind. In order that the poet, through his ego, might repress this experience and make it unrecognizable (unconscious), the whole arsenal of a pathological fantasy was brought into action. Moreover, this attempt to replace reality by fiction, being unsatisfactory, must be repeated in a long series of creative embodiments. This would explain the proliferation of imaginative forms, all monstrous, demonic, grotesque and perverse. On the one hand they are substitutes for the unacceptable experience, and on the other they help to conceal it.

Although a discussion of the poet's personality and psychic disposition belongs strictly to the second part of my essay, I cannot avoid taking up in the present connection the Freudian view of the visionary work of art. For one thing, it has aroused considerable attention. And then it is the only well-known attempt that has been made to give a "scientific" explanation of the sources of the visionary material or to formulate a theory of the psychic processes that underlie this curious mode of artistic creation. I assume that my own view of the question is not well known or generally understood. With this preliminary remark, I will now try to present it briefly.

If we insist on deriving the vision from a personal experience, we must treat the former as something secondary—as a mere substitute for reality. The result is that we strip the vision of its primordial quality and take it as nothing but a symptom. The pregnant chaos then shrinks to the proportions of a psychic disturbance. With this account of the matter we feel reassured and turn again to our picture of a well-ordered cosmos. Since we are practical and reasonable, we do not expect the cosmos to be perfect; we accept these unavoidable imperfections which we call abnormalities and diseases, and we take it for granted that human nature is not exempt from them. The frightening revelation of abysses that defy the human understanding is dismissed as illusion, and the poet is regarded as a victim and perpetrator of deception. Even to the poet, his primordial experience was "human—all too human," to such a degree that he could not face its meaning but had to conceal it from himself.

We shall do well, I think, to make fully explicit all the implications of that way of accounting for artistic creation which consists in reducing it to personal factors. We should see clearly where it leads. The truth is that it takes us away from the psychological study of the work of art, and confronts us with the psychic disposition of the poet himself. That the latter presents an important problem is not to be denied, but the work of art is something in its own right, and may not be conjured away. The question of the significance to the poet of his own creative work—of his regarding it as a trifle, as a screen, as a source of suffering or as an achievement—does not concern us at the moment, our task being to interpret the work of art psychologically. For this undertaking it is essential that we give serious consideration to the basic experience that underlies it—namely, to the vision. We must take it at least as seriously as we do the experiences that underlie the psychological mode of artistic creation, and no one doubts that they are both real and serious. It looks, indeed, as if the visionary experience were something quite apart from the ordinary lot of man, and for this reason we have difficulty in believing that it is real. It has about it an unfortunate suggestion of obscure metaphysics and of occultism, so that we feel called upon to intervene in the name of a well-intentioned reasonableness. Our conclusion is that it would be better not to take such things too seriously, lest the world revert again to a benighted superstition. We may, of course, have a predilection for the occult; but ordinarily we dismiss the visionary experience as the outcome of a rich fantasy or of a poetic mood—that is to say, as a kind of poetic licence psychologically understood. Certain of the poets encourage this interpretation in order to put a wholesome distance between themselves and their work. Spitteler, for example, stoutly maintained that it was one and the same whether the poet sang of an Olympian spring or to the theme: "May is here!" The truth is that poets are human beings, and that what a poet has to say about his work is often far from being the most illuminating word on the subject. What is required of us, then, is nothing less than to defend the importance of the visionary experience against the poet himself.

It cannot be denied that we catch the reverberations of an initial love-experience in *The Shepherd of Hermas,* in the *Divine Comedy* and in the *Faust* drama—an experience which is completed and fulfilled by the vision. There is no ground for the assumption that the second part of *Faust* repudiates or conceals the normal, human experience of the first part, nor are we justified in supposing that Goethe was normal at the time when he wrote *Part I,* but in a neurotic state of mind when he composed *Part II. Hermas,* Dante and Goethe can be taken as three steps in a sequence covering nearly two thousand years of human development, and in each of them we find the personal love-episode not only connected with the weightier visionary experience, but frankly subordinated to it. On the strength of this evidence which is furnished by the work of art itself and which throws out of court the question of the poet's particular psychic disposition, we must admit that the vision represents a deeper and more impressive experience than human passion. In works of art of this nature—and we must never confuse them with the artist as a person—we cannot doubt that the vision is a genuine, primordial experience, regardless of what reason-mongers may say. The vision is not something derived or secondary, and it is not a symptom of something else. It is true symbolic expression—that is, the expression of something existent in its own right, but imperfectly known. The love-episode is a real experience really suffered, and the same statement applies to the vision. We need not try to determine whether the content of the vision is of a physical, psychic or metaphysical nature. In itself it has psychic reality, and this is no less real than physical reality. Human passion falls within the sphere of conscious experience, while the subject of the vision lies beyond it. Through our feelings we experience the known, but our intuitions point to things that are unknown and hidden—that by their very nature are secret. If ever they become conscious, they are intentionally kept back and concealed, for which reason they have been regarded from earliest times as mysterious, uncanny and deceptive. They are hidden from the scrutiny of man, and he also hides himself from them out of *deisidaemonia*. He protects himself with the shield of science and the armour of reason. His enlightenment is born of fear; in the day-time he believes in an ordered cosmos, and he tries to maintain this faith against the fear of chaos that besets him by night. What if there were some living force whose sphere of action lies beyond our world of every day? Are there human needs that are dangerous and unavoidable? Is there something more purposeful than electrons? Do we delude ourselves in thinking that we possess and command our own souls? And is that which science calls the "psyche" not merely a question-mark arbitrarily confined within the skull, but rather a door that opens upon the human world from a world beyond, now and again allowing strange and unseizable potencies to act upon man and to remove him, as if upon the wings of the night, from the level of common humanity to that of a more than personal vocation? When we consider the visionary mode of artistic creation, it even seems as if the love-episode had served as a mere release—as if the personal experience were nothing but the prelude to the all-important "divine comedy."

It is not alone the creator of this kind of art who is in touch with the nightside of life, but the seers, prophets, leaders and enlighteners also. However dark this nocturnal world may be, it is not wholly unfamiliar. Man has known of it from time immemorial—here, there, and everywhere; for primitive man today it is an unquestionable part of his picture of the cosmos. It is only we who have repudiated it because of our fear of superstition and metaphysics, and because we strive to construct a conscious world that is safe and manageable in that natural law holds in it the place of statute law in a commonwealth. Yet, even in our midst, the poet now and then catches sight of the figures that people the night-world—the spirits, demons and gods. He knows that a purposiveness out-reaching human ends is the life-giving secret for man; he has a presentiment of incomprehensible happenings in the pleroma. In short, he sees something of that psychic world that strikes terror into the savage and the barbarian.

From the very first beginnings of human society onward man's efforts to give his vague intimations a binding form have left their traces. Even in the Rhodesian cliff-drawings of the Old Stone Age there appears, side by side with the most amazingly lifelike representations of animals, an abstract pattern—a double cross contained in a circle. This design has turned up in every cultural region, more or less, and we find it today not only in Christian churches, but in Tibetan monasteries as well. It is the so-called sunwheel, and as it dates from a time when no one had thought of wheels as a mechanical device, it cannot have had its source in any experience of the external world. It is rather a symbol that stands for a psychic happening; it covers an experience of the inner world, and is no doubt as lifelike a representation as the famous rhinoceros with the tick-birds on its back. There has never been a primitive culture that did not possess a system of secret teaching, and in many cultures this system is highly developed. The men's councils and the totem-clans preserve this teaching about hidden things that lie apart from man's daytime existence—things which, from primeval times, have always constituted his most vital experiences. Knowledge about them is handed on to younger men in the rites of initiation. The mysteries of the Graeco-Roman world performed the same office, and the rich mythology of antiquity is a relic of such experiences in the earliest stages of human development.

It is therefore to be expected of the poet that he will resort to mythology in order to give his experience its most fitting expression. It would be a serious mistake to suppose that he works with materials received at secondhand. The primordial experience is the source of his creativeness; it cannot be fathomed, and therefore requires mythological imagery to give it form. In itself it offers no words or images, for it is a vision seen "as in a glass, darkly." It is merely a deep presentiment that strives to find expression. It is like a whirlwind that seizes everything within reach and, by carrying it aloft, assumes a visible shape. Since the particular expression can never exhaust the possibilities of the vision, but falls far short of it in richness of content, the poet must have at his disposal a huge store of materials if he is to communicate even a few of his intimations. What is more, he must resort to an imagery that is difficult to handle and full of contradictions in order to express the weird paradoxicality of his vision. Dante's presentiments are clothed in images that run the gamut of Heaven and Hell; Goethe must bring in the Blocksberg and the infernal regions of Greek antiquity; Wagner needs the whole body of Nordic myth; Nietzsche returns to the hieratic style and recreates the legendary seer of prehistoric times; Blake invents for himself indescribable figures, and Spitteler borrows old names for new creatures of the imagination. And no intermediate step is missing in the whole range from the ineffably sublime to the perversely grotesque.

Psychology can do nothing towards the elucidation of this colourful imagery except bring together materials for comparison and offer a terminology for its discussion. According to this terminology, that which appears in the vision is the collective unconscious. We mean by collective unconscious, a certain psychic disposition shaped by the forces of heredity; from it consciousness has developed. In the physical structure of the body we find traces of earlier stages of evolution, and we may expect the human psyche also to conform in its make-up to the law of phylogeny. It is a fact that in eclipses of consciousness—in dreams, narcotic states and cases of insanity—there come to the surface psychic products or contents that show all the traits of primitive levels of psychic development. The images themselves are sometimes of such a primitive character that we might suppose them derived from ancient, esoteric teaching. Mythological themes clothed in modern dress also frequently appear. What is of particular importance for the study of literature in these manifestations of the collective unconscious is that they are compensatory to the conscious attitude. This is to say that they can bring a one-sided, abnormal, or dangerous state of consciousness into equilibrium in an apparently purposive way. In dreams we can see this process very clearly in its positive aspect. In cases of insanity the compensatory process is often perfectly obvious, but takes a negative form. There are persons, for instance, who have anxiously shut themselves off from all the world only to discover one day that their most intimate secrets are known and talked about by everyone.

If we consider Goethe's *Faust*, and leave aside the possibility that it is compensatory to his own conscious attitude, the question that we must answer is this: In what relation does it stand to the conscious outlook of his time? Great poetry draws its strength from the life of mankind, and we completely miss its meaning if we try to derive it from personal factors. Whenever the collective unconscious becomes a living experience and is brought to bear upon the conscious outlook of an age, this event is a creative act which is of importance to everyone living in that age. A work of art is produced that contains what may truthfully be called a message to generations of men. So *Faust* touches something in the soul of every German. So also Dante's fame is immortal, while *The Shepherd of Hermas* just failed of inclusion in the New Testament canon. Every period has its bias, its particular prejudice and its psychic ailment. An epoch is like an individual; it has its own limitations of conscious outlook, and therefore requires a compensatory adjustment. This is effected by the collective unconscious in that a poet, a seer or a leader allows himself to be guided by the unexpressed desire of his times and shows the way, by word or deed, to the attainment of that which everyone blindly craves and expects—whether this attainment results in good or evil, the healing of an epoch or its destruction.

It is always dangerous to speak of one's own times, because what is at stake in the present is too vast for comprehension. A few hints must therefore suffice. Francesco Colonna's book is cast in the form of a dream, and is the apotheosis of natural love taken as a human relation; without countenancing a wild indulgence of the senses, he leaves completely aside the Christian sacrament of marriage. The book was written in 1453. Rider Haggard, whose life coincides with the flowering-time of the Victorian era, takes up this subject and deals with it in his own way; he does not cast it in the form of a dream, but allows us to feel the tension of moral conflict. Goethe weaves the theme of Gretchen-Helen-Mater Gloriosa like a red thread into the colourful tapestry of *Faust*. Nietzsche proclaims the death of God, and Spitteler transforms the waxing and waning of the gods into a myth of the seasons. Whatever his importance, each of these poets speaks with the voice of thousands and ten thousands, foretelling changes in the conscious outlook of his time.

The Poet

Creativeness, like the freedom of the will, contains a secret. The psychologist can describe both these manifestations as processes, but he can find no solution of the philosophical problems they offer. Creative man is a riddle that we may try to answer in various ways, but always in vain, a truth that has not prevented modern psychology from turning now and again to the question of the artist and his art. Freud thought that he had found a key in his procedure of deriving the work of art from the personal experiences of the artist. It is true that certain possibilities lay in this direction, for it was conceivable that a work of art, no less than a neurosis, might be traced back to those knots in psychic life that we call the complexes. It was Freud's great discovery that neuroses have a causal origin in the psychic realm—that they take their rise from emotional states and from real or imagined childhood experiences. Certain of his followers, like Rank and Stekel, have taken up related lines of enquiry and have achieved important results. It is undeniable that the poet's psychic disposition permeates his work root and branch. Nor is there anything new in the statement that personal factors largely influence the poet's choice and use of his materials. Credit, however, must certainly be given to the Freudian school for showing how far-reaching this influence is and in what curious ways it comes to expression.

Freud takes the neurosis as a substitute for a direct means of gratification. He therefore regards it as something inappropriate—a mistake, a dodge, an excuse, a voluntary blindness. To him it is essentially a shortcoming that should never have been. Since a neurosis, to all appearances, is nothing but a disturbance that is all the more irritating because it is without sense or meaning, few people will venture to say a good word for it. And a work of art is brought into questionable proximity with the neurosis when it is taken as something which can be analyzed in terms of the poet's repressions. In a sense it finds itself in good company, for religion and philosophy are regarded in the same light by Freudian psychology. No objection can be raised if it is admitted that this approach amounts to nothing more than the elucidation of those personal determinants without which a work of art is unthinkable. But should the claim be made that such an analysis accounts for the work of art itself, then a categorical denial is called for. The personal idiosyncrasies that creep into a work of art are not essential; in fact, the more we have to cope with these peculiarities, the less is it a question of art. What is essential in a work of art is that it should rise far above the realm of personal life and speak from the spirit and heart of the poet as man to the spirit and heart of mankind. The personal aspect is a limitation—and even a sin—in the realm of art. When a form of "art" is primarily personal it deserves to be treated as if it were a neurosis. There may be some validity in the idea held by the Freudian school that artists without exception are narcissistic—by which is meant that they are undeveloped persons with infantile and auto-erotic traits. The statement is only valid, however, for the artist as a person, and has nothing to do with the man as an artist. In his capacity of artist he is neither auto-erotic, nor hetero-erotic, nor erotic in any sense. He is objective and impersonal—even inhuman—for as an artist he is his work, and not a human being.

Every creative person is a duality or a synthesis of contradictory aptitudes. On the one side he is a human being with a personal life, while on the other side he is an impersonal, creative process. Since as a human being he may be sound or morbid, we must look at his psychic make-up to find the determinants of his personality. But we can only understand him in his capacity of artist by looking at his creative achievement. We should make a sad mistake if we tried to explain the mode of life of an English gentleman, a Prussian officer, or a cardinal in terms of personal factors. The gentleman, the officer and the cleric function as such in an impersonal role, and their psychic make-up is qualified by a peculiar objectivity. We must grant that the artist does not function in an official capacity—the very opposite is nearer the truth. He nevertheless resembles the types I have named in one respect, for the specifically artistic disposition involves an overweight of collective psychic life as against the personal. Art is a kind of innate drive that seizes a human being and makes him its instrument. The artist is not a person endowed with free will who seeks his own ends, but one who allows art to realize its purposes through him. As a human being he may have moods and a will and personal aims, but as an artist he is "man" in a higher sense—he is "collective man"—one who carries and shapes the unconscious, psychic life of mankind. To perform this difficult office it is sometimes necessary for him to sacrifice happiness and everything that makes life worth living for the ordinary human being.

All this being so, it is not strange that the artist is an especially interesting case for the psychologist who uses an analytical method. The artist's life cannot be otherwise than full of conflicts, for two forces are at war within him—on the one hand the common human longing for happiness, satisfaction and security in life, and on the other a ruthless passion for creation which may go so far as to override every personal desire. The lives of artists are as a rule so highly unsatisfactory—not to say tragic—because of their inferiority on the human and personal side, and not because of a sinister dispensation. There are hardly any exceptions to the rule that a person must pay dearly for the divine gift of the creative fire. It is as though each of us were endowed at birth with a certain capital of energy. The strongest force in our make-up will seize and all but monopolize this energy, leaving so little over that nothing of value can come of it. In this way the creative force can drain the human impulses to such a degree that the personal ego must develop all sorts of bad qualities—ruthlessness, selfishness and vanity (so-called "auto-erotism")—and even every kind of vice, in order to maintain the spark of life and to keep itself from being wholly bereft. The auto-erotism of artists resembles that of illegitimate or neglected children who from their tenderest years must protect themselves from the destructive influence of people who have no love to give them—who develop bad qualities for that very purpose and later maintain an invincible egocentrism by remaining all their lives infantile and helpless or by actively offending against the moral code or the law. How can we doubt that it is his art that explains the artist, and not the insufficiencies and conflicts of his personal life? These are nothing but the regrettable results of the fact that he is an artist—that is to say, a man who from his very birth has been called to a greater task than the ordinary mortal. A special ability means a heavy expenditure of energy in a particular direction, with a consequent drain from some other side of life.

It makes no difference whether the poet knows that his work is begotten, grows and matures with him, or whether he supposes that by taking thought he produces it out of the void. His opinion of the matter does not change the fact that his own work outgrows him as a child its mother. The creative process has feminine quality, and the creative work arises from unconscious depths—we might say, from the realm of the mothers. Whenever the creative force predominates, human life is ruled and moulded by the unconscious as against the active will, and the conscious ego is swept along on a subterranean current, being nothing more than a helpless observer of events. The work in process becomes the poet's fate and determines his psychic development. It is not Goethe who creates *Faust*, but *Faust* which creates Goethe. And what is *Faust* but a symbol? By this I do not mean an allegory that points to something all too familiar, but an expression that stands for something not clearly known and yet profoundly alive. Here it is something that lives in the soul of every German, and that Goethe has helped to bring to birth. Could we conceive of anyone but a German writing *Faust* or *Also sprach Zarathustra*? Both play upon something that reverberates in the German soul—a "primordial image," as Jacob Burckhardt once called it—the figure of a physician or teacher of mankind. The archetypal image of the wise man, the saviour or redeemer, lies buried and dormant in man's unconscious since the dawn of culture; it is awakened whenever the times are out of joint and a human society is committed to a serious error. When people go astray they feel the need of a guide or teacher or even of the physician. These primordial images are numerous, but do not appear in the dreams of individuals or in works of art until they are called into being by the waywardness of the general outlook. When conscious life is characterized by one-sidedness and by a false attitude, then they are activated—one might say, "instinctively"—and come to light in the dreams of individuals and the visions of artists and seers, thus restoring the psychic equilibrium of the epoch.

In this way the work of the poet comes to meet the spiritual need of the society in which he lives, and for this reason his work means more to him than his personal fate, whether he is aware of this or not. Being essentially the instrument for his work, he is subordinate to it, and we have no reason for expecting him to interpret it for us. He has done the best that in him lies in giving it form, and he must leave the interpretation to others and to the future. A great work of art is like a dream; for all its apparent obviousness it does not explain itself and is never unequivocal. A dream never says: "You ought," or: "This is the truth." It presents an image in much the same way as nature allows a plant to grow, and we must draw our own conclusions. If a person has a nightmare, it means either that he is too much given to fear, or else that he is too exempt from it; and if he dreams of the old wise man it may mean that he is too pedagogical, as also that he stands in need of a teacher. In a subtle way both meanings come to the same thing, as we perceive when we are able to let the work of art act upon us as it acted upon the artist. To grasp its meaning, we must allow it to shape us as it once shaped him. Then we understand the nature of his experience. We see that he has drawn upon the healing and redeeming forces of the collective psyche that underlies consciousness with its isolation and its painful errors; that he has penetrated to that matrix of life in which all men are embedded, which imparts a common rhythm to all human existence, and allows the individual to communicate his feeling and his striving to mankind as a whole.

The secret of artistic creation and of the effectiveness of art is to be found in a return to the state of *participation mystique*—to that level of experience at which it is man who lives, and not the individual, and at which the weal or woe of the single human being does not count, but only human existence. This is why every great work of art is objective and impersonal, but none the less profoundly moves us each and all. And this is also why the personal life of the poet cannot be held essential to his art—but at most a help or a hindrance to his creative task. He may go the way of a Philistine, a good citizen, a neurotic, a fool or a criminal. His personal career may be inevitable and interesting, but it does not explain the poet.

LEV VYGOTSKY

The Psychology of Art *

We have seen from the foregoing that a work of art (such as a fable, a short story, a tragedy), always includes an affective contradiction, causes conflicting feelings, and leads to the short-circuiting and destruction of these emotions. This is the true effect of a work of art. We come now to the concept of *catharsis* used by Aristotle as the basis for his explanation of tragedy, and repeatedly mentioned by him with regard to the other arts. In his *Poetica* he says that "tragedy imitates an important and finished action of a certain magnitude, with a speech whose every part has a different ornament, or with action, not narration, that performs a purification of such affairs by means of pity and fear."

No matter what interpretation we assign the enigmatic term catharsis, we must be sure that it corresponds to Aristotle's. For our purposes, however, this is irrelevant. Whether we follow Lessing, who understands catharsis to be the moral action of the tragedy (the transformation of passions into virtues) or Müller, for whom it is the transition from displeasure to pleasure; whether we accept Bernays' interpretation of the term as healing and purification in the medical sense, or Zeller's opinion that catharsis appeases affect,—we will imperfectly and incompletely express the meaning we assign to this term. Despite the indefiniteness of its content, despite our failure to explain the meaning of this term in the Aristotelian sense, there is no other term in psychology which so completely expresses the central fact of aesthetic reaction, according to which painful and unpleasant affects are discharged and trans-

* Lev Vygotsky, *Psychology of Art* (Cambridge, Mass.: MIT Press, 1971), pp. 213-215, 259. (Footnotes omitted.)

formed into their opposites. Aesthetic reaction as such is nothing but catharsis, that is, a complex transformation of feelings. Though little is known at present about the process of catharsis, we do know, however, that the discharge
of nervous energy (which is the essence of any emotion) takes place in a
direction which opposes the conventional one, and that art therefore becomes
a most powerful means for important and appropriate discharges of nervous
energy. The basis for this process reveals itself in the contradiction which
inheres in the structure of any work of art. We have already mentioned
Ovsianiko-Kulikovskii, who believes Hector's farewell scene stirs in us contrasting and conflicting emotions. On the one hand, these are emotions we
would experience if the scene were described by Pisemskii; they are anything
but lyrical since the description is not a poem; on the other hand, the emotion
is stirred by the hexameters and a lyrical emotion par excellence. But then, in
any work of art there are emotions generated by the material as well as the
form; the question is: how do these two kinds of emotion interrelate to each
other? We already know the answer, for it derives from our preceding arguments. This relation is one of antagonism; the two kinds of emotion move in
opposite directions. The law of aesthetic response is the same for a fable as for
a tragedy: *it comprises an affect that develops in two opposite directions but reaches
annihilation at its point of termination.*

This is the process we should like to call catharsis. We have shown that
the artist always overcomes content with form, and we have found a corrob-
oration of this statement in the structures of the fable and the tragedy. If we
study the psychological effect of individual formal elements, we find that they
fit precisely the requirements set by the task. Wundt has shown that rhythm in
itself expresses only "a method of expressing feelings in terms of time." An
individual rhythmic form is the expression of a flow of feelings, but since the
temporal placement of the flow of feelings is part of the affect, the representation of this method in rhythm causes the affect as such. "Thus, the aesthetic significance of rhythm is its function as a cause affect. In other words,
rhythm generates the affect of which it is a part through the psychological laws
of emotional processes."

We see, therefore, that rhythm itself, as one of the formal elements, is
capable of generating the affects represented by it. If a poet selects a rhythm
whose effect is in contrast with, or opposite to, the effect of the content of his
work, we perceive this phenomenon of contrast. Bunin has described murder,
shooting, and passion with a rhythm of cold, detached calm. His rhythm generates an affect opposite to the one generated by his story's material. In the
end the aesthetic response becomes a feeling of catharsis; we experience a
complex discharge of feelings, their mutual transformation, and instead of the
painful experiences forming the content of the short story, we experience
the delicate, transparent feeling of a breath of fresh air. The same thing
occurs in fables and tragedies. Such a contrast of feelings exists also in the case
mentioned by Ovsianiko-Kulikovskii. Hexameters, if needed at all, and if
Homer is at all better than Pisemskii, do enlighten and cathartically purify the

emotions generated by the content of the *Iliad*. The contrast discovered by us in the structure of artistic form and that of artistic content is the basis of cathartic action in the aesthetic response. Schiller puts it like this: "The secret of a master is to destroy content by means of form; the more majestic and attractive the content, the more it moves to the fore, and the more the viewer falls under its spell, the greater the triumph of art which removes the content and dominates it."

A work of art always contains an intimate conflict between its content and its form, and the artist achieves his effect by means of the form, which destroys the content.

Let us now make some final statements. We can say that the basic aesthetic response consists of affect caused by art, affect experienced by us as if it were real, but which finds its release in the activity of imagination provoked by a work of art. This central release delays and inhibits the external motor aspect of affect, and we think we are experiencing only illusory feelings. Art is based upon the union of feeling and imagination. Another peculiarity of art is that, while it generates in us opposing affects, it delays (on account of the antithetic principle) the motor expression of emotions and, by making opposite impulses collide, it destroys the affect of content and form, and initiates an explosive discharge of nervous energy.

Catharsis of the aesthetic response is the transformation of affects, the explosive response which culminates in the discharge of emotions. . . .

Psychological investigation reveals that art is the supreme center of biological and social individual processes in society, that it is a method for finding an equilibrium between man and his world, in the most critical and important stages of his life. This view of course completely refutes the approach according to which art is an ornament, and thereby leads us to doubt the correctness of the above statement. Since the future has in store not only a rearrangement of mankind according to new principles, not only the organization of new social and economic processes, but also the "remolding of man," there seems hardly any doubt that the role of art will also change.

It is hard to imagine the role that art will play in this remolding of man. We do not know which existing but dormant forces in our organisms it will draw upon to form the new man. There is no question, however, that art will have a decisive voice in this process. Without new art there can be no new man. The possibilities of the future, for art as well as for life, are inscrutable and unpredictable. As Spinoza said, "That of which the body is capable has not yet been determined."

MARXISM AND THE
FRANKFURT SCHOOL

ONE OF THE MOST INTERESTING theoretical developments of the twentieth century has been that of "Critical Theory," largely an effort by a group of German philosophers and social theorists (the "Frankfurt School") of the 1920s and '30s to bring Marxist political economy and psychoanalysis together in a critique of modern society—of modern forms of power and desire. The Marxist view of art is very important, since its emphasis upon the relevance of the social context of artists and audiences is widely accepted, without however, equally widespread acceptance of Marxist normative conclusions.

The major figure of the Frankfurt School are Theodor Adorno, Walter Benjamin, Erich Fromm, Max Horkheimer, and Herbert Marcuse. Essays by Benjamin, Adorno, and Marcuse are included. Benjamin's essay is of great importance for addressing themes of authenticity and the "scientific technological order" found in both Marxist and Heideggerian traditions. Adorno's essay speaks to many of the same issues as Benjamin's, but with a penetrating if elitist critique of how collective powers influence the desire for art. Marcuse may be the most famous member of the Frankfurt School, largely the result of his political writings, and he offers in the selection here both a summary of the principles of Marxist aesthetics and a vehement criticism of their limitations.

WALTER BENJAMIN

The Work of Art in the Age of its Technical Reproducibility*

II

Even the most perfect reproduction of a work of art is lacking in one element: its presence in time and space, its unique existence at the place where it happens to be. This unique existence of the work of art determined the history to which it was subject throughout the time of its existence. This includes the changes which it may have suffered in physical condition over the years as well as the various changes in its ownership. The traces of the first can be revealed only by chemical or physical analyses which it is impossible to perform on a reproduction; changes of ownership are subject to a tradition which must be traced from the situation of the original.

The presence of the original is the prerequisite to the concept of authenticity. Chemical analyses of the patina of a bronze can help to establish this, as does the proof that a given manuscript of the Middle Ages stems from an archive of the fifteenth century. The whole sphere of authenticity is outside technical—and of course, not only technical—reproducibility. Confronted with its manual reproduction, which was usually branded as a

---

* Walter Benjamin, "The Work of Art in the Age of Mechanical Reproduction," *Illuminations,* ed. by Hannah Arendt, trans. by Harry Zohn (New York: Harcourt Brace & World, 1968) pp. 219-254, footnotes omitted. I have taken the liberty of re-translating the title to "The Work of Art in the Age of its Technical Reproducibility," both in the interest of greater accuracy and to heighten the resonances with the Greek sense of *technē* and Heidegger's view of technology. I owe this to a suggestion by Dennis J. Schmidt.

forgery, the original preserved all its authority; not so *vis à vis* technical reproduction. The reason is twofold. First, process reproduction is more independent of the original than manual reproduction. For example, in photography, process reproduction can bring out those aspects of the original that are unattainable to the naked eye yet accessible to the lens, which is adjustable and chooses its angle at will. And photographic reproduction, with the aid of certain processes, such as enlargement or slow motion, can capture images which escape natural vision. Secondly, technical reproduction can put the copy of the original into situations which would be out of reach for the original itself. Above all, it enables the original to meet the beholder halfway, be it in the form of a photograph or a phonograph record. The cathedral leaves its locale to be received in the studio of a lover of art; the choral production, performed in an auditorium or in the open air, resounds in the drawing room.

The situations into which the product of mechanical reproduction can be brought may not touch the actual work of art, yet the quality of its presence is always depreciated. This holds not only for the art work but also, for instance, for a landscape which passes in review before the spectator in a movie. In the case of the art object, a most sensitive nucleus—namely, its authenticity—is interfered with whereas no natural object is vulnerable on that score. The authenticity of a thing is the essence of all that is transmissible from its beginning, ranging from its substantive duration to its testimony to the history which it has experienced. Since the historical testimony rests on the authenticity, the former, too, is jeopardized by reproduction when substantive duration ceases to matter. And what is really jeopardized when the historical testimony is affected is the authority of the object.

One might subsume the eliminated element in the term "aura" and go on to say: that which withers in the age of mechanical reproduction is the aura of the work of art. This is a symptomatic process whose significance points beyond the realm of art. One might generalize by saying: the technique of reproduction detaches the reproduced object from the domain of tradition. By making many reproductions it substitutes a plurality of copies for a unique existence. And in permitting the reproduction to meet the beholder or listener in his own particular situation, it reactivates the object reproduced. These two processes lead to a tremendous shattering of tradition which is the obverse of the contemporary crisis and renewal of mankind. Both processes are intimately connected with the contemporary mass movements. Their most powerful agent is the film. Its social significance, particularly in its most positive form, is inconceivable without its destructive, cathartic aspect, that is, the liquidation of the traditional value of the cultural heritage. This phenomenon is most palpable in the great historical films. It extends to ever new positions. In 1927 Abel Gance exclaimed enthusiastically: "Shakespeare, Rembrandt, Beethoven will make films . . . all legends, all mythologies and all myths, all founders of religion, and the very religions . . . await their exposed resurrection, and the heroes crowd each other at the gate."[1] Presumably without intending it, he issued an invitation to a far-reaching liquidation.

III

During long periods of history, the mode of human sense perception changes with humanity's entire mode of existence. The manner in which human sense perception is organized, the medium in which it is accomplished, is determined not only by nature but by historical circumstances as well. The fifth century, with its great shifts of population, saw the birth of the late Roman art industry and the Vienna Genesis, and there developed not only an art different from that of antiquity but also a new kind of perception. The scholars of the Viennese school, Riegl and Wickhoff, who resisted the weight of classical tradition under which these later art forms had been buried, were the first to draw conclusions from them concerning the organization of perception at the time. However far-reaching their insight, these scholars limited themselves to showing the significant, formal hallmark which characterized perception in late Roman times. They did not attempt—and, perhaps, saw no way—to show the social transformations expressed by these changes of perception. The conditions for an analogous insight are more favorable in the present. And if changes in the medium of contemporary perception can be comprehended as decay of the aura, it is possible to show its social causes.

The concept of aura which was proposed above with reference to historical objects may usefully be illustrated with reference to the aura of natural ones. We define the aura of the latter as the unique phenomenon of a distance, however close it may be. If, while resting on a summer afternoon, you follow with your eyes a mountain range on a horizon or a branch which casts its shadow over you, you experience the aura of those mountains, of that branch. This image makes it easy to comprehend the social bases of the contemporary decay of the aura. It rests on two circumstances, both of which are related to the increasing significance of the masses in contemporary life. Namely, the desire of contemporary masses to bring things "closer" spatially and humanly, which is just as ardent as their bent toward overcoming the uniqueness of every reality by accepting its reproduction. Every day the urge grows stronger to get hold of an object at very close range by way of its likeness, its reproduction. Unmistakably, reproduction as offered by picture magazines and newsreels differs from the image seen by the unarmed eye. Uniqueness and permanence are as closely linked in the latter as are transitoriness and reproducibility in the former. To pry an object from its shell, to destroy its aura, is the mark of a perception whose "sense of the universal equality of things" has increased to such a degree that it extracts it even from a unique object by means of reproduction. Thus is manifested in the field of perception what in the theoretical sphere is noticeable in the increasing importance of statistics. The adjustment of reality to the masses and of the masses of reality is a process of unlimited scope, as much for thinking as for perception.

IV

The uniqueness of a work of art is inseparable from its being imbedded in the fabric of tradition. This tradition itself is thoroughly alive and extremely changeable. An ancient statue of Venus, for example, stood in a different traditional context with the Greeks, who made it an object of veneration, than with the clerics of the Middle Ages, who viewed it as an ominous idol. Both of them, however, were equally confronted with its uniqueness, that is, its aura. Originally the contextual integration of art in tradition found its expression in the cult. We know that the earliest art works originated in the service of a ritual—first the magical, then the religious kind. It is significant that the existence of the work of art with reference to its aura is never entirely separated from its ritual function. In other words, the unique value of the "authentic" work of art has its basis in ritual, the location of its original use value. This ritualistic basis, however remote, is still recognizable as secularized ritual even in the most profane forms of the cult of beauty. The secular cult of beauty, developed during the Renaissance and prevailing for three centuries, clearly showed that ritualistic basis in its decline and the first deep crisis which befell it. With the advent of the first truly revolutionary means of reproduction, photography, simultaneously with the rise of socialism, art sensed the approaching crisis which has become evident a century later. At the time, art reacted with the doctrine of *l'art pour l'art,* that is, with a theology of art. This gave rise to what might be called a negative theology in the form of the idea of "pure" art, which not only denied any social function of art but also any categorizing by subject matter. (In poetry, Mallarmé was the first to take this position.)

An analysis of art in the age of mechanical reproduction must do justice to these relationships, for they lead us to an all-important insight: for the first time in world history, mechanical reproduction emancipates the work of art from its parasitical dependence on ritual. To an ever greater degree the work of art reproduced becomes the work of art designed for reproducibility. From a photographic negative, for example, one can make any number of prints; to ask for the "authentic" print makes no sense. But the instant the criterion of authenticity ceases to be applicable to artistic production, the total function of art is reversed. Instead of being based on ritual, it begins to be based on another practice—politics.

V

Works of art are received and valued on different planes. Two polar types stand out: with one, the accent is on the cult value; with the other, on the exhibition value of the work. Artistic production begins with ceremonial objects destined to serve in a cult. One may assume that what mattered was their existence, not their being on view. The elk portrayed by the man of the Stone Age on the walls of his cave was an instrument of magic. He did expose it to his fellow men, but in the main it was meant for the spirits. Today the cult value would seem to demand that the work of art remain hidden. Certain statues of gods are accessible only to the priest in the cellar; certain Madonnas remain covered nearly all year round; certain sculptures on medieval cathedrals are invisible to the spectator on ground level. With the emancipation of the various art practices from ritual go increasing opportunities for the exhibition of their products. It is easier to exhibit a portrait bust that can be sent here and there than to exhibit the statue of a divinity that has its fixed place in the interior of a temple. The same holds for the painting as against the mosaic or fresco that preceded it. And even though the public presentability of a mass originally may have been just as great as that of a symphony, the latter originated at the moment when its public presentability promised to surpass that of the mass.

With the different methods of technical reproduction of a work of art, its fitness for exhibition increased to such an extent that the quantitative shift between its two poles turned into a qualitative transformation of its nature. This is comparable to the situation of the work of art in prehistoric times when, by the absolute emphasis on its cult value, it was, first and foremost, an instrument of magic. Only later did it come to be recognized as a work of art. In the same way today, by the absolute emphasis on its exhibition value the work of art becomes a creation with entirely new functions, among which the one we are conscious of, the artistic function, later may be recognized as incidental. This much is certain: today photography and the film are the most serviceable exemplifications of this new function.

VI

In photography, exhibition value begins to displace cult value all along the line. But cult value does not give way without resistance. It retires into an ultimate retrenchment: the human countenance. It is no accident that the portrait was the focal point of early photography. The cult of remembrance of loved ones, absent or dead, offers a last refuge for the cult value of the picture. For the last time the aura emanates from the early photographs in the fleeting expression of a human face. This is what constitutes their melancholy, incomparable beauty. But as man withdraws from the photographic image, the exhibition value for the first time shows its superiority to the ritual value. To have pinpointed this new stage constitutes the incomparable significance of Atget, who, around 1900, took photographs of deserted Paris streets. It has quite justly been said of him that he photographed them like scenes of crime. The scene of a crime, too, is deserted; it is photographed for the purpose of establishing evidence. With Atget, photographs become standard evidence for historical occurrences, and acquire a hidden political significance. They demand a specific kind of approach; free-floating contemplation is not appropriate to them. They stir the viewer; he feels challenged by them in a new way. At the same time picture magazines begin to put up signposts for him, right ones or wrong ones, no matter. For the first time, captions have become obligatory.

And it is clear that they have an altogether different character than the title of a painting. The directives which the captions give to those looking at pictures in illustrated magazines soon become even more explicit and more imperative in the film where the meaning of each single picture appears to be prescribed by the sequence of all preceding ones. . . .

IX

For the film, what matters primarily is that the actor represents himself to the public before the camera, rather than representing someone else. One of the first to sense the actor's metamorphosis by this form of testing was Pirandello. Though his remarks on the subject in his novel *Si Gira* were limited to the negative aspects of the question and to the silent film only, this hardly impairs their validity. For in this respect, the sound film did not change anything essential. What matters is that the part is acted not for an audience but for a mechanical contrivance—in the case of the sound film, for two of them. "The film actor," wrote Pirandello, "feels as if in exile—exiled not only from the stage but also from himself. With a vague sense of discomfort he feels inexplicable emptiness: his body loses its corporeality, it evaporates, it is deprived of reality, life, voice, and the noises caused by his moving about, in order to be changed into a mute image, flickering an instant on the screen, then in vanishing into silence. . . . The projector will play with his shadow before the public, and he himself must be content to play before the camera."[2] The situation might also be characterized as follows: for the first time—and this is the effect of the film—man has to operate with his whole living person, yet forgoing its aura. For aura is tied to his presence; there can be no replica of it. The aura which, on the stage, emanates from Macbeth, cannot be separated for the spectators from that of the actor. However, the singularity of the shot in the studio is that the camera is substituted for the public. Consequently, the aura that envelops the actor vanishes, and with it the aura of the figure he portrays.

It is not surprising that it should be a dramatist such as Pirandello who, in characterizing the film, inadvertently touches on the very crisis in which we see the theater. Any thorough study proves that there is indeed no greater contrast than that of the stage play to a work of art that is completely subject to or, like the film, founded in, mechanical reproduction. Experts have long recognized that in the film "the greatest effects are almost always obtained by 'acting' as little as possible. . . ." In 1932 Rudolf Arnheim saw "the latest trend . . . in treating the actor as a stage prop chosen for its characteristics and . . . inserted at the proper place." With this idea something else is closely connected. The stage actor identifies himself with the character of his role. The film actor very often is denied this opportunity. His creation is by no means all of a piece; it is composed of many separate performances. Besides certain fortuitous considerations, such as cost of studio, availability of fellow players, décor, etc., there are elementary necessities of equipment that split the actor's work into a series of mountable episodes. In particular, lighting and its installation require the presentation of an event that, on the screen, unfolds as a rapid and unified scene, in a sequence of separate shootings which may take hours at the studio; not to mention more obvious montage. Thus a jump from the window can be shot in the studio as a jump from a scaffold, and the ensuing flight, if need be, can be shot weeks later when outdoor scenes are taken. Far more paradoxical cases can easily be construed. Let us assume that an actor is supposed to be startled by a knock at the door. If his reaction is not satisfactory, the director can resort to an expedient: when the actor happens to be at the studio again he has a shot fired behind him without his being forewarned of it. The frightened reaction can be shot now and be cut into the screen version. Nothing more strikingly shows that art has left the realm of the "beautiful semblance" which, so far, had been taken to be the only sphere where art could thrive.

X

The feeling of strangeness that overcomes the actor before the camera, as Pirandello describes it, is basically of the same kind as the estrangement felt before one's own image in the mirror. But now the reflected image has become separable, transportable. And where is it transported? Before the public. Never for a moment does the screen actor cease to be conscious of this fact. While facing the camera he knows that ultimately he will face the public, the consumers who constitute the market. This market, where he offers not only his labor but also his whole self, his heart and soul, is beyond his reach. During the shooting he has as little contact with it as any article made in the factory. This may contribute to that oppression, that new anxiety which, according to Pirandello, grips the actor before the camera. The film responds to the shriveling of the aura with an artificial build-up of the "personality" outside the studio. The cult of the movie star, fostered by the money of the film industry, preserves not the unique aura of the person but the "spell of the personality," the phony spell of a commodity. So long as the movie-makers' capital sets the fashion, as a rule no other revolutionary merit can be accredited to today's film than the promotion of a revolutionary criticism of traditional concepts of art. We do not deny that in some cases today's films can also promote revolutionary criticism of social conditions, even of the distribution of property. However, our present study is no more specifically concerned with this than is the film production of Western Europe.

It is inherent in the technique of the film as well as that of sports that everybody who witnesses its accomplishments is somewhat of an expert. This is obvious to anyone listening to a group of newspaper boys leaning on their bicycles and discussing the outcome of a bicycle race. It is not for nothing that newspaper publishers arrange races for their delivery boys. These arouse great interest among the participants, for the victor has an opportunity to rise from delivery boy to professional racer. Similarly, the newsreel offers everyone the opportunity to rise from passer-by to movie extra. In this way any man might even find himself part of a work of art, as witness Vertoff's *Three Songs About Lenin* or Ivens' *Borinage*. Any man today can lay claim to being filmed. This claim can best be elucidated by a comparative look at the historical situation of contemporary literature.

For centuries a small number of writers were confronted by many thousands of readers. This changed toward the end of the last century. With the increasing extension of the press, which kept placing new political, religious, scientific, professional, and local organs before the readers, an increasing number of readers became writers—at first, occasional ones. It began with the daily press opening to its readers space for "letters to the editor." And today there is hardly a gainfully employed European who could not, in principle, find an opportunity to publish somewhere or other comments on his work, grievances, documentary reports, or that sort of thing. Thus, the distinction between author and public is about to lose its basic character. The difference becomes merely functional; it may vary from case to case. At any moment the reader is ready to turn into a writer. As expert, which he had to become willy-nilly in an extremely specialized work process, even if only in some minor respect, the reader gains access to authorship. In the Soviet Union work itself is given a voice. To present it verbally is part of a man's ability to perform the work. Literary license is now founded on polytechnic rather than specialized training and thus becomes common property.

All this can easily be applied to the film, where transitions that in literature took centuries have come about in a decade. In cinematic practice, particularly in Russia, this change-over has partially become established reality. Some of the players whom we meet in Russian films are not actors in our sense but people who portray *themselves*—and primarily in their own work process. In Western Europe the capitalistic exploitation of the film denies consideration to modern man's legitimate claim to being reproduced. Under these circumstances the film industry is trying hard to spur the interest of the masses through illusion-promoting spectacles and dubious speculations.

XI

The shooting of a film, especially of a sound film, affords a spectacle unimaginable anywhere at any time before this. It presents a process in which it is impossible to assign to a spectator a viewpoint which would exclude from the actual scene such extraneous accessories as camera equipment, lighting machinery, staff assistants, etc.—unless his eye were on a line parallel with the lens. This circumstance, more than any other, renders superficial and insignificant any possible similarity between a scene in the studio and one on the stage. In the theater one is well aware of the place from which the play cannot immediately be detected as illusionary. There is no such place for the movie scene that is being shot. Its illusionary nature is that of the second degree, the result of cutting. That is to say, in the studio the mechanical equipment has penetrated so deeply into reality that its pure aspect freed from the foreign substance of equipment is the result of a special procedure, namely, the shooting by the specially adjusted camera and the mounting of the shot together with other similar ones. The equipment-free aspect of reality here has become the height of artifice; the sight of immediate reality has become an orchid in the land of technology.

Even more revealing is the comparison of these circumstances, which differ so much from those of the theater, with the situation in painting. Here the question is: How does the cameraman compare with the painter? To answer this we take recourse to an analogy with a surgical operation. The surgeon represents the polar opposite of the magician. The magician heals a sick person by the laying on of hands; the surgeon cuts into the patient's body. The magician maintains the natural distance between the patient and himself; though he reduces it very slightly by the laying on of hands, he greatly increases it by virtue of his authority. The surgeon does exactly the reverse; he greatly diminishes the distance between himself and the patient by penetrating into the patient's body, and increases it but little by the caution with which his hand moves among the organs. In short, in contrast to the magician who is still hidden in the medical practitioner—the surgeon at the decisive moment abstains from facing the patient man to man; rather, it is through the operation that he penetrates into him.

Magician and surgeon compare to painter and cameraman. The painter maintains in his work a natural distance from reality, the cameraman penetrates deeply into its web. There is a tremendous difference between the pictures they obtain. That of the painter is a total one, that of the cameraman consists of multiple fragments which are assembled under a new law. Thus, for contemporary man the representation of reality by the film is incomparably more significant than that of the painter, since it offers, precisely because of the thoroughgoing permeation of reality with mechanical equipment, an aspect of reality which is free of all equipment. And that is what one is entitled to ask from a work of art.

XII

Mechanical reproduction of art changes the reaction of the masses toward art. The reactionary attitude toward a Picasso painting changes into the progressive reaction toward a Chaplin movie. The progressive reaction is characterized by the direct, intimate fusion of visual and emotional enjoyment with the orientation of the expert. Such fusion is of great social significance. The greater the decrease in the social significance of an art form, the sharper the distinction between criticism and enjoyment by the public. The conventional is uncritically enjoyed, and the truly new is criticized with aversion. With regard to the screen, the critical and the receptive attitudes of the public coincide. The decisive reason for this is that individual reactions are predetermined by the mass audience response they are about to produce, and this is nowhere more pronounced than in the film. The moment these responses become manifest they control each other. Again, the comparison with painting is fruitful. A painting has always had an excellent chance to be viewed by one person or by a few. The simultaneous contemplation of paintings by a large public, such as developed in the nineteenth century, is an early symptom of the crisis of painting, a crisis which was by no means occasioned exclusively by photography but rather in a relatively independent manner by the appeal of art works to the masses.

Painting simply is in no position to present an object for simultaneous collective experience, as it was possible for architecture at all times, for the epic poem in the past, and for the movie today. Although this circumstance in itself should not lead one to conclusions about the social role of painting, it does constitute a serious threat as soon as painting, under special conditions and, as it were, against its nature, is confronted directly by the masses. In the churches and monasteries of the Middle Ages and at the princely courts up to the end of the eighteenth century, a collective reception of paintings did not occur simultaneously, but by graduated and hierarchized mediation. The change that has come about is an expression of the particular conflict in which painting was implicated by the mechanical reproducibility of paintings. Although paintings began to be publicly exhibited in galleries and salons, there was no way for the masses to organize and control themselves in their reception. Thus the same public which responds in a progressive manner toward a grotesque film is bound to respond in a reactionary manner to surrealism.

XIII

The characteristics of the film lie not only in the manner in which man presents himself to mechanical equipment but also in the manner in which, by means of this apparatus, man can represent his environment. A glance at occupational psychology illustrates the testing capacity of the equipment. Psychoanalysis illustrates it in a different perspective. The film has enriched our field of perception with methods which can be illustrated by those of Freudian theory. Fifty years ago, a slip of the tongue passed more or less unnoticed. Only exceptionally may such a slip have revealed dimensions of depth in a conversation which had seemed to be taking its course on the surface. Since the *Psychopathology of Everyday Life* things have changed. This book isolated and made analyzable things which had herefore floated along unnoticed in the broad stream of perception. For the entire spectrum of optical, and now also acoustical, perception the film has brought about a similar deepening of apperception. It is only an obverse of this fact that behavior items shown in a movie can be analyzed much more precisely and from more points of view than those presented on paintings or on the stage. As compared with painting, filmed behavior lends itself more readily to analysis because of its incomparably more precise statements of the situation. In comparison with the stage scene, the filmed behavior item lends itself more readily to analysis because it can be isolated more easily. This circumstance derives its chief importance from its tendency to promote the mutual penetration of art and science. Actually, of a screened behavior item which is neatly brought out in a certain situation, like a muscle of a body, it is difficult to say which is more fascinating, its artistic value or its value for science. To demonstrate the identity of the artistic and scientific uses of photography which heretofore usually were separated will be one of the revolutionary functions of the film.

By close-ups of the things around us, by focusing on hidden details of familiar objects, by exploring commonplace milieus under the ingenious guidance of the camera, the film, on the one hand, extends our comprehension of the necessities which rule our lives; on the other hand, it manages to assure us of an immense and unexpected field of action. Our taverns and our metropolitan streets, our offices and furnished rooms, our railroad stations and our factories appeared to have us locked up hopelessly. Then came the film and burst this prison-world asunder by the dynamite of the tenth of a second, so that now, in the midst of its far-flung ruins and debris, we calmly and adventurously go traveling. With the close-up, space expands; with slow motion, movement is extended. The enlargement of a snapshot does not simply render more precise what in any case was visible, though unclear: it reveals entirely new structural formations of the subject. So, too, slow motion not only presents familiar qualities of movement but reveals in them entirely unknown ones "which, far from looking like retarded rapid movements, give the effect of singularly gliding, floating, supernatural motions."[3] Evidently a different nature opens itself to the camera than opens to the naked eye—if only because an unconsciously penetrated space is substituted for a space consciously explored by man. Even if one has a general knowledge of the way people walk, one knows nothing of a person's posture during the fractional second of a stride. The act of reaching for a lighter or a spoon is familiar routine, yet we hardly know what really goes on between hand and metal, not to mention how this fluctuates with our moods. Here the camera intervenes with the resources of its lowerings and liftings, its interruptions and isolations, its extensions and accelerations, its enlargements and reductions. The camera introduces us to unconscious optics as does psychoanalysis to unconscious impulses. . . .

Epilogue

The growing proletarianization of modern man and the increasing formation of masses are two aspects of the same process. Fascism attempts to organize the newly created proletarian masses without affecting the property structure, which the masses strive to eliminate. Fascism sees its salvation in giving these masses not their right, but instead a chance to express themselves. The masses have a right to change property relations; Fascism seeks to give them an expression while preserving property. The logical result of Fascism is the introduction of aesthetics into political life. The violation of the masses, whom

Fascism, with its *Führer* cult, forces to their knees, has its counterpart in the violation of an apparatus which is pressed into the production of ritual values.

All efforts to render politics aesthetic culminate in one thing: war. War and war only can set a goal for mass movements on the largest scale while respecting the traditional property system. This is the political formula for the situation. The technological formula may be stated as follows: Only war makes it possible to mobilize all of today's technical resources while maintaining the property system. It goes without saying that the Fascist apotheosis of war does not employ such arguments. Still, Marinetti says in his manifesto on the Ethiopian colonial war:

> For twenty-seven years we Futurists have revelled against the branding of war as antiaesthetic. . . . Accordingly we state: . . . War is beautiful because it establishes man's dominion over the subjugated machinery by means of gas masks, terrifying megaphones, flame throwers, and small tanks. War is beautiful because it initiates the dreamt-of metalization of the human body. War is beautiful because it enriches a flowering meadow with the fiery orchids of machine guns. War is beautiful because it combines the gunfire, the cannonades, the cease-fire, the scents, and the stench of putrefaction into a symphony. War is beautiful because it creates new architecture, like that of the big tanks, the geometrical formation flights, the smoke spirals from burning villages, and many others. . . . Poets and artists of Futurism! . . . remember these principles of an aesthetics of war so that your struggle for a new literature and a new graphic art . . . may be illumined by them!

This manifesto has the virtue of clarity. Its formulations deserve to be accepted by dialecticians. To the latter, the aesthetics of today's war appears as follows: If the natural utilization of productive forces is impeded by the property system, the increase in technical devices, in speed, and in the sources of energy will press for an unnatural utilization, and this is found in war. The destructiveness of war furnishes proof that society has not been mature enough to incorporate technology as its organ, that technology has not been sufficiently developed to cope with the elemental forces of society. The horrible features of imperialistic warfare are attributable to the discrepancy between the tremendous means of production and their inadequate utilization in the process of production—in other words, to unemployment and the lack of markets. Imperialistic war is a rebellion of technology which collects, in the form of "human material," the claims to which society has denied its natural material. Instead of draining rivers, society directs a human stream into a bed of trenches; instead of dropping seeds from airplanes, it drops incendiary bombs over cities; and through gas warfare the aura is abolished in a new way.

"Fiat ars—pereat mundus," says Fascism, and, as Marinetti admits, expects war to supply the artistic gratification of a sense perception that has been changed by technology. This is evidently the consummation of *"l'art pour l'art."* Mankind, which in Homer's time was an object of contemplation for the Olympian gods, now is one for itself. Its self-alienation has reached such a

degree that it can experience its own destruction as an aesthetic pleasure of the first order. This is the situation of politics which Fascism is rendering aesthetic. Communism responds to politicizing art.

NOTES

1. Abel Gance, "Le Temps de l'image est venu," *L'Art cinématographique,* Vol. 2, pp. 94 f. (Paris, 1927).

2. Luigi Pirandello, *Si Gira,* quoted by Léon Pierre-Quint, "Signification du cinéma," *L'Art cinématographique,* pp. 14-15.

3. Rudolf Arnheim, *loc. cit.,* p. 138.

THEODOR W. ADORNO

On the Fetish-Character in Music and the Regression of Listening*

The illusion of a social preference for light music as against serious is based on that passivity of the masses which makes the consumption of light music contradict the objective interest of those who consume it. It is claimed that they actually like light music and listen to the higher type only for reasons of social prestige, when acquaintance with the text of a single hit song suffices to reveal the sole function this object of honest approbation can perform. The unity of the two spheres of music is thus that of an unresolved contradiction. They do not hang together in such a way that the lower could serve as a sort of popular introduction to the higher, or the higher could renew its lost collective strength by borrowing from the lower. The whole can not be put together by adding the separated halves, but in both there appear, however distantly, the changes of the whole, which only moves in contradiction. If the flight from the banal becomes definitive, if the marketability of the serious product shrinks to nothing, in consequence of its objective demands, then on the lower level the effect of the standardization of successes means it is no longer possible to succeed in an old style, but only in imitation as such. Between incomprehensibility and inescapability, there is no third way; the situation has polarized itself into extremes which actually meet. There is no room between them for the "individual." The latter's claims, wherever they still occur, are illusory,

* Theodor W. Adorno, "On the Fetish-Character in Music and the Regression of Listening," from *The Essential Frankfurt School Reader*, edited by Andrew Arato and Eike Gebhardt (New York: Continuum, 1982), pp. 275-79, 287-88, 291-94, 297-99.

being copied from the standards. The liquidation of the individual is the real signature of the new musical situation.

If the two spheres of music are stirred up in the unity of their contradiction, the demarcation line between them varies. The advanced product has renounced consumption. The rest of serious music is delivered over to consumption for the price of its wages. It succumbs to commodity listening. The differences in the reception of official "classical" music and light music no longer have any real significance. They are only still manipulated for reasons of marketability. The hit song enthusiast must be reassured that his idols are not too elevated for him, just as the visitor to philharmonic concerts is confirmed in his status. The more industriously the trade erects wire fences between the musical provinces, the greater the suspicion that without these, the inhabitants could all too easily come to an understanding. Toscanini, like a second-rate orchestra leader, is called Maestro, if half ironically, and a hit song, "Music, maestro, please," had its success immediately after Toscanini was promoted to Marshal of the Air with the aid of the radio.

The world of that musical life, the composition business which extends peacefully from Irving Berlin and Walter Donaldson—"the world's best composer"—by way of Gershwin, Sibelius and Tchaikovsky to Schubert's B Minor Symphony, labeled *The Unfinished,* is one of fetishes. The star principle has become totalitarian. The reactions of the listeners appear to have no relation to the playing of the music. They have reference, rather, to the cumulative success which, for its part, cannot be thought of unalienated by the past spontaneities of listeners, but instead dates back to the command of publishers, sound film magnates and rulers of radio. Famous people are not the only stars. Works begin to take on the same role. A pantheon of best-sellers builds up. The programs shrink, and the shrinking process not only removes the moderately good, but the accepted classics themselves undergo a selection that has nothing to do with quality. In America, Beethoven's Fourth Symphony is among the rarities. This selection reproduces itself in a fatal circle: the most familiar is the most successful and is therefore played again and again and made still more familiar. The choice of the standard works is itself in terms of their "effectiveness" for progammatic fascination, in terms of the categories of success as determined by light music or permitted by the star conductors. The climaxes of Beethoven's Seventh Symphony are placed on the same level as the unspeakable horn melody from the slow movement of Tchaikovsky's Fifth. Melody comes to mean eight-beat symmetrical treble melody. This is catalogued as the composer's "idea" which one thinks he can put in his pocket and take home, just as it is ascribed to the composer as his basic property. The concept of the idea is far from appropriate to established classical music. Its thematic material, mostly dissected triads, does not at all belong to the author in the same specific sense as in a romantic song. Beethoven's greatness shows itself in the complete subordination of the accidentally private melodic elements of the form as a whole. This does not prevent all music, even Bach, who borrowed one of the most important themes of

The Well-Tempered Clavier, from being examined in terms of the category of ideas, with musical larceny being hunted down with all the zeal of the belief in property, so that finally one music commentator could pin his success to the title of tune detective.

At its most passionate, musical fetishism takes possession of the public valuation of singing voices. Their sensuous magic is traditional as is the close relation between success and the person endowed with "material." But today it is forgotten that it is material. For musical vulgar materialists, it is synonymous to have a voice and to be a singer. In earlier epochs, technical virtuosity, at least, was demanded of singing stars, the castrati and prima donnas. Today, the material as such, destitute of any function, is celebrated. One need not even ask about capacity for musical performance. Even mechanical control of the instrument is no longer really expected. To legitimate the fame of its owner, a voice need only be especially voluminous or especially high. If one dares even in conversation to question the decisive importance of the voice and to assert that it is just as possible to make beautiful music with a moderately good voice as it is on a moderately good piano, one will immediately find oneself faced with a situation of hostility and aversion whose emotional roots go far deeper than the occasion. Voices are holy properties like a national trademark. As if the voices wanted to revenge themselves for this, they begin to lose the sensuous magic in whose name they are merchandised. Most of them sound like imitations of those who have made it, even when they themselves have made it. All this reaches a climax of absurdity in the cult of the master violins. One promptly goes into raptures at the well-announced sound of a Stradivarius or Amati, which only the ear of a specialist can tell from that of a good modern violin, forgetting in the process to listen to the composition and the execution, from which there is still something to be had. The more the modern technique of the violin bow progresses, the more it seems that the old instruments are treasured. If the moments of sensual pleasure in the idea, the voice, the instrument are made into fetishes and torn away from any functions which could give them meaning, they meet a response equally isolated, equally far from the meaning of the whole, and equally determined by success in the blind and irrational emotions which form the relationship to music into which those with no relationship enter. But these are the same relations as exist between the consumers of hit songs and the hit songs. Their only relation is to the completely alien, and the alien, as if cut off from the consciousness of the masses by a dense screen, is what seeks to speak for the silent. Where they react at all, it no longer makes any difference whether it is to Beethoven's Seventh Symphony or to a bikini.

The concept of musical fetishism cannot be psychologically derived. That "values" are consumed and draw feelings to themselves, without their specific qualities being reached by the consciousness of the consumer, is a later expression of their commodity character. For all contemporary musical life is dominated by the commodity form: the late pre-capitalist residues have been eliminated. Music, with all the attributes of the ethereal and sublime which are generously accorded it, serves in America today as an advertisement for commodities which one must acquire in order to be able to hear music. If the advertising function is carefully dimmed in the case of serious music, it always breaks through in the case of light music. The whole jazz business, with its free distribution of scores to bands, has abandoned the idea that actual performance promotes the sale of piano scores and phonograph records. Countless hit song texts praise the hit songs themselves, repeating their titles in capital letters. What makes its appearance, like an idol, out of such masses of type is the exchange-value in which the quantum of possible enjoyment has disappeared. Marx defines the fetish character of the commodity as the veneration of the thing made by oneself which, as exchange-value, simultaneously alienates itself from producer to consumer—"human beings." "A commodity is therefore a mysterious thing, simply because in it the social character of men's labor appears to them as an objective character stamped upon the product of that labor: because the relation of the producers to the sum total of their own labor is presented to them as a social relation, existing not between themselves, but between the products of their labor." This is the real secret of success. It is the mere reflection of what one pays in the market for the product. The consumer is really worshipping the money that he himself has paid for the ticket to the Toscanini concert. He has literally "made" the success which he reifies and accepts as an objective criterion, without recognizing himself in it. But he has not "made" it by liking the concert, but rather by buying the ticket. To be sure, exchange-value exerts its power in a special way in the realm of cultural goods. For in the world of commodities this realm appears to be exempted from the power of exchange, to be in an immediate relationship with the goods, and it is this appearance in turn which alone gives cultural goods their exchange-value. But they nevertheless simultaneously fall completely into the world of commodities, are produced for the market, and are aimed at the market. The appearance of immediacy is as strong as the compulsion of exchange-value is inexorable. The social compact harmonizes the contradiction. The appearance of immediacy takes possession of the mediated, exchange-value itself. If the commodity in general combines exchange-value and use-value, then the pure use-value, whose illusion the cultural goods must preserve in completely capitalist society, must be replaced by pure exchange-value, which precisely in its capacity as exchange-value deceptively takes over the function of use-value. The specific fetish character of music lies in this *quid pro quo*. The feelings which go to the exchange-value create the appearance of immediacy at the same time as the absence of a relation to the object belies it. It has its basis in the abstract character of exchange-value. Every "psychological" aspect, every *ersatz* satisfaction, depends on such social substitution. . . .

The counterpart to the fetishism of music is a regression of listening. This does not mean a relapse of the individual listener into an earlier phase of his own development, nor a decline in the collective general level, since the millions who are reached musically for the first time by today's mass communications cannot be compared with the audience of the past. Rather, it is contemporary listening which has regressed, arrested at the infantile stage. Not only do the listening subjects lose, along with freedom of choice and responsibility, the capacity for conscious perception of music, which was from time immemorial confined to a narrow group, but they stubbornly reject the possibility of such perception. They fluctuate between comprehensive forgetting and sudden dives into recognition. They listen atomistically and dissociate what they hear, but precisely in this dissociation they develop certain capacities which accord less with the concepts of traditional aesthetics than with those of football and motoring. They are not childlike, as might be expected on the basis of an interpretation of the new type of listener in terms of the introduction to musical life of groups previously unacquainted with music. But they are childish; their primitivism is not that of the undeveloped, but that of the forcibly retarded. Whenever they have a chance, they display the pinched hatred of those who really sense the other but exclude it in order to live in peace, and who therefore would like best to root out the nagging possibility. The regression is really from this existent possibility, or more concretely, from the possibility of a different and oppositional music. Regressive, too, is the role which contemporary mass music plays in the psychological household of its victims. They are not merely turned away from more important music, but they are confirmed in their neurotic stupidity, quite irrespective of how their musical capacities are related to the specific musical culture of earlier social phases. The assent to hit songs and debased cultural goods belongs to the same complex of symptoms as do those faces of which one no longer knows whether the film has alienated them from reality or reality has alienated them from the film, as they wrench open a great formless mouth with shining teeth in a voracious smile, while the tired eyes are wretched and lost above. Together with sport and film, mass music and the new listening help to make escape from the whole infantile milieu impossible. The sickness has a preservative function. Even the listening habits of the contemporary masses are certainly in no way new, and one may readily concede that the reception of the prewar hit song "Puppchen" was not so very different from that of a synthetic jazz children's song. But the context in which such a children's song appears, the masochistic mocking of one's own wish for lost happiness, or the compromising of the desire for happiness itself by the reversion to a childhood whose unattainability bears witness to the unattainability of joy—this is the specific product of the new listening, and nothing which strikes the ear remains exempt from this system of assimilation. There are indeed social differences, but the new listening extends so far that the stultification of the oppressed affects the oppressors themselves, and they become the victims of the superior power of self-propelled wheels who think they are determining their direction.

Regressive listening is tied to production by the machinery of distribution, and particularly by advertising. Regressive listening appears as soon as advertising turns into terror, as soon as nothing is left for the consciousness but to capitulate before the superior power of the advertised stuff and purchase spiritual peace by making the imposed goods literally its own thing. In regressive listening, advertising takes on a compulsory character. For a while, an English brewery used for propaganda purposes a billboard that bore a deceptive likeness to one of those whitewashed brick walls which are so numerous in the slums of London and the industrial cities of the North. Properly placed, the billboard was barely distinguishable from a real wall. On it, chalk-white, was a careful imitation of awkward writing. The words said: "What we want is Watney's." The brand of the beer was presented like a political slogan. Not only does this billboard give an insight into the nature of up-to-date propaganda, which sells its slogans as well as its wares, just as here the wares masquerade as a slogan; the type of relationship suggested by the billboard, in which masses make a commodity recommended to them the object of their own action, is in fact found again as the pattern for the reception of light music. They need and demand what has been palmed off on them. They overcome the feeling of impotence that creeps over them in the face of monopolistic production by identifying themselves with the inescapable product. They thereby put an end to the strangeness of the musical brands which are at once distant from them and threateningly near, and in addition, achieve the satisfaction of feeling themselves involved in Mr. Know-Nothing's enterprises, which confront them at every turn. This explains why individual expressions of preference—or, of course, dislike—converge in an area where object and subject alike make such reactions questionable. The fetish character of music produces its own camouflage through the identification of the listener with the fetish. This identification initially gives the hit songs power over their victims. It fulfills itself in the subsequent forgetting and remembering. Just as every advertisement is composed of the inconspicuous familiar and the unfamiliar conspicuous, so the hit song remains salutarily forgotten in the half-dusk of its familiarity, suddenly to become painfully over-clear through recollection, as if in the beam of a spotlight. One can almost equate the moment of this recollection with that in which the title or the words of the initial verse of his hit song confront the victim. Perhaps he identifies himself with this because he identifies it and thereby merges with his possession. This compulsion may well drive him to recall the title of the hit song at times. But the writing under the note, which makes the identification possible, is nothing else but the trademark of the hit song. . . .

The ambivalence of the retarded listeners has its most extreme expression in the fact that individuals, not yet fully reified, want to extricate themselves from the mechanism of musical reification to which they have been handed over, but that their revolts against fetishism only entangle them more deeply in it. Whenever they attempt to break away from the passive status of compulsory consumers and "activate" themselves, they succumb to pseudoactivity. Types rise up from the mass of the retarded who differentiate themselves by pseudoactivity and nevertheless make the regression more strikingly visible. There are, first, the enthusiasts who write fan letters to radio stations and orchestras and, at well-managed jazz festivals, produce their own enthusiasm as an advertisement for the wares they consume. They call them-selves jitterbugs, as if they simultaneously wanted to affirm and mock their loss of individuality, their transformation into beetles whirring around in fascina-tion. Their only excuse is that the term jitterbugs, like all those in the unreal edifice of films and jazz, is hammered into them by the entrepreneurs to make them think that they are on the inside. Their ecstasy is without content. That it happens, that the music is listened to, this replaces the content itself. The ecstasy takes possession of its object by its own compulsive character. It is stylized like the ecstasies savages go into in beating the war drums. It has convulsive aspects reminiscent of St. Vitus' dance or the reflexes of muti-lated animals. Passion itself seems to be produced by defects. But the ecstatic ritual betrays itself as pseudoactivity by the moment of mimicry. People do not dance or listen "from sensuality" and sensuality is certainly not satisfied by lis-tening, but the gestures of the sensual are imitated. An analogue is the rep-resentation of particular emotions in the film, where there are physiognomic patterns for anxiety, longing, the erotic look; for smiling; for the atomistic expressivo of debased music. The imitative assimilation to commodity models is intertwined with folkloristic customs of imitation. In jazz, the relation of such mimicry to the imitating individual himself is quite loose. Its medium is caricature. Dance and music copy stages of sexual excitement only to make fun of them. It is as if desire's surrogate itself simultaneously turned against it; the "realistic" behavior of the oppressed triumphs over his dream of happiness while being itself incorporated into the latter. And as if to confirm the super-ficiality and treachery of every form of ecstasy, the feet are unable to fulfill what the ear pretends. The same jitterbugs who behave as if they were elec-trified by syncopation dance almost exclusively the good rhythmic parts. The weak flesh punishes the lies of the willing spirit; the gestural ecstasy of the infantile listener misfires in the face of the ecstatic gesture. The opposite type appears to be the eager person who leaves the factory and "occupies" himself with music in the quiet of his bedroom. He is shy and inhibited, per-haps has no luck with girls, and wants in any case to preserve his own special sphere. He seeks this as a radio ham. At twenty, he is still at the stage of a boy scout working on complicated knots just to please his parents. This type is held in high esteem in radio matters. He patiently builds sets whose most important parts he must buy ready-made, and scans the air for shortwave secrets, though there are none. As a reader of Indian stories and travel books, he once discovered unknown lands and cleared his path through the forest primeval. As radio ham he becomes the discoverer of just those industrial products which are interested in being discovered by him. He brings nothing home which would not be delivered to his house. The adventurers of pseu-doactivity have already organized themselves on a large scale; the radio ama-teurs have printed verification cards sent them by the shortwave stations they have discovered, and hold contests in which the winner is the one who can produce the most such cards. All this is carefully fostered from above. Of all fetishistic listeners, the radio ham is perhaps the most complete. It is irrelevant to him what he hears or even how he hears; he is only interested in the fact that he hears and succeeds in inserting himself, with his private equipment, into the public mechanism, without exerting even the slightest influence on it. With the same attitude, countless radio listeners play with the feedback or the sound dial without themselves becoming hams. Others are more expert, or at least more aggressive. These smart chaps can be found everywhere and are able to do everything themselves: the advanced student who in every gathering is ready to play jazz with machine-like precision for dancing and entertainment; the gas station attendant who hums his syncopation ingenuously while filling up the tank; the listening expert who can identify every band and immerses himself in the history of jazz as if it were Holy Writ. He is nearest to the sportsman: if not to the football player himself, then to the swaggering fellow who dominates the stands. He shines by a capacity for rough improvisations, even if he must practice the piano for hours in secret in order to bring the refractory rhythms together. He pictures himself as the individualist who whistles at the world. But what he whistles is its melody, and his tricks are less inventions of the moment than stored-up experiences from acquaintance with sought-after technical things. His improvisations are always gestures of nimble subordination to what the instrument demands of him. The chauffeur is the model for the listening type of the clever fellow. His agreement with everything dominant goes so far that he no longer produces any resistance, but of his own accord always does what is asked of him for the sake of the responsible functionary. He lies to himself about the completeness of his subordination to the rule of the reified mechanism. Thus, the sovereign routine of the jazz amateur is nothing but the passive capacity for adaptation to models from which to avoid straying. He is the real jazz subject; his improvisations come from the pattern, and he navigates the pattern, cigarette in mouth, as nonchalantly as if he had invented it himself. . . .

In the face of regressive listening, music as a whole begins to take on a comic aspect. One need only listen to the uninhibited sonority of a choral rehearsal from outside. This experience was caught with great force in a film by the Marx brothers, who demolish an opera set as if to clothe in allegory the insight of the philosophy of history on the decay of the operatic form, or in a most estimable piece of refined entertainment, break up a grand piano in order to take possession of its strings in their frame as the true harp of the future, on which to play a prelude. Music has become comic in the present phase primarily because something so completely useless is carried on with all the visible signs of the strain of serious work. By being alien to solid people, music reveals their alienation from one another, and the consciousness of alienation vents itself in laughter. In music—or similarly in lyric poetry—the society which judged them comic becomes comic. But involved in this laughter is the decay of the sacral spirit of reconciliation. All music today can very easily sound as *Parsifal* did to Nietzsche's ear. It recalls incomprehensible rites and surviving masks from an earlier time, and is provocative nonsense. The radio, which both wears out music and overexposes it, makes a major contribution to this. Perhaps a better hour may at some time strike even for the clever fellows: one in which they may demand, instead of prepared material ready to be switched on, the improvisatory displacement of things, as the sort of radical beginning that can only thrive under the protection of the unshaken real world. Even discipline can take over the expression of free solidarity if freedom becomes its content. As little as regressive listening is a symptom of progress in consciousness of freedom, it could suddenly turn around if art, in unity with the society, should ever leave the road of the always-identical.

Not popular music but artistic music has furnished a model for this possibility. It is not for nothing that Mahler is the scandal of all bourgeois musical aesthetics. They call him uncreative because he suspends their concept of creation itself. Everything with which he occupies himself is already there. He accepts it in its vulgarized form; his themes are expropriated ones. Nevertheless, nothing sounds as it was wont to; all things are diverted as if by a magnet. What is worn out yields pliantly to the improvising hand; the used parts win a second life as variants. Just as the chauffeur's knowledge of his old second-hand car can enable him to drive it punctually and unrecognized to its intended destination, so can the expression of a beat-up melody, straining under the pressure of clarinets and oboes in the upper register, arrive at places which the approved musical language could never safely reach. Such music really crystallizes the whole, into which it has incorporated the vulgarized fragments, into something new, yet it takes its material from regressive listening. Indeed, one can almost think that in Mahler's music this experience was seismographically recorded forty years before it permeated society. But if Mahler stood athwart the concept of musical progress, neither can the new and radical music whose most advanced practitioners give allegiance to him in a seemingly paradoxical way any longer be subsumed exclusively under the concept of progress. It proposes to consciously resist the phenomenon of regressive listening. The terror which Schönberg and Webern spread, today as in the past, comes not from their incomprehensibility but from the fact that they are all too correctly understood. Their music gives form to that anxiety, that terror, that insight into the catastrophic situation which others merely evade by regressing. They are called individualists, and yet their work is nothing but a single dialogue with the powers which destroy individuality—powers whose "formless shadows" fall gigantically on their music. In music, too, collective powers are liquidating an individuality past saving, but against them only individuals are capable of consciously representing the aims of collectivity.

The Aesthetic Dimension*

In a situation where the miserable reality can be changed only through radical political praxis, the concern with aesthetics demands justification. It would be senseless to deny the element of despair inherent in this concern: the retreat into a world of fiction where existing conditions are changed and overcome only in the realm of the imagination. However, this purely ideological conception of art is being questioned with increasing intensity. It seems that art as art expresses a truth, an experience, a necessity which, although not in the domain of radical praxis, are nevertheless essential components of revolution. With this insight, the basic conception of Marxist aesthetics, that is its treatment of art as ideology, and the emphasis on the class character of art, become again the topic of critical reexamination.[1]

This discussion is directed to the following theses of Marxist aesthetics:

1. There is a definite connection between art and the material base, between art and the totality of the relations of production. With the change in production relations, art itself is transformed as part of the superstructure, although, like other ideologies, it can lag behind or anticipate social change.
2. There is a definite connection between art and social class. The only authentic, true, progressive art is the art of an ascending class. It expresses the consciousness of this class.
3. Consequently, the political and the aesthetic, the revolutionary content and the artistic quality tend to coincide.

---

* Herbert Marcuse, *The Aesthetic Dimension* (Boston: Beacon Press, 1978), pp. 1-21, 75-77.

4. The writer has an obligation to articulate and express the interests and needs of the ascending class. (In capitalism, this would be the proletariat.)
5. A declining class or its representatives are unable to produce anything but "decadent" art.
6. Realism (in various senses) is considered as the art form which corresponds most adequately to the social relationships, and thus is the "correct" art form.

Each of these theses implies that the social relations of production must be represented in the literary work—not imposed upon the work externally, but a part of its inner logic and the logic of the material.

This aesthetic imperative follows from the base-superstructure conception. In contrast to the rather dialectical formulations of Marx and Engels, the conception has been made into a rigid schema, a schematization that has had devastating consequences for aesthetics. The schema implies a normative notion of the material base as the true reality and a political devaluation of nonmaterial forces particularly of the individual consciousness and subconscious and their political function. This function can be either regressive or emancipatory. In both cases, it can become a material force. If historical materialism does not account for this role of subjectivity, it takes on the coloring of vulgar materialism.

Ideology becomes mere ideology, in spite of Engels's emphatic qualifications, and a devaluation of the entire realm of subjectivity takes place, a devaluation not only of the subject as *ego cogito,* the rational subject, but also of inwardness, emotions, and imagination. The subjectivity of individuals, their own consciousness and unconscious tends to be dissolved into class consciousness. Thereby, a major prerequisite of revolution is minimized, namely, the fact that the need for radical change must be rooted in the subjectivity of individuals themselves, in their intelligence and their passions, their drives and their goals. Marxist theory succumbed to that very reification which it had exposed and combated in society as a whole. Subjectivity became an atom of objectivity; even in its rebellious form it was surrendered to a collective consciousness. The deterministic component of Marxist theory does not lie in its concept of the relationship between social existence and consciousness, but in the reductionistic concept of consciousness which brackets the particular content of individual consciousness and, with it, the subjective potential for revolution.

This development was furthered by the interpretation of subjectivity as a "bourgeois" notion. Historically, this is questionable.[2] But even in bourgeois society, insistence on the truth and right of inwardness is not really a bourgeois value. With the affirmation of the inwardness of subjectivity, the individual steps out of the network of exchange relationships and exchange values, withdraws from the reality of bourgeois society, and enters another dimension of existence. Indeed, this escape from reality led to an experience which could (and did) become a powerful force in *invalidating* the actually pre-

vailing bourgeois values, namely, by shifting the locus of the individual's realization from the domain of the performance principle and the profit motive to
that of the inner resources of the human being: passion, imagination, conscience. Moreover, withdrawal and retreat were not the last position. Subjectivity strove to break out of its inwardness into the material and intellectual
culture. And today, in the totalitarian period, it has become a political value as
a counterforce against aggressive and exploitative socialization.

Liberating subjectivity constitutes itself in the inner history of the individuals—their own history, which is not identical with their social existence. It
is the particular history of their encounters, their passions, joys, and sorrows—experiences which are not necessarily grounded in their class situation,
and which are not even comprehensible from this perspective. To be sure, the
actual manifestations of their history are determined by their class situation,
but this situation is not the ground of their fate—of that which happens to
them. Especially in its nonmaterial aspects it explodes the class framework. It
is all too easy to relegate love and hate, joy and sorrow, hope and despair to
the domain of psychology, thereby removing them from the concerns of radical praxis. Indeed, in terms of political economy they may not be "forces of
production," but for every human being they are decisive, they constitute
reality.

Even in its most distinguished representatives Marxist aesthetics has
shared in the devaluation of subjectivity. Hence the preference for realism as
the model of progressive art; the denigration of romanticism as simply reactionary; the denunciation of "decadent" art—in general, the embarrassment
when confronted with the task of evaluating the aesthetic qualities of a work
in terms other than class ideologies.

I shall submit the following thesis: the radical qualities of art, that is to
say, its indictment of the established reality and its invocation of the beautiful
image *(schöner Schein)* of liberation are grounded precisely in the dimensions
where art *transcends* its social determination and emancipates itself from the
given universe of discourse and behavior while preserving its overwhelming
presence. Thereby art creates the realm in which the subversion of experience
proper to art becomes possible: the world formed by art is recognized as a
reality which is suppressed and distorted in the given reality. This experience
culminates in extreme situations (of love and death, guilt and failure, but
also joy, happiness, and fulfillment) which explode the given reality in the
name of a truth normally denied or even unheard. The inner logic of the
work of art terminates in the emergence of another reason, another sensibility, which defy the rationality and sensibility incorporated in the dominant
social institutions.

Under the law of the aesthetic form, the given reality is necessarily *sublimated*: the immediate content is stylized, the "data" are reshaped and
reordered in accordance with the demands of the art form, which requires
that even the representation of death and destruction invoke the need for
hope—a need rooted in the new consciousness embodied in the work of art.

Aesthetic sublimation makes for the affirmative, reconciling component of art[3] though it is at the same time a vehicle for the critical, negating function of art. The transcendence of immediate reality shatters the reified objectivity of established social relations and opens a new dimension of experience: rebirth of the rebellious subjectivity. Thus, on the basis of aesthetic sublimination, a *desublimation* takes place in the perception of individuals—in their feelings, judgments, thoughts; an invalidation of dominant norms, needs, and values. With all its affirmative-ideological features, art remains a dissenting force.

We can tentatively define "aesthetic form" as the result of the transformation of a given content (actual or historical, personal or social fact) into a self-contained whole: a poem, play, novel, etc.[4] The work is thus "taken out" of the constant process of reality and assumes a significance and truth of its own. The aesthetic transformation is achieved through a reshaping of language, perception, and understanding so that they reveal the essence of reality in its appearance: the repressed potentialities of man and nature. The work of art thus re-presents reality while accusing it.[5]

The critical function of art, its contribution to the struggle for liberation, resides in the aesthetic form. A work of art is authentic or true not by virtue of its content (i.e., the "correct" representation of social conditions), nor by its "pure" form, but by the content having become form.

True, the aesthetic form removes art from the actuality of the class struggle—from actuality pure and simple. The aesthetic form constitutes the autonomy of art vis à vis "the given." However, this dissociation does not produce "false consciousness" or mere illusion but rather a counter-consciousness: negation of the realistic-conformist mind.

Aesthetic form, autonomy, and truth are inter-related. Each is a socio-historical phenomenon, and each *transcends* the socio-historical arena. While the latter limits the autonomy of art it does so without invalidating the *trans*historical truths expressed in the work. The truth of art lies in its power to break the monopoly of established reality (i.e., of those who established it) to *define* what is *real*. In this rupture, which is the achievement of the aesthetic form, the fictitious world of art appears as true reality.

Art is committed to that perception of the world which alienates individuals from their functional existence and performance in society—it is committed to an emancipation of sensibility, imagination, and reason in all spheres of subjectivity and objectivity. The aesthetic transformation becomes a vehicle of recognition and indictment. But this achievement presupposes a degree of autonomy which withdraws art from the mystifying power of the given and frees it for the expression of its own truth. Inasmuch as man and nature are constituted by an unfree society, their repressed and distorted potentialities can be represented only in an *estranging* form. The world of art is that of another *Reality Principle*, of estrangement—and only as estrangement does art fulfill a *cognitive* function: it communicates truths not communicable in any other language; *it contradicts*.

However, the strong affirmative tendencies toward reconciliation with the established reality coexist with the rebellious ones. I shall try to show that they are not due to the specific class determination of art but rather to the redeeming character of the *catharsis*. The catharsis itself is grounded in the power of aesthetic form to call fate by its name, to demystify its force, to give the word to the victims—the power of recognition which gives the individual a modicum of freedom and fulfillment in the realm of unfreedom. The interplay between the affirmation and the indictment of that which is, between ideology and truth, pertains to the very structure of art.[6] But in the authentic works, the affirmation does not cancel the indictment: reconciliation and hope still preserve the memory of things past.

The affirmative character of art has yet another source: it is in the commitment of art to Eros, the deep affirmation of the Life Instincts in their fight against instinctual and social oppression. The permanence of art, its historical immortality throughout the millennia of destruction, bears witness to this commitment.

Art stands under the law of the given, while transgressing this law. The concept of art as an essentially autonomous and negating productive force contradicts the notion which sees art as performing an essentially dependent, affirmative-ideological function, that is to say, glorifying and absolving the existing society.[7] Even the militant bourgeois literature of the eighteenth century remains ideological: the struggle of the ascending class with the nobility is primarily over issues of bourgeois morality. The lower classes play only a marginal role, if any. With a few notable exceptions, this literature is not one of class struggle. According to this point of view, the ideological character of art can be remedied today only by grounding art in revolutionary praxis and in the *Weltanschauung* of the proletariat.

It has often been pointed out that this interpretation of art does not do justice to the views of Marx and Engels.[8] To be sure, even this interpretation admits that art aims at representing the essence of a given reality and not merely its appearance. Reality is taken to be the totality of social relations and its essence is defined as the laws determining these relations in the "complex of social causality."[9] This view demands that the protagonists in a work of art represent individuals as "types" who in turn exemplify "objective tendencies of social development, indeed of humanity as a whole."[10]

Such formulations provoke the question whether literature is not hereby assigned a function which could only be fulfilled in the medium of theory. The representation of the social totality requires a conceptual analysis, which can hardly be transposed into the medium of sensibility. During the great debate on Marxist aesthetics in the early thirties, Lu Märten suggested that Marxist theory possesses a theoretical form of its own which militates against any attempt to give it an aesthetic form.[11]

But if the work of art cannot be comprehended in terms of social theory, neither can it be comprehended in terms of philosophy. In his discussion with Adorno, Lucien Goldmann rejects Adorno's claim that in order to understand a literary work "one has to transcend it towards philosophy, philosophical culture and critical knowledge." Against Adorno, Goldmann insists on the concreteness immanent in the work which makes it into an (aesthetic) totality in its own right: "The work of art is a universe of colors, sounds and words, and concrete characters. There is no death, there is only Phaedra dying."[12]

The reification of Marxist aesthetics depreciates and distorts the truth expressed in this universe—it minimizes the cognitive function of art as ideology. For the radical potential of art lies precisely in its ideological character, in its transcendent relation to the "basis." Ideology is not always *mere* ideology, false consciousness. The consciousness and the representation of truths which appear as abstract in relation to the established process of production are also ideological functions. Art presents one of these truths. As ideology, it opposes the given society. The autonomy of art contains the categorical imperative: "things must change." If the liberation of human beings and nature is to be possible at all, then the social nexus of destruction and submission must be broken. This does not mean that the revolution becomes thematic; on the contrary, in the aesthetically most perfect works, it does not. It seems that in these works the necessity of revolution is presupposed, as the *a priori* of art. But the revolution is also as it were surpassed and questioned as to how far it responds to the anguish of the human being, as to how far it achieves a rupture with the past.

Compared with the often one-dimensional optimism of propaganda, art is permeated with pessimism, not seldom intertwined with comedy. Its "liberating laughter" recalls the danger and the evil that have passed—this time! But the pessimism of art is not counterrevolutionary. It serves to warn against the "happy consciousness" of radical praxis: as if all of that which art invokes and indicts could be settled through the class struggle. Such pessimism permeates even the literature in which the revolution itself is affirmed, and becomes thematic; Büchner's play, *The Death of Danton*, is a classic example.

Marxist aesthetics assumes that all art is *somehow* conditioned by the relations of production, class position, and so on. Its first task (but only its first) is the specific analysis of this "somehow," that is to say, of the limits and modes of this conditioning. The question as to whether there are qualities of art which transcend specific social conditions and how these qualities are related to the particular social conditions remains open. Marxist aesthetics has yet to ask: What are the qualities of art which transcend the specific social content and form and give art its universality? Marxist aesthetics must explain why Greek tragedy and the medieval epic, for example, can still be experienced today as "great," "authentic" literature, even though they pertain to ancient slave society and feudalism respectively. Marx's remark at the end of *The Introduction to the Critique of Political Economy* is hardly persuasive; one simply cannot explain the attraction of Greek art for us today as our rejoicing in the unfolding of the social "childhood of humanity."

However correctly one has analyzed a poem, play, or novel in terms of its social content, the questions as to whether the particular work is good, beautiful, and true are still unanswered. But the answers to these questions cannot again be given in terms of the specific relations of production which constitute the historical context of the respective work. The circularity of this method is obvious. In addition it falls victim to an easy relativism which is contradicted clearly enough by the permanence of certain qualities of art through all changes of style and historical periods (transcendence, estrangement, aesthetic order, manifestations of the beautiful).

The fact that a work truly represents the interests or the outlook of the proletariat or of the bourgeoisie does not yet make it an authentic work of art. This "material" quality may facilitate its reception, may lend it greater concreteness, but it is in no way constitutive. The universality of art cannot be grounded in the world and world outlook of a particular class, for art envisions a concrete universal, humanity *(Menschlichkeit)*, which no particular class can incorporate, not even the proletariat, Marx's "universal class." The inexorable entanglement of joy and sorrow, celebration and despair, Eros and Thanatos cannot be dissolved into problems of class struggle. History is also grounded in nature. And Marxist theory has the least justification to ignore the metabolism between the human being and nature, and to denounce the insistence on this natural soil of society as a regressive ideological conception.

The emergence of human beings as "species beings"—men and women capable of living in that community of freedom which is the potential of the species—this is the subjective basis of a classless society. Its realization presupposes a radical transformation of the drives and needs of the individuals: an organic development within the socio-historical. Solidarity would be on weak grounds were it not rooted in the instinctual structure of individuals. In this dimension, men and women are confronted with psycho-physical forces which they have to make their own without being able to overcome the naturalness of these forces. This is the domain of the primary drives: of libidinal and destructive energy. Solidarity and community have their basis in the subordination of destructive and aggressive energy to the social emancipation of the life instincts.

Marxism has too long neglected the radical political potential of this dimension, though the revolutionizing of the instinctual structure is a prerequisite for a change in the system of needs, the mark of a socialist society as qualitative difference. Class society knows only the appearance, the image of the qualitative difference; this image, divorced from praxis, has been preserved in the realm of art. In the aesthetic form, the autonomy of art constitutes itself. It was forced upon art through the separation of mental and material labor, as a result of the prevailing relations of domination. Dissociation from the process of production became a refuge and a vantage point from which to denounce the reality established through domination.

Nevertheless society remains present in the autonomous realm of art in several ways: first of all as the "stuff" for the aesthetic representation which, past and present, is transformed in this representation. This is the historicity of the conceptual, linguistic, and imaginable material which the tradition transmits to the artists and with or against which they have to work; secondly, as the scope of the actually available possibilities of struggle and liberation; thirdly as the specific position of art in the social division of labor, especially in the separation of intellectual and manual labor through which artistic activity, and to a great extent also its reception, become the privilege of an "elite" removed from the material process of production.

The class character of art consists only in these objective limitations of its autonomy. The fact that the artist belongs to a privileged group negates neither the truth nor the aesthetic quality of his work. What is true of "the classics of socialism" is true also of the great artists: they break through the class limitations of their family, background, environment. Marxist theory is not family research. The progressive character of art, its contribution to the struggle for liberation cannot be measured by the artists' origins nor by the ideological horizon of their class. Neither can it be determined by the presence (or absence) of the oppressed class in their works. The criteria for the progressive character of art are given only in the work itself as a whole: in what it says and how it says it.

In this sense art is "art for art's sake" inasmuch as the aesthetic form reveals tabooed and repressed dimensions of reality: aspects of liberation. The poetry of Mallarmé is an extreme example; his poems conjure up modes of perception, imagination, gestures—a feast of sensuousness which shatters everyday experience and anticipates a different reality principle.

The degree to which the distance and estrangement from praxis constitute the emancipatory value of art becomes particularly clear in those works of literature which seem to close themselves rigidly against such praxis. Walter Benjamin has traced this in the works of Poe, Baudelaire, Proust, and Valéry. They express a "consciousness of crisis" *(Krisenbewusstsein):* a pleasure in decay, in destruction, in the beauty of evil; a celebration of the asocial, of the anomic—the secret rebellion of the bourgeois against his own class. Benjamin writes about Baudelaire:

> It seems of little value to give his work a position on the most advanced ramparts of the human struggle for liberation. From the beginning, it appears much more promising to follow him in his machinations where he is without doubt at home: in the enemy camp. These machinations are a blessing for the enemy only in the rarest cases. Baudelaire was a secret agent, an agent of the secret discontent of his class with its own rule. One who confronts Baudelaire with this class gets more out of him than one who rejects him as uninteresting from a proletarian standpoint.[13]

The "secret" protest of this esoteric literature lies in the ingression of the primary erotic-destructive forces which explode the normal universe of communication and behavior. They are asocial in their very nature, a subterranean rebellion against the social order. Inasmuch as this literature reveals the dominion of Eros and Thanatos beyond all social control, it invokes needs and gratifications which are essentially destructive. In terms of political praxis, this literature remains elitist and decadent. It does nothing in the struggle for liberation—except to open the tabooed zones of nature and society in which even death and the devil are enlisted as allies in the refusal to abide by the law and order of repression. This literature is one of the historical forms of critical aesthetic transcendence. Art cannot abolish the social division of labor which makes for its esoteric character, but neither can art "popularize" itself without weakening its emancipatory impact.

NOTES

1. Especially among the authors of the periodicals *Kursbuch* (Frankfurt: Suhrkamp, later Rotbuch Verlag), *Argument* (Berlin), *Literaturmagazin* (Reinbek: Rowohlt). In the center of this discussion is the idea of an autonomous art in confrontation with the capitalist art industry on the one hand, and the radical propaganda art on the other. See especially the excellent articles by Nicolas Born, H. C. Buch, Wolfgang Harich, Hermann Peter Piwitt, and Michael Schneider in volumes I and II of the *Literaturmagazin*, the volume *Autonomie der Kunst* (Frankfurt: Suhrkamp, 1972) and Peter Bürger, *Theorie der Avantgarde* (Frankfurt: Suhrkamp, 1974).

2. See Erich Köhler, *Ideal und Wirklichkeit in der Höfischen Epik* (Tübingen: Niemeyer, 1956; second edition 1970), especially chapter V, for a discussion of this in relation to the courtly epic.

3. See pp. 55f. [in original].

4. See my *Counterrevolution and Revolt* (Boston: Beacon Press, 1972), p. 81.

5. Ernst Fischer in *Auf den Spuren der Wirklichkeit; sechs Essays* (Reinbek: Rowohlt, 1968) recognizes in the "will to form" *(Wille zur Gestalt)* the will to transcend the actual: negation of that which is, and presentiment *(Ahnung)* of a freer and purer existence. In this sense, art is the "irreconcilable, the resistance of the human being to its vanishing in the [established] order and systems" (p. 67).

6. "Two antagonistic attitudes toward the powers that be are prevalent in literature: *resistance* and *submission.* Literature is certainly not mere ideology and does not merely express a social consciousness that invokes the illusion of harmony, assuring the individuals that everything is as it ought to be, and that nobody has the right to expect fate to give him more than he receives. To be sure, literature has time and again justified established social relationships; nevertheless, it has always kept alive that human yearning which cannot find gratification in the existing society. Grief and sorrow are essential elements of bourgeois literature" (Leo Lowenthal, *Das Bild des Menschen in der Literatur* [Neuwied: Luchterhand, 1966] pp. 14f.). (Published in English as *Literature and the Image of Man* [Boston: Beacon Press, 1957].)

7. See my essay "The Affirmative Character of Culture" in *Negations* (Boston: Beacon Press, 1968).

8. In his book *Marxistische Ideologie und allgemeine Kunsttheorie* (Tübingen: Mohr, 1970), Hans-Dietrich Sander presents a thorough analysis of Marx's and Engels' contribution to a theory of art. The provocative conclusion: most of Marxist aesthetics is not only a gross vulgarization—Marx's and Engels' views are also turned into their opposite! He writes: Marx and Engels saw "the essence of a work of art precisely not in its political or social relevance" (p. 174). They are closer to Kant, Fichte, and Schelling than to Hegel (p. 171). Sander's documentation for this thesis may well be too selective and minimize statements by Marx and Engels which contradict Sander's interpretation. However, his analysis does show clearly the difficulty of Marxist aesthetics in coming to grips with the problems of the theory of art.

9. Bertolt Brecht, "Volkstümlichkeit und Realismus," in *Gesammelte Werke* (Frankfurt: Suhrkamp, 1967), volume VIII, p. 323.

10. George Lukács, "Es geht um den Realismus," in *Marxismus und Literatur*, edited by Fritz J. Raddatz (Reinbek: Rowohlt, 1969), volume II, p. 77.

11. In *Die Linkskurve* III, 5 (Berlin: May 1931, reprinted 1970), p. 17.

12. *Colloque international sur la sociologie de la littérature* (Bruxelles: Institut de la Sociologie, 1974), p. 40.

13. Walter Benjamin, "Fragment über Methodenfrage einer Marxistischen Literatur-Analyse," in *Kursbuch* 20 (Frankfurt: Suhrkamp, 1970), p. 3.

POSTMODERNISM

GIVEN THAT WE DO NOT HAVE a clear sense of modernism, not least because it has different meanings in different disciplines and arts, it seems strange that so many contemporary writers should speak collectively of "postmodernism," a label that refuses to name itself. In one sense, postmodernism is another moment in modernism whereby the past is cast aside, for example, by the surrealists, futurists, and conceptualists. (See the writings by Marinetti Boccioni, Malevich, Kandinsky, Mondrian, and LeWitt.) In another sense, however, even as a moment within modernism, postmodernism appears to be emerging with sufficient clarity and coherence to define a genuine form of thought. The double question postmodernism poses is whether we find ourselves in a transformation of thought (at the "end" of the modern), and whether we can think of such a transformation from within.

The brief selection below sets forth one of two striking definitions Lyotard gives of postmodernism. In the other, from the Introduction to *The Postmodern Condition: A Report on Knowledge*, after arguing that a scientific or "magisterial" discourse requires a legitimating "meta-discourse" or "meta-narrative," he defines "*postmodern* as incredulity toward metanarratives" (p. xxiv). It is interesting to consider whether these two definitions are equivalent; it is far more important, however, to consider whether they name a theoretical phenomenon of our time.

The selection below on postmodernism should be read in conjunction with the selections in Part II from Goodman, Heidegger, and Merleau-Ponty; Part III from Gadamer, Ricoeur, Derrida, and Foucault; and in Part IV from Bakhtin, Göttner-Abendroth, Irigaray, and Owens, to get a satisfactory sense of the range of the phenomenon. What should be added, absent from all these selections, is the understanding found in Lyotard's other works that postmodernism is as much a result of contemporary technological developments as of a sensibility to language and discourse. What is involved is recognition of the profound relationship within discourse between knowledge and technology. Such a recognition may be enriched by comparison with the discussions by Adorno, Benjamin, and Foucault.

Perhaps the most interesting questions postmodernism poses for us, read in conjunction with feminist and multicultural theory, concern the variety of "post" ways of thinking that have emerged at the end of the twentieth century—postmodern, postpatriarchal, postcolonial, and so forth. Are these similar, do they converge, or do they oppose each other in fundamental respects? Despite their many similarities, many feminists and multiculturalists are suspicious of postmodernism as another male-dominated, Western development.

JEAN-FRANÇOIS LYOTARD

*What Is Postmodernism?**

I shall call modem the art which devotes its "little technical expertise" (son *"petit technique"*), as Diderot used to say, to present the fact that the unpresentable exists. To make visible that there is something which can be conceived and which can neither be seen nor made visible: this is what is at stake in modern painting. But how to make visible that there is something which cannot be seen? Kant himself shows the way when he names "formlessness, the absence of form," as a possible index to the unpresentable. He also says of the empty "abstraction" which the imagination experiences when in search for a presentation of the infinite (another unpresentable): this abstraction itself is like a presentation of the infinite, its "negative presentation." He cites the commandment, "Thou shalt not make graven images" *(Exodus)*, as the most sublime passage in the Bible in that it forbids all presentation of the Absolute. Little needs to be added to those observations to outline an aesthetic of sublime paintings. As painting, it will of course "present" something though negatively; it will therefore avoid figuration or representation. It will be "white" like one of Malevitch's squares; it will enable us to see only by making it impossible to see; it will please only by causing pain. One recognizes in those instructions the axioms or avant-gardes in painting, inasmuch as they devote themselves to making an allusion to the unpresentable by means of visible presentations. The systems in the name of which, or with which, this task has been able to support or to justify itself deserve the greatest attention; but they can originate only in the vocation of the sublime in order to legitimize it,

---

* Jean-François Lyotard, "What Is Postmodernism?," in *The Postmodern Condition: A Report on Knowledge* (Minneapolis: University of Minnesota Press, 1984) pp. 71-81.

that is, to conceal it. They remain inexplicable without the incommensurability of reality to concept which is implied in the Kantian philosophy of the sublime.

It is not my intention to analyze here in detail the manner in which the various avant-gardes have, so to speak, humbled and disqualified reality by examining the pictorial techniques which are so many devices to make us believe in it. Local tone, drawing, the mixing of colors, linear perspective, the nature of the support and that of the instrument, the treatment, the display, the museum: the avant-gardes are perpetually flushing out artifices of presentation which make it possible to subordinate thought to the gaze and to turn it away from the unpresentable. If Habermas, like Marcuse, understands this task of derealization as an aspect of the (repressive) "desublimation" which characterizes the avant-garde, it is because he confuses the Kantian sublime with Freudian sublimation, and because aesthetics has remained for him that of the beautiful.

The Postmodern

What, then, is the postmodern? What place does it or does it not occupy in the vertiginous work of the questions hurled at the rules of image and narration? It is undoubtedly a part of the modern. All that has been received, if only yesterday (*modo, modo,* Petronius used to say), must be suspected. What space does Cézanne challenge? The Impressionists'. What object do Picasso and Braque attack? Cézanne's. What presupposition does Duchamp break with in 1912? That which says one must make a painting, be it cubist. And Buren questions that other presupposition which he believes had survived untouched by the work of Duchamp: the place of presentation of the work. In an amazing acceleration, the generations precipitate themselves. A work can become modern only if it is first postmodern. Postmodernism thus understood is not modernism at its end but in the nascent state, and this state is constant.

Yet I would like not to remain with this slightly mechanistic meaning of the word. If it is true that modernity takes place in the withdrawal of the real and according to the sublime relation between the presentable and the conceivable, it is possible, within this relation, to distinguish two modes (to use the musician's language). The emphasis can be placed on the powerlessness of the faculty of presentation, on the nostalgia for presence felt by the human subject, on the obscure and futile will which inhabits him in spite of everything. The emphasis can be placed, rather, on the power of the faculty to conceive, on its "inhumanity" so to speak (it was the quality Apollinaire demanded of modern artists), since it is not the business of our understanding whether or not human sensibility or imagination can match what it conceives. The emphasis can also be placed on the increase of being and the jubilation which result from the invention of new rules of the game, be it pictorial, artistic, or any other. What I have in mind will become clear if we dispose very schematically a few names on the chessboard of the history of avant-gardes: on the side of melancholia, the German Expressionists, and on the side of *novatio,* Braque and Picasso, on the former Malevitch and on the latter Lissitsky, on the one Chirico and on the other Duchamp. The nuance which distinguishes these two modes may be infinitesimal; they often coexist in the same piece, are almost indistinguishable; and yet they testify to a difference *(un différend)* on which the fate of thought depends and will depend for a long time, between regret and assay.

The work of Proust and that of Joyce both allude to something which does not allow itself to be made present. Allusion, to which Paolo Fabbri recently called my attention, is perhaps a form of expression indispensable to the works which belong to an aesthetic of the sublime. In Proust, what is being eluded as the price to pay for this allusion is the identity of consciousness, a victim to the excess of time *(au trop de temps).* But in Joyce, it is the identity of writing which is the victim of an excess of the book *(au trop de livre)* or of literature.

Proust calls forth the unpresentable by means of a language unaltered in its syntax and vocabulary and of a writing which in many of its operators still belongs to the genre of novelistic narration. The literary institution, as Proust inherits it from Balzac and Flaubert, is admittedly subverted in that the hero is no longer a character but the inner consciousness of time, and in that the diegetic diachrony, already damaged by Flaubert, is here put in question because of the narrative voice. Nevertheless, the unity of the book, the odyssey of that consciousness, even if it is deferred from chapter to chapter, is not seriously challenged: the identity of the writing with itself throughout the labyrinth of the interminable narration is enough to connote such unity, which has been compared to that of *The Phenomenology of Mind.*

Joyce allows the unpresentable to become perceptible in his writing itself, in the signifier. The whole range of available narrative and even stylistic operators is put into play without concern for the unity of the whole, and new operators are tried. The grammar and vocabulary of literary language are no longer accepted as given; rather, they appear as academic forms, as rituals originating in piety (as Nietzsche said) which prevent the unpresentable from being put forward.

Here, then, lies the difference: modern aesthetics is an aesthetic of the sublime, though a nostalgic one. It allows the unpresentable to be put forward only as the missing contents; but the form, because of its recognizable consistency, continues to offer to the reader or viewer matter for solace and pleasure. Yet these sentiments do not constitute the real sublime sentiment, which is in an intrinsic combination of pleasure and pain: the pleasure that reason should exceed all presentation, the pain that imagination or sensibility should not be equal to the concept.

The postmodern would be that which, in the modern, puts forward the unpresentable in presentation itself; that which denies itself the solace of good forms, the consensus of a taste which would make it possible to share collectively the nostalgia for the unattainable; that which searches for new presentations, not in order to enjoy them but in order to impart a stronger sense of the unpresentable. A postmodern artist or writer is in the position of a philosopher: the text he writes, the work he produces are not in principle governed by preestablished rules, and they cannot be judged according to a determining judgment, by applying familiar categories to the text or to the work. Those rules and categories are what the work of art itself is looking for. The artist and the writer, then, are working without rules in order to formulate the rules of what *will have been done.* Hence the fact that work and text have the characters of an *event;* hence also, they always come too late for their author, or, what amounts to the same thing, their being put into work, their realization *(mise en oeuvre)* always begin too soon. *Post modern* would have to be understood according to the paradox of the future *(post)* anterior *(modo).*

It seems to me that the essay (Montaigne) is postmodern, while the fragment *(The Athaeneum)* is modern.

Finally, it must be clear that it is our business not to supply reality but to invent allusions to the conceivable which cannot be presented. And it is not to be expected that this task will effect the last reconciliation between language games (which, under the name of faculties, Kant knew to be separated by a chasm), and that only the transcendental illusion (that of Hegel) can hope to totalize them into a real unity. But Kant also knew that the price to pay for such an illusion is terror. The nineteenth and twentieth centuries have given us as much terror as we can take. We have paid a high enough price for the nostalgia of the whole and the one, for the reconciliation of the concept and the sensible, of the transparent and the communicable experience. Under the general demand for slackening and for appeasement, we can hear the mutterings of the desire for a return of terror, for the realization of the fantasy to seize reality. The answer is: Let us wage a war on totality; let us be witnesses to the unpresentable; let us activate the differences and save the honor of the name.

FEMINIST THEORY

AMONG THE MOST IMPORTANT DEVELOPMENTS of our time is that of
feminist theory, both in its social criticisms of the secondary status of women
in largely male-dominated societies throughout the world, and in its more
sweeping and provocative suggestion that the "patriarchal" or male-dominated structure of human social life has permeated thought and expression
throughout human history at every level. Not only have women been excluded
from centers of authority and expression throughout history, but the result
has been a largely one-sided, incomplete realization of human possibilities.
The "masculine" has been passed off as universal, neutral. This poses a
tremendous problem for feminist writing that would gain standing in a public
world.

Feminist writings have exploded in Western societies in the past twenty
years, including vociferous controversy and divergent points of view. Whatever one may think of such discussions in detail, their emergence defines an
important set of questions concerning the forms and limits of human expression. The selections below have been chosen for how successfully they define
the challenge feminist theory poses to our understanding of art. Among the
questions considered are whether there is a unique women's perspective on
art, a "matriarchal" aesthetic in contrast to traditional "patriarchal" aesthetics;
whether there is a feminist sensibility, grounded in women's relationship to
their bodies, unacknowledged in traditional societies in which the "subject" is
always "masculine"; and whether, consequently, only a diminished range of
artistic and human possibilities has been realized in the Western tradition.

To close the discussion opened by the selections by Göttner-Abendroth
and Irigaray, I include an essay by Craig Owens discussing the importance of
feminist theory to postmodernism.

HEIDE GÖTTNER-ABENDROTH

Nine Principles of a Matriarchal Aesthetic*

The principles of a matriarchal aesthetic can easily be derived from my description of matriarchal art of the past. But a matriarchal aesthetic is not a retreat into the distant past but a partly descriptive and partly prescriptive theory of a number of aspects of modern art. I shall apply this theory to art forms found in the work of contemporary female (and male) artists which already have matriarchal features. By means of a comparative analysis the meaning of these forms will become clear and from this clarity a programmatic structure may emerge. I shall also develop a matriarchal art utopia using these (already existing) forms as starting points.

But first I shall set out the nine principles of a matriarchal aesthetic, which I shall then go on to discuss in more detail.

First: Matriarchal art is located beyond the fictional, both in the past and in the present. Beyond the fictional art becomes magic. Magic intrudes into reality by means of symbols and has the effect of changing reality. Ancient matriarchal art tried to influence nature and to change it by using magic (ancient magic); modern matriarchal art attempts to change psychic and social reality using magic (modern magic).

Second: Matriarchal art has an enduring and predetermined framework: the structure of matriarchal mythology. This structure is universal as it is the basic pattern of all mythologies and all the later religions which developed from them. It is one of the fundamental objective categories of the human imagination.

* Heide Göttner-Abendroth, "Nine Principles of a Matriarchal Aesthetic," *Feminist Aesthetics,* ed. by Gisela Ecker and trans. by Harriet Anderson (Boston: Beacon Press, 1985) pp. 81-94.

But, like every structure, so the structure of matriarchal mythologies is not complete in itself. Each matriarchal society gave to the structure of its matriarchal mythology (religion, rituals, ways of living) a different reality. The result is that its concrete forms are as varied as the regional, individual and social conditions of those who created them. Matriarchal art which derives from the structure of matriarchal mythology is therefore diversity in unity, in which the unity is not dogmatic, the diversity not subjective.

Third: Matriarchal art transcends the traditional mode of communication which consists of: author-text (art product)-reader. Matriarchal art is not 'text', it is not limited to manufacturing art products. On the contrary, it is a process which gives a pre-existing inner structure, found in the ritual dance, external expression. It is a process in which all participate collectively to create this external expression; all are simultaneously authors and spectators.

The structure of matriarchal mythology is also not 'text' which a (woman) author produces and a (woman) reader fills with meaning—quite apart from the fact that female authors and readers do not feature in traditional communication theory at all. It exists as a fundamental category of the human imagination, the most ancient, the principal one from which all later religious and artistic artifacts of the imagination developed. This imagination is no undisciplined eclecticism, no arbitrary chain of associations—that is only its very late and degenerate aspect—rather, it follows its own inner rules, inscribed in the structure of matriarchal mythology. Its concrete forms continually give collective expression to this highly complex code of rules in many different ways. (In order to discover them, you don't need to delve into the unconscious for possible archetypes; you need only reveal the forgotten matriarchal traditions by analyzing past societies.)

Fourth: Matriarchal art demands the total commitment of all participants. As it does not recognize any divisions between author and audience in which the author creates the symbolic action and the audience (at the most) either identifies with it emotionally or contemplates it on a theoretical level (a patriarchal role division): in matriarchal art there is no division between emotion and thought. All participants operate simultaneously on the levels of emotional identification, theoretical reflection and symbolic action. In this way, the universal, objective nature of the structure of matriarchal mythology, which is known to all, prevents the identification from becoming subjective sentimentality, the theorizing from becoming abstract arbitrariness, and the action from becoming mere catharsis. Matriarchal art welds together feeling, thinking and doing in the form of the concrete mythological image and it is this totality which releases true ecstasy in the participants.

Fifth: Matriarchal art does not correspond to an extended model of communication with the elements: author-text-dealer-agent-audience. The dealer (art market) and agent (critic, interpreter, translator from one medium into another, archivist, art historian, etc.) are redundant. As it is a process which takes place between the participants matriarchal art cannot be evaluated and interpreted by outsiders nor sold as a commodity on the art market and later stored away in a dusty archive or exhibited in a museum. For matriarchal art cannot be objectified; that is, turned into an object. It is a dynamic process characterised by ecstasy and with a positive impact on reality (magic).

Sixth: Matriarchal art cannot be subdivided into genres because it cannot be objectified. The ritual dance ceremony embraces music, song, poetry, movement, decoration, symbol, comedy and tragedy, all for the purpose of invoking, imploring, praising the goddess.

The division between art and non-art is also redundant. On the one hand, matriarchal art breaks down the barrier between art and theory. In its ancient form, matriarchal art merges with mythology and astronomy; in its modern form with philosophy, the humanities, and with the natural and social sciences. At the same time, it breaks down the barrier between art and life. As ancient matriarchal art it merges with practical skills too, and with lifestyles which are opposed to the *status quo.* That is another reason why it cannot be applied to traditional communication models. For matriarchal art is not a simple one-way communication process, but a complex process of social interaction of which communication is only a part.

Seventh: As matriarchal art derives from the structure of matriarchal mythology which is a completely different value system—and not merely a reversed or contradictory one—from that of patriarchy, it too shares this different system of values. The erotic is the dominant force and not work, discipline, renunciation. The continuation of life as a cycle of re-births is its primary principle, and not war or heroic death for abstract, inhuman ideals. A sense of community, motherliness and sisterly love are the basic rules of the matriarchal society and not paternal authority, dominance of the husband, private and group egoism.

Modern matriarchal art, which gives these values expression and brings about changes in the psychic and social sphere, is a complex subversive process in a patriarchal society. It represents a subversive process which is not interested in power and control and therefore does not need a disguising ideology. In every patriarchy it constitutes a subversive force which proposes a revolutionary alternative.

Eighth: The social changes which matriarchal art brings about override the divisions in the aesthetic sphere. In patriarchal societies aesthetics is divided into a formalist, elitist, socially effective art on the one hand, and a popular, widespread but socially vilified and outcast art on the other. Overcoming this division would return to art its original public role, allowing it to emerge as the most important social activity and bringing about the aestheticisation of the whole of society. This was the reality of ancient matriarchal art; modern matriarchal art attempts to achieve it once again.

Ninth: Matriarchal art is not 'art'. For 'art' is necessarily defined in terms of the fictional; the principle of fictionality is the primary principle of every patriarchal theory of art (aesthetics). 'Art' is a concept and in its form as object has only existed since the aesthetic sphere was divided. 'Art' is therefore always artificial or denatured art.

Matriarchal art is independent of the fictional and is therefore not 'art' in the patriarchal sense of the word. Nor does it require any special technical know-how. It is rather the ability to shape life and so change it; it is itself energy, life, a drive towards the aestheticisation of society. It can never be divorced from complex social action because it is itself the center of that action.

Further Remarks About the Nine Principles
of a Matriarchal Aesthetic

These nine principles need a few further remarks so that the goddess can dance again.

ABOUT THE FIRST PRINCIPLE. It is the concept of 'modern magic' which may seem difficult to accept in this principle—it seems like a contradiction in terms. And what does an intrusion into reality by means of symbols with the effect of changing psychosocial reality mean?

It seems to us today that the problem with ancient magic was that it was believed it could interfere with natural forces by means of symbols; for example, that it could make the moon wax (moon dances) or bring rain (rain dances). However, this is to over-simplify things. The peoples of ancient cultures knew very well that the moon would wax again. After all, they had developed a calendar based on lunar phases which was in many cases (the Babylonians, the Maya) more accurate than the modern calendar. As far as the weather was concerned, they were well-versed in weather lore which was derived from close observation of the sky, cloud formation, the behavior of animals and plants, from which they could forecast the weather with great accuracy. Their use of magic, therefore, did not stem from their ignorance as today's arrogance would have it.

But they were convinced that this rational-technical knowledge was not enough in itself to influence the moon and the rain; emotion had to be involved as well. This belief was expressed in the moon dance which only took place at times carefully calculated using astronomy, or in the rain dance which was only performed when they could see from physical signs that rain really was on the way. They did not regard nature as merely quantifiable, but as a living being which could change its mind at the last moment. And so it was necessary to communicate with it via symbols in order to make themselves understood, to make it clear to nature that it should stand by its intentions. For it was, after all, still a goddess to them—a feeling which today we have completely lost.

Their belief in the role of magic in nature derives from the role magic played in people's everyday lives. They were familiar not only with natural magic but also with magic in psychosocial reality. They knew that an invalid would not recover with the aid of medicines alone—and they had plenty of these—but knew that there was also an important psychological element too—the belief in cure, the hope of recovery, the trust in the woman doctor, the witch doctor who fought the demon disease. It is well known that faith works wonders. This was the function of the complementary use of magic via symbols with medicinal cures (white magic, shamanism). It is a mistake and a distortion to believe that these peoples thought that symbolic treatment alone brought a cure. Their extensive knowledge of herbalism, a science which is almost totally lost to us today, proves otherwise.

Magic, which at that time was in effect psychology, could be found throughout the social matrix. Erotic and aggressive drives were not allowed simply to run wild. They were danced out and thus contained within a social context, that of the dance. The resulting change in social reality was a new, meaningful, communal living.

We encounter this involvement with psychosocial reality symbolically in all aspects of life today. It can be found in individual and social psychology, particularly in the psychology of the unconscious. However, this is now anything but healing, because the underlying ethos of magic has been lost. Instead, it merely serves the pressures of patriarchal society to conform, to disguise and to manipulate.

Magic, denounced as witchcraft, was a principal target for patriarchy when the latter was establishing itself. And for most people magic has still not lost its connotations with the primitive and evil, so it may sound strange when I talk of an 'ethos of magic'. But the difference between the practice of ancient magic in reality by means of symbols and modern manipulation by means of symbols is that the former was always based on the ideal of harmony. Its goal was always unity with reference both to the individual and society. Symbolic practices were always directed towards the individual's total powers of recovery or towards all the possibilities for the peaceful continued existence of a society. Not only were the intellect, feelings and ability to take action involved, but also the natural environment. Modern symbolic practices, on the other hand, serve only the very limited purposes of analysing people like machines and are only concerned with parts of the individual, not with the whole person. This is particularly the case when psychology is used to promote social conformity, commerce or war. The underlying 'ethos' is the opposite of the ethos of magic which tries to cure the individual or society by a harmonious combination of all capacities. The effect today is a corresponding chaos.

'Modern magic' means nothing other than symbolic practices which influence psychosocial reality but are based on an ethos of totality which does not succumb to private or sectarian interests. It differs from ancient magic in that there has been a considerable increase in knowledge in specific fields. It is the task of modern matriarchal art to develop a system of symbolic activities based on an 'ethos of magic' which corresponds to our present state of knowledge. This could help the fragmented, specialised, stereotyped and supervised individual of today to regain her/his totality.

ABOUT THE SECOND PRINCIPLE. The system of this unifying way of thinking was the structure of matriarchal mythology. I called this structure the fundamental category of the human imagination because it is not only ancient but also because it can be found amongst primitive peoples all over the world. It was the basis of the beliefs of all early complex cultures, and so had an impact even on the development of later patriarchal religions, philosophies and art and still exerts a covert influence today. I discussed this influence in my study of matriarchal mythology. [. . .][1]

Matriarchal cults and mythologies continued to be of great importance in the patriarchal epoch, for they did not disappear with the decline of the matriarchal society but survived for thousands of years either openly or as secret cults, or as images and ideas appropriated by the patriarchal religions. Later, they continued to be handed down in the form of folklore, festivals, fairy-tales, legends and even in 'great literature', although knowledge of their origin and significance increasingly declined. In my book mentioned above, I have described this process in Europe using the examples of folklore and literature.

In view of these historical trends I am certainly not exaggerating when I claim that the structure of matriarchal mythology is (or should be) the basis of modern matriarchal art. I am only demanding that something which has always existed in poetry and art but is now relegated to the unconscious should be consciously realized. There is nothing new about this structure in the sense that the connection with matriarchal art could not be re-established for us until its discovery. This connection has in fact always existed. It is just a question of a new awareness which will make the connection a living one for us again. It must become an explicit continuity after centuries of being merely implicit. This obscurity is not that of some mysterious, collective, unprovable archetype of the soul (in the sense of Jungian archetypes); it is the obscurity of every old and repressed cultural tradition which has been handed down divorced from its context, and whose patterns have petrified into mere ceremonies. There is no need for introspection in order to discover this cultural tradition; instead, we need a thorough ethnological and cultural-historical research. This will enable us to locate it precisely and follow it chronologically and geographically. In this way it will lose any aura of the mysterious and unprovable.

The analyses of art and literature in the next section show that such a structure of matriarchal mythology is appearing increasingly frequently and unambiguously. It is as though it were gradually re-emerging from a long oblivion to become part of our social consciousness. We only have to help it through the final stage for it to become an articulated body of knowledge and an example for artists.

ABOUT THE THIRD AND FIFTH PRINCIPLES. In these principles I presented the external expression of the structure of matriarchal mythology, that is, a matriarchal 'work of art', in terms of a negative description. As the basis for this negative description I used the general model of communication which has been used for patriarchal art. In this way I could establish precisely what matriarchal art is *not*.

It is not an object—a poetic, musical or optical 'text'; instead, it is a process. It does not need a commercial dealer or an agent; it does not acknowledge the distinction between author and spectator; it does not make a distinction between genres or between art and not-art. What is it then? Is it a kind of multi-media show? Certainly, but it is not only the staging of the combined effect of many media. Is it a performance? Perhaps, but it is not limited to the individual action of an artist whom others are only allowed to look at. Is it a happening? As the artistic expression of many people it is that too, but it is not a pattern that a few people worked out arbitrarily, for it has its given, enduring structure which contains the objective categories of the human imagination. Is it environmental art? As the artistic modification of the environment it is that too, but it does not find its full expression in the transformation of a flat, a house or the surrounding countryside, for it does not create passive, observable objects. Is it art at all? Yes, because it creates beauty, but not as the 'veil of appearance' but as reality. Isn't it then a new cult? No, because it does not stipulate any religious content, unlike religions which use dogmatic propositions. And anyway, this question assumes the patriarchal division of 'art' and 'cult' and is unanswerable. Can matriarchal art establish itself then outside a matriarchal society? No, because it was and is that society's direct expression. This form of society used to be that of the whole tribe and it was this which gave matriarchal art its accessibility. Today, it can best be found in small groups living in cultural isolation but even there it is not a different form of society but a different way of living. Matriarchal art practised there can only be anticipated through experimentation, which still has to find a valid form and full public accessibility.

My descriptions of moon dances and the structure of matriarchal mythology clearly show what matriarchal art is. It is exactly what the nine muses did: ritual dance festivals following the seasonal cycle representing initiation-marriage-death and return.

But today it seems impossible to revive ritual dance festivals of this sort. But didn't this appear to be the case with magic? Wouldn't these difficulties be overcome if we reminded ourselves that these ritual festivals merely symbolise fundamental categories of the human imagination? And these categories have not changed.

The question is only: how can these categories be symbolized today? The answer is completely open. Trial and error will show us and give us many different answers. The question of the possible shape and meaning of the matriarchal *Gesamtkunst*[2] today does not have only one answer. Every individual woman or every group responds to this question differently when giving these categories a living form. For the experiences, insights, conduct, and symbolic forms each woman or group invests, the meanings each gives to these categories, cannot be foreseen. Not even the participants know exactly, for it is only in the *process* of matriarchal art that the content becomes crystallized as form. The appearance of new meanings and new forms are certainly sought after but actually enter quite unpredictably. It is precisely this which enables matriarchal art to change reality. It is magic which is performed and experienced, and its spontaneous expressions can be so gripping that they lead to ecstasy.

Perhaps it has now become clear how fundamentally different matriarchal art is from patriarchal art. Matriarchal art is neither ornament nor commodity nor mere pleasure. Neither has it got anything to do with that unpleasant alternative between dogmatism in art on the one hand which still prescribes the themes, meanings and tone (as Christian art does), and subjectivity in art on the other which finds expression in any old theme or form (as bourgeois art does). Matriarchal art is coherent without being subjective because it follows the framework laid down by the categories. This explains its unexpected effects.

ABOUT THE FOURTH PRINCIPLE. From this we can easily see why this type of art makes demands on all human faculties and why these do not diminish during the art process but lead to the climax of ecstasy. This needs more discussion.

Our understanding of ecstasy today is just as vague and prejudiced as that of magic or ritual transformation. When these cultural forms declined at the beginning of the patriarchal era they were subsumed by a mass of polemic and intentional misunderstandings from which we still have not freed ourselves. Thus, for most people ecstasy is a kind of delirium leading to total incapacity, or at best a kind of gentle madness; to them, it is always something thoroughly irrational. This is wrong.

True ecstasy, however, is difficult to describe for it is the spontaneous meshing of all human forces, the emotional, intellectual and the active. We can evoke it but cannot direct it. Concepts like 'inspiration', 'illumination', 'intuitive seeing of connections' do, of course, indicate ecstasy at its intellectual level, but over-emphasise this at the expense of the active level. Similarly, the erotic will not do as an illustration either, although this implies action, because to do so is to neglect the spiritual-intellectual elements. The erotic is always involved, but if it is reduced to the emotional level—as is possible—it only generates delirium. This has nothing to do with the dynamic power of ecstasy.

True ecstasy unites the intellect, emotions and action in a climax where no one power is limited by another. They are not expressed consecutively but simultaneously, and each to its utmost capacity. Ecstasy is their transitory, inimitable collision at the moment of their fullest unfolding. For example, if we want to give expression to the elements of the imagination represented by the goddess-and-hero structure, then we need the intellect to recognise these elements, emotional strength to cope with experiencing them, and a large potential for action to bring them to completion. When these forces do succeed in this creative harmony—which does not happen very often—then there will be ecstatic moments: moments of rapture and liberty. They are like the chords of the harmony of the spheres played on the fragile instrument that is man and woman. No one can grasp and hold them—which is just as well as they could not be tolerated for any length of time.

Another decisive difference between matriarchal and patriarchal art emerges from this. For as an ecstatic process it is not a spectator art, not an art for voyeurs. Only by entering the process can one experience it.

ABOUT THE SIXTH PRINCIPLE. I probably do not need to say anything more about the suspension of the division between the genres. But here are a few remarks concerning the division into art and non-art.

I think it has become clear that entry into the process of matriarchal art presumes a theory, a knowledge of matriarchal forms of society, of the structure of mythology, and considerable thought about the possibilities of applying it to the present. But the process of matriarchal art always includes the transformation of forms of living for it encompasses all the practical skills as well. This disregard for the boundaries between theory and everyday life does not have to take place independently of the art process itself in the sense that you do the theory first and then apply it. They occur simultaneously.

Let us imagine that this process lasts for several days or weeks. Then the functions of daily life are necessarily involved: resting, sleeping, eating, drinking. Equally important are the elements of theory which are involved: speech, discussion, meditation. Without theory the elements of daily life lack a symbolic dimension. When combined, actions of daily life are integrated into a symbolic context and thus are no longer surface actions but become symbolic. This is why they can both emerge from and lead back to dance forms—giving the interpretation of dance a wider sense than that of today. Dance not only includes musical movement, but also parades, processions and dramatic interludes, all of which flow into one another. The kind of movement is varied just as at festivals. At festivals, too, there are ritual meals which are prepared, and enjoyed within a ritualized set of gestures, just as there are celebrations in which inspiring dramatic speeches are followed by dramatic interludes, while sleeping and waking are symbolic states of being which can be the stimulus for new and arcane festive acts. It would be inappropriate to isolate any single element, for it is only within the whole context of the process of matriarchal art that the individual elements gain their meaning. The process always takes place on many levels. It is only possible to isolate a single element when it no longer contains the symbolic value given it by the structure of matriarchal mythology as festival. . . .

ABOUT THE SEVENTH, EIGHTH AND NINTH PRINCIPLES. 'Life' is not confined to everyday life. It is clear from the last three principles that it encompasses political action too, for the changes in the ways of living which the process of matriarchal art brings do not only affect the lives of individuals, they also impinge on groups and whole societies. It is only when seen from this perspective that the full significance of symbolic actions of matriarchal art are understood.

After what has been said, this extension into politics may seem implausible; after all, isn't the process of matriarchal art in its assumptions and the course it takes essentially esoteric? Who knows what the structure of matriarchal mythology is? Who can reach true ecstasy? Who will allow their whole way of living to be transformed by an art process? And anyway, so far matriarchal art has only existed at an experimental stage and has been isolated in small cultural enclaves which do not appear to have any social impact.

This scenario is opposed to the nature of matriarchal art. For it is a ritual, public in character, taking place in the open, in the fields or in the city squares, accessible to all.

It should be public for another reason as well: nature is involved. In ancient matriarchal ceremonies the important elements were those natural phenomena such as the lunar cycle, sunrise, rain showers, and that is why the dates had to be calculated so accurately. If one can predict nature precisely then it does in fact cooperate and accomplish the most impressive 'symbolic feats'. These represented the climax of the ancient matriarchal ceremonies; the dancers had discoursed with nature and it had answered—and this, as a rule, inspired profound awe. That an astronomical calculation had determined the date of the event did not detract from the ecstasy, for the whole group had paid homage to nature by studying it so carefully, and it in turn had rewarded them with the right phenomenon at the right time.

The possibility of communicating with nature by means of symbolic acts is not out of the question today in spite of our denatured environment. It does, however, demand that we once again learn to adapt ourselves to nature instead of trying to force it to adapt to us. This starts with how we treat our own bodies, which also belong to nature, and goes on to how we treat our immediate, alterable environment. We cannot demand that the sun and the moon adapt to us, they demand that we adapt to them. If we do this then nature still favors us and cooperates with our symbols. The joy, the delight, which is thereby released can be tracked back to the harmonious correlation of a change in nature with a spiritual change in ourselves. The one is expressed by the other so that the whole act becomes symbolic. And it is precisely this obviously symbolic aspect which enables the uninitiated to understand completely what is taking place. It is unnecessary to explain at length not only because basic patterns such as initiation-marriage-death and return are known to everyone—for after these are the basic patterns of the human imagination which are expressed one way or another in all religions—but also because such fundamental processes occur simultaneously with visible natural phenomena. Nature itself explains the structure of matriarchal mythology by means of the seasons. It is not necessary for the uninitiated to be conscious of it. In this way the uninitiated are included in the ceremonies, and slowly become participants. Nature itself is the greatest ceremony. Anyone who has taken part in this process of matriarchal art in which every element in interaction becomes a symbol knows that they have not taken part in a new form of art, but in a new form of living.

This is exactly the reason why matriarchal art transcends the character of fiction, why as soon as it enters the public sphere it becomes provocative. It is an involuntary provocation. For matriarchal art encompasses a different set of values from patriarchy's and it lives according to this set of values without compounding it as the 'veil of appearance'. It demonstrates nature's unity with human beings as opposed to nature's exploitation and utilization by men. It demonstrates the harmony of the individual's capacities as opposed to their fragmented specialization which in most men leads to the most absurd excesses and in most women to equally absurd limitations. It shows the erotic to be the strongest creative force as opposed to devaluing and suppressing it as the ascetic patriarchal religions and moral systems have done. It demonstrates the finiteness of death and the infinity of life as opposed to the bleak scientific attitude to death and a cynical perfection of its machines. There is not a single aspect of the process which is not different from any corresponding patriarchal idea.

It is a tremendous challenge to live by the values which patriarchal societies have banished to the ghetto of the unreal. Patriarchal societies will fight matriarchal art because it does not allow itself to be domesticated either formally or socially. And thus this art finds itself involuntarily at the centre of political action. Its form will be the very unusual one of political confrontation, a totally unexpected tactic for the opponent who has not experienced this form of resistance before. The battle will not be an exchange of hostilities but an incessant ebb and flow/advance and retreat, an ungraspable symbolization, the creation of a completely new web of connections in the centre of this fragmented, atomized world. This symbolization cannot be anticipated—its phases, extent, forms will continually change. What can the opponent latch on to in this game of tag? He is bewitched and paralyzed.

This complex, socially subversive praxis cannot be fought with conventional weapons because the dominant social praxis is so totally irrelevant to it. It is a form of living which is self-contained, it is an effortless integration according to the rules of diversity and completion. It is beauty but not a commodity. It seeks to dissolve the divisions within the aesthetic and so aestheticize the whole of society. This means creating a meaningful social life together. Seen from this perspective, art is no longer a specialised technique, an exclusive know-how but the universal ability to shape a worthwhile life, both personally and socially.

In a patriarchal society this art, this beauty, is the prime opposition; but that is unimportant to beauty. And what weapons can be used against withdrawing and opposing, opposing and withdrawing beauty?

NOTES

1. *Die Göttin und ihr Heros* [The Goddess and her Demigod] (Munich 1980).

2. This is art which appeals to many senses and transcends traditional aesthetics.

LUCE IRIGARAY

*Any Theory of the "Subject" Has Always Been Appropriated by the "Masculine"**

We can assume that any theory of the subject has always been appropriated by the "masculine." When she submits to (such a) theory, woman fails to realize that she is renouncing the specificity of her own relationship to the imaginary. Subjecting herself to objectivization in discourse—by being "female." Re-objectivizing her own self whenever she claims to identify herself "as" a masculine subject. A "subject" that would re-search itself as lost (maternal-feminine) "object"?

Subjectivity denied to woman: indisputably this provides the financial backing for every irreducible constitution as an object: of representation, of discourse, of desire. Once imagine that woman imagines and the object loses its fixed, obsessional character. As a bench mark that is ultimately more crucial than the subject, for he can sustain himself only by bouncing back off some objectiveness, some objective. If there is no more "earth" to press down/repress, to work, to represent, but also and always to desire (for one's own), no opaque matter which in theory does not know herself, then what pedestal remains for the ex-sistence of the "subject"? If the earth turned and more especially turned upon herself, the erection of the subject might thereby be disconcerted and risk losing its elevation and penetration. For what would there be to rise up from and exercise his power over? And in?

* Luce Irigaray, *Speculum of the Other Woman*, trans. Gillian C. Gill (Ithaca: Cornell University Press, 1985), pp. 133-46.

The Copernican revolution has yet to have its final effects in the male imaginary. And by centering man outside himself, it has occasioned above all man's ex-stasis within the transcendental (subject). Rising to a perspective that would dominate the totality, to the vantage point of greatest power, he thus cuts himself off from the bedrock, from his empirical relationship with the matrix that he claims to survey. To specularize and to speculate. Exiling himself ever further (toward) where the greatest power lies, he thus becomes the "sun" if it is around him that things turn, a pole of attraction stronger than the "earth." Meanwhile, the excess in this universal fascination is that "she" also turns upon herself, that she knows how to re-turn (upon herself) but not how to seek outside for identity within the other: nature, sun, God . . . (woman). As things now go, man moves away in order to preserve his stake in the value of his representation, while woman counterbalances with the permanence of a (self)recollection which is unaware of itself as such. And which, in the recurrence of this re-turn upon the self—and its special economy will need to be located—can continue to support the illusion that the object is inert. "Matter" upon which he will ever and again return to plant his foot in order to spring farther, leap higher, although he is dealing here with a nature that is already self-referential. Already fissured and open. And which, in her circumvolutions upon herself, will also carry off the things confided to her for re-presentation. Whence, no doubt, the fact that she is said to be restless and unstable. In fact it is quite rigorously true that she is never exactly the same. Always whirling closer or farther from the sun whose rays she captures and sends curving to and fro in turn with her cycles.

Thus the "object" is not as massive, as resistant, as one might wish to believe. And her possession by a "subject," a subject's desire to appropriate her, is yet another of his vertiginous failures. For where he projects a something to absorb, to take, to see, to possess . . . as well as a patch of ground to stand upon, a mirror to catch his reflection, he is already faced by another specularization. Whose twisted character is her inability to say what she represents. The quest for the "object" becomes a game of Chinese boxes. Infinitely receding. The most amorphous with regard to ideas, the most obviously "thing," if you like, the most opaque matter, opens upon a mirror all the purer in that it knows and is known to have no reflections. Except those which man has reflected there but which, in the movement of that concave speculum, pirouetting upon itself, will rapidly, deceptively, fade.

And even as man seeks to rise higher and higher—in his knowledge too—so the ground fractures more and more beneath his feet. "Nature" is forever dodging his projects of representation, of reproduction. And his grasp. That this resistance should all too often take the form of rivalry within the hom(m)ologous, of a death struggle between two consciousnesses, does not alter the fact that at stake here somewhere, ever more insistent in its deathly hauteur, is the risk that the subject (as) self will crumble away. Also at stake, therefore, the "object" and the modes of dividing the economy between them. In particular the economy of discourse. Whereby the silent allegiance of the one guarantees the auto-sufficiency, the auto-nomy of the other as long as no questioning of this mutism as a symptom—of historical repression—is required. But what if the "object" started to speak? Which also means beginning to "see," etc. What disaggregation of the subject would that entail? Not only on the level of the split between him and his other, his variously specified alter ego, or between him and the Other, who is always to some extent *his* Other, even if he does not recognize himself in it, even if he is so overwhelmed by it as to bar himself out of it and into it so as to retain at the very least the power to promote his own forms. Others who will always already have been in the service of the same, of the presuppositions of the same logos, without changing or prejudicing its character as discourse. Therefore not really others, even if the one, the greatest, while holding back his reserves, perhaps contains the threat of otherness. Which is perhaps why he stands off-stage? Why he is repressed too? But high up, in "heaven"? Beyond, like everything else? Innocent in his exorbited empire. But once you get suspicious of the reasons for extrapolation, and at the same time interpret the subject's need to re-duplicate himself in a thought—or maybe a "soul"?—then the function of the "other" is stripped of the veils that still shroud it.

Where will the other spring up again? Where will the risk be situated which sublates the subject's passion for remaining ever and again the same, for affirming himself ever and again the same? In the *duplicity* of his speculation? A more or less conscious duplicity? Since he is only partially and marginally where he reflects/is reflected? Where he knows (himself)? As likeness whose price can be maintained by the "night" of the unconscious? The Other, lapsed within, disquieting in its shadow and its rage, sustaining the organization of a universe eternally identical to the self. The backside of (self)representation, of the visual plane where he gazes upon himself? Therefore, resemblance proliferates all the more in a swarm of analogues. The "subject" henceforth will be multiple, plural, sometimes di-formed, but it will still postulate itself as the cause of all the mirages that can be enumerated endlessly and therefore put back together again as one. A fantastic, phantasmatic fragmentation. A destruc(tura)tion in which the "subject" is shattered, scuttled, while still claiming surreptitiously that he is the reason for it all. Is reason feigned perhaps? Certainly, it is *one.* For this race of signifiers spells out again the solipsism of him who summons them, convokes them, even if only to disperse them. The "subject" plays at multiplying himself, even deforming himself, in this process. He is father, mother, and child(ren). And the relationships between them. He is masculine and feminine and the relationships between them. What mockery of generation, parody of copulation and genealogy, drawing its *strength* from the same model, from the model of the same: the subject. In whose sight everything *outside* remains forever a condition making possible the image and the reproduction of the self. A faithful, polished mirror, empty of altering reflections. Immaculate of all auto-copies. Other because wholly in the service of the same subject to whom it would present its surfaces, candid in their self-ignorance.

When the Other falls out of the starry sky into the chasms of the psyche, the "subject" is obviously obliged to stake out new boundaries for his field of implantation and to re-ensure—otherwise, elsewhere—his dominance. Where once he was on the heights, he is now entreated to go down into the depths. These changes in position are still postulated in terms of verticality, of course. Are phallic, therefore. But how to tame these uncharted territories, these dark continents, these worlds through the looking glass? How to master these devilries, these moving phantoms of the unconscious, when a long history has taught you to seek out and desire only clarity, the clear perception of (fixed) ideas? Perhaps this is the time to stress *technique* again? To renounce for the time being the sovereignty of thought in order to forge *tools* which will permit the exploitation of these resources, these unexplored mines. Perhaps for the time being the serene contemplation of empire must be abandoned in favor of taming those forces which, once unleashed, might explode the very concept of empire. A detour into *strategy, tactics, and practice* is called for, at least as long as it takes to gain vision, self-knowledge, self-possession, even in one's decenteredness. The "subject" sidles up to the truth, squints at it, obliquely, in an attempt to gain possession of what truth can no longer say. Dispersing, piercing those metaphors—particularly the photological ones—which have constituted truth by the premises of Western philosophy: virgin, dumb, and veiled in her nakedness, her vision still naively "natural," her viewpoint still resolutely blind and unsuspecting of what may lie beneath the blindness.

Now is the time to operate, before all is lost. That is, plow again those fields which had been assumed cultivated once and for all, but which now turn out to have merely lain fallow, capable of products that choke anything growing in their soil. The "subject" must dig his foundations deeper, extend the underground passages which assured the edifice of his determination, further dig out the cellars upon which he raises the monument of his identification, in order to prop up more securely his "dwelling": the system of his relationship to self, the closure of his auto-representations, focus of his lonely exile as "subject." Man's home has indeed become these/his theoretical elaborations, by means of which he has sought to reconstruct, in an impossible metaphorization, the matrix and the way that would lead to or back to it. But by wishing to reverse the anguish of being imprisoned within the other, of being placed inside the other, by making the very place and space of being his own, he becomes a prisoner of effects of symmetry that know no limit. Everywhere he runs into the walls of his palace of mirrors, the floor of which is in any case beginning to crack and break up. This in turn serves, of course, to sublate his activity, leading him to new tasks which for a time will distract him again from his specular imprisonment. A diversion from the depths of his madness, pretext for an increase in attentiveness, vigilance, mastery. The reason for the quakes must be sought out, these seismic convulsions in the self must be interpreted.

But man only asks (himself) questions that he can already answer, using the supply of instruments he has available to assimilate even the disasters in his history. This time at any rate he is prepared to lay odds again, and, give or take a few new weapons, he will make the unconscious into a property of his language. A disconcerting property, admittedly, which confuses everything he had long since assigned meaning to. But that, it seems, is not the most important thing at stake. The really urgent task is to ensure the colonization of this new "field," to force it, not without splintering, into the production of the same discourse. And since there can be no question of using the same plan/e for this "strange" speech, this "barbarous" language with which it is impossible to conduct a dialogue—read, monologue—the discovery will be set out hierarchically, in stages. Will be brought to order. By giving here a little more play to the system, here a little less. The forms of arrangement may vary, but they will all bear the paradox of forcing into the same representation—the representation of the self/same—that which insists upon its *heterogeneity*, its *otherness*.

Yet the fact that the dream can be interpreted only as a "rebus" should have persuaded the "reader" to turn it in all directions and positions, and not favor one type of inscription that would already prescribe a meaning to it: a linear, teleologically horizontal or vertical displacement, over a surface as yet unwritten, which it brands by cutting it up according to rules of repetition and recurrence, obeying processes that already paralyze the "body's" system of gestures within a given graphic order, etc. Why not rather have recalled those "pictures" made for children, pictographs in which the hunter and hunted, and their dramatic relationships, are to be discovered *between* the branches, *made out* from *between* the trees. From the spaces between the figures, or stand-in figures. Spaces that organize the scene, blanks that sub-tend the scene's structuration and that will yet not be read as such. Or not read at all? Not seen at all? Never in truth represented or representable, though this is not to say that they have no effect upon the present scenography. But fixed in oblivion and waiting to come to life. Turning everything upside down and back to front. If, that is, the interpreter-subject did not desire "this" (the id) to continue sustaining the proliferation of images (of self), as a trompe-l'oeil backcloth for the same's show, for a theater of the identical.

Dreams are also riddles in that—during "sleep," and in order to "keep" asleep—they recast the roles that history has laid down for "subject" and "object." Mutism that says without speech, inertia that moves without motion, or else only with the motions of another language, another script. Dream pictography, dream choreography, phonography, and pornography which compensate for the present *paralysis* of the sleeper. Who will/would awake—perhaps?—only if the "child," faced with such "riddles," did not have the overweening desire to "see" an other and same figure and form than the one that is already present for him. If it were enough for him to be entranced, let us say, by a *double syntax*, without claiming to regulate the second by the standard of representation, of re-presentation, of the first. If he were not "wounded," threatened by "castration," by anything he cannot see directly, anything he cannot perceive as like himself. Did not feel, as a result, the need to invent a new "theory," yet another in the series of optical instruments which, by means of the second—or hundred and second—sighting, moves in around the "man-ifestations" of the unconscious, under the protection of technological dis-tance. Prosthesis, which assists the horrified gaze to construct, laboriously, "consciously," concept by concept, the rationality of his repression. His estab-lished good. Session after session, in a procedure that is also regulated by visual—rememorative—laws, he repeats the same gesture reestablishing the bar, the barred. While all the while permissive, listening with benevolent neu-trality, collecting, on a carefully circumscribed little stage, the inter-dict. The lines between the lines of discourse. But he restricts himself to reframing, remarking, or "analyzing" its contours, re-stratifying its stages, so that order, good "conscious" order, may prevail. Elsewhere.

Now, let us imagine—for what else is there to do when rereading Freud but imagine a response, or else admit one's inability to survey such an imagi-nation—let us imagine that man (Freud in the event) had discovered that the rarest thing—the most exciting as well as the most scientifically rigorous, the most faithful to factual materiality and the most historically curative—would be to articulate directly, *without catacombs*, what we are calling these two syn-taxes. Irreducible in their strangeness and eccentricity one to the other. Com-ing out of different times, places, logics, "representations," and economies. In fact, of course, these terms cannot fittingly be designated by the number "two" and the adjective "different," if only because they are not susceptible to com-parison. To use such terms serves only to reiterate a movement begun long since, that is, the movement to speak of the "other" in a language already systematized by/for the same. Their distribution and demarcation and artic-ulation necessitate operations as yet nonexistent, whose complexity and sub-tlety can only be guessed at without prejudicing the results. Without a teleol-ogy already in operation somewhere. But had the man Freud preferred the play, or even the clash, of those two economies rather than their disposition in hierarchical stages by means of one barrier (or two), one censorship (or two), then perhaps he would not finally have cracked his head against all that remains irreducibly "obscure" to him in his speculations. Against the non-vis-ible, therefore not theorizable nature of woman's sex and pleasure. What-ever the explorations he attempts and which tempt him concerning this "dark continent," he always refers back to some still blind and incomprehensible "horizon" of investigation. And there, in what he recognizes as outside the range of his systematic prospecting (beyond the self?), Freud is in fact indi-cating a way off the historico-transcendental stage, at the very moment when his theory and his practice are perpetuating, in the mode of enunciation and the drama of enunciating, that very same stage, which we may now call the *hys-*

terico-transcendental. Announcing by this re-mark, by this effect of repetition—re-petitio principii—of recapitulation and, without his knowledge, of mimicry, that his breath is privileged. And he is out of breath.

For, when Freud reaffirms the incest taboo, he simply reannounces and puts back in place the conditions that constitute the speculative matrix of the "subject." He reinforces his positions in a fashion yet more "scientific," more imperious in their "objectivity." A demonstration he clearly needed himself if he is to "sublimate" in more universal interests his own desire for his/the mother. But as a result of using psychoanalysis (his psychoanalysis) only to scrutinize the history of his subject and his subjects, without interpreting *the historical determinants of the constitution of the "subject" as same*, he was restoring, yet again, that newly pressed down/repressed earth, upon which he stands erect, which for him, following tradition though in more explicit fashion, will be the body/sex of the mother/nature. He must challenge her for power, for productivity. He must resurface the earth with this floor of the idea. Identify with the law-giving father, with his proper names, his desires for making capital, in every sense of the word, desires that prefer the possession of territory, which includes language, to the exercise of his pleasures, with the exception of his pleasure in trading women—fetishized objects, merchandise of whose value he stands surety—with his peers. The ban upon returning, regressing to the womb, as well as to the language and dreams shared with the mother, this is indeed the point, the line, the surface upon which the "subject" will continue to stand, to advance, to unfold his discourse, even to make it whirl. Though he has barely escaped the ring, the vault, the snare of reconciling his end and his archives, those calls, resurgent, of his beginnings. Though that he-who-is-the-cause is barely keeping his balance. But since he now knows the reason for his wobbling. . . . And, after all, the acquisition of new riches is certainly part of this? Overdetermination, deferred action, dreams, fantasies, puns. . . . Language, by adopting its/these "annexes"—also ocular, uterine, embryonic—adds to its wealth, gains "depth," consistency, diversity, and multiplication of its processes and techniques. Was language once believed threatened? Here it is dancing, playing, writing itself more than ever, It is even claimed that language is "truer" than in the past, reimpregnated with its childhood. A consciousness yet more consciously pregnant with its relationship with the mother.

Whereas "she" comes to be unable to say what her body is suffering. Stripped even of the words that are expected of her upon that stage invented to listen to her. In an admission of the wear and tear on language or of its fetishistic denial? But hysteria, or at least the hysteria that is the privileged lot of the "female," *now has nothing to say.* What she "suffers," what she "lusts for," even what she "takes pleasure in," all take place upon another stage, in relation to already codified representations. Repression of speech, inter-dicted in "hieroglyphic" symptoms—an already suspicious designation of something prehistoric—which will doubtless never again be lifted into current history. Unless it be by making her enter, in contempt of her sex, into "masculine" games of tropes and tropisms. By converting her to a discourse that denies the specificity of her pleasure by inscribing it as the hollow, the intaglio, the negative, even as the censured other of its phallic assertions. By hom(m)osexualizing her. By perversely travestying her for the pederastic, sodomizing satisfactions of the father/husband. She shrieks out demands too innocuous to cause alarm, that merely make people smile. Just the way one smiles at a child when he shouts aloud the mad ambitions adults keep to themselves. And which one knows he can never realize. And when she also openly displays their power fantasies, this serves as a re-creation to them in their struggle for power. By setting before them, keeping in reserve for them, in her in-fancy, what they must of course keep clear of in their pursuit of mastery, but which they yet cannot wholly renounce for fear of going off course. So she will be the Pythia who apes induced desires and suggestions foreign to her still hazy consciousness, suggestions that proclaim their credibility all the louder as they carry her ever further from her interests. By resubmitting herself to the established order, in this role of delirious double, she abandons, even denies, the prerogative historically granted her: unconsciousness. She prostitutes the unconscious itself to the ever present projects and projections of masculine consciousness.

For whereas the man Freud—or woman, were she to set her rights up in opposition—*might have been able* to interpret what the overdetermination of language (its effects of deferred action, its subterranean dreams and fantasies, its convulsive quakes, its paradoxes and contradictions) owed to the repression (which may yet return) of maternal power—or of the matriarchy, to adopt a still prehistorical point of reference—whereas he might have been able also to interpret the repression of the history of female sexuality, we shall in fact receive only confirmation of the discourse of the same, through comprehension and extension. With "woman" coming once more to be embedded in, enclosed in, impaled upon an architectonic more powerful than ever. And she herself is sometimes happy to request a recognition of consciousness thereby, even an appropriation of unconsciousness that cannot be hers. Unconsciousness she is, but not for herself, not with a subjectivity that might take cognizance of it, recognize it as her own. Close to herself, admittedly, but in a total ignorance (of self). She is the reserve of "sensuality" for the elevation of intelligence, she is the matter used for the imprint of forms, gage of possible regression into naive perception, the representative representing negativity (death), dark continent of dreams and fantasies, and also eardrum faithfully duplicating the music, though not all of it, so that the series of displacements may continue, for the "subject." And she will serve to assure his determination only if she now seeks to reclaim his property from him: this (of his) elaborated as same out of this (of hers) foreclosed from specula(riza)tion. The same thing will always be at stake. The profiteering will barely have changed hands. A barter solution that she would adopt out of the void of her desire. And always one step behind in the process, the progress of history.

But if, by exploits of her hand, woman were to reopen paths into (once again) a/one logos that connotes her as castrated, especially as castrated of words, excluded from the work force except as prostitute to the interests of the dominant ideology—that is of hom(m)osexuality and its struggles with the maternal—then a certain sense, which still constitutes the sense of history also, will undergo unparalleled interrogation, revolution. But how is this to be done? Given that, once again, the "reasonable" words—to which in any case she has access only though mimicry—are powerless to translate all that pulses, clamors, and hangs hazily in the cryptic passages of hysterical suffering-latency. Then. . . . Turn everything upside down, inside out, back to front. *Rack it with radical convulsions*, carry back, reimport, those crises that her "body" suffers in her impotence to say what disturbs her. Insist also and deliberately upon those *blanks* in discourse which recall the places of her exclusion and which, by their *silent plasticity*, ensure the cohesion, the articulation, the coherent expansion of established forms. Reinscribe them hither and thither *as divergencies*, otherwise and elsewhere than they are expected, in *ellipses* and *eclipses* that deconstruct the logical grid of the reader-writer, drive him out of his mind, trouble his vision to the point of incurable diplopia at least. *Overthrow syntax* by suspending its eternally teleological order, by snipping the wires, cutting the current, breaking the circuits, switching the connections, by modifying continuity, alternation, frequency, intensity. Make it impossible for a while to predict whence, whither, when, how, why . . . something goes by or goes on: will come, will spread, will reverse, will cease moving. Not by means of a growing complexity of the same, of course, but by the irruption of other circuits, by the intervention at times of short-circuits that will disperse, diffract, deflect endlessly, making energy explode sometimes, with no possibility of returning to one single origin. A force that can no longer be channeled according to a given *plan/e*: a projection from a single source, even in the secondary circuits, with retroactive effects.

All this already applies to words, to the "lexicon" (as it is called), which is also connected up, and in the same direction. But we must go on questioning words as the wrappings with which the "subject," modestly, clothes the "female." Stifled beneath all those eulogistic or denigratory metaphors, she is unable to unpick the seams of her disguise and indeed takes a certain pleasure in them, even gilding the lily further at times. Yet, even more hemmed in, cathected by tropes, how could she articulate any sound from beneath this cheap chivalric finery? How find a voice, make a choice strong enough, subtle enough to cut through those layers of ornamental style, that decorative sepulcher, where even her breath is lost. Stifled under all those airs. She has yet to feel the need to get free of fabric, reveal her nakedness, her destitution in language, explode in the face of them all, words too. For the imperious need for her shame, her chastity—duly fitted out with the belt of discourse—, of her decent modesty, continues to be asserted by every man. In every kind of tone, form, theory, style, with the exception of a few that in fact rouse suspicion also by their pornographically, hom(m)osexual excess. Common stock, one may assume, for their production.

The (re)productive power of the mother, the sex of the woman, are both at stake in the proliferation of systems, those houses of ill fame for the subject, of fetish-words, sign-objects whose certified truths seek to palliate the risk that values may be recast into/by the other. But no clear univocal utterance, can in fact, pay off this mortgage since all are already trapped in the same credit structure. All can be recuperated when issued by the signifying order in place. It is still better to speak only in riddles, allusions, hints, parables. Even if asked to clarify a few points. Even if people plead that they just don't understand. After all, they never have understood. So why not double the misprision to the limits of exasperation? Until the ear tunes into another music, the voice starts to sing again, the very gaze stops squinting over the signs of auto-representation, and (re)production no longer inevitably amounts to the same and returns to the same forms, with minor variations.

This disconcerting of language, though anarchic in its deeds of title, nonetheless demands patient exactitude. The symptoms, for their part, are implacably precise. And if it is indeed a question of breaking (with) a certain mode of specula(riza)tion, this does not imply renouncing all mirrors or refraining from analysis of the hold this plan/e of representation maintains, rendering female desire aphasic and more generally atonic in all but its phallomorphic disguises, masquerades, and demands. For to dodge this time of interpretation is to risk its freezing over, losing hold, cutting back. All over again. But perhaps through this specular surface which sustains discourse is found not the void of nothingness but the dazzle of multifaceted speleology. A scintillating and incandescent concavity, of language also, that threatens to set fire to fetish-objects and gilded eyes. The recasting of their truth value is already at hand. We need only press on a little further into the depths, into that so-called dark cave which serves as hidden foundation to their speculations. For there where we expect to find the opaque and silent matrix of a logos immutable in the certainty of its own light, fires and mirrors are beginning to radiate, sapping the evidence of reason at its base! Not so much by anything stored in the cave—which would still be a claim based on the notion of the closed volume—but again and yet again by their indefinitely rekindled hearths.

But which "subject" up till now has investigated the fact that a *concave mirror* concentrates the light and, specifically, that this is not wholly irrelevant to woman's sexuality? Any more than is a man's sexuality to the convex mirror? Which "subject" has taken an interest in the anamorphoses produced by the conjunction of such curvatures? What impossible reflected images, maddening reflections, parodic transformations took place at each of their articulations? When the "it is" annuls them in the truth of a copula in which "he" still forever finds the resources of his identification as same. Not one subject has done so, on pain of tumbling from his ex-sistence. And here again, here too, one will rightly suspect any perspective, however surreptitious, that centers the subject, any autonomous circuit of subjectivity, any systematicity hooked back onto itself, any closure that claims for whatever reason to be metaphysical—or familial, social, economic even—, to have rightfully taken over, fixed, and framed that concave mirror's incandescent hearth. If this mirror—which, however, makes a *hole*—sets itself up pompously as an authority in order to give shape to the imaginary orb of a "subject," it thereby defends itself phobically in/by this inner "center" from the fires of the desire of/for woman. Inhabiting a securing morphology, making of its very structure some comfortable sepulcher from whence it may, possibly, by some hypothetical survival, be able to look out. (Re)g(u)arding itself by all sorts of windows-on-wheels, optical apparatuses, glasses, and mirrors, from/in this burning glass, which enflames all that falls into its cup.

But, may come the objection,—defending again the objective and the object—the speculum is not necessarily a mirror. It may, quite simply, be an instrument to *dilate* the lips, the orifices, the walls, so that the eye can penetrate the *interior*. So that the eye can enter, to see, notably with speculative intent. Woman, having been misinterpreted, forgotten, variously frozen in show-cases, rolled up in metaphors, buried beneath carefully stylized figures, raised up in different idealities, would now become the "object" to be investigated, to be explicitly granted consideration, and thereby, by this deed of title, included in the theory. And if this center, which fixed and immobilized metaphysics in its closure, had often in the past been traced back to some divinity or other transcendence invisible as such, in the future its ultimate meaning will perhaps be discovered by tracking down what there is to be *seen* of female sexuality.

Yes, man's eye—understood as substitute for the penis—will be able to prospect woman's sexual parts, seek there new sources of profit. Which are equally theoretical. By doing so he further fetishizes (his) desire. But the desire of the mystery remains, however large a public has been recruited of late for "hysteroscopy." For even if the place of origin, the original dwelling, even if not only the woman but the mother can be unveiled to his sight, what will he make of the exploration of this mine? Except usurp even more the right to look at everything, at the whole thing, thus reinforcing the erosion of his desire in the very place where he firmly believes he is working to reduce an illusion. Even if it should be a transcendental illusion. What will he, what will they, have *seen* as a result of that dilation? And what will they get out of it? A disillusion quite as illusory, since the transcendental keeps its secret. Between empirical and transcendental *a suspense will still remain inviolate*, will escape prospection, then, now, and in the future. The space-time of the risk that fetishes will be consumed, catch fire. In this fire, in this light, in the optical failure, the impossibility of gazing on their encounters in flame, the split (schize) founding and structuring the difference between experience and transcendental (especially phallic) eminence will burn also. *Exquisite/exschizoid crisis of ontico-ontological difference.* What manner of recasting all economy will ensue? To tell the truth, no one knows. And, to stay with truth, you can only fear the worst. For you may fear a general crisis in the value system, a foundering of the values now current, the devaluation of their standard and of their regimen of monopolies.

The copulative effusion, and fusion, melts down the mint's credit with each moment of bliss. Renews and redistributes the accepted stakes: between two crises, two explosions, two incandescences of fetish mineral. And it is no easy matter to foresee whether, in that game, the one—the man?—who has recouped the biggest pile of chips will be the winner. It is equally possible to imagine that the one—the woman—who has spent her time polishing her mine will carry the day. Since the abrasion of the stores entrusted to the reflecting surface renders that surface more likely to set aflame the supplies and capitalizations of the one who, under cover and pretext of seduction, puts his riches on display.

But, will come the objection once again—in the name of some other objectality—we are not fed by fire and flames. Maybe. But then neither are we by fetishes and gazes. And when will they cease to equate woman's sexuality with her reproductive organs, to claim that her sexuality has value only insofar as it gathers the heritage of her maternity? When will man give up the need or desire to drink deep in all security from his wife/mother in order to go and show off to this brothers and buddies the fine things he formed while suckling his nurse? And/or when will he renounce (reversing roles so as better to retain them) the wish to preserve his wife/child in her inability, as he sees it, to produce for the marketplace? With "marriage" turning out to be a more or less subtle dialectization of the nurturing relationship that aims to maintain, at the very least, the mother/child, producer/consumer distinction, and thereby perpetuate this economy?

To return to the gaze, it will be able to explore all the inner cavities. Although, in the case of the most secret, it will need the help of ancillary light and mirror. Of appropriate sun and mirrors. The instrumental and technical exploitation of sun and mirror will have shown the gaze, proved to it, that those mines contained no gold. Then the gaze, aghast at such bareness, will have concluded that at any rate all brilliance was its own preserve, that it could continue to speculate without competition. That the childish, the archaic credit accorded to the all-powerful mother was nothing, was but fable. But how is one to desire without fiction? What pleasure is there in stockpiling goods without risks, without expenditures?

You will have noted, in fact, that what polarizes the light for the exploration of internal cavities is, in paradigmatic fashion, *the concave mirror.* Only when that mirror has concentrated the feeble rays of the eye, of the sun, of the sun-blinded eye, is the secret of the caves illumined. Scientific technique will have taken up the condensation properties of the "burning glass," in order to pierce the mystery of woman's sex, in a new distribution of the power of the scientific method and of "nature." A new despecularization of the maternal and the female? Scientificity of fiction that seeks to exorcise the disasters of desire, that mortifies desire by analyzing it from all visual angles, but leaves it also intact. Elsewhere. Burning still.

CRAIG OWENS

*The Discourse of Others: Feminists and Postmodernism**

> Postmodern knowledge *[le savoir postmoderne]* is not simply an instrument of power. It refines our sensitivity to differences and increases our tolerence of incommensurability.
>
> —J. F. Lyotard, *La condition postmoderne*

Decentered, allegorical, schizophrenic . . .—however we choose to diagnose its symptoms, postmodernism is usually treated, by its protagonists and antagonists alike, as a crisis of cultural authority, specifically of the authority vested in Western European culture and its institutions. That the hegemony of European civilization is drawing to a close is hardly a new perception; since the mid-1950s, at least, we have recognized the necessity of encountering different cultures by means other than the shock of domination and conquest. Among the relevant texts are Arnold Toynbee's discussion, the eighth volume of his monumental *Study in History,* of the end of the modern age (an age that began, Toynbee contends, in the late 15th century when Europe began to exert its influence over vast land areas and populations not its own) and the beginning of a new, properly postmodern age characterized by the coexistence of different cultures. Claude Lévi-Strauss's critique of Western ethnocentrism could be cited in this context, as well as Jacques Derrida's critique of

---

* Craig Owens, "The Discourse of Others: Feminists and Postmodernism," *The Anti-Aesthetic: Essays on Postmodern Culture* (Port Townsend, Washington: Bay Press, 1983), pp. 57-77 (footnotes omitted).

this critique in *Of Grammatology*. But perhaps the most eloquent testimony to the end of Western sovereignty has been that of Paul Ricoeur, who wrote in 1962 that the discovery of the plurality of cultures is never a "harmless experience."

> When we discover that there are several cultures instead of just one and consequently at the time when we acknowledge the end of a sort of cultural monopoly, be it illusory or real, we are threatened with the destruction of our own discovery. Suddenly it becomes possible that there are just *others*, that we ourselves are an "other" among others. All meaning and every goal having disappeared, it becomes possible to wander through civilizations as if through vestiges and ruins. The whole of mankind becomes an imaginary museum: where shall we go this weekend—visit the Angkor ruins or take a stroll in the Tivoli of Copenhagen? We can very easily imagine a time close at hand when any fairly well-to-do person will be able to leave his country indefinitely in order to waste his own national death in an interminable, aimless voyage.

Lately, we have come to regard this condition as postmodern. Indeed, Ricoeur's account of the more dispiriting effects of our culture's recent loss of mastery anticipates both the melancholia and the eclecticism that pervade current cultural production—not to mention its much-touted pluralism. Pluralism, however, reduces us to being an other among others; it is not a recognition, but a reduction to difference to absolute indifference, equivalence, interchangeability (what Jean Baudrillard calls "implosion"). What is at stake, then, is not only the hegemony of Western Culture, but also (our sense of) our identity as a culture. These two stakes, however, are so inextricably intertwined (as Foucault has taught us, the positing of an Other is a necessary moment in the consolidation, the incorporation of any cultural body) that it is possible to speculate that what has toppled our claims to sovereignty is actually the realization that our culture is neither as homogeneous nor as monolithic as we once believed it to be. In other words, the causes of modernity's demise—at least as Ricoeur describes its effects—lie as much within as without. Ricoeur, however, deals only with the difference without. What about the difference within?

In the modern period the authority of the work of art, its claim to represent singularity, as is often said; rather, that authority was based on the universality modern aesthetics attributed to the *forms* utilized for the representation of vision, over and above differences in content due to the production of works in concrete historical circumstances. (For example, Kant's demand that the judgment of taste be universal—i.e., universally communicable—that it derive from "grounds deep-seated and shared alike by all men, underlying their agreement in estimating the forms under which objects are given to them.") Not only does the postmodernist work claim no such authority, it also actively seeks to undermine all such claims; hence, its generally deconstructive thrust. As recent analyses of the "enunciative apparatus" of visual representation—its poles of emission and reception—confirm, the representational systems of the West admit only one vision—that of the constitutive male subject—or, rather, they posit the subject of representation as absolutely centered, unitary, masculine.

The postmodernist work attempts to upset the reassuring stability of that mastering position. This same project has, of course, been attributed by writers like Julia Kristeva and Roland Barthes to the *modernist* avant-garde, which the introduction of heterogeneity, discontinuity, glossolalia, etc., supposedly put the subject of representation in crisis. But the avant-garde sought to transcend representation in favor of presence and immediacy; it proclaimed the autonomy of the signifier, its liberation from the "tyranny of the signified"; postmodernists instead expose the tyranny of the *signifier*, the violence of its law. (Lacan spoke of the necessity of submitting to the "defiles" of the signifier; should we not ask rather who in our culture is defiled by the signifier?) Recently, Derrida has cautioned against a wholesale condemnation of representation, not only because such a condemnation may appear to advocate a rehabilitation of presence and immediacy and thereby serve the interests of the most reactionary political tendencies, but more importantly, perhaps, because that which exceeds, "transgresses the figure of all possible representation," may ultimately be none other than . . . the law. Which obliges us, Derrida concludes, "to thinking altogether *differently*."

It is precisely at the legislative frontier between what can be represented and what cannot that the postmodernist operation is being staged—not in order to transcend representation, but in order to expose that system of power that authorizes certain representations while blocking, prohibiting or invalidating others. Among those prohibited from Western representation whose representations are denied all legitimacy are women. Excluded from representation by its very structure, they return within it as a figure for—a representation of—the unrepresentable (Nature, Truth, the Sublime, etc.). This prohibition bears primarily on woman as the subject, and rarely as the object of representation, for there is certainly no shortage of images *of* women. Yet in being represented by, women have been rendered an absence within the dominant culture as Michèle Montrelay proposes when she asks "whether psychoanalysis was not articulated precisely in order to repress femininity (in the sense of producing its symbolic representation)." In order to speak, to represent herself, a woman assumes a masculine position; perhaps this is why femininity is frequently associated with masquerade, with false representation, with simulation and seduction. Montrelay, in fact, identifies women as the "ruin of representation": not only have they nothing to lose; their exteriority to Western representation exposes its limits.

Here, we arrive at an apparent crossing of the feminist critique of patriarchy and the postmodernist critique of representation; this essay is a provisional attempt to explore the implication of that intersection. My intention is not to posit identity between these two critiques; nor is it to place them in a relation of antagonism or opposition. Rather, if I have chosen to negotiate the treacherous course between postmodernism and feminism, it is in order to introduce the issue of sexual difference into the modernism/postmodernism debate—a debate which has until now been scandalously in-different.

"A Remarkable Oversight"

Several years ago I began the second of two essays devoted to an allegorical impulse in contemporary art—an impulse that I identified as postmodernist—with a discussion of Laurie Anderson's multi-media performance *Americans on the Move*. Addressed to transportation as a metaphor for communication—the transfer of meaning from one place to another—*Americans on the Move* proceeded primarily as verbal commentary on visual images projected on a screen behind the performers. Near the beginning Anderson introduced the schematic image of a nude man and woman, the former's right arm raised in greeting, that had been emblazoned on the Pioneer spacecraft. Here is what she had to say about this picture; significantly, it was spoken by a distinctly male voice (Anderson's own processed through a harmonizer, which dropped it an octave—a kind of electronic vocal transvestism):

> In our country, we send pictures of our sign language into outer space. They are speaking our sign language in these pictures. Do you think they will think his hand is permanently attached that way? Or do you think they will read our signs? In our country, good-bye looks just like hello.

Here is my commentary on this passage:

> Two alternatives: either the extraterrestrial recipient of this message will assume that it is simply a picture, that is, an analogical likeness of the human figure, in which case he might logically conclude that male inhabitants of Earth walk around with their right arms permanently raised. Or he will somehow divine that this gesture is addressed to him and attempt to read it, in which case he will be stymied, since a single gesture signifies both greeting and farewell, and any reading of it must oscillate between these two extremes. The same gesture could also mean "Halt!" or represent the taking of an oath, but if Anderson's text does not consider these two alternatives that is because it is not concerned with ambiguity, with multiple meanings engendered by a single sign; rather, two *clearly defined but mutually incompatible* readings are engaged in blind confrontation in such a way that it is impossible to choose between them.

This analysis strikes me as a case of gross critical negligence. For in my eagerness to rewrite Anderson's text in terms of the debate over determinate versus indeterminate meaning, I had overlooked something—something that is so obvious, so "natural" that it may at the time have seemed unworthy of comment. It does not seem that way to me today. For this is, of course, an image of sexual difference or, rather, of sexual differentiation according to the distribution of the phallus—as it is marked and then re-marked by the man's right arm, which appears less to have been raised than erected in greeting. I was, however, close to the "truth" of the image when I suggested that men on

Earth might walk around with something permanently raised—close, perhaps, but no cigar. (Would my reading have been different—or less in-different—had I known then that, earlier in her career, Anderson had executed a work which consisted of photographs of men who had accosted her in the street?) Like all representations of sexual difference that our culture produces, this is an image not simply of anatomical difference, but of the values assigned to it. Here, the phallus is a signifier (that is, it represents the subject for another signifier); it is, in fact, the privileged signifier, the signifier of privilege, of the power and prestige that accrue to the male in our society. As such, it designates the effects of signification in general. For this (Lacanian) image, chosen to represent the inhabitants of Earth for the extraterrestrial Other, it is the man who speaks, who represents mankind. The woman is only represented; she is (as always) already spoken for.

If I return to this passage here, it is not simply to correct my own remarkable oversight, but more importantly to indicate a blind spot in our discussions of postmodernism in general: our failure to address the issue of sexual difference—not only in the objects we discuss, but in our own enunciation as well. However restricted its field of inquiry may be, every discourse on postmodernism—at least insofar as it seeks to account for certain recent mutations within that field—aspires to the status of a general theory of contemporary culture. Among the most significant developments of the past decade—it may well turn out to have been *the* most significant—has been the emergence, in nearly every area of cultural activity, of a specifically feminist practice. A great deal of effort has been devoted to the recovery and revaluation of previously marginalized or underestimated work; everywhere this project has been accompanied by energetic new production. As one engaged in these activities—Martha Rosler—observes, they have contributed significantly to debunking the privileged status modernism claimed for the work of art: "The interpretation of the meaning and social origin and rootedness of those (earlier) forms helped undermine the modernist tenet of the separateness of the aesthetic from the rest of human life, and an analysis of the oppressiveness of the seemingly unmotivated forms of high culture was companion to this work."

Still, if one of the most salient aspects of our postmodern culture is the presence of an insistent feminist voice (and I use the terms *presence* and *voice* advisedly), theories of postmodernism have tended either to neglect or to repress that voice. The absence of discussions of sexual difference in writings about postmodernism, as well as the fact that few women have engaged in the modernism/postmodernism debate, suggest that postmodernism may be another masculine invention engineered to exclude women. I would like to propose, however, that women's insistence on difference and incommensurability may not only be compatible with, but also an instance of postmodern thought. Postmodern thought is no longer binary thought (as Lyotard observes when he writes, "Thinking by means of oppositions does not correspond to the liveliest modes of postmodern knowledge *[le savoir postmod-*

ernej"). The critique of binarism is sometimes dismissed as intellectual fashion; it is, however, an intellectual imperative, since the hierarchical opposition of marked and unmarked terms (the decisive/divisive presence/absence of the phallus) is the dominant form both of representing difference and justifying its subordination in our society. What we must learn, then, is how to conceive difference without opposition.

Although sympathetic male critics respect feminism (an old theme: respect for women) and wish it well, they have in general declined the dialogue in which their female colleagues are trying to engage them. Sometimes feminists are accused of going too far, at others, not far enough. The feminist voice is usually regarded as one among many, its insistence on difference as testimony to the pluralism of the times. Thus, feminism is rapidly assimilated to a whole string of liberation or self-determination movements. Here is one recent list, by a prominent male critic: "ethnic groups, neighborhood movements, feminism, various 'countercultural' or alternative life-style groups, rank-and-file labor dissidence, student movements, single-issue movements." Not only does this forced coalition treat feminism itself as monolithic, thereby suppressing its multiple internal differences (essentialist, culturalist, linguistic, Freudian, anti-Freudian . . .); it also posits a vast, undifferentiated category, "Difference," to which all marginalized or oppressed groups can be assimilated, and for which women can then stand as an emblem, a *pars totalis* (another old theme: woman is incomplete, not whole). But the specificity of the feminist critique of patriarchy is thereby denied, along with that all other forms of opposition to sexual, racial and class discrimination. (Rosler warns against using woman as "a token for all markers of difference," observing that "appreciation of the work of women whose subject is oppression exhausts consideration of all oppressions.")

Moreover, men appear unwilling to address the issue placed on the critical agenda by women unless those issues have first been neut(e)ralized—although this, too, is a problem of assimilation: to the already known, the already written. In *The Political Unconscious*, to take but one example, Fredric Jameson calls for the "reaudition of the oppositional voices of black and ethnic cultures, women's or gay literature, 'naive' or marginalized folk art *and the like*" (thus, women's cultural production is anachronistically identified as folk art), but he immediately modifies this petition: "The affirmation of such non-hegemonic cultural voices remains ineffective," he argues, if they are not first *rewritten* in terms of their proper place in "the dialogical system of the social class." Certainly, the class determinants of sexuality—and of sexual oppression—are too often overlooked. But sexual inequality cannot be reduced to an instance in economic exploitation—the exchange of women among men—and explained in terms of class struggle alone; to invert Rosler's statement, exclusive attention to economic oppression can exhaust consideration of other forms of oppression.

To claim that the division of the sexes is irreducible to the division of labor is to risk polarizing feminism and Marxism; this danger is real, given the latter's fundamentally patriarchal bias. Marxism privileges the characteristically masculine activity of production as the *definitively human* activity (Marx: men "begin to distinguish themselves from animals as soon as they begin to produce their means of subsistence"); women, historically consigned to the spheres of unproductive or reproductive labor, are thereby situated outside the society of male producers, in a state of nature. (As Lyotard has written, "The frontier passing between the sexes does not separate two parts of the same social entity.") What is at issue, however, is not simply the oppressiveness of Marxist discourse, but its totalizing ambitions, its claim to account for every form of social experience. But this claim is characteristic of all theoretical discourse, which is one reason women frequently condemn it as phallocratic. It is not always theory *per se* that women repudiate, nor simply, as Lyotard has suggested, the priority men have granted to it, its rigid opposition to practical experience. Rather, what they challenge is the distance it maintains between itself and its objects—a distance which objectifies and masters.

Because of the tremendous effort of reconceptualization necessary to prevent a phallologic relapse in their own discourse, many feminist artists have, in fact, forged a new (or renewed) alliance with theory—most profitably, perhaps, with the writing of women influenced by Lacanian psychoanalysis (Luce Irigaray, Hélène Cixous, Montrelay . . .). Many of these artists have themselves made major theoretical contributions: film-maker Laura Mulvey's 1975 essay on "Visual Pleasure and Narrative Cinema," for example, has generated a great deal of critical discussion on the masculinity of the cinematic gaze. Whether influenced by psychoanalysis or not, feminist artists often regard critical or theoretical writing as an important arena of strategic intervention: Martha Rosler's critical texts on the documentary tradition in photography—among the best in the field—are a crucial part of her activity *as an artist*. Many modernist artists, of course, produced texts about their own production, but writing was almost always considered supplementary to their primary work as painters, sculptors, photographers, etc., whereas the kind of simultaneous activity on multiple fronts that characterizes many feminist practices is a postmodern phenomenon. And one of the things it challenges is modernism's rigid opposition of artistic practice and theory.

At the same time, postmodern feminist practice may question theory—and not only *aesthetic* theory. Consider Mary Kelly's *Post-Partum Document* (1973-79), a 6-part, 165-piece art work (plus footnotes) that utilizes multiple representational modes (literary, scientific, psychoanalytic, linguistic, archeological and so forth) to chronicle the first six years of her son's life. Part archive, part exhibition, part case history, the *Post-Partum Document* is also a contribution to as well as a critique of Lacanian theory. Beginning as it does with a series of diagrams taken from *Ecrits* (diagrams which Kelly presents as *pictures*), the work might be (mis)read as a straightforward application or illustration of psychoanalysis. It is, rather, a mother's interrogation of Lacan, an interrogation that ultimately reveals a remarkable oversight within the Lacanian narrative of the child's relation to the mother—the construction of the mother's fantasies vis-à-vis the child. Thus, the *Post-Partum Document* has proven to be a controversial work, for it appears to offer evidence of *female* fetishism (the various substitutes the mother invents in order to disavow separation from the child); Kelly thereby exposes a lack within the theory of fetishism, a perversion heretofore reserved for the male. Kelly's work is not anti-theory; rather, as her use of multiple representation systems testifies, it demonstrates that no one narrative can possibly account for all aspects of human experience. Or as the artist herself has said, "There's no single theoretical discourse which is going to offer an explanation for all forms of social relations or for every mode of political practice.". . .

In the visual arts we have witnessed the gradual dissolution of once fundamental distinctions—original/copy, authentic/inauthentic, function/ornament. Each term now seems to contain its opposite, and this indeterminacy brings with it an impossibility of choice or, rather, the absolute equivalence and hence interchangeability of choices. Or so it is said. The existence of feminism, with its insistence on difference, forces us to reconsider. For in our country good-bye may look just like hello, but only from a masculine position. Women have learned—perhaps they have always known—how to recognize the difference.

MULTICULTURAL THEORY

WHERE FEMINIST THEORY POSES the possibility for us that our understanding of art, theoretical and institutional, emerges from a history dominated by male institutions and standards, multicultural theory poses the possibility that our understanding of art is predominantly Western. Women have largely been excluded from the arts except as performers and consorts. Non-Western artists have largely been excluded from artistic canons as primitive, communal, or tribal. The consequences of such a critique are far-reaching, going far beyond art itself to the very structures of thought that define Western institutions. For the deepest and most sweeping claim is that Western rational and artistic standards pass themselves off as universal from within a very limited cultural perspective. In addition if from a more limited theoretical critique, important issues of the art market and the appropriation of nonWestern works for sale in Western markets suggest that changing perceptions of African and Pacific art may reflect economic and market considerations as much as aesthetic perceptions.

The selections included here address the ways in which African cultural institutions, including artistic productions, have been systematically distorted; the ways in which people from other cultures and their practices in Western society have found themselves in deeply problematic situations; and particular issues related to collecting artifacts from other cultures in a world economy.

These selections should be read in conjunction with the selections in Feminist Theory.

V. Y. MUDIMBE

*The Invention of Africa**

The colonializing structure, even in its most extreme manifestations—such as the crisis of South Africa (see, e.g., Seidman, 1985)—might not be the only explanation for Africa's present-day marginality. Perhaps this marginality could, more essentially, be understood from the perspective of wider hypotheses about the classification of beings and societies. It would be too easy to state that this condition, at least theoretically, has been a consequence of anthropological discourses. Since Turgot (who in the 1750s first classified languages and cultures according to "whether the peoples [are] hunters, shepherds, or husbandmen" [1913-1923, 1:172] and ultimately defined an ascending path from savagery to commercial societies), non-Western marginality has been a sign both of a possible absolute beginning and of a primitive foundation of conventional history. Rather than retracing an already too well-known evolutionary hallucination (Duchet, 1971; Hodgen, 1971), let us take a different angle by examining both the issues derived from a fifteenth-century painting and the allocation of an "African object" to nineteenth-century anthropology.

    Commenting upon *Las Meninas* of Velásquez, M. Foucault writes: "the painter is standing a little back from his canvas. He is glancing at his model; perhaps he is considering whether to add some finishing touch, though it is also possible that the first stroke has not yet been made . . ." (1973:3). The painter is at one side of the canvas working or meditating on how to depict his models. Once the painting is finished, it becomes both a given and a reflection

---

* V. Y. Mudimbe, *The Invention of Africa: Gnosis, Philosophy, and the Order of Knowledge* (Bloomington: Indiana University Press, 1988), pp. 6-12. (Some changes have been made in spelling.)

of what made it possible. And Foucault thinks that the order of *Las Meninas* seems to be an example of "a representation [which] undertakes to represent itself . . . in all its elements, with its images, the eyes to which it is offered, the faces it makes visible, the gestures that call it into being." Yet in the amazing complexity of this painting there is remarkable absence: "the person it resembles and the person in whose eyes it is only a resemblance" (Foucault, 1973:16).

Now let us consider Hans Burgkmair's painting *Exotic Tribe.* Is the painter sitting back contemplating his exotic models? How many? It is not even certain that a model is present in the room where Burgkmair is thinking about ways of subsuming particular versions of human beings. The year is 1508. Dürer is still alive. Burgkmair is by then a respected master of the new school of Augsburg he has founded. He would like to please the Fuggers and Welsers and has agreed to illustrate Bartolomäus Springer's book on his travels overseas (Kunst, 1967). He has carefully read Springer's diary, has probably studied some clumsy pencil or pen-and-ink sketches, and has decided to draw six pictures of "primitives."

The first picture of the series seems to represent a family. Let us imagine the painter at work. He has just read Springer's description of his voyage, and, possibly on the basis of some sketches, he is trying to create an image of blacks in "Gennea." Perhaps he has decided to use a model, presumably white but strongly built. The painter is staring at the pale body, imagining schemes to transform it into a black entity. The model has become a mirror through which the painter evaluates how the norms of similitude and his own creativity would impart both a human identity and a racial difference to his canvas. Perhaps the artist is already at work. Yet he has to stop regularly, walk around the model, leave the luminous space before the window, and retire into a discreet corner. His gaze addresses a point which is a question: how to superimpose the African characteristics described in Springer's narrative onto the norms of the Italian *contrapposto*? If he succeeds, the painting should be, in its originality, a celebration and a reminder of the natural link connecting human beings and, at the same time, an indication of racial or cultural differences. It should bear witness to the truth of similitudes, analogies, and possibly even the violence of antipathy. At any rate, Kunst notes that

> The nude African depicted from behind conforms to the classical rule of contraposto expressed in the compensatory balance of symmetrical parts of the body in movement: one shoulder leaning on one leg and the other, raised above the free leg. One guesses that this nude man was copied from a classic model to which the artist gave characteristics, jewelry and swords, of an exotic people still strongly attached to nature. (Kunst, 1967:19-20)

It is easy to dismiss my concern about similitude in this particular creative process. Am I not projecting a twentieth-century perspective onto the pictorial techniques of the early sixteenth century? The structure of figures is there in the first small painting, treated in a typical way. The fuss about similitude might just be, after all, only a contemporary hypothesis about the process of establishing links between beings and things from our present viewpoint. Yet it is possible to look for issues stemming from Burgkmair's representation. In effect, we can describe his artistic filiation and his dependence upon the classic ideals of the Renaissance (Kunst, 1967:20). We can also compare the principles of his technique with those apparent in some contemporary works directly or indirectly dealing with black figures, such as Erasmus Grasser's *Moor Dancers* (1480), Hieronymus Bosch's *Garden of Delights* (1500), *Katleen the Moor Woman* (1521) by Albrecht Dürer, and at the very end of the century, Cornelisz van Haarlem's *Batseba* (1594). Speculating about or analyzing the contrasts between white and black figures in these paintings, one could certainly search for a vision which refers to historically conventional explanations—for example, the sense of the characteristics and "the idea of design, that is to say, of expression by means of the pure disposition of contours and masses, and by the perfection and ordering of linear rhythm" (Fry, 1940:165). The complex play of colors in harmony and opposition, the order of shades between the white and the black, are obviously based on such intellectual and conscious references. But does not our understanding of the colorful economies of canvases refer, in a very insistent manner, to invisible traces?

The contrasts between black and white tell a story which probably duplicates a silent but powerful epistemological configuration. *Ex hypothesi* it might simply be a similitude interplay: "*Convenientia, aemulatio, analogy,* and *sympathy* tell us how the world must fold upon itself, duplicate itself, reflect itself, or form a chain with itself so that things can resemble one another. They tell us what the paths of similitude are and the directions they take; but not where it is, how one sees it, or by what mark it may be recognized" (Foucault, 1973:23-24).

Let us return to Burgkmair's finished painting. The three black figures— a boy, a man, a seated woman with a baby pressed to her breast—have the right proportions to one another and to the wider context. All are naked and have either bracelets around their arms or a string around their necks, clear signs that they belong to a "savage" universe (Kunst, 1967:20). The little boy is dancing, his oversized head turned toward the sky. At the center of the canvas, the man, presented in clear, strong lines, is staring at a faraway horizon, brandishing an arrow with his left hand and holding two other arrows in his right hand. He incarnates power, not only because he occupies the central place in the painting, but also because he is the most well-defined signifier in this scene. He is the locus defining the relationship between the boy at his left and the woman at his right, depicted with both a touch of hieratic sense and a slightly instinctual force. At the right, the woman with the baby is seated on a trunk. She seems to be staring pensively at the pelvic area of the man. The curves of her body are canonically executed.

The whole picture, in its simplicity and in the balanced rhythms of its lines, seems a truly charming and decorative painting. Yet what it really expresses is a discursive order. The structure of the figures, as well as the meaning of the nude bodies, proclaim the virtues of resemblances: in order to designate Springer's blacks, the painter has represented blackened whites. This was not rare during the sixteenth and the seventeenth centuries, as a great number of the drawings of the period reveal. That is the case for example, of the fifth picture in Filippo Pigafetta's 1591 edition of his *Relatione del Reame di Congo*, representing three Italianized African women, and that of the African king in the frontispiece of J. Ogilby's 1670 book on Africa. What is important in Burgkmair's painting, as well as in similar drawings, is their double representation.

The first, whose objective is to assimilate exotic bodies into sixteenth-century Italian painting methodology, reduces and neutralizes all differences into the sameness signified by the *white* norm, which, let us keep in mind, is more religious history than a simple cultural tradition. In concrete language this reference meant a "biblical solution to the problem of cultural differences [which] was regarded by most men as the best that reason and faith could propose" (Hodgen, 1971:254); that is, the same origin for all human beings, followed by geographical diffusion and racial and cultural diversification. And it was believed that the Bible stipulated that the African could only be the slave of his brethren.

There is another level, a more discreet one. It establishes a second representation that unites through similitude and eventually articulates distinctions and separations, thus classifying types of identities. Briefly, I can say that in Burgkmair's painting there are two representational activities: on the one hand, signs of an epistemological order which, silently but imperatively, indicate the processes of integrating and differentiating figures within the normative sameness; on the other hand, the excellence of an exotic picture that creates a cultural distance, thanks to an accumulation of accidental differences, namely, nakedness, blackness, curly hair, bracelets, and strings of pearls.

In their arrangements, these differences are pertinent signs. Because of the fundamental order which they reveal, and to which they bear witness, the virtues of resemblance erase physical and cultural variations, while maintaining and positing surface differences as meaningful of human complexity. Diego Velásquez's *Juan de Pareja* (1648) still actualizes this integrating reference, whereas major paintings such as Peter Paul Rubens's *Study of Four Blacks' Heads* (1620), Rembrandt's *Two Negroes* (1697), and Hyacinthe Rigaud's *Young Black* (1697) explicitly express and relate to another order. A new epistemological foundation was then functioning in the West. Theories of diversification of beings, as well as classificatory tables, explain the origins of constructing taxonomies and their objectives (Foucault, 1973:125-65). The framework of Linnaeus's *Systema Naturae* (1735) is just one of the paradigmatic classifications of species and varieties of *Homo Sapiens (europaeus, asiaticus, americanus, afer)* distinguished according to physical and temperamental characteristics (Count, 1950:355). It would be too easy to link it, *upstream,* to discursive formations about the great chain of beings and its hierarchy, and, *downstream,* first to Blumenbach's craniology and, second, to the general anti-African bias of the philosophical and scientific literature of the eighteenth and nineteenth centuries (Lyons, 1975:24-85).

Two very different discursive formations—the discovery of African art and the constitution of the object of African Studies, that is, the "invention" of Africanism as a scientific discipline—can illustrate the differentiating efficiency of such general classifying devices as pattern of reality, designation, arrangement, structure, and character. I have already suggested that resemblance has been pushed out of Rubens's, Rembrandt's, and Rigaud's perceptions of blacks. What is there, given in detailed description, might be considered as a naming and an analysis of an alterity and refers to a new epistemological ordering: a theory of understanding and looking at signs in terms of "the arrangement of identities and differences into ordered tables" (Foucault, 1973:72).

Portuguese sailors brought to Europe the first *feitiços,* African objects supposedly having mysterious powers, in the late fifteenth century. One finds them mostly in well-organized curio cabinets, along with Indian tomahawks or arrows, Egyptian artifacts, and Siamese drums. Some interpreters do consider them to be signs of a state of barbarism (Hodgen, 1971:162-203). Yet one can firmly state that more frequently they are seen as simple curiosities brought back in accordance with the tenth task of the traveler-observer in the table of Varenius's *Geographia generalis* (1650): to consider "famous Men, Artificers, and Inventions of the Natives of all countries" (Hodgen, 1971:167-68). On the whole, these objects are culturally neutral. Because of their shapes and styles, sometimes a bit terrifying, they account for the mysterious diversity of the Same (Bal, 1963:67). It is not until the eighteenth century that, as strange and "ugly" artifacts, they really enter into the frame of African art.

The black continent was still on the maps a *terra incognita,* but its peoples and their material productions were more familiar to travelers, students of the human species, merchants, and European states. From the beginning of the eighteenth century, there had been a tremendous increase in the slave trade and a profitable trans-Atlantic economy which involved most of the Western countries. In West Africa, Dahomey was a powerful commercial partner of European traders. The Ashanti empire expanded, dominating the Akans and the Oyo kingdom further to the east and increasing its power as it grew. Freed slaves and impoverished Africans were settled by European-sponsored organizations in present-day Sierra Leone. On the east coast, in 1729, Africans expelled the Portuguese from their fortresses in the northern region of Mozambique; and down south, in 1770, there was the first war between Dutch immigrants and Bantus. Two years later, James Bruce, traveling from North to Central Africa, reached the source of the White Nile in the very year that Chief Justice Mansfield declared in England that slavery was against the law (Verger, 1968).

In this atmosphere of intense and violent exchanges, *feitiços* became symbols of African art. They were viewed as primitive, simple, childish, and nonsensical. Mary H. Kingsley, at the beginning of this century, summed it up with an axiomatic evaluation: "The African has never made an even fourteenth-rate piece of cloth or pottery" (Kingsley, 1965:669). It seems to me that "a process of aesthetization" (Baudrillard, 1972) took place from the eighteenth century onward. What is called savage or primitive art covers a wide range of objects introduced by the contact between African and European during the intensified slave trade into the classifying frame of the eighteenth century. These objects, which perhaps are not art at all in their "native context," become art by being given simultaneously an aesthetic character and a potentiality for producing and reproducing other artistic forms. Taken in their initial function and significance, might they have created a radical *mise en perspective* of the Western culture wedded to classifications (Baudrillard, 1972)? That is precisely an impossibility. Arts are based on criteria, and it is difficult to imagine that these standards can emerge from outside the "power-knowledge" field of a given culture, a field which, at a historical period, establishes its artistic bible. Therefore it is obvious that fetishes and other "primitive" pieces of art are wonderful because their structure, character, and arrangement demand a designation (Laude, 1979; Wassing, 1969). They are "savage" in terms of the evolutionary chain of being and culture, which establishes a correspondence between advancement in the civilizing process and artistic creativity, as well as intellectual achievements.

At this point, paradoxically, it is a celebration of the African craftsmanship which confirms my analysis. Admiring the beauty of a "Negro sculpture," the late R. Fry was puzzled:

> It is curious that a people who produced such great artists did not produce also a culture in our sense of the word. This shows that two factors are necessary to produce the cultures which distinguish civilised peoples. There must be, of course, the creative artist, but there must also be the power of conscious critical appreciation and comparison. (Fry, 1940:90-91)

Fry is, I am afraid, utterly wrong. The two factors do not and cannot explicate types of cultures. They only constitute a basis for the production of art and its possible modifications over time (see Laude, 1979; Delange, 1967). They cannot completely account for the internal patterns of cultures. At any rate, it is the "power-knowledge" of an epistemological field which makes possible a domineering or humbled culture. From this perspective, the point that Fry makes immediately after has great sense: "It is likely enough that the Negro artist, although capable of . . . profound imaginative understanding of form, would accept our cheapest illusionist art with humble enthusiasm" (1940:91).

My thesis is confirmed, almost *ad absurdum*, by B. Jules-Rosette's study of contemporary African tourist art. She defines this art as an "art produced locally for consumption by outsiders" (1984:9) and strongly insists on the paradoxical interaction between its origin and its destination, that is, its production and its consumption:

> Although the concept of the tourist art system emphasizes how artists and their audiences perceive images and convert them into economic commodities, it does not neglect the expressive components of the interaction. Within the system, both images and actual objects constitute sources of exchange between producers and consumers. Although artists have a definite impression of the tourist audience, consumers often have little direct contact with the artists. (Jules-Rosette, 1984:10)

This concept of tourist art implies, in principle, a critique of the classical understanding of art. It also explicitly means a relativization of what the author calls "assumptions about the manner and quality of tourist art productions"; namely, its mass production character, the relative inexperience of present-day craftspeople, the collectivization in the artistic production, and the dominance of consumer demand over artistic creativity.

A limpid argument upholds the thesis of the study. Tourist art is both a symbolic and an economic exchange. This can be understood, according to Jules-Rosette, by reference to three models: First, the traditional African arts that have ceremonial and social significance may and do become objects produced primarily for external trade. Second, there are, in the very being of tourist art, signs of a major tension existing between "folk culture" and *"haute culture."* Or, as Jules-Rosette puts it: "Folk culture is implicitly contrasted with something else—*haute culture*. . . . There is an inherent tension and asymmetry between the ideals of high culture and the profit motives and new reproductive technologies that sustain the growth of the market of popular cultures" (1984:23). As to the horizons of this artistic production, Jules-Rosette insists on the fact of Western reading of African creativity and its propositions for innovations in African workshops.

> The international tourist art market depends upon the Western demand for "exotic" souvenir and gift items and the assumption that they should be procured abroad. The artists and craftspeople utilize this demand as a stimulus for creating new ideas and technologies to meet the needs of the expanding market. (Jules-Rosette, 1984:192)

TRINH T. MINH-HA

*Woman, Native, Other**

Freedom and the Masses

The notion of *art engagé* as defined by Jean-Paul Sartre, an influential apologist for socially effective literature, continues to grow and to circulate among contemporary engaged writers. It is easy to find parallels (and it is often directly quoted) in Third World literary discourses. "A free man addressing free men," the Sartrian writer "has only one subject—freedom." He writes to "appeal to the reader's freedom to collaborate in the production of his work" and paints the world "only so that free men may feel their freedom as they face it." The function of literary art, in other words, must be to remind us of that freedom and to defend it. Made to serve a political purpose, literature thus places itself within the context of the proletarian fight, while the writer frees himself from his dependence on elites—or in a wider sense, from any privilege—and creates, so to speak, an art for an unrestricted public known as "art for the masses." From the chain of notions dear to Sartre—choice, responsibility, contingency, situation, motive, reason, being, doing, having—two notions are set forth here as being most relevant to Third World engaged literary theories: freedom and the masses. What is freedom in writing? And what can writing-for-the-masses be? Reflecting on being a writer, "female, black, and free," Margaret Walker, for example, defines freedom as "a philosophical state of mind and existence." She proudly affirms:

---

* Trinh T. Minh-ha, *Woman, Native, Other: Writing Postcoloniality and Feminism* (Bloomington: Indiana University Press, 1989), pp. 3-5, 9, 28-39, 97-101. (Illustrations and notes omitted.)

> My entire career in writing . . . is determined by these immutable facts of my
> human condition. . . .
> Writing is my life, but it is an avocation nobody can buy. In this respect I believe
> I am a free agent, stupid perhaps, but *me* and still free. . . .
> The writer is still in the avant-garde for Truth and Justice, for Freedom, Peace,
> and Human Dignity. . . . Her place, let us be reminded, is anywhere she chooses
> to be, doing what she has to do, creating, healing, and always being herself.

These lines agree perfectly with Sartre's ideal of liberty. They may be said to
echo his concepts of choice and responsibility—according to which each person, being an absolute choice of self, an absolute emergence at an absolute
date, must assume her/his situation with the proud consciousness of being the
author of it. (For one is nothing but this "being-in-situation" that is the total
contingency of the world, of one's birth, past, and environment, and of the
fact of one's fellow wo/man.) By its own rationale, such a sense of responsibility (attributed to the lucid, conscientious, successful man of action) renders
the relationship between freedom and commitment particularly problematic.
Is it not, indeed, always in the name of freedom that My freedom hastens to
stamp out those of others? Is it not also in the name of the masses that My personality bestirs itself to impersonalize those of my fellow wo/men? Do the
masses become masses by themselves? Or are they the result of a theoretical
and practical operation of "massification"? From where onward can one say of
a "free" work of art that it is written for the infinite numbers which constitute
the masses and not merely for a definite public stratum of society?

For the People, By the People, and From the People

Like all stereotypical notions, the notion of the masses has both an upgrading
connotation and a degrading one. One often speaks of the masses as one
speaks of the people, magnifying thereby their number, their strength, their
mission. One invokes them and pretends to write on their behalf when one
wishes to give weight to one's undertaking or to justify it. The Guilt mentioned earlier is always lurking below the surface. Yet to oppose the masses to
the elite is already to imply that those forming the masses are regarded as an
aggregate of average persons condemned by their lack of personality or by
their dim individualities to stay with the herd, to be docile and anonymous.
Thus the notion of "art *for* the masses" supposes not only a split between the
artist and her/his audience—the spectator-consumer—but also a passivity on
the part of the latter. For art here is not attributed to the masses; it is ascribed
to the active few, whose role is precisely to produce *for* the great numbers.
This means that despite the shift of emphasis the elite-versus-masses opposition remains intact. In fact it must remain so, basically unchallenged, if it is to
serve a conservative political and ideological purpose—in other words, if (what
is defined as) "art" is to exist at all. One of the functions of this "art for the
masses" is, naturally, to contrast with the other, higher "art for the elite,"
and thereby to enforce its elitist values. The wider the distance between the

two, the firmer the stand of conservative art. One can no longer let oneself be deceived by concepts that oppose the artist or the intellectual to the masses and deal with them as with two incompatible entities. Criticisms arising from or dwelling on such a *myth* are, indeed, quite commonly leveled against innovators and more often used as tools of intimidation than as reminders of social interdependency. It is perhaps with this perspective in mind that one may better understand the variants of Third World literary discourse, which claims not exactly an "art for the masses," but an "art for the people, by the people, and from the people." In an article on "Le Poète noir et son peuple" (The Black Poet and His People), for example, Jacques Rabemananjara virulently criticized Occidental poets for spending their existence indulging in aesthetic refinements and subtleties that bear no relation to their peoples' concerns and aspirations, that are merely sterile intellectual delights. The sense of dignity, Rabemananjara said, forbids black Orpheus to go in for the cult of art for art's sake. Inspirer inspired by his people, the poet has to play the difficult role of being simultaneously the torch lighting the way for his fellowmen and their loyal interpreter. "He is more than their spokesman: he is their voice": his noble mission entitles him to be "not only the messenger, but the very message of his people." The concept of a popular and functional art is here poised against that of an intellectual and aesthetic one. A justified regression? A shift of emphasis again? Or an attempt at fusion of the self and the other, of art, ideology, and life? . . .

One may say of art for art's sake in general that it is itself a reaction against the bourgeois "functional" attitude of mind which sees in the acquisition of art the highest, purest form of consumption. By making explicit the gratuitousness of their works, artists show contempt for their wealthy customers, whose purchasing power allows them to subvert art in its subversiveness, reducing it to a mere commodity or a service. As a reaction, however, art for art's sake is bound to be "two-dimensional"—"one response to one stimulus" (Mphahlele)—and, therefore, to meet with no success among writers of the Third World. "I cannot imagine," says Wole Soyinka, "that our 'authentic black innocent' would ever have permitted himself to be manipulated into the false position of countering one pernicious Manicheism with another." An art that claims to be at the same time sender and bearer of a message, to serve the people and "to come off the street" (Cade Bambara), should then be altogether "functional, collective, and committing or committed" (Karenga). The reasoning circle closes on the notion of commitment, which again emerges, fraught with questions. . . .

Writing Woman

1) THE PRIEST-GOD SCHEME. Writing in the feminine. And on a colored sky. How do you inscribe difference without bursting into a series of euphoric narcissistic accounts of yourself and your own kind? Without indulging in a marketable romanticism or in a naive whining about your condition? In other

words, how do you forget without annihilating? Between the twin chasms of navel-gazing and navel-erasing, the ground is narrow and slippery. None of us can pride ourselves on being sure-footed there. Feminism can be iconoclastic, and all the more so when it calls itself Third World. But we have all let ourselves be infected with the leprosy of egotism, which remains the most difficult disease to cure, for what egotists, like lepers, inevitably undergo is a *loss of feeling* and are consequently apt to injure themselves without realizing it. I can let neither light nor air enter me when I close myself up and exist as a crystallized I, be this I feminine or masculine, female or male. Woman (with capital W) may therefore kill women if She loses the contact and speaks of Herself only according to what She wants to hear about Herself. A distinction needs to be made between "Write yourself. Write your body" and write about yourself, your body, your inner life, your fears, inhibitions, desires, and pleasures. The first refers to a scriptive act—the emergence of a writing-self—the second, to a consolidation of writing from the self. The two often overlap, but the type that consistently inundates the market is without doubt the second one: write-about biographies or novels, through whose stories the woman author constitutes an identity. A woman's room, despite its new seductive paneling, can become a prison as soon as it takes on the appearance of a lady's room (masculine notion of femininity) or a female's room (male's alter ego). The danger in going "the woman's way" is precisely that we may stop midway and limit ourselves to a series of reactions: instead of walking on, we are content with opposing woman('s emotion) to man('s abstraction), personal experience and anecdotes to impersonal invention and theory, in other words, with assuming the Quiller-Couch Syndrome. This is, obviously, not to say that the inner lives of women are of no interest nor that works dealing with women's feelings in a drawing room are less important than those dealing with war. No situation proves too small or too insignificant for a writer, since there is truly no narrow experience, only narrow representation. And narrow representation starts with the necessity of "I am God" or "I am Goddess" to create. The image of God alone making sky, earth, sea, and beings, transposed into writing, has led many of us to believe, as mentioned earlier, that the author exists *before* her/his own book, not simultaneously *with* it. The book perceived as an isolated materialization of something that precedes and exceeds it (the author's life, her/his thought or passion) is therefore bound to be a finished product, one whose content is expected to be entirely predetermined but whose form can always be ameliorated and further polished according to the ruling ideology of the "well written." Laying emphasis on the prestige of the individual and on the search for an explanation of the work in the wo/man who produces it (thereby perpetuating the myth of the original writer), literature remains completely dominated by the sovereignty of the author. On the one hand, the castrating objectivism of the "universal" writer; on the other hand, the obsessive personalism of the "singular" writer. Who is S/He? How does s/he create? How true, how authentic is her/his creation? How much of her/his real self has s/he inserted in her/his work? Writing, for the majority

of us who call ourselves writers, still consists of "expressing" the exalted emotions related to the act of creating and either appropriating language to ourselves or ascribing it to a subject who is more or less a reflection of ourselves.
The author's relation of antecedence, dependence, and possession to her/his
work resembles that of a mother/father to her/his child. Like father, like
son. Let us make man in our image, says the Bible. The writer is necessarily
either God or Priest. As long as the belief in the sacred origin of writing and
the religious principle of hidden meanings prevail, there will be a need for
"veracious" interpretation and commentary. The Priest's role is to transcribe
and/or explain as truthfully as possible God's confiding voice. The closer to
this voice s/he claims to stand, the more weight her/his vision or opinion is
likely to carry. Holy inspiration or faithful elucidation. Between critic and
author, the relationship is the same as between author and God or author and
imagination. Here the formula reads: The task of criticism is to bring to light
the enigmatic content of a work by reestablishing the ties between it and its
author or reconstituting the latter's thought and experience through her/his
works. God and Priest form an inseparable pair; the two often merge since the
Priest represents God and rarely hesitates to assert her/his claim to God's *message*. Thus, no matter how novel her work may appear to be, the woman who
writes about herself/others from the standpoint of the-one-who-knows delib-
erately/involuntarily carries on the conventions of the Priest-God scheme.
Omniscient and omnipresent, she is everywhere and understands everything
at the same time; she follows her own or her characters' outer expression
and inner conscience simultaneously; she sees the present, past, and future of
all events; and, above all, she has the power to dissolve the opacity of life.
Eager to create a meaningful world and/or to unveil her ignored/censored
deeper self, she adopts a series of strategies liable to ensure a transparency of
form through which content, intelligibly constructed, can travel unhindered.
Or she plays a hide-and-seek game with her readers, thus preserving the image
of the misunderstood genius and leaving the task of guessing-rediscovering-
clarifying to the critic. In many cases, she labors at confiding/confessing herself or at cutting herself sparingly into fragments and distributing them
amongst her characters, with whom the readers may in their turn identify
themselves. Charged with intentionality, writing is therefore disclosing (a
secret), and reading is believing. The writer as a personified releaser of meaning produces envelopes whose more or less brilliant colors serve to decorate
"the (theological) message." "Lost lady! Gentle fighter!" She sees God woman-
shaped, because she reacts when she is told "And if they will learn anything let
them ask their husbands at home: for it is a shame for women to speak in the
church" (I Corinthians 14:35).

2) "AND I GROW YOUNGER AS I LEAVE MY ME BEHIND." The to-and-fro movement
between the written woman and the writing woman is an endless one. "The
woman took a train/away away from herself, . . . and I/grow younger as I
leave/my me behind," Dilys Laing wrote, "They said: You took her with

you/and brought her back again./You look sick. Welcome home." Yes, welcome home, for she has the impudence to disbelieve, to live before god. And after. She is "woman enough" to slip out of herself and go, then to return almost without self and without denying the going. Writing, in a way, is listening to the others' language and reading with the others' eyes. The more ears I am able to hear with, the farther I see the plurality of meaning and the less I lend myself to the illusion of a single message. I say I write when I leave speech, when I lose my grip on it and let it make its way on its own. I am there only to provide it with a passageway. Why view these aspects of an individual which we imply in the term "writer" or "author" as projections of an isolated self and not of our common way of handling texts? For writing, like a game that defies its own rules, is an ongoing practice that may be said to be concerned, not with inserting a "me" into language, but with creating an opening where the "me" disappears while "I" endlessly come and go, as the nature of language requires. To confer an Author on a text is to close the writing. Eureka! It makes sense! *This is it!* I hold the key to the puzzle! Fear and seek. Fear and seek. The danger we fear most is forgetting to fear. Seek and lose. Lose, freely. When you are silent, it speaks; when you speak, it is silent. Writing is born when the writer is no longer. "In her own name she would have died of asphyxia. But once emerged from the membrane of self, spread out unto all the ways, coming to dwell at the brink of all sources." The greatest strength, Hélène Cixous further wrote, is "that of being no one, like a rose, of being pure joy before all naming. . . . How does the poet become self-strange to the point of the absolute innocence? Let herself be borne before thought, in thinking in preparation. . . . To become as simple as an apple, just like the goodness of an apple. . . . I am not ripe enough for innocence. Or yet too covered, too armed, too defended." I am so much that nothing can enter me or pass through me. I struggle, I resist, and I am filled with my own self. The "personal" may liberate as it may enslave. We set it up against "impersonal" as if the two were mutually exclusive of each other, then start asserting that emphasis on the personal, the intimate, and the domestic has always been determining to the Women's Movement, hence the importance, for instance, of the personal diary form, which remains an effective means of self-expression for women to whom other avenues are often closed. True, but looking at the diary exclusively as a means of self-expression is already a distortion and a confinement. When I say I die when writing is or that I die to live, I am not referring to the opposition of life and death. We create the dualism, not realizing that death, like life, is a process. The moment I am born, I enter the realm of death. Life and death are together one process, and we are dying every moment. Writing so as not to die, we hear. Or so as to die? Every moment, I/i ask. To disarm death? Or to kill immortality? That composite, inessential space where identity gives way to difference. She speaks about it as "images that shimmer around the edges," and she is lying low to let them develop. *She*, on the other hand, recalls it "as a voice fashioned out of shining darkness" and feels attracted toward "the tender light of an apple in the

night." She insists: "It tells you. You don't tell it."—"The picture tells you how
to arrange the words and the arrangement of the words tells you, or tells
me, what's going on in the picture." And *she* further specifies "their being glis-
tened, came to pass, I came to pass, beside them, in humility." Gleaming in
the dark. Beware! This is it again, may be it. The Revelation, the Vision, the
secret, the sacred origin of writing, that Holy Inspiration. *Not*-me should not
hide or yield to a Higher Me, for the question involved is *not* that of obliterating the self for a purer truth—*non*-self, hence *no* self to die. Diana Chang
wrote: "it wrote itself through me. I was driven and I drove the story
onward. . . . Things I was not aware, I knew . . . it was her voice which started
speaking through me. . . . I feel *she* wrote the novel. She knows what it means
to have once been an actress, not I." In her statement I read the anteriority of
language to the writer. That which emerges from silence may be revealing, but
it is revealing in the sense that language is always older than me. Never original, "me" grows indefinitely on ready-mades, which are themselves explainable
only through other ready-mades. Spontaneity-personality in such a context
does not guarantee more authenticity than stereotypy. Writing as an inconsequential process of sameness/otherness is ceaselessly re-breaking and re-
weaving patterns of ready-mades. The written bears the written to infinity.

3) "WRITE YOUR BODY." It wrote itself through me. "Women must write through
their bodies." Must not let themselves be driven away from their bodies. Must
thoroughly rethink the body to re-appropriate femininity. Must not however
exalt the body, not favor any of its parts formerly forbidden. Must perceive it
in its integrity. Must and must-nots, their absolution and power. When armors
and defense mechanisms are removed, when new awareness of life is brought
into previously deadened areas of the body, women begin to experience writ-
ing/the world differently. This is exciting and also very scary. For it takes
time to be able to tolerate greater aliveness. Hence the recurrence of musts
and must-nots. As soon as a barrier is destroyed, another is immediately
erected. Call it reform or expansion. Or else, well-defined liberation revolution. Closure and openness, again, are one ongoing process: we do not *have*
bodies, we *are* our bodies, and we are ourselves while being the world. Who
can endure constant open-endedness? Who can keep on living completely
exposed? We write—think and feel—(with) our entire bodies rather than only
(with) our minds or hearts. It is a perversion to consider thought the product
of one specialized organ, the brain, and feeling, that of the heart. The past
convention was that we desire because we are incomplete, that we are always
searching for that other missing half. More recently, we no longer desire-
because, we simply desire, and we desire as we are. "I am a being of desire,
therefore a being of words," said Nicole Brossard, "a being who looks for
her body and looks for the body of the other: for me, this is the whole history
of writing." Gathering the fragments of a divided, repressed body and reaching out to the other does not necessarily imply a lack or a deficiency. In writing themselves, women have attempted to render noisy and audible all that

had been silenced in phallocentric discourse. "Your body must be heard," Hélène Cixous insists, "[Women] must invent the impregnable language that will wreck partitions, classes and rhetorics, regulations and codes." Touch me and let me touch you, for the private is political. Language wavers with desire. It is "the language of my entrails," a skin with which I caress and feel the other, a body capable of receiving as well as giving: nurturing and pro-creating. Let it enter and let it go; writing myself into existence also means emptying myself of all that I can empty out—all that constitutes Old Sponta-neous/Premeditated Me—without ceasing from being. "Every woman is the woman of all women" (Clarice Lispector). Taking in any voice that goes through me, I/i will answer every time someone says: I. One woman within another, eternally. "Writing as a woman. I am becoming more and more aware of this," notes Anaïs Nin, "All that happens in the real womb, not in the womb fabricated by man as a substitute . . . woman's creation far from being like man's must be exactly like her creation of children, that is it must come out of her own blood, englobed by her womb, nourished by her own milk. It must be a human creation, of flesh, it must be different from man's abstrac-tions." Man is not content with referring to his creation as to his child, he is also keen on appropriating the life-giving act of childbearing. Images of men "in labor" and "giving birth" to poems, essays, and books abound in literature. Such an encroachment on women's domain has been considered natural, for the writer is said to be either genderless or bisexual. He is able to chat with both man's and woman's voices. This is how the womb is fabricated. Women began to be spoken of as if they were wombs on two feet when the fetus was described as a citizen, the womb was declared state property, legislation was passed to control it, and midwifery was kept under continual medical super-vision—in other words, when women were denied the right to create. Or not to create. With their bodies. "All that happens in the real womb": writing as an "intrinsic" child/birth process takes on different qualities in women's contexts. No man claims to speak from the womb, women do. Their site of fertilization, they often insist, is the womb, not the mind. Their inner gestation is in the womb, not in the mind. The mind is therefore no longer opposed to the heart; it is, rather, perceived as part of the womb, being "englobed by it." Men name "womb" to separate a part of woman from woman (to separate it from the rest that forms her: body and mind), making it possible to lay legal claim to it. By doing so, they create their own contradictions and come round to identifying her with their fabrication: a specialized, infant-producing organ. Women use "womb" to re-appropriate it and re-unite (or re-differ) them-selves, their bodies, their places of production. This may simply mean beating the master at his own game. But it may also mean asserting difference on differences. In the first case, the question is chiefly that of erecting inverted images and defying prohibitions. Annie Leclerc wrote:

> Let me first tell you where I get what I'm saying from, I get it from me, woman, and from my woman's belly. . . . Who would have told me, will I ever be able to

tell, from what words shall I weave the bewildering happiness of pregnancy, the very rending, overwhelming happiness of giving birth. . . .

So much the worst for him, I will have to speak of the joys of my sex, no, no, not the joys of my mind, virtue or feminine sensitivity, the joys of my woman's belly, my woman's vagina, my woman's breasts, sumptuous joys of which you have no idea at all.

I will have to speak of them since it is only from them that a new, woman speech will be born.

We will have to divulge what you have so relentlessly put in solitary confinement, for that is what all our other repressions build themselves upon.

Woman's writing becomes "organic writing," "nurturing-writing" *(nourri-criture)*, resisting separation. It becomes a "connoting material," a "kneading dough," a "linguistic flesh." And it draws its corporeal fluidity from images of water— a water from the source, a deep, subterranean water that trickles in the womb, a meandering river, a flow of life, of words running over or slowly dripping down the pages. This keeping-alive and life-giving water exists simultaneously as the writer's ink, the mother's milk, the woman's blood and menstruation. Logical backlash? An eye for an eye, a tooth for a tooth. Not quite, it seems. A woman's ink of blood for a man's ink of semen (an image found, for example, in Jacques Derrida's hymeneal fable: a sexual union in which the pen writes its in/dis/semination in the always folded/never single space of the hymen). In the second case—that of asserting difference on differences—the question of writing (as a) woman is brought a step further. Liquid/ocean associated with woman/mother is not just a facile play on words inherited from nineteenth-century Romantics (*mer-mère* in French). Motherhood as lived by woman often has little to do with motherhood as experienced by men. The mother cannot be reduced to the mother-hen, the wet-nurse, the year-round cook, the family maid, or the clutching, fear-inspiring matron. Mother of God, of all wo/mankind, she is role-free, non-Name, a force that refuses to be fragmented but suffocates codes (Cixous). In her maternal love, she is neither possessed nor possessive, neither binding nor detached nor neutral. For a life to maintain another life, the touch has to be infinitely delicate: precise, attentive, and swift, so as not to pull, track, rush, crush or smother. Bruised, half-alive, or dead is often the fate of what comes within the masculine grip. Woman, as Cixous defines her, is a whole—"whole composed of parts that are wholes"— through which language is born over and over again. (The One is the All and the All is the One; and yet the One remains the One and the All the All. Not two, not One either. This is what Zen has been repeating for centuries.) To the classic conception of bisexuality, the self-effacing, merger-type of bisexuality, Cixous opposes "The *other sexuality* . . . that is, each one's location in self (*repérage en soi*) of the presence—variously manifest and insistent according to each person, male or female—or both sexes, nonexclusion either of the difference or of one sex, and, from this 'self-permission,' multiplication of the effects of the inscription of desire, over all parts of my body and the other body." The notion of "bisexual, hence neuter" writing together with the fantasy of a "total" being are concepts that many men have actively promoted to do away with differentiation. Androgyny is another name for such a co-optation. Saying that a great mind is androgynous (and *God knows* how many times we have heard this line—supposedly from Coleridge—and in how many disguises it appears) is equivalent to saying that "the mind has no sex" (also read "no gender"). In the salvation theme of androgyny, the male is still seen as the active power of generation and the female as the passive one (a defective male, due to the absence of androgen). Thus Janice Raymond suggests as a substitute the word "integrity"; she expands it and redefines it as "an unfolding process of becoming. It contains within itself an insatiable generativeness, that is, a compulsion to reproduce itself in every diverse fashion." In every diverse fashion . . . Laying claim to the specificity of women's sexuality and the rights pertaining to it is a step we have to go through in order to make ourselves heard; in order to beat the master at his own game. But reducing everything to the order of sex does not, obviously, allow us to depart from a discourse directed within the apparatuses of sexuality. Writing does not translate bisexuality. It (does not express language but) fares across it. . . .

Third World?

To survive, "Third World" must necessarily have negative *and* positive connotations: negative when viewed in a vertical ranking system—"underdeveloped" compared to over-industrialized, "underprivileged" within the already Second sex—and positive when understood sociopolitically as a subversive, "non-aligned" force. Whether "Third World" sounds negative or positive also depends on *who* uses it. Coming from you Westerners, the word can hardly mean the same as when it comes from Us members of the Third World. Quite predictably, you/we who condemn it most are both we who buy in and they who deny any participation in the bourgeois mentality of the West. For it was in the context of such mentality that "Third World" stood out as a new semantic finding to designate what was known as "the savages" before the Independences. Today, hegemony is much more subtle, much more pernicious than the form of blatant racism once exercised by the colonial West. I/i always find myself asking, in this one-dimensional society, where I/i should draw the line between tracking down the oppressive mechanisms of the system and aiding their spread. "Third World" commonly refers to those states in Africa, Asia and Latin America which called themselves "non-aligned," that is to say, affiliated with neither the Western (capitalist) nor the Eastern (communist) power blocs. Thus, if "Third World" is often rejected for its judged-to-be-derogative connotations, it is not so much because of the hierarchical, first-second-third order implied, as some invariably repeat, but because of the growing threat "Third World" consistently presents to the Western bloc the last few decades. The emergence of repressed voices into the worldwide political arena has already prompted her (Julia Kristeva) to ask: "How will the West greet the awakening of the 'third world' as the Chinese call it? Can we [Westerners] participate, actively and lucidly, in this awakening when the center of the planet is in the process of moving toward the East?" Exploited, looked down upon, and lumped together in a convenient term that denies their individualities, a group of "poor" (nations), having once sided with neither of the dominating forces, has slowly learned to turn this denial to the best account. "The Third World to Third World peoples" thus becomes an empowering tool, and one which politically includes all non-whites in their solidarist struggle against all forms of Western dominance. And since "Third World" now refers to more than the geographically and economically determined nations of the "South" (versus "North"), since the term comprises such "developed" countries as Japan and those which have opted for socialist reconstruction of their system (China, Cuba, Ethiopia, Angola, Mozambique) as well as those which have favored a capitalist mode of development (Nigeria, India, Brazil), there no longer exists such a thing as a unified unaligned Third World bloc. Moreover, Third World has moved West (or North, depending on where the dividing line falls) and has expanded so as to include even the remote parts of the First World. What is at stake is not only the hegemony of Western cultures, but also their identities as unified cultures. Third World dwells on diversity; so does First World. This is our strength and our misery. The West is painfully made to realize the existence of a Third World in the First World, and vice versa. The Master is bound to recognize that His Culture is not as homogeneous, as monolithic as He believed it to be. He discovers, with much reluctance, He is just an other among others.

Thus, whenever it is a question of "Third World women" or, more disquietingly, of "Third World Women in the U.S.," the reaction provoked among many whites almost never fails to be that of annoyance, irritation, or vexation. "Why Third World in the U.S.?" they say angrily; "You mean those who still have relatives in South East Asia?" "Third World! I don't understand how one can use such a term, it doesn't mean anything." Or even better, "Why use such a term to defeat yourself?" Alternatives like "Western" and "non-Western" or "Euro-American" and "non-Euro-American" may sound a bit less charged, but they are certainly neither neutral nor satisfactory, for they still take the dominant group as point of reference, and they reflect well the West's ideology of dominance (it is as if we were to use the term "non-Afro-Asian," for example, to designate all white peoples). More recently, we have been hearing of the Fourth World which, we are told, "is a world populated by indigenous people who still continue to bear a spiritual relationship to their traditional lands." The colonialist creed "Divide and Conquer" is here again, alive and well. Often ill at ease with the outspoken educated natives who represent the Third World in debates and paternalistically scornful of those who remain reserved, the dominant thus decides to weaken this term of solidarity, both by invalidating it as empowering tool and by inciting divisiveness within the Third World—a Third World within the Third World. Aggressive Third World (educated "savages") with its awareness and resistance to domination must therefore be classified apart from gentle Fourth World (uneducated "savages"). Every unaligned voice should necessarily/consequently be either a personal or a minority voice. The (impersonal) majority, as logic dictates, has to be the (aligned) dominant.

> It is, apparently, inconvenient, if not downright mind stretching [notes Alice Walker], for white women scholars to think of black women as women, perhaps because "woman" (like "man" among white males) is a name they are claiming for themselves, and themselves alone. Racism decrees that if they are now women (years ago they were ladies, but fashions change) then black women must, perforce, be something else. (While they were "ladies" black women could be women and so on.)

Another revealing example of this separatist majority mentality is the story Walker relates of an exhibit of women painters at the Brooklyn Museum: when asked "Are there no black women painters represented here?" (none of them is, apparently), a white woman feminist simply replies "It's a *women's exhibit!*" Different historical contexts, different semantic contents . . .

"Woman" and the Subtle Power of Linguistic Exclusion

What is *woman*? Long ago, during one of the forceful speeches she delivered in defense of her people, Sojourner Truth was asked by a threatened white doctor in the audience to prove to all those present that she was truly a woman:

> "There are those among us," he began in a tone characteristic of institutional training, "who question whether or not you are a woman. Some feel that maybe you are a man in a woman's disguise. To satisfy our curiosity, why don't you show your breasts to the women [sic] in this audience?"

It seemed, indeed, profoundly puzzling for this man-child doctor's mind to see the Woman (or Breasts) in someone who had "never been helped into carriages, lifted over ditches, nor given the best places everywhere," who had "plowed, and planted, and gathered into barns," and who, beyond measure, triumphantly affirmed elsewhere: "Look at me! Look at my arm! . . . and no man could head me—and *ar'nt I a woman!*" Definitions of *"woman," "woman-hood," "femininity," "femaleness,"* and, more recently, of "female identity" have brought about the arrogance of such a sham anatomical curiosity—whose needs must be "satisfied"—and the legitimation of a shamelessly dehumanizing form of Indiscretion. Difference reduced to sexual identity is thus posited to justify and conceal exploitation. The Body, the most visible difference between men and women, the only one to offer a secure ground for those who seek the permanent, the feminine "nature" and "essence," remains thereby the safest basis for racist and sexist ideologies. The two merging themes of Otherness and the Identity-Body are precisely what Simone de Beauvoir discussed at length in *The Second Sex*, and continued until the time of her death to argue in the French journal she edited, *Questions Féministes*. The lead article written by the Editorial Collective under the title of "Variations on Common Themes" explains the purpose of the journal—to destroy the notion of differences between the sexes, "which gives a shape and a base to the concept of 'woman'":

> Now, after centuries of men constantly repeating that *we* were different, here are women screaming, as if they were afraid of not being heard and as if it were an exciting discovery: "We are different!" Are you going fishing? No, I am going fishing.

> The very theme of difference, whatever the differences are represented to be, is useful to the oppressing group. . . . any allegedly natural feature attributed to an oppressed group is used to imprison this group within the boundaries of a Nature which, since the group is oppressed, ideological confusion labels "nature of oppressed person" . . . to demand the right to Difference without analyzing its social character is to give back the enemy an effective weapon.

Difference as the Editorial Collective of *Questions Féministes* understands and condemns it is bound to remain an integral part of naturalist ideology. It is the very kind of colonized-anthropo-logized difference the master has always happily granted his subordinates. The search and the claim for an essential female/ethnic identity-difference today can never be anything more than a move within the male-is-norm-divide-and-conquer trap. The malady lingers on. As long as words of difference serve to legitimate a discourse instead of delaying its authority to infinity, they are, to borrow an image from Audre Lorde, "noteworthy only as *decorations*." In "An Open Letter to Mary Daly," Lorde reproaches Daly (whose vision of non-European women in *Gyn/Ecology* mainly results from her insistence on universalizing women's oppression) with utilizing Lorde's words "only to testify against myself as a woman of color." She further expands this comment by specifying:

> I feel you do celebrate differences between white women as a creative force towards change, rather than a reason for misunderstanding and separation. But you fail to recognize that, as women, those differences expose all women to various forms and degrees of patriarchal oppression, some of which we share, some of which we do not. . . . The oppression of women knows no ethnic nor racial boundaries, true, but that does not mean it is identical within those boundaries.

In other words,

> to imply . . . that all women suffer the same oppression simply because we are women, is to lose sight of the many varied tools of patriarchy.

Here you probably smile, for none of us is safe from such a critique, including I who quote Lorde in my attempts at disentangling Difference. The process of differentiation, however, continues, and speaking nearby or together with certainly differs from speaking for and about. The latter aims at the finite and dwells in the realm of fixed oppositions (subject/object difference; man/woman sexual difference), tending thereby to valorize the privileged father-daughter relationship.

On Collecting Art and Culture*

There is a Third World in every First World, and vice versa.
—Trinh T. Minh-ha

This essay is composed of four loosely connected parts, each concerned with the fate of tribal artifacts and cultural practices once they are relocated in Western museums, exchange systems, disciplinary archives and discursive traditions. The first part proposes a critical, historical approach to collecting, focusing on subjective, taxonomic, and political processes. It sketches the "art-culture system" through which in the last century exotic objects have been contextualized and given value in the West. This ideological and institutional system is further explored in the second part, where cultural description is presented as a form of collecting. The "authenticity" accorded to both human groups and their artistic work is shown to proceed from specific assumptions about temporality, wholeness, and continuity. The third part focuses on a revealing moment in the modern appropriation of non-Western works of "art" and "culture," a moment portrayed in several memoirs of Claude Lévi-Strauss of his wartime years in New York. A critical reading makes explicit the redemptive metahistorical narrative these memoirs presuppose. The general art-culture system supported by such a narrative is contested throughout the essay and particularly in the fourth part, where alternative "tribal" histories and contexts are suggested.

Collecting Ourselves

Entering
You will find yourselves in a climate of nut castanets,
A musical whip

---

* James Clifford, "On Collecting Art and Culture," in *Out There: Marginalization and Contemporary Cultures* (New York: New Museum of Contemporary Art and Cambridge: MIT Press, 1990), pp. 141-46, 151-65. (Notes omitted. Some changes have been made in spelling.)

> From the Torres Straits, from Mirzapur a sistrum
> Called Jumka, "used by Aboriginal
> Tribes to attract small game
> On dark nights," coolie cigarettes
> And mask of Saagga, the Devil Doctor,
> The eyelids worked by strings.

James Fenton's poem "The Pitt Rivers Museum, Oxford" from which this stanza is taken, rediscovers a place of fascination in the ethnographic collection. For this visitor even the museum's descriptive labels seem to increase the wonder (". . . attract small game / on dark nights") and the fear. Fenton is an adult-child exploring territories of danger and desire, for to be a child in this collection ("Please sir, where's the withered / Hand?") is to ignore the serious admonitions about human evolution and cultural diversity posted in the entrance hall. It is to be interested instead by the claw of a condor, the jaw of a dolphin, the hair of a witch, or "a jay's feather worn as a charm / in Buckinghamshire." Fenton's ethnographic museum is a world of intimate encounters with inexplicably fascinating objects: personal fetishes. Here collecting is inescapably tied to obsession, to recollection. Visitors "find the landscape of their childhood marked out / Here in the chaotic piles of souvenirs . . . boxroom of the forgotten or hardly possible."

> Go
> As a historian of ideas or a sex-offender,
> For the primitive art,
> As a dusty semiologist, equipped to unravel
> The seven components of that witch's curse
> Or the syntax of the mutilated teeth. Go
> In groups to giggle at curious finds.
> But do not step into the kingdom of your promises
> To yourself, like a child entering the forbidden
> Woods of his lonely playtime.

Do not step in this tabooed zone "laid with snares of privacy and fiction/And the dangerous third wish." Do not encounter these objects except as *curiosities* to giggle at, *art* to be admired, or *evidence* to be understood scientifically. The tabooed way, followed by Fenton, is a path of too-intimate fantasy, recalling the dreams of the solitary child "who wrestled with eagles for their feathers" or the fearful vision of a young girl, her turbulent lover seen as a hound with "strange pretercanine eyes." This path through the Pitt Rivers Museum ends with what seems to be a scrap of autobiography, the vision of a personal "forbidden woods"—exotic, desired, savage, and governed by the (paternal) law:

> He had known what tortures the savages had prepared
> For him there, as he calmly pushed open the gate

And entered the wood near the placard: "TAKE NOTICE MEN
MEN-TRAPS AND SPRING-GUNS ARE SET ON THESE
PREMISES."
For his father had protected his good estate.

Fenton's journey into otherness leads to a forbidden area of the self. His intimate way of engaging the exotic collection finds an area of desire, marked off and policed. The law is preoccupied with *property*.

C. B. Macpherson's classic analysis of Western "possessive individualism" traces the seventeenth-century emergence of an ideal self as owner: the individual surrounded by accumulated property and goods. The same ideal can hold true for collectivities making and remaking their cultural "selves." For example Richard Handler analyzes the making of a Québécois cultural "patrimoine," drawing on Macpherson to unravel the assumptions and paradoxes involved in "having a culture," selecting and cherishing an authentic collective "property." His analysis suggests that this identity, whether cultural or personal, presupposes acts of collection, gathering up possessions in arbitrary systems of value and meaning. Such systems, always powerful and rule governed, change historically. One cannot escape them. At best, Fenton suggests, one can transgress ("poach" in their tabooed zones) or make their self-evident orders seem strange. In Handler's subtly perverse analysis a system of retrospection—revealed by a Historic Monuments Commission's selection of ten sorts of "cultural property"—appears as a taxonomy worthy of Borges' "Chinese Encyclopedia": "(1) commemorative monuments; (2) churches and chapels; (3) forts of the French Regime; (4) windmills; (5) roadside crosses; (6) commemorative inscriptions and plaques; (7) devotional monuments; (8) old houses and manors; (9) old furniture; (10) 'les choses disparues.'" In Handler's discussion the collection and preservation of an authentic domain of identity cannot be natural or innocent. It is tied up with nationalist politics, with restrictive law, and with contested encodings of past and future.

Some sort of "gathering" around the self and the group—the assemblage of a material "world," the marking-off of a subjective domain that is not "other"—is probably universal. All such collections embody hierarchies of value, exclusions, rule-governed territories of the self. But the notion that this gathering involves the accumulation of possessions, the idea that identity is a kind of wealth (of objects, knowledge, memories, experience), is surely not universal. The individualistic accumulation of Melanesian "big men" is not possessive in Macpherson's sense, for in Melanesia one accumulates not to hold objects as private goods but to give them away, to redistribute. In the West, however, collecting has long been a strategy for the deployment of a possessive self, culture, and authenticity.

Children's collections are revealing in this light: a boy's accumulation of miniature cars, a girl's dolls, a summer-vacation "nature museum" (with labelled stones and shells, a hummingbird in a bottle), a treasured bowl filled with the bright shavings of crayons. In these small rituals we observe the channelings of obsession, an exercise in how to make the world one's own, to gather things around oneself tastefully, appropriately. The inclusions in all collections reflect wider cultural rules—of rational taxonomy, of gender, of aesthetics. An excessive, sometimes even rapacious need to *have* is transformed into rule-governed, meaningful desire. Thus the self that must possess but cannot have it all learns to select, order, classify in hierarchies—to make "good" collections.

Whether a child collects model dinosaurs or dolls, sooner or later she or he will be encouraged to keep the possessions on a shelf or in a special box or to set up a doll house. Personal treasures will be made public. If the passion is for Egyptian figurines, the collector will be expected to label them, to know their dynasty (it is not enough that they simply exude power or mystery), to tell "interesting" things about them, to distinguish copies from originals. The good collector (as opposed to the obsessive, the miser) is tasteful and reflective. Accumulation unfolds in a pedagogical, edifying manner. The collection itself—its taxonomic, aesthetic structure—is valued, and any private fixation on single objects is negatively marked as fetishism. Indeed a "proper" relation with objects (rule-governed possession) presupposes a "savage" or deviant relation (idolatry or erotic fixation). In Susan Stewart's gloss, "The boundary between collection and fetishism is mediated by classification and display in tension with accumulation and secrecy."

Stewart's wide-ranging study *On Longing* traces a "structure of desire" whose task is the repetitious and impossible one of closing the gap that separates language from the experience it encodes. She explores certain recurrent strategies pursued by Westerners since the sixteenth century. In her analysis the miniature, whether a portrait or doll's house, enacts a bourgeois longing for "inner" experience. She also explores the strategy of gigantism (from Rabelais and Gulliver to earthworks and the billboard), the souvenir, and the collection. She shows how collections, most notably museums—create the illusion of adequate representation of a world by first cutting objects out of specific contexts (whether cultural, historical, or intersubjective) and making them "stand for" abstract wholes—a "Bambara mask," for example, becoming an ethnographic metonym for Bambara culture. Next a scheme of classification is elaborated for storing or displaying the object so that the reality of the collection itself, its coherent order, overrides specific histories of the object's production and appropriation. Paralleling Marx's account of the fantastic objectification of commodities, Stewart argues that in the modern Western museum "an illusion of a relation between things takes the place of a social relation." The collector discovers, acquires, salvages objects. The objective world is given, not produced, and thus historical relations of power in the work of acquisition are occulted. The *making* of meaning in museum classification and display is mystified as adequate *representation*. The time and order of the collection erase the concrete social labor of its making.

Stewart's work, along with Phillip Fisher, Krzysztof Pomian, James Bunn, Daniel Defert, Johannes Fabian, and Rémy Saisselin, among others, brings collecting and display sharply into view as crucial processes of Western identity formation. Gathered artifacts—whether they find their way into curio cabinets, private living rooms, museums of ethnography, folklore, or fine art—function within a developing capitalist "system of objects." By virtue of this system a world of *value* is created and a meaningful deployment and circulation of artifacts is maintained. For Baudrillard collected objects create a structured environment that substitutes its own temporality for the "real time" of historical and productive processes: "The environment of private objects and their possession—of which collections are an extreme manifestation—is a dimension of our life that is both essential and imaginary. As essential as dreams."

A history of anthropology and modern art needs to see in collection both a form of Western subjectivity and a changing set of powerful institutional practices. The history of collections (not limited to museums) is central to an understanding of how those social groups that invented anthropology and modern art have *appropriated* exotic things, facts, and meanings. (*Appropriate*: "to make one's own," from the Latin *propius*, "proper," "property.") It is important to analyze how powerful discriminations made at particular moments constitute the general system of objects within which valued artifacts circulate and make sense. Far-reaching questions are thereby raised.

What criteria validate an authentic cultural or artistic product? What are the differential values placed on old and new creations? What moral and political criteria justify "good," responsible, systematic collecting practices? Why, for example, do Leo Frobenius' wholesale acquisitions of African objects around the turn of the century now seem excessive? How is a "complete" collection defined? What is the proper balance between scientific analysis and public display? (In Santa Fe a superb collection of Native American art is housed at the School of American Research in a building constructed, literally, as a vault, with access carefully restricted. The Musée de l'Homme exhibits less than a tenth of its collections; the rest is stored in steel cabinets or heaped in corners of the vast basement.) Why has it seemed obvious until recently that non-Western objects should be preserved in European museums, even when this means that no fine specimens are visible in their country of origin? How are "antiquities," "curiosities," "art," "souvenirs," "monuments," and "ethnographic artifacts" distinguished—at different historical moments and in specific market conditions? Why have many anthropological museums in recent years begun to display certain of their objects as "masterpieces?" Why has tourist art only recently come to the serious attention of the anthropologists? What has been the changing interplay between natural-history collecting and the selection of anthropological artifacts for display and analysis? The list could be extended.

The critical history of collecting is concerned with what from the material world specific groups and individuals choose to preserve, value, and exchange. Although this complex history, from at least the Age of Discovery, remains to be written, Baudrillard provides an initial framework for the deployment of objects in the recent capitalist West. In his account it is axiomatic that all categories of meaningful objects—including those marked off as scientific evidence and as great art—function within a ramified system of symbols and values.

To take just one example: the *New York Times* of December 8, 1984, reported the widespread illegal looting of Anasazi archeological sites in the American Southwest. Painted pots and urns thus excavated in good condition could bring as much as $30,000 on the market. Another article in the same issue contained a photograph of Bronze Age pots and jugs salvaged by archeologists from a Phoenician shipwreck off the coast of Turkey. One account featured clandestine collecting for profit, the other scientific collecting for knowledge. The moral evaluations of the two acts of salvage were sharply opposed, but the pots recovered were all meaningful, beautiful and old. Commercial, aesthetic, and scientific worth in both cases presupposed a given system of value. This system finds intrinsic interest and beauty in objects from a past time, and it assumes that collecting everyday objects from ancient (preferably vanished) civilizations will be more *rewarding* than collecting, for example, decorated thermoses from modern China or customized T-shirts from Oceania. Old objects are endowed with a sense of "depth" by their historically minded collectors. Temporality is reified and salvaged as origin, beauty, and knowledge.

This archaizing system has not always dominated Western collecting. The curiosities of the New World gathered and appreciated in the sixteenth century were not necessarily valued as antiquities, the products of primitive or "past" civilizations. They frequently occupied a category of the marvelous, of a present "Golden Age." More recently the retrospective bias of Western appropriations of the world's cultures has come under scrutiny. Cultural or artistic "authenticity" has as much to do with an inventive present as with a past, its objectification, preservation or revival.

Culture Collecting

Found in *American Anthropologist*, n.s. 34 (1932): 740:

Note from New Guinea
Aliatoa, Wiwiak District, New Guinea

April 21, 1932

We are just completing a culture of a mountain group here in the lower Torres Chelles. They have no name and we haven't decided what to call them yet. They are a very revealing people in spots, providing a final basic concept from which all the mother's brothers' curses and father's sisters' curses, etc. derive, and having articulate the attitude toward incest which Reo [Fortune] outlined as fundamental in his Encyclopedia article. They have taken the therapeutic measures which we recommended for Dobu and Manus—having a devil in addition to the neighbor sorcerer, and having got their dead out of the village and localized. But in other ways they are annoying: they have bits and snatches of all the rag tag and bob tail of magical and ghostly belief from the Pacific, and they are somewhat like the Plains in their receptivity to strange ideas. A picture of a local native reading the index to *The Golden Bough* just to see if they had missed anything, would be appropriate. They are very difficult to work, living all over the place with half a dozen garden houses, and never staying put for over a week at a time. Of course this offered a new challenge in method which was interesting. The difficulties incident upon being two days over impossible mountains have been consuming and we are going to do a coastal people next.

Sincerely yours,
Margaret Mead

"Cultures" are ethnographic collections. Since Tylor's founding definition of 1871 the term has designated a rather vague "complex whole" including everything that is learned group behavior, from body techniques to symbolic orders. There have been recurring attempts to define culture more precisely or, for example, to distinguish it from "social structure." But the inclusive use persists. For there are times when we still need to be able to speak holistically of Japanese or Trobriand or Moroccan culture in the confidence that we are designating something real and differentially coherent. It is increasingly clear, however, that the concrete activity of representing a culture, subculture, or indeed any coherent domain of collective activity is always strategic and selective. The world's societies are too systematically interconnected to permit any easy isolation of separate or independently functioning systems. The increased pace of historical change, the common recurrence of stress in the systems under study, forces a new self-consciousness about the way cultural wholes and boundaries are constructed and translated. The pioneering *élan* of Margaret Mead "completing a culture" in highland New Guinea, collecting a dispersed population, discovering its key customs, naming the result—in this case "the Mountain Arapesh"—is no longer possible.

To see ethnography as a form of culture collecting (not, of course, the *only* way to see it) highlights the ways that diverse experiences and facts are selected, gathered, detached from their original temporal occasions, and given enduring value in a new arrangement. Collecting—at least in the West, where time is generally thought to be linear and irreversible—implies a rescue of phenomena from inevitable historical decay or loss. The collection contains what "deserves" to be kept, remembered, and treasured. Artifacts and customs are saved out of time. Anthropological culture collectors have typically gathered what seems "traditional"—what by definition is opposed to modernity. From a complex historical reality (which includes current ethnographic encounters) they select what gives form, structure, and continuity to a world. What is hybrid or "historical" in an emergent sense has been less commonly collected and presented as a system of authenticity. For example in New Guinea Margaret Mead and Reo Fortune chose not to study groups that were, as Mead wrote in a letter, "badly missionized"; and it had been self-evident to Malinowski in the Trobriands that what most deserved scientific attention was the circumscribed "culture" threatened by a host of modern "outside" influences. The experience of the Melanesians becoming Christians for their own reasons—learning to play, and play with, the outsiders' games—did not seem worth salvaging.

Every appropriation of culture, whether by insiders or outsiders, implies a specific temporal position and form of historical narration. Gathering, owning, classifying, and valuing are certainly not restricted to the West; but elsewhere these activities need not be associated with accumulation (rather than redistribution) or with preservation (rather than natural or historical decay). The Western practice of culture collecting has its own local genealogy, enmeshed in distinct European notions of temporality and order. It is worth dwelling for a moment on this genealogy, for it organizes the assumptions being arduously unlearned by new theories of practice, process, and historicity.

A crucial aspect of the recent history of the culture concept has been its alliance (and division of labor) with "art." Culture, even without a capital c, strains toward aesthetic form and autonomy. I have already suggested that modern culture ideas and art ideas function together in an "art-culture system." The inclusive twentieth-century culture category—one that does not privilege "high" or "low" culture—is plausible only within this system, for while in principle admitting all learned human behavior, this culture with a small c orders phenomena in ways that privilege the coherent, balanced, and "authentic" aspects of shared life. Since the mid-nineteenth century, ideas of culture have gathered up those elements that seem to give continuity and depth to collective existence, seeing it whole rather than disputed, torn, intertextual, or syncretic. Mead's almost postmodern image of "a local native reading the index to *The Golden Bough* just to see if they had missed anything" is not a vision of authenticity.

Mead found Arapesh receptivity to outside influences "annoying." *Their* culture collecting complicated hers. Historical developments would later force her to provide a revised picture of these difficult Melanesians. In a new preface to the 1971 reprint of her three-volume ethnography *The Mountain Arapesh* Mead devotes several pages to letters from Bernard Narokobi, an Arapesh then studying law in Sydney, Australia. The anthropologist readily admits her astonishment at hearing from him: "How was it that one of the Arapesh—a people who had had such a light hold on any form of collective style—should have come further than any individual among the Manus, who had moved as a group into the modern world in the years between our first study of them, in 1928, and the beginning of our restudy, in 1953?" She goes on to explain that Narokobi, along with other Arapesh men studying in Australia, had "moved from one period in human culture to another" as "individuals." The Arapesh were "less tightly bound within a coherent culture" than Manus. Narokobi writes, however, as a member of his "tribe," speaking with pride of the values and accomplishments of his "clansfolk." (He uses the name Arapesh sparingly.) He articulates the possibility of a new multiterritorial "cultural" identity: "I feel now that I can feel proud of my tribe and at the same time feel I belong not only to Papua-New Guinea, a nation to be, but to the world community at large." Is not this modern way of being "Arapesh" already prefigured in Mead's earlier image of a resourceful native paging through *The Golden Bough*? Why must such behavior be marginalized or classed as "individual" by the anthropological culture collector?

Expectations of wholeness, continuity, and essence have long been built into the linked Western ideas of culture and art. A few words of recent background must suffice, since to map the history of these concepts would lead us on a chase for origins back at least to the Greeks. Raymond Williams provides a starting point in the early nineteenth century—a moment of unprecedented historical and social disruption. In *Culture and Society, Keywords*, and elsewhere Williams has traced a parallel development in usage for the words *art* and *culture*. The changes reflect complex responses to industrialism, to the specter of "mass society," to accelerated social conflict and change.

According to Williams in the eighteenth century the word *art* meant predominantly "skill." Cabinetmakers, criminals, and painters were each in their way artful. *Culture* designated a tendency to natural growth, its uses predominantly agricultural and personal: both plants and human individuals could be "cultured." Other meanings also present in the eighteenth century did not predominate until the nineteenth. By 1820s *art* increasingly designated a special domain of creativity, spontaneity, and purity, a realm of refined sensibility and expressive "genius." The "artist" was set apart from, often against, society—whether "mass" or "bourgeois." The term *culture* followed a parallel course, coming to mean what was most elevated, sensitive, essential, and precious—most uncommon—in society. Like art, culture became a general category; Williams calls it a "final court of appeal" against threats of vulgarity and leveling. It existed in essential opposition to perceived "anarchy."

Art and culture emerged after 1800 as mutually reinforcing domains of human *value*, strategies for gathering, marking off, protecting the best and most interesting creations of "Man." In the twentieth century the categories underwent a series of further developments. The plural, anthropological definition of culture (lower-case *c* with a possibility of a final *s*) emerged as a liberal alternative to racist classifications of human diversity. It was a sensitive means for understanding different and dispersed "whole ways of life" in a high colonial context of unprecedented global interconnection. *Culture* in its full evolutionary richness and authenticity, formerly reserved for the best creations of modern Europe, could now be extended to all the world's populations. In the anthropological vision of Boas' generation "cultures" were of equal value. In their new plurality, however, the nineteenth-century definitions were not entirely transformed. If they became less elitist (distinctions between "high" and "low" culture were erased) and less Eurocentric (every human society was fully "cultural"), nevertheless a certain body of assumptions were carried over from the older definitions. George Stocking shows the complex interrelations of nineteenth-century humanist and emerging anthropological definitions of culture. He suggests that anthropology owes as much to Matthew Arnold as to its official founding father, E. B. Tylor. Indeed much of the vision embodied in *Culture and Anarchy* has been transferred directly into relativist anthropology. A powerful structure of feeling continues to see culture, wherever it is found, as a coherent *body* that lives and dies. Culture is enduring, traditional, structural (rather than contingent, syncretic, historical). Culture is a process of ordering, not of disruption. It changes and develops like a living organism. It does not normally "survive" abrupt alterations.

In the early twentieth century, as *culture* was being extended to all the world's functioning societies, an increasing number of exotic, primitive, or archaic objects came to be seen as "art." They were equal in aesthetic and moral value with the greatest Western masterpieces. By midcentury the new attitude toward "primitive art" had been accepted by large numbers of educated Europeans and Americans. Indeed from the standpoint of the late twentieth century it becomes clear that the parallel concepts of art and culture did successfully, albeit temporarily, comprehend and incorporate a plethora of non-Western artifacts and customs. This was accomplished through two strategies. First, objects re-classified as "primitive art" were admitted to the imaginary museum of human creativity and, though more slowly, to the actual fine arts museums of the West. Second, the discourse and institutions of modern anthropology constructed comparative and synthetic images of Man drawing evenhandedly from among the world's authentic ways of life, however strange in appearance or obscure in origin. Art and culture, categories for the best creations of Western humanism, were in principle extended to all the world's peoples.

It is perhaps worth stressing that nothing said here about the historicity of these cultural or artistic categories should be construed as claiming that they are false or denying that many of their values are worthy of support. Like any successful discursive arrangement the art-culture authenticity system articulates considerable domains of truth and scientific progress as well as areas of blindness and controversy. By emphasizing the transience of the system I do so out of a conviction (it is more a feeling of the historical ground moving underfoot) that the classifications and generous appropriations of Western art and culture categories are now much less stable than before. This instability appears to be linked to the growing interconnection of the world's populations and to the contestation since the 1950s of colonialism and Eurocentrism. Art collecting and culture collecting now take place within a changing field of counterdiscourses, syncretisms, and reappropriations originating both outside and inside "the West." I cannot discuss the geopolitical causes of these developments. I can only hint at their transforming consequences and stress that the modern genealogy of culture and art that I have been sketching increasingly appears to be a local story. "Culture" and "art" can no longer be simply *extended* to non-Western peoples and things. They can at worst be *imposed*, at best *translated*—both historically and politically contingent operations.

Before I survey some of the current challenges to Western modes of collection and authentication, it may be worth portraying the still-dominant form of art and culture collecting in a more limited, concrete setting. The system's underlying historical assumptions will then become inescapable. For if collecting in the West salvages things out of non-repeatable time, what is the assumed direction of this time? How does it confer rarity and authenticity on the varied productions of human skill? Collecting presupposes a story; a story occurs in a "chronotope."

A Chronotope for Collecting

> *Dans son effort pour comprendre le monde, l'homme dispose donc toujours d'un surplus de signification.*

> —Claude Lévi-Strauss

The term *chronotope*, as used by Bakhtin, denotes a configuration of spatial and temporal indicators in a fictional setting where (and when) certain activities and stories *take place*. One cannot realistically situate historical detail—putting something "in its time"—without appealing to explicit or implicit chronotopes. Claude Lévi-Strauss's pointed, nostalgic recollections of New York during the Second World War can serve as a chronotope for modern art and culture collecting. The setting is elaborated in an essay whose French title, "New York post-et préfiguratif," suggests its underlying spatio-temporal predicament more strongly than the published English translation, "New York in 1941." The essay falls within a microgenre of Lévi-Strauss's writing, one he developed with virtuosity in *Tristes tropiques*. Specific places—Rio, Fire Island, new Brazilian cities, Indian sacred sites—appear as moments of intelligible human order and transformation surrounded by the destructive, entropic currents of global history.

In what follows I have supplemented the essay on New York with passages from other texts written by Lévi-Strauss either during the war years or in recollection of them. In reading them as a unified chronotrope, one ought to bear in mind that these are not historical records but complex literary commemorations. The time-space in question has been retrospectively composed by Lévi-Strauss and recomposed, for other purposes, by myself.

A refugee in New York during the Second World War, the anthropologist is bewildered and delighted by a landscape of unexpected juxtapositions. His recollections of those seminal years, during which he invented structural anthropology, are bathed in a magical light. New York is full of delightful incongruities. Who could resist

> the performances that we watched for hours at the Chinese opera under the first arch of the Brooklyn Bridge, where a company that had come long ago from

China had a large following. Every day, from mid-afternoon until past midnight, it would perpetuate the traditions of classical Chinese opera. I felt myself going back in time no less when I went to work every morning in the American room of the New York Public Library. There, under its neo-classical arcades and between walls paneled with old oak, I sat near an Indian in a feather headdress and a beaded buckskin jacket—who was taking notes with a Parker pen.

As Lévi-Strauss tells it, the New York of 1941 is an anthropologist's dream, a vast selection of human culture and history. A brief walk or a subway ride will take him from a Greenwich Village reminiscent of Balzac's Paris to the towering skyscrapers of Wall Street. Turning a corner in this jumble of immigrants and ethnic groups, the stroller suddenly enters a different world with its own language, customs, cuisine. Everything is available for consumption. In New York one can obtain almost any treasure. The anthropologist and his artistic friends André Breton, Max Ernst, André Masson, Georges Duthuit, Yves Tanguy, and Matta find masterpieces of pre-Colombian, Indian, Oceanic, or Japanese art stuffed in dealers' closets or apartments. Everything somehow finds its way here. For Lévi-Strauss New York in the 1940s is a wonderland of sudden openings to other times and places, of cultural matter out of place:

> New York (and this is the source of its charm and peculiar fascination) was then a city where anything seemed possible. Like the urban fabric, the social and cultural fabric was riddled with holes. All you had to do was pick one and slip through it if, like Alice, you wanted to get to the other side of the looking glass and find worlds so enchanting that they seemed unreal.

The anthropological *flâneur* is delighted, amazed, but also troubled by the chaos of simultaneous possibilities. This New York has something in common with the early-century dada-surrealist flea market—but with a difference. Its *objets trouvés* are not just occasions for reverie. This they surely are, but they are also signs of vanishing worlds. Some are treasures, works of great art.

Lévi-Strauss and the refugee surrealists were passionate collectors. The Third Avenue art dealer they frequented and advised, Julius Carlebach, always had several Northwest Coast, Melanesian, or Eskimo pieces on hand. According to Edmund Carpenter, the surrealists felt an immediate affinity with these objects' predilection for "visual puns"; their selections were nearly always of a very high quality. In addition to the art dealers another source for this band of primitive-art connoisseurs was the Museum of the American Indian. As Carpenter tells it: "The Surrealists began to visit the Bronx warehouse of that Museum, selecting for themselves, concentrating on a collection of magnificent Eskimo masks. These huge visual puns, made by the Kuskokwim Eskimo a century or more ago, constituted the greatest collection of its kind in the world. But the Museum Director, George Heye, called them "jokes" and sold half for $38 and $54 each. The Surrealists bought the best. Then they moved happily through Heye's Northwest Coast collection, stripping it of one masterwork after another." In 1946 Max Ernst, Barnett Newman, and several others mounted an exhibit of Northwest Coast Indian Painting at the Betty Parsons Gallery. They brought together pieces from their private collections and artifacts from the American Museum of Natural History. By moving the museum pieces across town, "the Surrealists declassified them as scientific specimens and reclassified them as art."

The category of primitive art was emerging, with its market, its connoisseurship, and its close ties to modernist aesthetics. What had begun with the vogue for *l'art nègre* in the twenties would become institutionalized by the fifties and sixties; but in wartime New York the battle to gain widespread recognition for tribal objects was not yet won. Lévi-Strauss recalls that as cultural attaché to the French Embassy in 1946 he tried in vain to arrange a trade: for a massive collection of American Indian art a few Matisses and Picassos. But "the French authorities turned a deaf ear to my entreaties, and the Indian collections wound up in American museums." The collecting of Lévi-Strauss and the surrealists during the forties was part of a struggle to gain aesthetic status for these increasingly rare masterworks.

New York seemed to have something unusual, valuable, and beautiful for everyone. Franz Boas liked to tell his European visitors about a Kwakiutl informant who had come to work with him in the city. As Roman Jakobson recalls:

> Boas loved to depict the indifference of this man from Vancouver Island toward Manhattan skyscrapers ("we built houses next to one another, and you stack them on top of each other"), toward the Aquarium, ("we throw such fish back in the lake") or toward the motion pictures which seemed tedious and senseless. On the other hand, the stranger stood for hours spellbound in the Times Square freak shows with their giants and dwarfs, bearded ladies and fox-tailed girls, or in the Automats where drinks and sandwiches appear miraculously and where he felt transferred to the universe of Kwakiutl fairy-tales.

In Lévi-Strauss's memory brass balls on staircase bannisters also figure in the collection of fascinating phenomena.

For a European New York's sheer space is vertiginous:

> I strode up and down miles of Manhattan avenues, those deep chasms over which loomed skyscrapers' fantastic cliffs. I wandered randomly into cross streets, whose physiognomy changed drastically from one block to the next: sometimes poverty-stricken, sometimes middle-class or provincial, and most often chaotic. New York was decidedly not the ultra-modern metropolis I had expected, but an immense, horizontal and vertical disorder attributable to some spontaneous upheaval of the urban crust rather than to the deliberate plans of builders.

Lévi-Strauss's New York is a juxtaposition of ancient and recent "strata," chaotic remnants of former "upheavals." As in *Tristes tropiques* metaphors from geology serve to transform empirical surface incongruities or faults into legible history. For Lévi-Strauss the jumble of Manhattan becomes intelligible as an overlay of past and future, legible as a story of cultural development. Old and new are side by side. The European refugee encounters scraps of his past as well as a troubling prefiguration of common destiny.

New York is a site of travel and reverie unlike the oneiric city of Breton's *Najda* or Aragon's *Paysan de Paris*. For Parisian emigrés finding their feet on its streets and avenues it is never a known place, something to be made strange by a certain surrealist and ethnographic attention. Instead they are ambushed by the familiar—an older Paris in Greenwich Village, glimpses of the European world in immigrant neighborhoods, medieval buildings reassembled at the Cloisters. But these reminders are masks, survivals, mere collectibles. In New York one is permanently away from home, *dépaysé*, both in space and in time. Post- and pre-figurative New York is fantastically suspended between a jumble of pasts and a uniform future.

> Whoever wanted to go hunting needed only a little culture, and flair, for doorways to open in the wall of industrial civilization and reveal other worlds and other times. Doubtless nowhere more than in New York at that time were there such facilities for escape. Those possibilities seem almost mythical today when we no longer dare to dream of doors: at best we may wonder about niches to cower in. But even these have become the stake in a fierce competition among those who are not willing to live in a world without friendly shadows or secret shortcuts known only to a few initiates. Losing its old dimensions one after another, this world has pushed us back into the one remaining dimension: one will probe it in vain for secret loopholes.

The resigned "entropologist" of *Tristes tropiques* remembers New York as the final glow and prophetic disintegration of all real cultural differences. Soon even the loopholes will be gone. Millennia of human diversity and invention seem to have been shipwrecked here, remnants and broken shards, good to evoke in escapist reveries, good to collect as art (or antiques), and "good to think with" in salvaging the cultural structures of a trans-historical *esprit humain*. The chronotope of New York prefigures anthropology.

Structuralist anthropology at least was conceived and written there. It is hard to imagine a better setting. Among New York's jumble of cultures, arts, and traditions, as a professor at the Ecole Libre des Hautes Etudes, Lévi-Strauss attended Roman Jakobson's celebrated lectures on sound and meaning. On many occasions he has testified to their revolutionary impact. Jakobson's demonstration that the bewildering diversity of meaningful human sounds could be reduced to discrete differential systems through the application of phonemic analysis offered an immediate model for studying the plethora of human kinship systems. More generally Jakobson's approach suggested a research program—that of discovering elementary cognitive structures behind the many "language-like" productions of human culture. Amid the cultural-historical jumble of wartime New York—too much in the same place at the same time—Lévi-Strauss glimpsed an underlying order.

The Elementary Structures of Kinship was researched in the New York Public Library reading room, where, beside what seemed to be a parody of a feathered Indian with a Parker pen, Lévi-Strauss pored over accounts of tribal marriage rules. The founding text of structural anthropology was drafted in a small, dilapidated studio in Greenwich Village, down the street from Yves Tanguy and a few yards (through the walls) from Claude Shannon, who, unknown to his neighbor, "was creating cybernetics."

Uptown at the American Museum of Natural History Lévi-Strauss could wander and wonder among the intimate, hyperreal dioramas of African animal species. Or he could marvel in the Hall of Northwest Coast Indians, where Kwakiutl and Tlingit masks in their glass cases whispered to him of Baudelairean *correspondences*. Indeed by the 1940s a deep correspondence between primitive and modern art was widely assumed in avant-garde milieux. The anthropologist friend of the surrealists saw these magical, archaic objects as luminous examples of human creative genius. He wrote in 1943 for the *Gazette des beaux arts*:

> These objects—beings transformed into things, human animals, living boxes—seem as remote as possible from our own conception of art since the time of the Greeks. Yet even here one would err to suppose that a single possibility of the aesthetic life had escaped the prophets and virtuosos of the Northwest Coast. Several of those masks and statues are thoughtful portraits which prove a concern to attain not only physical resemblance but the most subtle spiritual essence of the soul. The sculptor of Alaska and British Columbia is not only the sorcerer who confers upon the supernatural a visible form but also the creator, the interpreter who translates into eternal *chefs d'oeuvre* the fugitive emotions of man.

Human artistic creation transcends location and time. To communicate the incredible inventiveness he sees in the Northwest Coast Hall, Lévi-Strauss finds a revealing comparison: "This incessant renovation, this sureness which in no matter what direction guarantees definite and overwhelming success, this scorn of the beaten path, this ceaseless driving toward new feats which infallibly ends in dazzling results—to know this our civilization had to await the exceptional destiny of a Picasso. It is not futile to emphasize that the daring ventures of a single man which have left us breathless for thirty years, were known and practiced during one hundred and fifty years by an entirely indigenous culture." The passage is undoubtedly adapted to its occasion: the need to promote tribal works for an art-world public. (Elsewhere Lévi-Strauss would stress the systems limiting and making possible inventions by any local group or individual creator.) Here he insists only that tribal works are as inventive as that modern paragon of creativity, Picasso. Implicit in the conceit was a vision of human cultures as comparable to creative artists. As I have already argued, the twentieth-century categories of art and culture presupposed each other.

The categories were, however, institutionally separated. If the surrealists could reclassify tribal objects by moving them across town from an anthropology museum to an art gallery, the end points of the traffic were not thereby undermined. The discourses of anthropology and art were developing on separate but complementary paths. Their evolving relationship may be seen in a legendary surrealist journal of 1942-43 edited by David Hare and dominated by its "editorial advisors" André Breton, Max Ernst, and Marcel Duchamp. *VVV*, according to its subtitle, aspired to cover the fields of "poetry, plastic arts, anthropology, sociology, psychology." In fact it did justice to the first two with a sprinkling of the third. (Only four issues of *VVV* appeared in four years.) Number 1 contained two short articles by Lévi-Strauss, one on Kaduveo Indian face painting, the other an obituary for Malinowski. The following number contained a note by Alfred Métraux on two ancestral figurines from Eastern Island. And in the final issue Robert Allerton Parker fancifully interpreted complex line drawings from the New Hebrides (extracted from A. B. Deacon's ethnography) under the title "Cannibal Designs." In general material from non-Western cultures was included as exoticism or naive art. There were occasional photos of an Alaskan mask or a kachina.

In *VVV* anthropology was part of the décor of avant-garde art and writing. Serious cultural analysis made no real inroads into what were by now canonical surrealist notions of genius, inspiration, the irrational, the magical, the exotic, the primitive. Few of those around Breton (with the possible exception of Max Ernst) had any systematic interest in ethnological science. Lévi-Strauss's contributions to *VVV* seem out of place. Essentially a journal of art and literature, *VVV* was preoccupied with dreams, archetypes, genius, and apocalyptic revolution. It engaged in little of the unsettling, reflexive ethnography practiced by the dissidents of the earlier journal *Documents*. "Mainstream" surrealism did not typically bring cultural analysis to bear on its own categories.

Surrealist art and structural anthropology were both concerned with the human spirit's "deep" shared springs of creativity. The common aim was to transcend—not, as in *Documents*, to describe critically or subvert—the local orders of culture and history. Surrealism's subject was an international and elemental humanity "anthropological" in scope. Its object was Man, something it shared with an emerging structuralism. But a conventional division of labor was solidifying. Within the project of probing and extending humanity's creative esprit, the two methods diverged, one playing art to the other's science.

Modern practices of art and culture collecting, scientific and avant-garde, have situated themselves at the end of a global history. They have occupied a place—apocalyptic, progressive, revolutionary, or tragic—from which to gather the valued inheritances of Man. Concretizing this temporal set up, Lévi-Strauss's "post- and prefigurative" New York anticipates humanity's entropic future and gathers up its diverse pasts in de-contextualized, collectible forms. The ethnic neighborhoods, the provincial reminders, the Chinese Opera Company, the feathered Indian in the library, the works of art from other continents and eras that turn up in dealers' closets: all are survivals, remnants of threatened or vanished traditions. The world's cultures appear in the chronotope as shreds of humanity, degraded commodities, or elevated great art but always functioning as vanishing "loopholes" or "escapes" from a one-dimensional fate.

In New York a jumble of humanity has washed up in one vertiginous place and time, to be grasped simultaneously in all its precious diversity and emerging uniformity. In this chronotope the pure products of humanity's pasts are rescued by modern aesthetics only as sublimated art. They are salvaged by modern anthropology as consultable archives for thinking about the range of human invention. In Lévi-Strauss's setting the products of the present-becoming-future are shallow, impure, escapist, and "retro" rather than truly different—"antiques" rather than genuine Antiquities. Cultural invention is subsumed by a commodified "mass culture."

The chronotope of New York supports a global allegory of fragmentation and ruin. The modern anthropologist, lamenting the passing of human diversity, collects and values its survivals, its enduring works of art. Lévi-Strauss's most prized acquisition from a marvelous New York where everything seemed available was a nearly complete set of volumes 1 through 48 of the *Annual Reports* of the Bureau of American Ethnology. These were, he tells us in another evocation of the war years, "sacrosanct volumes, representing most of our knowledge about the American Indians. . . . It was as though the American Indian cultures had suddenly come alive and become almost tangible through the physical contact that these books, written and published before these cultures' definite extinction, established between their times and me." These precious records of human diversity had been recorded by an ethnology still in what he calls its "pure" rather than "diluted" state. They would form the authentic ethnographic material from which structuralism's metacultural orders were constructed.

Anthropological collections and taxonomies, however, are constantly menaced by temporal contingencies. Lévi-Strauss knows this. It is a disorder he always holds at bay. For example in *Tristes tropiques* he is acutely aware that focusing on a tribal past necessarily blinds him to an emergent present. Wandering through the modern landscape of New York, far from encountering less and less to know, the anthropologist is confronted with more and more—a heady mix-and-match of possible human combinations. He struggles to maintain a unified perspective; he looks for order in deep "geological" structures. But in Lévi-Strauss's work generally, the englobing "entropological" narrative barely contains a current history of loss, transformation, invention, and emergence.

Toward the end of his brilliant inaugural lecture at the Collège de France, "The Scope of Anthropology," Lévi-Strauss evokes what he calls "anthropological doubt," the inevitable result of ethnographic risktaking, the "buffetings and denials directed at one's most cherished ideas and habits by other ideas and habits best able to rebut them." He poignantly recalls Boas's Kwakiutl visitor, transfixed by the freaks and automats of Times Square, and he wonders whether anthropology may not be condemned to equally bizarre perceptions of the distant societies and histories it seeks to grasp. New York was perhaps Lévi-Strauss's only true "fieldwork": for once he stayed long enough and mastered the local language. Aspects of the place, such as Boas's Kwakiutl, have continued to charm and haunt his anthropological culture collecting.

But one New York native sits with special discomfort in the chronotope of 1941. This is the feathered Indian with the Parker pen working in the Public Library. For Lévi-Strauss the Indian is primarily associated with the past, the "extinct" societies recorded in the precious Bureau of American Ethnology *Annual Reports*. The anthropologist feels himself "going back in time." In modern New York an Indian can appear only as a survival or a kind of incongruous parody.

Another historical vision might have positioned the two scholars in the library differently. The decade just preceding Lévi-Strauss's arrival in New York had seen a dramatic turnaround in federal policy. Under John Collier's leadership at the Bureau of Indian Affairs a "New Indian Policy" actively encouraged tribal reorganization all over the country. While Lévi-Strauss studied and collected their pasts, many "extinct" Native American groups were in the process of reconstituting themselves culturally and politically. Seen in this context, did the Indian with the Parker pen represent a "going back in time" or a glimpse of another future? That is a different story.

Other Appropriations

To tell these other stories, local histories of cultural survival and emergence, we need to resist deep-seated habits of mind and systems of authenticity. We need to be suspicious of an almost-automatic tendency to relegate non-Western peoples and objects to the pasts of an increasingly homogeneous humanity. A few examples of current invention and contestation may suggest different chronotopes for art and culture collecting.

Anne Vitart-Fardoulis, curator at the Musée de l'Homme, has published a sensitive account of the aesthetic, historical, and cultural discourses routinely used to explicate individual museum objects. She discusses a famous intricately painted animal skin (its present name: M.H.34.33.5), probably originating among the Fox Indians of North America. The skin turned up in Western collecting systems some time ago in a "cabinet of curiosities"; it was used to educate aristocratic children and was much admired for its aesthetic qualities. Vitart-Fardoulis tells us that now the skin can be decoded ethnographically in terms of its combined "masculine" and "feminine" graphic styles and understood in the context of a probable role in specific ceremonies. But the meaningful contexts are not exhausted. The story takes a new turn:

> The grandson of one of the Indians who came to Paris with Buffalo Bill was searching for the [painted skin] tunic his grandfather had been forced to sell to pay his way back to the United States when the circus collapsed. I showed him all the tunics in our collection, and he paused before one of them. Controlling his emotion, he spoke. He told the meaning of this lock of hair, of that design, why this color had been used, the meaning of that feather. . . . This garment, formerly beautiful and interesting but passive and indifferent, little by little became meaningful, active testimony to a living moment through the mediation of someone who did not observe and analyze but who lived the object and for whom the object lived. It scarcely matters whether the tunic is really his grandfather's.

Whatever is happening in this encounter, two things are clearly *not* happening. The grandson is not replacing the object in its original or "authentic" cultural context. That is long past. His encounter with the painted skin is part of a modern recollection. And the painted tunic is not being appreciated as art, as an aesthetic object. The encounter is too specific, too enmeshed in family history and ethnic memory. Some aspects of "cultural" and "aesthetic" appropriation are certainly at work, but they occur within a *current tribal history*, a different temporality from that governing the dominant systems I diagrammed earlier. In the context of a present-becoming-future the old painted tunic becomes newly, traditionally meaningful.

The currency of "tribal" artifacts is becoming more visible to non-Indians. Many new tribal recognition claims are pending at the Department of the Interior. And whether or not they are formally successful matters less than what they make manifest: the historical and political reality of Indian survival and resurgence, a force that impinges on Western art and culture collections. The "proper" place of many objects in museums is now subject to contest. The Zuni who prevented the loan of their war god to the Museum of Modern Art were challenging the dominant art-culture system, for in traditional Zuni belief war god figures are sacred and dangerous. They are not ethnographic artifacts, and they are certainly not "art." Zuni claims on these objects specifically reject their "promotion" (in all senses of the term) to the status of aesthetic or scientific treasures.

I would not claim that the only true home for the objects in question is in "the tribe"—a location that, in many cases, is far from obvious. My point is just that the dominant, interlocking contexts of art and anthropology are no longer self-evident and uncontested. There are other contexts, histories, and futures in which non-Western objects and cultural records may "belong." The rare Maori artifacts that in 1984-85 toured museums in the United States normally reside in New Zealand museums. But they are controlled by the traditional Maori authorities, whose permission was required for them to leave the country. Here and elsewhere the circulation of museum collections is significantly influenced by resurgent indigenous communities.

What is at stake is something more than conventional museum programs of community education and "outreach." Current developments question the very status of museums as historical-cultural theaters of memory.

Whose memory? For what purposes? The Provincial Museum of British Columbia has for some time encouraged Kwakiutl carvers to work from models in its collection. It has lent out old pieces and donated new ones for use in modern potlatches. Surveying these developments, Michael Ames, who directs the University of British Columbia Museum, observes that "Indians, traditionally treated by museums only as objects and clients, add now the role of patrons." He continues: "The next step has also occurred. Indian communities establish their own museums, seek their own National Museum grants, install their own curators, hire their own anthropologists on contract, and call for repatriation of their own collections." The Quadra Island Kwakiutl Museum located in Quathraski Cove, British Columbia, displays tribal work returned from the national collections in Ottawa. The objects are exhibited in glass cases, but arranged according to their original family ownership. In Alert Bay, British Columbia, the U'mista Cultural Centre displays repatriated artifacts in a traditional Kwakiutl "big house" arranged in the sequence of their appearance at the potlatch ceremony. The new institutions function both as public exhibits and as cultural centers linked to ongoing tribal traditions. Two Haida museums have also been established in the Queen Charlotte Islands, and the movement is growing elsewhere in Canada and the United States.

Resourceful Native American groups may yet appropriate the Western museum—as they have made their own another European institution, the "tribe." Old objects may again participate in a tribal present-becoming-future. Moreover, it is worth briefly noting that the same thing is possible for written artifacts collected by salvage ethnography. Some of these old texts (myths, linguistic samples, lore of all kinds) are now being recycled as local history and tribal "literature." The objects of both art and culture collecting are susceptible to other appropriations.

This disturbance of Western object systems is reflected in a recent book by Ralph Coe, *Lost and Found Traditions: Native American Art: 1965-1985*. Coe's work is a collector's tour de force. Once again a white authority "discovers" true tribal art—but with significant differences. Hundreds of photographers document very recent works, some made for local use, some for sale to Indians or white outsiders. Beautiful objects—many formerly classified as curios, folk art, or tourist art—are located in ongoing, inventive traditions. Coe effectively questions the widespread assumption that fine tribal work is disappearing, and he throws doubt on common criteria for judging purity and authenticity. In his collection among recognizably traditional kachinas, totem poles, blankets, and plaited baskets we find skillfully beaded tennis shoes and baseball caps, articles developed for the curio trade, quilts, and decorated leather cases (peyote kits modeled on old-fashioned toolboxes).

Since the Native American Church, in whose ceremonies the peyote kits are used, did not exist in the nineteenth century, their claim to traditional status cannot be based on age. A stronger historical claim can in fact be made for many productions of the curio trade, such as the beaded "fancies" (hanging birds, mirror frames) made by Matilda Hill, a Tuscarora who sells at Niagara Falls:

> "Just try telling Matilda Hill that her 'fancies' are tourist curios," said Mohawk Rick Hill, author of an unpublished paper on the subject. "The Tuscarora have been able to trade pieces like that bird or beaded frame at Niagara since the end of the War of 1812, when they were granted exclusive rights, and she wouldn't take kindly to anyone slighting her culture!"

"Surely," Coe adds, "a trade privilege established at Niagara Falls in 1816 should be acceptable as tradition by now." He drives the general point home: "Another misconception derives from our failure to recognize that Indians have always traded both within and outside their culture; it is second nature to the way they operate in all things. Many objects are, and always have been, created in the Indian world without a specific destination in mind. The history of Indian trading predates any white influence, and trading continues today unabated. It is a fascinating instrument of social continuity, and in these modern times its scope has been greatly enlarged."

Coe does not hesitate to commission new "traditional" works, and he spends considerable time eliciting the specific meaning of objects both as individual possessions and as tribal art. We see and hear particular artists; the coexistence of spiritual, aesthetic, and commercial forces is always visible. Overall Coe's collecting project represents and advocates ongoing art forms that are both related to and separate from dominant systems of aesthetic-ethnographic value. In *Lost and Found Traditions* authenticity is something produced, not salvaged. Coe's collection, for all its love of the past, gathers futures.

A long chapter on "tradition" resists summary, for the diverse statements quoted from practice artists, old and young, do not reproduce prevailing Western definitions. "Whites think of our experience as the past," says one group of students discussing the topic. "We know it is right here with us."

> "We always begin our summer dances with a song that repeats only four words, over and over. They don't mean much of anything in English, 'young chiefs stand up.' To us those words demonstrate our pride in our lineage and our happiness in always remembering it. It is a happy song. Tradition is not something you gab about. . . . It's in the doing."

> "Your tradition is 'there' always. You're flexible enough to make of it what you want. It's always with you. I pray to the old pots at the ruins and dream about making pottery. I tell them I want to learn it. We live for today, but never forget the past."

> "Our job as artists is to go beyond, which implies a love of change, [always accomplished with] traditions in mind, by talking to the elders of the tribe and

by being with your grandparents. The stories they tell are just amazing. When you become exposed to them, everything becomes a reflection of those events. There's a great deal of satisfaction being an artist of traditions."

"We've always had charms: everything that's new is old with us."

TONY FRY AND ANNE-MARIE WILLIS

*Aboriginal Art: Symptom or Success?**

In the early 1980s, a number of major exhibitions and commercial ventures began to highlight tribal art. Among these exhibitions one of the most widely challenged was "'Primitivism' in 20th-Century Art: Affinity of the Tribal and the Modern" held at the Museum of Modern Art, New York, during the winter of 1984-85. In one review of that exhibition, ethnologist James Clifford critically questioned the ethnocentric practices of classification, recontextualization and presentation which project diverse cultures into a totalizing global narrative of the story of art. He argued that "we need exhibitions that question the boundaries of art and the art world, an influx of truly indigestible 'outside' artifacts. The relations of power whereby one portion of humanity can select, value, and collect the pure products of others needs to be criticized and transformed." It is this critique that needs to be brought to the recent exhibition and reception of Aboriginal art in the USA.

From such a perspective the contemporary political and economic drift towards cultural pluralism (multiculturalism) can be seen not so much as enlightened accommodation of other world views, but as a violent ripping of signs from the sites of their primary significance. Such operations are usually legitimized by the assumption that the curatorial enterprise is "saving" the tribal and the "primitive" from vanishing. A series of erasures occur as a result. First, culture is reified—it is declared dead and its material remains are taken over, embalmed and put on display. Then the living culture is overlooked and its own relation to its past is overridden. It is often treated not

* Tony Fry and Anne-Marie Willis, "Aboriginal Art: Symptom or Success," in *Art in America* (July 1989), pp. 111-16, 159-61. (Notes and illustration omitted. Some changes have been made in spelling.)

only as primitive, but as childlike in its "failure" to "responsibly" care for its own artifacts. The *right* of a culture, like Australian Aboriginal cultures, to treat many of its artifacts as ephemeral and subordinate to the continuity of symbolic performance (to ceremony, for example) is thus refused in the ahistorical drive to preserve objects as arrested signs of a commodified materiality.

It is clear from the recent presentations and public reception of Aboriginal work in the United States that the significant and often critical debates (in which Clifford's views are important) around the "Primitivism" show have made few lasting marks. Clifford's demonstration of the erroneous fiction of "affinities" between tribal and modern art, his exploration of the implication of recoding the culture of an "other" and of the historical inadequacy of the way art is dealt with are just some of the issues which have been overlooked in the recent promotion and reception of Aboriginal art. Instead, as we will show, the contextual milieu constituted around this work constantly obscures these critical issues and obstructs significant ways of engaging with the work. Furthermore, and with almost no exception, we believe that the critical comment the work has attracted in the United States over the past few years is wrongheaded, and actually makes an informed public perception more difficult to create. Thus, the existing critical writing needs to be challenged before it becomes the basis upon which dominant readings are established.

For one thing, we need to acknowledge the extreme inequality of economic and cultural exchange between Aboriginal peoples and the class of individual that owns the galleries and buys the work. There are no Aboriginal collectors of Aboriginal art. Since the 1970s the viability of Aboriginal art has been dependent upon a growing non-Aboriginal market and on a complex web of government-funded regional arts organizations. While these regional arts organizations are Aboriginal-controlled, the higher one moves up the arts-funding bureaucracy, the more the conflict between black and white value systems becomes evident, and the more the will of white heads of departments and government ministers tends to prevail. It is true that the sale of art work generates income for Aboriginal communities but there are losses as well as gains. The profits, variously measured, do not always, or in full, end up in black hands (either the artists or their families). Beside the normal network of art entrepreneurs, there are often other layers of intermediaries making a considerable amount of money off Aboriginal art. The artist sells to a community co-op or government-funded arts-marketing company; the co-op may have a gallery or it may sell to local dealers who, in turn, sell to the national and international trade. . . .

The unspecific designation "Aboriginal art" obscures a wide range of art-producing cultural milieus, from remote desert dwelling communities where artists consciously adapt traditional lifestyles to urban situations in which Aboriginal artists strategically work across black and white cultural modes. The meaning of Aboriginal art is not readable from the surfaces of the works themselves. Acutely aware of this ambiguity, its overwhelmingly non-Aboriginal promoters have been responsible for a whole new discourse which makes the work anew for the intended audience. Every press release, invitation, catalogue essay and review is implicated in this *production* of Aboriginal art for Western audiences. Of course, any new art form requires arguments as to why it should be considered worthy of attention, but this art in particular would have no public visibility were it not for the carefully managed flow of words that facilitate its circulation. Aboriginal art is promoted as something new simply because it is a new product in the art marketplace.

Most writers on Aboriginal art assume that providing information, commentary and criticism facilitates the appreciation of art objects produced by Aboriginal people. These critical efforts vary from the crude to the sophisticated, but all are flawed by a lack of awareness of ethnocentric speaking positions. Nearly all center on formal readings of the art object, with broader cultural considerations positioned as mere background illumination.

For contemporary art critics, the most obvious point of entry into the abstract forms of Aboriginal art is modernism. Thus the Western desert dot paintings (from the settlements such as Papunya, Yuendumu and Yuelemu), in which a complex and unknowable symbology of body painting and ground diagrams is transferred to canvas, often get read as abstract art. Typical of this Western response is what Kay Larson, art critic for *New York Magazine,* wrote: "Aboriginal art at its best is as powerful as any abstract painting I can think of. I kept remembering Jackson Pollock, who also spread the emotional weight of thought and action throughout the empty spaces of his canvases." This comparison naively maps modernist self-expression onto the cultural practices of non-Western artists. Larson went on to acknowledge a spiritual basis for Aboriginal art, adding that "Aboriginal painters receive their meaning as part of a legacy from the ancestors; within the strict identities of the dreamings, each artist can find a private latitude of expression." Here an attempt is made to reconcile the irreconcilable. But in traditional Aboriginal cultures, ancestors, kin, the past, the present, the animate, the inanimate are all linked in non-rationalist patterns of connection, in a way that makes nonsense of our binary oppositions of inside versus outside, private versus public, us versus them.

So a superficial formal comparison opens the door for multiple layerings of ethnocentric reading which try to acknowledge difference while obliterating its meaning. Thus Western knowledge confirms itself and its superiority. A more pertinent point of comparison to be made between Jackson Pollock's work and some Aboriginal art (the dot paintings from Central Australia, in particular) is that both share a strategy of concealment, the former as self-protection, the latter as cultural protection. In both cases the artists' codes are esoteric (which doesn't necessarily mean private), ambiguous and ultimately unknowable to the viewer. This makes the Aboriginal work very vulnerable to appropriation into other meaning systems, specifically those already embedded in the agendas of modernist criticism.

Often the deeper significance of Aboriginal art is explained by recourse to the notion of "the dreamings." The totality of the Aboriginal culture's way of constructing the world, that complex system of meaning designated by "Dreamings," is collapsed into such Western "translations" as legend, mythology, ancestors, gods or spirits. The "spirituality" of Aboriginal art that is invoked in nearly every text, ranging from newspaper reports to scholarly catalogues, needs to be understood as a textual device, a trope. For non-Aboriginals, the spiritual can never fully operate as part of the work's meaning, because that would require a sharing of belief systems between the producers, critics and viewers. As an alternative, the naming of the spiritual is a kind of shorthand, signalling the "deep," the "authentic," the "substantial," and assuring the viewer that although he or she may only be able to enter the work on a formal level, the work does in fact have deeper connections. The formalist reading remains the pivot for the Western viewer, but it avoids being dismissed as superficial pleasure in looking at patterns because "the spiritual" always hovering in the background.

The so-called cultural relativism of the First-World art world that encourages difference is in reality a type of ethnocentrism, for while the value system of the other is acknowledged as different, it is never allowed to function in a way that would challenge the dominant culture's values. For the anthropologist Peter Sutton, this is a problem of "appreciation": "Here lies yet another obstacle to the wider appreciation of Aboriginal art: the barrier of belief. While Aboriginal people may believe in the reality of the Dreamings, the spirits, and the monsters represented in their art, most others cannot." Yet this very language ("monsters," "most others do not") enfolds an assumed cultural superiority. On the other hand, the spirituality of Aboriginal art is also mobilized to chastise Western culture. As Robert Hughes writes, "It raises painful questions about the irreversible drainage from our own culture of spirituality, awe and connection to nature." Besides other flaws, such a lament fails to acknowledge that the commodity status and the function of the work of art under modernity participate in a long historical process that specifically divests art of spiritual meaning. Art criticism, with its hyperbolic claims for the exalted status of the art object, is an agency in this process, for in the last instance even critical "hype" functions to valorize the art object. The secularized spirituality that was reinvented under the rubric "pure esthetics" has flowed into every aspect of the process that shapes the exchange value of the commodity, becoming added value and contributing to the inflated prices of masterworks at art auctions. And art criticism, with its continual evocation of a hollowed-out spirituality, is now subjecting non-Western culture and its material forms to the same process in which the possibility for a continuity of belief and value is lost forever.

So one dimension of the ethnocentric discourse on Aboriginal art is the harnessing of it to the dominant culture's notions of art; another aspect is that "difference" is constructed almost exclusively on a binary model and is therefore bound up with the West's internal dialogues and is a manifestation of its crises and anxieties. A crude example of this can be found in a brochure for an exhibition of Aboriginal art called "Dreams and Life," the inaugural exhibition at the Caz Gallery in Los Angeles in September 1988. The unsigned brochure text claims, "The best thing about Aboriginal art is that it infuses a sense of proportion and calm into our technologically tied, electronic media bludgeoned existence. For it can never be duplicated or mass produced. It is, in essence, independent of the Western world—yet it is an art that is increasing in popularity all over the world." This statement suggests that the indigenous can simply be inducted into the technological without any change. To write that Aboriginal art "can never be duplicated or mass produced" alongside full-color reproductions of the work is myopic in the extreme. Aboriginal art, along with all contemporary and historical art, owes its very existence in the international world of contemporary art to electronic and printing technologies and to the specifically modern forms of publicity generated by them: the invitation, the press release, the scholarly catalogue, the glossy picture book, the postcard, the news story, the review and the TV and radio interview.

Historically, the language of esthetics has been used to "rescue" tribal artifacts from ethnography and anthropology. Ethnographic classification was seen as lowering the status of the object, reducing it to a functional component within a social system. And ethnographic museum display was seen to remove both use value and esthetic value. But to place non-Western artifacts next to Western art objects and to scrutinize them with a detached esthetic gaze is seen by Westerners as a "recognition" of the artifacts' inherent qualities. Only then can the objects be elevated to their "rightful" place and be honored. An unquestioned notion of the superiority of the esthetic has justified the lowering of this gaze onto disparate fields of cultural production from non-Western material objects and practices to many forms of popular culture of the West, thus enabling a cultural colonization which reduces all objects to an equivalence. At the same time, however, the critiques of art history in its formalist and style-based modes over the last decade have changed this situation. Demands for contextualization have now called the anthropologist back into favor; but this time the anthropologist serves the art critic. The anthropologist provides an "expert" reading of the visual codes of another culture in order for their richness to be enjoyed. However, such mediation is always transformation, with significance resting with the culture of secondary interpretation.

One of the most authoritative texts on Aboriginal art evidences the new hybrid anthropologized art criticism (or estheticized anthropology); it is *Dreamings: The Art of Aboriginal Australia,* the catalogue that accompanied the Asia Society exhibition. While exhibiting all the trappings of a conventional art catalogue, *Dreamings* contains six essays by five anthropologists (four from the South Australian Museum). On one level this provides a very sensitive and sophisticated exposition of Aboriginal art; the art is not reduced to one reading. Rather, connections are made between Aboriginal art and politics, and the texts show a degree of self-consciousness about European constructions of the Aborigine (there is even a chapter on the history of scholarship on Aboriginal art). But for all its expertise, *Dreamings* is bound by the same problems that hamper cruder examples. Peter Sutton, for example, speaks of "obstacles" to European "recognition" of the "cultural value" of Aboriginal art. On the whole, the catalogue acknowledges the major differences between the cultural traditions, but can only offer a bland pluralist notion of appreciating difference.

We could go on citing examples, but two points about Western approaches to Aboriginal art should be clear by now. First, that the non-Aboriginal relation to Aboriginal culture remains bound within an ethnocentric model. Western culture has invented a culture of difference: Aboriginal people are spoken about and spoken for, with the din of white voices drowning out any possibility for an Aboriginal presentation of their cultures on their own terms. Secondly, it should be clear that Aboriginal art objects are always approached esthetically in the West. In order to gain a richer and more complex understanding of the art object, it is implied that the non-Aboriginal viewer must regard every other aspect—including the object's economic, political, ideological dimensions— through the picture's framing devices.

What then is the way out of this ethnocentric bind? One answer could be to reverse the order of these things, to see the art as a symptom of contemporary conditions rather than as an expression of an erroneously romanticized 40,000-year-old culture. Aboriginal people constitute one percent of the total Australian population, but their life conditions are dramatically worse than for the rest of the population on every count, including infant mortality, life expectancy and general levels of health, housing and education. (As far as education is concerned, we might note that the noticeable absence of Aboriginal voices on Aboriginal art can be attributed in part to lack of access to the literary skills provided through tertiary education.) Aboriginal unemployment is endemic: in New South Wales, the most populous state, the unemployment level for Aborigines is 70 percent and in many rural areas across Australia it runs as high as 90 percent. Decades of colonization have led to situations of extreme despair, with a range of variously integrated and literally disintegrated Aboriginal lifestyles. Alcoholism, violent deaths and a hostile police presence are all part of everyday life. In recent years there has also been an alarming tendency toward suicides and unexplained deaths of Aboriginal men while in police custody (this situation is the subject of a Royal Commission). This distressing situation is reflected in the diminishing political position of Aboriginal people. There is no national representative coalition of Aboriginal groups. "Land rights" laws have been overturned and are only as secure as the whims of the politicians who control the state's government. And the Federal government has only made a tentative gesture (strategically, in 1988, the Bicentenary of white colonization) toward the possibility of a treaty with Aboriginal people, details of which remain vague.

It is into this situation of social, cultural and economic desperation that art-making has come as a form of economic salvation. It has been particularly significant for remote, welfare-dependent communities like Papunya, Yuen-dumu and Ramingining. The intervention of missionaries earlier in the century and of white art teachers in the 1970s transformed the impermanent material forms of cultural practices—body- and sand-painting and ceremonial dress/objects—into permanent and marketable forms such as sculptures, ochre paintings on bark and acrylics on canvas. Now, up to 7,000 producers in Northern, Central and Western Australia are involved in an industry which is worth up to $(Aust)25 million a year. It is cash-crop economy in which white and white-trained Aboriginal art advisers induct the producers into the demands of the art market, with its requirements of finish, controlled quantity of production and consistency with gradual innovation. In Australia all of these variables have been brought under control. Thus the marketing of contemporary Aboriginal art can be seen as a form of soft neo-colonialism, through which Aboriginal people are incorporated into commodity production (with the attendant reorganization of social relations). One result is that traditional beliefs and practices have to be reconfigured according to the relative success or failure of the commodity. There is thus no continuity of tradition, no 40,000-year-old culture, no "time before time." There are only objects, produced by a range of fragmented cultures with varying connections to tradition and economic necessity, posed against the homogenized readings of these objects according to the meaning systems of the culture of dominance.

Pierre Clastres wrote the first definition of ethnocide for the *Encyclopaedia Universalis* in 1974. Unlike genocide, the physical destruction of a people, ethnocide is defined as a people's cultural erasure. This is accomplished, according to Clastres, by "obliging them to transform themselves to the point of total identification, if possible, with the model proposed to or imposed upon them." Such processes are not implemented without resistance. But these processes and the resistance to them must be seen in their post-colonial context. For Australian Aboriginals, ethnocide followed genocide, and this history has had profound effects upon their nature and ability to resist the imposed models of colonized and recolonized selfhood. After 200 years of continuous destruction of many kinds, it is remarkable that any resistance is still possible. While Aboriginal peoples are proud of and celebrate their survival over 40,000 years, in fact the most substantial feat of survival has been in the last 200 years of colonial occupation.

Still, such an observation should not be cast in a romantic light. Yet, in the press coverage of Aboriginal art exhibitions in the United States, for instance, the standard line is that the work is a product of "primitive" cultures. If the more politically aware writers shun the actual word, the concepts that circulate around "the primitive" remain in, for example, such words as "nontechnological," "unchanging," "closer to nature," "ancient" and "survival from the past." Such designations are always imposed to place the other at the opposite end of a lineage of development to the classifier. The people and their culture are delivered as figures of fascination and inferiority.

Historically, the idea of the primitive, as it has been constituted in Western culture, has shifted since the epoch of initial colonization when non-white races were often regarded as not fully human. The subsequent pattern has been either to destroy the other (genocide) or to "civilize" them (ethnocide), and then make them into a spectacle. The "savage" thus was disarmed, neutralized and placed before the gaze of the culture of power. This "spectacular primitive" is intertwined with the history of colonialism. In reality, there are no "primitive artists" out *there* in the desert awaiting discovery by white art curators, nor does the role of "primitive artist" represent the latest expression and culmination of a 40,000-year-old culture. Rather, the "primitive artist" is an invented and imposed model, which becomes available as a role for the colonized subject. The keepers of traditional tribal knowledges and their forms of visual transmission are classified as artists, and what they produce is naturalized as "art." This is how it can be claimed that there are some 7,000 traditional artists in Northern, Central and Western Australia—an extraordinary figure for a total Aboriginal population that is measured only in the tens of thousands. Resistance in this context requires the refusal of the model quietly imposed by intermediaries.

The "spectacular primitive" takes a variety of forms—the artwork is one, another is the artist him- or herself. Aboriginal artists are literally being put on display. The Caz Gallery in Los Angeles, for instance, flew three artists from Australia to be present at their inaugural exhibition and to demonstrate their skills. The gallery applauded itself in its biography of Bobby Nganjerra, a bark and rock painter of advanced years, saying, "Now Caz Gallery is giving Bobby the most wonderful opportunity of his life—to talk to Americans about his culture and to demonstrate a skill which is fast vanishing." Such crass and patronizing banality—unfortunately all too common—demonstrates the diminishment of Aboriginals to a silenced and exoticized spectacle.

What the Caz Gallery did is not an isolated incident, either. When Aboriginal artists were invited to the "Dreamings" exhibition, the press continually harped on the enormity of the cultural distance between Australia and the New York art world. This slant served to reduce the artists to subjects under observation, rather than artists with whom one could communicate. The artists were never quoted as authorities on their own work; that was left to curators and anthropologists. Instead, the artists were *described* in much the same way as was the work. In the USA, Australia and other parts of the world the tribal artist is being reified, that is, turned into an object and then mobilized as a docile image of the primitive culture to be gazed upon. A major event in Paris this year, "Magiciens de la Terre" showed ". . . the indigenous art of peoples living traditional lifestyles in many parts of the world." As part of this event (in which art and tourism become indivisible), the power gallery of Sydney University (recently renamed the Museum of Contemporary Art, prior to moving to the tourist heartland of Sydney) took a group of Aboriginal artists from the Northern Territory to Paris to show their work at the Centre Georges Pompidou. Like many other participants put on display as part of that exhibition, the artists were described as "all traditional people who have little experience in cities."

Ironically the precedent for such an event already exists—exactly 100 years ago, during the Paris Exposition of 1889, the ethnocidal practices of the French Empire were put on display. In that case, "Rather than showing the effects of domination on conquered peoples, their dispossession and violation, the Exhibition put colonized peoples on display to the world in unprecedented numbers as an exotic spectacle." Not only was the power of the Empire demonstrated by such an exposition of the exotic, but the period's taste for the exotic was given great force and focus. (This taste culminated in Picasso's *Les Demoiselles d'Avignon* of 1907, the painting which has become an icon of the modern taste for the pre-modern and of modernist "primitivism.") Presumably more "sensitivity" and "good intentions" will be shown in 1989, but it is doubtful that the discernible changes will add up to progress. Indigenous culture is still being displayed for the gaze of the colonizer and on terms and conditions set by the dominant culture. This is not to say that this time there will not be some possibility of exchange, but the terms continue to be massively unequal.

One factor is that in the appropriation of Aboriginal culture, careers in "white" society are being made. The "experts" who trade in the knowledge of "the other" inherit the violent history of liberalism upon which colonialism was built. Their empathy for the people they speak for and "manage" is always overridden by their striving for a professional niche in the arts industry. Their career advancement depends upon the reproduction of "the primitive." Without the fetishized object and the dominated subject/creator, the "master" narrator has no narrative and thus no career. This does not imply that Aboriginals gain nothing; the trip to Paris, for instance, *may have* provided useful knowledge, income or pleasure. But it is always the professional elite, building their careers on Aboriginal backs, who gain much more.

In this process, "Aboriginal culture" is something manufactured within the parameters of the professional norms of the careerists; it becomes a culture from which Aboriginal people are excluded either literally or by having to assume subject positions made available only by "the oppressor." (Then, as the colonized they become colonizers of themselves and their own others.) Take this example—Peter Sutton writes on the study of Aboriginal art in *Dreamings*:

> Without a substantial and sophisticated literature it will remain difficult to design appropriate courses and to tempt talented scholars into the field. Philip Jones's chapter here on the history of Aboriginal art scholarship, which is the first of its kind, shows that an important beginning has been made but that thus far the record is thin. Much of the literature on Aboriginal art will continue to come from anthropologists. This is understandable, in the sense that the more exotic kinds of Aboriginal culture remain difficult to comprehend without the kind of comprehensive learning process anthropologists call fieldwork.

652   FRY AND WILLIS

Here, in the un-selfconscious prioritizing of conventional academic knowledge, is ethnocide in action. The practice advocated is predicated on the assumption that "we know best," that it is perfectly legitimate for the cultures of others to be remade in the image of the culture of domination. Sutton's statement also fails to recognize that this is now *the* issue in anthropology: "the sheer inexplicability and unjustifiability of the ethnographer's presence from the standpoint of the other."

Several years ago, the progressive position, white and black, argued that the political justification for the entry of Aboriginal art into the spaces of the establishment in Australia and abroad was that it would give Aboriginal people a platform from which to expose their plight and argue for a better deal, especially in terms of land rights as a prerequisite for autonomy and self-determination. Nowadays this idealism has all but disappeared. The art establishment's management of the discourses of art (including its creation of the ethnocidal "spectacular primitive"), linked with the negation of the potential of Aboriginal artists to politically exploit their increased profile because of the trade-off of economic expediency, has reinstated and ensured the complicity of the powerless. So, while Aboriginal people have acquired a global platform for the display of their work, this does not constitute a platform from which to express their political aspirations. This does not mean that the artists have abandoned their desire for greater self-determination. Many of them have simply realized the impossibility of breaking the bonds that maintain their structural position. Economic pragmatism, and in some cases the adoption of an artistic ego, have frequently taken the place of idealism.

Meanwhile, new spaces of resistance have been created, but of course, again, unevenly. There is not space here to digress into a major theory of resistance, but we could define it briefly as any action towards self-preservation. In this case, whether it is a private or public act of defiance, Aboriginal resistance opposes ethnocide. It should be clear that ethnocide does not necessarily displace the culture it seeks to destroy by a frontal assault. Its violence, its domination, arrives as much by seduction as by force. To sustain opposition a model counter to the one being imposed must be discovered or created. For Aboriginal people this has meant two choices, united by difference: the flight back into traditional culture and the attempt at the creation of a new culture.

As Shiva Naipaul argued, in Australia, the romantic recovery of the past as a pre-colonial life is impossible. The memory and the effect of genocide, ethnocide and the impact of the modern world are inescapable. Colonialism created a rift between past and present that can never be repaired. The desire to return to the past is directed toward a *conservative* utopia—that which it seeks to conserve is already transformed and is defined against the rejected present. The return to the old culture is therefore really a new culture built upon signs of the past.

Making a new culture which knowingly embraces the future is a more viable form of cultural bricolage (by this we mean the making of culture by a process of the selection and assembly of combined and recombined cultural forms). Resistance to ethnocide is not seen as trying simply to defend an existent cultural identity but the forging of a new one which rejects the models sought to be imposed. Radio, television and video have become significant media in this cultural strategy. And what is particularly significant is that these media break the circuit of producing products for circulation and consumption within the culture of dominance (as opposed to works of art). Aboriginal radio, video and TV producers are producing ideas and images that circulate in their own cultures.

Thus, the establishment of the Alice Springs-based Central Australian Aboriginal Media Association (CAAMA) eight years ago is significant. It operates one of the most widely listened to (by both blacks and whites) radio stations in the Northern Territory, with its country music and educational programming broadcasts in six Aboriginal languages and English. (The population of the Northern Territory is 22 percent Aboriginal, the highest of all the states, but this can be deceptive—the largest number of Aboriginal people live in New South Wales with Sydney comprising the greatest numbers, but there they are far less visible, being only around one percent of the population.) CAAMA mounted a successful campaign against commercial competitors for the one television broadcasting license for Central Australia and has now established Imparja TV station which, like the CAAMA radio broadcasts in six Aboriginal languages plus English, is owned by Aboriginal people and addresses social issues of concern to them. Imparja claims a cultural space in which innovation is possible; it has a future. This is a new symbol of power in a culture dominated by the media. It doesn't override the effects of the damaged culture in which it functions, but creates a fissure in which a new set of perceptions can seep in. Such comments do not imply such an operation is free from either the reach of ethnocidal agency or of more direct effects of unequal exchange—it is not judged by authority as a mainstream commercial channel and is dependent on government funding. It is neither beyond nor lacking in criticism, especially over the nature and quantity of Aboriginal-made content.

Aboriginal TV is an obvious outlet for Aboriginal-made video, and there are a number of production centers in the Northern Territory and other parts of Australia. Some, like the Warlpiri Media Association at Yuendumu, are based in art-producing communities. Video trades on the assumption that its application and cultural productions are a form of resistance. This is not because of its content, but rather because it is *occupied* as a cultural space from which the right to speak is asserted—a late-modern space to address the present and the future. Television's cultural and economic usefulness to Aboriginal people is great. For one thing, it is less easily accommodated into the international exchange of cultural commodities than are art works. More importantly, it can't be classified as easily and in the same ways as the 'spectacular primitive' (which isn't to say it is invulnerable).

The late Eric Michaels, an anthropologist who specialized in Aboriginal media, described one Aboriginal videomaker this way:

Jupurrurla, in his Bob Marley T-shirt and Adidas runners, armed with his video portapak, resists identification as a savage updating some archaic technology to produce curiosities of primitive tradition for the jaded modern gaze. Jupurrurla is indisputably a sophisticated cultural broker who employs videotape and electronic technology to express and resolve political, theological and aesthetic contradictions that arise in uniquely contemporary circumstances.

Such an image demonstrates that the contemporary and traditional art of Aboriginal people is not the art of a dead culture. If Aboriginal culture is dying, which in many ways it is, it is because it is being prevented from reconstituting itself. To make itself anew requires major advances in cultural, economic and political self-determination, and a cessation of cultural and economic exploitation. The continuous appropriation and exposure of the cultural forms of "the other" by the powers of dominant cultures is at the heart of this ethnocidal process.

The survival of Aboriginal culture is an omnipresent struggle that takes place wherever the signs of the culture appear—in the burnt desert of Central Australia or in the art galleries of North America and Europe. Where work such as Aboriginal art is shown, how it is presented, who sees it and all the other ways the boundaries are drawn and power is exercised needs to be criticized and transformed. Yet even this view, while correct, is nevertheless too timid. Rather there is an ongoing need for critique, contestation and challenge of current curatorial, institutional, critical and art-marketing practices. For, indeed, the situation is getting worse. It is time a line was drawn. Circumstances should be created that allow Aboriginal people to speak for themselves, in their own manner. At the same time, far greater awareness of the modes of exploitation, and of the subtle and complex ways by which exploitation operates and is reproduced, needs to be generated.

Artists' Declarations

The selections from twentieth-century artists here are primarily manifestoes asserting novel approaches to art. Most of these writings have a political character. Many twentieth-century avant-garde artists have regarded their works and writings as fundamental challenges to the nature of art and its traditions. Along with several of the selections above, these statements pose the question of whether contemporary art is a radical departure from the traditions of art or whether there is a continuity throughout the history of art and its theory, including the most radical works of this century. The ideas of "radical departures" and the "avant-garde" are associated with modernism and should be compared with postmodernism and considered in the light of the other selections in Part IV.

Futurism was an Italian movement in the first decade of the century claiming the aesthetic superiority of modern technology over traditional masterpieces of art. Suprematism, begun by Kasimir Malevich in 1913, was a Russian movement based on the theory that paintings should be composed exclusively of simple geometrical forms. The Russian painter Wassily Kandinsky is one of the major figures of modern art. He moved from relatively freeform abstract paintings to geometrical forms during his lifetime, and his influence on modern painting and sculpture was immense. Piet Mondrian was a Dutch painter whose grid-based, rectilinear paintings have been widely imitated. Sol LeWitt is an American artist, known for box-like geometrical forms and the use of dots and lines in predetermined structures. He moved later into conceptual art.

F. T. MARINETTI

Futurist Painting: Technical Manifesto *

On the 8th of March, 1910, in the limelight of the Chiarella Theater of Turin, we launched our first Manifesto to a public of three thousand people—artists, men of letters, students and others; it was a violent and cynical cry which displayed our sense of rebellion, our deep-rooted disgust, our haughty contempt for vulgarity, for academic and pedantic mediocrity, for the fanatical worship of all that is old and worm-eaten.

We bound ourselves there and then to the movement of Futurist Poetry which was initiated a year earlier by F. T. Marinetti in the columns of the *Figaro*.

The battle of Turin has remained legendary. We exchanged almost as many knocks as we did ideas, in order to protect from certain death the genius of Italian Art.

And now during a temporary pause in this formidable struggle we come out of the crowd in order to expound with technical precision our program for the renovation of painting, of which our Futurist Salon at Milan was a dazzling manifestation.[1]

Our growing need of truth is no longer satisfied with Form and Color as they have been understood hitherto.

---

* F. T. Marinetti "Futurist Painting: Technical Manifesto, April 11, 1910" in *Theories of Modern Art*, edited by Herschel B. Chipp (Berkeley and Los Angeles: University of California Press, 1968), p. 289-290, 292-293. Originally published as a pamphlet in Milan, 11 April 1910. This translation was made under Marinetti's guidance and published in the catalogue of the London exhibition. It differs in some minor points from the version published in the collected manifestoes of 1914 (*I Manifesti del Futurismo*, ed. F. T. Marinetti [Florence: "Lacerba," 1914]).

The gesture which we would reproduce on canvas shall no longer be a fixed *moment* in universal dynamism. It shall simply be the dynamic sensation itself (made eternal).

Indeed, all things move, all things run, all things are rapidly changing.

A profile is never motionless before our eyes, but it constantly appears and disappears. On account of the persistency of an image upon the retina, moving objects constantly multiply themselves; their form changes like rapid vibrations, in their mad career. Thus a running horse has not four legs, but twenty, and their movements are triangular.

All is conventional in art. Nothing is absolute in painting. What was truth for the painters of yesterday is but a falsehood today. We declare, for instance, that a portrait (to be a work of art) must not be like the sitter and that the painter carries in himself the landscapes which he would fix upon his canvas.

To paint a human figure you must not paint it; you must render the whole of its surrounding atmosphere.

Space no longer exists: the street pavement, soaked by rain beneath the glare of electric lamps, becomes immensely deep and gapes to the very center of the earth. Thousands of miles divide us from the sun; yet the house in front of us fits into the solar disk.

Who can still believe in the opacity of bodies, since our sharpened and multiplied sensitiveness has already penetrated the obscure manifestations of the medium? Why should we forget in our creations the doubled power of our sight capable of giving results analogous to those of the X-rays?

It will be sufficient to cite a few examples, chosen among thousands, to prove the truth of our arguments.

The sixteen people around you in a rolling motor bus are in turn and at the same time one, ten, four, three; they are motionless and they change places; they come and go, bound into the street, are suddenly swallowed up by the sunshine, then come back and sit before you, like persistent symbols of universal vibration.

How often have we not seen upon the cheek of the person with whom we were talking the horse which passes at the end of the street.

Our bodies penetrate the sofas upon which we sit, and the sofas penetrate our bodies. The motor bus rushes into the houses which it passes, and in their turn the houses throw themselves upon the motor bus and are blended with it.

The construction of pictures has hitherto been foolishly traditional. Painters have shown us the objects and the people placed before us. We shall henceforward put the spectator in the center of the picture.

As in every realm of the human mind, clear-sighted individual research has swept away the unchanging obscurities of dogma, so must the vivifying current of science soon deliver painting from academic tradition.

We would at any price re-enter into life. Victorious science has nowadays disowned its past in order the better to serve the material needs of our time;

we would that art, disowning its past, were able to serve at last the intellectual needs which are within us.

Our renovated consciousness does not permit us to look upon man as the center of universal life. The suffering of a man is of the same interest to us as the suffering of an electric lamp, which, with spasmodic starts, shrieks out the most heart-rending expressions of color.[2] The harmony of the lines and folds of modern dress works upon our sensitiveness with the same emotional and symbolical power as did the nude upon the sensitiveness of the old masters.

In order to conceive and understand the novel beauties of a Futurist picture, the soul must be purified (become again pure); the eye must be freed from its veil of atavism and culture, so that it may at last look upon Nature and not upon the museum as the one and only standard.

As soon as ever this result has been obtained, it will be readily admitted that brown tints have never coursed beneath our skin; it will be discovered that yellow shines forth in our flesh, that red blazes, and that green, blue, and violet dance upon it with untold charms, voluptuous and caressing.

How is it possible still to see the human face pink, now that our life, redoubled by noctambulism, has multiplied our perceptions as colorists? The human face is yellow, red, green, blue, violet. The pallor of a woman gazing in a jeweler's window is more intensely iridescent than the prismatic fires of the jewels that fascinate her like a lark.

The time has passed for our sensations in painting to be whispered. We wish them in future to sing and re-echo upon our canvases in deafening and triumphant flourishes.

Your eyes, accustomed to semidarkness, will soon open to more radiant visions of light. The shadows which we shall paint shall be more luminous than the highlights of our predecessors, and our pictures, next to those of the museums, will shine like blinding daylight compared with deepest night.

We conclude that painting cannot exist today without Divisionism. This is no process that can be learned and applied at will. Divisionism, for the modern painter, must be in INNATE COMPLEMENTARINESS, which we declare to be essential and necessary.

Our art will probably be accused of tormented and decadent cerebralism. But we shall merely answer that we are, on the contrary, the primitives of a new sensitiveness, multiplied hundredfold, and that our art is intoxicated with spontaneity and power.[3]

WE DECLARE:

1. THAT ALL FORMS OF IMITATION MUST BE DESPISED, ALL FORMS OF ORIGINALITY GLORIFIED.

2. THAT IT IS ESSENTIAL TO REBEL AGAINST THE TYRANNY OF THE TERMS "HAR-

MONY" AND "GOOD TASTE" AS BEING TOO ELASTIC EXPRESSIONS, BY THE HELP OF WHICH IT IS EASY TO DEMOLISH THE WORKS OF REMBRANDT, OF GOYA AND OF RODIN.

3. THAT THE ART CRITICS ARE USELESS OR HARMFUL.
4. THAT ALL SUBJECTS PREVIOUSLY USED MUST BE SWEPT ASIDE IN ORDER TO EXPRESS OUR WHIRLING LIFE OF STEEL, OR PRIDE, OF FEVER AND OF SPEED.
5. THAT THE NAME OF "MADMAN" WITH WHICH IT IS ATTEMPTED TO GAG ALL INNOVATORS SHOULD BE LOOKED UPON AS A TITLE OF HONOR.
6. THAT INNATE COMPLEMENTARINESS IS AN ABSOLUTE NECESSITY IN PAINTING, JUST AS FREE METER IN POETRY OR POLYPHONY IN MUSIC.
7. THAT UNIVERSAL DYNAMISM MUST BE RENDERED IN PAINTING AS A DYNAMIC SENSATION.
8. THAT IN THE MANNER OF RENDERING NATURE THE FIRST ESSENTIAL IS IN SINCERITY AND PURITY.
9. THAT MOVEMENT AND LIGHT DESTROY THE MATERIALITY OF BODIES.

WE FIGHT:

1. AGAINST THE BITUMINOUS TINTS BY WHICH IT IS ATTEMPTED TO OBTAIN THE PATINA OF TIME UPON MODERN PICTURES.
2. AGAINST THE SUPERFICIAL AND ELEMENTARY ARCHAISM FOUNDED UPON FLAT TINTS, AND WHICH, BY IMITATING THE LINEAR TECHNIQUE OF THE EGYPTIANS, REDUCES PAINTING TO A POWERLESS SYNTHESIS, BOTH CHILDISH AND GROTESQUE.
3. AGAINST THE FALSE CLAIMS TO BELONG TO THE FUTURE PUT FORWARD BY THE SECESSIONISTS AND THE INDEPENDENTS, WHO HAVE INSTALLED NEW ACADEMIES NO LESS TRITE AND ATTACHED TO ROUTINE THAN THE PRECEDING ONES.
4. AGAINST THE NUDE IN PAINTING, AS NAUSEOUS AND AS TEDIOUS AS ADULTERY IN LITERATURE.

We wish to explain this last point. Nothing is *immoral* in our eyes; it is the monotony of the nude against which we fight. We are told that the subject is nothing and that everything lies in the manner of treating it. That is agreed; we, too, admit that. But this truism, unimpeachable and absolute fifty years ago, is no longer so today with regard to the nude, since artists obsessed with the desire to expose the bodies of their mistresses have transformed the Salons into arrays of unwholesome flesh!

We demand, for ten years, the total suppression of the nude in painting.[4]

> Umberto Boccioni, painter (Milan)
> Carlo D. Carrà, painter (Milan)
> Luigi Russolo, painter (Milan)
> Giacomo Balla, painter (Rome)
> Gino Severini, painter (Paris)

Notes

1. The "Salon" referred to is the *"Mostra d'arte libera,"* opened 30 April 1911. In most versions of the manifesto the following significant paragraph took the place of the above: "We were concerned then with the relation between ourselves and society. Today, instead, with this second manifesto, we resolutely shake off all relative considerations and ascend to the highest expressions of the pictorial absolute."

2. In other publications this reads "expressions of grief."

3. In the publication of the collected manifestoes, in 1914, the following takes the place of this paragraph: "Finally, we reject the easy accusation of 'baroquism' with which some would like to confront us. The ideas we have presented here derive solely from our acute sensibility. While 'baroquism' signifies artificiality, irresponsible and devitalized virtuosity, the art we set forth is all spontaneity and power."

4. In the publication of the collected manifestoes in 1914 these final two paragraphs were omitted. In their place was the following:
"You think us mad. We are, instead, the primitives of a new, completely transformed sensibility.
"Outside the atmosphere in which we live are only shadows. We Futurists ascend towards the highest and most radiant peak and proclaim ourselves Lords of Light, for already we drink from the live founts of the sun."

Umberto Boccioni

Technical Manifesto of Futurist Sculpture *

In the monuments and exhibitions of every European city, sculpture offers a spectacle of such barbarism, clumsiness, and monotonous imitation, that my Futurist eye recoils from it with profound disgust!

The sculpture of every country is dominated by the blind and foolish imitation of formulas inherited from the past, an imitation encouraged by the double cowardice of tradition and facility. In Latin countries we have the burdensome weight of Greece and Michelangelo, which is borne in France and Belgium with a certain seriousness of skill, and in Italy with grotesque imbecility. In German countries we have a foolish Greek-ized Gothicism, industrialized in Berlin, and in Munich sweetened with effeminate care by German pedantry. In Slavic countries, on the other hand, there is a confused clash between archaic Greek and Nordic and Oriental monstrosities, a shapeless mass of influences that range from the excess of abstruse details deriving from Asia, to the childish and grotesque ingenuity of the Lapps and Eskimos.

In all these manifestations of sculpture, as well as in those with a larger measure of innovating audacity, the same error is perpetuated: the artist copies the nude and studies classical statuary with the simpleminded conviction that he can find a style corresponding to modern sensibility without

---

* Umberto Boccioni, "Technical Manifesto of Futurist Sculpture, 1912," in *Theories of Modern Art,* edited by Herschel B. Chipp (Berkeley and Los Angeles: University of California Press, 1968), pp. 298-304.

relinquishing the traditional concept of sculptural form. This concept, with its famous "ideal beauty" of which everybody speaks on bended knee, never breaks away from the Phidian period and its decadence.

And it is almost inexplicable why the thousands of sculptors who have continued from generation to generation to construct dummies have not as yet asked themselves why the galleries of sculpture, when not absolutely deserted, are visited with boredom and horror, and why the unveiling of monuments in squares all over the world meets with incomprehension and general hilarity. This does not happen with painting because of its continual renewal which, as slow as the process has been, is the clearest condemnation of the plagiarized and sterile works of all the sculptors of our epoch!

Sculptors must convince themselves of this absolute truth: to continue to construct and want to create with Egyptian, Greek, or Michelangelesque elements, is like wanting to draw water from a dry well with a bottomless bucket.

There can be no renewal in art whatever if the essence itself is not renewed, that is, the vision and concept of line and masses that form the arabesque. It is not simply by reproducing the exterior aspects of contemporary life that art becomes the expression of its own time; this is why sculpture as it has been understood to date by artists of the past century and the present is a monstrous anachronism!

Sculpture has failed to progress because of the limited field assigned to it by the academic concept of the nude. An art that has been completely to strip a man or woman in order to begin its emotive function is a dead art! Painting has taken on new life, profundity, and breadth through a study of landscape and the environment, which are made to react simultaneously in relationship to the human figures or objects, reaching the point of our Futurist INTERPENETRATION OF PLANES (*Technical Manifesto of Futurist Painting*, 11 *April* 1910). In the same way sculpture will find a new source of emotion, hence of style, extending its plastic quality to what our barbarous crudity has made us think of until now as subdivided, impalpable, and thus plastically inexpressible.

We have to start from the central nucleus of the object that we want to create, in order to discover the new laws, that is, the new forms, that link it invisibly but mathematically to the APPARENT PLASTIC INFINITE and to the INTERNAL PLASTIC INFINITE. The new plastic art will, then, be a translation into plaster, bronze, glass, wood, and any other material, of those atmospheric planes that link and intersect things. This vision that I have called PHYSICAL TRANSCENDENTALISM (*Lecture on Futurist Painting at the Circolo Artistico*, Rome, May 1911) will be able to give plastic form to the mysterious sympathies and affinities that the reciprocal formal influences of the planes of objects create.

Sculpture must, therefore, give life to objects by making their extension in space palpable, systematic, and plastic, since no one can any longer believe that an object ends where another begins and that our body is surrounded by anything—bottle, automobile, house, tree, road—that does not cut through it and section it in an arabesque of directional curves.

There have been two attempts at renewal in modern sculpture: one decorative, concentrating on style; and the other strictly plastic, concentrating on material. The first, anonymous and disordered, lacked a coordinating technical genius and, since it was too closely tied to the economic requirements of building, only produced pieces of traditional sculpture more or less decoratively synthesized and confined within architectural or decorative motives or schemes. All the buildings and houses constructed in accordance with modern criteria include such efforts in marble, cement, or in metal plate.

The second attempt, more pleasing, disinterested, and poetic, but too isolated and fragmentary, lacked a synthetic idea to give it law. In working towards renewal it is not enough just to believe with fervor; one must formulate and work out a norm that points the way. I am referring to the genius of Medardo Rosso [1858-1928], to an Italian, and to the only great modern sculptor who has attempted to open up a larger field to sculpture, rendering plastically the influences of an ambience and the atmospheric ties that bind it to the subject.

Of the three other great contemporary sculptors, Constantin Meunier [1831-1905] has contributed nothing new to sculptural sensibility. His statues are almost always agreeable fusions of the Greek heroic with the athletic humility of the stevedore, sailor, or miner. His plastic and constructional concept of the statue and of bas-relief is still that of the Parthenon or the classical hero, although it was he who first attempted to create and deify subjects that had been previously despised or relegated to lower types of realistic reproduction.

[Antoine] Bourdelle [1861-1929] brings to the sculptural block an almost fanatic severity of abstract architectural masses. Of passionate temperament, highly strung, sincerely looking for the truth, he none the less does not know how to free himself from a certain archaic influence and from the general anonymity of the stonecutters of the Gothic cathedrals.

Rodin is of vaster spiritual agility, which has allowed him to go from the Impressionism of the *Balzac* to the uncertainty of the *Burghers of Calais* and all the other Michelangelesque sins. He bears in his sculpture a restless inspiration and a sweeping lyrical drive, which would be truly modern if Michelangelo and Donatello had not already possessed the qualities in almost identical form four hundred or so years before, and if they were used to animate a completely re-created reality.

We thus have in the works of these three great sculptors influences coming from three different periods: Greek in Meunier, Gothic in Bourdelle, Italian Renaissance in Rodin.

The work of Medardo Rosso, on the other hand, is very modern and revolutionary, more profound and of necessity restricted. It involves neither heroes nor symbols, but the plane of a woman's brow, or of a child's, points towards a liberation of space, which will have a much greater importance in the history of the spirit than our times have given it. Unfortunately the impressionistic necessities of this attempt have limited Medardo Rosso's research to a kind of high or low relief, demonstrating that the human figure is still conceived of as a world in itself with traditional bases and an episodic goal.

The revolution of Medardo Rosso, although of the greatest importance, starts off from an external pictorial concept that overlooks the problem of a new construction of planes; while the sensual touch of the thumb, imitating the lightness of Impressionist brushstrokes, gives a sense of lively immediacy, it requires rapid execution from life and removes from the work of art its character of universal creation. It thus has the same strong points and defects as Impressionism in painting. Our aesthetic revolution also takes its start from these researches, but in continuing them it has gone on to reach an extreme opposite point.

In sculpture as in painting one cannot renovate without searching for THE STYLE OF THE MOVEMENT, that is, by making systematic and definitive in a synthesis what Impressionism has given us as fragmentary, accidental, and thus analytical. And this systematization of the vibrations of sculpture, whose foundation will be architectural, not only in the construction of the masses, but in such a way that the block of the sculpture will contain within itself the architectural elements of the SCULPTURAL ENVIRONMENT in which the subject lives.

Naturally we will bring forth a SCULPTURE OF ENVIRONMENT.

A Futurist composition in sculpture will embody the marvelous mathematical and geometrical elements that make up the objects of our time. And these objects will not be placed next to the statue as explanatory attributes or dislocated decorative elements but, following the laws of a new conception of harmony, will be embedded in the muscular lines of the body. Thus from the shoulder of a mechanic may protrude the wheel of a machine, and the line of a table might cut into the head of a person reading; and a book with its fan-like leaves might intersect the stomach of the reader.

Traditionally a statue is carved out or delineated against the atmospheric environment in which it is exhibited. Futurist painting has overcome this conception of the rhythmic continuity of the lines in a human figure and of the figure's isolation from its background and from its INVISIBLE INVOLVING SPACE. Futurist poetry, according to the poet Marinetti, "after having destroyed the traditional meter and created free verse, now destroys syntax and the Latin sentence. Futurist poetry is an uninterrupted and spontaneous flow of analogies, each one of which is intuitively related to the central subject. Thus, wireless imagination and free words." The Futurist music of Balilla Pratella breaks through the chronometrical tyranny of rhythm.

Why should sculpture remain behind, tied to laws that no one has the right to impose on it? We therefore cast all aside and proclaim the ABSOLUTE AND COMPLETE ABOLITION OF DEFINITE LINES AND CLOSED SCULPTURE. WE BREAK OPEN THE FIGURE AND ENCLOSE IT IN ENVIRONMENT. We proclaim that the environment must be part of the plastic block which is a world in itself with its own laws; that the sidewalk can jump up on your table and your head be transported across the street, while your lamp spins a web of plaster rays between one house and another.

We proclaim that the whole visible world must fall in upon us, merging with us and creating a harmony measurable only by the creative imagination; that a leg, an arm, or an object, having no importance except as elements of plastic rhythm, can be abolished, not in order to imitate a Greek or Roman fragment, but to conform to the harmony the artist wishes to create. A sculptural entity, like a picture, can only resemble itself, for in art the human figure and objects must exist apart from the logic of physiognomy.

Thus a human figure may have one arm clothed and the other bare, and the different lines of a vase of flowers might freely intervene between the lines of the hat and those of the neck.

Thus transparent planes, glass, sheets of metal, wires, outside or inside electric lights, can indicate the planes, inclinations, tones, and half tones of a new reality.

Thus a new intuitive coloring in white, in gray, in black, can increase the emotive strength of planes, while the note of a colored plane will accentuate with violence the abstract significance of the plastic reality!

What we have said about LINES/FORCES in painting (*Preface–Manifesto of the Catalogue of the First Futurist Exhibition,* Paris, October 1911[1]) can be said similarly of sculpture; the static muscular line can be made to live in the dynamic line/force. The straight line will predominate in this muscular line, since only it corresponds to the internal simplicity of the synthesis that we oppose to the external baroquism deriving from analysis.

But the straight line will not lead us to imitate the Egyptians, the primitives, and the savages as some modern sculptors have desperately attempted to do in order to free themselves from the Greeks. Our straight line is alive and palpitating; it will lend itself to all that is necessary for the infinite expressions of the material; and its bare, fundamental severity will symbolize the severity of steel that determines the lines of modern machinery.

Finally we can affirm that in sculpture the artist must not shrink from using any means that will allow him to achieve REALITY. There is no fear more stupid than that which makes us afraid to go beyond the bounds of the art we are practicing. There is no such thing as painting, sculpture, music, or poetry; there is only creation! Therefore if a composition is in need of a special rhythmical movement to aid or contrast with the static rhythm of the SCULPTURAL ENTITY (a necessity in a work of art), one can superimpose any structure whatsoever that is capable of giving the required movements to the planes or lines.

We cannot forget that the tick-tock and the moving hands of a clock, the in-and-out of a piston in a cylinder, the opening and closing of two cogwheels with the continual appearance and disappearance of their square steel cogs, the fury of a flywheel or the turbine of a propeller, are all plastic and pictorial elements of which a Futurist work in sculpture must take account. The opening and closing of a valve creates a rhythm just as beautiful but infinitely newer than the blinking of an animal eyelid.

CONCLUSIONS

1. We proclaim that sculpture is based on the abstract reconstruction of the planes and volumes that determine the forms, not their figurative value.
2. ABOLISH IN SCULPTURE as in every other art THE TRADITIONAL SUBLIMITY OF THE SUBJECT.
3. Deny to sculpture as an aim any "true-to-life" episodic construction, but affirm the absolute necessity of using all reality in order to return to the essential elements of plastic sensibility. Thus, in perceiving bodies and their parts as PLASTIC ZONES, a Futurist composition in sculpture will use metal or wood planes for an object, static or moved mechanically, furry spherical forms for hair, semicircles of glass for a vase, wire and screen for an atmospheric plane, etc.
4. Destroy the wholly literary and traditional nobility of marble and of bronze. Deny the exclusiveness of one material for the entire construction of a sculptural ensemble. Affirm that even twenty different materials can compete in a single work to effect plastic emotion. Let us enumerate some: glass, wood, cardboard, iron, cement, horsehair, leather, cloth, mirrors, electric lights, etc., etc.
5. Proclaim that in the intersection of the planes of a book with the angles of a table, in the lines of a match, in the frame of a window, there is more truth than in all the twisting of muscles, all the breasts and buttocks of the heroes and Venuses that inspire the modern idiocy in sculpture.
6. That only the most modern choice of subjects can lead to the discovery of new PLASTIC IDEAS.
7. That the straight line is the only means that can lead to the primitive virginity of a new architectural construction of sculptural masses or zones.
8. That there can be no renovation if not through a SCULPTURE OF ENVIRONMENT, for through this plasticity will be developed and, continuing, will be able to MODEL THE ATMOSPHERE that surrounds things.
9. The thing that one creates is nothing other than a bridge between the EXTERIOR PLASTIC INFINITE and the INTERIOR PLASTIC INFINITE; thus objects never end, and intersect with infinite combinations of sympathetic harmonies and clashing aversions.

NOTE

1. The exhibition was held in February 1912, although Boccioni noted he had earlier expounded on the ideas included in the preface to the catalogue.

KASIMIR MALEVICH

*Suprematism**

Under Suprematism I understand the supremacy of pure feeling in creative art.

To the Suprematist the visual phenomena of the objective world are, in themselves, meaningless; the significant thing is feeling, as such, quite apart from the environment in which it is called forth.

The so-called "materialization" of a feeling in the conscious mind really means a materialization of the *reflection* of that feeling through the medium of some realistic conception. Such a realistic conception is without value in Suprematist art. . . . And not only in Suprematist art but in art generally, because the enduring, true value of a work of art (to whatever school it may belong) resides solely in the feeling expressed.

Academic naturalism, the naturalism of the Impressionists, Cézanneism, Cubism, etc.—all these, in a way, are nothing more than dialectic methods which, as such, in no sense determine the true value of an art work.

An objective representation, having objectivity as its aim, is something which, as such, has nothing to do with art, and yet the use of objective forms in an art work does not preclude the possibility of its being of high artistic value.

Hence, to the Suprematist, the appropriate means of representation is always the one which gives fullest possible expression to feeling as such and which ignores the familiar appearance of objects.

---

* Kasimir Malevich, "Suprematism," in *Theories of Modern Art*, edited by Herschel B. Chipp (Berkeley and Los Angeles: University of California Press, 1968), pp. 341-346. From Malevich, *The Non-Objective World*, pp. 67-100 *passim*.

Objectivity, in itself, is meaningless to him; the concepts of the conscious mind are worthless.

Feeling is the determining factor . . . and thus art arrives at nonobjective representation—at Suprematism.

It reaches a "desert" in which nothing can be perceived by feeling.

Everything which determined the objective-ideal structure of life and "art"—ideas, concepts, and images—all this the artist has cast aside in order to heed pure feeling.

The art of the past which stood, at least ostensibly, in the service of religion and the state, will take on new life in the pure (unapplied) art of *Suprematism*, which will build up a new world—the world of feeling. . . .

When, in the year 1913, in my desperate attempt to free art from the ballast of objectivity, I took refuge in the square form and exhibited a picture which consisted of nothing more than a black square on a white field, the critics and, along with them, the public sighed, "Everything which we loved is lost. We are in a desert. . . . Before us is nothing but a black square on a white background!"

"Withering" words were sought to drive off the symbol of the "desert" so that one might behold on the "dead square" the beloved likeness of "reality" ("true objectivity" and a spiritual feeling).

The square seemed incomprehensible and dangerous to the critics and the public . . . and this, of course, was to be expected.

The ascent to the heights of nonobjective art is arduous and painful—but it is nevertheless rewarding. The familiar recedes ever further and further into the background. . . . The contours of the objective world fade more and more and so it goes, step by step, until finally the world—"everything we loved and by which we have lived"—becomes lost to sight.

No more "likenesses of reality," no idealistic images—nothing but a desert!

But this desert is filled with the spirit of nonobjective sensation which pervades everything.

Even I was gripped by a kind of timidity bordering on fear when it came to leaving "the world of will and idea," in which I had lived and worked and in the reality of which I had believed.

But a blissful sense of liberating nonobjectivity drew me forth into the "desert," where nothing is real except feeling . . . and so feeling became the substance of my life.

This was no "empty square" which I had exhibited but rather the feeling of nonobjectivity.

I realized that the "thing" and the "concept" were substituted for feeling and understood the falsity of the world of will and idea.

Is a milk bottle, then, the symbol of milk?

Suprematism is the rediscovery of pure art which, in the course of time, had become obscured by the accumulation of "things."

It appears to me that, for the critics and the public, the painting of Raphael, Rubens, Rembrandt, etc., has become nothing more than a *con-*

glomeration of countless "things," which conceal its true value—the feeling which gave rise to it. The virtuosity of the objective representation is the only thing admired.

If it were possible to extract from the works of the great masters the feeling expressed in them—the actual artistic value, that is—and to hide this away, the public, along with the critics and the art scholars, would never even miss it.

So it is not at all strange that my square seemed empty to the public.

If one insists on judging an art work on the basis of the virtuosity of the objective representation—the verisimilitude of the illusion—and thinks he sees in the objective representation itself a symbol of the inducing emotion, he will never partake of the gladdening content of a work of art.

The general public is still convinced today that art is bound to perish if it gives up the imitation of "dearly loved reality" and so it observes with dismay how the hated element of pure feeling—abstraction—makes more and more headway. . . .

Art no longer cares to serve the state and religion, it no longer wishes to illustrate the history of manners, it wants to have nothing further to do with the object, as such, and believes that it can exist, in and for itself, without "things" (that is, the "time-tested well-spring of life").

But the nature and meaning of artistic creation continue to be misunderstood, as does the nature of creative work in general, because feeling, after all, is always and everywhere the one and only source of every creation.

The emotions which are kindled in the human being are stronger than the human being himself . . . they must at all costs find an outlet—they must take on overt form—they must be communicated or put to work.

It was nothing other than a yearning for speed . . . for flight . . . which, seeking an outward shape, brought about the birth of the airplane. For the airplane was not contrived in order to carry business letters from Berlin to Moscow, but rather in obedience to the irresistible drive of this yearning for speed to take on external form.

The "hungry stomach" and the intellect which serves this must always have the last word, of course, when it comes to determining the origin and purpose of *existing* values—but that is a subject in itself.

And the state of affairs is exactly the same in art as in creative technology. . . . In painting (I mean here, naturally, the accepted "artistic" painting) one can discover behind a technically correct portrait of Mr. Miller or an ingenious representation of the flower girl at Potsdamer Platz not a trace of the true essence of art—no evidence whatever of feeling. Painting is the dictatorship of a method of representation, the purpose of which is to depict Mr. Miller, his environment, and his ideas.

The black square on the white field was the first form in which nonobjective feeling came to be expressed. The square = feeling, the white field = the void beyond this feeling.

Yet the general public saw in the nonobjectivity of the representation the demise of art and failed to grasp the evident fact that feeling had here assumed external form.

The Suprematist square and the forms proceeding out of it can be likened to the primitive marks (symbols) of aboriginal man which represented, in their combinations, *not ornament but a feeling of rhythm.*

Suprematism did not bring into being a new world of feeling but, rather, an altogether new and direct form of representation of the world of feeling.

The square changes and creates new forms, the elements of which can be classified in one way or another depending upon the feeling which gave rise to them.

When we examine an antique column, we are no longer interested in the fitness of its construction to perform its technical task in the building but recognize in it the material expression of a pure feeling. We no longer see in it a structural necessity but view it as a work of art in its own right.

"Practical life," like a homeless vagabond, forces its way into every artistic form and believes itself to be the genesis and reason for existence of this form. But the vagabond doesn't tarry long in one place and once he is gone (when to make an art work serve "practical purposes" no longer seems practical) the work recovers its full value.

Antique works of art are kept in museums and carefully guarded, not to preserve them for practical use but in order that their eternal artistry may be enjoyed.

The difference between the new, nonobjective ("useless") art and the art of the past lies in the fact that the full artistic value of the latter comes to light (becomes recognized) only after life, in search of some new expedient, has forsaken it, whereas the unapplied artistic element of the new art outstrips life and shuts the door on "practical utility."

And so there the new nonobjective art stands—the expression of pure feeling, seeking no practical values, no ideas, no "promised land". . . .

The Suprematists have deliberately given up objective representation of their surroundings in order to reach the summit of the true "unmasked" art and from this vantage point to view life through the prism of pure artistic feeling.

Nothing in the objective world is as "secure and unshakable" as it appears to our conscious minds. We should accept nothing as predetermined—as constituted for eternity. Every "firmly established," familiar thing can be shifted about and brought under a new and, primarily, unfamiliar order. Why then should it not be possible to bring about an artistic order? . . .

Our life is a theater piece, in which nonobjective feeling is portrayed by objective imagery.

A bishop is nothing but an actor who seeks with words and gestures, on an appropriately "dressed" stage, to convey a religious feeling, or rather the reflection of a feeling in religious form. The office clerk, the blacksmith, the soldier, the accountant, the general . . . these are all characters out of one stage play or another, portrayed by various people, who become so carried away that they confuse the play and their parts in it with life itself. We almost never get to see the *actual human face* and if we ask someone who he is, he answers, "an engineer," "a farmer," etc., or in other words, he gives the title of the role played by him in one or another effective drama.

The title of the role is also set down next to his full name, and certified in his passport, thus removing any doubt concerning the surprising fact that the owner of the passport is the engineer Ivan and not the painter Kasimir.

In the last analysis, what each individual knows about himself is precious little, because the "actual human face" cannot be discerned behind the mask, which is mistaken for the "actual face."

The philosophy of Suprematism has every reason to view both the mask and the "actual face" with skepticism, since it disputes the reality of human faces (human forms) altogether.

Artists have always been partial to the use of the human face in their representations, for they have seen in it (the versatile, mobile, expressive mimic) the best vehicle with which to convey their feelings. The Suprematists have nevertheless abandoned the representation of the human face (and of natural objects in general) and have found new symbols with which to render direct feelings (rather than externalized reflections of feelings), for *the Suprematist does not observe and does not touch—he feels.*

We have seen how art, at the turn of the century, divested itself of the ballast of religious and political ideas which had been imposed upon it and came into its own—attained, that is, the form suited to its intrinsic nature and became, along with the two already mentioned, a third independent and equally valid "point of view." The public is still, indeed, as much convinced as ever that the artist creates superfluous, impractical things. It never considers that these superfluous things endure and retain their vitality for thousands of years, whereas necessary, practical things survive only briefly.

It does not dawn on the public that it fails to recognize the real, true value of things. This is also the reason for the chronic failure of everything utilitarian. A true, absolute order of human society could only be achieved if mankind were willing to base this order on lasting values. Obviously, then, the artistic factor would have to be accepted in every respect as the decisive one. As long as this is not the case, the uncertainty of a "provisional order" will obtain, instead of the longed-for tranquillity of an absolute order, because the provisional order is gauged by current utilitarian understanding and this measuring-stick is variable in the highest degree.

In the light of this, all art works which, at present, are a part of "practical life" or to which practical life has laid claim, are in some senses devaluated. Only when they are freed from the encumbrance of practical utility (that is, when they are placed in museums) will their truly artistic, absolute value be recognized.

The sensations of sitting, standing, or running are, first and foremost, plastic sensations and they are responsible for the development of corresponding "objects of use" and largely determine their form.

A chair, bed, and table are not matters of utility but rather, the forms taken by plastic sensations, so the generally held view that all objects of daily use result from practical considerations is based upon false premises.

We have ample opportunity to become convinced that we are never in a position for recognizing any real utility in things and that we shall never succeed in constructing a really practical object. We can evidently only *feel* the essence of absolute utility but, since a feeling is always nonobjective, any attempt to grasp the utility of the objective is Utopian. The endeavor to confine feeling within concepts of the conscious mind or, indeed, to replace it with conscious concepts and to give it concrete, utilitarian form, has resulted in the development of all those useless, "practical things" which become ridiculous in no time at all.

It cannot be stressed too often that absolute, true values arise only from artistic, subconscious, or superconscious creation.

The new art of Suprematism, which has produced new forms and form relationships by giving external expression to pictorial feeling, will become a new architecture: it will transfer these forms from the surface of canvas to space.

The Suprematist element, whether in painting or in architecture, is free of every tendency which is social or otherwise materialistic.

Every social idea, however great and important it may be, stems from the sensation of hunger; every art work, regardless of how small and insignificant it may seem, originates in pictorial or plastic feeling. It is high time for us to realize that the problems of art lie far apart from those of the stomach or the intellect.

Now that art, thanks to Suprematism, has come into its own—that is, attained its pure, unapplied form—and has recognized the infallibility of nonobjective feeling, it is attempting to set up a genuine world order, a new philosophy of life. It recognizes the nonobjectivity of the world and is no longer concerned with providing illustrations of the history of manners.

Nonobjective feeling has, in fact, always been the only possible source of art, so that in this respect Suprematism is contributing nothing new but nevertheless the art of the past, because of its use of objective subject matter, harbored unintentionally a whole series of feelings which were alien to it.

But a tree remains a tree even when an owl builds a nest in a hollow of it.

Suprematism has opened up new possibilities to creative art, since *by virtue of the abandonment of so-called "practical consideration," a plastic feeling rendered on canvas can be carried over into space.* The artist (the painter) is no longer bound to the canvas (the picture plane) and can transfer his composition from canvas to space.

WASSILY KANDINSKY

Concrete Art*

All the arts derive from the same and unique root.

Consequently, all the arts are identical.

But the mysterious and precious fact is that the "fruits" produced by the same trunk are different.

The difference manifests itself by the means of each particular art—by the means of expression.

It is very simple at first thought. Music expresses itself by sounds, painting by colors, etc., facts that are generally recognized.

But the difference does not end here. Music, for example, organizes its means (sounds) within time, and painting its means (colors) upon a plane. Time and plane must be exactly "measured" and sound and color must be exactly "limited." These "limits" are the preconditions of "balance" and hence of composition.

Since the enigmatic but precise laws of composition are the same in all the arts, they obliterate differences.

I should like in passing to emphasize that the organic difference between time and plane is generally exaggerated. The composer takes the listener by the hand, makes him enter into his musical work, guides him step by step, and abandons him once the "piece" is finished. Exactitude is perfect. It is imper-

* Wassily Kandisky, "Concrete Art, 1938," in *Theories of Modern Art,* edited by Herschel B. Chipp (Berkeley and Los Angeles: University of California Press, 1968), pp. 346-349. From *XX' Sicèle* (Paris), No. 1 (1938), reprinted in No. 13 (Christmas, 1959), pp. 9-11. See also Kandinsky's essay "On the Problem of Form" *ca.* 1912 which, although written at the moment when he was commencing his first Abstract Expressionist paintings, anticipates in its ideology much abstract art of later years.

fect in painting. But—the painter does not possess this power to "guide." He can if he wishes force the spectator to commence here, to follow an exact path in the pictorial work, and to "leave" it there. These are questions that are excessively complicated, still very little known, and above all very seldom resolved.

I wish only to say that the affinity between painting and music is evident. But it manifests itself still more profoundly. You are well acquainted with the question of "associations" provoked by means of the different arts? Some scientists (especially physicists), some artists (especially musicians) have noticed long ago that a musical sound, for example, provokes an association of a precise color. (Note for example the correspondences established by Scriabin.) Stated otherwise, you "hear" the color and you "see" the sound.

Almost 30 years ago I published a small book which dealt with this question.[1] YELLOW, for example, possesses the special capacity to "ascend" higher and higher and to attain heights unbearable to the eye and the spirit; the sound of a trumpet played higher and higher becoming more and more "pointed," giving pain to the ear and to the spirit. BLUE, with the completely opposite power to "descend" into infinite depths, develops the sounds of the flute (when it is light blue), of the cello (when it has descended farther), of the double bass with its magnificent deep sounds; and in the depths of the organ you "see" the depths of blue. GREEN is well balanced and corresponds to the medium and the attenuated sounds of the violin. When skillfully applied, RED (vermillion) can give the impression of strong drum beats, etc. (*Über das Geistige in der Kunst* [Munich, 1912], pp. 64-71, English and American editions: *The Art of Spiritual Harmony*—W. K.)[2]

The vibrations of the air (sound) and of light (color) surely form the foundation of this physical affinity.

But it is not the only foundation. There is yet another: the psychological foundation. A problem of "spirit."

Have you heard or have you yourself used the expressions: "Oh, such cold music!" or "Oh, such frigid painting!"? You have the impression of frigid air entering through an open window in winter. And your entire body is uncomfortable.

But a skillful application of warm "tones" and "sounds" gives the painter and the composer an excellent possibility of creating warm works. They burn you directly.

Forgive me, but painting and music are able to make you (rather rarely, however) sick to the stomach.

You are also familiar with the case that, when you have the feeling of running your finger over several combinations of sounds or colors, you feel that your finger has been "pricked." As if by spines. But at other times your "finger" runs over painting or music as if over silk or velvet.

Finally, is not VIOLET less odoriferous than YELLOW, for example? And ORANGE? Light BLUE-GREEN?

And as "taste," are not these colors different? Such savory painting! Even the tongue of the spectator or the auditor commences to participate in the work of art.

These are the five known senses of man.

Do not deceive yourself; do not think that you "receive" painting by the eye alone. No, unknown to you, you receive it by your five senses.

Do you think that it could be otherwise?

What we understand by the word "form" in painting is not color alone. What we call "drawing" is inevitably another part of the means of pictorial expression.

To begin with a "point," which is the origin of all other forms, and of which the number is unlimited, the little point is a living being possessed of many influences upon the spirit of man. If the artist places it properly on his canvas, the little point is satisfied, and it pleases the spectator. He says, "Yes, that's me. Do you understand my little necessary sound in the great 'chorus' of the work?"

And how painful it is to see the little point where it should not be! You have the sensation of eating a meringue and tasting pepper on the tongue. A flower with the odor of rot.

Rot—that's the word! Composition transforms itself into decomposition. It is death.

Have you noted that in speaking so long of painting and its means of expression I have said not a single word about the "object"? The explanation of this fact is very simple: I have spoken of the essential pictorial means, that is, of inevitables.

One will never find the possibility to make painting without "colors" and "line," but painting without objects has existed in our time for more than 25 years.

As for the object, it can be *introduced* into a painting, or it can not.

When I think of all the *disputes* about this "not," those disputes which began almost 30 years ago and which today have not yet completely ended, I see the immense force of "habit." At the same time I see the immense force of the painting called "abstract" or "nonfigurative." I prefer to call this painting "concrete."

This art is a "problem" which some wanted to "bury" too often, which they said is definitely resolved (naturally, in the negative sense), but which will not let itself be buried.

It is too much alive.

There no longer exists a problem, neither of Impressionism, nor Expressionism (the Fauves!), nor of Cubism. All these "isms" are distributed into the different compartments of the history of art.

The compartments are numbered and bear labels corresponding to their contents. And, thus, the arguments are concluded.

It is the past.

But the arguments around "concrete art" do not yet allow an anticipation of their end. In good time! "Concrete art" is in full development, above all in the free countries, and the number of young artists participating in the "movement" increases in these countries.

The future!

Notes

1. See his essay "Wirkung der Farbe" (translated as: "Painting: the Effect of Color"), written in 1910 and published in 1912 in *Über das Geistige in der Kunst.*

2. Published in a new and better translation by Francis Golffing, Michael Harrison and Ferdinand Ostertag as *Concerning the Spiritual in Art* (New York: Wittenborn, Schultz, 1947.)

Plastic Art and Pure Plastic Art*

Although art is fundamentally everywhere and always the same, nevertheless two main human inclinations, diametrically opposed to each other, appear in its many and varied expressions. One aims at the *direct creation of universal beauty*, the other at the *aesthetic expression of oneself*, in other words, of that which one thinks and experiences. The first aims at representing reality objectively, the second subjectively. Thus we see in every work of figurative art the desire, objectively to represent beauty, solely through form and color, in mutually balanced relations, and, at the same time, an attempt to express that which these forms, colors, and relations arouse in us. This latter attempt must of necessity result in an individual expression which veils the pure representation of beauty. Nevertheless, both of the two opposing elements (universal-individual) are indispensable if the work is to arouse emotion. Art had to find the right solution. In spite of the dual nature of the creative inclinations, figurative art has produced a harmony through a certain coordination between objective and subjective expression. For the spectator, however, who demands a pure representation of beauty, the individual expression is too predominant. For the artist the search for a unified expression through the balance of two opposites has been, and always will be, a continual struggle.

Throughout the history of culture, art has demonstrated that universal beauty does not arise from the particular character of the form, but from the dynamic rhythm of its inherent relationships, or—in a composition—from

* Piet Mondrian, "Plastic Art and Pure Plastic Art" ("Figurative Art and Nonfigurative Art"), 1937, in *Theories of Modern Art*, edited by Herschel B. Chipp (Berkeley and Los Angeles: University of California Press, 1968), pp. 349-362. Title shortened.

677

the mutual relations of forms. Art has shown that it is a question of determining the relations. It has revealed that the forms exist only for the creation of relationships; that forms create relations and that relations create forms. In this duality of forms and their relations neither takes precedence.

The only problem in art is to achieve a balance between the subjective and the objective. But it is of the utmost importance that this problem should be solved, in the realm of plastic art—technically, as it were—and not in the realm of thought. The work of art must be "produced," "constructed." One must create as objective as possible a representation of forms and relations. Such work can never be empty because the opposition of its constructive elements and its execution arouse emotion.

If some have failed to take into account the inherent character of the form and have forgotten that this—untransformed—predominates, others have overlooked the fact that an individual expression does not become a universal expression through figurative representation, which is based on our conception of feeling, be it classical, romantic, religious, surrealist. Art has shown that universal expression can only be created by a *real equation of the universal and the individual.*

Gradually art is purifying its plastic means and thus bringing out the relationships between them. Thus, in our day two main tendencies appear: the one maintains the figuration, the other eliminates it. While the former employs more or less complicated and particular forms, the latter uses simple and neutral forms, or, ultimately, the free line and the pure color. It is evident that the latter (nonfigurative art) can more easily and thoroughly free itself from the domination of the subjective than can the figurative tendency; particular forms and colors (figurative art) are more easily exploited than neutral forms. It is, however, necessary to point out that the definitions "figurative" and "nonfigurative" are only approximate and relative. For every form, even every line, represents a figure; no form is absolutely neutral. Clearly, everything must be relative, but, since we need words to make our concepts understandable, we must keep to these terms.

Among the different forms we may consider those as being neutral which have neither the complexity nor the particularities possessed by the natural forms of abstract forms in general. We may call those neutral which do not evoke individual feelings or ideas. Geometrical forms being so profound an abstraction of form may be regarded as neutral; and on account of their tension and the purity of their outlines they may even be preferred to other neutral forms.

If, as a conception, nonfigurative art has been created by the mutual interaction of the human duality, this art has been *realized* by the mutual interaction of *constructive elements and their inherent relations.* This process consists in mutual purification; purified constructive elements set up pure relationships, and these in their turn demand pure constructive elements. Figurative art of today is the outcome of figurative art of the past, and nonfigurative art is the outcome of the figurative art of today. Thus the unity of art is maintained.

If nonfigurative art is born of figurative art, it is obvious that the two factors of human duality have not only changed, but have also approached one
another towards a mutual balance, towards unity. One can rightly speak of an
evolution in plastic art. It is of the greatest importance to note this fact, for it
reveals the true way of art; the only path along which we can advance. Moreover, the evolution of the plastic arts shows that the dualism which has manifested itself in art is only relative and temporal. Both science and art are discovering and making us aware of the fact that *time is a process of intensification,*
an evolution from the individual towards the universal, of the subjective
towards the objective; towards the essence of things and of ourselves.

A careful observation of art since its origin shows that artistic expression
seen from the outside is *not a process of prolongment but of intensifying one and the
same thing,* universal beauty; and that seen from the inside *it is a growth.* Extension results in a continual repetition of nature; it is not human and art cannot
follow it. So many of these repetitions which parade as "art" clearly cannot
arouse emotions.

Through intensification one creates successively on more profound
planes; extension remains always on the same plane. Intensification, be it
noted, is diametrically opposed to extension; they are at right angles to each
other as are length and depth. This fact shows clearly the temporal opposition
of nonfigurative and figurative art.

But if throughout its history art has meant a *continuous and gradual
change in the expression of one and the same thing,* the opposition of the two
trends—in our time so clear-cut—is actually an unreal one. It is illogical that the
two principal tendencies in art, figurative and nonfigurative (objective and
subjective) should be so hostile. Since art is in essence universal, its expression
cannot rest on a subjective view. Our human capacities do not allow of a perfectly objective view, but that does not imply that the plastic expression of art
is based on subjective conception. Our subjectivity realizes but does not create
the work.

If the two human inclinations already mentioned are apparent in a work
of art, they have both collaborated in its realization, but it is evident that the
work will clearly show which of the two has predominated. In general, owing
to the complexity of forms and the vague expression of relations, the two
creative inclinations will appear in the work in a confused manner. Although
in general there remains much confusion, today the two inclinations appear
more clearly defined as two tendencies: *figurative and nonfigurative art.* So-
called nonfigurative art often also creates a particular representation; figurative art, on the other hand, often neutralizes its forms to a considerable
extent. The fact that art which is really nonfigurative is rare does not detract
from its value; evolution is always the work of pioneers, and their followers are
always small in number. This following is not a clique; it is the result of all the
existing social forces; it is composed of all those who through innate or
acquired capacity are ready to represent the existing degree of human evolution. At a time when so much attention is paid to the collective, to the "mass,"

it is necessary to note that evolution, ultimately, is never the expression of the mass. The mass remains behind yet urges the pioneers to creation. For the pioneers, the social contact is indispensable, but not in order that they may know that what they are doing is necessary and useful, nor in order that "collective approval may help them to persevere and nourish them with living ideas." This contact is necessary only in an indirect way; it acts especially as an obstacle which increases their determination. The pioneers create through their reaction to external stimuli. They are guided not by the mass but by that which they see and feel. They discover consciously or unconsciously the fundamental laws hidden in reality, and aim at realizing them. In this way they further human development. They know that humanity is not served by making art comprehensible to everybody; to try this is to attempt the impossible. One serves mankind by enlightening it. Those who do not see will rebel, they will try to understand and will end up by "seeing." In art the search for a content which is collectively understandable is false; the content will always be individual. Religion, too, has been debased by that search.

Art is not made for anybody and is, at the same time, for everybody. It is a mistake to try to go too fast. The complexity of art is due to the fact that different degrees of its evolution are present at one and the same time. The present carries with it the past and the future. But we need not try to foresee the future; we need only take our place in the development of human culture, a development which has made nonfigurative art supreme. It has always been only one struggle, of only one real art: to create universal beauty. This points the way for both present and future. We need only continue and develop what already exists. The essential thing is that *the fixed laws of the plastic arts must be realized.* These have shown themselves clearly in nonfigurative art.

Today one is tired of the dogmas of the past, and of truths once accepted but successively jettisoned. One realizes more and more the relativity of everything, and therefore one tends to reject the idea of fixed laws, of a single truth. This is very understandable, but does not lead to profound vision. For there are "made" laws, "discovered" laws, but also laws—a truth for all time. These are more or less hidden in the reality which surrounds us and do not change. Not only science, but art also, shows us that reality, at first incomprehensible, gradually reveals itself, by the mutual relations that are inherent in things. Pure science and pure art, disinterested and free, can lead the advance in the recognition of the laws which are based on these relationships. A great scholar has recently said that pure science achieves practical results for humanity. Similarly, one can say that pure art, even though it appear abstract, can be of direct utility for life.

Art shows us that there are also constant truths concerning forms. Every form, every line has its own expression. This objective expression can be modified by our subjective view but it is no less true for that. Round is always round and square is always square. Simple though these facts are, they often appear to be forgotten in art. Many try to achieve one and the same end by different means. In plastic art this is an impossibility. In plastic art it is necessary to choose constructive means which are of one piece with that which one wants to express.

Art makes us realize that there are *fixed laws which govern and point to the use of the constructive elements, of the composition and of the inherent interrelationships between them*. These laws may be regarded as subsidiary laws to the *fundamental* law of equivalence which creates *dynamic equilibrium and reveals the true content of reality*.

We live in a difficult but interesting epoch. After a secular culture, a turning point has arrived; this shows itself in all the branches of human activity. Limiting ourselves here to science and art, we notice that, just as in medicine some have discovered the natural laws relating to physical life, in art some have discovered the artistic laws relating to plastics. In spite of all opposition, these facts have become movements. But confusion still reigns in them. Through science we are becoming more and more conscious of the fact that our physical state depends in great measure on what we eat, on the manner in which our food is arranged, and on the physical exercise which we take. Through art we are becoming more and more conscious of the fact that the work depends in large measure on the constructive elements which we use and on the construction which we create. We will gradually realize that we have not hitherto paid sufficient attention to constructive physical elements in their relation to the human body, nor to the constructive plastic elements in their relation to art. That which we eat has deteriorated through a refinement of natural produce. To say this, appears to invoke a return to a primitive natural state and to be in opposition to the exigencies of pure plastic art, which degenerates precisely through figurative trapping. But a return to pure natural nourishment does not mean a return to the state of primitive man; it means on the contrary that cultured man obeys the laws of nature discovered and applied by science.

Similarly in nonfigurative art, to recognize and apply natural laws is not evidence of a retrograde step; the pure abstract expression of these laws proves that the exponent of nonfigurative art associates himself with the most advanced progress and the most cultured minds, that he is an exponent of denaturalized nature, of civilization.

In life, sometimes the spirit has been overemphasized at the expense of the body, sometimes one has been preoccupied with the body and neglected the spirit; similarly in art content and forms have alternately been overemphasized or neglected because *their inseparable unity* has not been clearly realized.

To create this unity in art *balance of the one and the other must be created*.

It is an achievement of our time to have approached towards such balance in a field in which disequilibrium still reigns.

Disequilibrium means conflict, disorder. Conflict is also a part of life and of art, but it is not the whole of life or universal beauty. Real life is the *mutual interaction of two oppositions of the same value but of a different aspect and nature*. Its plastic expression is universal beauty.

In spite of world disorder, instinct and intuition are carrying humanity to a real equilibrium, but how much misery has been and is still being caused by primitive animal instinct. How many errors have been and are being committed through vague and confused intuition? Art certainly shows this clearly. But art shows also that in the course of progress, intuition becomes more and more conscious and instinct more and more purified. Art and life illuminate each other more and more; they reveal more and more their laws according to which a real and living balance is created.

Intuition enlightens and so links up with pure thought. They together become an intelligence which is not simply of the brain, which does not calculate, but which feels and thinks. Which is creative both in art and in life. From this intelligence there must arise nonfigurative art in which instinct no longer plays a dominating part. Those who do not understand this intelligence regard nonfigurative art as a purely intellectual product.

Although all dogma, all preconceived ideas, must be harmful to art, the artist can nevertheless be guided and helped in his intuitive researches by reasoning apart from his work. If such reasoning can be useful to the artist and can accelerate his progress, it is indispensable that such reasoning should accompany the observations of the critics who talk about art and who wish to guide mankind. Such reasoning, however, cannot be individual, which it usually is; it cannot arise out of a body of knowledge outside plastic art. If one is not an artist oneself one must at least know *the laws and culture of plastic art.* If the public is to be well informed and if mankind is to progress it is essential that the confusion which is everywhere present should be removed. For enlightenment, a clear demonstration of the *succession of artistic tendencies is necessary.* Hitherto, a study of the different styles of plastic art in their progressive succession has been difficult since the expression of the essence of art has been veiled. In our time, which is reproached for not having a style of its own, the content of art has become clear and the different tendencies reveal more clearly the progressive succession of artistic expression. Nonfigurative art brings to an end the ancient culture of art; at present therefore, one can review and judge more surely *the whole culture of art.* We are not at the turning-point of this culture; *the culture of particular form is approaching its end. The culture of determined relations has begun.*

It is not enough to explain the value of a work of art in itself; it is above all necessary to show *the place which a work occupies on the scale of the evolution of plastic art.* Thus in speaking of art, it is not permissible to say "this is how I see it" or "this is my idea." True art like true life takes a *single road.*

The laws which in the culture of art have become more and more determinate are *the great hidden laws of nature which art establishes in its own fashion.* It is necessary to stress the fact that these laws are more or less hidden behind the superficial aspect of nature. Abstract art is therefore opposed to a natural representation of things. But it *not opposed to nature* as is generally thought. It is opposed to the raw primitive animal nature of man, but it is one with true human nature. It is opposed to the conventional laws created during the culture of the particular form but it is one with the laws of the culture of pure relationships.

First and foremost there is the fundamental law of *dynamic equilibrium* which is opposed to the static equilibrium necessitated by the particular form.

The important task then of all art is to destroy the static equilibrium by establishing a dynamic one. Nonfigurative art demands an attempt to what is a consequence of this task, the *destruction* of particular form and the *construction* of a rhythm of mutual relations, of mutual forms of free lines. We must bear in mind, however, a distinction between these two forms of equilibrium in order to avoid confusion; for when we speak of equilibrium pure and simple we may be for, and at the same time against, a balance in the work of art. It is of the greatest importance to note the destructive-constructive quality of dynamic equilibrium. Then we shall understand that the equilibrium of which we speak in nonfigurative art is not without movement of action but is on the contrary a continual movement. We then understand also the significance of the name "constructive art."

The fundamental law of dynamic equilibrium gives rise to a number of other laws which relate to the constructive elements and their relations. These laws determine the manner in which dynamic equilibrium is achieved. The relations of *position* and those of *dimension* both have their own laws. Since the relation of the rectangular position is constant, it will be applied whenever the work demands the expression of stability; to destroy this stability there is a law that relations of a changeable dimension-expression must be substituted. The fact that all the relations of position except the rectangular one lack that stability, also creates a law which we must take into account if something is to be established in a determinate manner. Too often right and oblique angles are arbitrarily employed. All art expresses the rectangular relationship even though this may not be in a determinate manner; first by the height and width of the work and its constructive forms, then by the mutual relations of these forms. Through the clarity and simplicity of neutral forms, nonfigurative art has made the rectangular relation more and more determinate, until, finally, it has established it through free lines which intersect and appear to form rectangles.

As regards the relations of dimensions, they must be varied in order to avoid repetition. Although, as compared with the stable expression of the rectangular relationship, they belong to individual expression, it is precisely they that are most appropriate for the destruction of the static equilibrium of all form. By offering him a freedom of choice the relations of dimension *present the artist with one of the most difficult problems.* And the closer he approaches the ultimate consequence of his art the more difficult is his task.

Since the constructive elements and their mutual relations form an inseparable unity, the laws of the relations govern equally the constructive elements. These, however, have also their own laws. It is obvious that one cannot achieve the same expression through different forms. But it is often forgotten that varied forms or lines *achieve—in form—altogether different degrees in the evo-*

lution of plastic art. Beginning with natural forms and ending with the most abstract forms, *their expression becomes more profound.* Gradually form and line gain in tension. For this reason the straight line is a stronger and more profound expression than the curve.

In pure plastic art the significance of different forms and lines is very important; it is precisely this fact which makes it pure.

In order that art may be really abstract, in other words, that it should not represent relations with the natural aspect of things, the law of the *denaturalization of matter* is of fundamental importance. In painting, the primary color that is as pure as possible realizes this abstraction of natural color. But color is, in the present state of technique, also the best means for denaturalizing matter in the realm of abstract constructions in three dimensions; technical means are as a rule insufficient.

All art has achieved a certain measure of abstraction. This abstraction has become more and more accentuated until in pure plastic form art not only a transformation of form but also matter—be it through technical means or through color—a more or less natural expression is attained.

According to our laws, it is a great mistake to believe that one is practicing nonfigurative art by merely achieving neutral forms or free lines and determinate relations. For in composing these forms one runs the risk of a figurative creation, that is to say, one or more particular forms.

Nonfigurative art is created by establishing *a dynamic rhythm of determinate mutual relations* which *excludes the formation of any particular form.* We note thus, that to destroy particular form is only to do more consistently what all art has done.

The dynamic rhythm which is essential in all art is also the essential element of a nonfigurative work. In figurative art this rhythm is veiled.

Yet we all pay homage to clarity.

The fact that people generally prefer figurative art (which creates and finds its continuation in abstract art) can be explained by the dominating force of the individual inclination in human nature. *From this inclination arises all the opposition to art which is purely abstract.*

In this connection we note first the *naturalistic conception* and the *descriptive or literary orientation:* both a real danger to purely abstract art. From a purely plastic point of view, until nonfigurative art, artistic expression has been naturalistic or descriptive. To have emotion aroused by pure plastic expression one must abstract from figuration and so become "neutral." But with the exception of some artistic expressions (such as Byzantine art)[1] there has not been the desire to employ neutral plastic means, which would have been much more logical than to become neutral oneself in contemplating a work of art. Let us note, however, that the spirit of the past was different from the spirit of our own day, and that it is only tradition which has carried the past into our own time. In past times when one lived in contact with nature and when man himself was more natural than he is today, abstraction from figuration in thought was easy; it was done unconsciously. But in our more or less denaturalized period, such abstraction becomes an effort.

However that may be, the fact that figuration is a factor which is unduly taken into account, and whose abstraction in the mind is only relative, proves that today even great artists regard figuration as indispensable. At the same time these artists are already abstracting from figuration to a much greater extent than has been done before. More and more, not only the uselessness of figuration, but also obstacles which it creates, will become obvious. In this search for clarity, nonfigurative art develops.

There is, however, one tendency which cannot forgo figuration without losing its descriptive character. That is Surrealism. Since the predominance of individual thought is opposed to pure plastics it is also opposed to nonfigurative art. Born of a literary movement, its descriptive character demands figuration. However purified or deformed it may be, figuration veils pure plastics. There are, it is true, Surrealist works whose plastic expression is very strong and of a kind that if the work is observed at a distance, i.e., if the figurative representation is abstracted from, they arouse emotion by form, color and their relations alone. But if the purpose was nothing but plastic expression, why then use figurative representation? Clearly, there must have been the intention to express something outside the realm of pure plastics. This of course is often the case even in abstract art. There, too, there is sometimes added to the abstract forms something particular, even without the use of figuration; through the color or through the execution, a particular idea or sentiment is expressed. There is generally not the literary inclination but the naturalistic inclination which has been at work. It must be obvious that if one evokes in the spectator the sensation of, say, the sunlight or moonlight, of joy or sadness, or any other determinate sensation, one has not succeeded in establishing universal beauty, one is not purely abstract.

As for Surrealism, we must recognize that it deepens feeling and thought, but since this deepening is limited by individualism it cannot reach the foundation, the universal. So long as it remains in the realm of dreams, which are only a rearrangement of the events of life, it cannot touch true reality. Through a different composition of the events of life, it may remove their ordinary course but it cannot purify them. Even the intention of freeing life from its conventions and from everything which is harmful to the true life can be found in Surrealist literature. Nonfigurative art is fully in agreement with this intention but it achieves its purpose; it frees its plastic means and its art from all particularity. The names, however, of these tendencies, are only indications of their conceptions; it is the realization which matters. With the exception of nonfigurative art, there seems to have been a lack of realization of the fact that it is possible to express oneself profoundly and humanely by plastics alone, that is, by employing a neutral plastic means without the risk of falling into decoration or ornament. Yet all the world knows that even a single line can arouse emotion. But although one sees—and this is the artist's fault— few nonfigurative works which live by virtue of their dynamic rhythm and their execution, figurative art is no better in this respect. In general, people have not realized that one can express our very essence through neutral constructive elements; that is to say, we can express the essence of art. The essence of art of course is not often sought. As a rule, individualist human nature is so predominant, that the expression of the essence of art through a rhythm of lines, colors, and relationships appears insufficient. Recently, even a great artist has declared that "complete indifference to the subject leads to an incomplete form of art."

But everybody agrees that art is only a problem of plastics. What good then is a subject? It is to be understood that one should need a subject to expound something named "Spiritual riches, human sentiments, and thoughts." Obviously, all this is individual and needs particular forms. But at the root of these sentiments and thoughts there is one thought and one sentiment: these do not easily define themselves and have no need of analogous forms in which to express themselves. It is here that neutral plastic means are demanded.

For pure art then, the subject can never be an additional value; it is the line, the color and their relations which must "bring into play the whole sensual and intelligent register of the inner life . . . ," not the subject. Both in abstract art and in naturalistic art color expresses itself "in accordance with the form by which it is determined," and in all art it is the artist's task to make forms and colors living and capable of arousing emotion. If he makes art into an "algebraic equation," that is no argument against the art, it only proves that he is not an artist.

If all art has demonstrated that to establish the force, tension, and movement of the forms, and the intensity of the colors of reality, it is necessary that these should be purified and transformed; if all art has purified and transformed and is still purifying and transforming these forms of reality and their mutual relations, if all art is thus a continually deepening process: why then stop halfway? If all art aims at expressing universal beauty, why establish an individualist expression? Why then not continue the sublime work of the Cubists? That would not be a continuation of the same tendency, but on the contrary, *a complete breakaway from it and all that has existed before it.* That would only be going along the same road that we have already traveled.

Since Cubist art is still fundamentally naturalistic, the break which pure plastic art has caused consists in becoming abstract instead of naturalistic in essence. While in Cubism, from a naturalistic foundation, there sprang forcibly the use of plastic means, still half object, half abstract, the abstract basis of pure plastic art must result in the use of purely abstract plastic means.

In removing completely from the work all objects, "the world is not separated from the spirit," but is on the contrary *put into a balanced opposition* with the spirit, since the one and the other are purified. This creates a perfect unity between the two opposites. There are, however, many who imagine that they are too fond of life, particular reality, to be able to suppress figuration, and for that reason they still use in their work the object of figurative fragments which indicate its character. Nevertheless, one is well aware of the fact that in art one cannot hope to represent in the image things as they are, nor even as they manifest themselves in all their living brilliance. The Impressionists, Divisionists, and Pointillists have already recognized that. There are some today who, recognizing the weakness and limitation of the image, attempt to create a work of art through the objects themselves, often by composing them in a more or less transformed manner. This clearly cannot lead to an expression of their content nor of their true character. One can more or less remove the conventional appearance of things (Surrealism), but they continue nevertheless to show their particular character and to arouse in us individual emotions. To love things in reality is to love them profoundly; it is to see them as a microcosmos in the macrocosmos. *Only in this way can one achieve a universal expression of reality.* Precisely on account of its profound love for things, nonfigurative art does not aim at rendering them in their particular appearance.

Precisely by its existence nonfigurative art shows that "art" *continues always on its true road.* It shows that "art" is *not the expression of the appearances of reality such as we see it, nor of the life which we live,* but that *it is the expression of true reality and true life—indefinable but realizable in plastics.*

Thus we must carefully distinguish between two kinds of reality; one which has an individual and one which has a universal appearance. In art the former is the expression of space determined by particular things or forms, the latter establishes expansion and limitations—the creative factors of space— through neutral forms, free lines, and pure colors. While universal reality arises from determinate relations, particular reality shows only veiled relations. The latter must obviously be confused in just that respect in which universal reality is bound to be clear. The one is free, the other is tied to individual life, be it personal or collective. Subjective reality and relatively objective reality: this is the contrast. Pure abstract art aims at creating the latter, figurative art the former.

It is astonishing, therefore, that one should reproach pure abstract art with not being "real," and that one should envisage it as "arising from particular ideas."

In spite of the existence of nonfigurative art, one is talking about art today as if nothing determinate in relation to the new art existed. Many neglect the real nonfigurative art, and looking only at the fumbling attempts and at the empty nonfigurative works which today are appealing everywhere, ask themselves whether the time has not arrived "to integrate form and content" or "to unify thought and form." But one should not blame nonfigurative art for that which is only due to the ignorance of its very content. If the form is without content, without universal thought, it is the fault of the artist. Ignoring that fact, one imagines that figuration, subject, particular form, could add to the work that which the plastic itself is lacking. As regards the "content" of the work, we must note that our "attitude with regard to things, our organized individuality with its impulses, its actions, its reactions when in contact with reality, the lights and shades of our spirit," etc., certainly do modify the nonfigurative work, but they do not constitute its content. We repeat, that its content cannot be described, and that it is only through pure plastics and through the execution of the work that it can be made apparent. Through this indeterminable content, the nonfigurative work is "fully human." Execution and technique play an important part in the aim of establishing a more or less objective vision which the essence of the nonfigurative work demands. The less obvious the artist's hand the more objective will the work be. This fact leads to a preference for a more or less mechanical execution or to the employment of materials produced by industry. Hitherto, of course, these materials have been imperfect from the point of view of art. If these materials and their colors were more perfect and if a technique existed by which the artist could easily cut them up in order to compose his work as he conceives it, an art more real and more objective in relation to life than painting would arise. All these reflections evoke questions which have already been asked many years ago, mainly: is art still necessary and useful for humanity? Is it not even harmful to its progress? Certainly the art of the past is superfluous to the new spirit and harmful to its progress: just because of its beauty it holds many people back from the new conception. The new art is, however, still very necessary to life. In a clear manner it establishes the law according to which a real balance is reached. Moreover, it must create among us a profoundly human and rich beauty realized not only by the best qualities of the new architecture, but also by all that the constructive art in painting and sculpture makes possible.

But although the new art is necessary, the mass is conservative. Hence these cinemas, these radios, these bad pictures which overwhelm the few works which are really of our era.

It is a great pity that those who are concerned with the social life in general do not realize the utility of pure abstract art. Wrongly influenced by the art of the past, the true essence of which escapes them, and of which they only see that which is superfluous, they make no effort to know pure abstract art. Through another conception of the word "abstract," they have a certain horror of it. They are vehemently opposed to abstract art because they regard it as something ideal and unreal. In general they use art as a propaganda for collective or personal ideas, thus as literature. They are both in favor of the progress of the mass and against the progress of the elite, thus against the logical march of human evolution. Is it really to be believed that the evolution of the mass and that of the elite are incompatible? The elite rises from the mass; is it not therefore its highest expression?

To return to the execution of the work of art, let us note that it must contribute to a revelation of the subjective and objective factors in mutual balance. Guided by intuition, it is possible to attain this end. The execution is of the greatest importance in the work of art; it is through this, in large part, that intuition manifests itself and creates the essence of the work.

It is therefore a mistake to suppose that a nonfigurative work comes out of the unconscious, which is a collection of individual and prenatal memories. We repeat that it comes from pure intuition, which is at the basis of the subjective-objective dualism.

It is, however, wrong to think that the nonfigurative artist finds impressions and emotions received from the outside useless, and regards it even as necessary to fight against them. On the contrary, all that the nonfigurative artist received from the outside is not only useful but indispensable, because it arouses in him the desire to create that which he only vaguely feels and which he could *never represent in a true manner without the contact with visible reality and with the life which surrounds him.* It is precisely from this visible reality that he draws the objectivity which he needs in opposition to his personal subjectivity. It is precisely from this visible reality that he draws his means of expression; and, as regards the surrounding life, it is precisely this which has made his art nonfigurative.

That which distinguishes him from the figurative artist is the fact that in his creation he frees himself from individual sentiments and from particular impressions which he receives from outside, and that he breaks loose from the domination of the individual inclination within him.

It is therefore equally wrong to think that the nonfigurative artist creates through "the pure intention of his mechanical process," that he makes "calculated abstractions," and that he wishes to "suppress sentiment not only in himself but also in the spectator." It is a mistake to think that he retires completely into his system. That which is regarded as a system is nothing but constant obedience to the laws of pure plastics, to necessity, which art demands from him. It is thus clear that he has not become a mechanic, but that the progress of science, of technique, of machinery, of life as a whole, has only made him into a living machine, capable of realizing in a pure manner the essence of art. In this way, he is in his creation sufficiently neutral, that nothing of himself or outside of him can prevent him from establishing that which is universal. Certainly his art is art for art's sake . . . for the sake of the art *which is form and content at one and the same time.*

If all real art is the "sum total of emotions aroused by purely pictorial means" his art is the sum of the emotions aroused by plastic means.

It would be illogical to suppose that nonfigurative art will remain stationary, for this art contains *a culture* of the use of new plastic means and their determinate relations. Because the field is new there is all the more to be done. What is certain is that no escape is possible for the nonfigurative artist; he *must stay within his field and march towards the consequence of his art.*

This consequence brings us, in a future perhaps remote, towards the end of *art as a thing separated from our surrounding environment, which is the actual plastic reality.* But this end is at the same time a new beginning. Art will not only continue but will realize itself more and more. By the unification of architecture, sculpture, and painting, a new plastic reality will be created. Painting and sculpture will not manifest themselves as separate objects, nor as "mural art" which destroys architecture itself, nor as "applied" art, but *being purely constructive* will aid the creation of a surrounding not merely utilitarian or rational but also pure and complete in its beauty.

NOTE

1. As regards these works we must note that, lacking a dynamic rhythm, they remain, in spite of the profound expression of forms, more or less ornamental. [P.M.]

Sentences on Conceptual Art*

1. Conceptual Artists are mystics rather than rationalists. They leap to conclusions that logic cannot reach.
2. Rational judgments repeat rational judgments.
3. Illogical judgments lead to new experience.
4. Formal Art is essentially ʳ ₁tional.
5. Irrational thoughts should be followed absolutely and logically.
6. If the artist changes his mind midway through the execution of the piece he compromises the result and repeats past results.
7. The artist's will is secondary to the process he initiates from idea to completion. His wilfullness may only be ego.
8. When words such as painting and sculpture are used, they connote a whole tradition and imply a consequent acceptance of this tradition, thus placing limitations on the artist who would be reluctant to make art that goes beyond the limitations.
9. The concept and idea are different. The former implies a general direction while the latter are the components. Ideas implement the concept.
10. Ideas alone can be works of art; they are in a chain of development that may eventually find some form. All ideas need not be made physical.
11. Ideas do not necessarily proceed in logical order. They may set one off in unexpected directions but an idea must necessarily be completed in the mind before the next one is formed.

* Sol LeWitt, "Sentences on Conceptual Art," in *Six Years: The Dematerialization of the Art Object from 1966 to 1972,* edited by Lucy R. Lippard (New York: Praeger, 1973), pp. 75-76.

12. For each work of art that becomes physical there are many variations that do not.

13. A work of art may be understood as a conductor from the artist's mind to the viewer's. But it may never reach the viewer, or it may never leave the artist's mind.

14. The words of one artist to another may induce an idea chain, if they share the same concept.

15. Since no form is intrinsically superior to another, the artist may use any form, from an expression of words (written or spoken) to physical reality, equally.

16. If words are used, and they proceed from ideas about art, then they are art and not literature; numbers are not mathematics.

17. All ideas are art if they are concerned with art and fall within the conventions of art.

18. One usually understands the art of the past by applying the conventions of the present thus misunderstanding the art of the past.

19. The conventions of art are altered by works of art.

20. Successful art changes our understanding of the conventions by altering our perceptions.

21. Perception of ideas leads to new ideas.

22. The artist cannot imagine his art, and cannot perceive it until it is complete.

23. One artist may mis-perceive (understand it differently than the artist) a work of art but still be set off in his own chain of thought by that misconstrual.

24. Perception is subjective.

25. The artist may not necessarily understand his own art. His perception is neither better nor worse than that of others.

26. An artist may perceive the art of others better than his own.

27. The concept of a work of art may involve the matter of the piece or the process in which it is made.

28. Once the idea of the piece is established in the artist's mind and the final form is decided, the process is carried out blindly. There are many side-effects that the artist cannot imagine. These may be used as ideas for new works.

29. The process is mechanical and should not be tampered with. It should run its course.

30. There are many elements involved in a work of art. The most important are the most obvious.

31. If an artist uses the same form in a group of works, and changes the material, one would assume the artist's concept involved the material.

32. Banal ideas cannot be rescued by beautiful execution.

33. It is difficult to bungle a good idea.

34. When an artist learns his craft too well he makes slick art.

35. These sentences comment on art, but are not art.